The Principal Navigations, Voyages, Traffiques & Discoveries of the English Nation — Volume 14; America, Part III

Richard Hakluyt, (Editor: Edmund Goldsmid)

Alpha Editions

This edition published in 2024

ISBN 9789362512291

Design and Setting By
Alpha Editions
www.alphaedis.com
Email - info@alphaedis.com

As per information held with us this book is in Public Domain.
This book is a reproduction of an important historical work.
Alpha Editions uses the best technology to reproduce historical work
in the same manner it was first published to preserve its original nature.
Any marks or number seen are left intentionally to preserve.

Contents

(Continuation of Part II.)   - 2 -

Chap. XXV.   - 3 -

Chap. XXVI.   - 6 -

Chap. XXVII.   - 9 -

Chap. XXVIII.   - 12 -

Chap. XXIX.   - 15 -

Chap. XXX.   - 19 -

Chap. XXXI.   - 22 -

Chap. XXXII.   - 25 -

Chap. XXXIII.   - 27 -

Chap. XXXIV.   - 29 -

Chap. XXXV.   - 32 -

Chap. XXXVI.   - 35 -

Chap. XXXVII.   - 39 -

Chap. XXXVIII.   - 42 -

Chap. XXXIX.   - 44 -

Chap. XL.   - 47 -

Chap. XLI.   - 49 -

Chap. XLII.   - 51 -

Chap. XLIII.   - 53 -

Chap. XLIV.   - 55 -

Chap. 1.   - 65 -

Chap. 2.   - 69 -

Chap. 3.   - 72 -

Chap. 4.	- 75 -
Chap. 5.	- 78 -
Chap. 1.	- 109 -
Chap. 2.	- 112 -
Chap. 3.	- 117 -
Chap. 4.	- 120 -
Chap. 1.	- 172 -
Chap. 2.	- 174 -
Chap. 3.	- 180 -
Chap. 4.	- 187 -
Chap. 5.	- 192 -
Chap. 6.	- 197 -
Chap. 7.	- 204 -
VOL. XIV.	- 289 -
PART III.	- 290 -
Chap. 1.	- 291 -
Chap. 2.	- 294 -
Chap. 3.	- 297 -
Chap. 4.	- 300 -
Chap. 5.	- 303 -
Chap. 6.	- 306 -
Chap. 7.	- 310 -
Chap. 8.	- 313 -
Chap. 9.	- 319 -
Chap. 10.	- 323 -
Chap. 11.	- 328 -
Chap. 12.	- 332 -

Chap. 13.	- 337 -
Chap. 14.	- 341 -
Chap. 15.	- 345 -
Chap. 16.	- 348 -
Chap. 1.	- 352 -
Chap. 2.	- 357 -
Chap. 3.	- 358 -
Chap. 1.	- 362 -
Chap. 2.	- 366 -
Chap. 3.	- 370 -
Chap. 4.	- 374 -
Chap. 5.	- 378 -
Chap. 6.	- 382 -
Chap. 7.	- 385 -
Chap. 8.	- 388 -
Chap. 9.	- 391 -

NAUIGATIONS, VOYAGES, TRAFFIQUES, AND DISCOUERIES OF THE ENGLISH NATION IN AMERICA.

(Continuation of Part II.)

Virginia richly valued, by the description of the maine land of Florida, her next neighbour: out of the foure yeeres continuall trauell and discouerie, for aboue one thousand miles east and west, of Don Ferdinando de Soto and sixe hundred able men in his companie.—
(*Continued.*)

Chap. XXV.

How the Gouernour departed from Pacaha to Quigaute, and to Coligoa, and came to Cayas.

The Gouernour rested in Pacaha fortie daies. In all which time the two Caciques serued him with great store of fish, mantles and skinnes, and stroue who should doe him greatest seruice. At the time of his departure, the Cacique of Pacaha gaue him two of his sisters, saying that in signe of loue that hee might remember him, he should take them for his wiues: the ones name was Macanoche, and the others Mochila; they were well proportioned, tall of bodie, and well fleshed. Macanoche was of a good countenance, and in her shape and physiognimie looked like a Ladie; the other was strongly made. The Casiqui of Casqui commanded the bridge to be repaired, and the Gouernour returned through his Country, and lodged in a field neere his towne, whither hee came with great store of fish, and two women, which hee exchanged with two Christians for shirts. He gaue vs a guide and men for carriages. The Gouernour lodged at a towne of his, and the next day at another neere a Riuer, whither he caused canoes to be brought for him to passe ouer, and with his leaue returned. The Gouernour tooke his iourney toward Quigaute. The fourth of August, he came to the towne, where the Cacique vsed to keepe his residencie: on the way he sent him a present of many mantles and skinnes, and not daring to stay for him in the towne, he absented himselfe. The towne was the greatest that was seene in Florida. The Gouernour and his people lodged in the one halfe of it; and within few daies, seeing the Indians became liars, he commanded the other halfe to be burned, because it should not bee a shelter for them, if they came to assault him by night, nor an hindrance to his horsemen for the resisting of them. There came an Indian very well accompanied with many Indians, saying, that he was the Cacique. He deliuered him ouer to the men of his guard to look vnto him. There went and came many Indians, and brought mantles and skinnes. The counterfeit Cacique, seeing so little opportunitie to execute his euill thought, as hee went one day abroad talking with the Gouernour, he shewed him such a paire of heeles, that there was no Christian that could ouertake him, and he leaped into the Riuer, which was a crossebow shot from the towne: and assoone as hee was on the other side, many Indians that were thereabout making a great crie began to shoote. Coligoa neere to certaine mountaines Northwest. The Gouernour passed presently ouer to them with horsemen and footemen, but they durst not tarrie for him. Going forward on his way, hee came to a towne where the people were fled, and a little further to a lake, where the horses could not passe, and on the otherside were many women. The footemen passed, and tooke many of them, and much spoile. The Gouernour came to the Camp: And that night was a spie of the Indians taken by them of the watch. The Gouernour asked him, whether he would bring him where the Cacique was? he said, he would. And he went presently to seeke him with twentie horsemen, and fiftie footemen: and after he had sought him a day, and an halfe, hee found him in a strong wood: And a souldiour not knowing him, gaue him a wound on the head; and he cried out, that he should not kill him, saying, that he was the Cacique: so he was taken, and an hundred and fortie of his men with him. The Gouernour came againe to Quigaute, and willed him to cause his men to come to serue the Christians: and staying some daies for their comming, and seeing they came not, he sent two Captaines, euery one his way on both sides of the Riuer with horsemen and footemen. They tooke many men and women. Now seeing the hurt which they sustained for their rebellion, they came to see what the Gouernour would command them, and passed to and fro many times, and brought presents of cloth and fish. The Cacique and his two wiues were in the lodging of the Gouernour loose, and the halbardiers of his guard did keepe them. The Gouernour asked them which way the Countrie was most inhabited? They said, that toward the South downe the Riuer, were great townes and Caciques, which commanded great Countries, and much people: And that toward the Northwest there was a Prouince neere to certaine mountaines, that was called Coligoa. The Gouernour and all the rest thought good to goe first to Coligoa: saying, that peraduenture the mountains would make some difference of soile, and that beyond them there might be some gold or siluer: As for Quigaute, Casqui, and Pacaha, they were plaine Countries, fat grounds, and full of good medowes on the Riuers, where the Indians sowed large fields of Maiz. From Tascaluca to Rio grande, or the great Riuer, is about 300. leagues: it is a very low Countrie, and hath many lakes. From Pacaha to Quigaute may bee an hundred leagues. The Gouernour left the Cacique of Quigaute in his owne towne: And an Indian, which was his guide, led him through great woods without any way seuen daies iournie through a desert, where, at euery lodging, they lodged in lakes and pooles in verie shold water; there were such store of fish, that they killed them with cudgils; and the Indians which they carried in chaines, with the mud troubled the waters, and the fish being therewith, as it were astonied, came to the top of the water, and they tooke as much as they listed. The Indians of Coligoa had no knowledge of the Christians, and when they came so neere the towne, that the Indians saw them, they fled vp a Riuer, which passed neere the towne, and some leaped into it; but the Christians went on both sides of the Riuer, and tooke them. There were many men and women taken, and the Cacique with them. And by his commandement within three daies came many Indians with a present of mantles and Deeres skinnes, and two oxe hides: And they reported, that 5. or 6. leagues from thence toward the North, there were many of these oxen, and that because the Countrie was cold, it was euill inhabited. That the best Countrie which they knew, the most plentifull, and most inhabited, was a Prouince called Cayas, lying toward the South. From Quiguate to Coligoa may be 40. leagues. This towne of Coligoa stood at the foote of an hill, on the bank of a meane Riuer, of the bignesse of Cayas, the Riuer that passeth by Estremadura. It was a fat soile and so plentifull of Maiz, that they cast out the old, to bring in the new. There was also great plentie of French beanes and pompions. The French beanes were greater, and better than those of Spaine, and likewise the pompions, and being roasted, they haue almost the taste of chesnuts. The Cacique of Coligoa gaue a guide to Cayas, and staied behind in his owne towne. Wee trauelled fiue daies, and came to the Prouince of Palisema. The house of the Cacique was found couered with Deeres skinnes of Diuers colours and works drawne in them, and with the same in manner of carpets was the ground of the house couered. The Cacique left it so, that the Gouernour might lodge in it, in token that he sought peace and his friendship. But hee durst not tarrie his comming. The Gouernour, seeing he had absented himselfe, sent a Captaine with horsemen and footemen to seeke him. Hee found much people, but by reason of the roughnesse of the Countrie, he tooke none saue a few women and children. The towne was little and scattering, and had very little Maiz. For which cause the Gouernour speedilie departed from thence. Hee came to another towne called Tatalicoya, hee carried with him the Cacique thereof, which guided him to Cayas. From Tatalicoya are foure daies iournie to Cayas. When hee came to Cayas, and saw the towne scattered; hee thought they had told him a lie, and that it was not the Prouince of Cayas, because they had informed him that it was well inhabited: He threatned the Cacique, charging him to tell him where hee was: and he and other Indians which were taken neere about that place, affirmed that this was the towne of Cayas, and the best that was in that Countrie, and that though the houses were distant the one from the other, yet the ground that was inhabited was great, and that there was great store of people, and many fields of Maiz. The towne was called Tanico: he pitched his Campe in the best part of it neere vnto a Riuer. The same day that the Gouernour came thither, he went a league farther with certaine horsemen, and without finding any people, hee found many skinnes in a pathway, which the Cacique had left there, that they might bee found, in token of peace. For so is the custome in that Countrie.

Chap. XXVI.

How the Gouernour discouered the Prouince of Tulla, and what happened vnto him.

The Gouernour rested a moneth in the Prouince of Cayas. In which time the horses fattened and thriued more, then in other places in a longer time, with the great plentie of Maiz and the leaues thereof, which I thinke was the best that hath been seene, and they dranke of a lake of very hot water, and somewhat brackish, and they dranke so much, that it swelled in their bellies when they brought them from the watering. Vntill that time the Christians wanted salt, and there they made good store, which they carried along with them. The Indians doe carrie it to other places to exchange it for skinnes and mantles. They make it along the Riuer, which when it ebbeth, leaueth it vpon the vpper part of the sand. And because they cannot make it, without much sand mingled with it, they throw it into certain baskets which they haue for that purpose, broad at the mouth, and narrow at the bottom, and set it in the aire vpon a barre, and throw water into it, and set a small vessell vnder it, wherein it falleth: "Being strained and set to boile vpon the fire, when the water is sodden away, the salt remaineth in the bottome of the pan." On both sides of the Riuer the Countrie was full of sowne fields, and there was store of Maiz. The Indians durst not come ouer where wee were: and when some of them shewed themselues, the souldiers that saw them called vnto them; then the Indians passed the Riuer, and came with them where the Gouernor was. He asked them for the Cacique. They said, that he remained quiet, but that he durst not shew himselfe. The Gouernour presently sent him word, that he should come vnto him, and bring him a guide and an interpretour for his iournie, if he made account of his friendship: and if he did not so, he would come himselfe to seeke him, and that it would be the worse for him. Hee waited three daies, and seeing he came not, he went to seeke him, and brought him prisoner with 150. of his men. He asked him whether hee had notice of any great Cacique, and which way the Countrie was best inhabited. Hee answered, that the best Countrie thereabout was a Prouince toward the South, a day and an halfes iournie, which was called Tulla; and that he could giue him a guide, but no interpretour, because the speech of that Countrie was different from his, and because he and his ancestors had alwaies warres with the Lords of that Prouince: therefore they had no commerce, nor vnderstood one anothers language. Immediatly the Gouernour with certaine horsemen, and 50. footemen, departed toward Tulla, to see if the Countrie were such, as hee might passe through it with all his companie: and assoone as hee arriued there, and was espied of the Indians, the Countrie gathered together, and assoone as 15. or 20. Indians could assemble themselues, they set vpon the Christians: and seeing that they did handle them shrewdly, and that the horsemen ouertooke them when they fled, they gat vp into the tops of their houses, and sought to defend themselues with their arrowes: and being beaten downe from one, they gat vp vpon another. And while our men pursued some, others set vpon them another way. Thus the skirmish lasted so long, that the horses were tired, and they could not make them runne. The Indians killed there one horse, and some were hurt. There were 15. Indians slaine there, and 40. women and boies were taken prisoners. For whatsoeuer Indian did shoot at them, if they could come by him, they put him to the sword. The Gouernour determined to returne toward Cayas, before the Indians had time to gather a head; and presently that euening, going part of the night to leaue Tulla, he lodged by the way, and the next day came to Cayas: and within three daies after he departed thence toward Tulla with all his companie: He carried the Cacique along with him, and among all his men, there was not one found that could vnderstand the speech of Tulla. He staied three daies by the way, and the day that he came thither, he found the towne abandoned: for the Indians durst not tarrie his comming. But assoone as they knew that the Gouernour was in Tulla, the first night about the morning watch, they came in two squadrons two seuerall waies, with their bowes and arrowes, and long staues like pikes. Assoone as they were descried, both horse and foot sallied out vpon them, where many of the Indians were slaine: And some Christians and horses were hurt: Some of the Indians were taken prisoners, whereof the Gouernour sent sixe to the Cacique, with their right hands and noses cut off: and sent him word, that if he came not to him to excuse and submit himselfe, that hee would come to seeke him, and that hee would doe the like to him, and as many of his as hee could find, as hee had done to those which hee had sent him: and gaue him three daies respit for to come. And this he gaue them to vnderstand by signes, as well as hee could, for there was no interpretour. At the three daies end, there came an Indian laden with Oxe hides. He came weeping with great sobs, and comming to the Gouernour cast himselfe downe at his feet: He tooke him vp, and he made a speech, but there was none that vnderstood him. The Gouernour by signes commanded him, to returne to the Cacique, and to will him, to send him an interpretor, which could vnderstand the men of Cayas. The next day came three Indians laden with oxe hides; and within three daies after came 20. Indians, and among them one that vnderstood them of Cayas: Who, after a long oration of excuses of the Cacique, and praises of the Gouernour, concluded with this, that he and the other were come thither on the Caciques behalfe, to see what his Lordship would command him to doe, for he was readie at his commandement. The Gouernour and all his companie were verie glad. For in no wise could they trauell without an interpretour. The Gouernour commanded him to be kept safe, and bad him tell the men that came with him, that they should returne to the Cacique, and signifie vnto him, that he pardoned him for that which was past, and thanked him much for his presents and interpretour, which he had sent him, and that he would bee glad to see him, and that he should come the next day to talke with him. The Cacique of Tulla. After three daies, the Cacique came, and 80. Indians with him: and himselfe and his men came weeping into the Camp, in token of obedience and repentance for the errour passed, after the manner of that Countrie: He brought a present of many oxe hides: which, because the Countrie was cold, were verie profitable, and serued for couerlets, because they were very soft, and wolled like sheepe. Not farre from thence toward the North were many oxen. Gomara Histor. Gener. cap. 215. The Christians saw them not, nor came into the Countrie where they were, because those parts were euil inhabited, and had small store of Maiz where they were bred. The Cacique of Tulla made an oration to the Gouernour, wherein he excused himselfe, and offered him his Countrie, subiects, and person. Aswell this Cacique as the others, and all those which came to the Gouernour on their behalfe, deliuered their message or speech in so good order, that no oratour could vtter the same more eloquentlie.

Chap. XXVII.

How the Gouernour went from Tulla to Autiamque, where he passed the winter.

The Gouernour enformed himselfe of all the Countrie round about: and vnderstood, that toward the West was a scattered dwelling, and that toward the Southeast were great townes, especially in a Prouince called Autiamque, tenne daies iournie from Tulla; which might be about 80. leagues; and that it was a plentifull Countrie of Maiz. And because winter came on, and they could not trauell two or three moneths in the yeere for cold, waters, and snow: and fearing, that if they should stay so long in the scattered dwelling, they could not be susteined; and also because the Indians said, that neere to Autiamque was a great water, and according to their relation, the Gouernour thought it was some arme of the Sea: And because he now desired to send newes of himselfe to Cuba, that some supplie of men and horses might be sent vnto him: (for it was aboue three yeeres, since Donna Isabella, which was in Hauana, or any other person in Christendome had heard of him, and by this time he had lost 250. men, and 150. horses) he determined to winter in Autiamque, and the next spring, to goe to the sea coast, and make two brigantines, and send one of them to Cuba, and the other to Nueua Espanna, and that which went in safetie, might giue newes of him: Hoping with the goods which he had in Cuba, to furnish himselfe againe, and to attempt the discouery and conquest toward the West: for he had not yet come where Cabeça de Vaca had been. Quipana, fiue daies iournie from Tulla. Thus hauing sent away the two Caciques of Cayas and Tulla, he tooke his iournie toward Autiamque: Hee trauelled fiue daies ouer very rough mountaines, and came to a towne called Quipana, where no Indians could be taken for the toughnesse of the Countrie: and the towne being betweene hilles, there was an ambush laid, wherewith they tooke two Indians; which told them, that Autiamque was sixe daies iournie from thence, and that their was another Prouince toward the South, eight daies iournie off, plentiful of Maiz, and very well peopled, which was called Guahate. But because Autiamque was neerer, and the most of the Indians agreed of it, the Gouernour made his iournie that way. In three daies he came to a towne called Anoixi. He sent a Captaine before with 30. horsemen, and 50. footemen, and tooke the Indians carelesse, hee tooke many men and women prisoners. Within two daies after the Gouernour came to another towne called Catamaya, and lodged in the fields of the towne. Two Indians came with a false message from the Cacique to know his determination. Hee bad them tell their Lord, that hee should come and speake with him. The Indians returned and came no more, nor any other message from the Cacique. The next day the Christians went to the towne, which was without people: they tooke as much Maiz as they needed. That day they lodged in a wood, and the next day they came to Autiamque. Autiamque sixe daies iournie from Quipana. They found much Maiz laid vp in store, and French beanes, and walnuts, and prunes, great store of all sorts. They tooke some Indians which were gathering together the stuffe which their wiues had hidden. This was a champion Countrie, and well inhabited. The Gouernour lodged in the best part of the towne, and commanded presently to make a fense of timber round about the Campe distant from the houses, that the Indians might not hurt them without by fire. And measuring the ground by pases, hee appointed euery one his part to doe according to the number of Indians which he had: presently the timber was brought by them: and in three daies there was an inclosure made of very hie and thicke posts thrust into the ground, and many railes laid acrosse. Hard by this towne passed a Riuer, that came out of the Prouince of Cayas: and aboue and beneath it was very well peopled. Thither came Indians on the Caciques behalfe with a present of mantles and skinnes; and an halting Cacique, subiect to the Lord of Autiamque, Lord of a towne called Tietiquaquo, came many times to visit the Gouernour, and to bring him presents of such as hee had. The Cacique of Autiamque sent to know of the Gouernour, how long time hee meant to stay in this Countrie? And vnderstanding that he meant to stay aboue three daies, he neuer sent any more Indians, nor any other message, but conspired with the lame Cacique to rebell. Diuers inrodes were made, wherein there were many men and women taken, and the lame Cacique among the rest. The Gouernour respecting the seruices which he had receiued of him, reprehended and admonished him, and set him at libertie, and gaue him two Indians to carrie him in a chaire vpon their shoulders. The Cacique of Autiamque desiring to thrust the Gouernour out of his Countrie, set spies ouer him. And an Indian comming one night to the gate of the inclosure, a soldier that watched espied him, and stepping behind the gate, as he came in, he gaue him such a thrust, that he fell downe; and so he carried him to the Gouernour: and as he asked him wherefore he came, not being able to speake, hee fell downe dead. Great prouidence. The night following the Gouernour commanded a souldiour to giue the alarme, and to say that he had seene Indians, to see how ready they would be to answere the alarme. And hee did so sometimes as well there, as in other places, when he thought that his men were carelesse, and reprehended such as were slacke. And as well for this cause, as in regard of doing their dutie, when the alarme was giuen, euery one sought to be the first that should answere. They staied in Autiamque three moneths with great plentie of Maiz, French beanes, Walnuts, Prunes, and Conies: which vntill that time they knew not how to catch. And in Autiamque the Indians taught them how to take them: which was, with great springes, which lifted vp their feete from the ground: And the snare was made with a strong string, whereunto was fastened a knot of a cane, which ran close about the neck of the conie, because they should not gnaw the string. They tooke many in the fields of Maiz, especiallie when it freesed or snowed. The Christians staied there one whole moneth so inclosed with snow, that they went not out of the towne: and when they wanted firewood, the Gouernour with his horsemen going and coming many times to the wood, which was two crossebow shot from the towne, made a pathway, whereby the footemen went for wood. In this meane space, some Indians which went loose, killed many conies with their giues, and with arrowes. These conies were of two sorts, some were like those of Spaine, and the other of the same colour and fashion, and as big as great Hares, longer, and hauing greater loines.

Chap. XXVIII.

How the Gouernour went from Autiamque to Nilco, and from thence to Guacoya.

Vpon Monday the sixt of March 1542, the Gouernour departed from Autiamque to seeke Nilco, which the Indians said was neere the Great riuer, with determination to come to the Sea, and procure some succour of men and horses: for hee had now but three hundred men of warre, and fortie horses, and some of them lame, which did nothing but helpe to make vp the number: and for want of iron they had gone aboue a yeere vnshod: and because they were vsed to it in the plaine countrie, it did them no great harme. *The death of Iohn Ortiz, and the great misse of him being their interpretour.* Iohn Ortiz died in Autiamque; which grieued the Gouernour very much: because that without an Interpretour hee feared to enter farre into the land, where he might be lost. From thence forward a youth that was taken in Cutifachiqui did serue for Interpretour, which had by that time learned somewhat of the Christians language. The death of Iohn Ortiz was so great a mischiefe for the discouering inward, or going out of the land, that to learne of the Indians, that which in foure words hee declared, they needed a whole day with the youth: and most commonly hee vnderstood quite contrarie that which was asked him: whereby it often happened that the way that they went one day, and sometimes two or three daies, they turned backe, and went astray through the wood here and there. The Gouernour spent ten daies in trauelling from Autiamque to a prouince called Ayays; and came to a towne that stood neere the Riuer that passeth by Cayas and Autiamque. There hee commanded a barge to be made, wherewith he passed the Riuer. *Great snow about the twentieth of March.* When he had passed the Riuer there fell out such weather, that foure daies he could not trauell for snow. Assoone as it gaue ouer snowing, hee went three daies iourney through a Wildernesse, and a countrie so low, and so full of lakes and euill waies, that hee trauelled one time a whole day in water, sometimes knee deepe, sometimes to the stirrup, and sometimes they swamme. He came to a towne called Tutelpinco, abandoned, and without Maiz: there passed by it a lake, that entered into the riuer, which carried a great streame and force of water. Fiue Christians passing ouer it in a periagua, which the Gouernour had sent with a Captaine, the periagua ouerset: some tooke hold on it, some on the trees that were in the lake. One Francis Sebastian, an honest man of Villa noua de Barca Rota, was drowned there. The Gouernour went a whole day along the lake seeking passage, and could finde none, nor any way that did passe to the other side. Comming againe at night to the towne hee found two peaceable Indians, which shewed him the passage, and which way hee was to goe. There they made of canes and of the timber of houses thatched with canes, rafts wherewith they passed the lake. They trauelled three daies, and came to a towne of the territorie of Nilco, called Tianto. There they tooke thirtie Indians, and among them two principall men of this towne. The Gouernour sent a Captaine with horsemen and footmen before to Nilco, because the Indians might haue no time to carrie away the provision. They passed through three or foure great townes; and in the towne where the Cacique was resident, which was two leagues from the place where the Gouernour remained, they found many Indians with their bowes and arrowes, in manner as though they would haue staied to fight, which did compasse the towne; and assoone as they saw the Christians come neere them without misdoubting them, they set the Caciques house on fire, and fled ouer a lake that passed neere the towne, through which the horses could not passe. The next day being Wednesday the 29. of March the Gouernour came to Nilco: he lodged with all his men in the Caciques towne, which stood in a plaine field, which was inhabited for the space of a quarter of a league: and within a league and halfe a league were other very great townes, wherein was great store of Maiz, of French beanes, of Walnuts, and Prunes. *The best Countrie of Florida.* This was the best inhabited countrie, that was seene in Florida, and had most store of Maiz, except Coca, and Apalache. There came to the campe an Indian, accompanied with others, and in the Caciques name gaue the Gouernour a mantle of Marterns skinnes, and a cordon of perles. The Gouernour gaue him a few small Margarites, which are certaine beades much esteemed in Peru, and other things, wherewith he was very well contented. He promised to returne within two daies, but neuer came againe: but on the contrarie the Indians came by night in canoes, and carried away all the Maiz they could, and made them cabins on the other side of the Riuer in the thickest of the wood, because they might flee if wee should goe to seeke them. The Gouernour seeing hee came not at the time appointed, commanded an ambush to be laid about certaine store-houses neere the lake, whither the Indians came for Maiz: where they tooke two Indians, who told the Gouernour, that hee which came to visit him, was not the Cacique, but was sent by him vnder pretence to spie whether the Christians were carelesse, and whether they determined to settle in that country or to goe forward. Presently the Gouernour sent a Captaine with footmen and horsemen ouer the riuer; and in their passage they were descried of the Indians, and therefore he could take but tenne or twelue men and women, with whom hee returned to the campe. This Riuer which passed by Nilco, was that which passed by Cayas and Autiamque, and fell into Rio grande, or the Great Riuer, which passed by Pachaha and Aquixo neere vnto the prouince of Guachoya: and the Lord thereof came vp the Riuer in canoes to make warre with him of Nilco. On his behalf there came an Indian to the Gouernour and said vnto him, That he was his seruant, and prayed him so to hold him, and that within two daies hee would come to kisse his Lordships hands: and at the time appointed he came with some of his principal Indians, which accompanied him, and with words of great offers and courtesie hee gaue the Gouernour a present of many mantles and Deeres skinnes. The Gouernour gaue him some other things in recompense, and honoured him much. Hee asked him what townes there were downe the Riuer? He answered that he knew none other but his owne: and on the other side of the Riuer a prouince of a Cacique called Quigalta. So hee tooke his leaue of the Gouernour and went to his owne towne. Within few daies the Gouernour determined to goe to Guachoya, to learne there whether the Sea were neere, or whether there were any habitation neere, where hee might relieue his companie, while the brigantines were making, which he meant to send to the land of the Christians. As he passed the Riuer of Nilco, there came in canoes Indians of Guachoya vp the streame, and when they saw him, supposing that he came to seeke them to doe them some hurt, they returned downe the Riuer, and informed the Cacique thereof: who with all his people, spoiling the towne of all that they could carrie away, passed that night ouer to the other side of Rio grande, or the Great Riuer. The Gouernour sent a Captaine with fiftie men in sixe canoes downe the Riuer, and went himselfe by land with the rest: hee came to Guachoya vpon Sunday the 17. of April: he lodged in the towne of the Cacique, which was inclosed about, and seated a crossebow shot distant from the Riuer. Here the Riuer is called Tamaliseu, and in Nilco Tapatu, and in Coça Mico, and in the port or mouth Ri.

Foure names of Rio grande.

Chap. XXIX.

Of the message which the Gouernour sent to Quigalta, and of the answere which he returned; and of the things which happened in this time.

As soone as the Gouernour come to Guachoya, hee sent Iohn Danusco with as many men as could goe in the canoes vp the Riuer. For when they came downe from Nilco, they saw on the other side the Riuer new cabins made. Iohn Danusco went and brought the canoes loden with Maiz, French beanes, Prunes, and many loaues made of the substance of prunes. That day came an Indian to the Gouernour from the Cacique of Guachoya, and said, that his Lord would come the next day. The next day they saw many canoes come vp the Riuer, and on the other side of the great Riuer, they assembled together in the space of an houre: they consulted whether they should come or not; and at length concluded to come, and crossed the Riuer. In them came the Cacique of Guachoya, and brought with him manie Indians with great store of Fish, Dogges, Deeres skinnes, and Mantles: And assoone as they landed, they went to the lodging of the Gouernour, and presented him their gifts, and the Cacique vttered these words:

Mightie and excellent Lord, I beseech your Lordship to pardon mee the errour which I committed in absenting my selfe, and not tarrying in this towne to haue receiued and serued your Lordship; since, to obtaine this opportunitie of time, was, and is as much as a great victorie to me. But I feared that, which I needed not to haue feared, and so did that which was not reason to do; But as haste maketh waste, and I remoued without deliberation; so, as soone as I thought on it, I determined not to follow the opinion of the foolish, which is, to continue in their errour; but to imitate the wise and discreet, in changing my counsell, and so I came to see what your Lordship will command me to doe, that I may serue you in all things that are in my power.

The Gouernour receiued him with much ioy, and gaue him thankes for his present and offer. He asked him, whether hee had any notice of the Sea. Hee answered, no, nor of any townes downe the Riuer on that side; saue that two leagues from thence was one towne of a principall Indian a subiect of his; and on the other side of the Riuer, three daies iourney from thence downe the Riuer, was the Prouince of Quigalta, which was the greatest Lord that was in that Countrie. The Gouernour thought that the Cacique lied vnto him, to rid him out of his owne townes, and sent Iohn Danusco with eight horsemen downe the Riuer, to see what habitation there was, and to informe himselfe, if there were any notice of the Sea. Hee trauelled eight daies, and at his returne hee said, that in all that time he was not able to go aboue 14. or 15. leagues, because of the great creekes that came out of the Riuer, and groues of canes, and thicke woods that were along the banks of the Riuer, and that hee had found no habitation. The Gouernor falleth sick of thought. The Gouernour fell into great dumps to see how hard it was to get to the Sea: and worse, because his men and horses euery day diminished, being without succour to sustaine themselues in the country: and with that thought he fell sick. But before he tooke his bed hee sent an Indian to the Cacique at Quigalta to tell him, that hee was the Childe of the Sunne, and that all the way that hee came all men obeyed and serued him, that he requested him to accept of his friendship, and come vnto him; for he would be very glad to see him; and in signe of loue and obedience to bring something with him of that which in his countrie was most esteemed. The Cacique answered by the same Indian:

A most wittie and stout answere of the Cacique of Quigalta. That whereas he said he was the Child of the Sunne, if he would drie vp the Riuer he would beleeue him: and touching the rest, that he was wont to visit none; but rather that all those of whom he had notice did visit him, serued, obeyed and paid him tributes willingly or perforce: therefore if hee desired to see him, it were best he should come thither: that if hee came in peace, he would receiue him with speciall good will; and if in warre, in like manner hee would attend him in the towne where he was, and that for him or any other hee would not shrinke one foote backe.

By that time the Indian returned with this answere, the Gouernour had betaken himselfe to bed, being euill handled with feuers, and was much agrieued, that he was not in case to passe presently the Riuer and to seeke him, to see if he could abate that pride of his, considering the Riuer went now very strongly in those parts; for it was neere halfe a league broad, and 16. fathomes deep, and very furious, and ranne with a great current; and on both sides there were many Indians, and his power was not now so great, but that hee had need to helpe himselfe rather by slights then by force. The Indians of Guachoya came euery day with fish in such numbers, that the towne was full of them. The Cacique said, that on a certaine night hee of Quigalta would come to giue battell to the Gouernour. Which the Gouernour imagined that he had deuised, to driue him out of his countrey, and commanded him to bee put in hold: and that night and all the rest, there was good watch kept. Hee asked him wherefore Quigalta came not?

He said that hee came, but that he saw him prepared, and therefore durst not giue the attempt: and hee was earnest with him to send his Captaines ouer the Riuer, and that he would aide him with many men to set vpon Quigalta. The Gouernour told him that assoone as he was recouered, himselfe would seeke him out. And seeing how many Indians came daily to the towne, and what store of people was in that countrie, fearing they should al conspire together and plot some treason against him; and because the towne had some open gaps which were not made an end of inclosing, besides the gates which they went in and out by: because the Indians should not thinke he feared them, he let them all alone vnrepaired; and commanded the horsemen to be appointed to them, and to the gates: and all night the horsemen went the round; and two and two of euery squadron rode about, and visited the skouts that were without the towne in their standings by the passages, and the crossebowmen that kept the canoes in the Riuer. And because the Indians should stand in feare of him, hee determined to send a Captaine to Nilco, for those of Guachoya had told him that it was inhabited; that by vsing them cruelly, neither the one nor the other should presume to assaile him; and hee sent Nunnez de Touar with fifteene horsemen, and Iohn de Guzman Captaine of the footmen with his companie, in canoes vp the Riuer. The Cacique of Guachoya sent for many canoes and many warlike Indians to goe with the Christians: and the Captaine of the Christians, called Nunnez de Touar, went by land with his horsemen, and two leagues before he came to Nilco hee staied for Iohn de Guzman, and in that place they passed the Riuer by night: the horsemen came first, and in the morning by breake of day in sight of the towne they lighted vpon a spie; which assoone as he perceiued the Christians, crying out amaine fled to the towne to giue warning. Nunnez de Touar and his companie made such speed, that before the Indians of the towne could fully come out, they were vpon them: it was champion ground that was inhabited, which was about a quarter of a league. Five or sixe thousand people in Nilco. There were about fiue or sixe thousand people in the towne: and, as many people came out of the houses, and fled from one house to another, and many Indians came flocking together from all parts, there was neuer a horseman that was not alone among many. The Captaine had commanded that they should not spare the life of any male. Their disorder was so great, that there was no Indian that shot an arrow at any Christian. The shreekes of women and children were so great, that they made the eares deafe of those that followed them. There were slaine an hundred Indians, little more or lesse: and many were wounded with great wounds, whom they suffered to escape to strike a terror in the rest that were not there. There were some so cruell and butcherlike, that they killed old and young, and all that they met, though they made no resistance: and those which presumed of themselues for their valour, and were taken for such, brake through the Indians, bearing downe many with their stirrops and brests of their horses; and some they wounded with their lances, and so let them goe: and when they saw any youth or woman they tooke them, and deliuered them to the footmen. "These mens sinnes by Gods permission lighted on their own heads: who, because they would seeme valiant, became cruell; shewing themselues extreme cowards in the sight of all men, when as most neede of valour was required, and, afterward[1] they came to a shameful death." Of the Indians of Nilco were taken prisoners, fourescore women and children, and much spoile. The Indians of Guachoya kept back before they came at the towne, and staied without, beholding the successe of the Christians with the men of Nilco. And when they saw them put to flight, and the horsemen busie in killing of them, they hastened to the houses to rob, and filled their canoes with the spoile of the goods; and returned to Guachoya before the Christians; and wondring much at the sharpe dealing which they had seene them vse toward the Indians of Nilco, they told their Cacique all that had passed with great astonishment.

[1] Chap. 37.

Chap. XXX.

Of the death of the Adelantado Fernando de Soto: And how Aluarado was elected Gouernour in his stead.

The Gouernour felt in himselfe that the houre approched, wherein hee was to leaue this present life, and called for the Kings officers, Captaines and principall persons, to whom he made a speech, saying:

That now he was to goe to giue an account before the presence of God of all his life past: and since it pleased him to take him in such a time, and that the time was come that he knew his death, that he his most vnworthie seruant did yeeld him many thankes therefore; and desired all that were present and absent (whom he confessed himselfe to be much beholding vnto for their singular vertues, loue and loyaltie, which himselfe had well tried in the trauels, which they had suffered, which alwaies in his mind he did hope to satisfie and reward, when it should please God to giue him rest, with more prosperitie of his estate,) that they would pray to God for him, that for his mercie he would forgiue him his sinnes, and receiue his soule into eternall glorie: and that they would quit and free him of the charge which hee had ouer them, and ought vnto them all, and that they would pardon him for some wrongs which they might haue receiued of him: And to auoid some diuision, which vpon his death might fall out vpon the choice of his successour, he requested them to elect a principall person, and able to gouerne, of whom all should like well; and when he was elected, they should sweare before him to obey him: and that he would thanke them very much in so doing; because the griefe that he had, would somewhat be asswaged, and the paine that he felt, because he left them in so great confusion, to wit, in leauing them in a strange Countrie, where they knew not where they were.

Baltasar de Gallegos answered in the name of all the rest: And first of all comforting him, he set before his eies how short the life of this world was, and with how many troubles and miseries it is accompanied, and how God shewed him a singular fauor which soonest left it: telling him many other things fit for such a time. And for the last point, that since it pleased God to take him to himselfe, although his death did justly grieue them much, yet as wel he, as al the rest, ought of necessitie to conforme themselues to the will of God. And touching the Gouernour which he commanded they should elect, he besought him, that it would please his Lordship to name him which he thought fit, and him they would obey. And presently he named Luys de Moscoso de Aluarado his Captaine generall. And presently he was sworne by all that were present and elected for Gouernour. *The death of Don Ferdinando de Soto the 21. of May, 1542 at Guacoya.* The next day, being the 21. of May, 1542. departed out of this life, the valorous, virtuous, and valiant Captaine, Don Fernando de Soto, Gouernour of Cuba, and Adelantado of Florida: whom fortune aduanced, as it vseth to doe others, that hee might haue the higher fal. He departed in such a place, and at such time, as in his sicknesse he had but little comfort; and the danger wherein all his people were of perishing in that Countrie, which appeared before their eies, was cause sufficient, why euery one of them had need of comfort, and why they did not visit nor accompanie him as they ought to haue done. Luys de Moscoso determined to conceale his death from the Indians, because Ferdinando de Soto had made them beleeue, That the Christians were immortall; and also because they tooke him to be hardie, wise, and valiant: and if they should know that he was dead, they would bee bold to set vpon the Christians, though they liued peaceablie by them. *A wittie stratagem.* In regard of their disposition, and because they were nothing constant, and beleeued all that was tolde them, the Adelantado made them beleeue, that he knew some things that passed in secret among themselues, without their knowledge, how, or in what manner he came by them: and that the figure which appeared in a glasse, which he shewed them, did tell him whatsoeuer they practised and went about: and therefore neither in word nor deed durst they attempt any thing that might bee preiudiciall vnto him.

Assoone as he was dead, Luis de Moscoso commanded to put him secretly in an house, where hee remained three daies: and remoouing him from thence, commanded him to bee buried in the night at one of the gates of the towne within the wall. And as the Indians had seene him sick, and missed him, so did they suspect what might bee. And passing by the place where hee was buried, seeing the earth mooued, they looked and spake one to another. Luys de Moscoso vnderstanding of it, commanded him to be taken vp, by night, and to cast a great deale of sand into the mantles, wherein he was winded vp, wherein hee was carried in a canoe, and throwne into the middest of the Riuer. The Cacique of Guachoya inquired for him, demanding what was become of his brother and Lord, the Gouernour: Luys de Moscoso told him, that hee was gon to heauen, as many other times hee did: and because hee was to stay there certaine daies hee had left him in his place. The Cacique thought with himselfe that he was dead; and commanded two young and well proportioned Indians to be brought thither; *This is also the costome of the old Tartars.* and said, that the vse of that Countrie was, when any Lord died, to kill Indians to wait vpon him, and serue him by the way: and for that purpose by his commandement were those come thither: and prayed Luys de Moscoso to command them to be beheaded, that they might attend and serue his Lord and brother. Luys de Moscoso told him, that the Gouernour was not dead, but gone to heauen, and that of his owne Christian souldiers, he had taken such as he needed, to serue him, and praied him to command those Indians to be loosed and not to vse any such bad custome from thencefoorth: straightway hee commanded them to be loosed, and to get them home to their houses. And one of them would not goe; saying, that hee would not serue him, that without desert had judged him to death, but that hee would serue him as long as hee liued, which had saued his life. Seven hundred hogges. Luys de Moscoso caused all the goods of the Gouernor to be sold at an outcrie: to wit, two men slaues, and two women slaues, and three horses, and 700. hogges. For euery slaue or horse, they gaue two or three thousand ducats: which were to be paied at the first melting of gold or siluer, or at the diuision of their portion of inheritance. And they entered into bonds, though in the Countrie there was not wherewith, to pay it within a yeere after, and put in sureties for the same. Such as in Spaine had no goods to bind, gaue two hundred ducats for an hog, giuing assurance after the same maner. Those which had any goods in Spaine, bought with more feare, and bought the lesse. From that time forward, most of the companie had swine, and brought them vp, and fed vpon them; and obserued Fridaies and Saturdaies, and the euenings of feasts, which before they did not. For sometimes in two or three moneths they did eate no flesh, and whensoeuer they could come by it, they did eate it.

Chap. XXXI.

How the Gouernour Luys de Moscoso departed from Guachoya, and went to Chaguate; and thence to Aguacay.

Some were glad of the death of Don Ferdinando de Soto, holding for certaine, that Luys de Moscoso (which was giuen to his ease) would rather desire to be among the Christians at rest, then to continue the labours of the warre in subduing and discouering of Countries; whereof they were alreadie wearie, seeing the small profit that insued thereof. The Gouernour commanded the Captaines and principall persons to meet to consult and determine what they should doe. And being informed what peopled habitation was round about, he vnderstood that to the West, the Countrie was most inhabited, and that downe the Riuer beyond Quigalta was vninhabited, and had little store of food. He desired them all, that euerie one would giue his opinion in writing, and set his hand to it: that they might resolue by generall consent, whether they should goe downe the Riuer, or enter into the maine land. *Their general resolution to trauell by land Westward.* All were of opinion, that it was best to go by land toward the West, because Nueua Espanna was that way: holding the voyage by sea more dangerous, and of greater hazard, because they could make no ship of any strength to abide a storme, neither had they Master, nor Pilot, Compasse, nor Chart, neither knew they how farre the sea was off, nor had any notice of it: nor whether the Riuer did make any great turning into the land, or had any great fall the rocks, where all of them might be cast away. And some which had seene the sea-chart, did find, that from the place where they were by the sea coast to Noua Espanna, might bee 400. leagues, little more or lesse; and said, that though they went somewhat about by land in seeking a peopled Countrie, if some great wildernesse which they could not passe did not hinder them, by spending that sommer in trauell, finding prouision to passe the winter in some peopled Countrie, that the next summer after they might come to some Christian land, and that it might fortune in their trauel by land to find some rich Countrie, where they might doe themselves good. The Gouernour, although he desired to get out of Florida in shorter time, seeing the inconueniences they laid before him in trauelling by sea, determined to follow that which seemed good to them all. On Monday the fifth of Iune, he departed from Guachoya. The Cacique gaue him a guide to Chaguate, and staied at home in his owne towne. They passed through a prouince called Catalte: and hauing passed a wildernesse of sixe daies iournie, the twentieth day of the moneth he came to Chaguate. The Cacique of this Prouince had visited the Gouernour Don Ferdinando de Soto at Autiamque, whither he brought him presents of skinnes, and mantles and salt. And a day before Luys de Moscoso came to his towne, we lost a Christian that was sicke; which hee suspected that the Indians had slaine. Hee sent the Cacique word, that he should command his people to seeke him vp, and send him vnto him, and that he would hold him, as he did, for his friend: and if he did not, that neither he, nor his, should escape his hands, and that hee would set his Countrie on fire. Presently the Cacique came vnto him, and brought a great present of mantles and skinnes, and the Christian that was lost, and made this speech following:

Right excellent Lord, I would not deserue that conceit which you had of me, for all the treasure of the world. What inforced me to goe to visit and serue the excellent Lord Gouernour your father in Autiamque, which you should haue remembred, where I offered my selfe with all loyaltie, faith and loue, during my life to serue and obey him? What then could be the cause, I hauing receiued fauours of him, and neither you nor he hauing done me any wrong, that should mooue me to doe the thing, which I ought not? Beleeue this of mee, that neither wrong, nor any worldly interest, was able to make me to haue done it, nor shall be able to blind me. But as in this life it is a naturall course, that after one pleasure, many sorrowes doe follow: so by your indignation, fortune would moderate the ioy, which my heart conceiueth with your presence; and that I should erre, where I thought surest to haue hit the marke; in harboring this Christian which was lost, and vsing him in such manner, as he may tell himselfe, thinking that herin I did you service, with purpose to deliuer him vnto you in Chaguate, and to serue you to the vttermost of my power. If I deserue punishment for this, I will receiue it at your hands, as from my Lord, as if it were a fauour. For the loue which I did beare to the excellent Gouernour, and which I beare to you hath no limit. And like as you giue me chastisement, so will you also shew me fauour. And that which now I craue of you is this, to declare your will vnto me, and those things, wherein I may bee able to doe you the most and best seruice.

The Gouernour answered him, that because he did not find him in that towne, hee was incensed against him, thinking he had absented himselfe, as others had done: But seeing he now knew his loyaltie and loue, he would alwaies hold him as a brother, and fauour him in all his affaires. The Cacique went with him to the towne where he resided, which was a daies iournie from thence. Salt made of salt springs of water. They passed through a smal town, where there was a lake, where the Indians made salt: and the Christians made some one day while they rested there, of a brackish water, which sprang neere the towne in ponds like fountaines. The Gouernour staied in Chaguate sixe daies. There he was informed of the habitation that was toward the West. They told him, that three daies iournie from thence was a Prouince called Aguacay. The day that he departed from Chaguate, a Christian, called Francisco de Guzman, the base sonne of a Gentleman of Siuill, staied behind, and went to the Indians, with an Indian woman which he kept as his concubine, for feare he should be punished for gaming debts, that he did owe. The Gouernor had trauelled two daies before he missed him; hee sent the Cacique word to seeke him vp, and to send him to Aguacay, whither he trauelled: which hee did not performe. From the Cacique of Aguacay, before they came into the Countrie, there met him on the way 15. Indians with a present of skinnes, fish and rosted venison. The Gouernour came to his towne on Wednesday, the fourth of Iulie. He found the towne without people, and lodged in it: he staied there about a day; during which, he made some roades, and tooke many men and women. There they had knowledge of the South Sea. Here there was great store of salt made of sand, which they gather in a vaine of ground like peeble stones. And it was made as they make salt in Cayas.

Chap. XXXII.

How the Gouernour went from Aguacay to Naguatex, and what happened vnto him.

The same day that the Gouernour departed from Aguacay he lodged in a small towne subiect to the Lord of that prouince. The Campe pitched hard by a lake of salt water; and that euening they made some salt there. The day following hee lodged betweene two mountaines in a thinne groue of wood. The next day hee came to a small towne called Pato. The fourth day after his departure from Aguacay he came to the first habitation of a prouince called Amaye. There an Indian was taken, which said that from thence to Naguatex was a day and a halfes iourney: which they trauelled, finding all the way inhabited places. Hauing passed the peopled countrie of Amaye, on Saturday the 20. of Iulie they pitched their Campe at noone betweene Amaye and Naguatex along the corner of a groue of very faire trees. In the same place certaine Indians were discouered, which came to view them. The horsemen went out to them, and killed six, and tooke two; whom the Gouernour asked, wherefore they came? They said, to know what people hee had, and what order they kept; and that the Cacique of Naguatex their Lord had sent them, and that he, with other Caciques, which came to aide him, determined that day to bid him battell. While they were occupied in these questions and answeres, there came many Indians by two waies in two squadrons: and when they saw they were descried, giuing a great crie they assaulted the Christians each squadron by it selfe: but seeing what resistance the Christians made them, they turned their backes and betooke themselues to flight, in which many of them lost their liues: and most of the horsemen following them in chase, carelesse of the Camp, other two squadrons of Indians, which lay in ambush, set vpon the Christians that were in the Campe, which also they resisted, who also had their reward as the first. After the flight of the Indians, and that the Christians were retired, they heard a great noise a crossebow shot from the place where they were. The Gouernour sent twelue horsemen to see what it was. They found six Christians, foure footemen and two horsemen, among many Indians; the horsemen defending the footemen with great labour. These being of them that chased the first two squadrons, had lost themselues, and comming to recouer the Campe fell among those with whom they were fighting: and so they, and those that came to succour them, slew many of the Indians, and brought one aliue to the Campe: whom the Gouernour examined, who they were that came to bid him battell. He told him, that they were the Cacique of Naguatex, and of Amaye, and another of a prouince called Hacanac, a Lord of great Countries and many subiects: and that the Cacique of Naguatex came for Captaine and chiefest of them all. The Gouernour commanded his right arme and nose to be cut off, and sent him to the Cacique of Naguatex, charging him to tell him, that the next day hee would be in his countrey to destroy him; and if hee would withstand his entrance, hee should stay for him. That night he lodged there; and the next day hee came to the habitation of Naguatex, which was very scattering: he inquired where the Caciques chiefe towne was? They told him that it was on the other side of a Riuer, that passed thereby: hee trauelled thitherward, and came vnto it: and on the other side he saw many Indians, that taried for him, making shew as though they would defend the passage. And because hee knew not whether it could bee waded, nor where the passage was; and that some Christians and horses were hurt; that they might haue time to recouer, he determined to rest certaine daies in the towne where he was. So hee pitched his campe a quarter of a league from the Riuer, because the weather was very hot, neere vnto the towne, in a thinne groue of very faire and hie trees neere a brookes side: and in that place were certaine Indians taken; whom hee examined, whether the Riuer were wadeable or no? They said, yea, at some times, and in some places. August. They passe the Riuer. Within ten daies after he sent two Captaines with fifteene horsemen a peece vpward and downe the Riuer with Indians to shew them where they should goe ouer, to see what habitation was on the other side: And the Indians withstood them both, defending the passage of the Riuer as farre as they were able, but they passed in despite of them: and on the other side of the Riuer they saw great store of victuals; and with these newes returned to the Camp.

Chap. XXXIII.

How the Cacique of Naguatex came to visite the Gouernour: and how the Gouernour departed from Naguatex and came to Nondacao.

The Gouernour sent an Indian from Naguatex where hee lay, to command the Cacique to come to serue and obey him, and that hee would forgiue him all that was past; and if he came not, that he would seeke him, and giue him such punishment as he had deserued for that which he had done against him. Within two daies the Indian returned, and said that the Cacique would come the next day: which, the same day when he came, sent many Indians before him, among whom there were some principall men: hee sent them to see what countenance they found in the Gouernour, to resolue with himselfe whether hee should goe or not. The Indians let him vnderstand, that he was comming, and went away presently: and the Cacique came within two houres accompanied with many of his men: they came all in a ranke one before another on both sides, leauing a lane in the middest where hee came. Tulla not far from Naguatex, Eastward. They came where the Gouernour was, all of them weeping after the manner of Tulla, which was not farre from thence toward the East. The Cacique made his due obedience, and this speech following:

Right high and mightie Lord, whom all the world ought to serue and obey, I was bold to appeare before your Lordship, hauing committed so heinous and abominable an act, as only for me to haue imagined, deserued to be punished; trusting in your greatnes, that although I deserue to obtaine no pardon, yet for your owne sake only you will vse clemencie toward me, considering how small I am in comparison of your Lordship; and not to think vpon my weaknesses, which, to my griefe and for my greater good, I haue knowne. And I beleeue that you and yours are immortall; and that your Lordship is Lord of the land of nature, seeing that you subdue all things, and they obey you, euen the very hearts of men. For when I beheld the slaughter and destruction of my men in the battell, which, through mine ignorance, and the counsell of a brother of mine, which died in the same, I gaue your Lordship, presently I repented me in my heart of the error, which I had committed; and desired to serue and obey you: and to this end I come, that your Lordship may chastise and command mee as your owne.

The Gouernour answered him, that he forgaue him all which was past, that from thenceforth hee should do his dutie, and that he would hold him for his friend, and that he would fauour him in all things. *The Riuer growne vnpassable in August, at Naguatex.* Within foure daies hee departed thence, and comming to the Riuer he could not passe, because it was growne very bigge; which seemed to him a thing of admiration, being at that time that it was, and since it had not rained a moneth before. The Indians said, that it increased many times after that manner without raining in all the countrie. *Coniectures of a Sea to the Northward.* It was supposed, that it might be the tide that came into it. It was learned that the flood came alway from aboue, and that the Indians of all that countrie had no knowledge of the Sea. The Gouernour returned vnto the place where he had lodged before: and vnderstanding within eight daies after that the Riuer was passable, he departed. He passed ouer and found the towne without people: he lodged in the field, and sent the Cacique word to come vnto him, and to bring him a guide to goe forward. And some daies being past, seeing the Cacique came not, nor sent any bodie, hee sent two Captaines sundrie waies to burne the townes, and to take such Indians as they could finde: They burnt great store of victuals, and took many Indians. The Cacique seeing the hurt that he receiued in his countrie, sent six principall Indians with three men for guides which knew the language of the countrie, through which the Gouernour was to passe. Hee departed presently from Naguatex, and within three daies iourney came to a towne of foure or fiue houses, which belonged to the Cacique of that prouince, which is called Nissoone: it was euill inhabited and had little Maiz. Two daies iourney forward the guides which guided the Gouernour, if they were to goe Westward, guided him to the East; and sometimes went vp and downe through very great woods out of the way. The Gouernour commanded them to bee hanged vpon a tree: and a woman that they tooke in Nissoone guided him, and went backe againe to seeke the way. In two daies he came to another miserable towne called Lacane: an Indian was taken in that place, that said, that the countrie of Nondacao was a countrie of great habitation, and the houses scattering the one from the other, as they vse to bee in mountains, and had great store of Maiz. The Cacique came with his men weeping, like them of Naguatex: for this is their vse in token of obedience: hee made him a present of much fish, and offered to doe what he would command him. Hee tooke his leaue, and gaue him a guide to the prouince of Soacatino.

Chap. XXXIV.

How the Gouernour went from Nondacao to Soacatino and Guasco, and passed through a desert, from whence, for want of a guide, and an interpretour, he returned to Nilco.

The Gouernour departed from Nondacao toward Soacatino, and in fiue daies iournie came to a Prouince called Aays. The Indians which inhabited it, had no notice of the Christians: but assoone as they saw that they entred into their country, they assembled themselues: and as they came together 50. or 100. they came foorth to fight: while some fought, others came and charged our men another way, and while they followed some, others followed them. The fight lasted the greatest part of the day, till they came to their towne. Some horses and men were wounded, but not to any hurt of their trauelling: for there was no wound that was dangerous. There was a great spoile made of the Indians. That day that the Gouernour departed from thence, the Indian that guided him said, that in Nondacao he had heard say, that the Indians of Soacatino had seene other Christians, whereof they all were very glad: thinking it might be true, and that they might haue entred into those parts by Nueua Espanna; and that if it were so, it was in their owne hand to goe out of Florida, if they found nothing of profit: for they feared they should lose themselues in some wildernes. This Indian led him two daies out of the way. The Gouernour commanded to torture him. He said, that the Cacique of Nondacao, his Lord, had commanded him to guide them so, because they were his enemies, and that hee was to doe as his Lord commanded him. The Gouernour commanded him to be cast to the dogs: and another guided him to Soacatino, whither hee came the day following. It was a verie poore Countrie: there was great want of Maiz in that place. Hee asked the Indians, whether they knew of any other Christians. They said, that a little from thence toward the South they heard they were. 20. daies trauell toward the South. He trauelled 20. daies through a Countrie euill inhabited, where they suffered great scarcitie and trouble. For that little Maiz which the Indians had, they had hidden and buried in the woods, where the Christians, after they were well wearied with their trauell, at the end of their iournie went to seeke by digging what they should eat. Guasco: here they found some Turkie stones and mantles of cotton wooll. Chap. 35. At last, comming to a Prouince that was called Guasco, they found Maiz, wherewith they loaded their horses, and the

Indians that they had. From thence they went to another towne called Naquiscoça. The Indians said, they had no notice of any other Christians. The Gouernor commanded to torment them. They said, that they came first to another Lordship, which was called Naçacahoz, and from thence returned again to the West, from whence they came. The Gouernour came in two daies to Naçacahoz: Some women were taken there: among whom there was one, which said, that she had seene Christians, and had been taken by them, and had run away. The Gouernour sent a Captaine with 15. horsemen to the place where the women said she had seene them, to see if there were any signe of horses, or any token of their being there. After they had gone three or foure leagues the woman that guided them said, that all that she had told them was vntrue. And so they held all the rest that the Indians had said, of seeing Christians in the land of Florida. And, because the Countrie that way was poore of Maiz, and toward the West, there was no notice of any habitation, they returned to Guasco. The Indians told them there, that 10. daies iournie from thence toward the West, was a Riuer called Daycao; whither they went sometimes a hunting and killing of Deere: and that they had seene people on the other side, but knew not what habitation was there. The Riuer of Daycayo: which seemeth to be the Rio del oro. There the Christians tooke such Maiz as they found and could carrie, and, going 10. daies iournie through a wildernesse, they came to the Riuer which the Indians had told them of. Ten horsemen, which the Gouernour had sent before, passed ouer the same, and went in a way that led to the Riuer, and lighted vpon a companie of Indians that dwelt in verie little cabins: who, assoone as they saw them, tooke themselues to flight, leauing that which they had; all which was nothing but miserie and pouertie. The Countrie was so poore, that among them all there was not found halfe a peck of Maiz. The horsemen tooke two Indians, and returned with them to the Riuer, where the Gouernour staied for them. He sought to learne of them what habitation was toward the West. There was none in the Camp that could vnderstand their language. The Gouernour assembled the Captaines and principall persons, to determine with their aduice what they should doe. And the most part said, that they thought it best to returne backe to Rio grande, or the Great Riuer of Guachoya; because that in Nilco and thereabout was store of Maiz: saying, that they would make pinaces that winter, and the next sommer passe down the Riuer to seaward in them, and comming to the Sea they would goe along the coast to Nueua Espanna. For though it seemed a doubtfull thing and difficult, by that which they had already alleaged, yet it was the last remedie they had. No trauelling by land without an interpretour. For by land they could not goe for want of an Interpretour. And they held, that the countrie beyond the Riuer of Daycao, where they were, was that which Cabeça de Vaca mentioned in his relation that he passed of the Indians, which liued like the Alarbes, hauing no setled place, and fed vpon Tunas and rootes of the fields, and wilde beasts that they killed. Which if it were so, if they should enter into it and finde no victuals to passe the winter, they could not chuse but perish. For they were entred alreadie into the beginning of October: and if they staied any longer, they were not able to returne for raine and snowes, nor to sustaine themselues in so poore a countrey. The Gouernour (that desired long to see himselfe in a place where hee might sleepe his full sleep, rather then to conquer and gouerne a countrie where so many troubles presented themselues) presently returned back that same way that he came.

Chap. XXXV.

How they returned to Nilco, and came to Minoya, where they agreed to make ships to depart out of the land of Florida.

When that which was determined was published in the Campe, there were many that were greatly grieued at it: for they held the Sea voyage as doubtfull, for the euill meanes they had, and of as great danger, as the trauelling by land: and they hoped to finde some rich countrie before they came to the land of the Christians, by that which Cabeça de Vaca had told the Emperour: and that was this; Gold, siluer, and precious stones in Florida. That after hee had found clothes made of cotton wooll, hee saw gold and siluer, and stones of great value. And they had not yet come where hee had been. For vntill that place hee alwaies trauelled by the Sea coast: and they trauelled farre within the land; and that going toward the West, of necessitie they should come where hee had been. For he said, That in a certain place he trauelled many daies, and entred into the land toward the North. Turkie stones and mantles of cotton wooll found in Guasco. And in Guasco they had alreadie found some Turkie stones, and mantles of cotton wooll: which the Indians signified by signes that they had from the West: and that holding that course they should draw neere to the land of the Christians. But though they were much discontented with it, and it grieued many to goe backward, which would rather haue aduentured their liues and haue died in the land of Florida, then to haue gone poore out of it: yet were they not a sufficient part to hinder that which was determined, because the principall men agreed with the Gouernour. And afterward there was one that said, hee would put out one of his owne eyes, to put out another of Luis de Moscoso; because it would grieue him much to see him prosper: because aswell himself as others of his friends had crossed that which he durst not haue done, seeing that within two daies hee should leaue the gouernment. 150. leagues betweene the Riuer of Daycao, and Rio grande. From Daycao, where now they were, to Rio grande, or the Great Riuer, was 150. leagues: which vnto that place they had gone Westward. And by the way as they returned backe they had much adoe to find Maiz to eate: for where they had passed, the countrey was destroyed: and some little Maiz that was left the Indians had hidden. The townes which in Naguatex they had burned (whereof it repented them) were repaired againe, and the houses full of Maiz. *Fine earthen vessels.* This countrie is well inhabited and plentifull. In that place are vessels made of clay, which differ very little from those of Estremoz, or Monte-mor. In Chaguate the Indians by commandement of the Cacique came peaceably, and said, that the Christian which remained there would not come. The Gouernour wrote vnto him, and sent him inke and paper that he might answere. The substance of the words of the letter was to declare vnto him his determination, which was, to goe out of the land of Florida, and to put him in remembrance that he was a Christian, that hee would not remaine in the subiection of Infidels, that he pardoned him the fault which he had done in going away to the Indians, that hee should come vnto him: and if they did stay him, that hee would aduertise him thereof by writing. The Indian went with the letters and came againe without any more answere, then, on the back side, his name and his seale, that they might know he was aliue. The Gouernour sent twelue horsemen to seeke him: but he, which had his spies, so hid himselfe, that they could not find him. For want of Maiz the Gouernour could not stay any longer to seeke him. Hee departed from Chaguate, and passed the Riuer by Aays; going downe by it hee found a towne called Chilano, which as yet they had not seen. They came to Nilco, and found so little Maiz, as could not suffice till they made their ships; because the Christians, being in Guachoya in the seede time, the Indians for feare of them durst not come to sow the grounds of Nilco: and they knew not thereabout any other countrie where any Maiz was: and that was the most fruitfull soile that was thereaway, and where they had most hope to finde it. Euery one was confounded, and the most part thought it bad counsell to come backe from the Riuer of Dacayo, and not to haue followed their fortune, going that way that went ouer land. For by Sea it seemed impossible to saue themselues, vnlesse God would worke a miracle for them: for there was neither Pilot, nor Sea-chart, neither did they know where the Riuer entred into the Sea, neither had they notice of it, neither had they any thing wherewith to make sailes, nor any store of Enequem, which is a grasse whereof they make Okam, which grew there: and that which they found they saued to calke the Pinaces withall, neither had they any thing to pitch them withall: neither could they make ships of such substance, but that any storme would put them in great danger: and they feared much it would fall out with them, as it did with Pamphilo de Naruaez, which was cast away vpon that coast: And aboue all it troubled them most, that they could find no Maiz: for without it they could not bee sustained, nor could doe any thing that they had neede of. All of them were put to great confusion. Their chiefe remedy was to commit themselues to God, and to beseech him that he would direct them the way that they might saue their liues. And it pleased him of his goodnesse, that the Indians of Nilco came peaceablie, and told them, that two daies iourney from thence, neere vnto the Great Riuer, were two townes, whereof the Christians had no notice, and that the prouince was called Minoya, and was a fruitfull soile: that, whether at this present there was any Maiz or no, they knew not, because they had warre with them: but that they would be very glad with the fauour of the Christians to goe and spoyle them. The Gouernour sent a Captaine thither with horsemen and footmen, and the Indians of Nilco with him. Hee came to Minoya, and found two great townes seated in a plaine and open soile, halfe a league distant, one in sight of another, and in them hee tooke many Indians, and found great store of Maiz. Presently he lodged in one of them, and sent word to the Gouernour what hee had found: wherewith they were all exceeding glad. They departed from Nilco in the beginning of December; and all that way, and before from Chilano, they endured much trouble: for they passed through many waters, and many times it rained with a Northren winde, and was exceeding cold, so that they were in the open field with water ouer and vnderneath them: and when at the end of their daies iourney they found drie ground to rest vpon, they gaue great thanks to God. With this trouble almost all the Indians that serued them died. And after they were in Minoya, many Christians also died: and the most part were sicke of great and dangerous diseases, which had a spice of the lethargie. At this place died Andrew de Vasconcelos, and two Portugals of Eluas, which were very neere him: which were brethren, and by their surname called Sotis. The Christians lodged in one of the townes, which they liked best: which was fensed about, and distant a quarter of a league from the Great Riuer. The Maiz that was in the other towne was brought thither; and in all it was esteemed to bee 6000. hanegs or bushels. And there was the best timber to make ships, that they had seene in all the land of Florida: wherefore all of them gaue God great thankes for so singular a fauour, and hoped that that which they desired would take effect, which was, that they might safely bee conducted into the land of the Christians.

Chap. XXXVI.

How there were seuen Brigandines builded, and how they departed from Minoya.

Assoone as they came to Minoya, the Gouernor commanded them to gather all the chaines together, which euerie one had to lead Indians in; and to gather all the yron which they had for their prouision, and al the rest that was in the Camp: and to set vp a forge to make nailes, and commanded them to cut downe timber for the brigandines. And a Portugall of Ceuta, who hauing bin a prisoner in Fez, had learned to saw timber with a long saw, which for such purposes they had carried with them, did teach others, which helped him to saw timber. And a Genowis, whom it pleased God to preserue (for without him they had neuer come out of the countrie: for there has neuer another that could make ships but hee) with foure or fiue other Biscaine carpenters, which hewed his plancks and other timbers, made the brigandines: And two calkers, the one of Genua, the other of Sardinia did calke them with the tow of an hearb like hempe, whereof before I haue made mention, which there is named Enequen. And because there was not enough of it, they calked them with the flaxe of the Countrie, and with the mantles, which they rauelled for that purpose. A cooper which they had among them fell sicke, and was at the point of death: and there was none other that had any skill in that trade: it pleased God to send him his health: And albeit he was verie weake, and could not labour; yet 15. daies before they departed, he made for euery brigandine two halfe hogs heads, which the mariners call quarterets, because foure of them hold a pipe of water. Taguanate two daies iourney aboue Minoya. The Indians which dwelt two daies iournie aboue the Riuer in a Prouince called Taguanate, and likewise those of Nilco and Guacoya, and others their neighbours seeing the brigandines in making, thinking, because their places of refuge are in the water, that they were to goe to seeke them: and because the Gouernour demanded mantles of them, as necessarie for sailes, came many times, and brought many mantles, and great store of fish. And for certaine it seemed that God was willing to fauour them in so great necessitie, moouing the minds of the Indians to bring them: for to goe to take them, they were neuer able. For in the towne where they were, assoone as winter came in, they were so inclosed and compassed with water, that they could go no farther by land, then a league, and a league and an halfe. The great vse of horses. And if they would go farther, they could carrie no horses, and without them they were not able to fight with the Indians, because they were many: and so many for so many (numbers being equal) on foote they had the aduantage of them by water and by land, because they were more apt and lighter, and by reason of the disposition of the Countrie, which was according to their desire for the vse of their warre. They brought also some cords, and those which wanted for cables were made of the barkes of Mulberrie trees. They made stirrops of wood, and made ankers of their stirrops. The mightie increasing of the Riuer for two moneths space, to wit, all March and April. In the moneth of March, when it had not rained a moneth before, the Riuer grew so big, that it came to Nilco, which was nine leagues off: and on the other side, the Indians said, that it reached other nine leagues into the land. In the towne where the Christians were, which was somewhat high ground, where they could best goe, the water reached to the stirrops. They made certaine rafts of timber, and laid manie boughes vpon them, wheron they set their horses, and in the houses they did the like. But seeing that nothing preuailed, they went vp to the lofts: and if they went out of the houses, it was in canoes, or on horseback in those places where the ground was hiest. So they were two moneths, and could doe nothing, during which time the Riuer decreased not. The Indians ceased not to come vnto the brigantines as they were wont, and came in canoes. At that time the Gouernour feared they would set vpon him. Hee commanded his men to take an Indian secretly of those that came to the towne, and to stay him till the rest were gone: and they tooke one. The Gouernour commanded him to bee put to torture, to make him confesse, whether the Indians did practise any treason or no. The grand conspiracie of the Indians against the Christians. Hee confessed that the Caciques of Nilco, Guachoya, and Taguanate, and others, which in al were about 20. Caciques, with a great number of people, determined to come vpon him; and that three daies before, they would send a great present of fish to colour their great treason and malice, and on the verie day they would send some Indians before with another present. Note well. And these with those which were our slaues, which were of their conspiracie also, should set the houses on fire, and first of all possesse themselues of the lances which stood at the doores of the houses; and the Caciques with all their men should bee neere the towne in ambush in the wood, and when they saw the fire kindled, should come, and make an end of the conquest. The Gouernour commanded the Indian to be kept in a chaine, and the selfesame day that he spake of there came 30. Indians with fish. Thirtie Indians of the Cacique of Guachoya haue their right hands cut off. He commanded their right hands to be cut off, and sent them so backe to the Cacique of Guachoya, whose men they were. He sent him word, that he and the rest should come when they would, for he desired nothing more, and that hee should know, that they thought not any thing which he knew not before they thought of it. Hereupon they all were put in a very great feare: And the Caciques of Nilco and Taguanate came to excuse themselues: and a few daies after came he of Guachoya, and a principall Indian and his subiect, said, he knew by certaine information, That the Caciques of Nilco and Taguanate were agreed to come and make warre vpon the Christians. Assoone as the Indians came from Nilco, the Gouernour examined them, and they confessed it was true. Hee deliuered them presently to the principall man of Guachoya, which drew them out of the towne and killed them. Another day came some from Taguanate, and confessed it likewise. The right hands and noses of traitours cut off. The Gouernour commanded their right hands and noses to be cut off, and sent them to the Cacique, wherewith they of Guachoya remained very well contented: and they came oftentimes with presents of mantles and fish, and hogs, which bred in the Countrie of some swine that were lost by the way the last yeere. Assoone as the waters were slaked, they perswaded the Gouernour to send men to Taguanate: They came and brought canoes, wherein the footemen were conueied downe the Riuer, and a Captaine with horsemen went by land; and the Indians of Guachoya, which guided him, till they came to Taguanate, assaulted the towne, and tooke many men and women, and mantles, which with those that they had alreadie were sufficient to supplie their want. The Riuer increaseth but once a yeere when the snowes doe melt in March and Aprill. The brigandines being finished in the moneth of Iune, the Indians hauing told vs, That the Riuer increased but once a yeere, when the snowes did melt, in the time wherein I mentioned it had alreadie increased, being now in sommer, and hauing not rained a long time, it pleased God, that the flood came vp to the towne to seeke the brigandines, from whence they carried them by water to the Riuer. A miraculous accident. Which, if they had gone by land, had been in danger of breaking and splitting their keeles, and to bee all vndone; because that for want of iron, the spikes were short, and the planckes and timber very weake. The Indians of Minoya, during the time that they were there, came to serue them (being driuen thereunto by necessity) that of the Maiz which they had taken from them they would bestow some crummes vpon them. And because the Countrie was fertill, and the people vsed to feed of Maiz, and the Christians had gotten all from them that they had, and the people were many, they were not able to sustaine themselues. Those which came to the towne were so weake and feeble, that they had no flesh left on their bones: and many came and died neere the towne for pure hunger and weaknesse. The Gouernour commanded vpon grieuous punishments to giue them no Maiz. Yet, when they saw that the hogges wanted it not, and that they had yeelded themselues to serue them, and considering their miserie and wretchednes, hauing pity of them, they gaue them part of the Maiz which they had. And when the time of their embarkment came, there was not sufficient to serue their own turnes. That which there was, they put into the brigandines, and into great canoes tied two and two together. They shipped 22. of the best horses, that were in the Camp, the rest they made dried flesh of; and dressed the hogges which they had in like manner. They departed from Minoya the second day of Iulie, 1543.

Chap. XXXVII.

As the Christians went downe the great Riuer on their voyage, the Indians of Quigalta did set vpon them, and what was the successe thereof.

The day before they departed from Minoya, they determined to dismisse al the men and women of the Countrie, which they had detained as slaues to serue them, saue some hundred, little more or lesse, which the Gouernour embarked, and others whom it pleased him to permit. And because there were many men of qualitie, whom he could not deny that which he granted to others, he vsed a policy, saying, that they might serue them as long as they were in the Riuer, but when they came to the sea, they must send them away for want of water, because they had but few vessels. He told his friends in secret, that they should carrie theirs to Nueua Espanna: And all those whom hee bare no good will vnto (which were the greater number) ignorant of that which was hidden from them, which afterward time discouered, thinking it inhumanitie for so little time of seruice, in reward of the great seruice that they had done them, to carrie them with them, 500. Slaues left in the Countrie. to leaue them slaues to other men out of their owne Countries; left fiue hundred men and women: among whom were many boies and girles, which spake and vnderstood the Spanish tongue. The most of them did nothing but weepe: which mooued great compassion; seeing that all of them with good will would haue become Christians, and were left in state of perdition. They sailed down Rio Grande from Minoya 17. daies before they came to the mouth thereof. There went from Minoya 322. Spaniards in seuen brigandines, well made, saue that the plankes were thin, because the nailes were short, and were not pitched, nor had any decks to keep the water from comming in. In stead of decks they laid planks, whereon the mariners might runne to trim their sailes, and the people might refresh themselues aboue and below: The Gouernour made his Captaines, and gaue to euery one his brigandine, and took their oth and their word, that they would obey him, vntill they came to the land of the Christians. The Gouernour tooke one of the brigandines for himself, which he best liked. The same day that they departed from Minoya, they passed by Guachoya, where the Indians tarried for them in canoes by the Riuer. And on the shore, they had made a great arbour with boughes:

They desired him to come on shore; but he excused himselfe, and so went along: The Indians in their canoes accompanied him; and comming where an arme of the Riuer diclined on the right hand, they said, that the Prouince of Quigalta was neere vnto that place, and importuned the Gouernour to set vpon him, and that they would aide him. And because they had said, that he dwelt three daies journie down the Riuer, the Gouernour supposed that they had plotted some treason against him, and there left them; and went downe with the greatest force of the water. The current was very strong, and with the helpe of ores, they went very swiftly. The first day they landed in a wood on the left hand of the Riuer, and at night they withdrew themselues to the brigandines. The second day. The next day they came to a towne, where they went on shore, and the people that was in it durst not tarrie. A woman that they tooke there being examined, said, that that towne belonged to a Cacique named Huasene, subiect to Quigalta, and that Quigalta tarried for them below in the Riuer with many men. Certaine horsemen went thither, and found some houses, wherein was much Maiz. Immediately more of them went thither and tarried there one day, Another day. in which they did beate out, and tooke as much Maiz as they needed. While they were there, many Indians came from the nether part of the Riuer, and on the other side right against them somewhat carelessely set themselues in order to fight. The Gouernour sent in two canoes the crossebowmen that he had, and as many more as could goe in them. They ran away, and seeing the Spaniards could not ouertake them, they returned backe, and tooke courage; and coming neerer, making an outcrie, they threatned them: and assoone as they departed thence, they went after them, some in canoes, and some by land along the Riuer; and getting before, comming to a towne that stood by the Riuers side, they ioyned al together, making a shew that they would tarrie there. Euerie brigandine towed a canoe fastened to their sternes for their particular seruice. A town burned. Presently there entred men into euerie one of them, which made the Indians to flie, and burned the town. The same day they presently landed in a great field, where the Indians durst not tarrie. The third day. A fleet of an hundred faire and great canoes. The next day there were gathered together an hundred canoes, among which were some that carried 60. and 70. men, and the principall mens canoes had their tilts, and plumes of white and red feathers for their ensignes: and they came within two crossebow shot of the brigandines, and sent three Indians in a small canoe with a fained message to view the manner of the brigandines, and what weapons they had. And comming to the side of the Gouernours brigandine, one of the Indians entred, and said:

That the Cacique of Quigalta his Lord, sent him his commendations, and did let him vnderstand, that all the Indians of Guachoya had told him concerning himselfe, was false, and that they had incensed him, because they were his enemies; that he was his seruant, and should find him so.

The Gouernour answered him, that he beleeued all that he said was true, and willed him to tell him, that he esteemed his friendship very much. With this answer they returned to the place where the rest in their canoes were waiting for them, and from thence all of them fell downe, and came neere the Spaniards, shouting aloud, and threatning of them. The Gouernour sent Iohn de Guzman, which had been a Captaine of footemen in Florida, with 15. armed men in canoes to make them giue way. Assoone as the Indians saw them come towards them, they diuided themselues into two parts, and stood still till the Spaniards came nie them, and when they were come neere them, they ioyned together on both sides, taking Iohn de Guzman in the middest, and then they came first with him, and with great furie borded them: And as their canoes were bigger, and many of them leaped into the water to stay them, and to lay hold on the canoes of the Spaniards, and ouerwhelme them; so presently they ouerwhelmed them. The Christians fell into the water, and with the weight of their armour sunke downe to the bottome: and some few, that by swimming or holding by the canoe could haue saued themselues, with oares and staues, which they had, they strooke them on the head and made them sinke. When they of the brigandines saw the ouerthrow, though they went about to succour them, yet through the current of the Riuer they could not goe backe. Foure Spaniards fled to the brigandine that was neerest to the canoes; and only these escaped of those that came among the Indians. Eleuen Spaniards drowned. They were eleuen that died there: among whom Iohn de Guzman was one, and a sonne of Don Carlos, called Iohn de Vargas: the rest also were persons of account and men of great courage. Those that escaped by swimming, said that they saw the Indians enter the canoe of John de Guzman at the sterne of one of their canoes, and whether they carried him away dead or aliue they could not certainly tell.

Chap. XXXVIII.

Which declareth how they were pursued by the Indians.

The Indians, seeing that they had gotten the victorie, tooke such courage, that they assaulted them in the brigandines, which they durst not doe before. *25. Spaniards wounded.* They came first to that brigandine wherein Calderon went for Captaine, and was in the rereward: and at the first volie of arrowes they wounded 25. men. There were only foure armed men in this brigandine: these did stand at the brigandines side to defend it. Those that were vnarmed, seeing how they hurt them, left their oares and went vnder the deck: whereupon the brigandine began to crosse, and to goe where the current of the streame carried it. One of the armed men seeing this, without the commandement of the Captaine, made a footman to take an oare and stirre the brigandine, hee standing before him and defending him with his target. *The great vse of large targets.* The Indians came no neerer then a bowshot, from whence they offended and were not offended, receiuing no hurt: for in euery brigandine was but one crossebow, and those which wee had were very much out of order. So that the Christians did nothing else but stand for a butte to receiue their arrowes. Hauing left this brigandine they went to another, and fought with it halfe an houre; and so from one to another they fought with them all. *Strong mats a good defence against arrowes.* The Christians had mattes to lay vnder them, which were double, and so close and strong, that no arrow went thorow them. And assoone as the Indians gaue them leisure, they fensed the brigandines with them. And the Indians seeing that they could not shoote leuell, shot their arrowes at random vp into the aire, which fell into the brigandines, and hurt some of the men: and not therewith contented, they sought to get to them which were in the canoes with the horses. Those of the brigandines enuironed them to defend them, and tooke them among them. Thus seeing themselues much vexed by them, and so wearied that they could no longer endure it, they determined to trauell all the night following, thinking to get beyond the countrie of Quigalta, and that they would leaue them: but when they thought least of it, supposing they had now left them, they heard very neere them so great outcries, that they made them deafe, and so they followed vs all that night, and the next day till noone, by which time we were come into the countrie of others, whom they desired to vse vs after the same manner; and so they did. The men of Quigalta returned home; and the other in fiftie canoes fought with vs a whole day and a night: and they entred one of the brigandines, that came in the rereward by the canoe which she had at her sterne, and tooke away a woman which they found in it, and afterward hurt some of the men of the brigandines. Those which came with the horses in the canoes, being wearie with rowing night and day, lingered behind; and presently the Indians came vpon them, and they of the brigandines tarried for them. The Gouernour resolued to goe on shore and to kill the horses, because of the slow way which they made because of them. Assoone as they saw a place conuenient for it, they ⁚ Dried horseflesh for food. ⁚ went thither and killed the horses, and brought the flesh of them to drie it aboord. Foure or fiue of them remained on shore aliue: The Indians went vnto them, after the Spaniards were embarked. The horses were not acquainted with them, and began to neigh, and runne vp and downe, in such sort, that the Indians, for feare of them, leaped into the water: and getting into their canoes went after the brigandines, shooting cruelly at them. They followed vs that euening and the night following till the next day at tenne of the clocke, and then returned vp the Riuer. Presently from a small towne that stood vpon the Riuer came seuen canoes, and followed vs a little way downe the Riuer, shooting at vs: but seeing they were so few that they could do vs but little harme, they returned to their towne. From thence forward, vntill they came to the Sea, they had no encounter. They sailed downe the Riuer seuenteene daies, which may be two hundred and fifty leagues iourney, little more or lesse: and neere vnto the Sea the Riuer is diuided into two armes; each of them is a league and an halfe broad.

Chap. XXXIX.

How they came vnto the sea: and what happened vnto them in all their voiage.

Halfe a league before they came to the sea, they came to anker to rest themselues there about a day: for they were very weary with rowing and out of heart. For by the space of many daies they had eaten nothing but parched and sodden Maiz; which they had by allowance euery day an headpeece ful by strike for euery three men. While they rode there at anker seuen canoes of Indians came to set vpon those, which they brought with them. The Gouernor commanded armed men to go aboord them, and to driue them farther off. They came also against them by land through a thick wood, and a moorish ground, and had staues with very sharp forked heads made of the bones of fishes, and fought verie valiantly with vs, which went out to encounter them. And the other that came in canoes with their arrowes staid for them that came against them, and at their comming both those that were on land, and those in the canoes wounded some of vs: And seeing vs come neere them, they turned their backs, and like swift horses among footemen gat away from vs; making some returnes, and reuniting themselues together, going not past a bow shot off: for in so retiring they shot, without receiuing any hurt of the Christians. For though they had some bowes, yet they could not vse them; and brake their armes with rowing to ouertake them. And the Indians easily in their compasse went with their canoes, staying and wheeling about as it had been in a skirmish, perceiuing that those that came against them could not offend them. And the more they stroue to come neere them, the more hurt they receiued. Assoone as they had driuen them farther off they returned to the brigandines. They staied two daies there: And departed from thence vnto the place, where the arme of the Riuer entreth into the sea. They sounded in the Riuer neere vnto the Sea, and found 40. fathoms water. They staid there. And the Gouernour commanded al and singular persons to speake their minds touching their voiage, whether it were best to crosse ouer to Nueua Espanna, committing themselues to the hie sea, or whether they should keepe along the coast. There were sundry opinions touching this matter; wherein Iohn Danusco, which presumed much, and tooke much vpon him in the knowledge of nauigation, and matters of the sea, although hee had but little experience, mooued the Gouernour with his talke: and his opinion was seconded by some others. And they affirmed, that it was much better to passe by the hie sea, and crosse the gulfe, which was three of foure parts the lesser trauell, because in going along the coast, they went a great way about, by reason of the compasse, which the land did make. Iohn Danusco said, that he had seene the seacard, and that from the place where they were, the coast ran East and West vnto Rio de las Palmas; and from Rio de las Palmas to Nueua Espanna from North to South: and therefore in sailing alwaies in sight of land would bee a great compassing about and spending of much time; and that they would be in great danger to be overtaken with winter before they should get to the land of the Christians: and that in 10. or 12. daies space, hauing good weather, they might bee there in crossing ouer. The most part were against this opinion, and said, that it was more safe to go along the coast, though they staied the longer: because their ships were very weake and without decks, so that a very little storme was enough to cast them away: and if they should be hindred with calmes, or contrarie weather, through the small store of vessels which they had to carrie water in, they should likewise fall into great danger: and that although the ships were such as they might venture in them, yet hauing neither Pilot nor Seacard to guide themselues, it was no good counsell to crosse the gulfe. This opinion was confirmed by the greatest part: and they agreed to go along the coast. At the time wherein they sought to depart from thence, the cable of the anker of the Gouernours brigandine brake, and the anker remained in the Riuer. And albeit, they were neere the shore, yet it was so deepe, that the Diuers diuing many times could neuer find it: which caused great sadnes in the Gouernour, and in all those that went with him in his brigandine: But with a grindstone which they had, and certaine bridles which remained to some of the Gentlemen, and men of worship which had horses, they made a weight which serued in stead of an anker. They landed the 30. of May, 1539. Chap. 7. they went foorth to sea Iuly 18, 1543. The 18. of Iuly, they went foorth to sea with faire and prosperous weather for their voiage. And seeing that they were gone two or three leagues from the shore, the Captaines of the other brigandines ouertooke them, and asked the Gouernour, wherefore he did put off from the shore: and that if hee would leaue the coast, he should say so; and he should not do it without the consent of all: and that if hee did otherwise, they would not follow him, but that euery one would doe what seemed best vnto himselfe. The Gouernour answered, that hee would doe nothing without their counsell, but that hee did beare off from the land to saile the better and safer by night; and that the next day when time serued, he would returne to the sight of land againe. They sailed with a reasonable good wind that day and the night following, and the next day till euening song, alwaies in fresh water: whereat they wondred much: for they were very farre from land. But the force of the current of the Riuer is so great, and the coast there is so shallow and gentle, that the fresh water entreth farre into the

Sea. That euening on their right hand they saw certaine creekes, whither they went, and rested there that night: where Iohn Danusco with his reasons wonne them at last, that all consented and agreed to commit themselues to the maine Sea, alleaging, as he had done before, that it was a great aduantage, and that their voyage would be much shorter. They sailed two daies, and when they would haue come to sight of land they could not, for the winde blew from the shore. On the fourth day, seeing their fresh water began to faile, fearing necessitie and danger, they all complained of Iohn Danusco, and of the Gouernour that followed his counsell: and euery one of the Captaines said, that they would no more goe from the shore, though the Gouernour went whither he would. It pleased God that the winde changed though but a little: and at the end of foure daies after they had put to sea, being alreadie destitute of water, by force of rowing they got within sight of land, and with great trouble recouered it, in an open roade. That euening the winde came to the South, which on that coast is a crosse winde, and draue the brigandines against the shore, because it blew very hard, and the anchors weake, that they yeelded and began to bend. The Gouernour commanded all men to leape into the water, and going between them and the shore, and thrusting the brigandines into the Sea assoone as the waue was past, they saued them till the winde ceased.

Chap. XL.

How they lost one another by a storme, and afterward came together in a creeke.

Fresh water is commonlie found by diging in the sands on the sea side.
In the bay where they rode, after the tempest was past, they went on shore, and with mattockes, which they had, they digged certain pits, which grew full of fresh water, where they filled all the casks which they had. The next day they departed thence, and sailed two daies, and entred into a creeke like vnto a poole, fenced from the South winde, which then did blow, and was against them: and there they staied foure daies, not being able to get out: and when the Sea was calm they rowed out: they sailed that day, and toward euening the winde grew so strong that it draue them on the shore, and they were sorie that they had put foorth from the former harbour: for assoone as night approched a storme began to rise in the Sea, and the winde still waxed more and more violent with a tempest. The brigandines lost one another: two of them, which bare more into the Sea, entred into an arme of the Sea, which pearced into the land two leagues beyond the place where the other were that night. The fiue which staied behinde, being alwaies a league, and halfe a league the one from the other, met together, without any knowledge the one of the other, in a wilde roade, where the winde and the waues droue them on shore: for their anchors did strengthen and came home; and they could not rule their oares, putting seuen or eight men to every oare, which rowed to seaward: and all the rest leaped into the water, and when the waue was past that draue the brigandine on shore, they thrust it againe into Sea with all the diligence and might that they had. Others, while another waue was in comming, with bowles laued out the water that came in ouerboord. *A swarme of grieuous Moskitoes.* While they were in this tempest in great feare of being cast away in that place, from midnight forward they endured an intollerable torment of an infinite swarme of Moskitoes which fell upon them, which assoone as they had stung the flesh, it so infected it, as though they had bin venomous. In the morning the Sea was asswaged and the wind slaked, but not the Muskitoes: the sailes which were white seemed blacke with them in the morning. Those which rowed, vnless others kept them away, were not able to row. Hauing passed the feare & danger of the storme, beholding the deformities of their faces, and the blows which they gaue themselves to driue them away, one of them laughed at another. They met all together in the creek where the two

brigandines were, which outwent their fellowes. There was found a skumme, which they call Copee, which the Sea casteth vp, and it is like pitch, wherewith in some places, where pitch is wanting, they pitch their ships: there they pitched their brigandines. They rested two daies, and then eftsoones proceeded on their voyage. They sailed two daies more, and landed in a Bay or arme of the Sea, where they staied two daies. The same day that they went from thence sixe men went vp in a canoe toward the head of it, and could not see the end of it. They put out from thence with a South winde, which was against them: but because it was little, and for the great desire they had to shorten their voyage, they put out to sea by force of oares, and for all that made very little way with great labour in two daies, and went under the lee of a small Island into an arme of the Sea, which compassed it about. While they were there, there fell out such weather, that they gave God many thankes, that they had found out such an harbour. There was great store of fish in that place, which they tooke with nets, which they had, and hookes. Heere a man cast an hooke and a line into the Sea, and tied the end of it to his arme, and a fish caught it, and drew him into the water vnto the necke: and it pleased God that he remembered himselfe of a knife that he had, and cut the line with it. There they abode fourteen daies: and at the end of them it pleased God to send them faire weather, for which with great deuotion they appointed a procession, and went in procession along the strand, beseeching God to bring them to a land, where they might serue him in better sort.

Chap. XLI.

How they came to the Riuer of Panuco in Nueua Espanna.

In all the coast wheresoeuer they digged they found fresh water: there they filled their vessels; and the procession being ended, embarked themselues, and going alwaies in sight of the shore they sailed six daies. Iohn Danusco said that it would doe well to beare out to seaward: for he had seene the Seacard, and remembred that from Rio de las Palmas forward the coast did runne from North to South, and thitherto they had runne from East to West, and in his opinion, by his reckoning, Rio de las Palmas could not be farre off, from where they were. At the Northside of the Gulfe of Mexico is verie low land, saue in this one place. That same night they put to sea, and in the morning they saw Palme leaues floting, and the coast, which ranne North and South: from midday forward they saw great Mountaines, which vntill then they had not seene: for from this place to Puerto de Spiritu Santo, where they first landed in Florida, was a very plaine and low countrey: and therefore it cannot be descried, vnlesse a man come very neere it. By that which they saw, they thought that they had ouershot Rio de Palmas that night, which is 60. leagues from the Riuer of Panuco, which is in Nueua Espanna. They assembled all together, and some said it was not good to saile by night, lest they should ouershoot the Riuer of Panuco: and others said, it was not well to lose time while it was fauourable, and that it could not be so neere that they should passe it that night: and they agreed to take away halfe the sailes, and so saile all night. Two of the brigandines, which sailed that night with all their sailes, by breake of day had ouershot the Riuer of Panuco without seeing it. Of the fiue that came behind, the first that came vnto it was that wherein Calderan was Captaine. A quarter of a league before they came at it, and before they did see it, they saw the water muddie, and knew it to be fresh water: and comming right against the Riuer, they saw, where it entred into the Sea, that the water brake vpon a shold. And because there was no man there that knew it, they were in doubt whether they should goe in, or goe along, and they resolued to goe in: and before they came vnto the current, they went close to the shore, and entred into the port: and assoone as they were come in, they saw Indian men and women apparelled like Spaniards: whom they asked in what countrey they were? The Riuer of Panuca: the towne 15. leagues from the mouth of the Riuer. They answered in Spanish, that it was the Riuer of Panuco, and that the towne of the Christians was 15. leagues vp within the land. The ioy that all of them receiued vpon these newes cannot sufficiently be expressed: for it seemed vnto them, that at that instant they were borne again. And many went on shore and kissed the ground, and kneeling on their knees, with lifting vp their hands and eyes to heauen, they all ceased not to giue God thankes. Those which came after, assoone as they saw Calderon come to an anchor with his brigandine in the Riuer, presently went thither, and came into the hauen. The other two brigandines which had ouershot the place, put to sea to returne backe to seeke the rest, and could not doe it, because the wind was contrarie and the Sea growne: they were afraid of being cast away, and recouering the shore they cast anchor. While they rode there a storme arose: and seeing that they could not abide there, much lesse endure at Sea, they resolued to runne on shore; and as the brigandines were but small, so did they draw but little water; and where they were it was a sandie coast. By which occasion the force of their sailes draue them on shore, without any hurt of them that were in them. As those that were in the port of Panuco at this time were in great ioy, so these felt a double griefe in their hearts: for they knew not what was become of their fellowes, nor in what countrey they were, and feared it was a countrey of Indian enemies. They landed two leagues below the port: and when they saw themselues out of the danger of the Sea, euery one tooke of that which he had, as much as he could carrie on his backe: and they trauelled vp into the countrey, and found Indians, which told them where the fellowes were; and gaue them good entertainement: wherewith their sadnes was turned into ioy, and they thanked God most humbly for their deliuerance out of so many dangers.

Chap. XLII.

How they came to Panuco, and how they were receiued of the inhabitants.

From the time that they put out of Rio Grande to the sea, at their departure from Florida, vntil they arriued in the Riuer of Panuco, were 52 daies. They arriued in the Riuer of Panuco, 1543. Septem. 10. They came into the Riuer of Panuco the 10. of September 1543. They went vp the Riuer with their brigandines. They trauelled foure daies; and because the wind was but little, and many times it serued them not, because of the many turnings which the Riuer maketh, and the great current, drawing them vp by towing, and that in many places: for this cause they made very little way, and with great labour; and seeing the execution of their desire to be deferred, which was to come among Christians, and to see the celebration of diuine seruice, which so long time they had not seene; they left the brigandines with the mariners, and went by land to Panuco. All of them were apparrelled in Deeres skins tanned and died blacke, to wit, cotes, hose, and shooes. When they came to Panuco, presently they went to the Church to pray and giue God thankes, that so miraculously had saued them. The townesmen which before were aduertised by the Indians, and knew of their arriual, caried some of them to their houses, and entertained them, whom they knew, and had acquaintance of, or because they were their Countrimen. The Alcalde Mayor tooke the Gouernour home to his house: and commanded al the rest, assoone as they came, to be lodged 6. & 6. and 10. & 10. according to the habilitie of euery townesman. And all of them were prouided for by their hostes of many hennes and bread of Maiz, and fruites of the Countrie, which are such as be in the Isle of Cuba, whereof, before I haue spoken. The description of Panuco. The towne of Panuco may containe aboue 70 families; the most of their houses are of lime and stone, and some made of timber, and all of them are thatched. It is a poore Countrie, and there is neither gold nor siluer in it: The inhabitants live there in great abundance of victuals and seruants. The richest haue not aboue 500. crownes rent a yeere, and that is in cotton clothes and hennes and Maiz, which the Indians there seruants doe giue them for tribute. 311.

Christians arriued at Panuco. There arriued there; of those that came out of Florida, three hundred and eleuen Christians. Presently the Alcalde

Mayor sent one of the townesmen in post to aduertise the Viceroy, Don Antonio de Mendoça, which was resident in Mexico, that of the people that went with Don Ferdinando de Soto to discouer and conquer Florida, three hundred and eleuen men were arriued there, that seeing they were imploied in his Maiesties seruice, he would take some order to prouide for them. Whereat the Viceroy, and all the inhabitants of Mexico wondred. For they thought they were miscarried, because they had trauelled so farre within the maine land of Florida, and had no newes of them for so long a time: and it seemed a wonderfull thing vnto them, how they could saue themselues so long among Infidels, without any fort, wherein they might fortifie themselues, and without any other succour at all. Presently the Viceroy sent a warrant, wherein hee commanded, that whithersoeuer they went, they should giue them victuals, and as many Indians for their carriages as they needed: and where they would not furnish them, they might take those things that were necessarie perforce without incurring any danger of law. This warrant was so readilie obeyed, that by the way before they came to the townes, they came to receiue them with hennes, and victuals.

Chap. XLIII.

Of the fauour which they found at the hands of the Viceroy, and of the inhabitants of the Citie of Mexico.

From Panuco to the great Citie Temistitan Mexico is 60. leagues; and other 60. from Panuco to the Port de Vera Cruz, where they take shipping for Spaine, and those that come from Spaine do land to go for Nueua Espanna. These three townes stand in a triangle: to wit, Vera Cruz, to the South, Panuco to the North, and Mexico to the West, 60. leagues assunder. The Countrie is so inhabited with Indians, that from towne to towne, those which are farthest, are but a league, and halfe a league assunder. Some of them that came from Florida, staied a moneth in Panuco to rest themselues, others fifteene daies, and euery one as long as he listed: for there was none that shewed a sower countenance to his guests, but rather gaue them any thing that they had, and seemed to be grieued when they took their leaue. Which was to be beleeued. For the victuals, which the Indians doe pay them for tribute, are more than they can spend: and in that towne is no commerce; and there dwelt but few Spaniards there, and they were glad of their companie. The Alcalde Mayor diuided all the Emperours clothes which he had (which there they pay him for his tribute) among those that would come to receiue them. Those which had shirts of maile left, were glad men: for they had a horse for one shirt of maile: Some horsed themselues: and such as could not (which were the greatest part) tooke their iournie on foote: in which they were well receiued of the Indians that were in the townes, and better serued, then they could haue been in their owne houses, though they had been well to liue. For if they asked one hen of an Indian, they brought them foure: and if they asked any of the Countrie fruit, though it were a league off, they ran presently for it. This is the manner of China to carrie men chaires. And if any Christian found himselfe euill at ease, they carried him in a chaire from one towne to another. In whatsoeuer towne they came, the Cacique, by an Indian which carried a rod of Iustice in his hand, whom they call Tapile, that is to say, a sergeant, commanded them to prouide victuals for them, and Indians to beare burdens of such things as they had, and such as were needfull to carrie them that were sicke. The Viceroy sent a Portugall 20. leagues from Mexico, with great store of sugar, raisons of the Sunne, and conserues, and other things fit for sicke folkes, for such as had neede of them: and had giuen order to cloth them all at the Emperours charges. And their approch being knowne by the citizens of Mexico, they went out of the towne to receiue them: and with great courtesie, requesting them in fauour to come to their houses, euery one carried such as hee met home with him, and clothed them euery one the best they could: so that he which had the meanest apparrell, it cost aboue 30. ducats. As many as were willing to come to the Viceroyes house he commanded to be apparelled, and such as were persons of qualitie sate at his table: and there was a table in his house for as many of the meaner sort as would come to it: and he was presently informed who euery one was, to shew him the courtesie that he deserued. Some of the Conquerors did set both gentlemen and clownes at their owne table, and many times made the seruant sit cheeke by cheeke by his master: and chiefly the officers and men of base condition did so: for those which had better education did enquire who euery one was, and made difference of persons: but all did what they could with a good will: and euery one told them whom they had in their houses, that they should not trouble themselues, nor thinke themselues the worse, to take that which they gaue them: for they had bin in the like case, and had bin relieued of others, and that this was the custome of that countrey. God reward them all: and God grant, that those which it pleased him to deliuer out of Florida, and to bring againe into Christendome, may serue him: and vnto those that died in that countrey, and vnto all that beleeue in him and confesse his holy faith, God for his mercie sake grant the kingdome of heauen. Amen.

Chap. XLIV.

Which declareth some diuersities and particularities of the land of Florida: and the fruites, and beasts, and fowles that are in that Countrie.

Port de Spiritu Santo is in 29. degrees ½ on the West side of Florida.

From the Port de Spiritu Santo, where they landed when they entred into Florida, to the Prouince of Ocute, which may bee 400. leagues, little more or lesse, is a verie plaine Countrie, and hath many lakes and thicke woods, and in some places they are of wild pine trees; and is a weake soile: There is in it neither Mountaine nor hill. The Countrie of Ocute is more fat and fruitfull; it hath thinner woods, and very goodly medows vpon the Riuers. From Ocute to Cutifachiqui may be 130. leagues; 80. leagues thereof are desert, and haue many groues of wild Pine trees. Through the wildernesse great Riuers doe passe. From Cutifachiqui to Xuala, may be 250. leagues: it is al an hilly Countrie. Cutifachiqui and Xuala stand both in plaine grounds, hie, and haue goodly medows on the Riuers. From thence forward to Chiaha, Coça, and Talise, is plaine ground, dry and fat, and very plentifull of Maiz. From Xuala to Tascaluça may be 250. leagues. From Tascaluça to Rio Grande, or the Great Riuer, may be 300. leagues: the Countrie is low, and full of lakes. From Rio Grande forwarde, the Countrie is hier and more champion, and best peopled of all the land of Florida. And along this Riuer from Aquixo to Pacaha, and Coligoa, are 150. leagues: the Countrie is plaine, and the woods thinne, and in some places champion, very fruitfull and pleasant. From Coligoa to Autiamque are 250. leagues of hillie Countrie. From Autiamque to Aguacay, may be 230. leagues of plaine ground. From Aguacay to the Riuer of Daycao 120. leagues, all hillie Countrie.

Pagina 27. From the Port de Spiritu Santo vnto Apalache, they trauelled from East to West, and Northwest. From Cutifachiqui to Xuala from South to North. From Xuala to Coça from East to West. From Coça to Tascaluça, and to Rio Grande, as far as the Prouinces of Quizquiz and Aquixo from East to West. From Aquixo to Pacaha to the North. From Pacaha to Tulla from East to West: and from Tulla to Autiamque from North to South, to the Prouince of Guachoya and Daycao.

The bread which they eate in all the land of Florida is of Maiz, which is like course millet. And this maiz is common in all the Islandes and West Indies from the Antiles forward. There are also in Florida great store of Walnuts and Plummes, Mulberries, and Grapes. They sow and gather their Maiz euery one their seuerall crop. The fruits are common to all: for they grow abroad in the open fields in great abundance, without any neede of planting or dressing. Where there be Mountaines, there be chestnuts: they are somewhat smaller then the chestnuts of Spaine. Soft Walnuts Eastward from Rio Grande. Hard Walnuts Westward from Rio Grande. From Rio Grande Westward, the Walnuts differ from those that grow more Eastward: for they are soft, and like vnto Acornes: And those which grow from Rio Grande to Puerto del Spiritu Santo for the most part are hard; and the trees and Walnuts in shew like those of Spaine. There is a fruit through all the Countrie which groweth on a plant like Ligoacan, which the Indians doe plant. The fruit is like vnto Peares Riall: it hath a verie good smell, and an excellent taste. There groweth another plant in the open field, which beareth a fruit like vnto strawberries, close to the ground, which hath a verie good taste. The Plummes are of two kindes, red and gray, of the making and bignesse of nuts, and haue three or four stones in them. These are better than all the plummes of Spaine, & they make farre better Prunes of them. In the Grapes there is onelie want of dressing: for though they bee big, they have a great Kirnell. All other fruits are very perfect, and lesse hurtfull than those of Spaine.

Beasts. There are in Florida many Beares, and Lyons, Wolues, Deere, Dogges, Cattes, Marterns, and Conies. Fowles. There be many wild Hennes as big as Turkies, Partridges small like those of Africa, Cranes, Duckes, Pigeons, Thrushes and Sparrowes. There are certaine Blacke birds bigger then Sparrowes, and lesser then Stares. There are Gosse Hawkes, Falcons, Ierfalcons, and all Fowles of prey that are in Spaine.

The Indians are well proportioned. Those of the plaine Countries are taller of bodie, and better shapen, then those of the Mountaines. Those of the Inland haue greater store of Maiz, and commodities of the Countrie, then those that dwell vpon the sea coast. The Countrie along the sea coast is barren and poore: and the people more warlike. The coast runneth from Puerto del Spiritu Santo to Apalache, East and West; and from Apalache to Rio de las Palmas from East to West: from Rio de las Palmas vnto Nueua Espanna from North to South. It is a gentle coast, but it hath many sholdes, and great shelues of sand.

Deo gratias.

This relation of the discouerie of Florida was printed in the house of Andrew de Burgos, Printer and Gentleman of the house of my Lord Cardinall the Infante.

It was finished the tenth of Februarie in the yeere one thousand, fiue hundred, fiftie and seuen, in the noble and most loyall citie of Euora.

SVNDRY VOYAGES

MADE FROM NUEUA GALICIA, AND NUEUA VISCAIA IN NEW SPAINE, TO THE 15. PROUINCES OF NEW MEXICO, AND TO QUIUIRA AND CIBOLA, ALL SITUATE ON THE BACKESIDE OF GUASTECAN, FLORIDA, AND VIRGINIA, AS FARRE AS 37. DEGREES OF NORTHERLY LATITUDE: WITH A DESCRIPTION OF THE RIUERS, LAKES, CITIES, TOWNES, NATIONS, FERTILE SOYLE, AND TEMPERATE AYRE IN THOSE PARTES; AND MOST CERTAINE NOTICE OF MANY EXCEEDING RICH SILUER MINES, AND OTHER PRINCIPALL COMMODITIES.

A discourse of the famous Cosmographer Iohn Baptista Ramusius, concerning the three voyages of Frier Marco de Niça, Francis Vasquez de Coronado, and Ferdinando Alorchon next following: taken out of his third volume of Nauigations and Voyages.

The right honourable Don Antonio de Mendoça being sent by Charles the Emperour to be viceroy of Mexico and Nueua Espanna, and hauing vnderstood that Don Ferdinando Cortez had sent many ships along the coast of Nueua Espanna to discouer countries, and to find out the Isles of the Malucos, began himselfe to desire to do the like, as viceroy of Nueua Espanna; and hereupon they fell out: for Cortez said that he was general and discouerer of the South sea, and that it belonged to him to set forth those voyages. On the other side, the lord Don Antonio alledged that it belonged to him to make that discouery, as being viceroy of Nueua Espanna. So that they fell at great variance, and Cortez returned into Spaine to complaine vnto the Emperour. Don Antonio in the meane season hauing obteined knowledge of the voiage, which Andrew Dorantez (who was one of the company of Pamphilo Naruaez that escaped, as you may reade in the relation of Aluaro Nunnez, called Cabeça de Vaca) made; sent Frier Marco de Niça with a Negro of the said Dorantez to discouer that country. Which Frier Marco de Niça being returned, and hauing informed his lordship of all his discouery, he sent captain Francis Vasquez de Coronado with many Spaniards on horsebacke, and Indians on foot: likewise he sent a fleete by sea, whereof Ferdinando Alorchon was captaine, as may be seene in the relations following.

An extract of a letter of captaine Francis Vasques de Coronado, written to a Secretary of the right noble Don Antonio de Mendoça, viceroy of Nueua Espanna. Dated in Culiacan, the 8. of March 1539.

He saith that Frier Marcus de Niça arriued in the Prouince of Topira, where he found all the Indians fled vnto the mountaines for feare of the Christians, and that for his sake they came all downe to see him, with great ioy and gladnesse. They are men of good making and whiter then others, and their women are more beautifull then others of the neighbouring prouinces. Store of golde, siluer, and precious stones in Topira. There are no great cities there, yet are the houses built of stone, and are very good, and in them they haue great store of gold, which is as it were lost, because they know not what vse to put it to. The people weare Emeralds and other precious iewels vpon their bodies: they are valiant, hauing very strong armour made of siluer, fashioned after diuers shapes of beasts. They worship for their gods such things as they haue in their houses, as namely hearbes, and birdes, and sing songs vnto them in their language, which differeth but litle from that of Culiacan. They told the Frier that they were willing to become Christians, and the Emperors subjects, for they were without a gouernour; with condition that no man should hurt them: and that they would change their golde for such things as they wanted. Commandement was giuen, that they should bee receiued without doing them any displeasure. Neere vnto this countrey there is another Prouince heretofore discouered by our men, where the people go naked without any thing before them: they are very hardly reduced to Christianitie, and they are valiant and stoute. Their houses are couered with straw. They seeke no other riches but to feede cattel. They goe at certaine seasons to their sacrifices into a valley situate in that Prouince, which is inhabited with people, esteemed by those of the countrey as saints and priests, whom they call Chichimecas, which dwell in the woods without houses: and they eate such things as they of the countrey giue them of almes. They goe naked, and are tanned in the smoke, and tye their priuie member with a string vnto their knee, and the women likewise goe starke naked. They haue certaine temples couered with strawe, with small round windowes full of skuls of dead men; before their temple is a great round ditch, the brim whereof is compassed with the figure of a serpent made of gold and siluer, and with another mixture of vnknowen metals: and this serpent holdeth his tayle in his mouth. They of this valley from time to time cast lots, whose lucke it shal be to be sacrificed, and they make him great cheere, on whom the lotte falleth, and with great ioy they crowne him with flowers vpon a bed prepared in the sayd ditch all full of flowres and sweete hearbes, on which they lay him along, and lay great store of dry wood on both sides of him, and set on fire on eyther part, and so he dyeth. Where he continueth so quietly without being bound, as though hee did something, wherein he tooke great pleasure. And they say that hee is a Saint, and doe worshippe him for that yeere, and sing prayses, and Hymnes vnto him and afterward set vp his head with the rest in order within those windowes. Also they sacrifice their prisoners, whom they burn in another deeper ditch, and not with the foresayde ceremonies. The Spanyards which are in Xalisco write, that hauing good assistance, they hope that those people will become Christians. The Countrey is very good and fruitfull, and hath great store of good and wholesome waters.

A Letter of Francis Vazquez de Coronado, Gouernour of Nueua Galicia, to the lord Don Antonio de Mendoça, Viceroy of Nueua Espanna. Dated in Saint Michael of Culiacan, the 8. of March, 1539.

Of the hard passage from Saint Michael of Culiacan to Topira. The description of that Prouince, and of another neere vnto the same, very rich in gold and precious stones. The number, of the people which Vazquez caried with him in his iourney thither; and how greatly Frier Marcus of Niça is honoured by the Indians of Petatlan.

By the help of God I meane to set forward from this City of S. Michael of Culiacan toward Topira the 10. of April: neither can I any sooner set forward, because the powder and match which your Lordship sendeth mee, cannot be brought thither, before that time, and I thinke it be now in Compostella. Besides this, I am to passe many leagues ouer mightie high mountaines which reach vp to the skyes, and ouer a Riuer, which at this present is so bigge and swollen, that it can in no place be waded ouer. And if I depart at the time aforesayde, they say wee may wade ouer it. They tolde mee that from hence to Topira was not aboue 50 leagues; and I haue learned since that it is aboue foure score leagues. I doe not remember that I haue written to your Lordshippe the information which I haue of Topira: and though I had written thereof vnto you, yet because that since that time I haue learned something more, I thinke it meete to signifie them vnto your Lordshippe in these my letters. It may please your honour therefore to vnderstand, that they tell mee, that Topira is a very populous Prouince, lying betweene two riuers, and that there are aboue 50. inhabited townes therein. And that beyond the same there is another Countrey greater then it, the name whereof the Indians could not tell mee, wherein there is great store of victuals of Maiz, French peason, Axi or Pepper, Melons, and Gourds, and great store of Hennes of the countrey. These may seeme to be the Pintados mentioned by Frier Marco de Niza in his 2. Chap. The people weare on their bodies golde, Emeralds, and other precious stones, and are serued commonly in golde and siluer, wherewith they couer their houses: and the chiefe men weare great chaines of golde well wrought, about their necks and are apparelled with paynted garments, and haue store of wilde kine; and they say they enter not into their countrey, because themselues haue no great store of people: those Indians being many in number, and very valiant. That which here I say, I learned by two other relations of Indians dwelling neere vnto them. I meane to set forward at the time before mentioned, and I carrie with me 150 horsemen, and twelue spare horsemen, and 200. footmen, crossebowmen, and gunners. I take also with me liue hogs, sheepe and all such things as I can get for money: assure your Lordship that I meane not to returne to Mexico vntil I be able to informe your honour more perfectly, what the state of this place is: and if I find ought that we may doe good in, I will stay there, vntill I haue aduertised your Lordship, that you may command what you will haue done: and if it fall out so vnluckily, that there is nothing of importance, I will seeke to discouer 100. leagues farther, wherein (I hope in God) there will be something found in which your Lordship may imploy all these gentlemen and those which shall come hither hereafter. I thinke I cannot chuse but stay there: and the waters, the seasons, the disposition of the countrey, and other accidents wil direct mee what is best to be done. Frier Marco de Niça entred a good way into the countrey, accompanied with Stephan Dorantez, the 7. of February last past: when I departed from them, I left them with aboue 100. Indians of Petatlan, and from the time of their comming thither they greatly honoured the father, shewing him all the courtesies they could possibly. I cannot send you, nor describe vnto you his entrance among them better then I have done in all my relations which I wrote in my letters from Compostella, and I signified vnto you all things to the full from the citie of Michael: and though there is but the tenth part of those things it is a great matter. Herewithall I haue sent your Lordship a Letter, which I receiued from him: and I beleeue he may trauel many leagues farther in that sort. He saith, that if he finde any good countrey, he will write to mee thereof: I will not goe thither without informing your Lordship of my iourney. I hope in God that by one way or other wee shall discouer some good thing.

A Letter written by the most honourable Lord Don Antonio de Mendoça, Vice-roy of Nueua Espanna, to the Emperours Maiestie.

Of certaine Noblemen which sought to discouer the end of the firme land of Nueua Espanna toward the North. The arriuall of Vazquez de Coronado with Frier Marco at S. Michael of Culiacan, with commission to the Gouernours of those parts to pacifie the Indians, and not to make them slaues any more.

In the ships that went last from hence (whereof Michael de Vsnago was Admirall) I wrote vnto your Maiestie, how I sent two Franciscan Friers to discouer the ende of this firme land, which stretcheth to the North. And because their iourney fell out to greater purpose then was looked for, I will declare the whole matter from the beginning. It may please your Maiestie to call to minde how often I wrote vnto your Highnesse, that I desired to know the ende of this Prouince of Nueua Espanna, becavse it is so great a countrey, and that we haue yet no knowledge thereof. Neither had I onely this desire: for Nunno de Guzman departed out of this city of Mexico with 400 horsemen, and 14000. Indians footemen borne in these Indias, being the best men, and the best furnished, which haue beene seene in these parts: and he did so litle with them, that the most part of them were consumed in the enterprize, and could not enter nor discouer any more then already was discouered. After this the saide Nunno Guzman beeing Gouernour of Nueua Galacia, sent Captaines and Horsemen foorth diuers times, which sped no better then he had done. Likewise the Marques de valle Hernando Cortez sent a captaine with 2. ships to discouer the coast, which 2. ships and the captaine perished. After that he sent againe 2. other ships, one of which was diuided from her consort and the Master and certaine mariners slue the captaine, and vsurped ouer the ship. This was the Port of Santa Cruz in the Isle of California. After this they came to an

Island, where the Master with certaine mariners going on land, the Indians of the countrey slew them and tooke their boat: and the ship with those that were in it, returned to the coast of Nueua Galacia, where it ran on ground. By the men which came home in this ship, the Marques had knowledge of the countrey which they had discouered: and then, either for the discontentment which hee had with the bishop of Saint Domingo, and with the Iudges of this royal audience in Mexico, or rather because of his so prosperous successe in all things here in Nueua Espanna, without seeking any farther intelligence of the state of that Island, he set forward on that voyage with 3. Ships, and with certaine footemen and horsemen, not throughly furnished with things necessary; which fell out so contrary to his expectation, that the most part of the people which he carryed with him, dyed of hunger. And although he had ships, and a Countrey very neere him abounding with victuals, yet could hee neuer finde meanes to conquer it, but rather it seemed, that God miraculously did hide it from him: and so he returned home without atchieuing ought else of moment. After this, hauing heere in my company Andrew Dorantez, which is one of those who were in the voyage of Pamphilo Naruaez I often was in hand with him, supposing that he was able to doe your Maiestie great seruice, to imploy him with fortie or fiftie horses, to search out the secret of those parts: and hauing prouided all things necessary for his iourney, and spent much money in that behalfe, the matter was broken off, I wot not how, and that enterprise was giuen ouer. Yet of the things which were prouided for that purpose, I had left mee a Negro, which returned from the foresayde voyage of Naruaez, with Dorantez, and certaine slaues which I had bought, and certaine Indians which I had gathered together, who were borne in those North partes, whome I sent with Frier Marco de Niça, and his companion a Franciscan Frier, because they had bene long trauelled, and exercised in those partes, and had great experience in the affaires of the Indies, and were men of good life and conscience, for whom I obtained leaue of their superiours: and so they went with Frances Vazquez de Coronado, gouernour of Nueua Galicia vnto the Citie of Saint Michael of Culiacan, which is the last Prouince subdued by the Spaniards towarde that quarter, being two hundred leagues distant from this Citie of Mexico. Assoone as the Gouernour, and the Friers were come vnto that Citie, hee sent certaine of those Indians which I had giuen him, home into their Countrey, to signifie, and declare to the people of the same, That they were to vnderstand, that your Maiestie had commaunded they should not hereafter bee made slaues, and that they should not be afrayd any more, but might returne vnto their houses, and liue peaceably in them, (for before that time they had bin greatly troubled by the euill dealings which were vsed toward them) and that your Maiestie would cause them to be chastened, which were the causes of their vexation. With these Indians about twentie dayes after returned about 400 men; which comming before the gouernour said vnto him, that they came on the behalfe of al their Countrey-men, to tell him, that they desired to see and know those men which did them so great a pleasure as to suffer them to returne to their houses, and to sow Maiz for their sustenance: for by the space of many yeres they were driuen to flee into the mountaines, hiding themselues like wild beasts, for feare lest they should be made slaues, and that they and all the rest of their people were ready to doe whatsoeuer should bee commaunded them. Whom the gouernour comforted with good wordes, and gaue them victuals, and stayed them with him three or foure dayes, wherein the Friers taught them to make the signe of the Crosse, and to learne the name of our Lorde Iesus Christ, and they with great diligence sought to learne the same. After these dayes hee sent them home againe, willing them not to be afraid, but to be quiet, giuing them apparel, beades, kniues, and other such like things, which I had giuen him for such purposes. The sayde Indians departed very well pleased, and said, that whensoeuer hee would send for them, they and many others would come to doe whatsoeuer he would command them. The entrance being thus prepared, Frier Marco and his companion, with the Negro and other slaues, and Indians which I had giuen him, went forward on their voyage 10. or 12. dayes after. And because I had likewise aduertisement of a certaine Prouince called Topira situate in the mountaines, and had appointed the gouernour Vasquez de Coronado, that he should vse meanes to learne the state thereof: he supposing this to be a matter of great moment, determined himselfe to goe and search it, hauing agreed with the said Frier, that he should returne by that part of the mountaine, to meete with him in a certaine valley called Valle de los Coraçones, beeing 120. leagues distant from Culiacan. The gouernour trauelling into this prouince (as I haue written in my former letters) found great scarcity of victuals there, and the mountaines so craggy, that he could finde no way to passe forward, and was inforced to returne home to Saint Michael: so that aswell in chusing of the entrance, as in not being able to finde the way, it seemeth vnto all men, that God would shut vp the gate to all those, which by strength of humane force haue gone about to attempt this enterprise, and hath reuieled it to a poore and bare-footed Frier. And so the Frier beganne to enter into the Land, who because he found his entrance so well prepared, was very well receiued; and because he wrote the whole successe of his voyage, according to the instruction which I had giuen him to vndertake the same, I wil not write any more at large, but send your Maiestie this copy of all such things as he obserued in the same.

A relation of the reuerend father Frier Marco de Niça, touching his discouery of the kingdome of Ceuola or Cibola, situate about 30. degrees of latitude, to the North of Nueua Espanna.

Chap. 1.

Frier Marco de Nica departeth from Saint Michael in the Prouince of Culiacan, standing in 24. degrees of Northerly latitude: and comming to the Towne of Petatlan, receiueth many courtesies of the Indians there. Departing from thence, he had information of many Islands, and of a great countrey inhabited with ciuil people; he commeth to Vacupa: where during his aboad, he heard newes of Ceuola, and of the state of the 7. Cities, and of other prouinces, and of the rich Islands of perles, which extend northward vpon the coast.

I Frier Marco de Nica of the order of S. Francis, for the execution of the instruction of the right honourable lord Don Antonio de Mendoça, Vice-roy and Captaine Generall for the Emperors Maiestie in New Spaine, departed from the towne of S. Michael in the prouince of Culiacan on Friday the 7. of March, in the yeere 1539. hauing for my companion Frier Honoratus, and carying with me Stephan a Negro; belonging to Andrew Dorantez, and certaine of those Indians which the sayde lord Vice-roy had made free, and bought for this purpose: whom Frances Vazquez de Coronado gouernour of Nueua Galicia deliuered me, and with many other Indians of Petatlan, and of the towne called Cuchillo, which is some 50. leagues from Petatlan, who came to the valley of Culiacan, shewing themselues to bee exceeding glad, because they were certified by the Indians which had bin set free, whom the said gouernour had sent before to aduertise them of their libertie, that none of them from thenceforth should be made slaues, and that no man should inuade them, nor vse them badly; signifying vnto them, that <u>the Emperors Maiesty</u> had willed and commanded that it should be so. <u>Petatlan a towne.</u> With the foresaid company I went on my voyage vntill I came to the towne of Petatlan, finding all the way great intertainment, and prouision of victuals, with roses, flowres, and other such things, and bowers which they made for me of chalke and boughs platted together in all places where there were no houses. In this towne of Petatlan I rested 3. dayes, because my companion Honoratus fell so sicke, that I was constrained to leaue him there behinde.

Then, according to my said instruction, I followed my iourney as the holy Ghost did leade me without any merit of mine, hauing in my company the said Stephan the Negro of Dorantez, and certaine of the Indians which had bin set at liberty, and many of the people of the countrey, which gaue me great intertainment and welcome in all places where I came, and made mee bowers of trees, giuing me such victuals as they had, although they were but small: because (as they said) it had not rained there in 3 yeres, and because the Indians of this countrey sought means rather to hide themselues, then to sowe corne, for feare of the Christians of the Towne of S. Michael, which were wont to make in-roades euen to that place, and to warre vpon them, and to cary them away captiues. *The island of Saint Iago.* In all this way, which may be about 25 or 30. leagues from that part of Petatlan, I saw nothing worthy the noting, saue that there came to seeke me certaine Indians from the Island, where Fernando Cortez the Marques of the valley had bin, of whom I was informed, that it was an Island, and not firme land, as some suppose it to be. They came to the firme land vpon certaine rafts of wood: and from the maine to the island is but halfe a league by sea, litle more or lesse. *A great island, and 30. small islands, which seeme to be the new islands of California rich in pearles.* Likewise certaine Indians of another Island greater then this came to visit me, which island is farther off, of whom I was informed that there were 30. other smal islands, which were inhabited, but had smal store of victuals, sauing 2. which haue Maiz or corne of the countrey. These Indians had about their necks many great shels which were mother of Pearle. I shewed them pearles which I carryed with me for a shew, and they told me that there were in the Islands great store of them, and those very great: howbeit I saw none of them. I followed my voyage through a desert of 4. dayes iourney, hauing in my company both the Indians of the islands, and those of the mountaines which I *A desert foure daies iourney.* had passed, and at the end of this desert I found other Indians which maruelled to see me, because they had no knowledge of any Christians, hauing no traffike nor conuersation with those Indians which I had passed, in regard of the great desert which was between them. These Indians interteined me exceeding courteously, and gaue me great store of victuals, and sought to touch my garments, and called me Hayota, which in their language signifieth A man come from heauen. These Indians I aduertised by my interpreter, according to my instructions, in the knowledge of our Lord God in heauen, and of the Emperor. *This was the valley of Coraçones.* In these countries and in all places els by all wayes and meanes possible, I sought information where any Countreys were of more Cities and people of civilitie and vnderstanding, then those which I had found: and I could heare no newes of any such: howbeit they tolde mee, that foure or fiue dayes iourney within the Countrey, at the foote of the mountaines, there is a large and mightie plaine, wherein they tolde mee, that there were many great Townes, and people clad in Cotton: and when I shewed them certaine Metals which I carryed with mee, to learne what riche Metals were in the Lande, they tooke the minerall of Golde and tolde mee, that thereof were vesselles among the people of that plaine, and that they carryed certaine round greene stones hanging at their nostrilles, and at their eares, and that they haue certaine thinne plates of that Golde, wherewith they scrape off their sweat, and that the walles of their Temples are couered therewith, and that they vse it in all their household vessels. And because this Valley is distant from the Sea-coast, and my instruction was not to leaue the Coast, I determined to leaue the discouery thereof vntill my returne; at which time I might doe it more commodiously.

Vacupa a town 40. leagues from the Bay of California. Thus I trauelled three dayes iourney through townes inhabited by the sayde people, of whome I was receiued as I was of those which I had passed, and came vnto a Towne of reasonable bignesse, called Vacupa, where they shewed mee great courtesies, and gaue mee great store of good victuals, because the soyle is very fruitfull, and may bee watered. This Towne is fortie leagues distant from the Sea. And because I was so farre from the Sea, it being two dayes before Passion Sunday, I determined to stay there vntill Easter, to informe my selfe of the Islandes, whereof I sayde before that I had information. And so I sent certaine Indians to the Sea by three seuerall wayes, whom I commanded to bring mee some Indians of the Sea-coast, and of some of those Islandes, that I might receiue information of them: and I sent Stephan Dorantez the Negro another way, whom I commanded to goe directly Northward fiftie or threescore leagues, to see if by that way hee might learne any newes of any notable thing which wee sought to discouer, and I agreed with him, that if hee found any knowledge of any peopled and riche Countrey which were of great importance, that hee should goe no further, but should returne in person, or should sende mee certaine Indians with that token which wee were agreed vpon, to wit, that if it were but a meane thing, hee should sende mee a white Crosse of one handfull long; and if it were any great matter, one of two handfuls long; and if it were a Countrey greater and better then Nueua Espanna, hee should send mee a great crosse. So the sayde Stephan departed from mee on Passion-sunday after dinner: and within foure dayes after the messengers of Stephan returned vnto me with a great Crosse as high as a man, and they brought me word from Stephan, that I should forthwith come away after him, for hee had found people which gaue him information of a very mighty Prouince, and that he had certaine Indians in his company, which had bene in the sayd Prouince, and that he had sent me one of the said Indians. *From Vacupa to Ceuola are 32. dayes iourney.* This Indian told me, that it was thirtie dayes iourney from the Towne where Stephan was, vnto the first Citie of the sayde Prouince, which is called Ceuola. Hee affirmed also, that there are seuen great Cities in this Prouince, all vnder one Lord, the houses whereof are made of Lyme and Stone, and are very great, and the least of them with one lofte aboue head, and some of two and of three loftes, and the house of the Lorde of the Prouince of foure, and that all of them ioyne one vnto the other in good order, and that in the gates of the principall houses there are many Turques-stones cunningly wrought, whereof hee sayth they haue there great plentie: also that the people of this Citie goe very well apparelled: and that beyond this there are other Prouinces, all which (hee sayth) are much greater then these seuen cities. I gaue credite to his speach, because I found him to bee a man of good vnderstanding: but I deferred my departure to follow Stephan Dorantes, both because I thought hee would stay for mee, and also to attend the returne of my messengers which I had sent vnto the Sea, who returned vnto me vpon Easter day, bringing with them certaine inhabitants of the Sea-coast, and of two of the Islands. Of whom I vnderstoode, Great pearles and much gold in the Isles of California, which are 34. in number. that the Islandes aboue mentioned were scarce of victuals, as I had learned before, and that they are inhabited by people, which weare shelles of Pearles vpon their foreheads, and they say that they haue great Pearles, and much Golde. They informed mee of foure and thirtie Islandes, lying one neere vnto another: they say that the people on the Sea-coast haue small store of victuals, as also those of the Islandes, and that they traffique one with the other vpon raftes. This coast stretcheth Northward as is to bee seene. These Indians of the Coast brought me certaine Targets made of Cow-hydes very well dressed, which were so large, that they couered them from the head to the very foote, with a hole in the toppe of the same to looke out before: they are so strong that a Crossebow (as I suppose) will not pierce them.

Chap. 2.

He hath new information of the seuen Cities by certain Indians called Pintados, and of three other kingdomes called Marata, Acus, and Totonteac, being Countreys very rich in Turqueses and Hides of cattel. Following his voyage through those countries, he taketh possession thereof for the Emperors Maiestie, and of the Indians is much honoured and serued with victuals.

The same day came three Indians of those which I called Pintados, because I saw their faces, breasts and armes painted. These dwel farther vp into the countrey towards the East, and some of them border vpon the seuen cities, which sayd they came to see mee, because they had heard of me: and among other things, they gaue me information of the seuen cities, and of the other Prouinces, which the Indian that Stephan sent me had tolde me of, almost in the very same manner that Stephan had sent mee worde; and so I sent backe the people of the sea-coast; and two Indians of the Islandes sayde they would goe with mee seuen or eight dayes.

So with these and with the three Pintados aboue mentioned, I departed from Vacupa vpon Easter Tuesday, the same way that Stephan went, from whom I receiued new messengers with a Crosse of the bignesse of the first which he sent me: which hastened mee forward, and assured me that the land which I sought for, was the greatest and best countrey in all those partes. The sayd messengers told mee particularly without fayling in any one poynt, all that which the first messenger had tolde mee, and much more, and gaue mee more plaine information thereof. So I trauelled that day being Easter Tuesday, and two dayes more, the very same way that Stephan had gone; at the end of which 3 dayes they tolde mee, that from that place a man might trauell in thirtie dayes to the citie of Ceuola, which is the first of the seuen. Neither did one onely tell me thus much, but very many; who tolde me very particularly of the greatnesse of the houses, and of the fashion of them, as the first messengers had informed me. Also they tolde me, that besides these seuen Cities, there are 3 other kingdomes which are called Marata, Acus, and Totonteac. I enquired of them wherefore they trauelled so farre from their houses: They said that they went for Turqueses and Hides of kine, and other things; and that of all these there was great abundance in this Countrey. Likewise I enquired how, and by what meanes they obteined these things: They tolde me, by their seruice, and by the sweat of their browes, and that they went vnto the first citie of the Prouince which is called Ceuola, and that they serued them in tilling their ground, and in other businesses, and that they giue them Hydes of oxen, which they haue in those places, and turqueses for their seruice, and that the people of this city weare very fine and excellent turqueses hanging at their eares and at their nostrils. They say also, that of these turqueses they make fine workes vpon the principall gates of the houses of this citie. They tolde mee, that the apparell which the inhabitants of Ceuola weare, is a gowne of cotten downe to the foote, with a button at the necke, and a long string hanging downe at the same, and that the sleeues of these gownes are as broad beneath as aboue. They say, they gyrd themselues with gyrdles of turqueses, and that ouer these coates some weare good apparel, others hides of kine very well dressed, which they take to bee the best apparel of that countrey, whereof they haue there great quantitie. Likewise the women goe apparelled, and couered downe to the foote. These Indians gaue me very good intertainment, and curiously enquired the day of my departure from Vacupa, that at my returne they might prouide me of foode and lodging. They brought certaine sicke folkes before mee, that I might heale them, and sought to touch my apparell, and gaue mee certaine Cow-hydes so well trimmed and dressed, that by them a man might coniecture that they were wrought by ciuile people, and all of them affirmed, that they came from Ceuola.

The next day I followed my journey, and carrying with mee the Pintados, I came to another Village where I was well receiued by the people of the same: who likewise sought to touch my garments, and gaue mee as particular knowledge of the Lande aforesayde, as I had receiued of those which mette mee before: and also tolde mee, that from that place certaine people were gone with Stephan Dorantez, fours or fiue dies journey. And here I found a great crosse, which Stephan had left me for a signe, that the newes of the good Countrey increased, and left worde, that with all haste they should sende mee away, and that hee would stay for mee at the ende of the first Desert that he mette with. Heere I set vp two Crosses, and tooke possession according to mine instruction, because that the Countrey seemed better vnto mee then that which I had passed, and that I thought it meete to make an acte of possession as farre as that place.

In this maner I trauailed fiue dayes alwayes finding inhabited places with great hospitalitie and intertainments, and many Turqueses, and Oxe-hides, and the like report concerning the countrey. Heere I vnderstood, that after two dayes iourney I should finde a desert where there is no foode; but that there were certaine gone before to build mee lodgings, and to carrie foode for mee: whereupon I hastened my way, hoping to finde Stephan at the ende thereof, because in that place hee had left worde that he would stay for mee. Before I came to the desert, I mette with a very pleasant Towne, by reason of great store of waters conueighed thither to water the same.

Heere I mette with many people both men and women clothed in Cotton, and some couered with Oxe-hydes, which generally they take for better apparell then that of cotton. All the people of this Village goe in Caconados, that is to say, with Turqueses hanging at their nostrilles and eares: which Turqueses they call Cacona. Amongst others the Lord of this Village came vnto me, and two of his brethren very well apparelled in Cotton, who also were in Caconados, each of them hauing his Collar of Turqueses about his necke: and they presented vnto mee many wilde beastes, as Conies, Quailes, Maiz, nuttes of Pine trees, and all in great abundance, and offered mee many Turqueses and dressed Oxe-hydes and very fayre vessels to drinke in, and other things: whereof I would receiue no whit. Store of woollen cloth and sheepe in Totonteac. And hauing my garment of gray cloth, which in Spaine is called çaragoça, the Lord of this Village, and the other Indians touched my gowne with their handes, and tolde mee, that of such Cloth there was great store in Totonteac, and that the people of that Countrey wore the same. Whereat I laughed, and sayde that it was nothing else but such apparell of Cotton as they wore. And they replyed: We would haue thee thinke that we vnderstand, that apparell which thou wearest, and that which we weare are of diuers sortes. Vnderstand thou, that in Ceuola all the houses are full of that apparell which we weare, but in Totonteac there are certaine litle beasts, from whom they take that thing wherewith such apparell as thou wearest, is made. I prayed them to informe mee more playnely of this matter. And they tolde me that the sayde beastes were about the bignesse of the two braches or spaniels which Stephan carryed with him, and they say that there is great store of that cattell in Totonteac.

Chap. 3.

He entreth into a desert, and the Indians suffer him to want nothing necessary. Following his Voyage, he commeth into a fertile valley, and hath certaine knowledge giuen him (as he had before) of the state of Ceuola, and of Totonteac; and that the coast of the sea in 35. degrees trendeth much to the Westward: and also of the kingdomes of Marata and Acus.

A desert of foure dayes iourney. The next day I entred into the Desert, and where I was to dine, I found bowers made, and victuals in abundance by a riuers side; and at night I found bowers and victuals in like sort, and after that maner I found for 4 dayes trauell: all which time the wildernesse continueth.

A very populous valley. At the ende of these foure dayes, I entered into a valley very well inhabited with people. At the first Village there mette me many men and women with victuals, and all of them had Turqueses hanging at their nostrils and eares, and some had collars of turqueses like those which the Lord of the Village before I came to the Desert, and his two *Collars of turqueses two or three times double.* brethren wore: sauing that they ware them but single about their neckes, and these people weare them three or foure times double, and goe in good apparell, and skinnes or Oxen: and the women weare of the sayd Turqueses at there nostrils and ears, and very good wast-coats and other garments. Heere there was a great knowledge of Ceuola, as in Nueua Espanna of Temistitan, and in Peru of Cuzco: and they tolde vs particularly the maner of their houses, lodgings, streetes and market-places, as men that had bene oftentimes there, and as those which were furnished from thence with things necessary for the seruice of their housholde, as those also had done, which I already had passed. I tolde them it was impossible that the houses should be made in such sort as they informed mee, and they for my better vnderstanding tooke earth or ashes, and powred water thereupon, and shewed me how they layd stones vpon it, and how the buylding grew vp, as they continued laying stones thereon, vntill it mounted aloft. I asked them whether the men of that Countrey had wings to mount vp vnto those loftes: whereat they laughed, and shewed mee a Ladder in as good sort as I my selfe was able to describe it. Then they tooke a Staffe and helde it ouer their heads, and said that the lofts were so high one aboue another. Likewise heere I had information of the woollen cloth of Totonteac, where they say are houses like those of Ceuola, and better and more in number, and that it is a great Prouince, and hath no gouernour.

This graduation is mistaken by 6. or 7. degrees at the least. Here I vnderstand that the coast of the sea trended much toward the West: for vnto the entrance of this first desert which I passed, the coast still stretched Northward: and because the trending of the coast is a thing of great importance, I was desirous to knowe and see it: and I saw plainely, that in 35. degrees the coast stretcheth to the West, whereat I reioyced no lesse then of the good newes within land, and so I returned backe to proceede in my iourney.

Through the foresayd valley I trauailed fiue dayes iourney which is inhabited with goodly people, and so aboundeth with victuals, that it sufficeth to feede aboue three thousand horsemen: it is all well watered and like a garden: the burroughs and townes are halfe and a quarter of a league long, and in all these villages, I found very ample report of Ceuola, whereof they made such particular relation vnto me, as people which goe yeerely thither to earne their liuing. Heere I found a man borne in Ceuola, who told me that he came thither, hauing escaped from the gouernour or Lieutenant of the towne; for the Lord of these seuen Cities liueth and abideth in one of those townes called Ahacus, and in the rest he appoynteth lieu-tenants vnder him. This townesman of Ceuola is a white man of a good complexion, somewhat well in yeeres, and of farre greater capacitie then the inhabitants of this valley, or then those which I had left behind me. Hee sayde that he would goe with mee, that I might begge his pardon: and of him I learned many particulars: he tolde me that Ceuola was a great Citie, inhabited with great store of people, and hauing many Streetes and Market-places: and that in some partes of this Citie there are certaine very great houses of fiue stories high, wherein the chiefe of the Citie assemble themselues at certaine dayes of the yeere. He sayeth that the houses are of Lyme and Stone, according as others had tolde mee before, and that the gates, and small pillars of the principall houses are of Turqueses, and all the vessels wherein they are serued, and the other ornaments of their houses were of golde: and that the other sixe Cities are built like vnto *this, whereof some are bigger: and that Ahacus is the chiefest of them.* *Marata lieth toward the Southeast.* Hee sayth that toward the Southeast there is a kingdome called Marata, and that there were woont to be many, and those great Cities, which were all built of houses of Stone, with diuers lofts: and that these haue and doe wage warre with the Lord of the seuen cities, through which warre this kingdome of Marata is for the most part wasted, although it yet continueth and mainteineth warre against the other.

Totonteac lyeth West. Likewise he saith, that the kingdome called Totonteac lyeth toward the West, which he saith is a very mightie Prouince, replenished with infinite store of people and riches: and that in the sayde Kingdome they weare woollen cloth like that which I weare, and other finer sorts of woollen cloth made of the fleeces of those beastes which they described before vnto me: and that they are a very ciuile people. Moreouer hee tolde me, that there is another great Prouince and kingdome called Acus; for there is Acus, and Ahacus with an aspiration, which is the principall of the seuen cities: and Acus without an aspiration is a kingdome and Prouince of it selfe. He told me also, that the apparel which they weare in Ceuola is after the same maner as they before had certified me, and that all the inhabitants of the Citie lie vpon beddes raysed a good height from the ground, with quilts and canopies ouer them, which couer the sayde Beds: and hee tolde mee that he would goe with me to Ceuola and farther also, if I would take him with me. The like relation was giuen vnto me in this towne by many others, but not so particularly. I trauelled three dayes iourney through this valley: the inhabitants whereof made mee exceeding great cheere and intertainement. In this valley I saw aboue a thousand Oxe-hides most excellently trimmed and dressed. And here also I saw farre greater store of Turqueses and chaines made thereof, then in all places which I had passed; and they say, that all commeth from the city of Ceuola, whereof they haue great knowledge, as also of the kingdome of Marata, and of the kingdomes of Acus and Totonteac.

Chap. 4.

Of a very great beast with one horne vpon his forehead; and of the courtesies which the Indians shewed Frier Marcus of Niça, in his Voyage. Also how cruelly Stephan Dorantez and his companions were vsed vpon their arriuall at Ceuola, by the Lorde thereof.

Here they shewed me an hide halfe as bigge againe as the hide of a great oxe, and tolde me that it was the skin of a beast which had but one horne vpon his forehead, and that this horne bendeth toward his breast, and that out of the same goeth a point right forward, wherein he hath so great strength, that it will breake any thing how strong so euer it be, if he runne against it, and that there are great store of these beasts in that Countrey. The colour of the hide is of the colour of a great Goat-skin, and the haire is a finger thicke. Here I had messengers from Stephan which brought me word, that by this time he was come to the farthest part of the desert, and that he was very ioyfull, because the farther he went, the more perfect knowledge he had of the greatnesse of the countrey, and sent me word, that since his departure from me, hee neuer had found the Indians, in any lye; for euen vnto that very place he had found al in such maner as they had informed him, and hoped that he should find the like at his arriuall in the valley which he was going vnto, as he had found in the villages before passed. I set vp crosses, and vsed those acts and ceremonies, which were to be done according to my instructions. Fifteene daies iourney from the end of the desert to Ceuola or Ciuola. The inhabitants requested me to stay here three or foure daies, because that from this place there were foure dayes iourney vnto the desert, and from the first entrance in the same desert vnto the citie of Ceuola are 15 great dayes iourney more: also that they would prouide victuals for me and other necessaries for that voyage. Likewise they told me, that with Stephan the Negro were gone aboue 300 men to beare him company, and to carry victuals after him, and that in like sort many of them would go with me to serue me, because they hoped to returne home rich. I thanked them, and willed them to set things in order with speede, and so I rested there three dayes, wherein I always informed my selfe of Ceuola, and of as many other things as I could learne, and called many Indians vnto me, and examined them seuerally, and all of them agreed in one tale, and told me of the great multitude of people, and of the order of the streetes, of the greatnesse of the houses, and of the strength of the gates, agreeing altogether with that which the rest before had told me.

After three dayes many assembled themselues to goe with me, 30 of the principal of whom I tooke, being very well apparelled, and with chaines of turqueses, which some of them weare fiue or six times double, and other people to cary things necessary for them and me, and so set forward on my voyage.

Thus I entred into the second desert on the 9 of May, and trauelled the first day by a very broad and beaten way, and we came to diner vnto a water, where the Indians had made prouision for me: and at night we came to another water, where I found a house which they had fully made vp for me, and another house stood made where Stephan lodged when he passed that way, and many old cottages and many signes of fire which the people had made that trauelled to Ceuola by this way. In this sort I trauelled 12 dayes iourney being alway well prouided of victuals, of wild beasts, Hares, and Partridges of the same colour and tast with those of Spaine although they are not so big, for they be somewhat lesse.

Here met vs an Indian the sonne of one of the chiefe men that accompanied mee, which had gone before with Stephan, who came in a great fright, hauing his face and body all couered with sweat, and shewing exceeding sadnesse in his countenance; and he told mee that a dayes iourney before Stephan came to Ceuola he sent his great Mace made of a gourd by his messengers, as he was always woont to send them before him, that hee might knowe in what sort hee came vnto them, which gourd had a string of belles vpon it, and two feathers one white and another red, in token that he demanded safe conduct, and that he came peaceably. And when they came to Ceuola before the Magistrate, which the Lord of the citie had placed there for his Lieutenant, they deliuered him the sayde great gourd, who tooke the same in his hands, and after he had spyed the belles, in a great rage and fury hee cast it to the ground, and willed the messengers to get them packing with speed, for he knew well ynough what people they were, and that they should will them in no case to enter into the citie, for if they did hee would put them all to death. The messengers returned and tolde Stephan how things had passed, who answered them, that it made no great matter, and would needes proceed on his voyage till he came to the citie of Ceuola: where he found men that would not let him enter into the towne, but shut him into a great house which stoode without the citie, and streightway tooke all things from him which hee caried to truck and barter with them, and certaine turqueses, and other things which he had receiued of the Indians by the way, and they kept him there all that night without giuing him meate or drinke, and the next day in the morning this Indian was a thirst, and went out of the house to drinke at a riuer that was neere at hand, and within a little while after he saw Stephan running away, and the people followed him, and slew certaine of the Indians which went in his company. And when this Indian saw these things, he hid himselfe on the banks of the riuer, and afterward crossed the high way of the desert. The Indians that went with me hearing these newes began incontinently to lament, and I thought these heauie and bad newes would cost mee my life, neither did I feare so much the losse of mine owne life, as that I should not bee able to returne to giue information of the greatnesse of that Countrey, where our Lord God might be glorified: but streightway I cut the cords of my budgets which I carried with me ful of merchandise for traffique, which I would not doe till then, nor giue any thing to any man, and began to diuide all that I carried with mee among the principall men, willing them not to be afraid, but to goe forward with me, and so they did. And going on our way, within a dayes iourney of Ceuola wee met two other Indians of those which went with Stephan, which were bloody and wounded in many places: and assoone as they came to vs, they which were with mee began to make great lamentation. These wounded Indians I asked for Stephan, and they aggreeing in all poynts with the first Indian sayd, that after they had put him into the foresayd great house without giuing him meat and drinke all that day and all that night, they tooke from Stephan all the things which hee carried with him. The next day when the Sunne was lance high, Stephan went out of the house, and some of the chiefe men with him, and suddenly came store of people from the citie, whom assoone as hee sawe he began to run away, and we likewise, and foorthwith they shot at vs and wounded vs, and certaine dead men fell vpon vs, and so we lay till night and durst not stirre, and we heard great rumours in the citie, and saw many men and women keeping watch and ward vpon the walles thereof, and after this we could not see Stephan any more, and wee thinke they haue shot him to death, as they haue done all the rest which went with him, so that none are escaped but we onely.

Chap. 5.

The situation and greatnesse of the Citie of Ceuola, and how frier Marcus tooke possession thereof and of other prouinces, calling the same The new kingdome of S. Francis, and how after his departure from thence being preserued by God in so dangerous a voyage, he arriued at Compostella in Nueua Galicia.

Hauing considered the former report of the Indians, and the euill meanes which I had to prosecute my voyage as I desired, I thought it not good wilfully to lose my life as Stephan did; and so I told them, that God would punish those of Ceuola, and that the Viceroy when he should vnderstand what had happened, would send many Christians to chastise them: but they would not beleeue me, for they sayde that no man was able to withstand the power of Ceuola. And herewithall I left them, and went aside two or three stones cast, and when I returned I found an Indian of mine which I had brought from Mexico called Marcus, who wept and sayde vnto me: Father, these men haue consulted to kill vs, for they say, that through your and Stephans meanes their fathers are slaine, and that neither man nor woman of them shall remaine vnslaine. Then againe I diuided among them certaine other things which I had, to appease them, whereupon they were somewhat pacified, albeit they still shewed great griefe for the people which were slaine. I requested some of them to goe to Ceuola to see if any other Indian were escaped, with intent that they might learne some newes of Stephan; which I could not obtaine at their handes. When I saw this, I sayd vnto them, that I purposed to see the citie of Ceuola, whatsoeuer came of it. They sayde that none of them would goe with me. At the last when they sawe mee resolute, two of the chiefe of them sayde they would goe with me: with whome and with mine Indians and interpreters I followed my way, till I came within sight of Ceuola, which is situate on a plaine at the foote of a round hill, and maketh shew to bee a faire citie, and is better seated than any that I haue seene in these partes. The houses are builded in order, according as the Indians told me, all made of stone with diuers stories, and flatte roofes, as farre as I could discerne from a mountaine, whither I ascended to viewe the citie. The people are somewhat white, they weare apparell, and lie in beds, their weapons are bowes, they have Emralds and other jewels, although they esteeme none so much as turqueses, wherewith they adorn the walles of the porches of their houses, and their apparell and vessels, and they vse them in stead of money through all the Countrey. Their apparell is of cotton and of ox hides, and this is their most commendable and honourable apparell. Most rich mines of gold and siluer in the prouince of the Pintados. They vse vessels of gold and siluer, for they haue no other metall, whereof there is greater vse and more abundance then in Peru, and they buy the same for turqueses in the prouince of the Pintados, where there are sayd to be mines of great abundance. Of other kingdomes I could not obtaine so particular instruction. Diuers times I was tempted to goe thither, because I knewe I could but hazard my life, and that I had offered vnto God the first day that I began my iourney: in the ende I began to bee afraid, considering in what danger I should put my selfe, and that if I should dye, the knowledge of this countrey should be lost, which in my iudgement is the greatest and the best that hitherto hath been discouered: and when I told the chiefe men, what a goodly citie Ceuola seemed vnto mee, they answered me that it was the least of the seuen cities, and that Totonteac Totonteac the greatest and most populous prouince. is the greatest and best of them all, because it hath so many houses and people, that there is no ende of them. Hauing seene the disposition and situation of the place, I thought good to name that Countrey El Nueuo reyno de san Francisco: in which place I made a great heape of stones by the helpe of the Indians, and on the toppe thereof I set vp a small slender crosse because I wanted meanes to make a greater, and sayd that I set vp that crosse and heape in the name of the most honourable Lord Don Antonio de Mendoça Viceroy and Captaine generall of Nueua Espanna, for the Emperour our Lord, in token of possession, according to mine instruction. Which possession I sayd that I tooke in that place of all the seuen cities, and of the kingdomes of Totonteac, of Acus, and of Marata. Thus I returned with much more feare then victuals, and went vntill I found the people which I had left behind mee, with all the speede that I could make, whome I ouertooke in two dayes trauell, and went in their company till I had passed the desert, where I was not made so much of as before: for both men and women made great lamentation for the people which were slaine at Ceuola, and with feare I hastened from the people of this valley, and trauelled tenne leagues the first day, and so I went daily eight or ten leagues, without staying vntill I had passed the second desert. And though I were in feare, yet I determined to go to the great plaine, wherof I said before, that I had information, being situate at the foote of the mountaines, and in that place I vnderstoode that this plaine is inhabited for many dayes iourney toward the East, but I durst not enter into it, considering, that if hereafter wee shoulde inhabite this other Countrey of the seuen cities, and the kingdomes before mentioned, that then I might better discouer the same, without putting my selfe in hazard, and leaue it for this time, that I might giue relation of the things which I had now seene. At the entrance of this plaine I saw but seuen Townes onely of a reasonable bignesse, which were a farre off in a low valley beeing very greene and a most fruitfull soyle, out of which ranne many Riuers. I was informed that there was much golde in this valley, and that the inhabitants worke it into vessels and thinne plates, wherewith they strike and take off their sweat, and that they are people that will not suffer those of the other side of the plaine to traffique with them, and they could not tell me the cause thereof. Here I set vp two crosses, and tooke possession of the plaine and valley in like sort and order, as I did at other places before mentioned. Compostella in 21. degrees of latitude. And from thence I returned on my voyage with as much haste as I coulde make, vntill I came to the citie of Saint Michael in the prouince of Culiacan, thinking there to have found Francis Vazquez de Coronado gouernour of Nueua Galicia, and finding him not there, I proceeded on my iourney till I came to the Citie of Compostella, where I found him. I write not here many other particularities, because they are impertinent to this matter: I only report that which I haue seene, and which was told me concerning the Countreys through which I trauelled, and of those which I had information of.

EL VIAIE QVE HIZO ANTONIO

DE ESPEIO EN EL ANNO DE OCHENTA Y TRES: EL QUAL CON SUS COMPANNEROS DESCUBRIERON VNA TIERRA EN QUE HALLARON QUINZE PROUINCIAS TODAS LLENAS DE PUEBLOS, Y DE CASAS DE QUATRO Y CINCO ALTOS, A QUIEN PUSIERON POR NOMBRE EL NUEUO MEXICO, POR PARECERSE EN MUCHAS COSAS AL VIEJO. ESTA à LA PARTE DEL NORTE, Y SE CREE QUE POR ELLA, Y POR POBLADO, SE PUEDE VENIR HASTA LLEGAR A LA TIERRA QUE LLAMAN DEL LABRADOR.

Del Nueuo Mexico, y de su descubrimiento, y lo que del se sabe.

A.D. 1583. Ya dixe en el titulo del libro, que el anno de mil y quinientos y ochenta y tres, se auian descubierto quinze Prouincias, aquien los inuentores llamaron. *New Mexico.* El nueuo Mexico en la tierra firme de Nueua Espanna, y prometi de dar noticia del descubrimiento, como lo hare con la mayor breuedad que sea possible, porque si vuiera de poner diffusamente todo lo que vieron y supieron, fuera menester hazer dello nueua historia. *Friar Augustin Ruyz.* La substancia dello es, que el anno de mil y quinientos y ochenta y vno, teniendo noticia vn Religioso de la Orden de sant Francisco, que se llamaua fray Augustin Ruyz, que moraua en el valle de sant Bartholome, por relation de ciertos Indios. Conchos que se comunicauan con otros sus conuezinos llamados Passaguates: que hazia la parte del Norte (caminando siempre por tierra) auia ciertas poblaciones grandes, y nunca sabidas de nuestros Espannoles, ni descubiertas, con zelo de caridad, y de saluacion de las almas, pidio licencia al Conde de Corunna Viery de la dicha Nueua Espanna, y a sus mayores, para yr a ellas, a procurar aprendar su lengua, y sabida, bautizarlos, y predicarles el santo Euangelio. *His departure.* Alcançada la licencia de los sobredichos, tomando otros dos companneros de su mesma. Orden, se partio con ocho soldados, que de voluntad le quisieron acompannar, a poner en execution su Christiano y zeloso intento. Los quales a pocos dias de camino toparon con vna Prouincia, que se llamaua de los Tiguas, distante de las minas de sancta Barbora (de donde començaron la jornoda) dozientas y cinquenta leguas hazia el Norte, en la qual por cierta occasion los naturales le mataron al dicho padre vno de sus dos companeros. El qual, los soldados que yuan com el, viendo, y sintiendo el successo, y temiendo que del se podria seguir otro mayor danno, acordaron de comun consentimiento de boluerse a las minas de donde auian salido, con consideracion de que la gente que yua era muy poca para resistir a los successos que se podian offrecer en tanta distancia de la viuienda de los Espannoles, y tan lexos del necessario socorro. Los dos Religiosos que hauian quedado, no solo no vinieron en su parecer, mas antes viendo la ocasion para poner en execucion su buen desseo, y tanta mies madura para la mesa de Dios, viendo quo no podian persuadir a los soldados a passar adelante en el descubrimiento, se quedaron ellos en la dicha Prouincia con tres muchachos Indios, y vn mestizo, que auian lleuado consigo, pareciendoles que aunque quedassan solos, estauan alli seguros, por la affabilidad y amor con que los naturales della los tratauan. *The mines of Barbora 160 leagues from Mexico.* Llegados los ocho soldades adonde desseauan, embiaron luego la nueua al dicho Virey delo succedido a la ciuidad Mexico, que dista de las dichas minas de santa Barbora ciento y sesenta leguas. Sintieron mucho los religiosos de sant Francisco la quedada de sus hermanos: y timiendo no los matassen viendo los solos, començaron a mouer los animos de algunos soldados, para que en compannia de otro Religioso de la mesma Orden llamado fray Bernardino Beltran, tornassen à la dicha Prouincia, a sacar de peligro a los dichos dos Religiosos, y proseguir con la empresa començada.

Antonio de Espejo died in Havana in 1589. En esta sazon estaua en las dichas minas por cierta ocasion vn vezino de la ciuadad de Mexico, llamado Antonio de Espejo, hombre rico, y de mucho animo y industria, y zeloso del seruicio de la maiestad del Rey Don Philippe nuestro sennor, natural de Cordoua. El qual como enteniesse el desseo delos dichos religiosos, y la importancia del negocio, se offrecio a la jornada y a gastar en ella parte de su hazienda, y a riesgar su vida, siendo le para ello concedida licencia de alguna persona que representasse a su maiestad, la qual procurandola los dichos religiosos, le fue dada por el Capitan Iuan de Ontiueros Alcalde mayor por su maiestad en los pueblos que llaman las quatro Cienegas, que son en la gouernacion de la Nueua Vizcaya, setenta leguas de las dichas minas de santa Barbora, assi para que el pudiesse yr; como para que iuntasse la gente y soldados que pudiesse, para que le acompannassen, y ayudassen a conseguir su Christiano intento.

He sacrifices most of his wealth to assist the expedition. El dicho Antonio de Espejo tomo el negocio con tantas veras, que en muy pocos dias iunto los soldados y bastimentos necessarios para hazer la iornada, gastando en ello buena parte de su hazienda: y partio con todos ellos del valle de sant Bartholome a los diez de Nouiembre de mil y quinientos y ochenta y dos, lleuando para lo que se offreciesse ciento y quinze cauallos, y mulas, y muchas armas, municiones, y bastimentos, y alguna gente de seruicio.

Conchos. Endereço su camino hazia el Norte, y a dos jornados topo mucha cantidad de Indios de los que llaman Conchos en Rancherias o poblaciones de casas pagicas. Los quales como lo supiessen, y tuuiessen dello relacion muy de atras, los salieron a recebir con muestras de alegria.

Their food. La comida destos, y delos de la Prouincia, que es grande, es de carne de conejos, liebres, y venados que matan, y lo ay todo en grandissima cantidad. *Their customs.* Tienen mucho maiz, que es el trigo de las Indias calabaças, y melones, y en abundancia: y ay muchos rios que crian mucha cantidad de pescado muy bueno, y de diuersas suertes: andan casi todos desnudos, y las armas que vsan son arco y flecha, y viuen debaxo de gouierno, y sennorio de Caciques, como los Mexicanos, y no les hallaron Idolos, ni pudieron entender que adorassen à nadie, por lo qual facilmente consintieron en que les pusiessen los Christianos cruzes, y quedaron muy contentos con ellas, despues de auersido informados de los nuestros dela significacion dellas, que se hizo por interpretes que lleuauan, por cuyo medio supieron de otras poblaciones, para adonde los dichos Conchos los guiaron, accompannandolos mas de veinte y quatro leguas, que todas estauan pobladas de gente de su nacion, y los salian a recebir de paz, por auiso que embiauan los Caciques de vnos pueblos a otros.

Passaguates. Andadas las veinte y quatro leguas dichas, toparon otra nacion de Indios, llamados Passaguates, los quales viuian al modo que los ya dichos. *Silver.* Conchos sus conuezinos, y hizieron con ellos lo proprio, guiandolos adelante otras quarto jornados, con los auisos de los Caciques, de la manera ya dicha: hallaron los nuestros en este camino muchas minas de plata, al parecer de los que lo entendian, de mucho, y muy rico metal.

Tobosos. Vna jornada destas toparon otra nacion, llamada los Tobosos, los quales en viendo el rastro de los nuestros, se huyeron a las sierras, dexando sus casas y pueblos desiertos. Supose despues que algunos annos antes auian acudido por alli ciertos soldados que yuan en busca de minas, y auian lleuado cautiuos a ciertos naturales, lo qual tenia temerosos y abispados a los demas. El Capitan dio orden como los fuessen a llamar, assegurandolos de que no los seria hecho ningun mal, y diose tan buena manea que hizo venir a muchos, aquien regalo, y dio dones, acariciandolos, y declarandoles por el interprete, que no yuan a hazer mal a nadie, con lo qual se boluieron todos a sossegar, y consintieron les pusiessen Cruzes, y declarassen el mysterio dellas, mostrando reciber dello gran contentamiento, en cuya demonstracion los fueron acompannando, como lo auian hecho sus vezinos, hasta que los metieron en tierra problada de otra nacion differente, que distantan de la suya cosa de doze leguas: vsan arco, y flecha, y andan desnudos.

Prosiguese del descubrimiento del Nueuo Mexico.

Iumanos. *Rio del Norte.* La nacion hasta donde los dicho Tobosos los guiaron se llanaua Iumanos, a quien porotro nombre laman los Espannoles Patarabuyes: tienen vna Prouincia grande, y de muchos pueblos con mucha gente, y las casas eran con açoteas, y de calicanto, y los pueblos traçados por buen orden: tienen todos los hombres y mugeres los rostros rayados, y los braços, y piernas: es gente corpulenta, y de mas policia, que los que hasta alli auian visto, y tenian muchos mantenimientos, y mucha caça de pie y de buelo, y gran cantitad de pescado, a causa de tener grandes rios que vienen de hazia el Norte, y alguno tan grande como Guadalquiuir, el qual entra en la propria mar del Norte. *Good salt.* Tiene muchas lagunas de agur salida que se quaja cierto tiempo del anno, y se haze muy buena sal. Es gente bellicosa, y mostraronlo luego, porque la primera noche que los nuestros assentaron real, les flecharon, y mataron cinco cauallos, hiriendo muy mal otros tantos, y no dexaran ninguno a vida, sino por las guardas que los defendieron. *Rio Grande. Twelve days journey.* Hecho este mal racado, despoblaron el lugar, y se subieron a vna sierra que estaua cerca, adonde fue luego por la mannana el Capitan con otros cinco soldados bien armados con vn interprete llamado Pedro, Indio de su mesma nacion, y con buenas razones los quieto y dexo de paz, haziendolos baxar a su pueblo y casas, y persuadiendolos a que diestien auiso asus vezinos de que no eran hombres que hazian mal a nadie, ni les yuan a tomar sus haziendas: que lo alcanço facilmente con su prudencia, y con darles a los Caciques algunas sartas de quentas de vidrio que llenaua para este effeto, y sombreros, y otras ninnerias: con este, y con el buen tratamiento que les hazian, se fueron muchos dellos en compannia de los nuestros algunos dias, caminando siempre por la ribera del rio grande arriba dicho, portoda la qual hauia muchos pueblos di Indios desta nacion, que duraron por espacio de doze jornadas, en todas las quales auisados los vnos Caciques de los otros salian a recebir a los nuestros sin arcos, ni flechas, y les trayan muchos mantenimientos, y otros regalos y dadiuos, en especial cueros y camuças muy bien adereçados, y que no les excedian en esto las de Flandes. *Apalito.* Es gente toda vestida y hallaron que tenian alguna lumbre de nuestra sancta Fee, porque sennalauan a Dios mirando al cielo, y le llaman en sul lengua Apalito, y le conocen por sennor, de cuya larga mano, y misericordia confiessan auer recibido la vida, y el ser natural, y los bienes temporales. Venian muchos dellos y les mugeres y ninnos, a que el Religioso, que diximos que yua con el dicho Capitan y soldados, los santiguasse, y echasse la benedicion: el qual como les preguntasse de quien auian entendido aquel conocimiento de Dios que tenian: respondieron, que de tres Christianos, y vn negro, que auian passado por alli, y detenidose algunos dias en su tierra, que segun las sennas que dieron, eran Aluar Nunnes Cabeça de Vaca, y Dorantes, y Castillo Maldonado, y vn negro, que todos ellos auian escapado de la armida con que entro Panfilo de Narbaez en la Florida, y despues de auer sido muchos dias esclauos, vinieron a dar a estos pueblos, haziendo Dios por medio dellos muchos milagros, y sanando con el tocamento solo de sus manos muchos infermos, por lo qual dexaron gran nombre en toda aquella tierra. Toda esta Prouincia quedo de paz, y muy sossegada, en cuya demonstracion fueron acompannando y siruiendo a los nuestros algunos dias por la orilla del rio que diximos arriba.

A pocas dias toparon con vna gran poblacion de Indios, adonde los salieron a recebir por nueua que tuuieron de sus vezinos, y les sacaron muchas cosas muy curiosas de pluma de differentes colores, y muchas mantas de algodon barretadas de azul y blanco, como las que traen de la China, para rescatarlas, y trocarlas por otras cosas. Yuan todos, assi hombres como mugeres, y ninnos vestidos de camuças muy buenas y bien adobadas, y nancapudieron los nuestros entender que nacion era por falta de interprete que intendiesse su lengua, aunque por sennas tratauan con ellos, à los quales como les mostrassen algunas piedras de metal rico, y les preguntassen si hauiade aquello en su tierra: Respondieron por las mesmas sennas que cinco dias de comino de alli hazia el Poniente, auia de aquello en muy gran cantidad, y que ellos los guiarian para alla, y se lo mostrarian, como lo cumplieron despues, acompannandolos por espacio de veynte y dos leguas, todas pobladas de gente de su mesma nacion: a quien immediatamente se seguia por el mesmo rio arriba otra de mucha mas gente que la de la passada, de quien fueron bien recibidos, y regalados con muchos presentes especialmente de pescado que hauia infinito, *Great lakes.* a causa de vnas lagunas grandes que cerca de alli hauia, que lo crian en la abundancia dicha. Estuuieron entre estos tres dias, en los quales de dia, y de noche les hizieron muchos bayles a su modo, con particular signification de algeria: no se supo como se llamaua esta nacion por falta de interprete, aunque entendieron que se extendia mucho, y que era muy grande. Entre estos hallaron vn Indio Concho de nacion, que les dixo, y sennalo, que quinze iornadas de alli hazia el Poniente hauia vna laguna muy ancha, y cerca della muy grandes pueblos, y casas de tres y quatro altos, y la gente bien vestida, y la tierra de muchos bastimentos, el qual se offrecio de lleuarlos alla, y holgaran los nuestros dello, y solo lo dexaron de poner en effecto, pro proseguir el intento con que auian començado la jornada, que era yr al Norte a dar socorra a los Religiosos arriba dichos.

Rich ores. En esta Prouincia lo que particularmente notaron fue, que hauia muy buyen temple, y muy ricas tierras, y mucha caça de pie y buelo, y muchos metales ricos, y otras cosas particulares, y de prouecho.

Desta Prouincia fueron siguiendo su derrota por espacio de quinze dias, sin topar en todos ellos ninguna gente por entre grandes pinales de pinnas y pinnones, como los de Castilla: al cabo de los quales auiendo caminado a su parecer ochenta leguas, toparon vna pequenna Rancheria, o pueblo de poca gente, y en sus casas, que eran pobres, y de paja, gran cantidad de cueros de venados tan bien adereçados como los de Flandes, *Salt.* y mucha sal blanca, y muy buena. Hizieronles muy buen hospedaje dos dias que alli estuuieron, despues delos quales los acompannaron como doze leguas a vnas poblaciones grandes, caminando siempre por el rio del Norte ya dicho, hasta llegar a la tierra que llaman el Nueuo Mexico. Estaua toda la ribera del dicho rio llena de grandissimas alamedas de alamos blancos y en partes tomauan quatro leguas de ancho, y ansi mesmo de muchos nogales, y parrales como los de Castilla. Auiendo caminado dos dias por estas alamedas y nogueralles, toparon diez pueblos que estauan assentados en la ribera del dicho rio por ambas partes, sin otros que se mostrauan mas desuiados, en los quales les parecio auia mucha gente, y la que ellos vieron passauan en numero de diez mil animas. En esta Prouincia los regalaron mucho con recebimientos, y con lleuarlos a sus pueblos, don de les dauan mucha comida, y gallinas de la tierra, y otras cosas, y todo con gran voluntad. *Houses of four stories.* Aqui hallaron casas de quatro altos, y bien edificadas, y con galanos aposentos, y en las mas dellas auia estufas para tiempo de inuierno. *Clothing of the Natives.* Andauan vestidos de algodon, y de cuero de venado, y el traje, assi de los hombres, como de las mugeres, es al modo del de los Indios del reyno de Mexico: y lo que les causo mas estranneza, fue ver que todos ellos, y ellas andauan calçados conçapatos y botas de buen cuero con suelas de vaca, cosa que hazta alli nunca la auian visto. Las mugeres trayan el cabello muy peynado, y compuesto, y sin cosa sobre la cabeça. En todos estos pueblos auia Caciques que los gouernauan como entre los Indios Mexicanos, con Alguaziles para executar sus mandamientos, los quales van por el pueblo, diziendo à vozes la voluntad de los Caciques, y que la pongan por obra. *Idols.* En esta Prouincia hallaron los nuestros muchos Idolos que adorauan, y en especial que tenian en cada casa vn templo para el Demonio, donde le lleuan de ordinario de comer, y otra cosa, que de la manera que entre los Christianos tenemos en los caminos cruzes: assi tienen ellos vnas como capillas, altas, donde dizen, descansa, y se recrea el Demonio, quando va de vn pueblo a otro: las quales estan muy adornadas y pintadas. En todas las sementeras, o labranças, que las tienen muy grandes, tienen a vn lado dellas vn portal con quatro pilares, donde comen los trabajadores, y passan la siesta, porque es la gente muy dada ala labor, y estan de ordinario en ella: es tierra de muchos montes y pinales. *Arms.* Las armas que vsan son arcos muy fueres, y flechas con las puntas de pedernal con que passan vnta cota, y macanas, que son vnos palos de media vara de largo, y llanos todos de pedernales agudos, que bastan a partir por medio vn hombre, y ansi mesmo vnas como adargas de cuero de vaca crudio.

Prosiguese del Nueuo Mexico, y de las cosas que en el se vieron.

Tiguas. Despues de auer estado en esta Prouincia quatro dias, y a poca distancia toparon con otra, que se llamaua la Prouincia de los Tiguas, en la qual auia diez y seys pueblos: en el vno de los quales, llamado por nombre Poala, hallaron que auian muerto los indios à los dichos dos padres fray Francisco Lopez, y fray Augustin a quien yuan a buscar, y juntamene a tres muchachos, y vn mestizo. Quando los deste pueblo, y sus conuezinos vieron a los nuestros, remordiendo les la propria consciencia, y temiendose que yuan a castigarlos, y tomar vengança de las muertes de los dichos padres, no los osaron esperar, antes dexando sus casas deseirtas se subieron a las sierras mas cercanas, de donde nunca los pudieron hazer baxar, anunque lo procuraron con alagos y mannas. Hallaron en los pueblos y casas muchos mantenimientos, y gran infinidad de gallinas de la tierra, y muchas suertes de metales, y algunos que parecian muy buenos. No se pudo entender claramente que tanta gente fuesse la desta Prouincia, por causa de auerse (como ya dixe) subido a la sierra.

A debate. Auiendo hallado muertos a los que buscauan, entraron en consulta sobre si se boluerian à la Nueua Vizcaya, de donde hauian salido, o passarian adelante: en lo qual vno diuersos pareceres: pero como alli entendiessen, que a la parte de Oriente de aquella Prouincia, y muy distante de alli hauian grandes pueblos y ricos, hallandose alli tan cerca, acordo el dicho Capitan Antonio de Espejo de consentimiento de Religioso ya dicho, llamado fray Bernardino Beltran, y de la mayor parte de sus soldados, y companneros, de proseguir con el descubrimiento hasta ver en que paraua, para poder der dello noticia cierta y clara a su Magestad, como testigos de vista: y assi conformes determinaron que quedandose alli el Real, fuessen el Capitan con dos companneros en demanda de su desseo, que lo pusieron por obra. Y a dos dias de camino toparon con vna Prouincia donde vieron onze pueblos, y en ellos mucha gente, que a su parecer passaua en numero de quarenta mil animas: era tierra muy fertil y bastecida, cuyos confines estan immediatamente juntas con las tierras de Cibola, donde ay muchas vacas, de cuyos cueros se visten, y de algodon: siguiendo en la manera del gouierno el orden que guarden sus conuezinos: ay sennales de muchas minas ricas, y assi hallauan metales dellas en algunas casas de los Indios, los quales tienen, y adoran Idolos: recibieronlos de paz, y dieron les de comer. Visto esto, y la disposicion de la tierra, se boluieron al real de donde auian salido, a dar noticia a sus companneros de todo lo sobredicho.

Quires. Llegados al Real (como esta dicho) tuuieron noticia de otra Prouincia, llamada los Quires, que estaua el rio del Norte arriba seys leguas de distancia, y como se partiessen para alla, y llegassen vna legua della, les salieron a recebir de paz mucha cantidad de Indios, y a rogar que se fuessen con ellos a sus pueblos, que como lo hiziessen, fueron muy bien recebidos y regalados. Vieron solamente cinco pueblos en esta Prouincia, en los quales auia muy gran cantidad de gente, y la que ellos vieron passaua de quinze mil animas, y adoran Idolos como sus vezinos. Hallaron en vno destos pueblos vna Vrraca en vna jaula, como se vsa en Castilla, y tira soles, como los que se traen de la China, pintados en ellos el sol y la luna, y muchas estrellas. Donde come tomassen la altura, se hallaron en treynta y siete grados y medio debaxo del Norte.

Cunames. Salieron desta Prouincia, y caminando por el proprio rumbo, y a catorze leguas, hallaron otra Prouincia, llamada los Cunames donde vieron otros cinco pueblos, y el principal dellos, *City of Cia.* y mas grande se llamaua Cia, que era tan grande que tenia ocho placas, cuyas casas eran encaladas, y pintadas de colores, y mejores que las que hauian visto en las Prouincias atras: parecioles que la gente que vieron passauan de veynte mil animas: hizieron presente a los nuestros de muchas mantas curiosas, y de cosas de comer muy bien guisadas, y juzgaron ser la gente mas curiosa, y de mayor policia, de quantas hasta alli hauian visto, y de mejor gouierno: monstraronles ricos metales, y vnas sierras alli cerca de donde de los sacauan. Aqui tuuieron noticia de otra Prouincia, que staua hazia el Nordueste, que se determinaron de yra ella.

Amejes. Come vuiessen andado como seys leguas, toparon con la dicha Prouincia, que se llamaua de los Amejes, en la qual hauia siete pueblos muy grandes, y en ellos a su entender mas de treynta mil animas. Vno destos siete pueblos dixeron era muy grande y hermoso, que la dexaron de yr a ver, assi por estar de tras vna sierra, como por temor de algun ruyn successo, si a caso se diuidian los vnos de los otros. Es gente al modo de la Prouincia su vezina, y tan abastada como ella, y de tan buen gouierno.

Acoma. A quinze leguas desta Prouincia, caminando siempre hazia el Poniente, hallaron vn pueblo grande llamado Acoma, era de mas de seys mil animas, y estaua essentado sobre vno penna alta que tenia mas de cinquenta estados en alto, no teniendo otra entrada sino per vna escalera que estaua hecha en la propria penna, cosa que admiro mucho alos nuestros: toda el agua que en el pueblo auia era de cisternas.

Vinieron los principales de paz a ver a los Espannoles, y traxeron les muchas mantas, y camucas muy bien adere cadas, y gran cantidad de bastimentos. Tienen sus sembrados dos leguas de alli, y sacan el agua para regarlos de vn rio pequenno que esta cerca, en cuya ribera vieron muy grandes rosales como los de aca de Castilla. *Bellicose Natives.* Ay muchas sierras con sennales de metales, aunque no subieron a verlo, por ser los Indios dellas muchos, y muy bellicosos. Estuuieron los nuestros en este lugar tres dias, en vno de los quales los naturales les hizieron vn bayle muy solenne, saliendo a el con galannos vestidos, y con juegos muy ingeniosos, con que holgaron en se estremo.

Veynte y quatro leguas de aqui, hazia el Poniente dieron con vna Prouincia, que se nombra en lengua de los naturales Zuny, *Zuny or Cibola.* y la llaman los Espannoles Cibola, ay en ella gran cantidad de Indios, en la qual estuuo Francisco Vazquez Coronado, y dexo muchas Cruzes puestas y otras sennales de Christianidad que siempre se estauan en pie. Hallaron ansi mesmo tres Indios, Christianos que se auian quedado de aquella jornada, cuyos nombres eran Andres de Cuyoacan, Gaspar de Mexico, y Antonio de Guadalajara, los quales renian casi oluidada su misma lengua, y sabian muy bien la delos naturales, aunque a pocas bueltas que les hablaron se entendieron facilmente. *A great lake.* De quien supieron que sesenta jornadas de alli auia vna laguna, o lago muy grande, en cuyas riberas estauan muchos pueblos grandes y buenos, *Much gold.* y que los naturales tenian mucho oro, de lo qual era indicion el traer todos braceletes y orejeras dello: y que como el sobredicho Francisco Vazquez Coronado tuuiesse noticia muy cierta dello, hauia salido desta Prouincia de Cibola para yr alla, y auiendo andado doze jornadas le falto el agua, y se determino de boluer, como lo hizo, con determinacion de tornar otra vez mas de proposito a ello, que despues no lo puso an execucion, porque la muerte le atajo los passos y pensamientos.

Prosiue del Nueuo Mexico.

Another debate. A la nueua de la riqueza dicha, quiso a cudir el dicho Capitan Antonio de Espejo, y aunque eran de su parecer algunos de sus companneros, la mayor parte, y el Religioso fue de contrario: diziendo, era ya tiempo de boluerse a la nueua Viscaya de donde hauian salido, a dar cuenta de lo que auian visto: que lo pusieron por obra dentro de pocos dias la mayor parte, dexando al Capitan con nueue companneros que le quisieron seguir: el qual, despues de hauerse certificado muy por entero de la riqueza arriba dicha, y de mucha abundancia de metales que en ello auia muy buenos, salio con los dichos sus companneros desta prouincia, y caminando hazia el proprio Poniente, despues de hauer andado veinte y ocho leguas, hallaron otra muy grande en la qual les parecio hauia mas de cinquenta mil animas, cuyos moradores como supiessen su llegada, les embiaron vn recado, diziendo, que si no querian que los matassen, no se acercassen mas a sus pueblos; a lo qual respondio el dicho Capitan, que ellos no les yuan a hazer mal, como lo verian, y que assi les rogauan no se pusiessen en lleuar adelante su intento, dando al mensajero algunas cosas de las que lleuaua: el qual supo tan bien obonar a los nuestros, y allanar los pechos alborotados de los Indios, que les dieron lugar de voluntad para que entrassen, que lo hizieron con ciento y cinquenta Indios amigos de la prouincia de Cibola ya dicha, y los tres Indios Mexicanos, de quien queda hecha mencion. Vna legua antes que llegassen al primer pueblo, les salieron a recibir mas de dos mil Indios cargados de bastimentos, a quien el dicho Capitan dio algunas cosas de poco precio, que a ellos les parecio ser de mucho, y las estimaron masque si fueran de oro. *Zaguato or Ahuato.*

Llegando mas cerca del pueblo, que se llamaua Zaguato, salio a recebirlos gran muche numbre de Indios, y entre ellos los Caciques, haziendo tanta demostracion de plazer y regozijo, que echauan mucha farina de maiz por el suelo, para que la pisassen los cauallos: con esta fiesta entraron en el, y fueron muy bien hospedados, y regalados, que se lo pago en parte el Capitan, con dar a todos los mas principales sombreros, y quentas de vidrio, y otras muchas cosas que lleuaua para semejantes offrecimientos.

Despacharon luego los dichos Caciques recados a todos los de aquella Prouincia, dandoles noticia de la venida de los huespedes, y de como eran hombres muy corteses, y no les hazian mal: lo qual fue bastante para hazer los venir a todos cargados de presentes para los nuestros, y de que los importunassen, fuessen con ellos a holgarse a sus pueblos, que lo hizieron, aunque siempre con recado de lo que podia succeder. Por lo qual el dicho Capitan vso de vna cautela, y fue dezir a los Caciques, que por quanto los cauallos eran muy brauos, y les auian dicho que los querian matar, seria necessario hazer vn fuerte de calicanto donde meter los para euitar el danno que querian hazer en los Indios. Creyeronlo los Caciques tan de veras que dento de pocas horas juntaron tanta gente que hizieron el dicho fuerte que los nuestros querion con vna presteza increyble. Demas desto, diziendo el Capitan que se queria yr, le traxeron vn presente de 40. mil. mantas de algodon pintadas y blancas, y mucha cantidad de pannos de manos con borlas en las puntas, y otras muchas cosas, y entre ellas metales ricos, y que mostrauan tener mucha plata. Halaron entre estos Indios muy gran noticia de la laguna grande arriba dicha, y conformaron con los otros en lo tocante a las riquezas, y mucha abundancia de oro.

Fiado el Capitan desta gente, y de sus buenos animos, a cordo a cabo de algunos dias de dexar alli cinco de sus companneros con los demas Indios amigos, para que se boluiessen a la prouincia de Zuny con el bagaje, y de yrse el con los quatro que quedauan a la ligera en descubrimiento de cierta noticia que tenia de vnas minas muy ricas. *The mines discovered.* Lo qual puesto por obra se partio con las guias que lleuaua, y como vuiesse caminado hazia el proprio Poniente quarenta y cinco leguas, topo con las dichas minas, y saco con sus proprias manos riquissimos metales, y de mucha plata y las minas, que eran de vna veta muy ancha, estauan en vna sierra adonde se podia subir con facilidad, a causa de hauer para ello camino abierto. Cerca delas auia algunos pueblos de Indios serranos que les hizieron amistad, y los salieron a recebir con Cruzes en las cabeças, y otras sennales de paz. *A great river.* Aqui cerca toparon dos rios razonables, a cuyas orillas hauia muchas patras de vnas muy buenas, y grandes noguerales, y mucho lino como lo de Castilla, y dixeron por sennas que detras de aquellas sierras estaua vno que tenia mas de ocho leguas de ancho, pero no se pudo entender que tan cerca, *North Sea.* aunque hizieron demonstracion que corria hazia la mar del Norte, y que en las riberas del de vna y otra banda ay muchas pueblos tan grandes, que en su comparacion a quellos en que est aua eran barrios.

Despues de hauer tomado toda esta relacion, se partio el dicho Capitan para la Prouincia de Zuny, adonde hauia mendado yr a los dichos companneros: y como llegasse a ella con salud, hauiendo ydo por muy buen camino, hallo con ella a sus cinco companneros, y al dicho padre Fray Bernardino con los soldados que se auian determinado de boluer, como ya diximos, que aun no se auian partido, por ciertas ocasiones: a los quales los naturales hauian hecho muy buen tratamiento, y dadoles todo lo necessario muy complida mente, haziendo despues lo mesmo con el capitan, y los que con el venian, a quien salieron a recebir con demonstracion de alegria, y dieron muchos bastimentos para la jornada que hauian de hazar, rogandoles que boluissen con breuedad, y traxessen muchos Castillas (que assi llaman a los Espannoles) y que a todos les darian de comer. Por lo qual para poderlo hazer con comodidad auian sembrado a quel anno mas trigo y semillas, que en todos los passados.

En este tiempo se retificaron en su primera determinacion el dicho religioso, y los soldados arriba dichos, y accordaron de boluerse a la prouincia de donde auian salido con el designio que queda dicho, a quien se junto Gregorio Hernandez que auia sido Alferez en la jornada: *They resolve to return.* los quales partidos, quedando el Capitan con solos ocho soldados, se resoluio de seguir lo començado y correr por el Rio del norte arriba, que lo puso por obra. *Hubates.* Y hauiendo caminado como sesenta leguas hazia la prouincia de los Quires ya dicha, doze leguas de alli hazia la parte del Oriente, hallaron vna prouincia que se llamaua los Hubates, donde los indios los receibieron de paz, y les dieron muchos mantenimientos, y noticia de que cerca de alli hauia vnas minas muy ricas, que las hallaron, y sacaron dellas metales reluzientes y buenos, con los quales se boluieron al pueblo de donde auian salido. Iuzgaron esta prouincia por de hasta veynte y cinco mil animas, todos muy bien vestidos de mantas de algodon pintadas, y camuças muy bien adere cadas. Tienen muchos montes de pinales y cedros, y las casas de los pueblos son de quatro y cinco altos. *Tamos.* *They return.* Aqui tuuieron noticia que otra prouincia que estaua vna jornada de alli, que se llamaua de los Tamos, en qui hauia mas de quarenta mil animas, donde como llegasen no les quisieron dar de comer los moradores della, ni admitirlos en sus pueblos: por lo qual, y por el peligro en que estauan, y *1583.* estar algunos soldados enfermos, y ser tan pocos (como hauemos dicho) se determinaron de yrse saliendo para tierra de Christianos, y lo pusieron en execucion a principio de Iulio del anno de ochenta y tres, siendo guiados por vn Indio que se fue con ellos, y los lleuo por camino differente del que a la venida hauian traydo, por vn rio abaxo, a quien llamaron de las vacas, por auer gran muche dumbre dellas en toda su ribera, por donde caminaron ciento y veynte leguas, topando las ordinariamente: de aqui salieron al rio de los Conchos por donde auian entrado, y del al Valle de Sant Bertholme de donde hauian salido para dar principio al descubrimiento: y ya quando llegaron, hallaron que el dicho fray Bernardino Beltran, y sus companneros auian llegado a saluamento al dicho pueblo muchos dias hauia, y que de alli se auian ydo a la villa de Guadiana. Hizo en este pueblo el dicho Capitan Antonio de Espejo informacion muy cierta de todo lo arriba dicho, laqual embio luego al Conde de Corunna Virey de aquel Reyno, y el a su Magestad, y a los Sennores, de su Real Consejo de las Indias, para que ordenassen lo que fuessen seruidos, que lo han ya hecho con mucho cuydado. *A pious wish.* Nuestro Sennor de situa de ayudar este negocio, de modo que tantas almas rededimas con su sangre no se condenen, de cuyos buenos ingenios (en que exceden alos de Mexico y Peru, segun se antendio de los que los trataron) se puede presumir, abraçaran con facilidad la ley Euangelica, dexando la idolatria, que agora la mayor parte dellos tiene: quo lo haga Dios como puede para honor y gloria suya, y augmento de la sancto fe Catholica.

A briefe relation of two notable voyages, the first made by frier Augustin Ruyz a Franciscan, in the yeere 1581: the second by Antonio de Espejo in the yere 1583: who together with his company discouered a land wherein they found fifteene prouinces all full of townes, conteining houses of foure and fiue stories high, which they named New Mexico; for that in many respects it resembleth the prouince of olde Mexico. This land is situate to the North of Nueua Espanna, and stretcheth from 24 to 34 degrees and better: by the which and by other inhabited lands it is thought that men may trauell euen to Terra de Labrador. Taken out of the history of China written by Frier Iuan Gonzales de Mendoça, and printed in Madrid 1586.

I haue now declared in the title of this present discourse, that in the yeere 1583 there were discouered fifteene prouinces, which the discouerers called New Mexico, situate on the firme land of Nueua Espanna, and I promised to giue notice of the sayd discouery which I will do with as much breuity as is possible: for if I should record at large all particulars which they saw and came to the knowledge of, it would require a full history. The substance thereof is as followeth.

The first voyage made by Frier Augustin Ruiz to the prouince de los Tiguas. In the yere of our Lord 1581, a certaine Franciscan frier called Augustin Ruiz which dwelt in the valley of S. Bartholomew, being informed by the report of certaine Indians called Conchos, which had dealings and conuersation with other of their neighbours called Passaguates; that toward the North, trauelling always by land, there were certaine great townes not hitherto knowen nor discouered by our Spanyards; moued with a zeale of charity and a desire to saue soules, craued licence of the Conde of Corunna as then Viceroy of Nueua Espanna, and of his superiors, to go to the sayd townes, and to indeuour to learne their language, and hauing learned the same to baptise them and to preach the holy Gospel vnto them. After he had obtained licence of the parties aforesayd, taking with him other two companions of his owne order, and eight souldiers, who of their owne good will offered to beare him company, he departed to put in execution his Christian and zealous intent. *The chiefe of these 8 soldiers was Francisco Sanchez Xamuzeado which made a map of these prouinces, which being intercepted is come to our hands.* Who after certeine dayes trauell came vnto a countrey called The prouince de los Tiguas distant from the mines of Santa Barbara, from whence they began their iourney, 250 leagues towards the North: in which prouince the inhabitants, vpon a certaine occasion, slew one of the sayd friers two companions. The souldiers that went with him seeing this mishap, and perceiuing the successe, and likewise fearing, that thereof might happen some greater danger, determined with a common consent to return vnto the mines from whence they departed: considering that their company was too small to resist the dangers that might happen, being so farre distant from the dwellings of the Spanyards, and from all necessary succour. But the two friers which remained aliue did not onely refuse their determination, but rather seeing fit occasion to put their good desire in execution, and so great a haruest ripe for the Lords table, because they could not persuade the souldiers to proceed any further in that discouery, remained behinde in the sayd prouince with three Indian boyes and one Mestiço whom they had carried with them; thinking that although they remained alone, yet should they be there in securitie, by reason of the great affability and loue which the people of that place shewed vnto them.

The eight souldiours being returned to their wished home, immediatly sent newes of all that had passed to the Viceroy vnto the city of Mexico, which is distant from the sayd mines of Santa Barbara 160 leagues.

The friers of Sant Francis were much agrieued at the staying of their brethren behinde in the countrey, and fearing least the Sauages would kill them seeing them left alone, they began to mooue the minds of certaine souldiers to make another voyage to the sayd prouince in the company of another Frier of the foresayd Order called Frier Bernardin Beltran, to deliuer the aforesayd two religious men out of danger, and to prosecute their former enterprise.

The second voyage. At the same time there was at the foresayd mines vpon some occasion a citizen of Mexico called Antonio de Espejo, a rich man, and of great courage and industry, and very zealous in the seruice of king Philip his souereigne, and was borne in Cordoua. Who vnderstanding the desire of the foresayd friers, and the importance of the action, offered himselfe to go on that voyage, and also to spend part of his substance, and to aduenture his life therein; conditionally that licence might be granted him to the same purpose from some person sufficiently authorised by his

Maiestie. Which licence at the sayd friers procurement was granted vnto him by the gouernour Iuan de Ontiueros the kings Alcade mayór or chiefe Iustice in the towns called Las quatro Cienegas situate within the iurisdiction of Nueua Biscaya seuenty leagues from the sayd mines of Santa Barbara; authorizing him both to take in hand the sayd voyage, and also to assemble such people and souldiers as he could, which might accompany and ayde him in the performance of this his Christian intent.

The sayd Antonio de Espejo was so earnest in this matter, that in very few dayes he had gathered a company of souldiers, and made prouision of things necessary for his voyage, spending therein a good part of his substance. And he departed with his whole company from the valley of S. Bartholomew the tenth of Nouember 1582; taking with him (for whatsoeuer should happen) 115 horses and mules, with great store of weapons, munition, and victuals, and some Indians to serue him in his iourney.

Directing his course toward the North, after two dayes iourney he met with great store of the foresayd Indians called Conchos, which dwell in villages or hamlets of cottages couered with straw. Who, assoone as they vnderstood of his approch, hauing newes thereof long before, came foorth to receiue him with shewes of great ioy. The food of this people and of all the rest of that prouince, which is great, are conies, hares, and deere which they kill, of all which they haue great abundance. Also they haue great store of Maiz or Indian wheat, gourds, and melons very good and plentifull: and there are many riuers full of excellent fish of diuers sorts. They goe almost naked, and the weapons that they vse are bowes and arrowes, and liue vnder the gouernment and lordship of Caçiques like those of Mexico: they found no idols among them, neither could they vnderstand that they worshipped any thing, whereupon they easily consented that the Spanyards should set vp crosses, and were very well content therewith, after they were informed by our friers of the signification thereof, which was done by the interpreters that they caried with them; by whose meanes they vnderstood of other townes, whither the said Conchos did conduct them, and bare them company aboue foure and twenty leagues, all which way was inhabited with people of their owne nation: and at all places where they came they were peaceably receiued by aduice that was sent by the Caçiques from one towne to another.

Hauing passed the foure and twenty leagues aforesayd, they came vnto another nation of Indians called Passaguates, who liue after the maner of the foresayd Conchos their borderers, and did vnto them as the others had done, conducting them forward other foure dayes iourney, with aduice of the Caciques as before. Very great and rich siluer mines. The Spanyards found in this iourney many mines of siluer, which according to the iudgement of skilfull men, were very plentifull and rich in metall.

A dayes iourney from thence they met with another nation called Tobosos, who so soone as they beheld the countenance of our people fledde vnto the mountaines, leauing their townes and houses desolate. Afterward wee vnderstood that certeine yeeres past there came vnto that place certaine souldiers to seeke mines, who caried away captiue certaine of the people of the countrey, which caused the rest of them to be so shey and fearefull. The captaine sent messengers to call them backe againe, assuring them that they should not sustaine any harme, and handled the matter so discreetly, that many of them returned, whom he made much of, and gaue them gifts, vsing them kindly, and declaring vnto them by the interpreter, that their comming was not to hurt any man: whereupon they were all quieted, and were content that they should set vp crosses, and declare the mystery of the same, making shew that they were highly pleased therewith. For proofe whereof they accompanied them on their voyage, as their neighbours had done, vntill they had brought them to a countrey inhabited by another nation, which was distant from theirs some 12 leagues. They vse bowes and arrowes and go naked.

Iumanos or Patarabueyes. The nation vnto which the sayd Tobosos conducted them, is called Iumanos, whom the Spanyards by another name call Patarabueyes: their prouince is very great, conteining many townes and great store of people: their houses are flat roofed, and built of lime and stone, and the streets of their townes are placed in good order. All the men and women haue their faces, armes and legges raced and pounced: they are a people of great stature, and of better gouernment, then the rest which they had seene in their former iourneys: and are well prouided of victuals, and furnished with plenty of wilde beasts, fowles and fishes, *Rio turbioso del Norte.* by reason of mighty riuers from the North, whereof one is as great as Guadalquiuir, which falleth into the North sea or bay of Mexico. Here also are many lakes of salt water, which at a certeine time of the yere waxeth hard, and becommeth very good salt. They are a warlike people, and soone made shew thereof: for the first night that our people incamped there, with their arrowes they slew fiue horses, and wounded fiue other very sore, nor would not haue left one of them aliue, if they had not beene defended by our guard. *Rio del Norte.* Hauing done this mischiefe, they abandoned the towne, and withdrew themselues to a mountaine which was hard by, whither our captaine went betimes in the morning, taking with him fiue souldiers well armed, and an interpreter called Peter an Indian of their owne nation, and with good persuasions appeased them, causing them to descend to their towne and houses, and persuading them to giue aduice vnto their neighbours, that they were men that would hurt no body, neither came they thither to take away their goods: which he obtained easily by his wisedome, and by giuing vnto the Caciques certeine bracelets of glasse beads, with hats and other trifles, which he caried with him for the same purpose; so by this meanes, and by the good interteinment which they gaue them, many of them accompanied our Spanyards for certeine dayes, alwayes trauelling along the banke of the great riuer abouesayd; along the which there were many townes of the Indians of this nation, which continued for the space of twelue dayes trauel, all which time the Caciques having receiued aduice from one to another, came forth to interteine our people without their bowes and arrowes, and brought them plenty of victuals, with other presents and gifts, especially hides and chamois-skins wery well dressed, so that those of Flanders do nothing exceed them. These people are all clothed, and seemed to haue some light of our holy faith: for they made signes to God, looking vp towards heauen, and call him in their language Apalito, and acknowledge him for their Lord, from whose bountifull hand and mercy they confesse that they haue receiued their life and being, and these worldly goods. Many of them with their wiues and children came vnto the frier (which the captaine and souldiers brought with them) that hee might crosse and blesse them. :Pamphilo de Naruaez: :entred into Florida 1527.: Who demanding of them, from whom they had receiued that knowledge of God, they answered, from three Christians and one Negro which passed that way, and remained certaine dayes among them, who by the signes which they made, were Aluaro Nunnez, Cabeca de Vaca, and Dorantes, and Castillo Maldonado, and a Negro; all which escaped of the company which Pamphilo de Naruaez landed in Florida; who after they had bene many dayes captiues and slaues, escaped and came to these townes, by whom God shewed many miracles, and healed onely by the touching of their hands many sicke persons, by reason wherof they became very famous in all that countrey. :Rio del Norte. Another: :prouince.: All this prouince remained in great peace and security; in token wherof, they accompanied and serued our men certaine dayes, trauelling along by the great riuer aforesayd.

Within few days after they came vnto another great prouince of Indians, from whence they came forth to receiue them, vpon the newes which they had heard of their neighbors, and brought them many curious things made of feathers of diuers colours, and many mantles of cotton straked with blew and white, like those that are brought from China, to barter and trucke them for other things. All of them both men, women and children were clad in chamois skinnes very good and wel dressed. Very great quantity of siluer. Our people could neuer vnderstand what nation they were for lacke of an interpreter: howbeit they dealt with them by signes; and hauing shewed vnto them certaine stones of rich metall, and inquired whether there were any such in their countrey: they answered by the same signes, that fiue dayes iourney Westward from thence there was great quantity therof, and that they would conduct them thither, and shew it vnto them; as afterward they performed their promise, and bare them company 22 leagues, which was all inhabited by people of the same nation.

Next vnto the foresayd prouince they came vnto another further vp the great riuer aforesayd, being much more populous then the former, of whom they were well receiued, and welcomed with many presents, especially of fish, whereof they haue exceeding great store, by reason of certaine great lakes not far from thence, wherein they are bred in foresayd plenty. They stayed among these people three days; all which time both day and night they made before them many dances, according to their fashion, with signification of speciall ioy. They could not learne the name of this nation for want of an interpreter, yet they vnderstood that it extended very farre, and was very great. Among these people they found an Indian of the foresayd nation of the Conchos, who told them, and shewed them by signes, that fifteene dayes iourney from thence toward the West there was a very broad lake, and nere vnto it very great townes, and in them houses of three or foure stories high, and that the people were well apparelled, and the countrey full of victuals and prouision. This Concho offered himselfe to conduct our men thither; whereat our company reioyced, but left off the enterprise, onely to accomplish their intent for which they vndertook the voyage, which was to go Northward to giue ayd vnto the two friers aforesayd. The chiefe and principall thing that they noted in this prouince was, that it was of very good temperature, and a very rich soile, and had great store of wilde beasts, and wild fowle, and abundance of rich metals, and other excellent things, and very profitable.

From this prouince they folowed their iourney for the space of fifteene dayes without meeting any people all that while, passing thorow great woods and groues of pine trees bearing such fruit as those of Castile: at the end whereof, having trauelled, to their iudgement, fourescore leagues, they came vnto a small hamlet or village of fewe people, in whose poore cottages couered with straw they found many deeres-skinnes as well dressed as those of Flanders, with great store of excellent white salt. They gave our men good entertainment for the space of two dayes while they remained there, after which they bare them company about twelue leagues, vnto certaine great townes, alwayes travelling by the riuer called Rio del Norte abouesayd, till such time as they came vnto the countrey called by them New Mexico. Here all along the shore of the sayd riuer grew mighty woods of poplar being in some places foure leagues broad, and great store of walnut trees, and vines like those of Castillia.

Hauing trauelled two dayes thorow the said woods of Poplar and Walnut trees, they came to ten townes situate on both sides of the sayd riuer, besides others which they might see further out of the way, wherein they seemed to be great store of people, and those which they saw were aboue ten thousand persons. In this prouince they received them very courteously, and brought them to their townes, whereas they gaue them plenty of victuals and hennes of the countrey, with many other things, and that with great good will. Here they found houses of foure stories high, very well built, with gallant lodgings, and in most of them were Stooues for the Winter season. Their garments were of Cotton and of deere-skinnes, and the attire both of the men and women is after the maner of the Indians of the kingdome of Mexico. But the strangest thing of all was to see both men and women weare shooes and boots with good soles of neats leather, a thing which they never sawe in any other part of the Indies. The women keepe their haire well combed and dressed, wearing nothing els vpon their heads. In all these townes they had Caciques, which gouerned their people like the Caciques of Mexico, with Sergeants to execute their commandments, who goe thorow the townes proclaiming with a loud voice the pleasure of the Caciques, commanding the same to be put in execution. In this prouince our men found many idols which they worshipped, and particularly they had in euery house an Oratory for the diuell, whereinto they ordinarily cary him meat: and another thing they found, that as it is an vse among the Christians to erect crosses vpon the high wayes, so haue this people certain high chapels, in which they say the diuell vseth to take his ease, and to recreat himselfe as he traueleth from one towne to another; which chapels are maruellously well trimmed and painted. In all their arable grounds, wherof they haue great plenty, they erect on the one side a little cottage or shed standing vpon foure studdes, vnder which the labourers do eat, and passe away the heat of the day, for they are a people much giuen to labour, and doe continually occupy themselues therein. These high mountains are a cause of the coldness of the countrey. This countrey is full of mountaines and forrests of Pine trees. The weapons that they vse are strong bowes and arrowes headed with flints, which will pierce thorow a coat of male, and macanas which are clubs of halfe a yard long, so beset with sharpe flints, that they are sufficient to cleaue a man asunder in the midst: they vse also a kinde of targets made of raw hides.

Hauing remained foure dayes in this prouince, not farre off they came to another called The prouince of Tiguas conteining sixteene townes, in one wherof, called Poala, they vnderstood that the inhabitants had slaine the two fathers aforesayd, to wit, frier Francis Lopez, and frier Augustus Ruyz whom they went to seeke, together with the three Indian boyes, and the mestiço. So soone as the people of this towne and their neighbours saw our men there, their own consciences accusing them, and fearing that our men came to punish them, and to be auenged of the death of the foresaid fathers, they durst not abide their comming, but leauing their houses desolate they fled to the mountaines next adioyning, from whence they could neuer cause them to descend, although our men attempted the same by diuers deuises and entisements. They found in the townes and houses good store of victuals, with infinite number of hennes in the countrey, and many sorts of metals, wherof some seemed to be very good. They could not perfectly vnderstand what numbers of people this prouince might conteine, by reason they were fled into the mountains, as I haue said before.

Hauing found those to be slaine which they went to seeke, they entred into consultation, whether they should returne to Nueua Biscaya, from whence they came, or should proceed further in their iourney; whereabout there were diuers opinions: howbeit, vnderstanding there, that toward the Orient or East parts of that prouince, ⸨This draweth toward Virginia.⸩ and very far distant from thence, there were great and rich townes: and finding themselues so far on the way, the sayd captaine Antonio de Espeio with the consent of the foresaid frier called Frier Bernardine Beltron, and the greater part of his souldiers and companions determined to proceed on the discouery, till such time as they did see to what end it would come; to the end they might giue certeine and perfect knowledge thereof to his Maiesty, as eye-witnesses of the same. And so with one accord they determined, that while the army lay still there, the captaine and two more of his company should prosecute their desire, which they did accordingly. And within two dayes iourney they came vnto another prouince, where they found eleuen townes, and much people in them; which in their iudgement were aboue forty thousand persons. The country was very fertile and plentifull, whose confines bordered vpon the territories of Cibola, where there are great store of kine, with whose hides and with cotton they apparell themselues, imitating in the forme of their gouernment their next neighbours. In this place are signes of very rich mines, some quantity of the metals whereof they found in the houses of the Indians; which Indians haue and doe worship idols. They receiued our men peaceably, and gaue them victuals. Hauing seene this much, and the disposition of the countrey, they returned to the campe, from whence they departed, to informe their companions of the things aboue mentioned.

Being returned to the campe they had intelligence of another prouince called Los Quires, Quires bordering vpon Rio del Norte. which stood six leagues higher vp the riuer called Rio del Norte. And in their iourney thitherward, being arriued within a league of the place, there came forth very many Indians to receiue them in peace, requesting them to beare them company to their townes: which they did, and were maruellous well interteined and cherished. In this prouince they found fiue townes only. Wherein were great store of people, and those which they saw were aboue 14000 soules, who worship idols as their neighbours do. In one of these townes they found a pie in a cage after the maner of Castile, and certaine shadowes or canopies like vnto those which are brought from China, wherein were painted the Sunne, the Moone, and many Starres. Where hauing taken the height of the pole-starre, they found themselues to be in 37 degrees and ½ of Northerly latitude.

Cunames, or Punames. Cia a great city. They departed out of this prouince, and keeping still the same Northerly course, fourteene leagues from thence they found another prouince called The Cunames, where they saw other fiue townes, the greatest whereof was called Cia, being so large, that it conteined eight market-places, the houses whereof being plaistered and painted with diuers colours, were better then any which they had seene in the prouinces before mentioned: the people which they heere saw, they esteemed to be aboue twenty thousand persons. They presented to our men many curious mantles, and victuals excellently well dressed; so that our men deemed this nation to be more curious, and of greater ciuility, and better gouernment, then any other that hitherto they had seene. They shewed them rich metals, and the mountaines also not farre off whereout they digged them. Heere our people heard of another prouince standing toward the Northwest, whereunto they purposed to goe.

Ameies, or Emexes. Hauing trauelled about six leagues, they came to the sayd prouince, the people whereof were called Ameies, wherin were seuen very great townes, conteining, to their iudgement, aboue thirty thousand soules. They reported that one of the seuen townes was very great and faire, which our men would not go to see, both because it stood behinde a mountaine, and also for feare of some mishappe, if in case they should be separated one from another. This people are like vnto their neighbours of the former prouince, being as well prouided of all necessaries as they, and of as good gouernment.

Acoma or Acoman a towne conteining aboue 6000 persons. About fifteene leagues from this prouince, trauelling alwayes toward the West, they found a great towne called Acoma, conteining aboue sixe thousand persons, and situate vpon an high rocke which was aboue fifty paces hie, hauing no other entrance but by a ladder or paire of staires hewen into the same rocke, whereat our people maruelled not a little: all the water of this towne was kept in cisternes. The chiefe men of this towne came peaceably to visit the Spanyards, bringing them many mantles and chamois-skinnes excellently dressed, and great plenty of victuals. Their corne-fields are two leagues from thence, and they fetch water out of a small riuer nere thereunto, to water the same, on the brinks whereof they saw many great banks of Roses like those of Castile. Here are many mountaines that beare shewes of mettals, but they went not to see them, because the Indians dwelling vpon them are many in number, and very warlike. Our men remained in this place three dayes, vpon one of the which the inhabitants made before them a very solemne dance, comming foorth in the same with gallant apparell, vsing very witty sports, wherewith our men were exceedingly delighted.

Zuny or Sunne. Twenty foure leagues from hence toward the West, they came to a certaine prouince called by the inhabitants themselues *Zuny*, and by the Spanyards Cibola, containing great numbers of Indians; *Vasquez de Coronado was here 1540 and 1541.* in which prouince Francisco Vasquez de Coronado had bene, and had erected many crosses and other tokens of Christianity, which remained as yet standing. Heere also they found three Indian Christians which had remained there euer since the said iourny, whose names were Andrew de Culiacan, Gaspar de Mexico, and Antonio de Guadalajara, who had almost forgotten their owne language, but could speake that countrey speech very well; howbeit after some small conference with our men, they easily vnderstood one another. *A mighty lake 60 daies iourney from Cibola.* By these three Indians they were informed, that threescore dayes iourney from this place there was a very mighty lake, vpon the bankes whereof stood many great and good townes, and that the inhabitants of the same had plenty of golde, an euident argument wherof was their wearing of golden bracelets and earrings: and also that after the sayd Francis Vasquez de Coronado had perfect intelligence thereof, hee departed out of this prouince of Cibola to goe thither, and that hauing proceeded twelue dayes iourney, he began to want water; and thereupon determined to returne, as he did indeed, with intention to make a second voyage thither at his better opportunity; which afterward he performed not, being preuented of his determined iourney by death.

Another mightie prouince Westward of Cibola 28. leagues, called Mohotze. Vpon the newes of these riches the sayd Captaine Antony de Espeio was desirous to go thither; and though some of his companions were of his opinion, yet the greater part and the frier were of the contrary, saying that it was now high time to returne home to New Biscay from whence they came, to giue account of that which they seene: which the sayd greater part within few dayes put in execution, leauing the captaine with nine companions onely that willingly followed him: who after hee had fully certified himselfe of the riches abouesayd, and of the great quantity of excellent mettals that were about that lake, departed out of this prouince of Cibola with his companions; and travelling directly toward the West, after hee had passed 28 leagues, he found another very great prouince, which by estimation contained aboue 5000 soules: the inhabitants whereof assoone as they vnderstood of their approch, sent them word, vpon paine of death to come no neerer to their townes: whereto the captaine answered, that their comming was in no wise to hurt them, as they should well perceiue, and therefore requested them not to molest him in his intended voyage, and withall gaue to the messenger a reward of such things as they brought with them: who thereupon made so good report of our people, and so appeased the troubled minds of the Indians, that they granted them free accesse vnto their townes, and so they went thither with 15. Indians their friends of the prouince of Cibola aforesaid, and the three Mexican Indians before mentioned. When they were come within a league of the first towne, there came forth to meete them aboue 2000. Indians laden with victuals, whom the Captaine rewarded with some things of small value, which they made great accompt of, and esteemed more precious than gold. Zaguato, or Ahuxto a towne. As they approched neere vnto the towne which was named Zaguato, a great multitude of Indians came forth to meete them, and among the rest their Caçiques, with so great demonstration of ioy and gladnes, that they cast much meale of Maiz vpon the ground for the horses to tread vpon: with this triumph they entred the towne, where they were very wel lodged and much made of, which the Captaine did in part requite, giuing to the chiefest among them hats, and beads of glasse, with many such trifles, which he caried with him for the like purpose. The said Caciques presently gaue notice to the whole prouince of the arriual of these new guests, whom they reported to bee a courteous people, and such as offered them no harme: which was occasion sufficient to make them all come laden with presents vnto our people, and to intreat them to goe and make merry with them in their townes; which they yeelded vnto, though always with great foresight what might follow. *A witty policie to be vsed by the English in like cases.* Whereupon the Captaine vsed a certaine policie, making the Caciques beleeue, that forasmuch as his horses were very fierce (for they had told the Indians that they would kill them) therefore it was necessary to make a Fort of lime and stone to inclose them, for the auoyding of such inconueniences as otherwise might happen vnto the Indians by them. This tale was so steadfastly beleeued by the Caciques, that in fiue houres they assembled such store of people together, that with incredible celeritie they built the said Fort which our men required.

Moreouer, when the Captaine saide that he would depart, they brought vnto him a present of 40000. mantles of cotton, both white and other colours, and great store of hand towels, with tassels at the corners, with diuers other things, and among the rest rich mettals, which seemed to holde much siluer. Among these Indians they learned very much concerning The great Lake aforesaide, whose report agreed wholly with relation of the former, as touching the riches and great abundance of gold about that lake.

The Captaine reposing great confidence in this people and in their good disposition toward him determined after certaine dayes, to leaue there fiue of his companions with the rest of his Indian friends, that they might returne with his cariages to the prouince of Zuni, while himselfe with the foure other which remained should ride in post to discouer certaine very rich Mines, whereof he had perfect information. And putting this purpose in execution he departed with his guides, and hauing traueiled due-west 45. leagues he came vnto the said Mines, and tooke out of the same with his owne hands exceeding rich metals holding great quantitie of siluer: and the mines which were of a very broad veine were in a mountaine whereon they might easily ascend, by reason of an open way that led vp to the same. Neere vnto these mines were certaine townes of Indians dwelling upon the mountaine whereon they might easily ascend, by reason of an open way that led vp to the same. Neere vnto these mines were certaine townes of Indians dwelling vpon the mountaines, who shewed them friendship, and came forth to receiue them with crosses on their heads, and other tokens of peace. Hereabout they found two riuers of a reasonable bignesse, vpon the banks whereof grew many vines bearing excellent grapes, and great groues of walnut trees, and much flaxe like that of Castile: and they shewed our men by signes, that behinde those mountaines there was a riuer about 8. leagues broad, *Perhaps this Riuer may fall into the Chesepiouk bay, or into the great lake of Tadoac.* but they could not learne how neere it was: howbeit the Indians made demonstration that it ran towards the North sea, and that vpon both sides thereof stood many townes of so great bignesse, that in comparison thereof those wherein they dwelt were but small hamlets.

After he had receiued all this information, the said Captaine returned toward the prouince of Zuni, whither he had sent his said companions: and being arriued there in safety, hauing trauailed vpon a very good way, he found in the same place his 5. companions, and the said father Frier Bernardin Beltran, with the souldiers which were determined to returne, as is aforesaid, but vpon certaine occasions were not as yet departed: whom the inhabitants had most friendly treated, and furnished with all things necessary in abundance as afterward likewise they vsed the Captaine, and those that came with him, comming foorth to meete them with shew of great ioy, and giuing them great store of victuals to serue them in their iourney homewards, and requesting them to returne againe with speed, and to bring many Castilians with them (for so they call the Spaniards) to whom they promised food sufficient. For the better performance wherof they sowed that yeere more graine and other fruits, then they had done at any time before.

At this present the Frier and souldiers aforesaid resolued themselues in their former determination, and agreed to returne vnto the prouince from whence they came with intention before mentioned, to seeke the two Friers that were slaine, to whom also Gregorio Hermandez who had bene standard-bearer in the iourney, ioyned himselfe. Who being departed, the Captaine accompanied onely with 8. souldiers, determined to prosecute his former attempt, and to passe vp higher the saide riuer called Rio del Norte, which he did accordingly. And hauing traueiled about 60. leagues toward the prouince of the Quires aforesaid, 12 leagues from thence toward the Orient or East they found a prouince of Indians called Hubates, who receiued them peaceably, and gaue them great store of victuals, informing them also of very rich Mines which they found whereout they got glistening and good metal, and therewith returned to the towne from whence they came. This prouince contained by their estimation 25000. persons all very well apparelled in coloured mantles of cotton, and Chamois-skins very well dressed. They haue many mountaines full of Pines *and Cedars, and the* houses of their townes are of 4. and 5. stories high. *Their returne.* Here they had notice of another prouince distant about one dayes iourney from thence inhabited by certaine Indians called Tamos, and containing aboue 40000 soules: whither being come the inhabitants would neither giue them any victuals, nor admit them into their townes: for which cause, and in regard of the danger wherein they were, and because some of the souldiers were not well at ease, and for that they were so fewe (as we haue said) they determined to departe thence, and to returne toward the land of the Christians, which they put in execution in the beginning of Iuly 1583, being guided by an Indian that went with them, who led them another way then they went forth by, downe a riuer, which they called Rio de las vacas; that is to say, The riuer of oxen, in respect of the great multitudes of oxen or kine that fed vpon the bankes therof, by the which they traueiled for the space of 120. leagues, still meeting with store of the said cattell. From hence they went forward to the riuer of Conchos by which they entered, and thence to the valley of S. Bartholomew, from whence they first entered into their discouerie. Vpon their coming thither they found that the said Frier Bernardin Beltran and his company were safely arriued at the said towne many dayes before, and were gone from thence to the towne of Guadiana. In this towne the foresaid captaine Anthony de Espeio made most certaine relation of all that is aforesaid, which relation presently hee sent vnto the Conde of Corunna Vizroy of Nueua Espanna, who sent the same to his Maiestie, and the Lords of his royal counsel in the Indies, to the end they might take such order as they thought best, which they haue already performed with great care and circumspection.

Almighty God vouchsafe his assistance in this busines, that such numbers of soules redeemed by his blood may not vtterly perish, of whose good capacitie, wherein they exceed those of Mexico and Peru (as we be giuen to vnderstand by those that haue delt with them) we may boldly presume that they will easily embrace the Gospel, and abandon such idolatrie as now the most of them doe liue in: which Almightie God graunt for his honour, and glory, and for the increase of the holy Catholique faith.

A letter of Bartholomew Cano from Mexico the 30. of May 1590. to Francis Hernandes of Siuil, concerning the speedy building of two strong Forts in S. Iohn de Vllua, and in Vera Cruz, as also touching a notable new and rich discouery of Cibola or New Mexico 400. leagues Northwest of Mexico.

It may please you Sir, to be aduertised that I haue receiued your letters, whereby I vnderstand that our ship with the treasure is safely arriued, God be praised therefore. The frigate arriued here in safetie which brought the letters of Aduise from the King to the Viceroy. She arriued in S. Iohn de Vllua the 29. of May, and departed from S. Lucar in Spaine the 6. of April. By which his Maiestie writeth vnto the Viceroy, what time the Fleete shall depart from hence, and what course they shall take, not as they had wont for to do: by reason that there are great store of men of war abroad at the sea, which mean to encounter with the Fleete. I pray God sende them well to Spaine: for here wee were troubled very sore with men of warre on this coast. His Maiestie hath sent expresse commandement vnto the Marques of Villa Manrique his cosen, Viceroy of Noua Hispania, that immediatly vpon sight of his letters he shall command to be builded in S. Iohn de Vulla, and in Vera Cruz two strong Forts for the defence of these countries, of his Maiesties charges: And that there shalbe garisons in both the Forts for the defence of the ships which ride there, and for the strength of the countrey.

500. Spaniards sent to conquer the great citie of Cibola which is 400. leagues from Mexico Northwestward. There are departed out of Mexico and other townes hereabout by the commaundement of the Viceroy 500. souldiers Spaniards, vnder the conduct of Rodrigo del Rio the gouernour of Nueua Biscaia which are gone to win a great City called Cibola, which is 400. leagues beyond Mexico to the Northwest, and standeth vp in the maine land. It is by report a very great citie, as bigge as Mexico, and a very rich countrey both of golde Mines and siluer Mines: and the King of the countrey is a mighty King, and he will not become subiect to his Maiestie. There were certaine Spaniards sent to that king from the Viceroy in an ambassage: It is thought that they are slaine, for we can here no newes of them.

The other newes that I can certifie you of at this instant is, that there is a Iudge of the city of Guadalajara called don Nunno de villa Inscensia lately maried. Also the kings Atturney of Guadalajara maried his daughter of 8. yeres old with a boy of 12. yeres old. But the Viceroy saith that he hath a warrant from his Maiestie, that if any Iudge whatsoeuer dwelling in that kingdome of Guadalajara should mary any sonne in that iurisdiction, that then the said Viceroy is to depriue him of his office. And therefore he went about to depriue the Iudge and the kings Attourney of their offices. A dangerous rebellion in Guadalajara a prouince of Noua Hispania. Whereupon the people of that prouince would not thereunto consent, nor suffer them to be dismissed of their offices, nor to be arrested, nor caried prisoners to Mexico. When the viceroy had intelligence thereof, and that the Countrey did resist his commandement, and would not suffer them to be apprehended, he sent certaine Captaines with souldiers to goe and apprehend the Iudge, the kings Attourney, and as many as did take their parts. So the citizens of Guadalajara withstood the viceroies forces, and put themselues in defence; and are up in armes against the viceroy: yet they do not rebel against the king, but say: God saue king Philip, and will submit themselues to his Maiestie, but not to the viceroy. So that all the kingdome of Guadalajara is vp in armes, and are all in a mutinie against vs of Mexico. I beseech Almighty God to remedy it, and that it may be qualified in time: or else all Noua Spania will be vtterly spoiled. I write this thing, because it is publiquely knowen in all places. And thus I rest, from Mexico the 30. of May 1590.

Bartholomew Cano.

The relation of Francis Vasquez de Coronado, Captaine general of the people which were sent in the name of the Emperours maiestie to the Countrey of Cibola newly discouered, which he sent to Don Antonio de Mendoça Viceroy of Mexico, of such things as happened in his voyage from 22. of Aprill in the yeere 1540. which departed from Culiacan forward, and of such things as hee found in the Countrey which he passed.

Chap. 1.

Francis Vasquez departeth with his armie from Culiacan, and after diuers troubles in his voyage, arriueth at the valley of the people called Los Caracones, which he findeth barren of Maiz: for obtaining whereof hee sendeth to the valley called The valley of the Lord: he is informed of the greatnesse of the valley of the people called Caracones, and of the nature of those people, and of certaine Islands lying along that coast.

The 22. of the moneth of Aprill last past I departed from the prouince of Culiacan with part of the army, and in such order as I mentioned vnto your Lordship, and according to the successe I assured my selfe, by all likelihood that I shall not bring all mine armie together in this enterprise: because the troubles haue bene so great and the want of victuals, that I thinke all this yeere wil not be sufficient to performe this enterprise, and if it should bee performed in so short a time, it would be to the great losse of our people. This was but 200. leagues from Mexico. For as I wrote vnto your Lordship, I was fourescore dayes in trauailing to Culiacan, in all which time I and three Gentlemen my companions which were horsemen, carried on our backs, and on our horses, a little victuall, so that from henceforward wee carried none other needefull apparell with vs, that was aboue a pound weight: and all this notwithstanding and though wee put our selues to such a small proportion of victuals which wee carried, for all the order that possibly wee could take, wee were driuen to our ships. And no maruayle, because the way is rough and long: and with the carriage of our Harquebuses downe the mountaine and hilles, and in the passage of Riuers, the greater part of our corne was spoyled. And because I send your Lordship our voyage drawen in a Mappe, I will speake no more thereof in this my letter.

Frier Marcus of Niza. Thirtie leagues before wee arriued at the place which the father prouinciall tolde vs so well of in his relation, I sent Melchior Diaz before with fifteene horses, giuing him order to make but one dayes iourney of two, because hee might examine all things, against mine arriuall: who trauiled foure dayes iourney through exceeding rough Mountaines where hee found neither victuals, nor people nor information of any things, sauing that hee found two or three poore little villages, containing 20. or 30. cottages a piece, and by the inhabitants thereof hee vnderstoode that from thence forward there were nothing but exceeding rough mountaines which ran very farre, vtterly disinhabited and voyd of people. And because it was labour lost, I would not write vnto your Lordship thereof.

It grieued the whole company, that a thing so highly commended, and whereof the father had made so great bragges, should be found so contrary, and it made them suspect that all the rest would fall out in like sort. Which when I perceiued I sought to encourage them the best I coulde, telling them that your Lordshippe alwayes was of opinion, that this voyage was a thing cast away, and that we should fixe our cogitation vpon those seuen Cities, and other prouinces, whereof wee had knowledge: that there should bee the ende of our enterprise: and with this resolution and purpose wee all marched cheerefully through a very badde way which was not passible but one by one, or else wee must force out with Pioners the path which wee founde, wherewith the Souldiours were not a little offended, finding all that the Frier had sayde to bee quite contrary: for among other things which the father sayde and affirmed, this was one, that the way was plaine and good, and that there was but one small hill of halfe a league in length. And yet in trueth there are mountaines which although the way were well mended could not bee passed without great danger of breaking the horses neckes: and the way was such, that of the cattel which your Lordship sent vs for the prouision of our armie wee lost a great part in the voyage through the roughnesse of the rockes. The lambes and sheepe lost their hoofes in the way: and of those which I brought from Culiacan, I left the greater part at the Riuer of Lachimi, because they could not keepe company with vs, and because they might come softly after vs, foure men on horsebacke remained with them which are nowe come vnto vs, and haue brought vs not past foure and twentie lambes, and foure sheepe, for all the rest were dead with trauailing through that rough passage, although they trauailed but two leagues a day, and rested themselues euery day.

The valley of the people called Caracones. At length I arriued at the valley of the people called Caracones, the 26. day of the moneth of May: and from Culiacan vntill I came thither, I could not helpe my selfe, saue onely with a great quantitie of Maiz: for seeing the Maiz in the fieldes, were not yet ripe, I was constrained to leaue them all behind me. In this valley of the Caracones wee found more store of people then in any other part of the Countrey which wee had passed, and great store of tillage. *Valle del Senor.* But I vnderstood that there was store there of in another valley called The Lords valley, which I woulde not disturbe with force, but sent thither Melchior Diaz with wares of exchange to procure some, and to giue the sayde Maiz to the Indians our friendes which wee brought with vs, and to some others that had lost their cattell in the way, and were not able to carry their victuals so farre which they brought from Culiacan. It pleased God that wee gate some small quantitie of Maiz with this traffique, whereby certaine Indians were relieued and some Spanyards.

And by that time that wee were come to this valley of the Caracones, some tenne or twelue of our horses were dead through wearinesse: for being ouercharged with great burdens, and hauing but little meate, they could not endure the trauaile. Likewise some of our Negros and some of our Indians dyed here: which was no small wante vnto vs for the performance of our enterprise. *The valley de los Caracones distant fiue dayes journey from the Westerne sea.* They tolde me that this valley of the Coracones is fiue dayes journey from the Westerne Sea. *Seuen or eight Isles, which are the Isles of California. A ship scene on the sea coast.* I sent for the Indians of the Sea coast to vnderstand their estate, and while I stayed for them the horses rested: and I stayed there foure dayes, in which space the Indians of the Sea coast came vnto mee: which told mee, that, two dayes sayling from their coast of the Sea, there were seuen or eight Islands right ouer against them well inhabited with people, but badly furnished with victuals, and were a rude people: And they told mee, that they had seene a Shippe passe by not farre from the shore: which I wote not what to thinke whether it were one of those that went to discouer the Countrey, or else a Ship of the Portugals.

Chap. 2.

They come to Chichilticale: after they had rested themselues two dayes there, they enter into a Countrey very barren of victuals, and hard to trauaile for thirtie leagues, beyond which they found a Countrey very pleasant, and a riuer called Rio del Lino, they fight with the Indians being assaulted by them, and with victorie vanquishing their citie, they relieued themselues of their pinching hunger.

I Departed from the Caracones, and alwayes kept by the Sea coast as neere as I could iudge, and in very deed I still found my selfe the farther off: in such sort that when I arriued at Chichilticale I found myselfe tenne dayes iourney from the Sea: and the father prouinciall sayd that it was onely but fiue leagues distance, and that hee had seene the same. Wee all conceiued great griefe and were not a little confounded, when we saw that wee found euery thing contrary to the information which he had giuen your Lordship.

The Indians of Chichilticale say, that if at any time they goe to the Sea for fish, and other things that they carry, they goe trauersing, and are tenne dayes iournie in going thither. And I am of opinion that the information which the Indians giue me should be true. The sea returneth toward the West right ouer against the Coracones the space of tenne or twelue leagues. The Chichilticale is indeede but in 28. deg. Where I found that your Lordships ships were seene, which went to discouer the hauen of Chichilticale, which father Marcus of Niça sayd to bee in fiue and thirtie degrees. God knoweth what griefe of mind I haue sustained: because I am in doubt that some mishappe is fallen vnto them: and if they follow the coast, as they sayde they would, as long as their victuals last which they carry with them, whereof I left them store in Culiacan, and if they be not fallen into some misfortune, I hope well in God that by this they haue made some good discouerie, and that in this respect their long staying out may be pardoned.

The 24. of Iune. I rested myselfe two dayes in Chichilticale, and to haue done well I should haue stayed longer, in respect that here wee found our horses so tyred; but because wee wanted victuals, we had no leasure to rest any longer: I entred the confines of the desert Countrey on Saint Iohns eue, and to refresh our former trauailes, the first dayes we founde no grasse, but worser way of mountaines and badde passages, then wee had passed alreadie: and the horses being tired, were greatly molested therewith: so that in this last desert we lost more horses than we had lost before: and some of my Indians which were our friends dyed, and one Spanyard whose name was Spinosa; and two Negroes, which dyed with eating certaine herbes for lacke of victuals. From this place I sent before mee one dayes iourney the master of the fielde Don Garcia Lopez de Cardenas with fifteene horses to discouer the Countrey, and prepare our way: wherein hee did like himselfe, and according to the confidence which your Lordship reposed in him. And well I wote he fayled not to do his part: for as I have informed your Lordship, it is most wicked way, at least thirtie leagues and more, because they are inaccessible mountaines.

A godly and fruitfull countrey found. But after wee had passed these thirtie leagues, wee found fresh riuers, and grasse like that of Castile, and specially of that sort which we call Scaramoio, many Nutte trees and Mulberrie trees but the Nutte trees differ from those of Spayne in the leafe: and there was Flaxe, but chiefly neere the bankes of a certayne riuer which therefore we called El Rio del Lino, that is to say, the riuer of Flaxe: wee found no Indians at all for a dayes trauaile, but afterward foure Indians came out vnto vs in peaceable maner, saying that they were sent euen to that desert place to signifie vnto vs that wee were welcome, and that the next day all the people would come out to meet vs on the way with victuals: and the master of the fielde gaue them a crosse, willing them to signifie to those of their citie that they should not feare, and they should rather let the people stay in their houses, because I came onely in the name of his Majestie to defend and ayd them.

And this done, Fernando Aluarado returned to aduertise mee that certaine Indians were come vnto them in peaceable maner, and that two of them stayed for my comming with the master of the fielde. Whereupon I went vnto them and gave them beades and certaine short clokes, willing them to returne vnto their citie, and bid them to stay quiet in their houses and feare nothing. *A wise forecast.* And this done I sent the master of the field to search whether there were any bad passage which the Indians might keepe against vs, and that hee should take and defend it vntill the next day that I shoulde come thither. *The treason of the Indians.* So hee went, and found in the way a very bad passage, where wee might haue sustayned very great harme: wherefore there hee seated himselfe with his company that were with him: and that very night the Indians came to take that passage to defend it, and finding it taken, they assaulted our men there, and as they tell mee, they assaulted them like valiant men; although in the ende they retired and fledde away; for the master of the fielde was watchfull, and was in order with his company: the Indians in token of retreate sounded on a certaine small trumpet, and did no hurt among the Spanyards. *Great forecast and diligence of the Campe-master.* The very same night the master of the fielde certified mee hereof. Whereupon the next day in the best order that I could I departed in so great want of victuall, that I thought that if wee should stay one day longer without foode, wee should all perish for hunger, especially the Indians, for among vs all we had not two bushels of corne: wherefore it behooued mee to pricke forward without delay. The Indians here and there made fires, and were answered againe afarre off as orderly as wee for our liues could haue done, to giue their fellowes vnderstanding, how wee marched and where we arriued.

They arriue at the citie of Cibola. Assoone as I came within sight of this citie of Grenada, I sent Don Garcias Lopez Campe-master, frier Daniel, and frier Luys, and Fernando Vermizzo somewhat before with certaine horsemen, to seeke the Indians and to aduertise them that our comming was not to hurt them, but to defend them in the name of the Emperour our Lord, according as his maiestie had giuen vs in charge: which message was deliuered to the inhabitants of that countrey by an interpreter. *The arrogancie of the people of Cibola.* But they like arrogant people made small account thereof; because we seemed very few in their eyes, and that they might destroy vs without any difficultie: and they strooke frier Luys with an arrow on the gowne, which by the grace of God did him no harme.

Commandement to vse gentlenesse to the Sauages. In the meane space I arriued with all the rest of the horsemen, and footemen, and found in the fieldes a great sort of the Indians which beganne to shoote at vs with their arrowes: and because I would obey your will and the commaund of the Marques, I woulde not let my people charge them, forbidding my company, which intreated mee that they might set vpon them, in any wise to prouoke them, saying that that which the enemies did was nothing, and that it was not meete to set vpon so fewe people. On the other side the Indians perceiuing that we stirred not, tooke great stomacke and courage vnto them: insomuch that they came hard to our horses heeles to shoote at vs with their arrowes. Whereupon seeing that it was now time to stay no longer, and that the friers also were of the same opinion, I set vpon them without any danger: for suddenly they fled part to the citie which was neere and well fortified; and other vnto the field, which way they could shift: and some of the Indians were slaine, and more had beene if I would haue suffered them to haue bene pursued.

> There were 800 men within the towne. Gomara, Hist. gen. cap. 213.

But considering that hereof wee might reape but small profite, because the Indians that were withoute, were fewe, and those which were retired into the citie, with them which stayed within at the first were many, where the victuals were whereof wee had so great neede, I assembled my people, and diuided them as I thought best to assault the citie, and I compassed it about: and because the famine which wee sustained suffered no delay my selfe with certaine of these gentlemen and souldiers put our selues on foote, and commaunded that the crossebowes and harquebusiers shoulde giue the assault, and shoulde beate the enemies from the walles, that they might not hurt vs, and I assaulted the walles on one side, where they told me there was a scaling ladder set vp, and that there was one gate but the crossebowmen suddenly brake the strings of their bowes, and the harquebusiers did nothing at all: for they came thither so weake and feeble, that scarcely they coulde stand on their feete: and by this meanes the people that were aloft on the wals to defend the towne were no way hindered from doing vs all the mischiefe they could:

> They defend the wals with stones like those of Hochelaga.

so that twise they stroke mee to the ground with infinite number of great stones, which they cast downe: and if I had not beene defended with an excellent good headpiece which I ware, I thinke it had gone hardly with mee: neuerthelesse my companie tooke mee vp with two small wounds in the face, and an arrowe sticking in my foote, and many blowes with stones on my armes and legges, and thus I went out of the battell very weake. I thinke that if Don Garcias Lopez de Cardenas the second time that they strooke mee to the ground had not succoured mee with striding ouer mee like a good knight, I had beene in farre greater danger then I was. But it pleased God that the Indians yeelded themselues vnto vs, and that this citie was taken: and such store of Maiz was found there in, as our necessitie required. The Master of the fielde, and Don Pedro de Touar, and Fernando de Aluarado, and Paul de Melgosa Captaines of the footemen escaped with certaine knocks with stones: though none of them were wounded with arrowes, yet Agoniez Quarez was wounded in one arme with the shot of an arrowe, and one Torres a townesman of Panuca was shot in the face with another, and two footemen more had two small woundes with arrowes. And because my armour was gilded and glittering, they all layd load on mee, and therefore I was more wounded then the rest, not that I did more then they, or put my selfe forwarder then the rest, for all these Gentlemen and souldiers carried themselues as manfully as was looked for at their hands. I am nowe well recouered I thanke God, although somewhat bruised with stones. Likewise in the skirmish which wee had in the fieldes, two or three other souldiers were hurt, and three horses slaine, one of Don Lopez, the other of Viliega and the third of Don Alonso Manrique, and seuen or eight other horses were wounded; but both the men and horses are whole and sound.

Chap. 3.

Of the situation and state of the seuen cities called the kingdome of Cibola, and of the customes and qualities of those people, and of the beasts which are found there.

It remaineth now to certifie your Honour of the seuen cities, and of the kingdomes and prouinces whereof the Father prouincial made report vnto your Lordship. And to bee briefe, I can assure your honour, he sayd the trueth in nothing that he reported, but all was quite contrary, sauing only the names of the cities, and great houses of stone: for although they be not wrought with Turqueses, nor with lyme, nor brickes, yet are they very excellent good houses of three or foure or fiue lofts high, wherein are good lodgings and faire chambers with lathers instead of staires, and certaine cellers vnder the ground very good and paued, which are made for winter, they are in manner like stooues: and the lathers which they have for their houses are all in a maner mooueable and portable, which are taken away and set downe when they please, and they are made of two pieces of wood with their steppes, as ours be. The seuen cities are seuen small townes, all made with these kinde of houses that I speake of: and they stand all within foure leagues together, and they are called the kingdome of Cibola, and euery one of them haue their particular name and none of them is called Cibola, but altogether they are called Cibola. And this towne which I call a citie, I haue named Granada, as well because it is somewhat like vnto it, as also in remembrance of your lordship. In this towne where I now remain, there may be some two hundred houses, all compassed with walles, and I think that with the rest of the houses which are not so walled, they may be together fiue hundred. There is another towne neere this, which is one of the seuen, and it is somewhat bigger than this, and another of the same bignesse that this is of, and the other foure are somewhat lesse: and I send them all painted vnto your lordship with the voyage. *A painter necessarie in a new discouery.* And the parchment wherein the picture is, was found here with other parchments. The people of this towne seeme vnto me of a reasonable stature, and wittie, yet they seeme not to bee such as they should be, of that iudgment and wit to builde these houses in such sort as they are. For the most part they goe all naked, except their priuie parts which are couered: and they haue painted mantles like those which I send vnto your Lordship. They haue no cotton wooll growing, because the countrey is colde, yet they weare mantels thereof as your honour may see by the shewe thereof: and true it is that there was found in their houses certaine yarne made of cotton wooll. *Store of Turqueses.* They weare their haire on their heads like those of Mexico, and they are well nurtured and condicioned: And they haue Turqueses I thinke good quantitie, which with the rest of the goods which they had, except their corne, they had conueyed away before I came thither: for I found no women there, nor no youth vnder fifteene yeeres olde, nor no olde folkes aboue sixtie, sauing two or three olde folkes, who stayed behinde to gouerne all the rest of the youth and men of warre. There were found in a certaine paper two poynts of Emralds, and certaine small stones broken which are in colour somewhat like Granates very bad, and other stones of Christall, which I gaue one of my seruants to lay vp to send them to your lordship, and hee hath lost them as hee telleth me. We found heere Guinie cockes, but fewe. The Indians tell mee in all these seuen cities, that they eate them not, but that they keepe them onely for their feathers. I beleeue them not, for they are excellent good, and greater then those of Mexico. The season which is in this countrey, and the temperature of the ayre is like that of Mexico: or sometime it is hotte, and sometime it raineth; but hitherto I neuer sawe it raine, but once there fell a little showre with winde, as they are woont to fell in Spaine.

Gomora hist. gen. Cap. 213. sayth that the colde is by reason of the high mountaines. The snow and cold are woont to be great, for so say the inhabitants of the Countrey: and it is very likely so to bee, both in respect to the maner of the Countrey, and by the fashion of their houses, and their furres and other things which this people have to defend them from colde. There is no kind of fruit nor trees of fruite. The Countrey is all plaine, and is on no side mountainous: albeit there are some hillie and bad passages. There are small store of Foules: the cause whereof is the colde, and because the mountains are not neere. Heere is no great store of wood, because they haue wood for their fuell sufficient foure leagues off from a wood of small Cedars. There is most excellent grasse within a quarter of a league hence, for our horses as well to feede them in pasture, as to mow and make hay, whereof wee stoode in great neede, because our horses came hither so weak and feeble. The victuals which the people of this countrey haue, is Maiz, whereof they haue great store, and also small white Pease: and Venison, which by all likelyhood they feede vpon, (though they say no) for wee found many skinnes of Deere, of Hares, and Conies. They eate the best cakes that euer I sawe, and euery body generally eateth of them. They haue the finest order and way to grinde that we euer saw in any place. And one Indian woman of this countrey will grinde as muche as foure women of Mexico. They have most excellent salte in kernell, which they fetch from a certaine lake a dayes iourney from hence. The Westerne sea within 150 leagues from Cibola. They haue no knowledge among them of the North Sea, nor of the Westerne Sea, neither can I tell your lordship to which wee bee neerest; But in reason they should seeme to be nearest to the Westerne Sea: and at the least I thinke I am an hundred and fiftie leagues from thence: and the Northerne Sea should bee much further off. Your lordship may see how broad the land is here. Here are many sorts of beasts, as Beares, Tigers, Lions, Porkespicks, and certaine Sheep as bigge as an horse, with very great hornes and little tailes, I haue seene their hornes so bigge, that it is a wonder to behold their greatnesse. Here are also wilde goates whose heads likewise I haue seene, and the pawes of Beares, and the skins of wilde Bores. There is game of Deere, Ounces, and very great Stagges: and all men are of opinion that there are some bigger then that beast which your Lordship bestowed upon me, which once belonged to Iohn Melaz. Oxe hides dressed and painted very cunningly. They trauell eight dayes iourney vnto certaine plaines lying toward the North Sea. In this countrey there are certaine skinnes well dressed, and they dresse them and paint them where they kill their Oxen, for so they say themselues.

Chap. 4.

Of the state and qualities of the kingdomes of Totonteac, Marata, and Acus, quite contrary to the relation of Frier Marcus. The conference which they haue with the Indians of the citie of Granada which they had taken, which had fiftie yeres past foreseene the comming of the Christians into their countrey. The relation which they haue of other seuen cities, whereof Tucano is the principall, and how he sent to discouer them. A present of divers things had in these countreys sent vnto the Viceroy Mendoça by Vasques de Coronado.

The kingdome of Totonteac so much extolled by the Father prouinciall, which sayde that there were such wonderfull things there, and such great matters, and that they made cloth there, the Indians say is an hotte lake, about which are fiue or six houses: and that there were certaine other, but that they are ruinated by warre. The kingdome of Marata is not to be found, neither haue the Indians any knowledge thereof. Tadouac seemeth because it is a lake, and endeth in ac to haue some affinitie herewith. The kingdome of Acus is one onely small citie, where they gather cotton which is called Acucu. And I say that this is a towne. For Acus with an aspiration nor without is no word of the countrey. And because I gesse that they would deriue Acucu of Acus, I say that it is this towne whereinto the kingdom of Acus is conuerted. Beyond this towne they say there are other small townes which are neere to a riuer which I haue seene and haue had report of by the relation of the Indians. I would to God I had better newes to write vnto your lordship: neuerthelesse I must say the truth: And as I wrote to your lordship from Culiacan, I am now to aduertise your honour as wel of the good as of the bad. Yet this I would haue to bee assured, that if all the riches and the treasures of the world were heere, I could haue done no more in the seruice of his Maiestie and of your lordshippe, then I haue done in comming hither whither you haue sent mee, my selfe and my companions carrying our victuals vpon our shoulders and vpon our horses three hundred leagues; and many dayes going on foote trauailing ouer hills and rough mountains, with other troubles which I cease to mention, neither purpose I to depart vnto the death, if it please his Maiestie and your lordship that it shall be so.

Three dayes after this citie was taken, certaine Indians of these people came to offer mee peace, and brought mee certaine Turqueses and badde mantles, and I received them in his Maiesties name with all the good speaches that I could deuise, certifying them of the purpose of my comming into this countrey, which is in the name of his Maiestie, and by the commaundment of your Lordship, that they and all the rest of the people of this prouince should become Christians, and should knowe the true God for their Lorde, and receiue his Maiestie for their King and earthly Soueraigne: And herewithall they returned to their houses, and suddenly the next day they set in order all their goods and substance, their women and children, and fled to the hilles, leauing their townes as it were abandoned, wherein remained very fewe of them. A citie greater than Granada. When I sawe this, within eight or tenne dayes after being recouered of my woundes, I went to the citie, which I sayde to be greater then this where I am, and found there some fewe of them, to whom I sayde that they should not bee afrayd, and that they should call their gouernour vnto mee: Howbeit forasmuch as I can learne or gather, none of them hath any gouernour: for I sawe not there any chiefe house, whereby any preeminence of one ouer another might bee gathered. After this an olde man came, which sayd that hee was their lord, with a piece of a mantle made of many pieces, with whom I reasoned that small while that hee stayed with mee, and hee sayd that within three dayes after, hee and the rest of the chiefe of that towne would come and visite mee, and giue order what course should bee taken with them. Which they did: for they brought mee certaine mantles and some Turqueses. I aduised them to come downe from their holdes, and to returne with their wiues and children to their houses, and to become Christians, and that they would acknowledge the Emperours maiestie for their King and lorde. And euen to this present they keepe in those strong holdes their women and children, and all the goods which they haue. Two tables painted by the Indians, one of beasts another of birdes and fishes. I commaunded them that they should paint mee out a cloth of all the beastes which they knowe in their countrey: And such badde painters as they are, foorthwith they painted mee two cloths, one of their beastes, another of their birdes and fishes. An old prophecie that those parts should be subdued by Christians. They say that they will bring their children, that our religious men may instruct them, and that they desire to knowe our lawe: And they assure vs, that aboue fiftie yeeres past it was prophecied among them, that a certaine people like vs should come, and from that part that wee came from, and that they should subdue all that countrey.

They worship the water. That which these Indians worship as farre as hitherto wee can learne, is the water: for they say it causeth their corne to growe, and maintaineth their life; and that they know none other reason, but that their ancesters did so. I haue sought by all meanes possible to learne of the inhabitants of these townes, whether they haue any knowledge of other people, countreys and cities: *Seuen cities farre from Granada.* And they tell mee of seuen cities which are farre distant from this place, which are like vnto these, though they haue not houses like vnto these but they are of earth, and small: and that among them much cotton is gathered. The chiefe of these townes whereof they haue any knowledge, they say is called Tucano: and they gaue mee no perfect knowledge of the rest. And I thinke they doe not tell me the trueth, imagining that of necessitie I must speedily depart from them, and returne home. But herein they shall soone finde themselues deceiued. I sent Don Pedro de Touar with his companie of footemen and with certaine other horsemen to see this towne: And I would not haue despatched this packet vnto your lordship, vntill I had knowen what this towne was, if I had thought that within twelue or fifteene dayes I might haue had newes from him: for hee will stay in this iourney thirtie dayes at least. And hauing examined that the knowledge hereof is of small importance, and that the colde and the waters approch: I thought it my duety to doe according as your lordship gaue me charge in your instructions, which is, that immediatly vpon mine arriuall here, I should signifie so much vnto your lordship, and so I doe, sending withall the bare relation of that which I haue seene. I haue determined to send round about the countrey from hence to haue knowledge of all things, and rather to suffer all extremitie, then to leaue this enterprise to serue his maiestie, if I may find any thing wherein I may performe it, and not to omit any diligence therein, vntill your lordship send mee order what I shall doe. Wee haue great want of pasture: *The Spaniards victualling in discoueries.* and your Lordship also shall vnderstand, that among all those which are here, there is not one pound of raisins, nor suger, nor oyle, nor any wine, saue only one pinte which is saued, to say Masse: for all is spent and spilt by the way. Now your lordship may prouide vs what you thinke needefull. And if your honour meane to send vs cattell, your lordship must vnderstand that they will bee a sommer in comming vnto vs: for they will not be able to come vnto vs any sooner. *A garment excellently imbroidered with needle worke.* I would haue sent your lordshippe with this dispatch many musters of things which are in this countrey: but the way is so long and rough, that it is hard for me to doe so: neuerthelesse I send you twelue small mantles, such as the people of the countrey are woont to weare, and a certaine garment also, which seemeth vnto me to bee well made: I kept the same, because it seemed to mee to bee excellent well wrought, because I beleeue that no man euer sawe any needle worke in these Indies, except it were since the Spaniards inhabited the same. I send your Lordshippe also two clothes painted with the beasts of this country, although as I haue sayde, the picture be very rudely done, because the painter spent but one day in drawing of the same. I haue seene other pictures on the walles of the houses of this citie with farre better proportion, and better made. I send your honour one Oxe-hide, certaine Turqueses, and two eare-rings of the same, and fifteene combes of the Indians, and certain tablets set with these Turqueses, and two small baskets made of wicker, whereof the Indians haue great store. I send your Lordship also two rolles which the women in these parts are woont to weare on their heads when they fetch water from their welles, as wee vse to doe in Spaine. And one of these Indian women with one of these rolles on her head, will carie a pitcher of water without touching the same vp a lather. I send you also a muster of the weapons wherewith these people are woont to fight, a buckler, a mace, a bowe, and certaine arrowes, among which are two with points of bones, the like whereof, as these conquerours say, haue neuer beene seene. I can say nothing vnto your lordshippe touching the apparell of their women. For the Indians keepe them so carefully from vs, that hitherto I haue not seene any of them, sauing only two olde women, and these had two long robes downe to the foote open before, and girded to them, and they are buttoned with certaine cordons of cotton. I requested the Indians to giue me one of these robes, which they ware, to send your honour the same, seeing they would not shewe mee their women. And they brought mee two mantles which are these, which I send you as it were painted: they haue two pendents like the women of Spaine, which hang somewhat ouer their shoulders. ·The death of Stephan the Negro. · The death of the Negro is most certaine: for here are many of the things found which hee carried with him: And the Indians tell me that they killed him here, because the Indians of Chichilticale tolde them that hee was a wicked villaine, and not like vnto the Christians: because the Christians kill no women: and hee killed women: and also he touched their women, which the Indians loue more then themselues; therefore they determined to kill him: But they did it not after such sort as was reported, for they killed none of the rest of those that came with him: neither slewe they the young lad which was with him of the prouince of Petatlan, but they tooke him and kept him in safe custodie vntill nowe. And when I sought to haue him, they excused themselues two or three dayes to giue him mee, telling mee that hee was dead, and sometimes that the Indians of Acucu had carried him away. But in conclusion when I tolde them that I should bee very angry if they did not giue him mee, they gaue him vnto me. Hee is an interpreter, for though hee cannot well speake their language, yet hee vnderstandeth the same very well. *Gold and siluer found in Cibola.* In this place there is found some quantitie of golde and siluer, which those which are skilful in minerall matters esteeme to be very good. To this houre I could neuer learne of these people from whence they haue it: And I see they refuse to tell mee the trueth in all things imagining, as I haue sayde, that in short I would depart hence, but I hope in God they shall no longer excuse themselues. I beseech your lordship to certifie his Maiestie of the successe of his voyage. For seeing wee haue no more then that which is aforesayd, and vntil such time as it please God that wee finde that which wee desire, I meane not to write my selfe. Our Lorde God keepe and preserue your excellencie.

From the Prouince of Cibola, and from this citie of Granada the third of August 1540. Francis Vasques de Coronado kisseth the hands of your Excellencie.

The rest of this voyage to Acuco, Liguex, Cicuic, and Quiuira, and vnto the Westerne Ocean, is thus written in the generall historie of the West Indies by Francis Lopez de Gomera, Chap. 214.

Because they would not returne to Mexico without doing something, nor with emptie hands, they agreed to passe further into the countrey, which was tolde them to bee better and better. So they came to Acuco a towne vpon an exceeding strong hill. *The Westerne sea discouered.* And from thence Don Garcias Lopez de Cardenas with his companie of horsemen went vnto the Sea: and Francis Vasques went to Tiguex, which standeth on the banke of a great riuer. There they had newes of Axa and Quiuira. There they sayde was a King whose name was Tartatrax, with a long beard, horie headed, and rich, which was girded with a Bracamart, which prayed vpon a payre of beades, which worshipped a Crosse of golde, and the image of a woman, the Queene of heauen. This newes did greatly reioyce and cheere vp the armie: although some thought it to bee false, and the report of the Friers. They determined to goe thither, with intention to winter in so rich a countrey as that was reported to bee. One night the Indians ranne away, and in the morning they found thirtie horses dead, which put the armie in feare. In their iourney they burnt a certaine towne: And in another towne which they assaulted, they killed certaine Spaniards, and wounded fiftie horses and the inhabitants drewe into their towne Francis de Ouando wounded or dead, to eate and sacrifice him as they thought, or peraduenture to see more perfectly, what maner of them the Spaniards were: for there was not found there any signe of sacrificing men. Our people layde siege vnto the towne, but could not take it in more then fiue and fortie dayes space. The townesmen that were besieged, dranke snowe in stead of water: and seeing themselues forlorne they made a fire, wherein they cast their mantles, feathers, Turqueses and precious things, that those strangers might not enioy them. They issued out in a squadron with their women and children in the middest, to make way by force, and to saue themselues, but fewe escaped the edge of our swordes and the horses, and a certaine riuer which was neere the towne. Seuen Spaniards were slaine in this conflict, and fourescore were wounded, and many horses: whereby a man may see of what force resolution is in necessitie. Many Indians returned to the towne with the women and children, and defended themselues, vntill our men set fire on the towne. In this countrey there are melons, and white and redde cotton, whereof they make farre larger mantels, then in other parts of the Indies. From Tigues they went in foure dayes iourney to Cicuic, which is a small towne, and foure leagues from thence they met with a new kind of oxen wild and fierce, whereof the first day they killed fourescore, which sufficed the armie with flesh. From Cicuic they went to Quiuira, which after their accompt, is almost three hundred leagues distant, through mighty plaines, and sandie heathes so smooth, and wearisome, and bare of wood, that they made heapes of oxe-dung for want of stones and trees, that they might not lose themselues at their returne: for three horses were lost on that plaine, and one Spaniard, which went from his companie on hunting. All that way and plaines are as full of crookebacked oxen, as the mountaine Serena in Spaine is of sheepe: but there is no people but such as keepe those cattell. They were a great succour for the hunger and want of bread which our people stoode in. One day it rayned in that plaine a great showre of haile, as bigge as Orenges, which caused many teares, weakenesse, and vowes. At length they came to Quiuira and found Tatarrax, whome they sought, an hoarie headed man, naked, and with a iewell of copper hanging at his necke, which was all his riches. The Spaniards seeing the false report of so famous riches, returned to Tiguex, without seeing either crosse or shew of Christianitie: and from thence to Mexico. The Spaniards would haue inhabited the countrey. In the ende of March of the yeere 1542. Francis Vasquez fell from his horse in Tiguex, and with the fall fell out of his wits, and became madde. Which some tooke to bee for griefe, and others thought it to be but counterfeited: for they were much offended with him, because hee peopled not the countrey.

Quiuira is in fortie degrees: it is a temperate countrey, and hath very good waters, and much grasse, plummes, mulberries, nuts, melons and grapes, which ripen very well. There is no cotton: and they apparell themselues with oxe-hides and deeres skinnes. They sawe shippes on the sea coast, which bare Alcatrarzes or Pellicanes of golde and siluer in their prows, and were laden with marchandises, and they thought them to bee of Cathaya, and China, because they shewed our men by signes that they had sayled thirtie dayes.

Frier Iohn de Padilla stayed behinde in Tigues, with another of his companions called Frier Francis, and returned to Quiuira, with some dozen Indians of Mechuacan, and with Andrew de Campo a Portugall, the gardiner of Francis de Solis: He tooke with him horses and mules with prouision. He tooke sheepe and hennes of Castile, and ornaments to say Masse withall. The people of Quiuira slewe the Friers, and the Portugall escaped with certaine Indians of Mechuacan. Who albeit at that time he escaped death, yet could hee not free himselfe out of captiuitie: for by and by after they caught him againe. But ten monenths after he was taken captiue, hee fled away with a couple of dogs. As hee trauiled, hee blessed the people with a crosse, whereunto they offered much, and wheresoeuer hee came, they giue him almes, lodging, and foode. Andrew de Campo trauailed from Quiuira to Panuco. He came to the countrey of the Chichimechas and arriued at Panuco. When he came to Mexico, hee ware his haire very long, and his beard tyed up in a lace, and reported strange things of the lands, riuers and mountaines that he had passed.

It grieued Don Antonio de Mendoca very much that the army returned home: for he had spent aboue threescore thousand pesos of golde in the enterprise, and ought a great part thereof still. The cause why the Spaniards peopled not in Cibola. Many sought to haue dwelt there; but Francis Vasquez de Coronado, which was rich, and lately married to a faire wife, would not consent, saying, that they could not maintaine nor defend themselues in so poore a countrey, and so farre from succour. They trauailed aboue nine hundred leagues in this countrey.

The foresayd Francis Lopez de Gomara in his generall historie of the West Indies, Chap. 215. writeth in maner following of certaine great

and strange beasts neuer seene nor heard of in our knowen world of Asia, Europe, and Africa: which somewhat resembling our oxen, hauing high bunches on their backes like those on the backes of Camels, are therefore called by him Vacas corcobados, that is to say, Crooke-backed oxen, being very deformed and terrible in shewe, and fierce by nature: which notwithstanding for foode, apparell, and other necessarie vses, are most seruiceable and beneficiall to the inhabitants of those countreys. He reporteth also in the same chapter of certaine strange sheepe as bigge as horses, and of dogs which vse to carie burthens of 50. pound weight vpon their backes.

All the way betweene Cicuic and Quiuira is a most plaine soyle, without trees and stones, and hath but fewe and small townes. These are much like the people that Captain Frobisher brought into England from Meta Incognita. The men clothe and shooe themselues with lether; and the women which are esteemed for their long lockes, couer their heads and secrets with the same. They haue no bread of any kinde of graine, as they say: which I account a very great matter. Their chiefest foode is flesh, and that oftentimes they eate raw, either of custome or for lacke of wood. They eate the fatte as they take it out of the Oxe, and drinke the blood hotte, and die not therewithall, though the ancient writers say that it killeth, as Empedocles and others affirmed, they drinke it also colde dissolued in water. They seeth not the flesh for lacke of pots, but rost it, or to say more properly, warme it at a fire of Oxe-dung: when they eate, they chawe their meate but little, and rauen vp much, and holding the flesh with their teeth, they cut it with rasors of stone, which seemeth to be great bestialitie: but such is their maner of liuing and fashion. They goe together in companies, and mooue from one place to another, as the wilde Moores of Barbarie called Alarbes doe, following the seasons and the pasture after their Oxen.

The description of the oxen of Quiuira. These Oxen are of the bignesse and colour of our Bulles, but their hornes are not so great. They haue a great bunch vpon their fore shoulders, and more haire on their fore part then on their hinder part: and it is like wooll. They haue as it were an horse-manne vpon their backe bone, and much haire and very long from the knees downward. They haue great tuffes of haire hanging downe their foreheads, and it seemeth that they haue beardes, because of the great store of haire hanging downe at their chinnes and throates. The males haue very long tailes, and a great knobbe or flocke at the end: so that in some respect they resemble the Lion, and in some other the Camell. They push with their hornes, they runne, they ouertake and kill an horse when they are in their rage and anger. Finally, it is a foule and fierce beast of countenance and forme of bodie. The horses fledde from them, either because of their deformed shape, or else because they had neuer seene them. Their masters haue no other riches nor substance: of them they eat, they drink, they apparel, they shooe themselues: and of their hides they make many things, as houses, shooes, apparell and ropes: of their bones they make bodkins: of their sinewes and haire, threed: of their hornes, mawes, and bladders, vessels; of their dung, fire: and of their calues-skinnes, budgets, wherein they drawe and keepe water. To bee short, they make so many things of them as they haue neede of, or as many as suffice them in the vse of this life.

There are also in this countrey other beastes as big as horses, which because they haue hornes and fine wool, they cal them sheepe, and they say that euery horne of theirs weigheth is fiftie pound weight.

There are also great dogs which will fight with a bull, and will carrie fiftie pound weight in sackes when they goe on hunting, or when they remooue from place to place with their flockes and heards.

DIVERS VOYAGES MADE BY ENGLISHMEN TO THE FAMOUS CITIE OF MEXICO, AND TO ALL OR MOST PART OF THE OTHER PRINCIPALL PROUINCES, CITIES, TOWNES AND PLACES THROUGHOUT THE GREAT AND LARGE KINGDOM OF NEW SPAINE, EUEN AS FARRE AS NICARAGUA AND PANAMA, AND THENCE TO PERU: TOGETHER WITH A DESCRIPTION OF THE SPANIARDS FORME OF GOUERNMENT THERE: AND SUNDRY PLEASANT RELATIONS OF THE MANERS AND CUSTOMES OF THE NATURAL INHABITANTS, AND OF THE MANIFOLD RICH COMMODITIES AND STRANGE RARITIES FOUND IN THOSE PARTES OF THE CONTINENT: AND OTHER MATTERS MOST WORTHY THE OBSERUATION.

The voyage of Robert Tomson Marchant, into Noua Hispania in the yeere 1555. with diuers obseruations concerning the state of the Countrey: And certaine accidents touching himselfe.

Robert Tomson borne in the towne of Andouer in Hampshire began his trauaile out of England in An. 1553. in the moneth of March: who departing out of the citie of Bristoll in a good ship called The barke yong, in companie of other Marchants of the sayd citie, within 8. dayes after arriued at Lisbone in Portugall, where the sayd Robert Tomson remained 15. dayes, at the end of which he shipped himselfe for Spaine in the sayd shippe, and within 4. dayes arriued in the bay of Cadiz in Andalusia, which is vnder the kingdome of Spaine, and from thence went vp to the citie of Siuil by land, which is 20. leagues, and there hee repaired to one Iohn Fields house an English Marchant, who had dwelt in the said city of Siuil 18. or 20. yeres maried with wife and children: In whose house the said Tomson remained by the space of one whole yeere or thereabout, for two causes: The one to learn the Castillian tongue, the other to see the orders of the countrey, and the customes of the people. At the end of which time hauing seene the fleetes of shippes come out of the Indies to that citie, with such great quantitie, of gold and siluer, pearles, precious stones, suger, hides, ginger, and diuers other rich commodities, he did determine with himselfe to seeke meanes and opportunitie to passe ouer to see that rich countrey from whence such great quantitie of rich commodities came. And it fell out that within short time after, the said Iohn Field (where the sayd Tomson was lodged) did determine to passe ouer into the West Indies, himselfe, with his wife, children, and familie, and at the request of the sayde Tomson, he purchased a licence of the King to passe into the Indies, for himselfe, his wife and children, and among them also for the sayde Tomson to passe with them: so that presently they made preparation of victuall and other necessarie prouision for the voyage. But the shippes which were prepared to perfourme the voyage being all ready to depart, vpon certaine considerations by the kings commandment were stayed and arrested till further should bee knowen of the Kings pleasure. Whereupon the said Iohn Field, with Robert Tomson departed out of Siuil and came down to S. Lucar 15. leagues off, and seeing the stay made vpon the ships of the said fleet, and being not assured when they would depart, determined to ship themselues for the Iles of the Canaries, which are 250. leagues from S. Lucar, and there to stay till the said fleet should come thither: for that is continually their port to make stay at 6. or 8. daies, to take in fresh water, bread, flesh, and other necessaries.

So that in the moneth of February in An. 1555. the sayde Robert Tomson with the said Iohn Field and his companie, shipped themselues out of the towne of S. Lucar in a caruel of the citie of Cadiz, and within 6. dayes they arriued at the port of the Grand Canaria, where at our comming the ships that rode in the said port began to cry out of all measure with loud voyces, in so much that the castle which stood fast by began to shoot at vs, and shot 6. or 7. shot at vs, and strooke downe our maine maste, before we could hoise out our boat to goe on land, to know what the cause of the shooting was, seeing that we were Spanish ships, and were comming into his countrey. So that being on lande, and complaining of the wrong and damage done vnto us; they answered, that they had thought we had bene French rouers, that had come into the said port to do some harme to the ships that were there. For that 8. dayes past there went out of the port a caruell much like vnto ours, laden with sugers and other marchandise for Spaine and on the other side of the point of the sayd Iland, met with a Frenchman of warre, who tooke the said caruell, and vnladed out of her into the said French ship both men and goods. And being demanded of the said Spaniards what other ships remained in the port whence they came, they answered that there remained diuers other ships, and one laden with sugers (as they were) and ready to depart for Spaine: vpon the which newes the Frenchmen put 30. tall men of their ship well appointed into the said caruel which they had taken, and sent her backe againe to the said port from whence she had departed the day before. And somewhat late towards the euening came into the port, not shewing past 3. or 4. men, and so came to an anker hard by the other ships that were in the said port, and being seene by the castle and by the said ships, they made no reconing of her, because they knew her, and thinking that she had found contrary windes at the sea, or had forgot something behinde them, they had returned backe againe for the same, and so made no accompt of her, but let her alone riding quietly among the other ships in the said port: So that about midnight the said caruel with the Frenchmen in her went aboord the other ship that lay hard by laden with sugers, and droue the Spaniards that were in her vnder hatches, and presently let slip her cables and ankers, and set saile and carried her cleane away, and after this sort deceiued them: And they thinking or fearing that we were the like did shoote at vs as they did.

English factors in the Grand Canaria. This being past, the next day after our arriuall in the sayd port, wee did vnbarke our selues and went on lande vp to the citie or head towne of the great Canaria, where we remained 18. or 20. dayes: and there found certaine Englishmen marchants servants of one Anthony Hickman and Edward Castelin, marchants of the citie of London that lay there in traffique, of whom wee receiued great courtesie and much good cheere. After the which 20. dayes being past, in the which we had seene the countrey, the people, and the disposition thereof, wee departed from thence, and passed to the next Ile of the Canaries 18. leagues off; called Teneriffe, and being come on land, went vp to the citie called La Laguna, where we remained 7. moneths, attending the comming of the whole fleete, which in the ende came, and there hauing taken that which they had neede of, wee shipped our selues in a ship of Cadiz, being one of the saide fleete, which was belonging to an Englishman maried in the citie of Cadiz in Spaine, whose name was Iohn Sweeting, and there came in the sayd ship for captain also an Englishman maried in Cadiz, and sonne in law to the sayde Iohn Sweeting, whose name was Leonard Chilton: there came also in the said ship another Englishman which had beene a marchant of the citie of Exeter, one of 50. yeeres or thereabout, whose name was Ralph Sarre. So that we departed from the sayd Ilands in the moneth of October the foresayd yeere, 8. ships in our companie, and so directed our course towards the bay of Mexico, and by the way towardes the Iland of S. Domingo, otherwise called Hispaniola. So that within 32. dayes after we departed from the Iles of Canaries wee arriued with our ship at the port of S. Domingo, and went in ouer the barre where our ship knocked her keele at her entrie: and there our ship rid before the towne, where wee went on land, and refreshed our selues 16. dayes, where we found no bread made of wheat, but biscuit brought out of Spaine, and out of the bay of Mexico: for the countrey it selfe doeth yeelde no kinde of bread to make graine withall. But the bread they make there, is certaine cakes made of rootes called Cassaui, which is something substantiall, but it hath but an vnsauorie taste in the eating thereof. Flesh of beefe and mutton they haue great store: for there are men that haue 10000. head of cattell, of oxen, bulles and kine, which they doe keepe onely for the hides; for the quantitie of flesh is so great, that they are not able to spend the hundreth part. Hogs flesh is there good store, very sweete and sauorie, and so holesome, that they giue it to sick folkes to eat in stead of hennes and capons, although they haue good store of poultrie of that sort, as also of Guinycocks and Guinyhens. At the time of our being there, the citie of S. Domingo was not of aboue 500. housholds of Spaniards, but of the Indians dwelling in the suburbs there were more. The countrey is most part of the yere very hot, and very ful of a kind of flies or gnats with long bils, which do pricke and molest the people very much in the night when they are asleepe, in pricking their faces and hands, and other parts of their bodies that lie vncouered, and make them to swel wonderfully. Many of our men died of these wormes at the taking of Puertorico. Also there is another kind of small worme which creepeth into the soles of mens feet and especially of the black Moores and children which vse to go barefoot, and maketh their feet to grow as big as a mans head, and doth so ake that it would make one run mad. They haue no remedy for the same, but to open the flesh sometimes 3. or 4. inches and so dig them out. The countrey yeeldeth great store of suger, hides of oxen, buls and kine, ginger, Cana fistula and Salsa perilla: mines of siluer and gold there are none, but in some riuers there is found some smal quantitie of gold. The principal coine that they do trafique withal in that place, is blacke money made of copper and brasse: and this they say they do vse not for that they lacke money of gold and siluer to trade withall out of the other parts of India, but because if they should haue good money, the marchants that deale with them in trade, would cary away their gold and siluer, and let the countrey commodities lie still. And thus much for S. Domingo. So we were comming from the yles of Canaries to S. Domingo, and there staying vntil the moneth of December, which was 3. moneths. About the beginning of Ianuary we departed thence towards the bay of Mexico and new Spaine, toward which we set our course, and so sailed 24. dayes till we came within 15. leagues of S. Iohn de Vllua, which was the port of Mexico of our right discharge: And being so neere our said port, there rose a storme of Northerly windes, which came off from Terra Florida, which caused vs to cast about into the sea, againe, for feare least that night we should be cast vpon the shoore before day did breake, and so put our selues in danger of casting away: the winde and sea grew so foule and strong, that within two houres after the storme began, eight ships that were together were so dispersed, that we could not see one another. One of the ships of our company being of the burthen of 500. tun called the hulke of Carion, would not cast about to sea as we did, but went that night with the land, thinking in the morning to purchase the port of S. Iohn de Vllua, but missing the port went with the shoare and was cast away. There were drowned of that ship 75. persons, men, women and children, and 64. were saved that could swim, and had meanes to saue themselves: among those that perished in that ship, was a gentlemen who had bene present the yere before in S. Domingo, his wife and 4. daughters with the rest of his seruants and household. We with the other 7. ships cast about into the sea, the storme during 10. dayes with great might, boisterous winds, fogs and raine: our ship being old and weake was so tossed, that she opened at the sterne a fadome vnder water, and the best remedy we had was to stop it with beds and pilobiers, and for feare of sinking we threw and lightned into the sea all the goods we had or could come by: but that would not serue. Then we cut our maine mast, and threw all our Ordinance into the sea sauing one piece, which early in a morning when wee thought wee should haue sunke, we shot off, and as pleased God there was one of the ships of our company neere vnto vs, which we saw not by meanes of the great fogge, which hearing the sound of the piece, and vnderstanding some of the company to be in great extremitie, began to make toward vs, and when they came within hearing of vs, we desired them for the loue of God to helpe to saue vs, for that we were all like to perish. They willed vs to hoise our foresaile as much as we could and make towards them, for they would do their best to saue vs, and so we did. And we had no sooner hoised our foresaile, but there came a gale of winde and a piece of a sea, strooke in the foresaile, and caried saile and maste all ouerboord, so that then we thought there was no hope of life. And then we began to imbrace one another, euery man his friend, euery wife her husband, and the children their fathers and mothers, committing our soules to Almighty God, thinking neuer to escape aliue: yet it pleased God in the time of most need when all hope was past, to aide vs with his helping hand, and caused the winde a little to cease, so that within two houres after, the other ship was able to come aboord vs, and tooke into her with her boat man, woman and child, naked without hose or shoe vpon many of our feete. I do remember that the last person that came out of the ship into the boat was a woman blacke Moore, who leaping out of the ship into the boat with a yong sucking childe in her armes, lept too short and fell into the sea, and was a good while vnder the water before the boat could come to rescue her, and with the spreading of her clothes rose aboue water againe, and was caught by the coat and pulled into the boate hauing still her child vnder her arme, both of them halfe drowned, and yet her natural loue towards her child would not let her let the childe goe. And when she came aboord the boate she helde her childe so fast vnder her arm still, that two men were scant able to get it out. So we departed out of our ship and left it in the sea: it was worth foure hundreth thousand ducats, ship and goods when we left it. And within three dayes after we arriued at our port of S. Iohn de Vllua in New Spaine. I do remember that in the great and boysterous storme of this foule weather, in the night, there came vpon the toppe of our maine yarde and maine maste, a certaine little light, much like vnto the light of a little candle, which the Spaniards called the Cuerpo santo, and saide it was S. Elmo, whom they take to bee the aduocate of Sailers. At the which sight the Spaniards fell downe vpon their knees and worshipped it, praying God and S. Elmo to cease the torment, and saue them from the perill that they were in with promising him that on their comming on land, they would repaire vnto his Chappell, and their cause Masses to be saide, and other ceremonies to be done. The friers cast reliques into the sea, to cause the sea to be still, and likewise said Gospels, with other crossings and ceremonies vpon the sea to make the storme to cease: which (as they said) did much good to weaken the furie of the storme. But I could not perceiue it, nor gaue no credite to it, till it pleased God to send vs the remedie and deliuered vs from the rage of the same, His Name be praised therefore. This light continued aboord our ship about three hours, flying from maste to maste, and from top to top: and sometime it would be in two or three places at once. I informed my selfe of learned men afterward what that light should be, and they said, that it was but a congelation of the winde and vapours of the Sea congealed with the extremitie of the weather, which flying in the winde, many times doeth chance to hit on the masts and shrowds of the ships that are at sea in foule weather. And in trueth I do take it to be so: for that I haue seene the like in other ships at sea, and in sundry ships at once. By this men may see how the Papists are giuen to beleeue and worship such vaine things and toyes, as God, to whom all honour doth appertaine and in their neede and necessities do let to call vpon the liuing God, who is the giuer of all good things.

> His arriuall at Vera Cruz.

The 16. of April in Anno 1556. we arrived at the port of S. Iohn de Vllua in new Spaine, very naked and distressed, of apparell, and all other things, by meanes of the losse of our foresaid ship and goods, and from thence we went to the new Towne called Vera Cruz, fiue leagues from the said port of S. Iohn de Vllua, marching still by the sea side, where wee found lying vpon the sands great quantitie of mightie great trees with roots and all, some of them of foure, fiue, and sixe cart load by our estimation, which, as the people told vs, were in the great stormy weather, which we endured at sea,

> Florida 300. leagues from San Iuan de Vllua.

rooted out of the ground in Terra Florida, which is three hundredth leagues ouer by Sea, and brought thither. So we came to the saide Towne of Vera cruz, where wee remained a moneth: and there the said Iohn Field chanced to meete with an olde friend of his acquaintance in Spaine, called Gonçalo Ruiz de Cordoua, a very rich man of the saide Towne of Vera cruz: who hearing of his comming thither with his wife and family, and of his misfortune by Sea, came vnto him and receiued him and all his household into his house, and kept vs there a whole moneth, making vs very good cheere, and giuing vs good entertainment, and also gaue vs that were in all eight persons, of the said Iohn Fields house, double apparell new out of the shop of very good cloth, coates, cloakes, hose, shirts, smocks, gownes for the women, hose, shoes, and al other necessary apparel, and for our way vp to the Citie of Mexico, horses, moiles, and men, and money in our purses for the expenses by the way, which by our accompt might amount vnto the summe of 400. Crownes. And after wee were entred two dayes iourney into the Countrey, I the saide Robert Tomson fell so sicke of an ague, that the next day I was not able to sit on my horse, but was faine to be caried vpon Indians backes, from thence to Mexico. And when wee came within halfe a dayes iourney of the Citie of Mexico, the saide Iohn Field also fell sicke, and within three dayes after we arriued at the said Citie, hee died: And presently sickened one of his children, and two more of his houshold people, and within eight days died. So that within tenne dayes after we arriued at the Citie of Mexico, of eight persons that were of vs of the saide company, there remained but foure aliue, and I the said Tomson was at the point of death of the sicknes that I got vpon the way, which continued with mee the space of sixe moneths. At the end of which time it pleased Almightie God to restore me my health againe, although weake and greatly disabled. And being some thing strong, I procured to seeke meanes to liue, and to seeke a way how to profite my selfe in the Countrey, seeing it had pleased God to sende vs thither in safetie. Then by friendship of one Thomas Blake a Scottishman borne, who had dwelt and had bene married in the said Citie aboue twentie yeeres before I came to the saide Citie, I was preferred to the seruice of a gentleman a Spaniard dwelling there, a man of great wealth, and one of the first conquerours of the said Citie, whose name was Gonçalo Cerezo, with whom I dwelt twelue monethes and a halfe. At the ende of which I was maliciously accused by the Holy house for matters of Religion, and so apprehended and caried to prison, where I lay close prisoner seuen monethes, without speaking to any creature, but to the Iailer that kept the said prison, when he brought me my meat and drinke. In the meane time was brought into the saide prison one Augustin Boacio an Italian of Genoua also for matters of Religion, who was taken at Sacatecas 80. leagues to the Northwest of the Citie of Mexico: At the ende of the said seuen monethes, we were both caried to the high Church of Mexico, to doe open penance vpon an high scaffold, made before the high Alter, vpon a Sunday, in presence of a very great number of people, who were at the least fiue or sixe thousand. For there were that came one hundreth mile off, to see the said Auto (as they call it) for that there were neuer none before, that had done the like in the said Countrey, nor could not tell what Lutheranes were, nor what it meant: for they neuer heard of any such thing before. We were brought into the Church, euery one with a S. Benito vpon his backe, which is halfe a yard of yellow cloth, with a hole to put in a mans head in the middest, and cast ouer a mans head: both flaps cast one before, and another behinde, and in the middest of euery flap, a S. Andrewes crosse, made of red cloth, sowed on vpon the same, and that is called S. Benito. The common people before they sawe the penitents come into the Church, were giuen to vnderstand that wee were heretiques, infidels, and people that did despise God, and his workes, and that wee had bene more like deuils than men, and thought wee had had the fauour of some monsters, or heathen people. And when they saw vs come into the Church in our players coates, the women and children beganne to cry out, and made such a noise, that it was strange to see and heare, saying, that they neuer sawe goodlier men in all their liues, and that it was not possible that there could be in vs so much euill as was reported of vs, and that we were more like Angels among men, then such persons of such euill Religion as by the Priestes and friers wee were reported to be, and that it was great pitie that wee should bee so vsed for so small an offence. So that being brought into the said high Church, and set vpon the scaffold which was made before the high Alter, in the presence of all the people, vntil high Masse was done, and the sermon made by a frier, concerning our matter, they did put vs in all the disgrace they could, to cause the people not to take so much compassion vpon vs, for that wee were heretiques, and people that were seduced of the deuill, and had forsaken the faith of the Catholique Church of Rome, with diuers other reprochfull wordes, which were too long to recite in this place. High Masse and Sermon being done, our offences, as they called them, were recited, euery man what he had said and done, and presently was the sentence pronounced against vs. That was that the said Augustine Boacio was condemned to wear his S. Benito all the dayes of his life, and put into perpetuall prison, where hee should fulfill the same, and all his goods confiscated and lost. And I the saide Tomson to weare the S. Benito for three yeeres, and then to be set at libertie. And for the accomplishing of this sentence or condemnation, we must be presently sent downe from Mexico, to Vera Cruz, and from thence to S. Iohn de Vllua, and there to be shipped for Spaine, which was 65. leagues by land, with strait commandement, that vpon paine of 1000. duckets, the Masters euery one should looke straitly vnto vs, and carry vs to Spaine, and deliver vs vnto the Inquisitors of the Holy house of Siuill, that they should put vs in the places, where we should fulfill our penances, that the Archbishop of Mexico had enioyned vnto us, by his sentence there giuen. For performance of the which, we were sent downe from Mexico, to the Sea side, which was 65. leagues, with fetters upon our feete, and there deliuered to the Masters of the ships, to be carried for Spaine, as before is said. And it was so, that the Italian, fearing that if he had presented himselfe in Spaine before the Inquisitors, that they would haue burned him, to preuent that danger when wee were comming homeward, and were arriued at the yland of Terçera, one of the ysles of the Açores, the first night that we came into the said port to an ancker, about midnight he found the meanes to get him naked out of the ship into the sea, and swam naked a shoare, and so presently got him to the further side of the yland, where hee found a little Caruel ready to depart for Portugal, in the which he came to Lisbone, and passed into France, and so into England, where hee ended his life in the Citie of London. And I for my part kept still aboord the ship, and came into Spaine, and was deliuered to the Inquisitors of the Holy house of Siuill, where they kept me in close prison, till I had fulfilled the three years of my penance. Which time being expired, I was freely put out of prison, and set at libertie: and being in the Citie of Siuil a casher of one Hugh Typton, an English marchant of great doing, by the space of one yeere, it fortuned that there came out of the Citie of Mexico, a Spaniard, called Iohn de la Barrera, that had bene long time in the Indies, and had got summes of golde and siluer, and with one onely daughter shipped himselfe for to come for Spaine, and by the way chanced to die, and giue all that hee had vnto his onely daughter, whose name was Marie de la Barrera, and being arriued at the Citie of Siuil, it was my chance to marry with her. The marriage was worth to mee 2500. pounds in barres of golde and siluer, besides iewels of great price. This I thought good to speake of, to shew the goodnes of God to all them that put their trust in him, that I being brought out of the Indies, in such great misery and infamy to the world, should be prouided at Gods hand in one moment, of more then in all my life before I could attaine vnto by my owne labour.

After we departed from Mexico, our S. Benitoes were set vp in the high Church of the said Citie, with our names written in the same, according to there vse and custome, which is and will be a monument and a remembrance of vs, as long as the Romish Church doth raigne in that country. The same haue bene seene since by one Iohn Chilton, and diuers others of our nation, which were left in that countrey long since, by Sir Iohn Hawkins. And because it shalbe knowen wherefore it was that I was so punished by the Clergies hande, as before is mentioned, I will in briefe words declare the same.

It is so, that being in Mexico at the table, among many principall people at dinner, they began to inquire of me being an Englishman, whether it were true, that in England they had ouerthrowen all their Churches and houses of Religion, and that all the images of the Saints of heauen that were in them were thrown downe, broken, and burned, and in some places high wayes stoned with them, and whether the English nation denied their obedience to the Pope of Rome, as they had bene certified out of Spaine by their friends. To whom I made answere, that it was so, that in deed they had in England put downe all the Religious houses of friers and monks that were in England, and the images that were in their Churches and other places were taken away, and vsed there no more: for that (as they say) the making of them, and putting of them where they were adored, was cleane contrary to the expresse commandement of Almighty God, Thou shalt not make to thy selfe any grauen image, &c. and that for that cause they thought it not lawfull that they should stand in the Church, which his the house of adoration. One that was at the declaring of these words who was my master Gonsalo Cereso, answered and said, if it were against the commandement of God to haue images in the Churches, that then he had spent a great deale of money in vaine, for that two yeres past he had made in the monastery of Santo Domingo, in the said citie of Mexico, an image of our Lady of pure siluer and golde, with pearles and precious stones, which cost him 7000. and odde pesos, and euery peso is 4.s. 8.d. of our money: which indeed was true, for that I haue seene it many times my selfe where it stands. At the table was another gentleman, who presuming to defend the cause more then any other that was there, saide, that they knew well ynough that they made but of stockes and stones, and that to them was no worship giuen, but that there was a certaine veneration due vnto them after they were set vp in the Church, and that they were set there to a good intent: the one, for that they were books for the simple people, to make them vnderstand the glory of the saints that were in heauen, and a shape of them to put vs in remembrance to cal vpon them, to be our intercessors vnto God for vs, for that we are such miserable sinners, that we are not worthy to appeare before God, and that vsing deuotion to saints in heauen, they may obtaine at Gods hands the sooner the thing that we demand of him. As for example, said he, imagin that a subiect hath offended his king vpon the earth in any kind of respect, is it for the party to go boldly to the king in person, and to demand pardon for his offences? No, saith he, the presumption were two great, and possibly he might be repulsed, and haue a great rebuke for his labour. Better it is for such a person to seek some priuate man neere the king in his Court, and make him acquainted with his matter, and let him be a mediator to his Maiesty for him, and for the matter he hath to do with him, and so might he the better come to his purpose, and obteine the thing which he doeth demand: euen so saith he, it is with God and his saints in heauen: for we are wretched sinners, and not worthy to appeare nor present our selues before the Maiesty of God to demand of him the thing that we haue need of: therefore thou hast need to be deuout, and have deuotion to the mother of God, and the saints of heauen, to be intercessors to God for thee, and so mayest thou the better obtaine of God the thing that thou dost demand. To this I answered, and said, sir, as touching the comparison you made of the intercessors to the king, how necessary they were, I would but aske you this question. Set the case that this king you speake of, if he be so merciful, as, when he knoweth that one, or any of his subiects hath offended him, he send for him to his owne towne, or to his owne house, or palace, and say vnto him, come hither, I know that thou hast offended many lawes, if thou doest know thereof, and doest repent thee of the same, with ful intent to offend no more, I wil forgiue thy trespasse, and remember it no more: said I, if this be done by the kings owne person, what then hath this man need to go seeke friendship at any of the kings priuat seruants hands, but go to the principal, seeing that he is readier to forgive thee, then thou art to demand forgiuenes at his hands? Euen so is it with our gracious God, who calleth and crieth out vnto vs throughout all the world, by the mouth of his Prophets, Apostles, and by his owne mouth, saying, Come vnto me al ye that labour and are ouer laden, and I wil refresh you: besides 1000. other offers and proffers which hee doth make vnto vs in his holy Scriptures. What then haue we need of the saints helpe that are in heauen, whereas the Lord himselfe doth so freely offer himselfe vnto vs? At which sayings, many of the hearers were astonied, and said, that by that reason, I would giue to vnderstand, that the inuocation of Saints was to be disanulled, and by the Lawes of God not commanded. I answered, that they were not my words but the words of God himselfe: looke into the Scriptures your selfe, and you shall so finde it. The talk was perceiued to be preiudiciall to the Romish doctrine, and therefore it was commanded to be no more entreated of, and all remained vnthought vpon, had it not bene for a villanous Portugal that was in the company, who said, Basta ser Ingles para saber todo esto y mas: who the next day, without imparting any thing to any body, went to the Bishop of Mexico, and his Prouisor, and said, that in a place where he had bene the day before, was an Englishman, who had said, that there was no need of Saints in the Church, nor of any inuocation of Saints, vpon whose denomination I was apprehended for the same words here rehearsed, and none other thing, and thereupon was vsed, as before is written.

Sant Iuan de Vllua. Now to speake somewhat of the description of the countrey, you shall vnderstand, that the port of S. Iohn de Vllua is a very little Island low by the water side, the broadest or longest part thereof not aboue a bow-shoote ouer, and standeth within two furlongs of the firme land. In my time there was but one house, and a little Chappel to say masse in, in all the Island: the side to the land wards is made by mans handes, with free-stone and grauel, and is 4. fadome deepe downe right, wherefore the great ships that come in there do ride so neere the shoare of the land, that you may come and goe aland vpon their beake noses. They vse to put great chaines of yron in at their halsers, and an ancker to the land ward, and all little ynough to more well their shippes for feare of the Northerly winds, which come of the coast of Florida, that sometimes haue caried ships, and houses, and all away to the shoare. The king was wont to haue 20. great mightie Negroes, who did serue for nothing else, but onely to repaire the said Island, where the foule weather doeth hurt it. The Countrey all thereabout is very plaine ground, and a mile from the sea side a great wildernes, with great quantitie of red Deere in the same, so that when the mariners of the ships are disposed, they go vp into the wildernes, and do kil of the same, and bring them aboard to eate, for their recreation.

The way and distance from San Iuan de Vllua to Vera Cruz, is five leagues. From this port to the next towne, which is called Vera Cruz, are 5. leagues almost by the Sea side, till you come within one league of the place, and then you turne vp towards the land, into a wood, till you come to a litle riuer hard by the said townes side, which sometimes of the yere is dry without water. The towne of Vera Cruz in my time, had not past 300. housholds, and serued out but for the folke of the ships, to buy and bring there goods aland, and deliuer it to their owners, as also the owners and their factors to receiue there goods of the Masters of the ships. This town standeth also in a very plaine on the one side the riuer, and the other side is enuironed with much sande blowen from the sea side with the tempest of weather, many times comming vpon that coast. This town also is subiect to great sicknes, and in my time many of the Mariners and officers of the ships did die with those diseases, there accustomed, and especially those that were not vsed to the countrey, nor knew the danger thereof, but would commonly go in the Sunne in the heat of the day, and did eat fruit of the countrey with much disorder, and especially gaue themselues to womens company at their first comming: whereupon they were cast into a burning ague, of the which few escaped.

Venta de Rinconado. Halfe a dayes iourney from Vera Cruz, towards Mexico, is a lodging of fiue or sixe houses, called the Rinconado, which is a place, where is a great pinacle made of lime and stone, fast by a riuer side, where the Indians were wont to doe their sacrifices vnto their gods, and it is plaine and low ground betwixt that and Vera Cruz, and also subiect to sicknes: but afterward halfe a dayes iourney that you do begin to enter into the high land, you shall find as faire, good, and sweet countrey, as any in the world, and the farther you go, the goodlier and sweeter the countrey is, till you come to Pueblo de los Angeles, which may be some 43 leagues from Vera Cruz, which was in my time a towne of 600. housholds, or thereabout, standing in a goodly soile. Beteene Vera Cruz and that you shall come through many townes of the Indians, and villages, and many goodly fields of medow grounds, Riuers of fresh waters, forrests, and great woods, very pleasant to behold. From Pueblo de los Angeles, to Mexico, is 20 leagues of very faire way and countrey, as before is declared. Mexico was a Citie in my time, of not aboue 1500. housholds of Spaniards inhabiting there, but of Indian people in the suburbs of the said city, dwelt aboue 300000. as it was thought, and many more. This City of Mexico is 65 leagues from the North sea, and 75 leagues from the South sea, so that it standeth in the midst of the maine land, betwixt the one sea and the other. It is situated in the middest of a lake of standing water, and enuironed round about with the same, sauing in many places, going out of the Citie, are many broad wayes through the said lake or water. This lake and Citie is enuironed also with great mountaines round about, which are in compasse aboue thirtie leagues, and the said Citie, and lake of standing water, doeth stand in a great plaine in the middest of it. This lake of standing water doeth proceed from the shedding of the raine, that falleth upon the saide mountaines, and so gather themselues together in this place.

All the whole proportion of this Citie doeth stand in a very plaine ground, and in the middest of the said Citie is a square place of a good bow-shoote ouer from side to side: and in the middest of the said place is the high Church, very faire and well builded all through, at that time not halfe finished, and round about the said place, are many faire houses built: on the one side, are the houses where Mutezuma the great king of Mexico that was, dwelt, and now there lye always the viceroyes that the king of Spaine sendeth thither euery three yeeres. And in my time there was for viceroy a gentleman of Castil, called Don Luis de Velasco. And on the other side of the saide place, ouer against the same, is the Bishops house, very faire built, and many other houses of goodly building. And hard by the same, are also other very faire houses, built by the Marques de Valle, otherwise called Hernando Cortes, who was hee that first conquered the saide Citie and Countrey, who after the said conquest which hee made with great labour and trauaile of his person, and danger of his life, and being growen great in the Countrey, the King of Spaine sent for him, saying that he had some particular matters to impart vnto him. This is to be vnderstood of his second comming into Spaine. And when he came home, he could not bee suffered to returne backe againe, as the King before had promised him. With the which, for sorrow that he tooke, he died; and this he had for the reward of his good seruice.

The said Citie of Mexico hath the streetes made very broad, and right, that a man being in the high place, at the one ende of the street, may see at the least a good mile forward, and in all the one part of the streets of the North part of their Citie, there runneth a pretie lake of very cleare water, that euery man may put into his house as much as he will, without the cost of any thing, but of letting in. Also there is a great caue or ditch of water that commeth through the Citie, euen vnto the high place, where come euery morning at the break of the day twentie or thirtie Canoas, or troughes of the Indians, which bring in them all manner of prouision for the citie, which is made, and groweth in the Countrey, which is a very good commoditie for the inhabitants of that place. And as for victuals in the said Citie, of beefe, mutton, and hennes, capons, quailes, Guiny-cockes, and such like, all are very good cheape: To say, the whole quarter of an oxe, as much as a slaue can carry away from the Butchers, for fiue Tomynes, that is, fiue Royals of plate, which is iust two shillings and sixe pence, and a fat sheepe at the Butchers for three Royals, which is 18. pence and no more. Bread is as good cheape as in Spaine, and all other kinde of fruites, as apples, peares, pomegranats, and quinces, at a reasonable rate. The Citie goeth wonderfully forwards in building of Frieries and Nunneries, and Chappels, and is like in time to come, to be the most populous Citie in the world, as it may be supposed. The weather is there always very temperate, the day differeth but one houre of length all the yere long. The fields and the woods are alwayes greene. The woods full of popinjayes, and many other kinde of birdes, that make such an harmonie of singing, and crying, that any man will reioyce to heare it. In the fields are such odoriferous smels of flowers and hearbs, that it giueth great content to the senses. About the Citie of Mexico two, three, or foure leagues off, are diuers townes of Indians, some of 4000. or 6000. housholds, which doe stand in such a goodly soyle, that if Christians had the inhabitation thereof, it would be put to a further benefite. In my time were dwelling and aliue in Mexico, many ancient men that were of the conquerours at the first conquest with Hernando Cortes: for then it was about 36. yeeres agoe, that the said Countrey was conquered.

About Mexico there are diuers Mines of siluer, and also in other places there about, but the principall Mines that are in all New Spaine are in Sacatecas, 80. leagues from Mexico, and the Mines of S. Martin, thirtie leagues, both to the Westward of Mexico, where is great store of gold and siluer. Also there is a place called the Misteca, fiftie leagues to the Northwest, which doth yeeled great store of very good silke, and Cochinilla. Wine and oyle there is none growing in the Countrey, but what commeth out of Spaine. Also there are many goodly fruits in that Countrey, whereof we haue none such, as Plantanos Guyaues, Lapotes, Tunas, and in the wilderness great store of blacke cheries, and other wholesome fruites. The Cochinilla is not a worme, or a flye, as some say it is, but a berrie that groweth vpon certaine bushes in the wilde field, which is gathered in time of the yeere, when it is ripe. Also the Indico that doeth come from thence to die blew, is a certaine hearbe that groweth in the wilde fieldes, and is gathered at one time of the yeere, and burnt, and of the ashes thereof, with other confections put thereunto, the said Indico is made. Balme, Salsa perilla, Cana fistula, suger, oxe hides, and many other good and seruiceable things the Countrey doeth yeeld, which are yeerely brought into Spaine, and there solde and distributed to many nations.

ROBERT TOMSON.

A voyage made by M. Roger Bodenham to S. Iohn de Vllua in the bay of Mexico, in the yeere 1564.

A new trade begun in the city of Fez by Roger Bodenham. I Rodger Bodenham hauing a long time liued in the city of Siuil in Spaine, being there married, and by occasion thereof vsing trade and traffique to the parts of Barbary, grew at length to great losse and hinderance by that new trade begun by me in the city of Fez: whereupon being returned into Spaine, I began to call my wits about mee, and to consider with my selfe by what meanes I might recover and renew my state; and in conclusion, by the ayde of my friends, I procured a ship called The Barke Fox perteining to London, of the eight or nine score tunnes; and with the same I made a voyage to the West India, hauing obteined good fauour with the Spannish merchants, by reason of my long abode, and marriage of the countrey. My voyage was in the company of the Generall Don Pedro Melendes for Noua Hispania: who being himselfe appointed Generall for Terra Firma and Peru, made his sonne Generall for New Spaine, although Pedro Melendes himselfe was the principall man and director in both fleets. We all departed from Cadiz together the last day of May in the yere 1564: and I with my ship being vnder the conduct of the sonne of Don Pedro aforesayd, arriued with him in Noua Hispania, where immediately I tooke order for the discharge of my merchandise at the port of Vera Cruz, otherwise called Villa Rica, to be transported thence to the city of Mexico, which is sixty and odde leagues distant from the sayd port of Villa Rica. In the way are many good townes, as namely, Pueblo de los Angeles, and another called Tlaxcalan. The city of Mexico hath three great causeyes to bring men to it, compassed with a lake, so that it needeth no walles, being so defended by the water. It is a city plentifull of all necessary things, hauing many faire houses, churches, and monasteries. I hauing continued in the countrey the space of nine moneths, returned againe for Spaine with the Spanish fleet, and deliuered the merchandise and siluer which I had in the ship into the Contratation house, and there receiued my fraight, which amounted outwards and homewards to the value of 13000 ducats and more. I obserued many things in the time of my abode in Noua Hispania, aswell touching the commodities of the countrey as the maners of the people both Spaniards and Indians: but because the Spanish histories are full of these obseruations, I omit them, and referre the readers to the same: onely this I say, that the commodity of Cochinalla groweth in greatest abundance about the towne of Pueblo de los Angeles, and is not there woorth aboue forty pence the pound.

A notable discourse of M. Iohn Chilton, touching the people, maners, mines, cities, riches, forces, and other memorable things of New Spaine, and other prouinces in the West Indies, seene and noted by himselfe in the time of his trauels, continued in those parts, the space of seuenteene or eighteene yeeres.

In the yeere of our Lord 1561, in the moneth of Iuly, I Iohn Chilton went out of this city of London into Spaine, where I remained for the space of seuen yeres, and from thence I sailed into Noua Hispania, and so trauelled there, and by the South sea, vnto Peru, the space of seuenteene or eighteene yeeres: and after that time expired, I returned into Spaine, and so in the yere 1586 in the moneth of Iuly, I arriued at the foresayd city of

London: where perusing the notes which I had taken in the time of my trauell in those yeeres, I haue set downe as followeth.

In the yeere 1568, in the moneth of March, being desirous to see the world, I embarked my selfe in the bay of Cadiz in Andaluzia, in a shippe bound for the Isles of the Canaries, where she tooke in her lading, and set forth from thence for the voyage, in the moneth of Iune, the same yere. Within a moneth after, we fell with the Isle of S. Domingo, and from thence directly to Noua Hispania, and came into the port of S. Iohn de Vllua, which is a little Island standing in the sea, about two miles from the land, where the king mainteineth about 50 souldiers, and captaines, that keepe the forts, and about 150 negroes, who all the yeere long are occupied in carying of stones for building, and other vses, and to helpe to make fast the ships that come in there, with their cables. There are built two bulwarkes at ech ende of a wall, that standeth likewise in the sayde island, where the shippes vse to ride, made fast to the sayd wall with their cables, so neere, that a man may leape ashore. From this port I iourneyd by land to a towne called Vera Cruz, standing by a riuers side, where all the factours of the Spanish merchants dwell, which receiue the goods of such ships as come thither, and also lade the same with such treasure and merchandize as they returne backe into Spaine. They are in number about foure hundred, who onely remaine there during the time that the Spanish fleet dischargeth, and is loden againe, which is from the end of August to the beginning of April following. And then for the vnwholesomnesse of the place they depart thence sixteene leagues further vp within the countrey, to a towne called Xalapa, a very healthfull soile. There is neuer any woman deliuered of childe in this port of Vera Cruz: for so soone as they perceiue themselues conceiued with child, they get them into the countrey, to auoid the perill of the infected aire, although they vse euery morning to driue thorow the towne aboue two thousand head of cattell, to take away the ill vapours of the earth. From Xalapa seuen leagues I came to another place, named Perota, wherein are certaine houses builded of straw, called by the name of ventas, the inhabitants whereof are Spaniards, who accustome to harbour such trauellers as are occasioned to iourney that way vp into the land. It standeth in a great wood of Pine and Cedar trees, the soile being very colde, by reason of store of snow which lieth on the mountaines there all the yere long. There are in that place an infinite number of deere, of bignesse like vnto great mules, hauing also hornes of great length. From Perota nine leagues, I came to the Fuentes of Ozumba, which fuentes are springs of water issuing out of certeine rocks into the midst of the high wayes, where likewise are certaine ranges, and houses, for the vses before mentioned.

Pueblo de los Angeles eight leagues. Eight leagues off from this place I came to the city of the Angels, so called by that name of the Spanyards, which inhabit there to the number of a thousand, besides a great number of Indians. This city standeth in very plaine fields, hauing neere adioyning to it many sumptuous cities, as namely the city of Tlaxcalla, a city of two hundred thousand Indians, tributaries to the king, although he exacteth no other tribute of them then a handfull of wheat a piece, which amounteth to thirteene thousand hanneges yeerely as hath appeared by the kings books of account. And the reason why he contenteth himselfe with this tribute, onely for them, is, because they were the occasion that he tooke the city of Mexico, with whom the Tlaxcallians had warre at the same time when the Spanyards came into the countrey. The gouernour of this city is a Spanyard, called among them the Alcade mayor, who administreth chiefest causes of iustice both vnto the Christians and Indians, referring smaller and lighter vices, as drunkennesse and such like to the iudgement and discretion of such of the Indians as are chosen euery yeere to rule amongst them, called by the name of Alcades. These Indians from fourteene yeeres olde vpwards, pay vnto the king for their yerely tribute one ounce of siluer, and an hannege of maiz, which is valued among them commonly at twelue reals of plate. The widowes among them pay halfe of this. The Indians both of this city, and of the rest, lying about Mexico, goe clothed with mantles of linnen cloth made of cotton wooll, painted thorowout with works of diuers and fine colours. Tlaxcalla foure leagues northward from los Angeles. It is distant from the city of the Angels foure leagues to the Northward, and fourteene from Mexico. There is another city a league from it, called Chetula, consisting of more then sixty thousand Indians, tributaries, and there dwell not aboue twelue Spanyards there. Vulcan is a hill that continually burneth with fire. From it, about two leagues, there is another, called Acassingo, of aboue fifty thousand Indians, and about eight or twelue Spanyards, which standeth at the foot of the Vulcan of Mexico, on the East side. There are besides these, three other great cities, the one named Tapiaca, a very famous city, Waxazingo, and Tichamachalcho: all these in times past belonged to the kingdome of Tlaxcalla: and from these cities they bring most of their Cochinilla into Spaine. Pueblo de los Angeles 20. leagues from Mexico. The distance from the city of the Angels, to the city of Mexico is twenty leagues. The city of Mexico is the city of greatest fame in all the Indies, hauing goodly and costly houses in it, builded all of lime and stone, and seuen streets in length, and seuen in breadth, with riuers running thorow euery second street, by which they bring their prouision in canoas. It is situated at the foot of certaine hilles, which conteine in compasse by estimation aboue twenty leagues, compassing the sayd city on the one side, and a lake which is fourteene leagues about on the other side. Vpon which lake there are built many notable and sumptuous cities, as the city of Tescuco, where the Spanyards built sixe frigats, at that time when they conquered Mexico, and where also Fernando Cortes made his abode fiue or six moneths in curing of the sicknesse of his people, which they had taken at their comming into the countrey. There dwell in this city about sixty thousand Indians, which pay tribute to the king. In this city the sayd Fernando built the finest church that euer was built in the Indies, the name whereof is S. Peters.

The voyage from Mexico to Nueua Biscaia. After I had continued two yeeres in this city, being desirous to see further the countreys, I imployed that which I had, and tooke my voyage towards the prouinces of California, in the which was discouered a certeine countrey by a Biscaine, whose name was Diego de Guiara, and called it after the name of his countrey, New Biscay, where I solde my merchandise for exchange of siluer, for there were there certaine rich mines discouered by the aforesayd Biskaine. *The Siluer mines of Tamascaltepec.* Going from Mexico I directed my voyage somewhat toward the Southwest, to certaine mines, called Tamascaltepec, and so traueled forward the space of twenty dayes thorow desert places vnhabited, till I came to the valley of S. Bartholomew, which ioyneth to the prouince of New Biscay. In all these places, the Indians for the most part go naked, and are wilde people. Their common armour is bowes and arrowes: they vse to eate vp such Christians as they come by. *The hauen where the ships of China and the Philippinas arriue.* From hence departing, I came to another prouince named Xalisco, and from thence to the port of Nauidad, which is 120 leagues from Mexico, in which port arriue always in the moneth of April, all the ships that come out of the South sea from China, and the Philippinas, and there they lay their merchandise ashore. The most part whereof is mantles, made of Cotton wooll, Waxe, and fine platters gilded, made of earth, and much golde.

The next Summer following, being in the yeere 1570 (which was the first yeere that the Popes Buls were brought into the Indies) I vndertooke another voyage towards the prouince of Sonsonate, which is in the kingdome of Guatimala, whither I caried diuers marchandize of Spaine, all by land on mules backs. The way thitherward from Mexico is to the city of the Angels, and from thence to another city of Christians 80 leagues off, called Guaxaca, in which there dwelt about 50 Spanyards, and many Indians. All the Indians of this prouince pay their tribute in mantles, of

Cotton wooll, and Cochinilla, whereof there groweth abundance thorowout this countrey. Neere to this place there lieth a port in the South sea, called Aguatulco, in the which there dwell not aboue three or foure Spanyards, with certaine Negroes, which the king mainteineth there: in which place Sir Francis Drake arriued in the yeere 1579, in the moneth of April, where I lost with his being there aboue a thousand duckets, which he tooke away with much other goods of other merchants of Mexico from one Francisco Gomes Rangifa, factour there for all the Spanish merchants that then traded in the South sea: for from this Port they vse to imbarke all their goods that goe for Peru, and to the kingdome of Honduras. From Guaxaca I came to a towne named Nixapa, which standeth vpon certaine very high hilles in the prouince of Sapotecas, wherein inhabit about the number of twenty Spanyards, by the King of Spaines commandement, to keepe that country in peace: for the Indians are very rebellious: and for this purpose hee bestowed on them the townes and cities that be within that prouince. From hence I went to a city called Tecoantepec, which is the farthest towne to the Eastward in all Noua Hispania, which some time did belong to the Marques de Valle, and because it is a very fit port, standing in the South sea, the king of Spaine, vpon a rebellion made by the sayd Marques against him, tooke it from him, and doth now possesse it as his owne. Heere in the yeere 1572 I saw a piece of ordinance of brasse, called a Demy culuerin, which came out of a ship called the Iesus of Lubeck, which captaine Hawkins left in S. Iohn de Vllua, being in fight with the Spanyards in the yeere 1568; which piece they afterwards carried 100 leagues by land ouer mighty mountaines to the sayd city, to be embarked there for the Philippinas. Leauing Tecoantepec, I went still along by the South sea about 150 leagues in the desolate prouince of Soconusco, in which prouince there groweth cacao, which the Christians cary from thence into Noua Hispania, for that it will not grow in any colde countrey. The Indians of this countrey pay the king their tribute in cacao, giuing him four hundred cargas, and euery carga is 24000 almonds, which carga is worth in Mexico thirty pieces of reals of plate. They are men of great riches, and withall very proud: and in all this prouince thorowout, there dwell not twenty Christians. I trauelled thorow another prouince called Suchetepec; and thence to the prouince of Guasacapan: in both which prouinces are very few people, the biggest towne therein hauing not aboue two hundred Indians. The chiefest merchandise there, is cacao. Hence I went to the city of Guatimala, which is the chiefe city of all this kingdome: in this city doe inhabit about 80 Spanyards: and here the king hath his gouernours, and councell, to whom all the people of the kingdome repaire for iustice. This city standeth from the coast of the South sea 14 leagues within the land, and is very rich, by reason of the golde that they fetch out of the coast of Veragua. From this city to the Eastward 60 leagues lieth the prouince Sonsonate, where I solde the merchandize I caried out of Noua Hispania. The chiefest city of this prouince is called S. Saluador, which lieth 7 leagues from the coast of the South sea, and hath a port lying by the sea coast, called Acaxutla, where the ships arriue with the merchandize they bring from Noua Hispania; and from thence lade backe againe the cacao: there dwell here to the number of threescore Spanyards. Nicoia a port where ye ships which goe to the Philippinas are builded. From Sonsonate I trauelled to Nicoia, which is in the kingdome of Nicaragua, in which port the king buildeth all the shipping that trauell out of the Indies to the Malucos. Puerto de Cauallos a rich place. I went forward from thence to Costa rica, where the Indians both men and women go all naked, and the land lieth betweene Panama, and the kingdome of Guatimala: and for that the Indians there liue as warriers, I durst not passe by land, so that here in a towne called S. Saluador I bestowed that which I caried in annile (which is a kinde of thing to die blew withall) which I caried with me to the port of Cauallos, lying in the kingdome of Honduras, which port is a mighty huge gulfe, and at the comming in on the one side of it there lieth a towne of little force without ordinance or any other strength, hauing in it houses of straw: at which towne the Spanyards vse yeerely in the moneth of August to vnlade foure ships which come out of Spaine laden with rich merchandize, and receiue in heere againe their lading of a kinde of merchandise called Annile and Cochinilla (although it be not of such value as that of Noua Hispania) and siluer of the mines of Tomaangua, and golde of Nicaragua, and hides, and Salsa perilla, the best in all the Indies: all which merchandize, they returne, and depart from thence alwayes in the moneth of April following, taking their course by the Island of Iamaica, in which Island there dwell on the West side of it certeine Spanyards of no great number. The description of Hauana at large. From this place they go to the cape of S. Anthony, which is the vttermost part of the Westward of the Island of Cuba, and from thence to Hauana lying hard by, which is the chiefest port that the king of Spaine hath in all the countreys of the Indies, and of greatest importance: for all the ships, both from Peru, Honduras, Porto rico, S. Domingo, Iamaica, and all other places in his Indies, arriue there in their returne to Spaine, for that in this port they take in victuals and water, and the most part of their lading: here they meet from all the foresayd places alwayes in the beginning of May by the kings commandement: at the entrance of this port it is so narrow, that there can scarse come in two ships together, although it be aboue six fadome deepe in the narrowest place of it. In the North side of the comming in there standeth a tower, in which there watcheth euery day a man to descrie the sailes of ships which hee can see on the sea; and as many as he discouereth, so many banners he setteth vpon the tower, that the people of the towne (which standeth within the port about a mile from the tower) may vnderstand thereof. Vnder this tower there lieth a sandy shore, where men may easily go aland: and by the tower there runneth a hill along by the waters side, which easily with small store of ordinance subdueth the towne and port. The port within is so large that there may easily ride a thousand saile of ships without anker or cable, for no wind is able to hurt them. The smol force of Hauana. There inhabit within the towne of Hauana about three hundred Spanyards, and about threescore souldiers, which the king mainteineth there for the keeping of a certeine castle which hee hath of late erected, which hath planted in it about twelue pieces of small ordinance, and is compassed round with a small ditch, wherethorow at their pleasure they may let in the sea. About two leagues from Hauana their lieth another towne called Wanabacoa, in which there is dwelling about an hundred Indians, and from this place 60 leagues there lieth another towne named Bahama, situate on the North side of the Island. The chiefest city of this Island of Cuba (which is aboue 600 leagues in length) is also called Sant Iago de Cuba, where dwelleth a bishop and about two hundred Spanyards; which towne standeth on the South side of the Island about 100 leagues from Hauana. The commodities of Cuba. All the trade of this Island is cattell, which they kill onely for the hides that are brought thence into Spaine: for which end the Spanyards mainteine there many negroes to kil their cattell, and foster a great number of hogs, which being killed, and cut into smal pieces, they dry in the Sun, and so make it prouision for the ships which come for Spaine.

Hauing remained in this Island two moneths, I tooke shipping in a frigat, and went ouer to Nombre de Dios, and from thence by land to Panama, which standeth vpon the South sea. From Nombre de Dios to Panama is 17 leagues distance: from which towne there runneth a riuer which is called the riuer of Chagre, which runneth within 5 leagues of Panama, to a place called Cruzes, thorow which riuer they cary their goods, and disimbarke them at the sayd Cruzes, and from thence they are conueyed on mules backs to Panama by land: where they againe imbarke them in certeine small shippes in the South sea for all the coast of Peru. In one of these ships I went to Potossie, and from thence by land to Cusco, and from thence to Paita.

Here I remained the space of seuen moneths, and then returned into the kingdome of Guatimala, and arriued in the prouince of Nicoia, and Nicaragua. From Nicaragua I trauelled by land to a prouince called Nicamula (which lieth toward the North sea in certaine high mountaines) for that I could not passe thorow the kingdome of Guatimala at that time for waters, wherewith all the Low countreys of the prouince of Soconusco, lying by the South sea, are drowned with the raine that falleth aboue the mountaines, enduring always from April to September: which reason for that they call their Winter. From this prouince I came into another called De Vera Paz, in which the chiefest city is also called after that name, where there dwelleth a bishop and about forty Spanyards. Among the mountaines of this country toward the North sea, there is a prouince called La Candona, where are Indian men of war which the king can not subdue, for that they haue townes and forts in a great lake of water aboue the sayd mountaines: the most part of them goe naked, and some weare mantles of cotton wooll. Chiapa 300 leagues from Mexico. Distant from this about 80 leagues, I came into another prouince called the prouince of Chiapa, wherein the chiefest city is called Sacallan, where there dwelleth a bishop and about an hundred Spanyards. In this countrey there is great store of Cotten wooll, whereof the Indians make fine linnen cloth, which the Christians buy and carry into Noua Hispania. The people of this prouince pay their tribute to the king all in Cotton wooll and Feathers. Fourteene leagues from this city there is another called Chiapa, where are the finest gennets in all the Indies, which are carried hence to Mexico, 300 leagues from it. Ecatepec an hill nine leagues high. From this city I trauelled still thorow hilles and mountaines, till I came to the end of this prouince, to a hill called Ecatepec, which in English signifieth The hill of winde: for that they say, it is the highest hill that euer was discouered: for from the top of it may be discovered both the North and the South seas; and it is in height supposed to be nine leagues. They which trauell ouer it, lie always at the foot of it ouer night, and begin their iourney about midnight, to trauell to the top of it before the Sunne rise the next day, because the winde bloweth with such force afterwards, that it is impossible for any man to goe vp: from the foot of this hill to Tecoantepec, the first towne of Noua Hispania, are about fifteene leagues. And so from hence I iourned to Mexico.

By and by after I came to Mexico (which was in the yere 1572) in the company of another Spanyard, which was my companion in this iourney, we went together toward the prouince of Panuco, which lieth vpon the coast of the North sea, and within three dayes iourney we entred a city called Mestitlan, where there dwelt twelue Spanyards: the Indian inhabitants there were about thirty thousand. This city standeth vpon certaine hie mountaines, which are very thicke planted with townes very holesome and fruitfull, hauing plentifull fountaines of water running thorow them. The high wayes of these hilles are all set with fruits, and trees of diuers kindes, and most pleasant. In euery towne as we passed thorow, the Indians presented vs with victuals. Within twenty leagues of this place there is another city called Clanchinoltepec, belonging to a gentleman, where there inhabit about fourty thousand Indians; and there are among them eight or nine friers of the order of Saint Augustine, who haue there a Monastery. Within three dayes after we departed from this place, and came to a city called Guaxutla, where there is another Monastery of friers of the same Order: there dwell in this towne about twelue Spanyards. From this place forwards beginneth a prouince called Guastecan, which is all plaine grounds without any hilles. The first towne we came vnto is called Tancuylabo, in which there dwell many Indians, high of stature, hauing all their bodies painted with blew, and weare their haire long downe to their knees, tied as women vse to do with their haire-laces. When they goe out of their doores, they cary with them their bowes and arrowes, being very great archers, going for the most part naked. Salt a principal merchandize. In those countreys they take neither golde nor siluer for exchange of any thing, but only Salt, which they greatly esteeme, and vse it for a principall medicine for certaine wormes which breed in their lips and in their gummes. After nine dayes trauell from this place, we came to a towne called Tampice, which is a port towne vpon the sea, wherein there dwell, I thinke, forty Christians, of which number whilest wee abode there, the Indians killed foureteene, as they were gathering of Salt, which is all the trade that they haue in this place: it standeth vpon the entrie of the riuer of Panuco, which is a mighty great riuer; and were it not for a sand that lieth at the mouth of it, ships of fiue hundred tonne might goe vp into it aboue three score leagues. From hence we went to Panuco, foureteen leagues from Tampice, which in times past had bene a goodly city, where the king of Spaine had his gouernour: but by reason that the Indians there destroyed the Christians, it lieth in a maner waste, conteining in it not aboue tenne Christians with a priest. In this towne I fell sicke, where I lay one and forty dayes, hauing no other sustenance then fruit and water, which water I sent for aboue sixe leagues off within the countrey. Here I remained till my companion came to me, which had departed from me another way, reteining in my company onely a slaue, which I brought with me from Mexico. And the last day in Easter weeke my companion came to me, finding me in a very weake state, by reason of the vnholesomenesse of the place. Notwithstanding my weakenesse, I being set on an horse, and an Indian behinde mee to holde mee, we went forward on our voyage all that day till night. The next day in the morning we passed ouer the riuer in a canoa; and being on the other side, I went my selfe before alone: and by reason there met many wayes traled by the wilde beasts, I lost my way, and so trauelled thorow a great wood about two leagues: and at length fell into the hands of certaine wilde Indians, which were there in certaine cottages made of straw; who seeing me, came out to the number of twenty of them, with their bowes and arrowes, and spake vnto mee in their language, which I vnderstood not: and so I made signes vnto them to helpe mee from my horse; which they did by commandement of their lord, which was there with them: and lighted downe. They caried me vnder one of their cottages, and layed me vpon a mat on the ground: and perceiuing that I could not vnderstand them, they brought vnto mee a little Indian wench of Mexico, of fifteene or sixteene yeeres of age, whom they commanded to ask me in her language from whence I came, and for what intent I was come among them: for (sayth she) doest thou not know Christian, how that these people will kill and eat thee? To whom I answered, let them doe with me what they will; heere now I am. Shee replied, saying, thou mayest thank God thou art leane; for they feare thou hast the pocks: otherwise they would eate thee. So I presented to the king a little wine which I had with me in a bottle; which he esteemed aboue any treasure: for wine they will sell their wiues and children. Afterwards the wench asked me what I would haue, and whether I would eat any thing. I answered that I desired a little water to drinke, for that the countrey is very hote: and shee brought me a great Venice glasse, gilded, full of water. And maruelling at the glasse, I demanded how they came by it. She tolde me that the Casique brought it from Shallapa, a great towne distant 30 leagues from this place on the hilles, whereas dwelt certeine Christians, and certeine friers of the Order of S. Augustine, which this Casique with his people on a night slew: and burning the friers monasterie, among other things reserued this glasse: and from thence also brought me. Hauing now bene conuersant with them about three or four houres, they bid her aske me if I would goe my way. I answered her, that I desired nothing els. So the Casique caused two of his Indians to leade me forward in my way; going before me with their bowes and arrowes, naked, the space of three leagues, till they brought me into an high way: and then making a signe vnto me, they signified that in short time I should come to a towne where Christians inhabited, which was called S. Iago de los valles, standing in plaine fields, walled about with a mud wall: the number of the Christians that dwelt therein, were not aboue foure or fiue and twenty, vnto which the king of Spaine giueth Indians and townes, to keepe the countreys subiect vnto him. Here the Christians haue their mighty mules, which they cary for all the parts of the Indies, and into Peru, for that all their merchandize are carried by this meanes by land. In this towne aforesayd, I found my company which I had lost before, who made no other account of me but that I had beene slaine: and the Christians there likewise maruelled to heare that I came from those kinde of Indians aliue, which was a thing neuer seene nor heard of before: for they take a great pride in killing a Christian, and to weare any part of him where he hath any haire growing, hanging it about their necks, and so are accounted for valiant men. *Don Henrico Manriques viceroy of Mexico.* In this towne I remained eighteene dayes, till I recouered my health, and in the meane space there came one Don Francisco de Pago, whom the viceroy Don Henrico Manriques had sent for captaine generall, to open and discouer a certeine way from the sea side to the mines of Sacatecas, which were from this place 160 leagues, for to transport their merchandize by that way, leauing the way by Mexico, which is seuen or eight weeks trauell. So this captaine tooke me and my company, with the rest of his souldiers, to the number of forty, which he had brought with him, and fiue hundred Indians, which we tooke out of two towns in this prouince called Tanchipa, and Tamaclipa, all good archers and naked men, and went thence to the riuer de las Palmas, which is of great bignesse, parting the kingdome of Noua Hispania and Florida: and going still along by this riuer the space of three dayes, seeking passage to passe ouer; and finding none, we were at length inforced to cut timber to make a balsa or raft, which when we had made, we sate on it, the Indians swimming in the water, and thrusting it before them to the other side. Within thirty dayes after, trauelling thorow woods, hiles, and mountaines, we came to the mines of Sacatecas, which are the richest mines in all the Indies, and from thence they fetch most siluer: at which mines there dwelt aboue three hundred Christians: and there our Captaine gaue vs leaue to depart. So we came to the valley of S. Michael toward Mexico; and from thence to Pueblo nouo; and from that place to the prouince of Mechuacan, after which name the chiefest city of that place is called; where there dwelles a bishop, and aboue an hundred Spanyards in it: it aboundeth with all kind of Spanish fruits, and hath woods full of nut trees, and wild vines. Heere are many mines of copper, and great store of cattell. It lieth 60 leagues from Mexico, whither we came within foure dayes after. The Indians of this countrey are very mighty and big men.

Afterwards I returned another way to the prouince of Sonsonate by Vera Cruz, and so to Rio Aluarado, and from thence to the prouince of Campeche, which lieth on the South side of the bay of Mexico; the chiefe towne of this prouince is called Merida, in which is a bishop and almost 100 Spanyards. The Indians of this prouince pay all their tribute in mantles of cotton wooll and cacao. There is no port in all this prouince for a ship of 100 tun to ride in, but onely in the riuer of Tabasco, by which riuer this city of Merida standeth. The chiefest merchandize which they lade there in small frigats, is a certeine wood called campeche, (wherewith they vse to die) as also hides and annile. By this there lieth the prouince of Iucatan, nere the Honduras by the North sea coast, where there is also another bishop, and a towne likewise named Iucatan, where there dwell a few Spanyards. They haue no force at all in all this coast to defend themselues withall, saue only that the land is low, and there is no port to receiue any shipping, vnlesse they be frigats, which cary from thence to the port of S. Iohn de Vllua, waxe, cacao, hony, and also mantles of cotton wool, whereof they make there great store, and of which kind of merchandize there is great trade thence to Mexico: of the same also they pay their tribute to the king.

The greatnesse of the king of Spaines tribute out of the West Indies. The king hath tribute brought him yerely out of the Indies into Spaine betweene nine and ten millions of gold and siluer: for he receiueth of euery Indian which is subiect vnto him (excepting those which do belong to the Incommenderos, which are the children of those Spanyards, who first conquered the land, to whom the king gaue and granted the gouernment of the cities and townes subdued for three liues) twelue reals of plate, and a hannege of maiz, which is a wheat of the countrey, (fiue of them making a quarter of English measure) and of euery widow woman he hath sixe reals, and halfe a hannege of maiz. And so if any Indian haue twenty children in his house, he payeth for euery one of them, being aboue fifteene yeres old, after that rate. This Wheat being duely brought to the gouernour of euery prouince and city, is sold in Mexico by the kings gouernours there every yeere; so that the money receiued for it, is put into the kings Treasurie there, and is so yeerely caried from thence into Spaine. The quinta. Of the Spanyards which are owners of the mines of gold and siluer, he receiueth the fift part of it, which he calleth his quintas, which being taken out of the heape, there is his armes set on it; for otherwise it may not be brought out of the land into Spaine, vnder paine of death. The marke of siluer, which is eight ounces, when it commeth out of the mines, not hauing the kings seale vpon it, is woorth three and forty reals of plate, and so it is current: and when they will bring it for Spaine, they cary it to the kings Treasure house, where his seale is set vpon it; and so it is raised in value thereby to threescore and foure reals of plate: and so the king hath for his custome of euery marke of plate one and twenty reals.

From the yere of 1570, which was the yeere that the Popes buls came into the Indies, as is afore mentioned, he hath receiued both of the Indians which are tributaries vnto him, and also of all others belonging to the Incommenderos, of euery one being aboue twelue yeeres of age, foure reals of euery bull. Also they cary other pardons with them into the Indies, for such as be dead, although an hundred yeres before the Spanyards came into the countrey: which pardons the friers in their preachings perswaded the poore Indians to take, telling them that with giuing foure reals of plate for a Masse, they would deliuer their soules out of purgatory. Of the Christians likewise dwelling there he hath foureteene reals for euery bull: and there be certeine buls brought thither for the Christians besides the former, which serue for pardoning all such faults wherein they haue trespassed either against the king, by keeping backe his customes, or one against another by any other injury; for euery hundred crownes whereof a mans conscience doth accuse him that he hath deceiued the king or any other, he must giue ten for a bull, and so after that rate for euery hundred which he hath any way stollen, and so is pardoned the fault. *The reuenue of the kings buls and pardons came yerely to three millions.* The reuenue of his buls after this maner yeeldeth vnto his treasury yeerely aboue three millions of gold, as I haue bene credibly informed, although of late both the Spanyards and Indians do refuse to take the buls; for that they perceiue he doth make a yeerely custome of it: onely ech Indian taketh one pardon for all his householde, (whereas in former time euery Indian vsed to take one for euery person in his house) and teareth the same into small pieces, and giueth to euery one of his householde a little piece, saying thus, they need now no more, seeing in that which they bought the yeere before they had aboue ten thousand yeres pardon. These pieces they sticke vp in the wall of the houses where they lie. *Rebellions in Noua Hispania by two great exactions.* Both the Christians and Indians are weary with these infinite taxes and customes, which of late he hath imposed vpon them, more than in the yeeres before: so as the people of both sorts did rebell twise in the time that I was among them, and would have set vp another king of themselues: for which cause the king hath commanded vpon paine of death, that they should not plant either oile or wine there, but should alwayes stand in need of them to be brought out of Spaine, although there would more grow there in foure yeeres then there groweth in Spaine in twenty, it is so fertile a countrey.

The reasons which mooue the kings of Spaine to forbid foren traffike in the West Indies. And the king to keepe the countrey alwayes in subiection, and to his owne vse, hath streightly prouided by lawe, vpon paine of death, and losse of goods, that none of these countreys should traffique with any other nation, although the people themselues doe much now desire to trade with any other then with them, and would vndoubtedly doe, if they feared not the perill ensuing thereupon.

About Mexico, and other places in Noua Hispania, there groweth a certaine plant called magueis, which yeeldeth wine, vineger, hony, and blacke sugar, and of the leaues of it dried they make hempe, ropes, shooes which they vse, and tiles for their houses: and at the ende of euery leafe there groweth a sharpe point like an awle, wherewith they vse to bore or pearce thorow any thing.

Thus to make an end, I have heere set downe the summe of all the chiefest things that I haue obserued and noted in my seventeene yeres trauell in those parts.

A relation of the commodities of Noua Hispania, and the maners of the inhabitants, written by Henry Hawkes merchant, which liued fiue yeeres in the sayd countrey, and drew the same at the request of M. Richard Hakluyt Esquire of Eton in the county of Hereford, 1572.

Saint Iohn de Vilua is an Island not high aboue the water, where as now the Spanyards vpon M. Iohn Hawkins being there, are in making a strong fort. In this place all the ships that come out of Spaine with goods for these parts, do vnlade: for they haue none other port so good as this is. The comming into this place hath three chanels, and the best of all is the Northermost, which goeth by the maine land: and on euery side of the chanels there are many small rocks, as big as a small barrell: they wil make men stand in doubt of them, but there is no feare of them. There is another Island there by, called The Island of sacrifices, whereas the Spanyards did in times past vnlade their goods: and for that, they say, there are vpon it spirits or deuils, it is not frequented as it hath bene. In these places the North wind hath so great dominion, that oftentimes it destroyeth many ships and barks. This place is giuen to great sicknesse. These Islands stand in 18 degrees and a halfe, and about the same is great plenty of fish.

Fiue leagues from S. Iohn de Vllua is a faire riuer: it lieth Northwest from the port, and goeth to a little towne of the Spanyards called Vera Cruz, and with small vessels or barks, which they call frigats, they cary all their merchandize which commeth out of Spaine, to the said towne: and in like maner bring all the gold, siluer, cochinilla, hides, and all other things that the shippes cary into Spaine vnto them. And the goods being in Vera Cruz, they carry them to Mexico, and to Pueblo de los Angeles, Sacatecas, and Saint Martin, and diuers other places so farre within the countrey, that some of them are 700 miles off, and some more, and some lesse, all vpon horses, mules, and in waines drawen with oxen, and in carres drawen with mules.

In this towne of Vera Cruz within these twenty yeres, when women were brought to bed, the children new borne incontinently died; which is not now in these dayes, God be thanked.

This towne is inclined to many kinde of diseases, by reason of the great heat, and a certeine gnat or flie which they call a mosquito, which biteth both men and women in their sleepe: and assoone as they are bitten, incontinently the flesh swelleth as though they had bene bitten with some venimous worme. And this musquito or gnat doth most follow such as are newly come into the countrey. Many there are that die of this annoyance.

This towne is situated vpon the riuer aforesayd, and compassed with woods of diuers maners and sorts, and many fruits, as orenges and limons, guiaues, and diuers others, and birds in them, popinjayes both small and great, and some of them as big as a rauen, and their tailes as long as the taile of a fezant. There are also many other kinde of birds of purple colour, and small munkeys, maruellous proper.

This hote or sicke countrey continueth fiue and forty miles towards the city of Mexico; and the fiue and forty miles being passed, then there is a temperate countrey, and full of tillage: but they water all their corn with riuers which they turn in upon it. And they gather their Wheat twise a yere. And if they should not water the ground where as their corne is sowen, the country is so hote it would burne all.

Before you come to Mexico, there is a great towne called Tlaxcalla, which hath in it aboue 16000 households. All the inhabitants thereof are free by the kings of Spaine: for these were the occasion that Mexico was woone in so short time, and with so little losse of men. Wherefore they are all gentlemen, and pay no tribute to the king. In this towne is all the cochinilla growing.

Mexico is a great city; it hath more then fifty thousand households, whereof there are not past fiue or six thousand houses of Spanyards: all the other are the people of the countrey, which liue vnder the Spanyards lawes. There are in this city stately buildings, and many monasteries of friers and nunnes, which the Spanyards haue made. And the building of the Indians is somewhat beautifull outwardly, and within full of small chambers, with very small windowes, which is not so comly as the building of the Spanyards. This city standeth in the midst of a great lake, and the water goeth thorow all or the most part of the streets, and there come small boats, which they call canoas, and in them they bring all things necessary, as wood, and coales, and grasse for their horses, stones and lime to build, and corne.

This city is subject to many earthquakes, which oftentimes cast downe houses, and kil people. This city, is very well prouided of water to drinke, and with all maner of victuals, as fruits, flesh and fish, bread, hennes and capons, Guiny cocks and hennes and all other fowle. There are in this city euery weeke three Faires or Markets, which are frequented with many people, aswell Spanyards as the people of the countrey. There are in these Faires or Markets all maner of things that may be inuented, to sell, and in especiall, things of the countrey. The one of these Faires is vpon the Munday; which is called S. Hypolitos faire, and S. Iames his faire is vpon the Thursday, and vpon Saturday is S. Iohns faire. In this city is alwayes the kings gouernour or viceroy, and there are kept the Termes or Parliaments. And although there be other places of iustice, yet this is aboue all: so that all men may appeale vnto this place, and may not appeale from this city, but onely into Spaine before the king: and it must be for a certeine sum: and if it be vnder that summe, then there is no appellation from them. Many riuers fall into this lake which the city standeth in: but there was neuer any place found wither it goeth out.

The Indians know a way to drowne the city, and within these three yeeres they would haue practised the same: but they which should haue bene the doers of it were hanged: and euer since the city hath bene well watched both day and night, for feare lest at some time they might be deceiued: for the Indians loue not the Spanyards. Round about the towne there are very many gardens and orchards of the fruits of the countrey, maruellous faire, where the people haue great recreation. The men of this city are maruellous vicious; and in like maner the women are dishonest of their bodies, more then they are in other cities or townes in this countrey.

There are neere about this city of Mexico many riuers and standing waters, which haue in them a monstrous kinde of fish, which is maruellous rauening, and a great deuourer of men and cattell. He is woont to sleepe vpon the drie land many times, and if there come in the meane time any man or beast and wake or disquiet him, he speedeth well if he get from him. He is like vnto a serpent, sauing that he doth not flie, neither hath he wings.

There is West out of Mexico a port towne which is on the South sea, called Puerto de Acapulco, where as there are shippes which they haue ordinarily for the nauigation of China, which they haue newly found. This port is threescore leagues from Mexico.

There, is another port towne which is called Culiacan, on the South sea, which lieth West and by North out of Mexico, and is 200 leagues from the same: and there the Spanyards made two ships to goe seeke the streight or gulfe, which, as they say, is betweene the Newfoundland and Groenland; and they call it the Englishmens streight: which as yet was neuer fully found. They say, that streight lieth not farre from the maine land of China, which the Spanyards account to be maruellous rich.

Toward the North from Mexico there are great store of siluer mines. There, is greater quantitie of siluer found in these mines toward the North, then there is any other parts: and as the most men of experience sayde alwayes, they finde the richer mines the more Northerly. These mines are commonly vpon great hilles and stony ground, maruellous hard to be laboured and wrought.

Out of some of the mines the Indians finde a certeine kinde of earth of diuers colours, wherewith they paint themselues in times of their dances, and other pastimes which they vse.

In this countrey of Noua Hispania there are also mines of golde, although the golde be commonly found in riuers, or very neere vnto riuers. And nowe in these dayes there is not so much golde found as there hath bene heretofore.

There are many great riuers, and great store of fish in them, not like vnto our kindes of fish. And there are maruellous great woods, and as faire trees as may be seene, of diuers sorts, and especially firre trees, that may mast any shippe that goeth vpon the sea, oakes and pineapples, and another tree which they call Mesquiquez: it beareth a fruit like vnto a peascod, maruellous sweet, which the wilde people gather, and keepe it all the yere, and eat it in stead of bread.

The Spanyards haue notice of seuen cities which old men of the Indians shew them should lie towards the Northwest from Mexico. They haue vsed and vse dayly much diligence in seeking of them, but they cannot find any one of them. They say that the witchcraft of the Indians is such, that when they come by these townes they cast a mist vpon them, so that they cannot see them.

Pedro Morales and Nicolas Burgignon write the like of Copalla. They haue understanding of another city which they call Copalla: and in like maner, at my beeing in the countrey, they haue vsed much labour and diligence in the seeking of it: they haue found the lake on which it should stand, and a canoa, the head whereof was wrought with copper curiously, and could not finde nor see any man nor the towne, which to their vnderstanding should stand on the same water, or very neere the same.

The strange oxen of Cibola. There is a great number of beasts or kine in the countrey of Cibola, which were neuer brought thither by the Spanyards, but breed naturally in the countrey. They are like vnto our oxen, sauing that they haue long haire like a lion, and short hornes, and they haue upon their shoulders a bunch like a camell, which is higher then the rest of their body. They are maruellous wild and swift in running. They call them the beasts or kine of Cibola.

Cibola abandoned. This Cibola is a city which the Spanyards found now of late, without any people in the same, goodly buildings, faire chimneys, windowes made of stone and timber excellently wrought, faire welles with wheeles to draw their water, and a place where they had buried their dead people, with many faire stones vpon the graues. And the captaine would not suffer his souldiers to brake vp any parte of these graues, saying, he would come another time to do it.

A great riuer near Cibola. They asked certeine people which they met, whither the people of this city were gone: and they made answer, they were gone downe a riuer, which was there by, very great, and there builded a city which was more for their commodity.

This captaine lacking things necessary for himselfe and his men, was faine to return backe againe, without finding any treasure according to his expectation: neither found they but fewe people, although they found beaten wayes, which had beene much haunted and frequented. The captaine at his comming backe againe, had a great checke of the gouernour, because he had not gone forwards, and seene the end of that riuer.

They haue in the countrey, farre from the sea side, standing waters, which are salt: and in the moneths of April and May the water of them congealeth into salt, which salt is all taken for the kings vs and profit.

Dogs of India described. Their dogs are all crooked backt, as many are of the countrey breed, and cannot run fast: their faces are like the face of a pig or an hog, with sharpe noses.

In certeine prouinces which are called Guatimala, and Soconusco, there is growing great store of cacao, which is a berry like vnto an almond: it is the best merchandize that is in all the Indies. The Indians make drinke of it, and in like maner meat to eat. It goeth currently for money in any market or faire, and may buy an flesh, fish, bread or cheese, or other things.

There are many kinde of fruits of the countrey, which are very good, as plantans, sapotes, guianes, pinas, aluacatas, tunas, mamios, limons, grapes which the Spanyards brought into the countrey, and also wild grapes, which are of the country, and very small, quinses, peaches, figs, and but few apples, and very small, and no peares: but there are melons and calabaçs or gourds.

There is much hony, both of bees and also of a kind of tree which they call magueiz. This hony of magueiz is not so sweet as the other hony, but it is better to be eaten only with bread, then the other is; and the tree serueth for many things, as the leaues make threed to sowe any kind of bags, and are good to couer and thatch houses, and for diuers other things.

They haue in diuers places of the countrey many hote springs of water: as aboue all other, I haue seen one in the prouince of Mechuacan. In a plaine field without any mountaine, there is a spring which hath much water, and it is so hot, that if a whole quarter of beefe be cast into it, within an halfe houre it will be as well sodden as it will be ouer a fire in halfe a day. I haue seene halfe a sheepe cast in it, and immediately it hath bene sodden, and I haue eaten part of it.

There are many hares, and some conies. There are no partridges, but abundance of quailes.

They haue great store of fish in the South sea, and many oisters, and very great. The people do open the oisters, and take out the meat of them, and dry it as they do any other kinde of fish, and keepe them all the yeere: and when the times serue, they send them abroad into the country to sell, as all other fish. They haue no salmon, nor trowt, nor pele, nor crape, tench, nor pike in all the countrey.

There are in the countrey mighty high mountaines, and hilles, and snow upon them: they commonly burne; and twise every day they cast out much smoke and ashes at certeine open places, which are in the tops of them.

There is among the wilde people much manna. I haue gathered of the same, and haue eaten it, and it is good: for the Apothecaries send their seruants at certeine times, to gather of the same for purgations and other vses.

There are in the mountaines many wilde hogs, which all men kill, and lions and tygres; which tygres do much harm to men that trauell in the wildernesse.

Mines discouered, not found againe. In this countrey, not long since, there were two poore men that found a maruellous rich mine; and when these men went to make a register of the same (according to the law and custom) before the kings officers, they thought this mine not meet for such men as they were: and violently took the sayd mine for the king; and gaue no part thereof vnto the two poore men. And within certaine dayes the kings officers resorted thither to labor in the mine, and they found two great mighty hilles were come together; so they found no place to worke in.

The authour fiue yeeres in Nueua Espanna. And in the time while I was among them, which was fiue yeeres, there was a poore shepheard, who keeping his sheepe, happened to finde a well of quicke-siluer; and he went in like maner to manifest the same, as the custome and maner is; the kings officers dealt in like order as they did with the two poore men that found the rich mine, taking it quite from the shepheard: but when they went to fetch home the quicke-siluer, or part thereof, they could neuer finde it againe. So these things haue bene declared vnto the king, who hath giuen commandement, that nothing being found in the fields, as mines, and such like, shall be taken away from any man. And many other things haue bene done in this countrey, which men might count for great maruels.

There is a great abundance of sugar here, and they make diuers conserues, and very good, and send them to Peru, where as they sell them maruellous well, because they make none in those parts.

Description of the Indians person and maner. The people of the countrey are of good stature, tawny coloured, broad faced, flat nosed, and giuen much to drinke both wine of Spaine and also a certeine kind of wine which they make with hony of Maguiez, and roots, and other things which they vse to put into the same. They call the same wine Pulco. They are soone drunke, and giuen to much beastlinesse, and void of all goodnesse. In their drunkennesse, they vse and commit Sodomy; and with their mothers and daughters they haue their pleasures and pastimes. Whereupon they are defended from the drinking of wines, vpon paines of money, aswell he that selleth the wines as the Indian that drinketh the same. And if this commandement were not, all the wine in Spaine and in France were not sufficient for the West Indies onely.

The people of Nueua Espanna great cowards. They are of much simplicity, and great cowards, voide of all valour, and are great witches. They vse diuers times to take with the diuell, to whom they do certaine sacrifices and oblations: many times they haue bene taken with the same, and I haue seene them most cruelly punished for that offence.

The people are giuen to learn all maner of occupations and sciences, which for the most part they learned since the coming of the Spanyards: I say all maner of arts. They are very artificiall in making of images with feathers, or the proportion or figure of any man, in all kind of maner as he is. The finenesse and excellency of this is woonderfull, that a barbarous people as they are, should giue themselues to so fine an arte as this is. They are goldsmiths, blackesmiths, and coppersmiths, carpenters, masons, shoomakers, tailors, sadlers, imbroderers, and of all other kind of sciences: and they will do worke so good cheape, that poore young men that goe out of Spaine to get their liuing, are not set on worke: which is the occasion there are many idle people in the countrey. For the Indian will liue all the weeke with lesse then one groat: which the Spanyard cannot do, nor any man els.

The Indians ignorance from whence they came. They say, that they came of the linage of an olde man which came thither in a boat of wood, which they call a canoa. But they cannot tell whether it were before the flood or after, neither can they giue any reason of the flood, nor from whence they came. And when the Spanyards came first among them, they did certeine sacrifice to an image made in stone, of their owne inuention. The stone was set vpon a great hill, which they made of bricks of earth: they call it their Cowa. And certeine dayes in the yere they did sacrifice, certeine olde men, and yoong children: and onely beleeued in the Sunne and the Moone, saying, that from them they had all things that were needful for them. They haue in these parts great store of cotton wool, with which they make a maner of linen cloth, which the Indians weare, both men and women, and it serueth for shirts and smocks, and all other kind of garments, which they weare vpon their bodies: and the Spanyards vse it to all such purposes, especially such as cannot buy other. And if it were not for this kind of cloth, all maner of cloth that goeth out of Spaine, I say linnen cloth, would be solde out of all measure.

The wilde Indians. The wilde people go naked, without any thing vpon them. The women weare the skinne of a deere before their priuities, and nothing els vpon all their bodies. They haue no care for any thing, but onely from day to day for that which they haue need to eat. They are big men, and likewise the women. They shoot in bowes which they make of a cherry tree, and their arrowes are of cane, with a sharpe flint stone in the end of the same; they will pierce any coat of maile: and they kill deere, and cranes, and wilde geese, ducks, and other fowle, and wormes, and snakes, and diuers other vermin, which they eat. They liue very long: for I haue seene men that haue beene an hundred yeres of age. They haue but very litle haire in their face, nor on their bodies.

The Indians haue the friers in great reuerence: the occasion is, that by them and by there meanes they are free and out of bondage; which was so ordeined by Charles the emperor: which is the occasion that now there is not so much gold and siluer comming into Europe as there was while the

Indians were slaues. For when they were in bondage they could not chuse but doe their taske euery day, and bring their master so much metall out of their mines: but now they must be well payed, and much intreated to haue them worke. So it hath bene, and is a great hinderance to the owners of the mines, and to the kings quinto or custome.

There are many mines of copper in great quantity, whereof they spend in the countrey as much as serueth their turnes. There is some golde in it, but not so much as will pay the costs of the fining. The quantity of it is such, and the mines are so farre from the sea, that it will not be worth the fraight to cary it into Spaine. On the other side, the kings officers will giue no licence to make ordinance thereof; whereupon the mines lie vnlaboured, and of no valuation.

There is much lead in the countrey; so that with it they couer churches, and other religious houses: wherefore they shall not need any of our lead, as they haue had need thereof in times past.

The pompe and liberalitie of the owners of the mines is maruellous to beholde: the apparell both of them and of their wiues is more to be compared to the apparell of noble persons then otherwise. If their wiues go out of their houses, as vnto the church, or any other place, they goe out with great maiesty, and with as many men and maids as though she were the wife of some noble man. I will assure you, I haue seene a miners wife goe to the church with an hundred men, and twenty gentlewomen and maids. They keepe open house: who will, may come and eat their meat. They call men with a bell to come to dinner and supper. They are princes in keeping of their houses, and bountifull in all maner of things.

Things necessary to mines of siluer and golde. A good owner of mines must haue at the least an hundred slaues to cary and to stampe his metals; he must haue many mules, and men to keepe the mines; he must haue milles to stampe his metals; he must haue many waines and oxen to bring home wood to fine the oare; he must haue much quicke-siluer, and a maruellous quantity of salt-brine for the metals; and he must be at many other charges. And as for this charge of quicke-siluer, it is a new inuention, which they finde more profitable then to fine their oare with lead. Howbeit the same is very costly: for there is neuer a hundred of quicke-siluer but costeth at the least threescore pounds sterling. And the mines fall dayly in decay, and of lesse value: and the occasion is, the few Indians that men haue to labour their mines.

There is in New Spaine a maruellous increase of cattle, which daily do increase, and they are of a greater growth then ours are. You may haue a great steere that hath an hundred weight of tallow in his belly for sixteene shillings; and some one man hath 2000 head of cattel of his owne. They sell the hides vnto the merchants, who lade into Spaine as many as may be well spared. They spend many in the countrey in shoes and boots, and in the mines: and as the countrey is great, so is the increase of the cattell woonderfull. In the Island of Santo Domingo they commonly kill the beasts for their hides and tallow; and the fowles eat the carkeises: and so they do in Cuba and Porto Rico, whereas there is much sugar, and cana fistula, which dayly they send into Spaine. They have great increase of sheep in like maner, and dayly do intend to increase them. They have much wooll, and as good as the wooll of Spaine. They make cloth as much as serueth the countrey, for the common people, and send much cloth into Peru. I haue seene cloth made in the city of Mexico, which hath beene solde for tenne pezos a vare, which is almost foure pounds English, and the vare is less then our yard. They haue woad growing in the countrey, and allum, and brasill, and diuers other things to die withall, so that they make all colours. In Peru they make no cloth: but heereafter our cloth will be little set by in these parts, vnlesse it be some fine cloth. The wools are commonly foure shillings euery roue, which is fiue and twenty pounds: and in some places of the countrey that are farre from the places where as they make cloth, it is woorth nothing, and doth serue but onely to make beds for men to lie on.

They make hats, as many as do serue the Countrey, very fine and good, and sell them better cheape, then they can be brought out of Spaine, and in like maner send them into Peru.

Many people are set on worke both in the one and in the other: they spin their wooll as we doe, and in steed of oyle, they haue hogs grease: they twist not their threed so much as wee doe, neither worke so fine a threed. They make kersies, but they make much cloth, which is course, and sell it for lesse than 12. pence the vare. It is called Sayall.

They haue much silke, and make all maner of sorts thereof, as Taffataes, Sattins, Veluets of all colours, and they are as good as the silkes of Spaine, sauing that the colours are not so perfect: but the blackes are better then the blackes that come out of Spaine.

They haue many horses, and mares, and mules, which the Spaniards brought thither. They haue as good Iennets, as any are in Spaine, and better cheape then they bee in Spaine. And with their mules they cary all their goods from place to place.

There is raine vsually in this Countrey, from the moneth of May, to the midst of October, euery day, which time they call their winter, by reason of the said waters. And if it were not for the waters which fall in these hot seasons, their Maiz, which is the greatest part of their sustenance, would be destroyed. This Maiz is the greatest maintenance which the Indian hath, and also all the common people of the Spaniards. And their horses and mules which labour, cannot be without the same. This graine is substantiall, and increaseth much blood. If the Miners should bee without it, they coulde not labour their mines: for all their seruants eate none other bread, but onely of this Maize, and it is made in cakes, as they make oaten cakes, in some places of England.

An Hanega is a bushel and an halfe. The Indians pay tribute, being of the age of 20. yeeres, 4. shillings of money, and an hanege of Maiz, which is worth 4. shillings more vnto the king euery yeere. This is payd in all Noua Hispania, of as many as be of the age of 20. yeeres, sauing the citie of Tlascalla, which was made free because the citizens thereof were the occasion that Cortes tooke Mexico in so little a time.[2] And although at the first they were freed from painment of tribute, yet the Spaniards now begin to vsurpe vpon them, and make them to till a great field of Maiz, at their owne costes euery yeere for the King, which is as beneficial vnto him, and as great cost vnto them, as though they paid their tribute, as the others doe.

[2] The Republic of Tlascala had at first opposed the Spaniards on their advance to Mexico, but being defeated, became their allies and remained true to them throughout the troublous period of the evacuation and siege of the Capital.

The ships which goe out of Spaine with goods for Peru, goe to Nombre de Dios, and there discharge the said goods: and from thence they be carried ouer the necke of a land, vnto a port towne in the South sea, called Panama, which is 17. leagues distant from Nombre de Dios. And there they doe ship their goods againe and so from thence goe to Peru. They are in going thither three monethes, and they come backe againe in 20. dayes. They haue seldome foule weather, and fewe ships are lost in the South sea.

Salomons Islands, sought and found in the South Sea 1588. Foure yeeres past, to wit 1568, there was a ship made out of Peru, to seeke Salomons Islands, and they came somewhat to the South of the Equinoctial, and found an Island with many blacke people, in such number that the Spaniards durst not go on land among them. And because they had bene long vpon the voyage, their people were very weake, and so went not on land, to know what commoditie was vpon it. And for want of victuals, they arriued in Noua Hispania, in a port called Puerto de Nauidad, and thence returned backe againe vnto Peru, whereas they were euil entreated, because they had not knowen more of the same Island.

China found by the West. They haue in this port of Nauidad ordinarily their ships, which goe to the Islands of China,[3] which are certaine Islands which they haue found within these 7. yeres. They haue brought from thence gold, and much Cinamon, and dishes of earth, and cups of the same, so fine, that euery man that may haue a piece of them, will giue the weight of siluer for it. There was a Mariner that brought a pearle as big as a doues egge from thence, and a stone, for which the Viceroy would haue giuen 3000 duckets. Many things they bring from thence, most excellent. There are many of these ylands, and the Spaniards haue not many of them as yet: *This is to be understood of the time when this discourse was written, Anno 1572.* for the Portugals disturbe them much, and combate with them euery day, saying, it is part of their conquest, and to the maine land they cannot come at any hand. There are goodly people in them, and they are great Mariners, richly apparelled in cloth of gold, and siluer, and silke of all sorts, and goe apparelled after the maner of the Turkes. This report make such as come from thence. *China ships with one saile.* The men of the maine land haue certeine traffique with some of these ylanders, and come thither in a kind of ships, which they haue with one saile, and bring of such marchandize as they haue need of. And of these things there haue bene brought into New Spaine both cloth of gold and siluer, marueilous to be seene. So by their saying, there is not such a countrey in the whole world. The maine land is from the ylands 190. leagues: and the ylands are not farre from the Malucos Northwards. And the people of these ylands, which the Spaniards haue, say, that if they would bring their wiues and children, that then they should haue among them what they would haue. So there goe women dayly, and the king payeth all the charges of the maried men and their wiues, that go to these ylands. And there is no doubt but the trade will be marueilous rich in time to come. It was my fortune to be in company with one Diego Gutieres, who was the first Pilot that euer went to that countrey of the Phillippinas. Hee maketh report of many strange things in that Countrey, as well riches as other, and saith, if there bee any Paradise vpon earth, it is in that countrey: and addeth, that sitting vnder a tree, you shall haue such sweet smels, with such great content and pleasure, that you shall remember nothing, neither wife, nor children, nor haue any kinde of appetite to eate or drinke, the odoriferous smels wil be so sweete. This man hath good liuings in Noua Hispania, notwithstanding hee will returne thither, with his wife and children, and as for treasure there is abundance, as he maketh mention. In this countrey of Noua Hispania there are many buckes and does, but they haue not so long hornes as they haue here in England. The Spaniards kill them with hand guns, and with greyhounds, and the Indians kill them with their bowes and arrowes, and with the skins they make chamoyce, such as we in England make doublets and hose of, as good as the skins that are dressed in Flanders and likewise they make marueilous good Spanish leather of them. Indian Rauens not killed, to deuoure carrion. There is a bird which is like vnto a Rauen, but he hath some of his feathers white: there is such abundance of them, that they eate all the corrupt and dead flesh which is in the countrey. Otherwise the abundance of carren is so much, that it would make a marueilous corrupt aire in all the countrey, and be so noisome, that no man could abide it. Therefore it is commanded there shall none of them be killed. These birds are always about cities and townes, where there is much flesh killed.

[3] The Philippines.

Wrong done to the Indians punished. The Indians are much favoured by the Iustices of the Countrey, and they call them their orphanes. And if any Spaniard should happen to doe any of them harme, or to wrong him in taking any thing from him, as many times they doe, or to strike any of them, being in any towne, whereas iustice is, they are as well punished for the same, as if they had done it one Spaniard to another. When a Spaniard is farre from Mexico, or any place of iustice, thinking to doe with the poore Indian what he list, considering he is so farre from any place of remedy, he maketh the Indian do what he commandeth him, and if he will not doe it, hee beateth and misuseth him, according to his owne appetite. The Indian holdeth his peace, vntill he finde an opportunitie, and then taketh a neighbor with him, and goeth to Mexico, although it be 20. leagues off and maketh his complaint. This his complaint is immediately heard, and although it be a knight, or a right good gentleman, he is forthwith sent for, and punished, both by his goods, and also his person is imprisoned, at the pleasure of the Iustice. Iustice the cause of ciuilitie. This is the occasion that the Indians are so tame and ciuil, as they are: and if they should not haue this fauour, the Spaniards would soone dispatch all the Indians, or the Indians would kill them. But they may call them dogs and vse other euil words, as much they will, and the Indian must needes put it vp, and goe his way.

The poore Indians wil go euery day two or three leagues to a faire or market with a childe vpon their necks, with as much fruit or rootes, or some kind of ware, as cotton wooll, or cadis of all colours, as shall be not worth a pennie: and they will mainteine themselues vpon the same. For they liue with a marueillous small matter.

They are in such pouertie, that if you neede to ride into the Countrey, you shall haue an Indian to goe with you all the day with your bed vpon his backe, for one royall of plate: and this you shall haue from one towne to another. Here you are to vnderstand, that all men that traueile by the way, are always wont to carry their beds with them. They are great theeues, and wil steale all that they may, and you shall haue no recompence at their hands.

The apparel of the Indians. The garments of the women, are in this maner. The vppermost part is made almost like to a womans smocke, sauing that it is as broade aboue as beneath, and hath no sleeues, but holes on eche side one to put out their armes. It is made of linnen cloth made of cotton wooll, and filled full of flowers, of red cadis and blew, and other colours. This garment commeth downe to the knees, and then they haue cloth made after the same maner, and then they goeth rounde about their waste, and reacheth to their shooes and ouer this a white fine sheet vpon their heads, which goeth downe halfe the legge. Their haire is made vp round with an haire lace about their head. And the men haue a small paire of breaches of the same cotton wooll, and their shirts which hang ouer their breeches, and a broad girdle about their middles, and a sheete with flowers vpon their backes, and with a knot vpon one shoulder and an hat vpon their heads, and a paire of shoes. And this is all their apparell, although it be a Casique, which they vse in all the Countrey.

The wals of the houses of the Indians, are but plaine, but the stones are layd so close, that you shall not well perceiue the ioynts betweene one stone and another, they are so finely cut: and by the meanes that the stones are so workmanly done, and finely ioyned together, there is some beautie in their wals. They are marueilous small and light, as Pumic stones. They make their doores very little, so that there can go in but one man at a time. Their windowes and roomes within their houses are small, and one roome they haue reserued for their friends, when they come to talke one with another, and that is always faire matted, and kept marueilous cleane, and hanged full of images, and their chaires standing there to sit in. They eate their meate vpon the ground, and sleepe on the ground vpon a mat, without any bed, both the gentlemen, and other.

The Indians strike their fire with one sticke in another, aswell the tame people, as the wilde. For they know not how to do it with an yron, and a stone.

Diuers speeches. In Noua Hispania, euery 10. or 12. leagues they haue a contrary speach, sauing onely about Mexico: so there is a number of speeches in the Countrey.

Mutezuma, and his riches. Mutezuma which was the last King of this Countrey, was one of the richest princes which haue bene seene in our time, or long before. He had all kinde of beasts which were then in the countrey, and all maner of birdes, and fishes, and all maner of wormes, which creepe vpon the earth, and all trees, and flowers, and herbes, all fashioned in siluer and golde, which was the greatest part of al his treasure, and in these things had he great ioy, as the old Indians report. And vnto this day, they say that the treasure of Mutezuma is hidden, and that the Spaniards haue it not. This King would giue none of his people freedome, nor forgiue any of them that should pay him tribute, though he were neuer so poore. For if it had bene told him that one of his tributaries was poore, and that he was not able to pay his tribute according to the custome, then he would haue him bound to bring at such times as tributes should be payd, a quill full of Lice, saying, hee would haue none free, but himselfe. He had as many wiues or concubines, as hee would haue, and such as liked him.

The Indians wash themselues euery day. Alwayes whensoeuer he went out of his Court to passe the time, he was borne vpon 4 of his noble mens shoulders set vpon a table, some say, of golde, and very richly dressed with feathers of diuers and many colours and flowers. He washed all his body euery day, were it neuer so cold. And vnto this day so do all the Indians, and especially the women.

The Spaniards keepe the Indians in great subjection. They may haue in their houses no sword nor dagger, nor knife with any point, nor may weare vpon them any maner of armes, neither may they ride vpon any horse nor mules, in any sadle nor bridle, neither may they drinke wine, which they take for the greatest paine of all. They haue attempted diuers times to make insurrections, but they haue bene ouerthrowen immediatly by their owne great and beastly cowardlinesse.[4]

[4] This cannot be said of the aboriginal Mexicans, as nothing could have surpassed the determination and courage they showed during the great siege of Mexico.

Cannybals. There remaine some among the wild people, that vnto this day eate one another. I haue seene the bones of a Spaniard that haue been as cleane burnished, as though it had been done by men that had no other occupation.

And many times people are caried away by them, but they neuer come againe, whether they be men or women.

They haue in the Sea ylands of red salt in great abundance, whereas they lade it from place to place about the Sea coast: and they spend very much salt with salting their hides and fish: and in their mines they occupie great quantitie. They haue much Alume, and as good as any that is in all the Leuant, so that they neede none of that commoditie. They have also of their owne growing, much Cana fistula, and much Salsa Perilla, which is marueilous good for many kind of diseases.

There are in Florida many Iarrefalcons, and many other kinde of hawkes, which the gentlemen of Noua Hispania send for euery yeere. The Spaniards haue two forts there, chiefly to keepe out the Frenchmen from planting there.

A discourse written by one Miles Philips Englishman, one of the company put on shoare Northward of Panuco, in the West Indies, by M. Iohn Hawkins 1568. conteining many special things of that countrey and of the Spanish gouernment, but specially of their cruelties vsed to our Englishmen and amongst the rest to himselfe for the space of 15. or 16 yeres together, vntil by good and happy means he was deliuered from their bloody hands, and returned into his owne Countrey. An. 1582.[5]

[5] This account differs in some slight particulars from that given by Sir John Hawkins himself, which will be found in Volume XV. of this edition.

Chap. 1.

Wherein is shewed the day and time of our departure from the coast of England, with the number and names of the ships, their Captaines and Masters, and of our trafique and dealing vpon the coast of Africa.

This fleet consisted of 6 ships. Vpon Munday the second of October 1567. the weather being reasonable faire, our Generall M. Iohn Hawkins, hauing commanded all his Captaines and Masters to be in a readinesse to make sail with him, hee himselfe being imbarked in the Iesus, whereof was appointed for Master Robert Barret, hoised saile, and departed from Plymouth vpon his intended voyage for the parts of Africa, and America, being accompanied with fiue other saile of ships, as namely the Mynion, wherein went for Captaine M. Iohn Hampton, and Iohn Garret Master. The William and Iohn, wherein was Captaine Thomas Bolton, and Iames Raunce Master. The Iudith, in whom was Captaine M. Francis Drake afterward knight, and the Angel, whose Master, as also the Captaine and Master of the Swallow I now remember not. And so sayling in company together vpon our voyage vntil the tenth of the same moneth, an extreeme storme then tooke vs neere vnto Cape Finister, which dured for the space of foure dayes, and so separated our ships, that wee had lost one another, and our Generall finding the Iesus to bee but in ill case, was in minde to giue over the voyage, and to returne home. Howbeit the eleuenth of the same moneth the Seas waxing calme, and the winde comming faire, he altered his purpose, and held on the former intended voyage: And so comming to the yland of Gomera being one of the ylands of the Canaries, where according to an order before appointed, we met with all our ships which were before dispersed, wee then took in fresh water and departed from thence the fourth of Nouember, and holding on our course, vpon the eightenth day of the same moneth wee came to an ancker vpon the coast of Africa, at Cape Verde in twelue fadome water; and here our Generall landed certaine of our men, to the number of 160. or thereabout, seeking to take some Negros. And they going vp into the Countrey for the space of sixe miles, were encountred with a great number of the Negros: who with their enuenomed arrowes did hurt a great number of our men, so that they were inforced to retire to the ships, in which conflict they recouered but a few Negros, and of these our men which were hurt with their enuenomed arrowes, there died to the number of seuen or eight in very strange maner, with their mouths shut, so that wee were forced to put stickes and other things into their mouths to keepe them open,[6] and so afterward passing the time vpon the coast of Guinea, until the twelfth of Ianuary, we obteined by that time the number of 150. Negros. And being ready to depart from the Sea coast, there was a Negro sent as an Ambassadour to our Generall, from a King of the Negros, which was oppressed with other Kings his bordering neighbours, desiring our Generall to grant him succour and ayde against those his enemies, which our Generall granted vnto, and went himselfe in person a lande, with the number of two hundreth of our men or thereabouts, and the said King which had requested our ayde, did ioyne his force with ours, so that thereby our Generall assaulted, and set fire vpon a Towne of the said King his enemies, in which there was at the least the number of eight or ten thousand Negros, and they perceiuing that they were not able to make any resistance sought by flight to saue themselues, in which their flight there were taken prisoners to the number of eight or nine hundreth, which our Generall ought to haue had for his share: howbeit the Negro King which requested our ayde, falsifying his word and promise, secretly in the night conueyed himselfe away with as many prisoners as he had in his custodie: but our Generall notwithstanding finding himselfe to haue nowe very neere the number of 500. Negros thought it best without longer abode to depart with them, and such marchandize as hee had from the coast of Africa, towards the West Indies,[7] and therefore commanded with all diligence to take in fresh water and fewel, and so with speed to prepare to depart. The William and Iohn separated and neuer after met with the fleete. Howbeit before we departed from thence, in a storme that wee had, wee lost one of our ships, namely the William and Iohn, of which ship and of her people, we heard no tidings during the time of our voyage.

[6] They died of tetanus.

[7] All three voyages made by Hawkins to the West, in 1562, 1564 and 1567 were for the purpose of trading in slaves.

Chap. 2.

Wherein is shewed the day and time of our departure from the coast of Africa, with the day and time of our arriuall in the West Indies, also of our trade, and trafique their, and also of the great crueltie that the Spaniards vsed towards vs, by the Vice-roy his direction, and appointment, falsifying his faith and promise giuen, and seeking to haue intrapped vs.

All things being made in a readinesse, at our Generall his appointment, vpon the thirde day of Februarie 1568, wee departed from the coast of Africa, hauing the weather somewhat tempestuous, which made our passage the more hard; and sayling so for the space of 52. dayes, vpon the 27 of March 1568. we came in sight of an yland called Dominica, vpon the coast of America in the West Indies, situated in 14. degrees latitude,[8] and 322. of longitude: from thence our Generall coasted from place to place, euer making trafique with the Spaniards and Indians as hee might, which was somewhat hardly obtained, for that the King had straightly charged all his gouernours in those parts not to trade with any: yet notwithstanding, during the moneths of April and May, our Generall had reasonable trade and trafique, and courteous entertainement in sundry places, as at Margarita, Coraçao, and else where, til we came, to Cape de la vela,[9] and Rio de Hacha,[10] (a place from whence all the pearles doe come:) the gouernour there would not by any meanes permit vs to haue any trade or trafique, nor yet suffer vs to take in fresh water: by meanes whereof our Generall for the auoyding of famine and thirst about the beginning of Iune, was enforced to land two hundreth of our men, and so by maine force and strength to obtaine that which by no faire meanes hee could procure: And so recouering the Towne with the losse of two of our men, there was a secret and peaceable trade admitted, and the Spaniards came in by night, and bought of our Negroes to the number of 200. and vpwards, and of our other merchandize also. From thence we departed for Carthagena, where the Gouernour was so straight, that wee could not obteine any trafique there, and so for that our trade was neere finished, our Generall thought it best to depart from thence the rather for the auoyding of certaine dangerous stormes called the Huricanos, which accustomed to begin there about that time of the yere, and so the 24. of Iuly 1568. we departed from thence directing our course North: and leauing the yland of Cuba vpon our right hand, to the Eastward of vs, and so sayling toward Florida, vpon the 12. of August an extreeme tempest arose, which dured for the space of 8.

dayes, in which our ships were most dangerously tossed and beaten hither, and thither, so that we were in continuall feare to be drowned by reason of the shallownes of the coast, and in the end we were constrained to flee for succour to the port of S. Iohn de Vllua, or Vera Cruz, situated in 19. degrees of latitude, and in 279. degrees of longitude, which is the port that serueth for the Citie of Mexico: in our seeking to recouer this port our Generall met by the way three small ships that caried passengers, which hee tooke with him, and so the sixtenth of September 1568. wee entered the saide port of S. Iohn de Vllua. The Spaniards there supposing vs to haue bene the King of Spaines Fleete, the chiefe officers of the Countrey thereabouts came presently aboord our Generall, where perceiuing themselues to haue made an vnwise aduenture, they were in great feare to haue bene taken and stayed: howbeit our Generall did vse them all very courteously. Mexico 60. leagues from S. Iuan de Vllua. In the said port there were twelue ships which by report had in them in treasure to the value of two hundreth thousand pound, all which being in our Generall his power and at his deuotion, he did freely set at libertie, as also the passengers which he had before stayed, nor taking from any of them all the value of one groat: onely hee stayed two men of credite and accompt, the one named Don Laurenzo de Alua, and the other Don Pedro de Riuera, and presently our Generall sent to the Viceroy to Mexico which was threescore leagues off, certifying him of our arriuall there by force of weather, desiring that forasmuch as our Queene his Soueraigne, was the king of Spaine his louing sister and friend, that therefore hee would, considering our necessities and wants, furnish vs with victuals for our Nauie, and quietly suffer vs to repaire and amend our ships. And furthermore that at the arriual of the Spanish Fleet which was there dayly expected and looked for, to the ende that there might no quarell arise betweene them, and our Generall and his company for the breach of amitie, he humbly requested of his excellencie, that there might in this behalfe some special order be taken. This message was sent away the 16. of September 1568. it being the very day of our arriual there.

[8] Should be 18 degrees.

[9] In Venezuela.

[10] In Colombia.

The next morning being the seuententh of the same moneth, wee descried 13. saile of great shippes: and after that our Generall vnderstood, that it was the king of Spaines Fleete then looked for, he presently sent to aduertise the Generall hereof, of our being in the sayd port, and giuing him further to vnderstand, that before he should enter there into that harbour, it was requisite that there should passe betweene the two Generals some orders and conditions to bee obserued on either part, for the better contriuing of peace betweene them and theirs, according to our Generals request made vnto the Viceroy. And at this instant our Generall was in a great perplexitie of minde, considering with himselfe that if hee shoulde keepe out that Fleete from entring into the port, a thing which hee was very well able to doe with the helpe of God, then should that Fleete be in danger of present shipwracke and losse of all their substance, which amounted vnto the value of one million and eight hundreth thousand pounds. It is put downe 6. millions in Sir Iohn Hawkins his relation. Againe he saw that if he suffered them to enter, hee was assured that they would practise by all maner of meanes to betray him and his, and on the other side the hauen was so little, that the other Fleete entring, the shippes were to ride one hard aboord of another. Also hee saw that if their Fleete should perish by his keeping of them out, as of necessitie they must if he should haue done so, then stood hee in great feare of the Queene our Soueraignes displeasure in so waightie a cause: therefore did he choose the least euill, which was to suffer them to enter vnder assurance, and so to stand vpon his guard, and to defend himselfe and his from their treasons which we were well assured they would practise, and so the messenger being returned from Don Martin de Henriques, the newe Viceroy, who came in the same Fleete, and had sufficient authoritie to command in all cases both by Sea and by lande in this prouince of Mexico or new Spaine, did certifie our Generall, that for the better maintenance of amitie betweene the king of Spaine and our Soueraigne, all our requests should bee both fauourably granted, and faithfully perfourmed: signifying further that he heard and vnderstood of the honest and friendly dealing of our Generall, toward the king of Spaines subjects in all places where he had bene, as also in the said port: so that to bee briefe our requests were articled, and set downe in writing. Viz.

4. Articles concluded vpon, betwixt the English and the Spaniards; although the treacherous Spaniards kept none of them.

1. The first was that wee might haue victuals for our money, and licence to sell as much wares, as might suffice to furnish our wants.

2. The second, that we might be suffered peaceably to repaire our ships.

3. The thirde that the yland might bee in our possession during the time of our abode there, In which yland our Generall for the better safetie of him and his had alreadie planted and placed certaine Ordinance which were eleuen pieces of brasse, therefore he required that the same might so

continue, and that no Spaniard should come to lande in the saide yland, hauing or wearing any kinde of weapon.

4. The fourth and the last, that for the better and more sure performance and maintenance of peace, and of all the conditions, there might twelue gentlemen of credite bee deliuered of either part as hostages.

These conditions were concluded and agreed vpon in writing by the Viceroy and signed with his hand, and sealed with his seale, and 10. hostages vpon either part were receiued. And further it was concluded that the two Generals should meet, and giue faith ech to other for the performance of the premisses. Al which being done, the same was proclaimed by the sound of a trumpet, and commandement was giuen that none of either part should violate or breake the peace vpon paine of death: thus at the ende of three dayes all was concluded, and the Fleete entred the port, the ships saluting one another as the maner of the Sea doth require: the morrow after being Friday we laboured on all sides in placing the English ships by themselues, the Captaines and inferiour persons of either part, offering, and shewing great courtesie one to another, and promising great amity vpon all sides. Howbeit as the sequel shewed, the Spaniards meant nothing lesse vpon their parts. For the Viceroy and gouernour thereabout had secretly at land assembled to the number of 1000. chosen men, and wel appointed, meaning the next Thursday being the 24. of September at dinner time to assault vs, and set vpon vs on all sides. But before I go any further, I thinke it not amisse briefly to discribe the matter of the yland as it then was, and the force and strength, that it is now of.

A faire castle and bulwarke builded vpon the yland of San Iuan de Vllua.

For the Spaniards since the time of our Generals being there, for the better fortifying of the same place, haue vpon the same yland built a faire Castle and bulwarke very well fortified: this port was then at our being there, a little yland of stones, not past three feet aboue water in the highest place, and not past a bow-shotte ouer any way at the most, and it standeth from the maine land, two bowshootes or more: and there is not in all this coast any other place for ships safely to arriue at: also the North windes in this coast are of great violence and force, and vnlesse the shippes bee safely moored in, with their anckers fastened in this yland, there is no remedie, but present destruction and shipwracke. All this our generall wisely foreseeing, did prouide that he would haue the said yland in his custody, or els the Spaniards might at their pleasure, haue but cut our cables, and so with the first Northwinde that blewe, we had our passport, for our ships had gone a shoore. But to returne to the matter.

The value of a Spanish viceroy his faith. The time approching that their treason must be put in practise, the same Thursday morning, some appearance thereof began to shewe it selfe, as shifting of weapons from shippe to shippe, and planting, and bending their Ordinance against our men that warded vpon the lande, with great repaire of people: which apparent shewes of breach of the Viceroyes faith caused our Generall to sende one to the Viceroy, to enquire of him what was meant thereby, which presently sent and gaue order, that the Ordinance aforesayde, and other things of suspicion should bee remooued, returning answer to our Generall in the faith of a Viceroy, that hee would bee our defence and safetie from all villanous treacherie: this was vpon Thursday in the morning. Our Generall not being therewith satisfied, seeing they had secretly conueyed a great number of men aboord a great hulke or ship of theirs of sixe hundreth tunne, which shippe rode hard by the Mynion, hee sent againe to the Viceroy Robert Barret the Master of the Iesus, a man that could speake the Spanish tongue very well, and required that those men might bee vnshipt againe, which were in that great hulke. The Viceroy then perceiuing that their treason was throughly espied, stayed our Master, and sounded the Trumpet, and gaue order that his people should vpon all sides charge vpon our men, which warded on shoore, and else where, which strooke such a mase, and sudden feare among vs, that many gave place, and sought to recouer our shippes for the safetie of themselues. *The villanous treacherie of the Spaniards and their crueltie.* The Spaniards which secretly were hid in ambush at lande were quickly conueyed ouer to the yland in their long boates, and so comming to the yland, they slewe all our men that they could meete with, without mercy. The Minion which had somewhat before prepared her selfe to auoyd the danger, haled away and abode the first brunt of the 300 men that were in the great hulke: then they sought to fall aboord the Iesus, where was a cruel fight, and many of our men slaine: but yet our men defended themselues, and kept them out: so the Iesus also got loose, and ioyning with the Minion, the fight waxed hote vpon all sides: but they hauing woon and got our ordinance on shore, did greatly annoy vs. In this fight there were two great shippes of the Spaniards sunke, and one burnt, so that with their shippes they were not able to harme vs, but from the shore they beat vs cruelly with our owne ordinance, in such sort that the Iesus was very sore spoyled: and suddenly the Spaniards hauing fired two great ships of their owne, they came directly against vs, which bred among our men a marueilous feare. Howbeit the Minion which had made her sayles ready, shifted for her selfe, without consent of the Generall, Captaine or Master, so that very hardly our Generall could be receiued into the Minion: the most of our men that were in the Iesus shifted for themselues, and followed the Minion in the boat, and those which that small boat was not able to receiue, were most cruelly slaine by the Spaniards. Of our ships none escaped sauing the Minion and the Iudith: and all such of our men as were not in them were inforced to abide the tyrannous cruelty of the Spaniards. Copstowe one of M. Hawkins men returned from Nueua Espanna. For it is a certaine trueth, that whereas they had taken certaine of our men ashore, they tooke and hung them vp by the armes vpon high postes vntill the blood burst out of their fingers ends: of which men so vsed, there is one Copstow, and certaine others yet aliue who by the mercifull prouidence of the almighty, were long since arriued here at home in England, carying still about with them (and shall to their graues) the marks and tokens of those their inhumane and more then barbarous cruell dealings.

Chap. 3.

Wherein is shewed, how that after we were escaped from the Spaniards, wee were like to perish with famine at the Sea, and how our Generall, for the auoiding thereof was constrained to put halfe of his men on land, and what miseries wee after that sustained amongst the Sauage people, and how againe we fell into the hands of the Spaniards.

After that the Viceroy, Don Martin Henriques had thus contrary to his faith and promise most cruelly dealt with our Generall master Hawkins, at S. Iohn de Vllua, where most of his men were by the Spaniards slaine and drowned, and all his ships sunke and burned, sauing the Minion, and the Iudith, which was a small barke of fiftie tunne, wherein was then Captaine master Francis Drake aforesayd: the same night the said barke lost vs, we being in great necessitie, and inforced to remoue with the Minion two bow-shoote from the Spanish fleete, where we ankered all that night: and the next morning wee weyed anker, and recouered an island a mile from the Spaniards, where a storme tooke vs with a North winde, in which we were greatly distressed, hauing but two cables and two ankers left: for in the conflict before we had lost three cables and two ankers. The morrow after, the storme being ceased and the weather faire, we weied, and set sayle, being many men in number, and but small store of victuals to suffice vs for any long time: by meanes whereof we were in despaire and feare that we should perish through famine, so that some were in minde to yeelde themselues to the mercy of the Spaniards, other some to the Sauages or Infidels, and wandring thus certaine daies in these vnknowen seas, hunger constrained vs to eate hides, cats and dogs, mice, rats, parrats and munkies: to be short, our hunger was so great, that wee thought it sauorie and sweete whatsoeuer wee could get to eate.

And on the eight of October wee came to land againe, in the bottome of the bay of Mexico, where we hoped to haue found some inhabitants, that wee might haue had some reliefe of victuals, and a place where to repaire our ship, which was so greatly bruised, that we were scarse able with our weary armes to keepe foorth the water: being thus oppressed with famine on the one side and danger of drowning on the other, not knowing where to find reliefe, wee began to bee in wonderfull despaire, and wee were of many mindes, amongst whom there were a great many that did desire our Generall to set them on land, making their choise rather to submit themselues to the mercie of the Sauages or Infidels, then longer to hazard themselues at sea, where they very well sawe, that if they should remaine together, if they perished not by drowning, yet hunger would inforce them in the ende to eate one another: to which request our Generall did very willingly agree, considering with himselfe that it was necessary for him to lessen his number, both for the safetie of himselfe and the rest: and thereupon being resolued to set halfe his people ashore that he had then left aliue, it was a world to see how suddenly mens minds were altered: for they which a little before desired to be set on land, were now of another minde, and requested rather to stay: by meanes whereof our Generall was inforced for the more contentation of all mens minds, and to take away all occasions of offence, to take this order: First he made choice of such persons of seruice and account, as were needefull to stay, and that being done, of those which were willing to goe he appointed such as he thought might be best spared, and presently appointed that by the boate they should bee set on shore, our Generall promising vs that the next yeere he would either come himselfe, or else send to fetch vs home. Here againe it would haue caused any stony heart to haue relented to heare the pitifull mone that many did make, and howe loth they were to depart: the weather was then somewhat stormy and tempestuous, and therefore we were to passe with great danger, yet notwithstanding there was no remedy, but we that were appointed to goe away, must of necessitie doe so. They were put on land 25 leagues northward of Panuco the 8 of October 1568. Howbeit those that went in the first boat were safely set on shore, but of them which went in the second boate, of which number I my selfe was one, the seas wrought so high, that we could not attaine to the shore, and therefore we were constrained through the cruell dealing of Iohn Hamptone captaine of the Minion, and Iohn Sanders boat-swaine of the Iesus, and Thomas Pollard his mate, to leape out of the boate into the maine sea, hauing more then a mile to shore, and so to shift for ourselues, and either to sinke or swimme. And of those that so were (as it were) throwen out, and compelled to leape into the sea, there were two drowned, which were of captaine Blands men.

In the euening Of the same day, it being Munday the eight of October, 1568, when we were all come to shore, we found fresh water, whereof some of our men drunke so much, that they had almost cast themselues away, for wee could scarse get life of them for the space of two or three houres after: other some were so cruelly swollen, what with the drinking in of the salt water, and what with the eating of the fruit which wee found on land hauing a stone in it much like an almond (which fruit is called Capule) that they were all in very ill case, so that we were in a maner all of vs both feeble, faint and weake.

The next morning being Tewsday, the ninth of October, we thought, it best to trauell along by the sea coast, to seeke out some place of habitation: (whether they were Christians or Sauages, we were indifferent, so that we might haue wherewithall to sustaine our hungry bodies) and so departing from an hill where we had rested all night, not hauing any drie threed about vs, (for those that were not wet being not throwen into the sea, were thorowly wet with raine, for all the night it rained cruelly:) As we went from the hil, and were come into the plaine, we were greatly troubled to passe for the grasse and weedes that grewe there higher then any man. On the left hand we had the sea, and vpon the right hand great woods, so that of necessitie we must needs passe on our way Westward, through those marshes; and going thus, suddenly we were assaulted by the Indians, a warlike kind of people, which are in a maner as Canibals, although they doe not feede vpon mans flesh as Canibals doe.

Chichimici a warlike and cruell people. These people are called Chichimici, and they vse to weare their haire long, euen down to their knees, they doe also colour their faces greene, yellow, red and blew, which maketh them to seeme very ougly and terrible to beholde. These people doe keepe warres against the Spaniards, of whom they haue bene oftentimes very cruelly handled: for with the Spaniards there is no mercy.

Our men assailed by the Chichemici. They perceiuing vs at our first comming on land, supposed vs to haue bene their enemies, the bordering Spaniards, and hauing by their forerunners descried what number we were, and how feeble and weake without armour or weapon, they suddenly according to their accustomed maner, when they encounter with any people in warlike sorte, raised a terrible and huge crie, and so came running fiercely vpon vs, shooting off their arrowes as thicke as haile, vnto whose mercy we were constrained to yeeld, not hauing amongst vs any kind of armour, nor yet weapon, sauing one caliuer, and two old rustie swords, whereby to make any resistance, or to saue ourselues: which when they perceiued that wee sought not any other then fauour and mercie at their handes, and that we were not their enemies the Spaniards, they had compassion on vs, and came and caused vs all to sit down: and when they had a while surueyed, and taken a perfect view of vs, they came to all such as had any coloured clothes amongst vs, and those they did strip starke naked, and tooke their clothes away with them, but those that were apparelled in blacke they did not meddle withall, and so went there wayes, and left vs without doing vs any further hurt, onely in the first brunt they killed eight of our men.

Eight of our men slaine. And at our departure, they perceiuing in what weake case we were, pointed vs with their hands which way we should go to come to a towne of the Spaniards, which as we afterwards perceiued, was not past ten leagues from thence, vsing these words: Tampice, Tampice Christiano, Tampice Christiano, which is as much (we thinke) as to say in English, at Tampice you shall find the Christians. The weapons that they vse are no other but bowes and arrowes, and their aime is so good, that they very seldome misse to hit any thing that they shoote at. Shortly after they had left vs stript (as aforesayd) we thought it best to diuide our selues into two companies, and so being separated, halfe of vs went vnder the leading of one Anthony Godard, who is yet a man aliue, and dwelleth at this instant in the towne of Plimmouth, whom before we chose to be captaine ouer vs all, and those which went vnder his leading, of which number I Miles Philips was one, trauailed Westward that way which the Indians with their hands had before pointed vs to go. The other halfe went vnder the leading of one Iohn Hooper, whom they did choose for their captain, and with the company that went with him, Dauid Ingram was one, and they tooke their way and trauelled Northward, and shortly after, within the space of two dayes, they were againe incountered with the sauage people, and their captaine Hooper and two more of his company were slaine: then againe they diuided themselues, and some held on their way still Northward, and other some, knowing that we were gone Westward, sought, to meet with vs againe, as in truth there was about the number of 25 or 26 of them that met with vs in the space of foure dayes againe, and then we began to reckon amongst our selues, how many wee were that were set on shore, and we found the number to be an hundred and foureteene, whereof two were drowned in the sea and eight were slaine at the first incounter, so that there remained an hundred and foure, of which 25 went Westward with vs, and 52 to the North with Hooper and Ingram: and as Ingram since hath often told me, there were not past three of their company slaine, and there were but sixe and twenty, of them that came againe to vs, so that of the company that went Northward, there is yet lacking, and not certainely heard of, the number of three and twenty men. And verely I doe thinke that there are of them yet aliue, and married in the said countrey, at Cibola, as hereafter I purpose (God willing) to discourse of more particularly, with the reason and causes that make mee so to thinke of them that were lacking, which were Dauid Ingram, Twide, Browne, and sundry others, whose names wee could not remember. And being thus met againe together, we trauelled on still Westward, sometime thorow such thicke woods, that we were inforced with cudgels to breake away the brambles and bushes from tearing our naked bodies: other sometimes we should trauell thorow the plaines, in such high grasse that we could scarse see one another, and as we passed in some places, we should haue of our men slaine, and fall downe suddenly, being strooken by the Indians, which stood behinde trees and bushes, in secret places, and so killed our men as they went by, for wee went scatteringly in seeking of fruites to relieue our selues. We were also oftentimes greatly annoyed with a kind of flie, which in the Indian tongue is called Tequani, and the Spaniards called them Muskitos. There are also in the sayd countrey a number of other kinde of flies, but none so noysome as these Tequanies bee: you shall hardly see them they be so small, for they are scarse so big as a gnat: they will sucke ones blood marueilously, and if you kill them while they are sucking, they are so venimous that the place will swell extremely, euen as one that is stoong with a Waspe or Bee: but if you let them sucke their fill, and to goe away of themselues, then they doe you no other hurt, but leaue behind them a red spot somewhat bigger then a flea-biting. At the first wee were terribly troubled with these kinde of flies, not knowing their qualities, and resistance wee could make none against them, being naked: as for cold wee feared not any, the countrey there is alwayes so warme. And as we trauelled thus for the space of tenne or twelue dayes, our captaine did oftentimes cause certaine to goe vp into the toppes of high trees, to see if they could descrie any towne or place of inhabitants, but they could not perceiue any, and vsing often the same order to climbe vp into high trees, at the length they descried a great riuer that fell from the Northwest into the maine sea, and presently after, we heard an harquebuze shot off, which did greatly incourage vs, for thereby wee knew that we were neere to some Christians, and did therefore hope shortly to finde some succour and comfort, and within the space of one houre after, as we trauelled, we heard a cocke crowe, which was also no small ioy vnto vs, and so we came to the North side of the riuer of Panuco, where the Spaniards haue certaine Salines, at which place it was that the harquebuze was shot off, which before we heard: to which place we went not directly, but missing thereof, we left it about a bowshot vpon our left hand: of this riuer wee dranke very greedily, for wee had not met with any water in six dayes before, and as we were here by the riuer side resting our selues, and longing to come to the place where the cocke did crowe, and where the harquebuze was shot off, we perceiued many Spaniards vpon the other side of the riuer, riding vp and downe on horsebacke, and they perceiuing vs, did suppose that we had beene of the Indians their bordering enemies, the Chichimeci: the riuer was not past halfe a bowe shoot ouer: and presently one of the Spaniards tooke an Indian boate called a Canoa, and so came ouer, being rowed by two Indians, and hauing taken the view of vs, did presently rowe ouer backe againe to the Spaniards, who without any delay made out about the number of twenty horsemen, and imbarking themselues in the Canoas, they led their horses by the reines swimming ouer after them, and being come ouer to that side of the riuer where we were, they sadled their horses, and being mounted vpon them with their lances charged, they came very fiercely running at vs. Our captaine Anthony Godard seeing them come in that order, did perswade vs to submit and yeelde our selues vnto them, for being naked, as we at this time were, and without weapon, we could not make any resistance, whose bidding we obeied, and vpon the yeelding of our selues, they perceiued vs to be Christians, and did call for more Canoas, and caried vs ouer by foure and foure in a boat, and being come on the other side, they vnderstanding by our captaine how long we had bene without meate, imparted between two and two a loafe of bread made out of that countrey wheat, which the Spaniards call Maiz, of the bignesse of our halfepenie loaues, which bread is named in the Indian tongue Clashacally. This bread was very sweete and pleasant vnto vs, for we had not eaten any in a long time before: and what is it that hunger doth not make to haue a sauory and delicate taste? And hauing thus parted the bread amongst vs, those which were men they sent afore to the towne, hauing also many Indians inhabitants of that place to garde them: they which were yong, as boyes, and some such also as were feeble, they tooke vp vpon their horses, behind them, and so caried vs to the towne where they dwelt, which was very neere distant a mile from the place where, we came ouer.

This towne is well situated, and well replenished with all kindes of fruits, as Orenges, Limons, Pomegranates, Apricoks, and Peaches, and sundry others, and is inhabited with a great number of tame Indians, or Mexicans, and had in it also at that time about the number of two hundred Spaniards, men, women, and children, besides Negros. *The Salines of Panuco.* Of their Salines, which lie upon the West side of the riuer, more then a mile distant from thence, they make a great profit, for it is an excellent good merchandize there: the Indians doe buy much thereof, and cary it vp into the countrey, and there sell it to their owne countrey people, in doubling the price. Also much of the Salt made in this place, is transported from thence by sea to sundry other places, as to Cuba, S. Iohn de Vllua, and the other ports of Tamiago, and Tamachos, which are two barred hauens West and by South aboue threescore leagues from S. Iohn de Vllua. When we were all come to the towne, the Gouernor there shewed himselfe very seuere vnto vs, and threatened to hang vs all: and then he demanded what money wee had, which in trueth was very little, for the Indians which we first met withall, had in a maner taken all from vs, and of that which they left, the Spaniards which brought vs ouer, tooke away a good part also: howbeit, from Anthony Godard the Gouernour here had a chaine of gold, which was giuen vnto him at Carthagena, by the Gouernour there, and from others he had some small store of money: so that we accounted that amongst vs all he had the number of fiue hundred Pezos, besides the chaine of gold.

And hauing thus satisfied himselfe, when he had taken all that we had, he caused vs to be put into a little house much like a hogstie, where we were almost smoothered: and before we were thus shut vp into that little coat, they gaue vs some of the countrey wheate, called Mayz, sodden, which they feede their hogs withall. But many of our men which had bene hurt by the Indians at our first comming on land, whose wounds were very sore and grieuous, desired to haue the helpe of their Surgeons to cure their wounds. The gouernour, and most of them all answered, that wee should haue none other Surgeon but the hangman, which should sufficiently heale vs of all our griefes: and thus reuiling vs, and calling vs English dogs, and Lutheran heretikes, we remained the space of three dayes in this miserable state, not knowing what should become of vs, waiting euery houre to be bereaued of our liues.

Chap. 4.

Wherein is shewed how we were vsed in Panuco, and in what feare of death we were there, and how we were caried to Mexico to the Viceroy, and of our imprisonment there and at Tescuco, with the courtesies and cruelties wee receiued during that time, and how in the end wee were by proclamation giuen to serue as slaues to sundry gentlemen Spaniards.

Vpon the fourth day after our comming thither, and there remaining in a perplexitie, looking euery houre when we should suffer death, there came a great number of Indians and Spaniards weaponed to fetch vs out of the house, and amongst them we espied one that brought a great many of new halters, at the sight whereof we were greatly amazed, and made no other account but that we should presently haue suffered death, and so crying and calling to God for mercie and forgiuenesse of our sinnes, we prepared our selues, making vs ready to die: yet in the end, as the sequel shewed, their meaning was not so: for when wee were come out of the house, with those halters they bound our armes behind vs, and so coupling vs two and two together, they commanded vs to march on through the towne, and so along the countrey from place to place toward the citie of Mexico, which is distant from Panuco West and by South the space of ninetie leagues, hauing onely but two Spaniards, to conduct vs, they being accompanied with a great number of Indians warding on either side with bowes and arrowes, lest we should escape from them. And trauelling in this order, vpon the second day at night we came vnto a towne which the Indians call Nohele, and the Spaniards call it Santa Maria: in which towne there is a house of white friers, which did very courteously vse vs, and gaue vs hote meat, as mutton and broath, and garments also to couer our selues withal, made of white bayes: we fed very greedily of the meat, and of the Indian fruit, called Nochole, which fruit is long and small, much like in fashion to a little cucumber. Our greedy feeding caused vs to fall sicke of hote burning agues. And here at this place one Thomas Baker one of our men died of a hurt: for he had bene before shot with an arrow into the throat at the first incounter.

The next morrow about ten of the clocke, we departed from thence, bound two and two together, and garded as before, and so trauailed on our way toward Mexico, till we came to a towne within forty leagues of Mexico, named Mestitlan, where is a house of blacke friers: and in this towne there are about the number of three hundred Spaniards, both men, women, and children. The friers sent vs meat from the house ready dressed, and the friers, and the men and women vsed vs very courteously, and gaue vs some shirts and other such things as we lacked. Here our men were very sicke of their agues, and with eating of another fruit called in the Indian tongue, Guiaccos, which fruit did binde vs so sore, that for the space of tenne or twelue dayes we could not ease our selues. The next morning we departed from thence with our two Spaniards and Indian gard, as aforesayd. Of these two Spaniards the one was an aged man, who all the way did very courteously intreate vs, and would carefully go before to prouide for vs both meat and things, necessary to the vttermost of his power: the other was a yong man who all the way trauelled with vs, and neuer departed from vs, who was a very cruell caitiue, and he caried a iaueline in his hand, and sometimes when as our men with very feeblenesse and faintnesse were not able to goe so fast as he required them, he would take his iauelin in both his handes, and strike them with the same betweene the necke and the shoulders so violently, that he would strike them downe; then would he cry, and say, Marchad, marchad Ingleses perros, Luterianos, enemigos de Dios: which is as much to say in English, as March, march on you English dogges, Lutherans, enemies to God. And the next day we came to a towne called Pachuca, and there are two places of that name: as this towne of Pachuca, and the mines of Pachuca, which are mines of siluer, and are about six leagues distant from this towne of Pachuca towards the Northwest.

Here at this towne the good olde man our Gouernour suffered vs to stay two dayes and two nights, hauing compassion of our sicke and weake men, full sore against the minde of the yoong man his companion. From thence we tooke our iourney, and trauelled foure or fiue dayes by little villages, and Stantias, which are farmes or dairie houses of the Spaniards, and euer as wee had neede, the good olde man would still prouide vs sufficient of meates, fruites, and water to sustaine vs. At the end of which fiue dayes wee came to a towne within fiue leagues of Mexico, which is called Quoghliclan, were wee also stayed one whole day and two nights, where was a faire house of gray friers, howbeit wee saw none of them. Here wee were told by the Spaniards in the towne, that wee had not past fifteene English miles from thence to Mexico, whereof wee were all very ioyfull and glad, hoping that when we came thither, we should either be relieued, and set free out of bonds, or els bee quickly dispatched out of our liues: for seeing our selues thus caried bound from place to place, although some vsed vs courteously, yet could wee neuer ioy, nor be merrie till wee might perceiue our selues set free from that bondage, either by death or otherwise.

The next morning we departed from thence on our iourney towards Mexico, and so trauelled till wee came within two leagues of it, where there was built by the Spaniards a very faire church, called our Ladyes church, in which there is an image of our Lady of siluer and gilt, being as high, and as large as a tall woman, in which church, and before this image, there are as many lamps of siluer as there be dayes in the yeere, which vpon high dayes are all lighted. Whensoeuer any Spaniards passe by this church, although they be on horse backe, they will alight, and come into the church, and kneele before this image, and pray to our Lady to defend them from all euil; so that whether he be horseman or footman he will not passe by, but first goe into the Church, and pray as aforesayd, which if they doe not they thinke and beleeue that they shall neuer prosper: which image they call in the Spanish tongue, Nuestra sennora de Guadalupe. At this place there are certain cold baths, which arise, springing vp as though the water did seeth: the water thereof is somewhat brackish in taste, but very good for any that have any sore or wound, to wash themselues therewith, for as they say, it healeth many: and euery yeere once vpon our Lady day the people vse to repair thither to offer, and to pray in that Church before the image, and they say that our Lady of Guadalupe doeth work a number of miracles. About this Church there is not any towne of Spaniards that is inhabited, but certaine Indians doe dwell there in houses of their own countrey building.

Here we were met with a great number of Spaniards on horsebacke, which came from Mexico to see vs, both gentlemen, and men of occupations, and they came as people to see a wonder: we were still called vpon to march on: and so about foure of the clocke in the afternoone of the said day we entered into the citie of Mexico, by the way or street called la calle Santa Catherina: and we stayed not in any place till we came to the house or palace of the Vice Roy, Don Martin Henriques, which standeth in the middest of the city, hard by the market place, called La plaça del Marquese.

Certaine Englishmen taken prisoners at the fight at Sant Iuan de Vllua.

We had not stayed any long time at this place, but there was brought vs by the Spaniards from the market place great store of meat, sufficient to haue satisfied fiue times so many as we were: some also gaue vs hats, and some gaue vs money: in which place we stayed for the space of two houres, and from thence we were conueyed by water in two large Canoas to an hospital where as certaine of our men were lodged, which were taken before the fight at S. Iohn de Vllua: wee should haue gone to our Ladies hospitall, but that there were also so many of our men taken before at that fight that there was no roome for vs. After our coming thither, many of the company that came with me from Panuco dyed within the space of fourteene dayes: soone after which time we were taken foorth from that place, and put altogether into our Ladies hospitall, in which place we were courteously vsed, and visited oftentimes by vertuous gentlemen and gentlewomen of the citie, who brought vs diuers things to comfort vs withall, as succats and marmilads, and such other things, and would also many times giue vs many things, and that very liberally. In which hospitall we remained for the space of sixe moneths, vntill we were all whole and sound of body, and then we were appointed by the Vice Roy to be caried vnto the towne of Tescuco, which is from Mexico Southwest distant eight leagues:[11] in which towne there are certaine houses of correction and punishment for ill people called Obraches, like to Bridewell here in London: into which place diuers Indians are sold for slaues, some for ten yeeres, and some for twelue. It was no small griefe vnto vs when we vnderstood that we should be caried thither, and to bee vsed as slaues, we had rather be put to death: howbeit there was no remedy, but we were caried to the prison of Tescuco, where we were not put to any labour, but were very straitly kept, and almost famished, yet by the good prouidence of our mercifull God, we happened there to meet with one Robert Sweeting, who was the sonne of an Englishman, borne of a Spanish woman; this man could speake very good English, and by his means wee were holpen very much with victuals from the Indians, as mutton, hennes, and bread. And if we had not bene so relieued, we had surely perished: and yet all the prouision that wee had gotten that way was but slender. And continuing thus straightly kept in prison there for the space of two moneths, at the length wee agreed amongst our selues to breake forth of prison, come of it what would, for we were minded rather to suffer death then longer to liue in that miserable state. And so hauing escaped out of prison, we knew not what way to flie for the safetie of ourselues, the night was darke, and it rained terribly, and not hauing any guide, we went we knew not whither, and in the morning, at the appearing of the day, we perceiued our selues to be come hard to the city of Mexico, which is 24 English miles from Tescuco. The day being come we were espied by the Spaniards, and pursued, and taken, and brought before the Vice Roy and head iustices, who threatned to hang vs for breaking of the kings prison. Almost an hundred Englishmen prisoners in Mexico. Yet in the end they sent vs into a garden belonging to the Vice Roy, and comming thither, we found there our English gentlemen which were deliuered as hostages when as our General was betrayed at S. Iohn de Vllua, as is aforesaid, and with them wee also found Robert Barret, the Master of the Iesus, in which place we remained labouring and doing such things as we were commanded, for the space of 4 moneths, hauing but two sheepe a day allowed to suffice vs all, being very neere a hundred men, and for bread we had euery man two loaues a day, of the quantity of one halfe-peny loafe. At the end of which foure moneths, they hauing remooued our gentlemen hostages, and the Master of the Iesus to a prison in the Vice Roy his own house, did cause it to be proclaimed, that what gentleman Spaniard soeuer was willing or would haue any English man to serue him, and be bound to keepe him forth comming, to appeare before the Iustices within one moneth after notice giuen, that they should repaire to the said garden, and there take their choice: which proclamation was no sooner made, but the gentlemen came and repaired to the garden amaine, so that happie was he that could soonest get one of vs.

[11] It is nothing of the kind, being 16 miles East North East of Mexico, on the banks of Lake Tezcuco.

Chap. 5.

Wherein is shewed in what good sort, and how wealthily we liued with our masters vntil the comming of the Inquisition, when as againe our sorrows began a fresh: Of our imprisonment in the holy house, and of the seuere iudgement, and sentences giuen against vs, and with what rigour and crueltie the same were executed.

The gentlemen that thus tooke vs for their seruants or slaues, did new apparell vs through out, with whom we abode, doing such service as they appointed vs vnto, which was for the most part to attend vpon them at the table, and to be as their chamberlaines, and to waite vpon them when they went abroad, which they greatly accounted of; for in that countrey no Spaniard will serue one another, but they are all of them attended and serued by Indians weekly, and by Negroes which be their slaues during their life. In this sort we remained and serued in the said citie of Mexico, and thereabouts for the space of a yeere and somewhat longer. Afterwards many of vs were by our masters appointed to go to sundry of their Mines where they had to doe, and to be as ouerseers of the Negroes and Indians that laboured there. In which mines many of vs did profite and gaine greatly: for first we were allowed three hundred Pezos a man for a yeere, which is threescore pound sterling and besides that the Indians and Negroes which wrought vnder our charge, vpon our well using and intreating of them, would at times as vpon Saturdayes when they had left worke, labour for vs, and blow as much siluer as should be worth vnto vs 3 markes or there abouts, euery marke being worth 6 Pezos, and a halfe of their money, which 19 Pezos and a halfe, is worth 4li. 10s. of our money. Sundry weeks we did gaine so much by this means besides our wages, that many of vs became very rich, and were worth three thousand, or foure thousand Pezos, for we liued and gained thus in those Mines some three or foure yeeres. As concerning those Gentlemen which were deliverd as hostages, and that were kept in prison, in the Viceroy his house, after that we were gone from out the garden to serue sundry gentlemen as aforesaid, they remained prisoners in the said house for the space of 4 moneths after their comming thither, at the end whereof the fleete being readie to depart from S. Iohn de Vllua, to goe for Spaine, the said Gentlemen were sent away into Spaine with the fleete, where as I haue heard it credibly reported, many of them died with the cruell handling of the Spaniards in the Inquisition house, as those which haue bene deliuered home after they had suffered the persecution of that house can more perfectly declare. Robert

Barret also master of the Iesus, was sent away with the fleete into Spaine the next yeere following, where afterwards he suffered persecution in the Inquisition, and at the last was condemned to be burnt, and with him one more of our men whose name was Iohn Gilbert.

Now after that sixe yeeres were fully expired since our first coming into the Indies, in which time we had bene imprisoned and serued in the said countreys as is before truely declared. In the yeere of our Lord one thousand fiue hundred seuenty foure, the Inquisition began to be established in the Indies, very much against the mindes of many of the Spaniards themselues: for neuer vntil this time since their first conquering and planting in the Indies, were they subiect to that bloodie and cruell Inquisition. The chiefe Inquisitor was named Don Pedro Moya de Contreres, and Iohn de Bouilla his companion, and Iohn Sanches the Fischall, and Pedro de los Rios the Secretary: they being come and setled, and placed in a very faire house neere vnto the white Friers, considering with themselues that they must make an entrance and beginning of that their most detestable Inquisition here in Mexico, to the terror of the whole countrey, thought it best to call vs that were Englishmen first in question, and so much the rather, for that they had perfect knowledge and intelligence that many of vs were become very rich, as hath bene alreadie declared, and therefore we were a very good booty and pray to the Inquisitors: so that now againe began our sorrowes a fresh, for we were sent for, and sought out in all places of the countrey, and proclamation made vpon paine of losing of goods and excommunication that no man should hide or keepe secret any Englishmen or any part of their goods. By means whereof we were all soone apprehended in all places, and all our goods seized and taken for the Inquisitors vse, and so from all parts of the countrey we were conueied and sent as prisoners to the citie of Mexico, and there committed to prison, in sundry darke dungeons, where we could not see but by candle light, and were neuer past two together in one place, so that we saw not one another, neither could one of vs tell what was become of another. Thus we remained close imprisoned for the space of a yeere and a halfe, and others for some lesse time, for they came to prison euer as they were apprehended. During which time of our imprisonment, at the first beginning we were often called before the Inquisitors alone, and there seuerely examined of our faith, and commanded to say the Pater noster, the Aue Maria, and the Creed in Latin, which God knoweth great number of vs could not say, otherwise then in the English tongue. And hauing the said Robert Sweeting who was our friend at Tescuco alwayes present with them for an interpreter, he made report for vs, that in our own countrey speech we could say them perfectly, although not word for word as they were in Latin. Then did they proceede to demand of vs vpon our othes what wee did beleeue of the Sacrament, and whether there did remaine any bread or wine after the words of consecration, yea or no, and whether we did not beleeue that the host of bread which the priest did hold vp ouer his head, and the wine that was in the chalice, was the very true and perfect body and blood of our Sauiour Christ, yea or no: To which if we answered not yea, then was there no way but death. Then they would demand of vs what we did remember of our selues, what opinions we had held, or had bin taught to hold contrary to the same whiles we were in England: to which we for the safety of our liues were constrained to say, that we neuer did beleeue, nor had bene taught otherwise then as before we had sayd. Then would they charge vs, that we did not tell them the truth, that they knew the contrary, and therefore we should cal our selues to remembrance, and make them a better answer at the next time, or els we should be rackt, and made to confesse the trueth whether we would or no. And so comming againe before them the next time, we were still demanded of our beliefe whiles we were in England, and how we had bin taught, and also what we thought or did know of such of our owne company as they did name vnto vs, so that we could neuer be free from such demands, and at other times they would promise vs, that if we would tell them trueth, then should we haue fauour and be set at libertie, although we very wel knew their fair speeches were but means to entrap vs, to the hazard and losse of our liues: howbeit God so mercifully wrought for vs by a secret means that we had, that we kept vs still to our first answer, and would stil say that we had told the trueth vnto them, and knew no more by our selues nor any other of our fellows then as we had declared, and that for our sinnes and offences in England against God and our Lady, or any of his blessed Saints, we were heartily sory for the same, and did cry God mercy, and besought the Inquisitors for Gods sake, considering what we came into those countreyes by force of weather, and against our wils, and that neuer in all our lives we had either spoken or done any thing contrary to their lawes, that therefore they would haue mercy vpon vs. *Our men are cruelly rackt.* Yet all this would not serue; for still from time to time we were called upon to confesse and about the space of 3 moneths before they proceeded to their seuere iudgement, we were al rackt, and some enforced to vtter that against themselves, which afterwards cost them their liues. And thus hauing gotten from our own mouthes matter sufficient for them to proceed in iudgement against vs, they caused a large scaffold to be made in the middest of the market place in Mexico right ouer against the head church, and 14 or 15 daies before the day of their iudgement with the sound of a trumpet, and the noise of their Attahalies, which are a kind of drummes, they did assemble the people in all parts of the citie: before whom it was then solemnely proclaimed that whosoeuer would vpon such a day repaire to the market place, they should heare the sentence of the holy Inquisition against the English heretikes,

Lutherans, and also see the same put in execution. Which being done, and the time approching of this cruell judgement, the night before they came to the prison where we were, with certaine officers of that holy hellish house, bringing with them certaine fooles coats which they had prepared for vs, being called in their language S. Benitos, which coats were made, of yellow cotton and red crosses vpon them, both before and behind: they were so busied in putting on their coats about vs, and bringing vs out into a large yard, and placing and pointing vs in what order we should go to the scaffold or place of iudgment vpon the morrow, that they did not once suffer vs to sleepe all that night long. The next morning being come, there was giuen to every one of vs for our breakfast a cup of wine, and a slice of bread fried in honie, and so about eight of the clocke in the morning, we set foorth of the prison, euery man alone in his yellow coat, and a rope about his necke, and a great greene Waxe candle in his hand vnlighted, hauing a Spaniard appointed to goe vpon either side of euery one of vs: and so marching in this order and maner toward the scaffold in the market place, which was a bow shoot distant or thereabouts, we found a great assembly of people all the way, and such a throng, that certain of the Inquisitors officers on horseback were constrained to make way, and so comming to the scaffold, we went vp by a pairs of stayres, and found seates readie made and prepared for vs to sit downe on, euery man in order as he should be called to receiue his iudgement. We being thus set downe as we were appointed, presently the Inquisitors came vp another paire of staires, and the Viceroy and all the chiefe Iustices with them. When they were set downe and placed vnder the cloth of estate agreeing to their degrees and calling; then came vp also a great number of Friers, white, blacke and gray, about the number of 300 persons, they being set in the places for them appointed. Then was there a solemne Oyes made, and silence commanded, and then presently beganne their seuere and cruell iudgement.

The cruell iudgements of the Spanish Inquisitors vpon our poore countrey-men. The first man that was called was one Roger the chiefe Armourer of the Iesus, and hee had iudgement to haue three hundred stripes on horsebacke, and after condemned to the gallies as a slaue for 10 yeeres.

After him were called Iohn Gray, Iohn Brown, Iohn Moone, Iames Collier, and one Thomas Browne: these were adiudged to haue 200 stripes on horsebacke, and after to be committed to the gallies for the space of 8 yeeres.

Then was called Iohn Keyes, and was adiudged to have 100 stripes on horsebacke, and condemned to serue in the gallies for the space of 6 yeeres.

Then were seuerally called the number of 53 one after an other, and euery man had his seueral iudgement, some to haue 200 stripes on horseback, and some 100, and condemned for slaues to the gallies, some for 6 yeeres, some for 8 and some for 10.

And then was I, Miles Philips, called, and was adiudged to serue in a monasterie for 5 yeeres, without any stripes, and to weare a fooles coat, or S. Benito, during all that time.

Then were called Iohn Storie, Richard Williams, Dauid Alexander, Robert Cooke, Paul Horsewell and Thomas Hull: these six were condemned to serue in monasteries without stripes, some for three yeeres and some for foure, and to weare the S. Benito during all the said time. Which being done, and it now drawing toward night, George Riuelly, Peter Momfrie, and Cornelius the Irishman, were called and had their iudgement to be burnt to ashes, and so were presently sent away to the place, of execution in the market place but a little from the scaffold, where they were quickly burnt and consumed. And as for vs that had receiued our iudgement, being 68 in number, we were caried backe that night to prison againe. And the next day in the morning being good Friday, the yeere of our Lord 1575; we were all brought into a court, of the Inquisitors pallace, where we found a horse in a readinesse for euery one of our men which were condemned to haue stripes, and to be committed to the gallies, which were in number 60 and so they being inforced to mount vp on horsebacke naked from the middle vpward, were caried to be shewed as a spectacle for all the people to behold throughout the chiefe and principall streetes of the citie, and had the number of stripes to euery one of them appointed, most cruelly laid vpon their naked bodies with long whips by sundry men appointed to be the executioners thereof: and before our men there went a couple of criers which cried as they went: Behold these English dogs, Lutherans, enemies to God, and all the way as they went there were some of the Inquisitors themselues, and of the familiars of that rakehel order, that cried to the executioners, Strike, lay on those English hereticks, Lutherans, Gods enemies: and so this horrible spectacle being shewed round about the citie, they returned to the Inquisitors house with their backes all gore blood, and swollen with great bumps, and were then taken from their horses, and carried againe to prison, where they remained vntill they were sent into Spaine to the gallies, there to receiue the rest of their martirdome: and I and the 6 other with me which had iudgement, and were condemned amongst the rest to serue an apprentiship in the monastery, were taken presently and sent to certaine religious houses appointed for the purpose.

Chap. 6.

Wherein is shewed how we were vsed in the religious houses, and that when the time was expired, that we were adiudged to serue in them, there came newes to Mexico of M. Francis Drakes being in the South Sea, and what preparation was made to take him, and how I seeking to escape, was againe taken, and put in prison at Vera Cruz, and how againe I made mine escape from thence.

I Miles Philips and William Lowe were appointed to the blacke Friers, where I was appointed to be an ouerseer of Indian workmen, who wrought there in building of a new church: amongst which Indians I learned their language of Mexican tongue very perfectly, and had great familiaritie with many of them, whom I found to be a courteous and louing kind of people, ingenious, and of great vnderstanding, and they hate and abhorre the Spaniards with all their hearts, they haue vsed such horrible cruelties against them, and do still keepe them in such subiection and seruitude, that they and the Negros also doe daily lie in waite to practise their deliuerance out of that thraldome and bondage, that the Spaniards doe keepe them in. William Lowe he was appointed to serue the Cooke in the kitchen, Richard Williams and Dauid Alexander were appointed to the Grey Friers, Iohn Story and Robert Cooke to the white Friers: Paul Horsewel the Secretary tooke to be his seruant: Thomas Hull was sent to a Monastery of priests, where afterward he died. Thus we serued out the yeeres that we were condemned for, with the vse of our fooles coates, and we must needs confesse that the Friers did vse very courteously: for euery one of vs had his chamber with bedding and diet, and all things cleane and neat: yea many of the Spaniards and Friers themselues do vtterly abhorre and mislike of that cruell Inquisition, and would as they durst bewaile our miseries, and comfort vs the best they could, although they stood in such feare of that diuelish Inquisition, that they durst not let the left hande know what the right doth. Now after that the time was expired for which we were condemned to serue in those religious houses, we were then brought againe before the chief Inquisitor, and had all our fooles coates pulled off and hanged vp in the head church, called Ecclesia Maior, and euery mans name and iudement written thereupon with this addition, An heretike Lutheran reconciled. And there are also all their coates hanged vp, which were condemned to the gallies, with their names and iudgements, and vnderneath his coat, Heretike Lutheran reconciled. And also the coats and names of the three that were burned, whereupon were written, An obstinate heretike Lutheran burnt. Then were we suffered to goe vp and downe the countrey, and to place our selues as we could, and yet not so free, but that we very well knew that there was good espiall alwayes attending vs and all our actions, so that we durst not once speake or looke awry. Dauid Alexander and Robert Cooke returned to serue the Inquisitor, who shortly after maried them both to two of his Negro women: Richard Williams maried a rich widow of Biskay with 4000 Pezos. Paul Horsewell is maried to a Mestisa, as they name those whose fathers were Spaniards, and their mothers Indians, and this woman which Paul Horsewell hath maried, is sayd to be the daughter of one that came in with Hernando Cortes the conquerour, who had with her in mariage foure thousand Pezos, and a faire house: Iohn Storie is maried to a Negro woman: William Lowe had leaue and licence to goe into Spaine where he is now maried: for mine owne part I could neuer throughly settle my selfe to marry in that countrey, although many faire offers were made vnto me of such as were of great abilitie and wealth, but I could haue no liking to liue in that place, where I must euery where see and know such horrible idolatrie committed, and durst not once for my life speake against it: and therefore I had alwayes a longing and desire to this my natiue countrey: and, to returne and serue againe in the Mines where I might haue gathered great riches and wealth, I very well saw that at one time or another I should fall againe into the danger of that diuelish Inquisition, and so be strip of all, with losse of life also, and therefore I made my choice rather to learne to weaue Grogranes and Taffaties, and so compounding with a Silke-weauer, I bound my selfe for three yeeres to serue him, and gaue him an hundred and fiftie Pezos to teach me the science, otherwise he would not haue taught mee vnder seuen yeeres prentiship, and by this meanes I liued the more quiet, and free from suspition. Howbeit I should many times be charged by familiars of that diuelish house, that I had a meaning to runne away into England, and to be an heretike Lutheran againe: To whom I would answere that they had no neede to suspect any such thing in mee, for that they knew all very well that it was impossible for me to escape by any maner of meanes: yet notwithstanding I was called before the Inquisitor, and demanded why I did not marrie: I answered that I had bound myselfe at an occupation. Well said the Inquisitor, I knowe thou meanest to runne away, and therefore I charge thee here vpon paine of burning as an heretike relapsed, that thou depart not out of this citie, nor come neere to the port of S. Iohn de Vllua, nor to any other port: To the which I answered that I would willingly obey. Yea said he, see thou doe so, and thy fellowes also, they shall haue the like charge.

So I remained at my science the full time, and learned the Art, at the end wherof there came newes to Mexico that there were certaine Englishmen landed with a great power at the port of Acapulco, vpon the South sea, and that they were comming to Mexico to take the spoyle thereof, which wrought a marueilous great feare amongst them, and many of those that were rich began to shift for themselues, their wiues and children: vpon which hurlie burlie the Viceroy caused a generall muster to be made of all the Spaniards in Mexico, and there were found to be the number of 7000 and odde householders of Spaniards in the citie and suburbs, and of single men vnmaried, the number of 3000 and of Mestizoes, which are counted to be the sonnes of Spaniards, borne of Indian women, twenty thousand persons, and then was Paul Horsewel and I Miles Philips sent for before the Viceroy, and were examined if we did know an English man named Francis Drake, which was brother to Captaine Hawkins: to which we answered, that Captaine Hawkins had not any brother but one, which was a man of the age of threescore yeeres or thereabouts, and was now gouernour of Plimmouth in England. And then he demanded of vs if we knewe one Francis Drake, and we answered, no.

While these things were in doing, there came newes that all the Englishmen were gone, yet were there eight hundred men made out vnder the leading of seueral Captains, whereof two hundred were sent to the port of S. Iohn de Vllua, vpon the North Sea vnder the conduct of Don Luys Suares, two hundred were sent to Guatimala in the South sea, who had for their captaine Iohn Cortes, two hundred more were sent to Guatulco, a port of the South sea, ouer whom went for captaine Don Pedro de Robles, and two hundred more were sent to Acapulco, the port where it was said that Captaine Drake had bene. And they had for Captaine doctor Robles Alcalde de Corte, with whom I Miles Philips went as interpreter, hauing licence giuen by the Inquisitors. When we were come to Acapulco, we found that Captaine Drake was departed from thence, more then a moneth before we came thither. But yet our captaine Alcalde de Corte there presently embarked himselfe in a small ship of threescore tunne or thereabout, hauing also in companie with him two other small barkes, and not past two hundred men in all, with whom I went as interpreter in his owne ship, which God knoweth was but weake and ill appointed, so that for certaine, if we had met with Captaine Drake, he might easily haue taken vs all: We being imbarked kept our course and ranne Southward towards Panama, keeping still as nigh the shore as we could, and leauing the land vpon our left hand, and hauing coasted thus for the space of eighteene or twentie dayes, and being more to the South then Guatimala, we met at last with other ships which came from Panama, of whom we were certainly informed that he was cleane gone off the coast more then a moneth before: and so we returned backe to Acapulco againe, and there landed, our

Captaine being thereunto forced, because his men were very sore sea-sicke: All the while that I was at Sea with them I was a glad man, for I hoped that if we met with master Drake, we should all be taken, so that then I should haue beene freed out of that danger and miserie wherein I liued, and should returne to mine owne countrey of England againe. But missing thereof, when I sawe there was no remedie but that we must needes come on lande againe, little doeth any man know the sorow and griefe that inwardly I felt, although outwardly I was constrained to make faire weather of it. And so being landed, the next morow after, we began our iourney towardes Mexico, and past these townes of name in our way, as first the towne of Tuatepec, 50 leagues from Mexico, from thence to Washaca, 40 leagues from Mexico: from thence to Tepiaca 24 leagues from Mexico, and from thence to Pueblo de los Angeles, where is a high hill which casteth out fire three times a day, which hill is 18 leagues in maner directly West from Mexico, from thence we went to Stapelapa, 8 leagues from Mexico, and there our captaine and most of his men tooke boat, and came to Mexico againe, hauing bene forth about the space of seuen weekes or thereabouts. Our captaine made report to the Viceroy what he had done, and how farre he had trauelled, and that for certaine he was informed that Captaine Drake was not to be heard of. The Spanish Viceroy prophecied, but falsely. To which the Viceroy replied and said, Surely we shall haue him shortly come into our hands driuen a land through necessitie in some one place or other, for he being now in these seas of Sur, it is not possible for him to get out of them againe, so that if he perish not at sea, yet hunger wil force him to land. And then againe I was commanded by the Viceroy that I should not depart the citie of Mexico, but alwaies be at my masters house in a readinesse at an houres warning, when soeuer I should be called: for that notwithstanding within one moneth after certaine Spaniards going to Mecameca, 18 leagues from Mexico, to send away certaine hides and Cochinilla, that they had there at their Stantias or dairie houses, and my master hauing leaue of the Secretarie for me to go with them, I tooke my iourney with them being very well horsed and appointed, and comming thither and passing the time there at Mecameca certaine dayes till we had perfect intelligence that the fleete was readie to depart, I not being past 3 daies iourney from the port of S. John de Vllua, thought it to be the meetest time for me to make an escape, and I was the bolder, presuming vpon my Spanish tongue, which I spake as naturally as any of them all, thinking with my selfe, that when I came to S. Iohn de Vllua, I would get to be entertained as a souldiour, and so go home into Spaine in the same Fleete, and therefore secretly one euening late, the moone shining faire, I conueyed my selfe away, and riding so for the space of two nights and two dayes, sometimes in, and sometimes out, resting very little all that time, vpon the second day at night I came to the towne of Vera Cruz, distant from the port of S. Iohn de Vllua, where the ships rode, but only 5 leagues, and here purposing to rest my selfe a day or two, I was no sooner alighted, but within the space of one halfe houre after, I was by ill hap arrested, and brought before Iustices there, being taken and suspected to be a gentlemans sonne of Mexico, that was runne away from his father, who in trueth was the man they sought for: So I being arrested, and brought before the Iustices, there was a great hurly burly about the matter, euery man charging me that I was the sonne of such a man dwelling in Mexico, which I flatly denied, affirming that I knewe not the man, yet would they not beleeue me, but vrged stil vpon me that I was he that they sought for, and so I was conueied away to prison. And as I was thus going to prison, to the further increase of my griefe, it chanced that at that very instant there was a poore man in the presse that was come to towne to sell hennes, who told the Iustices that they did me wrong, and that in truth he knew very well that I was an Englishman and no Spaniard. They then demanded of him how he knew that, and threatned him that he said so, for that he was my companion, and sought to conuey me away from my father, so that he also was threatned to be laid in prison with me: he for the discharge of himselfe stood stifly in it, that I was an Englishman, and one of captain Hawkins men, and that he had knowen me weare the S. Benito in the Blacke-friers at Mexico, for 3 or 4 whole yeres together: which when they heard, they forsooke him, and began to examine me a new, whether that speech of his were true, yea or no, which when they perceiued that I could not denie, and perceiuing that I was run from Mexico, and came thither of purpose to conuey my selfe away with the fleete, I was presently committed to prison with a sorrowfull heart, often wishing my selfe that that man which knew me had at that time bene further off: howbeit he in sinceritie had compassion of my distressed estate, thinking by his speech, and knowing of me, to haue set me free from that present danger which he sawe me in: howbeit, contrary to his expectation, I was thereby brought into my extreme danger, and to the hazard of my life, yet there was no remedy but patience perforce. And I was no sooner brought into prison, but I had a great paire of bolts clapt on my legs, and thus I remained in that prison for the space of 3 weekes where were also many other prisoners which were thither committed for sundry crimes and condemned to the gallies. During which time of imprisonment there, I found amongst those my prison-fellowes some that had knowen me before in Mexico, and truely they had compassion of me, and would spare of their victuals and any thing els that they had to doe me good: amongst whom there was one of them that told me that he vnderstood by a secret friend of his which often came to the prison to him, that I should be shortly sent backe againe to Mexico by wagon, so soone as the fleete was gone from S. Iohn de Vllua, for Spaine.

This poore man my prison fellow of himselfe, and without any request made by me, caused his said friend which came often vnto him to the grate of the prison, to bring him wine and victuals, to buy for him 2 kniues which had files in their backes, which files were so wel made that they would serue and suffice any prisoner to file off his irons, and of those kniues or files he brought one to me, and told me that he had caused it to be made for me, and let me haue it at that very price it cost him, which was 2 Pezos, the value of 8.s. of our money: which knife when I had it, I was a ioyfull man, and conueied the same into the foote of my boot, vpon the inside of my left leg, and so within 3 or 4 dayes after that I had thus receiued my knife, I was suddenly called for, and brought before the head Iustice which caused those my irons with the round bolt to be stricken off and sent to a Smiths in the towne, where was a new paire of bolts made ready for me of another fashion, which had a broad iron barre comming betweene the shackles, and caused my hands to be made fast with a paire of manacles; and so was I presently laid in a wagon all alone, which was there readie to depart with sundry other wagons, to the number of 60. towardes Mexico, and they all were laden with sundry merchandise which came in the fleete out of Spaine.

The wagon that I was in was foremost in all the companie, and as we trauelled I being alone in the wagon, began to trie if I could plucke my hands out of the manacles, and as God would, although it were somewhat painefull for me, yet my hands were so slender that I could pull them out, and put them in againe, and euer as we went, when the wagon made most noyse, and the men were busiest, I would be working to file off my bolts, and traueling thus for the space of 8 leagues from Vera Cruz, we came to an high hill, at the entring vp of which (as God would) one of the wheeles of the waggon wherein I was, brake, so that by that means the other wagons went afore, and the wagon man that had charge of me set an Indian Carpenter a worke to mend the wheele: and here at this place they baited at an hostrie that a Negro woman keepes: and at this place, for that the going vp of the hill is very steepe, for the space of two leagues and better, they doe alwaies accustome to take the moiles of 3 or 4 wagons, and to place them altogether for the drawing vp of one wagon, and so to come downe againe, and fetch vp others in that order. *Miles Philips his last wonderful escape.* All which came very well to pass: for as it drew towards night when most of the Wagoners were gone to draw vp their wagons, in this sort I being alone had quickly filed off my bolts, and so espying my time in the darke of the euening before they returned downe the hill againe, I conueyed my selfe into the woods there adioyning, carrying my bolts and manacles with me, and a few biscuits, and two small cheeses. And being come into the woods, I threw my yrons into a thicke bush, and then couered them with mosse and other things, and then shifted for myself as I might all that night. And thus by the good prouidence of Almightie God, I was freed from mine yrons all sauing the collar that was about my necke, and so got my libertie the second time.

Chap. 7.

Wherein is shewed how I escaped to Guatimala, vpon the South sea, and from thence to the port of Cauallos, where I got passage to goe into Spaine, and of our arriuall at Hauana, and our comming to Spaine, where I was againe like to haue bene committed prisoner, and how through the great mercy of God I escaped, and came home in safetie into England in February 1582.

The next morning (day light being come) I perceiued by the Sunne rising what way to take to escape their hands, for when I fleede, I tooke the way into the woods vpon the left hand: and hauing left that way that went to Mexico vpon my right hand, I thought to keepe my course as the woods and mountaines lay, still direct South as neere as I could: by meanes whereof I was sure to conuey myselfe farre ynough from that way that went to Mexico. And as I was thus going in the woods, I saw many great fires made to the North not past a league from the mountaine where I was, and trauelling thus in my bootes with mine yron collar about my necke, and my bread and cheese, the very same forenoon I mette with a company of Indians which were hunting of Deere for their sustenance: to whom I spake in the Mexican tongue, and told them how that I had of a long time bin kept in prison by the cruel Spanyards, and did desire them to helpe me to file off mine yron collar, which they willingly did: reioycing greatly with me, that I was thus escaped out of the Spanyards hands. Then I desired that I might haue one of them to guide mee out of those desert mountaines towards the South, which they also most willingly did: and so they brought mee to an Indian towne 8. leagues distant from thence, named Shalapa, where I stayed three dayes, for that I was somewhat sickely. At which towne (with the gold that I had quilted in my dublet) I bought me an horse of one of the Indians, which cost me 6. pezos and so trauelling South, within the space of 2. leagues I happened to ouertake a gray Frier, one that I had bene familiar withall in Mexico, whom then I knew to be a zealous good man, and one that did much lament the crueltie vsed against vs by the Inquisitors, and truely hee vsed me very courteously: and I having confidence in him did indeed tel him, that I was minded to aduenture to see if I could get out of the sayd countrey if I could finde shipping, and did therefore pray him of his ayde, direction, and aduise herein, which he faithfully did, not only in directing me which was my safest way to trauaile, but he also of himselfe kept me company for the space, of three dayes, and euer as we came to the Indian houses (who vsed and intertained vs well) hee gathered among them in money to the value of 20. pezos, which at my departure from him hee freely gaue vnto mee. So came I to the citie of Guatimala vpon the South sea, which is distant from Mexico about 250. leagues, where I stayed 6. dayes, for that my horse was weake. And from thence I trauailed still South and by East seuen dayes iourney, passing by certaine Indian townes, vntill I came to an Indian towne distant from Mexico, direct South 309. leagues. And here at this towne enquiring to go to the Port de Cauallos in the Northeast sea, it was answered that in trauailing thither I should not come to any towne in 10. or 12. dayes iourney: so heere I hired two Indians to be my guides, and I bought hennes, and bread to serue vs so long time, and tooke with vs things to kindle fire euery night, because of wilde beastes, and to dresse our meate: and euery night when we rested, my Indian guides would make two great fires, betweene the which we placed our selues, and my horse. And in the night time we should heare the Lions roare, with Tigres, Ounces, and other beastes, and some of them we should see in the night, which had eyes shining like fire. And trauailing thus for the space of twelue dayes, wee came at last to the port of Cauallos vpon the East sea, distant from Guatimala South and by East, two hundred leagues, and from Mexico 450. or thereabouts.[12] This is a good harborough for shippes, and is without either castle or bulwarke. I hauing dispatched away my guides, went downe to the Hauen, where I saw certaine ships loden chiefly with Canary-wines, where I spake with one of the Masters, who asked me what Countrey man I was, and I told him that I was borne in Granado, and he said, that then I was his countreyman. I required him that I might passe home with him in his ship, paying for my passage: and he said yea, so that I had a safe conduct, or letter testimonial to shew, that he might incurre no danger; for said be, it may be that you haue killed some man, or be indebted, and would therefore run away. To that I answered, that there was not any such cause. Wel, in the end we grew to a price, that for 60. pezos he would cary me into Spaine: a glad man was I at this good hap, and I quickly solde my horse, and made my prouision of hennes and bread to serue me in my passage; And thus within 2. dayes after we set saile, and neuer stayed vntill we came to Hauana, which is distant from puerto de Cauallos by sea 500. leagues: where we found the whole fleete of Spaine, which was bound home from the Indies. And heere I was hired for a souldier to serue in the Admiral ship of the same fleete, wherein the General himself went. There landed while I was here 4. ships out of Spaine, being all full of souldiers and ordinance, of which number there were 200 men landed here, and 4. great brasse pieces of ordinance, although the castle were before sufficiently prouided: 200. men more were sent to Campeche, and certaine ordinance: 200. to Florida with ordinance: and 100. lastly to S. Iohn de Vllua. As for ordinance there they haue sufficient, and of the very same which was ours, which we had in the Iesus, and those others which we had planted in the place, where the Vice-roy betrayed M. Hawkins our general, as hath bene declared. The sending of those souldiers to euery of those Ports, and the strengthening of them, was done by commandement from the king of Spaine, who wrote also by them to the general of his flcctc, giuing him in charge so to doe, as also directing him what course he should keepe in his comming home into Spaine, charging him in any hand not to come nigh to the yles of Açores, but to keepe his course more to the Northward, advertising him withal, what number and power of French ships of warre, and other, Don Antonio had at that time at Terçera, and the yles aforesaid: which the general of the fleete wel considering, and what great store of riches he had to bring home with him into Spaine, did in all very duetifully observe and obey: for in trueth he had in his said fleete 37. saile of ships, and in euery of them there was as good as 30. pipes of silver one with another, besides great store of gold, Cochinilla, sugars, hides, and Cana Fistula, with other apothecary drugs. This our general, who was called Don Pedro de Guzman, did prouidently take order for, for their most strength and defence, if neede should be, to the vttermost of his power, and commanded vpon paine of death, that neither passenger nor souldier should come aboord without his sword and harquebush, with shot and powder, to the end that they might be the better able to encounter the fleete of Don Antonio, if they should hap to meete with them, or any of them: and euer as the weather was faire, the said general would himselfe go aboord from one ship to another, to see that every man had his ful prouision according to the commandement giuen. Yet to speake truly what I thinke, two good tall ships of warre would have made a foule spoil amongst them. For in all this fleete there were not any that were strong and warlike appointed, sauing only the Admiral, and Vice-admiral: And againe ouer and besides the weaknesse and the ill furnishing of the rest, they were all so deeply laden, that they had not bene able (if they had bene charged) to haue held out any long fight. Wel, thus we set saile, and had a very ill passage home, the weather was so contrary. We kept our course in maner Northeast, and brought our selues to the height of 42. degrees of latitude, to be sure not to meete with Don Antonio his fleete, and were vpon our voyage from the 4. of Iune, vntil the 10. of September, and neuer saw land till we fell with the Arenas Gosdas hard by S. Lucar.[13] And there was an order taken that none should goe on shoare vntill he had licence: as for me, I was knowen by one in the ship, who told the Master that I was an Englishman, which (as God would) it was my good hap to heare: for if I had not heard it, it had cost me my life. Notwithstanding, I would not take any knowledge of it, and seemed to be mery and pleasant, that we were all come so wel in safety. Presently after, licence came that we should go on shoare, and I pressed to be gone with the first: howbeit, the Master came vnto me, and said, Sirra, you must goe with me to Siuil by water: I knew his meaning well enough, and that he meant there to offer me vp as a sacrifice to the Holy house. For the ignorant zeal of a number of these superstitious Spaniards is such, that they thinke that they haue done God good seruice, when they haue brought a Lutheran heretike to the fire to be burnt: for so do they account of vs. Wel, I perceiuing all this, took vpon me not to suspect anything, but was still iocund and mery: howbeit, I knew it stood me vpon to shift for my selfe. And so wayting my time when the Master was in his cabbin asleepe, I conueyed my selfe secretly downe by the shrowds into the ship boate, and made no stay but cut the rope wherewithal she was moared, and so by the cable haled on shore, where I leapt on land, and let the boate goe whither it would. Thus by the helpe of God I escaped that day, and then neuer stayed at S. Lucar, but went all night by the way which I had seene other take toward Siuil: so that the next morning I came to Siuil, and sought me out a workemaster, that I might fall to my science, which was weauing of taffataes; and being intertained I set my selfe close to my worke, and durst not for my life once to stirre abroad for fear of being knowen: and being thus at my worke, within 4 dayes after I heard one of my fellows say, that he heard there was great inquiry made for an Englishman that came home in the fleete: what an heretique Lutheran (quoth I) was it, I would to God I might knowe him, surely I would present him to the Holy house. And thus I kept still within doores at my worke, and fained my selfe not well at ease, and that I would labour as I might to get me new clothes. And continuing thus for the space of 3. moneths I called for my wages, and bought me all things new, different from the apparell that I did weare at sea, and yet durst not be ouerbold to walke abroad: and after vnderstanding that there were certaine English ships at S. Lucar bound for England, I tooke a boat and went aboord one of them, and desired the Master that I might haue passage with him to goe into England, and told him secretly that I was one of those which Captaine Hawkins did set on shore in the Indies: he very courteously prayed me to haue him excused, for he durst not meddle with me, and prayed me therefore to returne from whence I came. Which when I perceiued, with a sorrowful heart, God knoweth, I tooke my leaue of him, not without watry cheekes. *He commeth home in an English ship from Maiorca.* And then I went to S. Mary port, which is 3. leagues from S. Lucar, where I put my selfe to be a souldier to goe in the king of Spaines Gallies, which were bound for Maiorca, and comming thither in the end of the Christmas holidayes, I found there two English ships, the one of London, and the other of the West countrey, which were ready freighted and stayed but for a faire winde. To the Master of the one, which was of the West countrey went I, and told him that I had bene 2. yeeres in Spaine to learne the language, and that I was now desirous to goe home and see my friends, for that I lacked maintenance: and so hauing agreed with him for my passage, I tooke shipping. And thus through the prouidence of Almighty God, after 16. yeeres absence, hauing sustained many and sundry great troubles and miseries, as by this discourse appeareth, I came home to this my natiue countrey of England in the yeere 1582. in the moneth of February, in the ship called the Landret, and arriued at Poole.

[12] Caballos or Port Cortez is a town of Honduras, on the North Coast, 56 miles north of Santiago.

[13] San Lucar de Barrameda, 18 miles north of Cadiz.

The trauailes of Iob Hortop, which Sir Iohn Hawkins set on land within the bay of Mexico, after his departure from the Hauen of S. Iohn de Vllua in Nueua Espanna, the 8. of October 1568.

Not vntruely nor without cause said Iob the faithfull seruant of God (whom the sacred Scriptures tell vs, to haue dwelt in the land of Hus) that man being borne of a woman, liuing a short time, is replenished with many miseries: which some know by reading of histories, many by the view of others calamities, and I by experience in my selfe, as this present Treatise insuing shall shew.

It is not vnknowen vnto many, that I Iob Hortop poudermaker was borne at Bourne, a towne in Lincolnshire, from my age of twelue yeeres brought vp in Redriffe neere London, with M. Francis Lee, who was the Queenes Maiesties powdermaker, whom I serued, vntil I was prest to goe on the 3. voyage to the West Indies, with the right worshipful Sir Iohn Hawkins, who appointed me to be one of the Gunners in her Maiesties ships called the Iesus of Lubeck, who set saile from Plimmouth in the moneth of October 1567. hauing with him another ship of her Maiesties, called the Minion, and foure ships of his owne, namely the Angel, the Swallow, the Iudith, and the William and Iohn. He directed his Vice-admiral, that if foule weather did separate them, to meete at the Iland of Tenerif. After which by the space of seuen dayes and seuen nights, we had such stormes at sea, that we lost our long boats and a pinnesse, with some men: comming to the Isle of Tenerif, there our Generall heard that his Vice-admirall with the Swallow, and the William and Iohn were at the Iland called Gomera, where finding his Vice-admirall, he anchored, tooke in fresh water, and set saile for Cape Blank, where in the way wee tooke a Portugal carauel, laden with fish called Mullets: from thence we sailed to cape Verde. In our course thither we met a Frenchman of Rochel called captaine Bland, who had taken a Portugal carauel, whom our vice admiral chased and tooke. Captaine Drake, now Sir Francis Drake was made master and captaine of the Carauel, and so we kept our way till we came to cape Verde, and there we anchored, tooke our boates, and set souldiers on shore. Our Generall was the first that leapt on land, and with him Captaine Dudley: there we tooke certaine Negroes, but not without damage to our selues. For our Generall, Captaine Dudley, and 8. other of our company were hurt with poysoned arrowes: about nine dayes after, the 8. that were wounded died.

A remedie against poysoned arrowes. Our general was taught by a Negro, to draw the poyson out of his wound with a cloue of garlike, whereby he was cured. From thence wee went to Sierra leona, where be monstrous fishes called Sharkes, which will deuoure men. I amongst others was sent in the Angell with two Pinnesses into the riuer called Calousa, to seeke two Carauels that were there trading with the Negros: wee tooke one of them with the Negros, and brought them away.

In this riuer in the night time we had one of our pinnesses bulged by a sea-horse, so that our men swimming about the riuer were all taken into the other pinnesses, except two that tooke hold one of another, and were caried away by the sea-horse. This monster[14] hath the iust proportion of a horse, sauing that his legs be short, his teeth very great, and a span in length: hee vseth in the night to goe on land into the woods, seeking at vnawares to deuoure the Negroes in their cabbins, whom they by their vigilancie preuent, and kill him in this maner. The Negroes keepe watch, and diligently attend their comming, and when they are gone into the woods, they forthwith lay a great tree ouerthwart the way, so that at their returne, for that their legs be so short, they cannot goe ouer it: then the Negroes set vpon them with their bowes, arrowes and darts, and so destroy them.

[14] Hippopotamus.

From thence we entred the riuer called the Casserroes, where there were other Carauels trading with the Negroes, and them we tooke. In this Iland betwixt the riuer and the maine, trees grow with Oisters vpon them. There grow Palmito trees, which bee as high as a ships maine mast, and on their tops grow nuts, wine and oyle, which they call Palmito wine and Palmito oyle. The Plantan tree also groweth in that countrey; the tree is as bigge is a mans thigh, and as high as a firre pole, the leaues thereof be long and broad, and on the top grow the fruit which are called Plantanos: they are crooked and a cubite long, and as bigge as a mans wrist, they growe on clusters: when they be ripe they be very good and daintie to eate: Sugar is not more delicate in taste then they be.

From thence with the Angel, the Iudith, and the two pinnesses, we sailed to Sierra leona, where our Generall at that time was, who with the captaines and souldiers went vp into the riuer called Taggarin, to take a towne of the Negroes, where he found three kings of that countrie with fiftie thousand Negroes besieging the same towne, which they could not take in many yeeres before when they had warred with it. Our General made a breach, entred, and valiantly tooke the towne, wherein we found fiue Portugals which yeelded themselues to his mercie, and hee saued their liues: we tooke and caried thence for traffique to the West Indies 500. Negroes. The three kings droue 7000. Negroes into the sea at low water, at the point of the land, where they were all drowned in the Oze, for that they could not take their canoas to saue themselues. Wee returned backe againe in our pinnesses to the ships, and there tooke in fresh water, and made ready sayle towards Rio grande. At our comming thither we entred with the Angel, the Iudith, and the 2. pinnesses, and found there seuen Portugal Caruels, which made great fight with vs. In the ende by Gods helpe wee wonne the victory, and droue them to the shore, from whence with the Negroes they fled, and we fetcht the caruels from the shore into the riuer. The next morning M. Francis Drake with his caruel, the Swallow, and the William and Iohn came into the riuer, with captaine Dudley and his souldiers, who landed being but a hundred souldiers, and fought with seuen thousand Negroes, burned the towne, and returned to our Generall with, the losse of one man.

In that place there be many muske-cats, which breed in hollow trees: the Negroes take them in a net, and put them in a cage, and nourish them very daintily, and take the muske from them with a spoone.

Now we directed our course from Guinea towards the West Indies.

And by the way died Captaine Dudley.

In sayling towards the Indies, the first land that we escryed, was the Iland called Dominica, where at our comming we anchored, and tooke in fresh water and wood for our prouision: which done, we sayled towards the Iland called Margarita, where our Generall in despite of the Spaniards anchored, landed, and tooke in fresh victuals. A mile off the Iland there is a rocke in the sea, wherein doe breede many fowles like vnto Barnacles: in the night we went out in our boates, and with cudgels we killed many of them, and brought them with many of their egs aboord with vs: their egges be as bigge as Turkies egges, and speckled like them. We did eate them, and found them very good meate.

From thence wee sayled to Burboroata, which is in the maine land of the West Indies: there we came in, mored our ships, and taried two moneths trimming and dressing our ships, and in the meane time traded with certaine Spanyards of that countrey. There our Generall sent vs vnto a towne called Placencia, (which stood on a high hil) to haue intreated a Bishop that dwelt there for his fauour and friendship in their lawes, who hearing of our comming, for feare forsooke the town.

In our way vp the hil to Placencia, wee found a monstrous venomous worme with two heads: his body was as bigge as a mans arme, and a yard long: our master Robert Barret did cut him in sunder with his sword, and it made it as blacke as if it were coloured with ynke.

Heere be many Tygers, monstrous and furious beasts, which by subtiltie deuoure and destroy many men: they vse the traded wayes, and wil shew themselues twise or thrise to the trauellers, and so depart secretly, lurking till they be past, then suddenly and at vnawares they leape vpon them and deuoure them: they had so vsed two of our company, had not one of them, looked behind. Our Generall sent three ships vnto the Iland called Coraçao,[15] to make prouision for the rest, where they remayned vntill his comming. ⁚ Rio de la Hacha taken. ⁚ Hee sent from thence the Angel and the Iudith to Rio de Hacha,[16] where we anchored before the town. The Spaniards shot three pieces at vs from the shore, whom we requited with two of ours, and shotte through the Gouernours house: we wayed anchor, and anchored againe without shot of the towne, where wee rid fiue dayes in despite of the Spanyards, and their shot. In the meane space there came a Caruel of aduise from S. Domingo, whom with the Angel, and the Iudith wee chased and droue to the shore: we fetcht him from thence in spite of 200. Spaniards hargubush shot, and anchored againe before the towne, and rid there with them, till our Generals comming, who anchored, landed his men, and valiantly tooke the Towne, with the losse of one man, whose name was Thomas Surgeon: wee landed and planted on the shore for our safeties, our field ordinance: we droue the Spaniards vp into the country aboue two leagues whereby they were inforced to trade with our General, to whom he sold most part of his Negros.

[15] Situated 75 miles from the Venezuelan coast.

[16] At the mouth of the Hacha river, Magdalena State, Columbia.

In this riuer we killed a monstrous Lagarto or Crocodile in this port at sunne set: seuen of vs went in the pinnesse vp into the Riuer, carying with vs a dogge, vnto whom with ropeyarn we bound a great hooke of steele, with a chaine that had a swiuel, which we put vnder the dogs belly, the point of the hooke comming ouer his back fast bound, as aforesaid: we put him ouer board, and veered out our rope by litle and litle, rowing away with our boate: the Lagarto came and presently swallowed vp the dogge, then did we rowe hard till we had choked him: he plunged and made a wonderfull stirre in the water: we leapt on shore, and haled him on land: he was 23. foote by the rule, headed like a hogge, in body like a serpent, full of scales as broad as a sawcer: his taile long and full of knots as bigge as a fawcon shotte: he hath foure legs, his feete haue long nailes like vnto a dragon: we opened him, tooke out his guts, flayed him; dried his skinne, and stuffed it with straw, meaning to haue brought it home, had not the ship bin cast away. This, monster will cary away and deuoure both men and horse.

From hence we shaped our course to Santa Martha,[17] where we landed, traded and sold certaine Negroes: there two of our company killed a monstrous adder, going towards his caue with a Conie in his mouth: his body was as bigge as any mans thigh, and seuen foote long, vpon his tayle he had sixteene knottes, euery one as bigge as a great walnut, which they say, doe shew his age: his colour was greene and yellow: they opened him; and found two conies in his belly.

From thence wee sayled to Cartagena,[18] where we went in, mored our Shippes, and would haue traded with them, but they durst not for feare of the King: wee brought vp the Minion against the Castle, and shotte at the Castle and Towne: then we landed in an Iland, where were many gardens: there in a caue we found certaine Botijos of wine, which wee brought away with vs, in recompence whereof, our Generall commanded, to be set on shore woollen and linnen cloth, to the value thereof. From hence by foule weather wee were forced to seeke the Port of Saint Iohn de Vllua. In our way thwart of Campeche we met with a Spaniard, a small ship, who was bound for Santo Domingo: he had in him a Spaniard called Augustin de villa nueua, who was the man that betrayed all the Noble men in the Indies, and caused them to be beheaded, wherefore he with two Friers fled to S. Domingo: them we tooke and brought with vs into the Port of S. Iohn de Vllua. Our Generall made great account of him, and vsed him like a Noble man: howbeit in the ende he was one of them that betrayed vs. When wee had mored our ships, and landed, we mounted the Ordinance that wee found there in the Ilande, and for our safeties kept watch and warde.

Don Martin de Henriquez the trecherous Vice-roy. The next daye after wee discouered the Spanish fleete, whereof Luçon a Spanyard was Generall: with him came a Spanyard called Don Martin Henriquez, whom the king of Spaine sent to be his Vice-roy of the Indies. He sent a Pinnesse with a flagge of truce vnto our Generall, to knowe of what Countrey those Shippes were that rode there in the King of Spaines Port: who sayd they were the Queene of Englands ships, which came in there for victuals for their money: wherefore if your Generall will come in here, he shall giue me victuals and all other necessaries, and I will goe out on the one side of the Port, and he shall come in on the other side. The Spanyard returned for answere, that he was a Vice-roy, and had a thousand men, and therefore he would come in. Our Generall sayd, If he be a Vice-roy, I represent my Queenes person, and I am a Vice-roy as well as he: and if he haue a thousand men, my powder and shot will take the better place. Then the Vice-roy after counsell among themselues, yeelded to our Generals demand, swearing by his King and his Crowne, by his commission and authority that he had from his King, that hee would performe it, and thereupon pledges were giuen on both parts. Our Generall bearing a godly and Christian minde, voyde of fraude and deceit, iudged the Spanyards to haue done the like, deliuered to them sixe gentlemen, not doubting to haue receiued the like from them: but the faithlesse Spanyardes, in costly apparell gaue of the basest of their company, as afterwardes it was well knowen. These things finished, proclamation was made on both sides, that on payne of death no occasion should be giuen, whereby any quarrel should grow to the breach of the league, and then they peaceably entred the port, with great triumph on both sides.

[17] Capital of the State of Magdalena.

[18] Lat. 10 degrees 25 North; lon. 75.34 West. Capital of Bolivar.

The Spaniards presently brought a great Hulke, a ship of sixe hundred, and mored her by the side of the Minion, and they cut out ports in their other ships, planting their ordinance towards vs, in the night they filled the Hulke with men, to lay the Minion aboord, as the sequel did shew, which made our General doubtful of their dealings: wherefore, for that he could speake the Spanish tongue, he sent Robert Barret aboord the Vice-roy, to knowe his meaning in those dealings, who willed him with his company to come in to him, whom he commanded presently to be set in the bilbowes, and forthwith a Cornet (for a watchword among the false Spaniards) was sounded <u>for the enterprising of their pretended treason against our Generall, Augustine de villa nueua a most thanklesse traytour.</u> whom Augustine de villa noua sitting at dinner with him, should then presently haue killed with a poynado which hee had priuily in his sleeue, was espyed and preuented by one Iohn Chamberlayne, who tooke the poynado out of his sleeue. Our General hastily rose vp, and commanded him to be put prisoner in the Stewards roome, and to be kept with two men. The faithlesse Spanyards, thinking all things to their desire had bene finished, suddenly sounded a Trumpet, and therewith three hundred Spaniards entred the Minion, whereat our General with a loude and fierce voyce called vnto vs, saying, God and Saint George, vpon those traiterous villaines, and rescue the Minion, I trust in God the day shalbe ours: and with that the Mariners and souldiers leapt out of the Iesus of Lubeck into the Minion, and beat out the Spanyards, and with a shot out of her fiered the Spaniards Vice admirall, where the most part of 300. Spanyards were spoyled, and blowen ouer boord with powder. Their Admirall also was on fire halfe an houre: we cut our cables, wound off our ships, and presently fought with them: they came vpon vs on euery side, and continued the fight from ten of the clocke vntill it was night: they killed all our men that were on shore in the Iland, sauing three, which by swimming got aboord the Iesus of Lubeck. One of those three was Iob Hortop the reporter hereof. Four Spanish ships sunke. They sunke the Generals ship called the Angel, and tooke the Swallow: the Spaniards Admirall had aboue threescore shot through her: many of his men were spoyled: four other of their ships were sunke. There were in that fleete, and that came from the shore to rescue them, fifteene hundred: we slew of them fiue hundred and fourtie, as we were credibly informed by a note that came to Mexico. In this fight the Iesus of Lubeck had fiue shotte through her mayne Mast: her foremast was shotte in sunder vnder the bounds with a chayne shotte, and her hull was wonderfully pearced with shotte, therefore it was vnpossible to bring her away. They set two of their owne Shippes on fire, intending therewith to haue burnt the Iesus of Lubeck, which we preuented by cutting our cables in the halse, and winding off by our sternefast.

The Minion was forced to set saile and stand off from vs, and come to an anker without shot of the Island. Our Generall couragiously cheered vp his souldiers and gunners, and called to Samuel his page for a cup of Beere, who brought it him in a siluer cup, and hee drinking to all men willed the gunners to stand by their Ordinance lustily like men. He had no sooner set the cup out of his hand, but a demy Culuerin shot stroke away the cup and a Coopers plane that stoode by the main mast, and ranne out on the other side of the ship: which nothing dismaid our Generall, for he ceased not to incourage vs, saying, feare nothing, for God, who hath preserued me from this shot, will also deliuer vs from these traitours and villaines. Then Captaine Bland meaning to haue turned out of the port, had his maine mast stroke ouer boord with a chaine shot that came from the shore, wherefore he ankered, fired his ship, tooke his pinnesse with all his men, and came aboord the Iesus of Lubek to haue runne away from him, he answered, that he was not minded to haue run away from him, but his intent was to haue turned vp, our Generall, who said vnto him, that he thought he would not and to haue laid the weathermost ship of the Spanish fleete aboord, and fired his ship in hope therewith to haue set on fire the Spanish fleete, hee said if he had done so he had done well. With this, night came on. Our Generall commanded the Minion, for safegard of her masts to be brought vnder the Iesus of Lubecks lee: he willed M. Francis Drake to come in with the Iudith, and to lay the Minion aboord, to take in men and other things needfull, and to goe out, and so he did.

At night when the wind came off the shore, wee set sayle, and went out in dispite of the Spanyards and their shot, where wee ankered, with two ankers vnder the Island, the wind being Northerly, which was wonderfull dangerous, and wee feared euery houre to be driuen with the lee shore. In the end when the wind came larger, we waied anker, and set saile, seeking the riuer of Panuco for water, whereof we had very little, and victuals were so scarce, that we were driuen to eate hides, cats, rats, parrats, monkies, and dogges: wherefore our Generall was forced to diuide his company into two parts, for there was a mutinie among them for want of victuals: and some said that they had rather be on the shore to shift for themselues amongst the enemies, then to serue on ship-boord. He asked them who would go on shore, and who would tarry on ship-boord, those that would goe on shore, he willed to goe on foremast, and those that would tarrie, on baft mast: fourescore and sixteene of vs were willing to depart. Our Generall gaue vnto euery one of vs sixe yards of Roane cloth, and money to them that demanded it. About an hundred Englishmen landed. When we were landed, he came vnto vs, where friendly imbracing euery one of vs, he was greatly grieued that he was forced to leaue vs behind him, he counselled vs to serue God, and to loue one another, and thus courteously he gaue vs a sorowful farewell, and promised if God sent him safe home, he would do what he could, that so many of vs as liued should be brought into England, and so he did.

Since my returne into England I haue heard that many misliked that he left vs so behind him, and brought away Negroes: but the reason is this, for them he might haue had victuals, or any other thing needfull, if by foule weather hee had bene driuen vpon the Islands, which for gold nor siluer he could not haue had.

And thus our Generall departed to his ship, and we remained on land, where for our safeties, fearing the wild Indians that were about vs, we kept watch all night, and at Sunne rising wee marched on our way, three and three in a ranke, vntill that we came into a fielde vnder a groue, where the Indians came vpon vs, asking vs what people we were, and how we came there. Two of our company, namely Anthony Goddard and Iohn Cornish, for that they could speake the Spanish tongue, went to them and said wee were Englishmen, that neuer came in that countrey before, and that we had fought with the Spaniards, and for that we lacked victuals, our Generall set vs on shore: they asked vs whither we intended to goe, we said to Panuco. The Captaine of the Indians willed vs to giue vnto them some of our clothes and shirts, which we did: then he bad vs giue them all, but we would not so doe, whereupon Iohn Cornish was then slaine with an arrow, which an Indian boy that stoode by the Captaine shot at him, wherefore hee stroke the boy on the necke with his bow, that he lay for dead, and willed vs to follow him, who brought vs into a great fielde where we found fresh water: hee bad vs sit downe about the pond and drinke, and he with his company would goe in the meane space to kill fiue or sixe Deere, and bring them vs. We taryed there till three of the clocke, but they came not: there one of our company whose name was Iohn Cooke, with foure other departed from vs into a groue to seeke reliefe, where presently they were taken by the Indians, and stript as naked as euer they were borne, and so returned to vs.

Then we diuided ourselues into two parts, halfe to Anthony Goddard, and the rest to Iames Collier, and thus seuerally we sought for Panuco. Anthony Goddard with his company bid vs farewell, they passed a riuer, where the Indians robbed many of them of their clothes, and so passing on their way, came to a stony hill, where they stayed. 8. Englishmen slaine. Iames Collier with his company that day passed the same riuer, and were also robbed, and one of them slaine by chance: wee came that night vnto the hill, where Anthony Goddard and his company rested, there we remained til morning, and then we marched altogether from thence, entring betweene two groues, where the Indians robbed vs of all our clothes, and left vs naked, they hurt many, and killed eight of vs. Three dayes after we came to another riuer, there the Indians shewed vs the way to Panuco, and so left vs: we passed the riuer into the wildernes, where we made wreaths of greene grasse, which we wound about our bodies, to keepe vs from the Sunne, and gnats of that Countrey. We trauelled there seuen dayes, and seuen nights, before we came to Panuco, feeding on nothing but roots, and Guiauos,[19] a fruit like figs. At our comming to the riuer of Panuco two Spanish horsemen came ouer vnto vs in a Canowe: they asked vs how long we had bene in the wildernesse, and where our generall was, for they knewe vs to be of the company that had fought with their countrimen: we told them seuen dayes and seuen nights, and for lacke of victuals our Generall set vs on shore, and he was gone away with his ships. They returned to their Gouernour, who sent them with fiue Canowes to bring vs all ouer, which done, they set vs in aray, where a hundred horsemen with their lances, came forceably vpon vs, but did not hurt vs, they carried vs prisoners to Panuco, where we remained one night. In the riuer of Panuco there is a fish like a calfe, the Spanyards call it a Mollatin, hee hath a stone in his head, which the Indians vse for the disease of the Collicke, in the night he commeth on land and eateth grasse. I haue eaten of it, and it eateth not much vnlike to bacon. From thence we were sent to Mexico, which is 90 leagues from Panuco. In our way thither, 20 leagues from the sea side, I did see white Crabs running vp and downe the sands, I haue eaten of them, and they be very good meat. There groweth a fruit which the Spanyards call Auocottes, it is proportioned like an egge, and as blacke as a cole, hauing a stone in it, and it is an excellent good fruit. A manifold Magueis. There also groweth a strange tree which they call Magueis, it serueth them to many vses, below by the root they make a hole, whereat they do take out of it twise euery day a certeine kind of licour, which they seeth in a great kettle, till the third part be consumed, and that it waxe thick, it is as sweet as any hony, and they do eat it. Within 20. daies after that they haue taken al the licour from it, it withereth, and they cut it down, and vse it as we vse our hempe here in England, which done, they conuert it to many vses: of some part they make mantles, ropes, and threed: of the ends they make needles to sow their saddles, pannels, and other furniture for their horses: of the rest they make tyles, to couer their houses, and they put it to many other purposes.

[19] Guavas.

And thus we came to Mexico, which is seuen or eight miles about, seated in a great fen, inuironed with 4 hils, it hath but two wayes of entrance, and it is full of creeks, in the which in their Canowes they passe from place to place, and to the Islands there within. In the Indies ordinarily three times a yeere bee wonderfull earthquakes, which put the people in great feare and danger: during the time of two yeeres that I was in Mexico, I saw them sixe times; when they come they throw downe trees, houses, and Churches. There is a citie 25. leagues from Mexico, called Tlaxcalla, which is inhabited with an hundred thousand Indians, they goe in white shirts, linnen breeches, and long mantles, and the women weare about them a garment much like vnto a flannell petticote. The kings pallace was the first place wee were brought vnto in Mexico, where without we were willed to sit downe. Much people, men, women, and children came wondring about vs, many lamented our misery, and some of their clergy asked vs if we were Christians, we said, we praised God, we were as good Christians as they: they asked how they might know that, we said by our confessions. From thence we were caried in a Canow to a Tanners house, which standeth a little from the citie: the next morning two friers and two priests came thither to vs, and willed vs to blesse our selues, and say our prayers in the Latin tongue, that they might vnderstand vs, many of our company did so, wherevpon they returned to the viceroy, and told him that we were good Christians, and that they liked vs well, and then they brought vs much reliefe, with clothes, our sicke men were sent to their Hospitals, where many were cured, and many died. From the Tanners house we were led to a gentlemans place, where vpon paine of death we were charged to abide, and not to come into the citie, thither we had all things necessary brought vs: on Sundayes and holy dayes much people came, and brought vs great reliefe.

The viceroy practised to hang vs, and caused a paire of new gallowes to be set vp, to haue executed vs, whereunto the noblemen of that countrey would not consent, but prayed him to stay vntil the ship of aduise brought newes from the king of Spaine, what should be done with vs, for they said they could not find any thing by vs, whereby they might lawfully put vs to death.

The viceroy then commanded vs to be sent to an Island there by, and he sent for the Bishop of Mexico, who sent foure priests to the Island, to examine and confesse vs, who said, that the viceroy would burne vs, when wee were examined and confessed according to the lawes of the countrey. They returned to the Bishop, and told him that we were very good Christians. The Bishop certified the viceroy of our examinations and confessions, and said that wee were good Christians, therefore he would not meddle with vs. Then the viceroy sent for our master R. Barret, whom he kept prisoner in his pallace, vntill the fleete was departed for Spaine. The rest of vs he sent to a towne seuen leagues from Mexico called Tescuco, to card wooll among the Indian slaues, which drudgery we disdained, and concluded to beat our masters, and so we did: wherefore they sent to the viceroy, desiring him for Gods sake and our Ladies, to send for vs, for they would not keepe vs any longer, they said that we were deuils and no men.

The viceroy sent for vs, and imprisoned vs in a house in Mexico, from thence he sent Anthony Goddard, and some other of our company with him into Spaine with Luçon, the Generall that tooke vs: the rest of vs staied in Mexico two yeres after, and then were sent prisoners into Spaine, with Don Iuan de Valesco de Varre, admirall and generall of the Spanish fleet, who caried with him in his ship, to be presented to the King of Spaine, the anatomie of a giant, which was sent from China to Mexico, to the Viceroy Don Martin Henriquez, to bee sent to the king of Spaine for a great wonder. It did appere by the anatomie, that he was of a monstrous size, the skull of his head was neere as bigge as halfe a bushel, his necke-bones, shoulder plates, arme bones, and all other lineaments of his other partes, were huge and monstrous to behold, the shanke of his legge from the ankle to the knee, was as long as from any mans ankle vp to his wast, and of bignesse accordingly.

A description of ginger. At this time, and in this ship, were also sent to be presented to the king of Spaine, two chestes full of earth with ginger growing in them, which were also sent from China, to be sent to the king of Spaine. The ginger runneth in the ground like to liccoras, the blades grow out of it in length and proportion like vnto the blades of wild garlicke, which they cut euery fifteene dayes, they vse to water them twise a day, as we doe our herbes here in England, they put the blades in their pottage, and vse them in their other meates, whose excellent sauour and tast is very delightfull, and procureth a good appetite.[20]

[20] Ginger is the underground stem (rhizome) of *Zingiber officinal.* The rhizome throws up barren leafy reed like stems 3 or 4 feet high, and occasionally flowering stems. The flowers are arranged in a cone-shaped spike, each in the axil of a large greenish-yellow bract. The corolla is orange-yellow, divided into three long segments. One of the staminodes forms a large purple three-lobed lip. Ginger is probably a native of tropical Asia, but is now cultivated in all warm countries. The name occurs in a list of imports into Alexandria in the second century, and during the middle ages was evidently an important article of commerce. It is often mentioned in the Old English leech-books of the eleventh century; and during the thirteenth and fourteenth centuries it was the commonest spice, next to pepper, though 1 lb. of it cost as much as a sheep, 1*s.* 7*d.* (Rogers, "History of Agriculture and Prices in England.")

1570. When we were shipped, in the Port of S. Iohn de Vllua, the Generall called our master Robert Barret and vs with him into his cabbin, and asked vs if wee would fight against Englishmen, if we met them at the sea, we said that we would not fight against our Crowne, but if we met with any other, we would do what we were able. He said if we had said otherwise, he would not haue beleeued vs, and for that we should be the better vsed, and haue allowance as other men had: and he gaue a charge to euery one of vs, according to our knowledge, Robert Barret was placed with the pilote, I was put in the gunners roome, William Cawse with the boat-swaine, Iohn Beare with the quarter-masters, Edward Rider and Geffrey Giles, with the ordinary mariners, Richard the masters boy attended on him and the pilote: shortly after we departed from the port of S. Iohn de Vllua with all the fleete of Spaine, for the port called Hauana: wee were 26. dayes sayling thither. There wee came in, ankered, tooke in fresh water, and stayed 16. dayes for the fleete of Nombre de Dios, which is the fleet that brings the treasure from Peru.

The Generall of that fleet was called Diego Flores de Valdes. After his comming, when he had watred his ships, both the fleetes ioyned in one, and Don Iuan de Velasco de Varre was the first fifteen daies Generall of both the fleets, who turning through the chanell of Bahama, his pilote had like to haue cast away all the fleet vpon the Cape called Cannaueral, which was preuented by me Iohn Hortop, and our master Robert Barret: for I being in the second watch escried land, and called to Robert Barret, bidding him looke ouer boord, for I saw land vnder the lee-bow of the ship: he called to the boat-swaine, and bid him let flie the fore saile sheat, and lay the helm vpon the lee, and cast the ship about. When we were cast about, we were but in seuen fathome water: we shot off a piece, giuing aduice to the fleet to cast about, and so they did: For this we were beloued of the Generall, and all the fleet. The Generall was in a great rage, and swore by the king, that he would hang his pilote: for he said, that twise before he had almost cast away the Admirall. When it was day, he commanded a piece to be shot off to call to councill: the other Admirall in his ship came vp to him, and asked what the matter was, he said, that his pilote had cast away his ship and all the fleet, had it not bene for two of the Englishmen, and therefore he would hang him. The other Admirall with many faire words perswaded him to the contrary.

A sea-monster in the shape of a man. When we came in the height of Bermuda, we discouered a monster in the sea, who shewed himselfe three times vnto vs from the middle vpwards, in which parts hee was proportioned like a man, of the complection of a Mulato, or tawny Indian. The Generall did commaund one of his clearks to put it in writing, and hee certified the King and his Nobles thereof. Presently after this, for the space of sixteene dayes we had wonderful foule weather, and then God sent vs a faire wind, vntill such time as we discouered the Iland called Faial.

On S. Iames day we made rackets, wheeles, and other fireworkes, to make pastime that night, as it is the order of the Spaniards. When we came neere the land, our master R. Barret conferred with vs, to take the pinnesse one night, when we came on the Iland called Terçera, to free our selues from the danger and bondage that we were going into, whereunto we agreed: none had any pinnesse asterne then but our ship, which gaue great courage to our enterprize: we prepared a bagge of bread, and a Botijo of water, which would haue serued vs nine dayes, and prouided our selues to goe: our Master borrowed a small compasse of the Master gunner of the ship, who lent it him, but suspected his intent, and closely made the Generall priuy to it, who for a time dissembled the matter. In the ende seeing our pretense, he called R. Barret, commanding his head to bee put in the stocks, and a great payre of yron bolts on his legs, and the rest of vs, to be set in the stocks by the legs. Then he willed a peece to be shot off, and he sent the pinnesse for the other Admirall, and all the captaines, masters, and pilotes of both fleetes to come aboord of him. He commanded the maine-yard to be strooke downe, and to put 2. pullies, on euery yard-arme one; the hangman was called, and we were willed to confesse our selues, for he swore by the king that he would hang vs.

When the other Admiral, and the rest were come aboord, he called them into his counsel-chamber, and told them that he would hang the master of the Englishmen, and all his company. The Admirall, whose name was Diego Flores de Valdes, asked him wherefore: he sayd, that we had determined to rise in the night with the pinnesse, and with a ball of fire-worke to set the ship on fire, and goe our wayes: therefore, sayd he, I will haue you the Captaines, Masters, and Pilotes, to set your hands vnto that, for I sweare by the king that I will hang them, Diego Flores de Valdes answered, I nor the Captaines, Masters, and Pilotes wil not set our hands to that, for hee said, if he had bin prisoner as we were, he would haue done the like himselfe. He counselled him to keepe vs fast in prison, till he came into Spaine, and then send vs to the Contratation house in Siuil, where, if we had deserued death the law would passe on vs, for hee would not haue it said that in such a fleet as that was, sixe men and a boy should take the pinnesse, and goe away, and so he returned to his ship againe.

When he was gone, the Generall came to the maine mast to vs, and swore by the king, that we should not come out of the stocks til we came into Spaine: within 16. dayes after we came ouer the Bar of S. Lucar, and came vp to the Hurcados, then he put vs into a pinnesse in the stocks, and sent vs prisoners to the Contratation house in Siuil. From thence after one yere we brake prison, on S. Steuens day at night, 7. of our company escaped, Robert Barret, I Iob Hortop, Iohn Emerie, Humphrey Roberts, and Iohn Gilbert were taken, and brought backe to the contratation house, where we remained in the stocks till twelfe tide was past. Then our keeper put vp a petition to the Iudge of the contratation house, that we might be sent to the great prison house in Siuil, for that we broke prison, whereupon we were presently led thither, where we remained one moneth, and from thence to the castell of the Inquisition house in Triana, where wee continued one yere: which expired, they brought vs out in procession, euery one of vs hauing a candle in his hand, and the coate with S. Andrewes crosse on our backs: they brought vs vp on an high scaffold, that was set vp in the place of S. Francis, which is in the chiefe street of Siuill: there they set vs downe vpon benches: euery one in his degree, and against vs on another scaffold sate all the Iudges, and the Clergy on their benches: the people wondered, and gazed on vs, some pittying our cases, others said, burne those heretikes.

Robert Barret and Iohn Gilbert burned. When we had sit there two houres, we had a sermon made to vs: after which one called Bresinia, secretarie to the Inquisition, went vp into the pulpit with the processe, and called Robert Barret and Iohn Gilbert, whom two familiars of the

Inquisition brought from the scaffold before the Iudges, where the secretarie read the sentence, which was that they should be burnt, and so they returned to the scaffold, and were burnt.

Job Hortop his condemnation. Then I Job Hortop, and Iohn Bone were called, and brought to the place, as before, where we heard our sentence, which was, that we should go to the Gallies, and there row at the oares ende ten yeeres, and then to be brought backe to the Inquisition house, to haue the coate with S. Andrewes crosse put on our backs, and from thence to goe to the euerlasting prison remedilesse, and so we were returned from the scaffold from whence we came. Thomas Marks, and Thomas Ellis were called, and had sentence to serue in the Galleys eight yeeres, and Humphrey Roberts, and Iohn Emery to serue fiue yeeres, and so were returned to the benches on the scaffold, where we sate till foure of clocke in the afternoone. Then we were led againe to the Inquisition house, from whence we were brought. The next day in the morning Bresinia the treasurer came thither to vs, and deliuered to euery one of vs his sentence in writing. I with the rest were sent to the Gallies, where we were chained foure and foure together: euery mans daily allowance was 26 ounces of course blacke bisket and water, our clothing for the whole yeere two shirts, two paire of breeches of course canuas, a red coat of course cloth, soone on, and soone off, and a gowne of haire with a friers hood: our lodging was on the bare boords, and banks of the Gallies, our heads and beards were shauen euery month, hunger, thirst, cold, and stripes we lacked none, til our seueral times expired. And after the time of 12. yeeres, for I serued two yeeres aboue my sentence, I was sent backe to the Inquisition House in Siuill, and there hauing put on the coat with S. Andrewes crosse, I was sent to the euerlasting prison remedilesse, where I wore the coat 4. yeeres, and then vpon great suit, I had it taken off for 50 duckets, which Hernando de Soria treasurer of the kings mint lent me, whom I serued for it as a drudge 7. yeres, and vntil the moneth of October last, 1590. and then I came from Siuill to S. Lucar, where I made meanes to come away in a flie-boat, that was laden with wines and salt, which were Flemings goods, the king of Spaines subiects, dwelling in Siuil, maried to Spanish women, and sworne to their king. In this moneth of October last departing from S. Lucar, at sea, off the southermost Cape, we met an English ship, called the Galeon Dudley, who took the Flemming, and me out of him, and brought me to Portsmouth, where they set me on land, the 2. day of December last past, 1590. From thence I was sent by M. Muns the lieutenant of Portsmouth, with letters to the R. honourable the Earle of Sussex, who commanded his secretary to take my name and examination, how long I had bene out of England, and with whom I went, which he did. And on Christmas euen I took my leaue of his honour, and came to Redriffe.

The Computation of my imprisonment.

I suffered imprisonment in Mexico two yeeres.

In the Contratation house in Siuill one yeere.

In the Inquisition house in Triana one yeere.

I was in the Gallies twelue yeeres.

In the euerlasting prison remediles, with the coat with S. Andrews crosse on my back 4. yeres.

And at libertie I serued as a drudge Hemando de Soria 3. yeeres, which is the full complement of 23. yeeres.

Since my departure from England, vntill this time of my returne, I was fiue times in great danger of death, besides the many perils I was in, in the Gallies.

First in the Port of Saint John de Vllua, where being on shore, with many other of our company, which were all slaine sauing I, and two other that by swimming got aboord the Jesus of Lubek.

Secondly, when we were robbed by the wild Indians.

Thirdly, after we came to Mexico, the vice roy would haue hanged vs.

Fourthly, because he could not haue his mind to hang vs, he would haue burnt vs.

Fiftly, the Generall that brought vs into Spaine, would haue hanged vs at sea.

Thus hauing truely set downe vnto you my trauels, misery and dangers, endured the space of 23. yeeres, I ende.

A relation of the Hauen of Tecuanapa, a most conuenient place for building of ships, situate vpon the South sea not farre from Nicaragua, which was sent vnto the viceroy of Mexico or to the king of Spaine: wherein are described the riuers of Ometepec, Tlacamama, and Tlacolula falling into the said Hauen, with the townes, people, and mountaines adioyning to the said riuers, and other things fit for the building and victualling of ships.

The Port and small harbour of Tecuanapa hath in the driest time of Sommer in the chanell little lesse then one fathome at low water, and at full sea one fathome and an halfe: in the time of raine, with the increasing of the land-water it hath three fathoms and more. It lyeth toward the West, and there the Bishopricks of Guaxacan and Tlarcali are separated. From hence toward the point called Punta de Intla and Dordaci there is a Bay 2. leagues distant, which though it be no special harbour, yet vpon an extremity ships may come and ride there, as in times past they haue done. This Bay on the right hand toward the North maketh a lake somewhat large towards the midst of the chanell, and in some parts deepe, but specially on the side of Cuahintla, but on either side it is but shallow. As you passe betweene the sea and certaine great and large woods of orenge trees, and trees of other nature which grow along the sea coast, which are of no great bredth, al the countrey appeareth very open: howbeit on the side of Cuahintla the mountaines haue many creeks and a small lake called Tulaningo, and the countrey cannot be trauelled, except you take the way betweene the sea and the end of this lake, which may be about two leagues of sandy way. And on the North side there is another small creeke. And going by the sands side one quarter of a league, you come to the way that leadeth vnto Quacapotla a mansion of Intla.

The riuer of Ometepec being the principal riuer which commeth to this hauen hath his head in the mountaines of Xicayan de Touer about 24 leagues from this hauen from diuers brooks which come out of the mountaines of Cacatepec, and beneath a towne called Suchistlahuaca litle more then 3. leagues all the brooks ioyne together: and from that place you may passe downe to the sea with Canoas and Lighters; and you might come farther but for the fall of a furious streame or current which runeth between two great rocks, passing from Cocahulapa a mansion of Ometepec vnto Yanguitle a mansion of the said Ometepec. These inconueniences being past (which in my iudement may be about one league) the Riuer is more nauigable, so that you may sayle in the same about 12. leagues. During the space of which 12 leagues, about a league and a halfe distance from the waters side, and in many other parts of the same riuer it hath great quantitie of woods which vse to grow in hot soiles, fit for ship-timber, as Huber-trees, and Suchicuhitil, whereof they of Nicaragua make great profit. Also there be white okes and Tehegurtes in great quantitie, and many other kinds of timber: and in the mountaines there be firre-trees, okes, and cork-trees, which easily may bee caried downe the riuer, because they may be cut some 2, 3, 4, and 5. leagues from the riuer, and may be brought downe to the waters side with the seruice and helpe of those that dwell in the townes thereabout.

At the head of these brooks where the riuer beginneth is the towne which is called Xicaian, belonging to the heires of Francis de Touer y de Guillen, containing about 350 Indians of rude speech and of little policie, being 24. leagues from the sea, little more or lesse. The place it selfe is hot, although the mountaines round about be cold.

Aionapa. A little from this is the towne of Aioanapa possessed by the heires of Perez Gomez, hauing in it about 300. Indians of the selfe same speach and qualitie. The countrey is more subiect to heate then cold; yet hath it neere it cold countrey and mountaines. It is distant from Xicaian de Touer 4. leagues, and from the sea 20. leagues.

Sixe leagues downeward toward the South is the towne of Suchistlahuaca on the said riuer, and the inhabitants are of the same speach and qualities. The countrey is more subiect to heate then cold. It is in the charge of Gonzaluo Fernandez a citizen of Mexico, and hath about 150. Indians, and is 15. leagues distant from the sea.

From this towne vnto the towne of Ometepec are 6 leagues. The place is very hot, and in the same gouernment, and is situate betweene certaine hils one league from the riuer: he and his followers haue vnder them about 700. Indians, which speake the Ayacastecan, Amusgan, and Niciecan tongues, and this place is from the sea nine leagues.

From this towne vnto Ihualapa are two great leagues: it is in the gouernment of the heires of Laurence de Castro, of the foresaid temperature, and the people vse the said language, and are of the like stature: and it standeth three leagues from the riuer, and from the sea ten leagues.

These are the best townes, and of the best traffique that are vpon all this coast. The Indians are rich in Cacao and victuals, and in these townes doe the Indians of Niciecan principally trade. And in the towns of Ihualapa the chiefe Aguazil of the prouince is resident for the most part of the yeere.

More lowe beneath the riuer of Tlacolula, about a league or a league and an halfe from the towne of Ometepec is the towne called Pio, which was wont to be a towne of Tlacolula, and was a frontier towne against the Mexicans. There be in it about 50. Indians of the ancient inhabitants: one Grauiel de Chiauez a citizen of Mexico hath the gouernement thereof: it is 4. leagues from Ihualapa, and 6. from the sea.

A little below this is the towne of Huehuatlan in the selfe same gouernement standing one league from the riuer on certaine high hils: it hath 10. Indians, and is from the sea 5. leagues.

And one league from this towne stands the towne of Cuahacapotla a mansion of Antla or Intla: it hath to the number of 15. Indians; it standeth one league and a halfe from the riuer, and 4. leagues, from the mouth thereof.

At the fountaines or heads of the rest of the brooks is the towne of Cacatepec being in the gouernment of Raphael de Treyo: he and his tenants haue vnder them some 700. Indians of Niciecan: it is from the sea some 22. leagues.

The riuer which is called Tlacamama commeth from the mountains of Atoyaque and Amusgos, which are some 17. leagues from the sea. There it maketh a formed riuer, so big, that it is nauigable to the sea with canoas and lighters: I say from a litle below Tolistlahuaca a mansion of Xicaian. It is nauigable 8 moneths in the yeere, and the other 4. not, because that the sands of the plaines do soke and drink vp the water in such wise, that there remaineth so little, that there is no passage: howbeit in small lighters timber may bee brought downe this riuer one league from the place where it is cut, vnto the place that I haue spoken of; whereas bigger vessels may bee made; for nigh vnto that place other brooks and running waters doe ioyne and meet, which make it a maine riuer. It hath nigh vnto it in the mountaines of Atoyaque, Cacatepec, and Amusgos many woods of pine-trees, cork-trees, and okes of great bignesse: and beneath those mountaines in the warme countrey, neere vnto the riuers there is much timber of those sorts which I mentioned before to be about the riuer of Ometepec, which may easily be cut and carried downe vnto Tecuanapa in the time before specified.

This riuer hath likewise townes adioyning to it; the first at the foote of the mountaines is the town of Atoiaque belonging to the king, and to the heires of Pronetto: their language is Niciecan, the countrey hot, the people politique, and it is from the sea 15. leagues. It hath about 200. Indians.

One league from this towne, and 14. from the sea is the towne of Xicaian belonging likewise to the king, and to the heires of Pronetto. They are Niciecan people and very comely, and in a hot countrey. It hath by account 300. Indians. There are resident in it the Vicar and Iustice; it is from the riuer a league and a halfe.

A league from this towne, and 14. from the sea is situate the mansion of Pinotespan subiect to Tututepec, which hath with the manors subject vnto it 500. Indians.

Two leagues from the towne, and one from Xicayan, and 13. from Tecuanapa, and 3. from the riuer is the towne of Tlacamama: the people are very comely, and politique. It containeth some 100. Indians, and belongeth to the king.

More toward the South 5. leagues from the riuer, and two from this towne, and 14. from the sea is the towne called Pinotespan del Rey: They are handsome people, but of slow speach: this towne conteineth about 100. Indians like the former. They be wealthie, because they make great quantitie of salte; for they haue a lake in which salte groweth vnder the water, (a thing repugnant to nature, that two contraries doe grow and are conserued together) whereout they take it in breaking it with stones vpon the ground vnder the water.

It hath also the towne of Amusgos, which is in the gouernment of Fernando de Auila, which may be from Tecuanapa 18. leagues. They speake the Amusgan tongue. The countrey is hotte: it standeth on the highway from Nicieca: it hath 400. Indians, few more or lesse.

These are all the townes of account situate neere this riuer.

Neere vpon this riuer are two farmes, the one belonging to Pedro Brauo, and the other to him that maketh this relation vnto your Excellencie, which may be from the sea some 8. or 9. leagues all plaine ground. And in this territorie there is but one towne called Quesala situate vpon the riuer, and 6. leagues from the sea; which in times past hath beene a great towne, and now hath but three Indians onely, and it is from the farmes 3. leagues.

The mansion house of Don Mattheo is more toward the South, standing in a mountainous and waste countrey, which aboundeth with cattell being 3. leagues from the riuer; and as farre from Tecuanapa, as from the place where all the cattel is; and the sea that way is from it but one league.

A little below this mansion about 4. leagues, and 7. leagues from the sea, is a garden of Alonso Pedraza which beareth Cacao.

And 2. leagues from this garden, and 6. leagues from the sea standeth the towne of Cuahintlan belonging to the king a towne of 19 housholds, but very rich, for they gather much Cacao and the best in that countrey. They speake the Tlapanecan tongue. This towne hath the sea that way within halfe a league.

Huatulco or Guatulco in 15. deg and 50. minutes. And this coast from Cuahintlan to Tecuanapa, and the coast which runneth to Huatulco is a coast of much pearle, for in olde time the Indians gathered much pearle there.

And 2 leagues from Cuahintlan and 4. from Tecuanapa is a garden of Cacao in the landes of Francisco Maldonado, which is called Cacahu-Atoyaque.

These are the things worthy of relation from the head springs of this riuer of Tlacamama vnto the sea: and this foresaid riuer entreth into the riuer of Ometepec 5. leagues from Tecuanapa.

The riuer of Tlacolula springeth within the boundes of Chilsiztlahuaca subiect to Comastlahuaca a towne of Suchistlahuaca, neere which are many mountaines. This riuer is nauigable little more then 2. leagues before it entreth into the riuer of Ometepec, where it is 5. leagues from the sea.

Hard by it is the towne of Tlacolula abouenamed; and 3. leagues from it is the towne of Azoyoque an olde manour of Tlapa. The towne of Chilsiztlahuaca hath but 3. Indians; and the towne of Azoyoque hath more then 300. Indians. But because in this hauen must bee the building of ships, the prouince of Talpa and Tututepec may stand them in great stead; the prouince of Tututepec being neighbour to the riuer of Tlacamama, and the prouince of Tlapa to the riuer of Tlacolula. For they may, as I haue sayd, carrie the timber in lighters or rafts downe the riuers, and may vse the Indians in the townes thereabout to fell and draw the same out of the cold mountaines; for in the warm countreys the most is plaine ground, whereas with very fewe men and oxen it may be brought vnto the place where it should be imbarqued.

There may come flat bottomes, and canoas vnto the townes thereabout, and lade themselues with victuals: For they haue already come by that riuer to the rode of Ometepec, and made there prouision at the mansion of Don Mattheo, and at the farmes, at that time when his Maiestie did people the plaines which are betweene these riuers, conteining a large and voyde countrey sufficient for the erecting of 20. manours, being a countrey well furnished with water and pasture without any danger or perill, according to the description hereunto annexed.

This small harbour of Tecuanapa being seene and viewed, seemeth very commodious to build shippes in, by reason of the great abundance of mountaines full of good timber for that purpose, with the commodities of riuers, and with the seruice and victuals from the townes thereabout, which be very good for coast townes.

The desire of him that made this relations, hath bene with zeale to serue your excellencie; who therewithall desireth the Lord God to giue the successe.

CERTAINE VOYAGES

NAVIGATIONS AND TRAFFIQUES BOTH ANCIENT AND OF LATE, TO DIUERS PLACES VPON THE COAST OF BRASIL: TOGETHER WITH A RUTTIER FOR ALL THAT COAST, AND TWO INTERCEPTED LETTERS WHICH REUEALE MANY SECRETS OF THE STATE OF THAT COUNTREY: THE REST OF OUR VOYAGES TO BRASIL WHICH HAUE BENE EITHER INTENDED OR PERFORMED TO THE RIUER OF PLATE, THE STREIGHT OF MAGELLAN, THE SOUTH SEA, OR FARTHER THAT WAY, BEING RESERUED FOR THE GENERALL HEADES NEXT INSUING.[21]

[21] The Voyages of circumnavigation by the Straits of Magellan will be found in Vol. XV of this Edition.

A briefe relation of two sundry voyages made by the worshipful M. William Haukins of Plimmouth, father to Sir Iohn Haukins knight, late Treasurer of her Majesties Nauie, in the yeere 1530 and 1532.

Olde M. William Haukins of Plimmouth, a man for his wisedome, valure, experience, and skill in sea causes much esteemed, and beloued of K. Henry the 8, and being one of the principall Sea-captaines in the West parts of England in his time, not contented with the short voyages commonly then made onely to the knowne coasts of Europe, armed out a tall and goodly shippe of his owne of the burthen of 250 tunnes called the Paule of Plimmouth, wherewith he made three long and famous voyages vnto the coast of Brasil, a thing in those dayes very rare, especially to our Nation. In the course of which voyages he touched at the riuer of Sestos vpon the coast of Guinea, where hee traffiqued with the Negros, and tooke of them Elephants teeth, and other commodities which that place yeeldeth: and so arriuing on the coast of Brasil, he vsed there such discretion, and behaued himselfe so wisely with those sauage people, that he grew into great familiarity and friendship with them. A king of Brasil brought into England. Insomuch that in his second voyage, one of the sauage kings of the countrey of Brasil, was contented to take ship with him, and to be transported hither into England: whereunto M. Haukins agreed, leauing behinde in the Countrey as a pledge for his saftie and returne againe, one Martin Cockeram of Plimmouth. This Brasilian king being arriued, was brought vp to London and presented to K. Henry the 8, lying as then at White-hall: at the sight of whom the King and all the Nobilitie did not a litle maruaile, and not without cause: for in his cheekes were holes made according to their sauage maner, and therein smalle bones were planted, standing an inch out from the said holes, which in his owne Countrey was reputed for a great brauerie. He had also another hole in his nether lip wherein was set a precious stone about the bignes of a pease: All his apparel, behauiour, and gesture, were very strange to the beholders.

Hauing remained here the space almost of a whole yeere, and the king with his sight fully satisfied, M. Hawkins according to his promise and appointment, purposed to conuey him againe into his countrey: but it fell out in the way, that by change of aire and alteration of diet, the said Sauage King died at sea, which was feared would turn to the losse of the life of Martin Cockeram his pledge. Neuerthelesse, the Sauages being fully perswaded of the honest dealing of our men with their prince, restored againe the said pledge, without any harme to him, or any man of the company: which pledge of theirs they brought home againe into England, with their ship fraighted, and furnished with the commodities of the countrey. Which Martin Cockeram, by the witnesse of Sir Iohn Hawkins, being an officer in the towne of Plimmouth, was liuing within these fewe yeeres.[22]

[22] This Martin Cockeram is introduced by Kingsley in Chapter XXX of "Westward Ho!" Indeed the principal incidents of that novel are nothing but extracts from Hakluyt's Collection; in many passages, the only difference being the use of modern phraseology.

An ancient voyage of M. Robert Reniger and M. Thomas Borey to Brasil in the yeere of our Lord 1540.

I Haue bene certainly informed by M. Anthony Garrard an ancient and worshipfull marchant of the citie of London, that this commodious and gainefull voyage to Brasil was ordinarily and vsually frequented by M. Robert Reniger, M. Thomas Borey, and diuers other substantial and wealthy merchants of Southampton, about 60. yeeres past, that is to say in the yeere 1540.

A voyage of one Pudsey to Baya in Brasil anno 1542.

A fort built in Brasil by the English. Also the worshipfull M. Edward Cotton of Southampton Esquire gaue mee more particularly to vnderstand, how that one Pudsey of Southampton, a man of good skill and resolution in marine causes, made a voyage in like maner 62. yeeres agoe to Baya de todos los Santos the principall towne of all Brasil, and the seate of the Portugal vice-roy and of the bishop, and that he built a fort not farre distant from that place in the foresaid yeere 1542. [23]

[23] If the voyage of Pudsey took place 62 years before Hakluyt published his third volume, the date of it must have been 1538, not 1542.

A letter written to M. Richard Staper by Iohn Whithal from Santos in Brasil, the 26. of Iune 1578.

Worshipfull sir, and welbeloued friend M. Staper, I haue me most heartily commended vnto you, wishing your health euen as mine owne.

These few words may bee to let you vnderstand, that whereas I wrote vnto you not many dayes past by the way of Lisbon, howe that I determined to bee with you very shortly, it is in this countrey offered mee to marry, and to take my choice of three or foure: so that I am about three dayes agoe consorted with an Italian gentleman to marry with his daughter within these foure dayes. This my friend and father in law Signor Ioffo Dore is borne in the citie of Geneua in Italy: [24] his kindred is well knowen amongst the Italians in London: also hee hath but onely this childe which is his daughter, which hee hath thought better bestowed vpon mee then on any Portugal in all the countrey, and doeth giue with her in marriage to me part of an Ingenio which he hath, that doeth make euery yeere a thousand roues of sugar. This my mariage will be worth to me two thousand duckets, little more or lesse. Also Signor Ioffo Dore my father in law doeth intende to put into my handes the whole Ingenio with sixtie or seuentie slaues, and thereof to make me factor for vs both. I giue my liuing Lord thankes for placing me in such honour and plentifulnesse of all things.

[24] Of course this it intended for Genoa.

Also certaine dayes past I talked with the Prouedor and the Captaine, and they haue certified me, that they haue discouered certaine Mines of siluer and gold, and looke euery day for Masters to come to open the said Mines: which when they be opened will inrich this countrey very much. Mines of gold and siluer newly discouered at S. Vincent. This place is called S. Vincent, and is distant from you two thousand leagues, and in 24. degrees of latitude on the South side of the Equinoctial line, and almost vnder the Tropike of Capricorne. A countrey it is very healthful without sicknesse.

Moreouer, I haue talked with the Captaine and Prouedor, and my father in law, who rule all this countrey, for to haue a ship with goods to come from London hither, which haue promised mee to giue mee licence, saying that nowe I am free denizen of this countrey. To cause a ship to come hither with such commodities as would serue this countrey, would come to great gaines, God sending in safety the profite and gaines. In such wares and commodities as you may ship hither from London is for euery one commoditie deliuered here three for one, and then after the proceed may be imployed in white sugar at foure hundred reis the roue.

The voyage to S. Vincent worth three for one outward only. I meane also to haue a friend in London to send mee a ship of 60. or 70. tunnes, little more or lesse, with such commodities as I shall giue aduise for. This voyage is as good as any Peru-voyage. If you and Master Osborne will deale here, I will deale with you before any other, because of our old friendly friendship in time past. If you haue any stomacke thereto, in the name of God do you espie out a fine barke of seuentie or eightie tunnes, and send her hither with a Portugall Pilot to this port of S. Vincent in Brasil, bordering vpon the borders of Peru.

Also I herewith write vnto you in what forme and maner you shall furnish this voyage both in commodities and otherwise.

In what maner a voyage to S. Vincent with a ship of 70. or 80. tunnes is to be made. First you must lade in the said ship certaine Hampshire and Deuonshire karsies: for the which you must let her depart from London in October, and to touch in the Canaries, and there to make sale of the saide karsies, and with the proceed thereof to lade fifteene tunnes of wines that be perfect and good, and six dozen of Cordouan skinnes of these colours, to wit, orenge, tawnie, yellow, red, and very fine black. I thinke you shall not finde such colours there. Therefore you must cause them that shall goe vpon this voyage, to take saffron with them, to cause the same skinnes to bee put into the saide colours. Also I thinke you shall finde oyles there. Three hogsheads of sweete oyle for this voyage are very necessary, or a hundred and fiftie iarres of oyle. Also in London you may lade in the said ship these parcels of commodities or wares, as followeth:

In primis, Foure peeces of hollands of middle sort.

Item, One peece of fine holland.

Foure hundred elles of osenbriges very fine.

Foure dozen of sizzors of all sorts.

Sixteene kintals of pitch of the Canaries.

Twentie dozen of great kniues which be made in fardles, of a low price.

Foure dozen of a small sort.

Sixe peeces of bayes of the lowest sort.

One very fine peece of bayes.

Four hundred elles of Manchester-cottons, most blacke, greene, some yellow.

Eight or tenne dozen of hats, the one halfe trimmed with taffata, the other plaine with the bands of Cypresse.

Sixe dozen of course shirts.

Three dozen of doublets of canuas.

Three dozen of doublets of stiched canuas.

One piece of fine Millan fustian barred.

Sixe dozen of locks for doores and chests.

Sixe thousand of all maner of fish hooks

Four dozen reames of paper.

Two dozen of glasses of diuers sorts.

Two dozen of Venice glasses, the one halfe great, the other middle sort.

Two dozen of mantles of frize, of the lowest price that can be.

Three dozen of frize gownes.

Foure hundred pound of tinne of the vse of Portugall, most smal dishes and trenchers.

Foure pound of silke of all colours.

Twentie pound of spices, cloues, cinamon, pepper, and saffron.

Two kintals of white sope.

Three pound of threed, white, black, and blew.

Three pound of fine white threed.

Item, halfe a dozen of Northerne karsies of diuers colours.

Foure sorting clothes, blew, red, yellow, and green.

Sixe Northerne dozens of diuers colours.

One fine blew cloth of eight pound.

One fine stamell of tenne or twelue pound.

One fine sheeps coloured cloth of twelue pound.

One fine blacke karsie. One fine stamell karsie.

Sixe yards of blacke veluet.

Three barrels of nailes for chests.

Two barrels of nailes for ships and barks.

Sixe kintals of Occom.

Two dozen of veluet girdles without hangers.

Foure yards of taffata red, blacke, and blew, with some greene.

Two dozen of leather girdles.

Sixe dozen of axes, hatches, and small billes to cut wood.

Foure mases of gitterne strings.

Foure hundred or fiue hundreds elles of some linnen cloth that is of a low price to make shirts and sheets.

Foure tunne of yron.

These be such sort of wares as I would you should send. If you meane to deale, or send any ship hither, haue you no doubt, but by the helpe of God I shall put all things in good order according to your contentment and profit: for my father in lawe with the Captaine and Prouedor doe rule this countrey.

My father in law and I shal (God willing) make a good quantitie of sugar euery yeere, which sugar we intend to ship for London from henceforth, if we can get such a trustie and good friend as you to deale with vs in this matter. I pray you presently after the receit of this my letter to write mee answere thereof and send your letter to M. Holder to Lisbone, and he wil conuey it to me out of hand.

Besides the premisses send sixe yards of skarlet, parchment lace of diuers colours.

Sixe yards of crimosin veluet.

Sixe yards of crimosin satten.

Twelue yards of fine puke blacke.

Here in this countrey in stead of Iohn Whithall they haue called me Iohn Leitoan: so that they haue vsed this name so long time, that at this present there is no remedie but it must remaine so. When you write vnto me, let the superscription be vnto Iohn Leitoan.

Thus I commit you with all yours to the holy Ghost for euer.

If you send this ship, I would haue you giue order that she touch in no part of the coast of Guinie nor any other coast, but to come directly hither to the port of S. Vincent, and from the Canaries let her be dispatched in my name, to wit, Iohn Leitoan.

Also a dozen shirts for my wearing let be sent, if you send the ship.

Item, sixe or eight pieces of sayes for mantles for women, which is the most necessary thing that can be sent.

By your assured friend Iohn Whithall.

A copie of the letters of the Aduenturers for Brasill sent to Iohn Whithall dwelling in Santos, by the Minion of London, Anno 1580. the 24. of October in London.

Master Whithall, as vnacquainted wee commend vs vnto you, etc. vnderstanding by your friends, M. Iohn Bird, M. Robert Walkaden, and your brother Iames Whithall of certaine letters that they haue receiued of yours from Santos, which wee haue seene and read, wherein from time to time you doe require, and desire them to send a good ship to Santos, with such wares and commodities as you did write for, whereby you did not onely promise that they should haue good intertainment, but also should sell the saide commodities to make three of one outward at the least in euery thing, and that for to relade their ship backe, they should haue of the best, finest, and whitest drie sugars 32. pound of our weight for a ducket at the most. The premises considered, with the great credit that they and we doe giue to your writing and promise, haue caused vs, whose names be hereunder written, to ioyne our selues in company together, and to be at great charges purposely to send this good ship the Minion of London, not onely with such marchandizes as you wrote for, but also with as many other things as we thought might any wayes pleasure you, or profit the country.

And we craue of you, that we and our factors may haue so much credite of you, as we haue in you and of your letters, which is to beleeue vs that we haue taken this voyage vpon vs, with no other minde or purpose, then to deale faithfully and truely in the trade by sea and land, so as you shall not onely haue cause to reioyce, and deserue thanks for our comming, but also you wil procure the magistrates there to be bound, as they vse in Galicia, that we may be preserued and defended from all reprisals and imbargements of princes or subiects for any causes or matters whatsoeuer, whereby wee may bee incouraged by them, giuing vs this securitie of good intertainment, to continue the trade yeerely henceforth: and for our parts we promise upon our credits and fidelities, to commit no outrage at the sea nor land, nor suffer any to be done in our company that we may let, but rather to defend and protect all other such peaceable marchants as we are, with their ships and goods.

And to the ende that you and others shall know that wee meane as we say, we haue giuen order to our factors to giue you good hostages for your assurance of our good fidelities: and further we haue sent a testimoniall of our owne true meaning in writing vnder the seales of this honourable Citie of London, which we wil not discredite by our behauiours for all the treasure that you haue: and so we haue written to your magistrates of your port, and others in Spanish, the copy whereof we send you herewith enclosed in English. And if the time should fal out so contrary to our expectations, that there should not be fine white sugar sufficient to lade our ship in due time at Santos, then we pray you direct our factours where they may goe with the shippe in safetie to supply their want, and helpe them to a good sure Pilot for that purpose, and write your letters to your friends where the best sugar is made in their fauors, and helpe our factours to haue a testimoniall from Santos, that they and you traded together friendly, and so departed in good and perfect amitie, and shew them that the iust cause of our comming is to trade as marchants peaceably, and not as Pirates to commit any offence to one or other.

Also we pray you, if there be any store of waxe, or salt-peeter, whereby the price there may yeeld vs as much profit as the white sugars at a ducket the roue, or any other commodity of like profite, then to procure that we may lade it without danger of lawe, be it oare of golde or siluer or whatsoeuer else.

We haue sent you copper cauldrons for your Ingenios, with iron and all other necessaries for your purpose, and artificers to set the same: and as wee haue at your request bene at great charges in sending these men, so we pray you let vs haue lawful fauour in like courtesie to further all our causes. And if any of our Mariners or passengers in any respect of displeasure against their company, or in hope of preferment of mariage or otherwise would procure to tary and dwell there, and leaue his charge and office, that then you will bee a meane to the Iustice that such fugitives should be sent abord the ship as prisoners: for as you know, without our men wee cannot bring home our ship.

Wee haue giuen order to our factours to vse your counsell and helpe in their affaires, and to gratifie you for the same as to your courtesie and faithfull friendship shall appertaine to your good liking: and in the meane time for a token of our good willes towards you, we haue sent you a fieldbed of walnut tree, with the canopy, valens, curtaines, and gilt knops. And if there be any commoditie else that may pleasure you or your friends, wee haue giuen order that they shall haue the refusing of it before any other, giuing for it as it is worth.

And thus to conclude, promising to performe all the foresaide things on our parts in euery condition, we commit you to God, who euer preserue you with all his blessings.

Your louing friends: Christopher Hodsdon.[25], Anthonie Garrard, Thomas Bramlie, Iohn Bird, William Elkin.

[25] For a very curious account of the family of "Hodsdon" or "Hudson," consult the "Life of Henry Hudson" in the publications of the Clarendon Historical Society for 1883.

Certaine notes of the voyage to Brasil with the Minion of London aforesaid, in the yere 1580. written by Thomas Grigs Purser of the said ship.

The thirde day of Nouember in the yeere abouesaid we departed in the Minion of London from Harwich, from which time no great thing worth the knowledge or regard of others happened vntil the 22. of December the next moneth, which day for our owne learning and vse wee obserued the setting of the Sunne, which was West southwest, we then being vnder the line Equinoctiall, where we found the aire very temperate, and the winde for the most part Southeast and East southeast. The same day we also obserued the rising of the moone, being one day after the full, which rose at East northeast.——

The first land that wee fell with vpon the coast of Brasill was the yland of S. Sebastian, where we arriued the 14. day of Ianuary in the yeere 1581.[26]

[26] South West of Rio de Janeiro.

The 16. day Thomas Babington, and others in our pinnesse, went a shoare to Guaybea, where they met with Iohn Whithall his father and mother in lawe, who hauing receiued letters from thence to be deliuered at Santos, came abord, and then we weyed and set saile, and the 28. day wee arriued at the yland of Santa Catelina, neere the entrance of Santos.

Our course from S. Sebastian was Southwest and by West, and betwixt the Southwest and by West, and West southwest.

This yland of Santa Catelina seemeth at the first to be a part of the yland of Girybia. Wee ankered at nine fathome blacke osie ground.

Vpon the yland there grow many Palmito-trees, but no fresh water is there to be found.

The third day of February we arriued before the towne of Santos, and were there well received and intertained of the Captaine, the kings officers, and all the people.

The fourth day we tooke into our ship a beefe aliue, which for the victualling of the ship, and the refreshing of our men, and to make vs the merrier at Shrouetide.

The eight day we deliuered to M. Iohn Whithall a bedstead with the appurtenances, which were sent to him from our marchants of London.

The 18. day the captaine of Santos came abord our ship, by whom we had knowledge of foure great French ships of warre, that had bene at the riuer of Ienero, which there tooke three Canoas, but were driuen from thence by their castles and forts, and were looked for here at Santos. Whereupon the Captaine requested vs to lend them some armour and artillery, and we lent them twentie caliuers and two barrels of powder.

The yle of Alcatrarzas or Pelicanes. The 19. day our skiffe which we had sent to Alcatrarzas, and had bene away sixe dayes, came againe, and brought good store of great and good fish, and tolde vs that there was good store of fish to be taken there by the hooke, and as much wood as we would haue of the Palmito-tree.

The 20. day at night Nicholas Gale, one of our company, fell ouer our shippes side, and was drowned in the port of Santos before the towne, where our ship rode at anker.

The 22. day two of the Canoas which the Frenchmen tooke in the riuer of Ienero, returned to Santos, and reported that the foure French ships were past to the southwards, as they thought, for the Straights of Magellan, and so into the South sea.

The 23. day the aforesaid Nicholas Gale, who fell ouerboard two days before, was found againe, and taken vp three miles from our ship, and our company went to his buriall in the Church at Santos.

This day the Captaine and Iustices of Santos wished vs to tary in their road till the last of April, for they had sent a barke of Santos to Baya at the kings charges, to know whether we should haue trade there or no, and this barke could not returne before that time.

About this time there arriued at Fernambuck [27] a shippe from Portugall, which brought newes that the Islands, Indies, and Portugall it selfe was molested and troubled by the Spaniards, and that the Portugales had both English and Frenchmen to Lisbone to defend them against Spaine.

[27] Pernambuco.

The 25. day wee sent two of our men, namely Thomas Michael and Simon Thorne to Baya in a barke that went thither from Santos.

The two and twentie day of April our Master and Thomas Babington hauing some talke and conference with the Padres of Santos, they (our men being ready to go to the Riuer of Ienero) tolde them, that they were sorry for our banishment from the Church, and that the Ministrador had written from Rio de Ienero, that forasmuch as these twentie yeres or more the English nation had denied the Church of Rome and her proceedings, therefore the Ministrador commanded that none of vs should come to their Church: the Padres willed vs herein to haue patience, and to take it in good part, and promised to stand our friends in their word and writing, both to the Ministrador and to the bishop at Baya, and further requested all our English company to haue no ill opinion of them.

The 28. of April we laded sugars into our ship.

The 21. of May we tooke in fresh victuals from Santos.

The 10. day of Iune we gratified one Iosto Thorno, dwelling in Santos, with some of our English victuals, and intertained him in good sort in our ship, and this day wee were promised to haue a Pilot at Santos to cary vs to Baya.

Leaks in the Minion made by wormes. The 11. day we went to fish, to make prouision for our ship and men, and from that time til the eighteenth day wee fet water, and cut wood for our fire, and trimmed our ship of the harmes and leakes which the wormes had made in her while wee ridde at the yland of S. Sebastian, and in the meane time we departed from before the towne of Santos. Our Master sent his skiffe from the barre of Santos, thinking to haue brought Thomas Babington and William Euet with the

Pilot, which wee had tarried for three dayes: and as the skiffe was going, William Euet being by the Riuers side, called to our pinnesse, and sent a letter to our Master, Whose name was Stephen Hare. which Thomas Babington had written, wherein were no newes, but that the Ministrador was arriued at Santos from the Riuer of Ienero, and would speake with our Master, but he willed that whatsoeuer Thomas Babington did write, no credit should be giuen to it. And further he wished vs presently to depart for Sant Sebastian, and there to dispatch our businesse, and then to sende backe for Babington and himselfe to Guaybea, where he (if he were well) would giue his attendance to come abord.

Their departure from Santos. As we rid two leagues a sea-bord the barre of Santos, wee broke a cable in the open sea, which happened the 15. day of this moneth.

We arriued at S. Sebastian the 15. day, and there shifted our balast, and had in stones, and halled our ship a ground to stop our leakes, and caried our casks a shoare to be hooped for water, which indeed might better haue bene done in Santos, before the Ministrador came thither: yet we finished all things pertaining to our ship, by the 22 of this moneth, at S. Sebastian.

The first day of Iuly Thomas Babington came abord with William Euet, in our pinnesse, and the rest of our men that went for them: but there was no Pilot brought according to promise to cary vs to Baya.

The things that we obserued and noted in the time of our being at Santos, were these.

All such wares and marchandizes as owe no custome in Brasill, their vse is, to set a price vpon the same, how they shalbe sold: which is done by the magistrates of the towne, according to the ordinances of their King.

But for all such marchandizes as do owe custome there, the marchants are to sell them according as they may, to the greatest profit and aduantage that they can.

Concerning the prouince of Peru, wee learned that one part of it by land and water is but twelue dayes iourney from the towne of Santos, and from thence it may be about foure or fiue dayes iourney by water to the maine riuer of Plate.[28]

From the head of the riuer of Plate, and from their chiefe townes there, they do trade and trafique by land into Peru by waggons, and horses or mules.

The said riuer of Plate is so full of sands and dangers, and the fresh so fierce sometimes, that no shipping dares to deale with it, small barks to their knowledge may go vp it, and not els.

The Portugales here cannot be suffered to vse their Mines of treasure in these parts, vpon paine of death, the contrary being commanded by the king and the Vice-roy, who is as their king in place of authoritie.

About twentie leagues from Santos there is a certaine kinde of wilde Sauages, lying in the mountaines, which are in friendship with the Portugales, and they haue continuall warres with certaine other Sauages that dwell towards the borders of Peru, which is distant from Santos about 400. or 500. leagues. Those Sauages of Peru haue store of gold and siluer, but they knowe not the vse of it.

Looke what Sauages of their enemies they take, they sell them to the Portugales for kniues, combes, axes or hatchets, and other trifles: they will sell one for a pennie-knife to a Portugal, and after two yeeres they are worth twentie or thirtie duckets to the Portugal.

This people haue also continuall warres with the Spaniards: and this was tolde vs by one of those Sauages, which hath dwelt among the Portugales these seuen yeeres, with his master called Sennor Manoel Veloso. And this fellowe would willingly haue come with vs for England.

[28] Paraguay is probably meant. The river of that name, which ultimately flows into the Sea as Rio de la Plata, is about 700 miles distant from Santos.

The yle of Alcatrarzas or Pelicanes dangerous for rocks. There are certaine rockes that lie off betweene the yle of Alcatrarzas and S. Sebastian, about two leagues, which are to be taken heed of, which a farre off in faire weather shewe like the sailes of ships.

There are other rocks that lie off S. Catelina also fiue leagues to the East and by south into the sea off the yland.

At our comming vp to Santos we found foure fadom and a halfe water in the shallowest place, and the like we found within a league after we were departed from S. Catelina, litle more or lesse, but after you haue runne in the depth of foure fadome and a halfe, about a mile or lesse, then you shall haue it deeper againe more and more.

Before the towne of Santos we rode in eight or tenne fadome water.

A letter of Francis Suares to his brother Diego Suares dwelling in Lisbon, written from the riuer of Ienero in Brasill in Iune 1596. concerning the exceeding rich trade newly begunne betweene that place and Peru, by the way of the Riuer of Plate, with small barks of 30. and 40. tunnes.

Sir, we set saile from Lisbon the fourth of April 1596. and arriued here in this riuer of Ienero the twentie seuenth of Iune next ensuing. And the same day the Visitadores did visit our ship with great ioy, thinking that those commodities which wee brought with vs, had bene for the marchants of this countrey: but it prooued to the contrary.

Wine solde at an excessiue rate. The pilot brought with him in the sayd shippe two pipes of wine which were taken from him, and solde by the Iustice for foure and twenty reals euery gallon. But I solde mine for two and thirty and sixe and thirty reals the gallon. If I had brought any great store of wine, I should haue made a great gaine of it: for I should haue gotten eight reals for one.

The next day in the morning we went all on shore, and gaue God thanks for our prosperous voyage, and good successe which he had sent vs. And because the gouernour of this countrey was gone from this Towne to another house of his, three leagues vp into the riuer beyond the place where we rode at anker, I desired the captaine of our shippe after dinner, that we might take the shippe boat, and goe to the place where the gouernour did lie. And so going vp the riuer, we met with a canoa which was comming downe the riuer, and going aboard our shippe; which canoa was laden with fresh victuals, and in the same was one Portugall, which met vs, and tolde vs that the gouernour of that captaine shippe had sent vs a present, which we receiued very thankefully, and sent it aboord. And we went vp the riuer, to the place where the gouernour did dwell; and comming to the place where we landed, hard by the riuers side, the gouernour came thither and receiued vs very courteously. So we remained at his house two days, talking of many matters of Portugall: then we departed from him, and came downe the riuer.

Three dayes after, I hired a ware-house by my selfe, and landed my commodities. And now I am selling them as fast as I can; and sell them very well, and to great profit: for I haue sold all our hats. I would I had brought forty or fifty dozen, by reason of the great vtterance of them vp into Peru, and into the new kingdome of Granada, by the way of the riuer of Plate. *A rich trade from the riuer of Ienero by the riuer of Plate into*

Peru, etc. For here is passage euery three or foure moneths with barks of thirty and forty tunnes a piece, which are laden with sugars, rice, taffataes, hats, and other kindes of commodities of this countrey, which are caried vp the sayd riuer of Plate in the sayd barks, and thence are conueyed vp into Peru. And these barks are but tenne or twelue days going vp the sayd riuer to Peru. And within foure and fiue moneths after, the sayd barkes come downe this riuer againe laden with reals of plate, and bring downe from those places no other commodities but treasure. *The shortnesse of the returne of the voyage to Peru.* It is a woonderfull thing to behold the great gaine and profit which is gotten in this riuer and in this countrey. I am ashamed to write it, fearing that I shall not be beleeued. For the imployment of one hundred ducats in spaine, being brought hither, will yeeld twelue hundred and fifteene hundred ducats profit. This trade hath beene vsed but within this yeere. *The rich trade was begunne in the yere 1595.* For wee can goe vp to the mines of Potosi, which are the best and the richest mines in all Peru.[29] If the merchants of Spaine and Portugall did know this trade, they would not send nor venture so much merchandise to Cartagena as they doe. For vp this riuer is a great deale the neerer way, and the easier to go to Peru. For the Peruleros or merchants of Peru, which dwell there, come downe to this harbour and riuer of Ienero, and bring with them fifteene thousand and twentie thousand ducats in reals of plate and gold, and imploy it heere in this riuer in commodities: and when heere are no commodities to be had for money in this place, then these merchants of Peru, are constrained to go to Baia and Fernambuc, and there to imploy their money. *The voyage of Angola in Africa.* I would I had brought good store of silks, and not these kinde of commodities which I did bring. For here is more profit to be had a great deale then in the voyage of Angola. For heere with fiue hundred ducats in fiue moneths space a man may get sixe thousand ducats. And this is no fable, but most true, and a great deale more then I can expresse. For a rapier Which doeth cost in Spaine foure and twenty and sixe and twenty reals, is sold heere for forty and fifty ducats: a bridle for a horse is solde for fifteene ducats; a lock of a doore and the key is solde for ten ducats: a pound of beniamin is solde for fifteene ducats: a yard of veluet is solde for twenty and fiue and twenty ducats: taffataes are solde for sixe and seuen ducats the vare: an ownce of muske, is solde for forty ducats: and all kinde of commodities after this rate. *Gaine of ten thousand ducats for the laying out of one thousand.* So one thousand ducats of Spanish commodities will gaine tenne thousand ducats. Thus I hope in God to make more profit and gaine this voyage, then in two voyages to Angola: for I haue solde most of my hats for two duckets and a halfe and for three ducats. The rest I will cary to Angola, to helpe to sell the rest of my commodities, which I cannot sell in this riuer. And I haue solde an hundred cubits of broad cloth for fiue hundred and fiue hundred and fifty and sixe hundred reys the cubit. A trade of buying Negros in Angola. If I would haue solde all my cloth for ready money tolde downe for foure hundred and fifty and fiue hundred reyes, the merchants would haue bought it all of me: but I would sell no more, because I meant to exchange it in Angola for Negros. Howbeit with ready money in hand in Angola a man shall buy better Negros, and better cheape. The captaine of our ship solde all his cloth for ready money for fore hundred and fifty reys the cubit, and thought that he had made a good market, but he hath deceiued himselfe. I solde six broad clothes for fiue hundred and fifty reys the cubit: and I was offered thirty thousand reys for a cloth. Vineger is solde for two and thirty, sixe and thirty, and forty reals a iarre, by reason there is great store of limmons and orenges in the countrey: but in Angola it is more woorth. Oliues are solde for halfe a reall a piece: wherefore I hope to sell the hogshead for twenty thousand reys. In taffataes and veluets there will be gotten two hundred and fifty and three hundred for one hundred. If I had brought great store, I could haue solde it all at this rate. I haue already gotten great store of reals of plate: for it is tolde mee that money is a good commodity in Angola. But I must imploy some in meale, which is in the grinding. All the rest of my money I will send you by billes of exchange, and some part I wil imploy in sugars: for I haue sent order to Baia for that purpose. For from this place there is no shipping that doth go that way. So these letters I do send by the way of Fernambuc, and haue directed them to my cousin: for I do determine to settle my selfe here in this countrey. There is come downe from Peru, by this riuer of Plate, a merchant called Alonso Ramires, and he hath brought downe with him ten or twelue thousand ducats in reals of plate, and is come downe to this place to build him a ship to returne into Spaine; and there is come in his company a bishop. And thus Iesus Christ send you long health.

Your louing brother Francis Suares.

[29] By Peru, Bolivia is here meant, Potosi can be reached from Rio de la Plata by ascending the river Paraguay to its junction with the Pilcomayo, and thence ascending that river.

The well gouerned and prosperous voyage of M. Iames Lancaster, begun with three ships and a galley-frigat from London in October 1594, and intended for Fernambuck, the porte-towne of Olinda in Brasil. In which voyage (besides the taking of nine and twenty ships and frigats) he surprized the sayd port-towne, being strongly fortified and manned; and held possession thereof thirty dayes together (notwithstanding many bolde assaults of the enemy both by land and water) and also prouidently defeated their dangerous and almost ineuitable fireworks. Heere he found the cargazon or freight of a rich East Indian carack; which together with great abundance of sugars, Brasil-wood, and cotton he brought from thence; lading therewith fifteene sailes of tall ships and barks.

In September 1594 the worshipfull M. Iohn Wats, alderman, M. Paul Banning, alderman, and others of worship in the city of London, victualled three good ships; to wit, The Consent, of the burden of 240 tunnes or thereabout, The Salomon, of 170 tunnes, and the Virgin, of 60 tunnes: and appointed for commanders in this voyage, M. Iames Lancaster of London, gentleman, admirall of the fleet, M. Edmund Barker of London, viceadmirall, and M. Iohn Audely of Poplar neere London rereadmirall, hauing in their sayd ships to the number of 275 men and boyes.

Being fully furnished with all needfull prouision, wee departed from Blackwall in October following, keeping our owne coast, vntill we came into the West countrey, where we met with such gusts and stormes, that the Salomon spending her mast at the Range of Dartmouth, put into harbour; but by the earnest care and industry of the generall and others hauing charge, she was shortly againe prouided. Which done, hauing a pleasant gale for our purpose, we put foorth from Dartmouth the last of Nouember following. But contrary to our expectation, not fifty leagues from our owne coast, we lost the Salomon and the Virgin, by a storme of contrary winde that fell vpon vs: yet being alone, in hope to meet them about the Canaries or Cape Blank, we kept on our course to the Canaries, but could heare no tidings of our consorts, which greatly grieued vs.

Thence we went, bearing for the isle of Tenerif, where in the morning early we had sight of a saile, which being becalmed vnder the shore, was towing with their boat a head, hauing one other at her sterne. For this saile we manned our boat, appointing our men wel for fight, if need should require. The Spaniards seeing our boat come, entred theirs, and leauing the ship, sought to saue themselues by flight: but our men pursued them so fast, that they boorded them, and brought them with their shippe to our Generall. This ship was laden with 80 tunnes of Canary-wine, which came not vnto vs before it was welcome. We kept and manned it, plying that day, and the next night thereabout. The very next morning we had sight of one other; to whome in like maner wee sent our boat: but their gunner made a shot at her, and strooke off a propper yoong mans arme; yet we inforced her to yeeld, and found 40 tunnes of wine in her. The Spaniards hauing their free passage, and an acquaintance for the deliuery of their wines, were all set on shore vpon Tenerif, making a quicke returne of their long voyage intended into the West Indies.

Hence we departed toward Cape Blank; and before wee came thither, we met againe with the Virgin our rereadmirall, whose men tolde vs for very truth, that the Salomon was returned for England; inforced so to doe, by spending her mast the second time. Which when our men vnderstood, they were all in a maze, not knowing what to doe, and saying among themselues that their force was but small when all our strength were together, and now we had lost the one halfe of our strength, we were not able to performe the voyage: and therefore some of them came to the captain, asking him what he would now do, seeing the Salomon was now lost, the one halfe of our strength, giuing him counsell to beare vp for the West Indies, and proue there to make his voyage, because his first plat for want of strength was cleane ouerthrown. The captaine hearing this new nouelty, as not vnacquainted with the variable pretenses of mariners, made them this answere: Sirs, I made knowen to you all at my comming out of England what I pretended, and that I meant to go to Fernambuck, and although at the present we want one of our ships, yet (God willing) I mean to go forward, not doubting but to meet her at the appointed places, which are either at Cape Blank or the islands of Cape Verde: for I am assured that M. Barker the captaine is so resolute to performe this voyage, that his mast being repaired, he will not faile to meet vs, and it were no wisdome for vs to diuert our course, till we haue sought him at those places where our appointed meeting is: for the diuerting of courses is the ouerthrow of most of our actions. And I hope you will be all contented herewith: for to go any other course then I haue determined (by Gods helpe) I will not be drawen vnto. With these reasons and many others shewed, they rested all satisfied: and at our comming to Cape Blank (God be praised) we met with the Salomon with no small ioy to vs all; and there she had taken of Spaniards and Portugals 24 saile of ships and carauels, fisher-men, and had taken out of them such necessaries as she had neede of. Of these ships our Captaine tooke foure along with him, with another that he had taken himselfe, meaning to imploy them as occasion should serue. At this place he vnderstood one of the pilots of those ships, that one of the caracks that came out of the East Indies, was cast away in the rode of Fernambuc, and that all her goods were layd vpon the Arracife which is the lower towne. Of these newes we were all glad, and reioyced much; for our hopes were very good, seeing such a booty before vs.

A gally-frigat carried out of England in pieces. Of this good company and happy successe we were all ioyful, and had great hope of the blessing of God in performance of our intended voyage, and so after some parle and making frolike for ioy of our meeting one with the other (praising God for all) we plied for Maio: where coming to anker, our generall and the rest of the captaines went ashore to view the place where we might in best safety set our gally-frigat together; which frame wee brought from England of purpose to land men in the country of Brasil. Here we discharged our great prize of wine, and set her on fire: but before our coming thither, you shall vnderstand we had sight of four sailes, which was captaine Venner in his ship the Peregrine, and a proper Biskaine which he tooke at Cape Blank, the Welcome of Plymmouth and her pinnesse: all which stood with vs. But they seeing our flags, not expecting such good fellowes as we, did beare from vs all they might; which our people tooke very vnkindly, that being all friends, they would neither enquire, nor tell vs any newes of our friends, but without making any shew of kindness would so depart. *The gally-frigat set vp.* As before I haue said, the choice being made for the place to build the gally-frigat, ashore it was brought, where the carpenters applied their worke, still cheered vnto it by the generals good gifts bestowed among them, and kind vsage of the rest of the commanders, not without great care of the captaine for the safety of them all, by keeping good watch: yet one negligent fellow, which had no knowledge of the countrey, straying from his company, was by the Portugals taken, and very kindly vsed, and brought againe vnto vs: for which good the generall rewarded them well with gifts very acceptable, which they tooke as kindly. While wee were thus busily imployed about the foresayd galley, we descried at sea foure sailes, which we had good hope would haue prooued Indies men, or some to haue brought vs what wee looked for: but they proued captaine Venner with his fleete, as aforesayd, who, seeing vs at anker, ankered also; where spending some time, and being acquainted with our generals determination for landing, consorted with vs, and their bils, according to the maner of the sea, were made and signed on either part, we to haue three parts, and he the fourth, of all that should be taken, whereby our strength was increased, to all our comforts. Three weeks or thereabouts we stayd in this place before the gally was finished; which done, putting men into her, and fitting her with oares, hauing fourteene banks on a side, a mast and saile, the commandement of her was committed vnto M. Wats, an honest skilful mariner.

From thence we put againe to sea, and went for the ile Braua, where we watered: which done, we made no long stay after, but bent our course as directly as we could for the place, making our first fall with the land to the Southward of Cape S. Augustine; from whence wee plied still to our desired port of Fernambuck, and did so much, that about midnight we came before the harbour; where some plied vp and downe, holding that the best policy, to forebeare the entring till day might giue them light, the harborow being hard, and therefore the more perillous. The 29 of March. Our ships being in safety well arriued, God was praised: and the generall in his boat went from ship to ship, willing them to made ready such men as they could spare, with muskets, pikes, billes, bowes, arrowes, and what weapons they had to follow him. Himself, with 80 men from his owne ship, imbarked himselfe in the gally, which carried in her prow a good sacar, and two murdering pieces.

Our admiral spent all the night in giuing directions to euery ship to haue their men ready shipped in their boats, for he intended to enter the harborow at the breake of day, and to leaue his ships without, till he had gotten the fort and the towne: for he would not aduenture the ships in, till the harborow was gotten. Also he prouided fiue ships, which he brought from Cape Blank, and put men in them as many as could conueniently saile them, and no more, giuing them charge to enter the harborow with his boats: for at the entrance of the harborow rode three great Holland ships, which our admirall doubted would impeach his going in; and therefore he gaue order to the men of these fiue small ships, which were not aboue 60 tunnes a piece, if the Hollanders did offer any resistance, to run aboord of them, and to set their owne ships on fire, and scape in their boats, which they had for the same purpose, that by this meanes they might not impeach our entrance. But when the morning was come, we were fallen aboue halfe a mile downe to the Northward, below the harborow, which was a great inconuenience vnto vs: so that before wee could get vp againe, the ebbe was come vpon vs, and thereby we were forced to houer before the harborow till two of the clocke in the afternoone, in the sight of all the towne. In this meane time, our ships rode before the fort without the harborow, about a demy-coluering shot off: in the which time passed many shot betweene the fort and the ships, and especially betweene the admirals ship and them: but no great harme was done on either part. All this while our admirall kept the men ready houering in the gally and the boats. The Hollanders that rode in the mouth of the harborow, seeing our resolution, layd out haulsers, and wound themselues out of the way of vs. Our admirall was very ioyfull, and gaue great incouragement to all his men: for, to passe these three great Hollanders, he held it the greatest danger of all. About 12 of the clocke the gouernor of the towne sent a Portugall aboord the admirals ship, to know what he would haue, and wherefore he came. He returned him this answere: That he wanted the caracks goods, and for them he came, and them he would haue, and that he should shortly see. In this processe of time, the townes-men and inhabitants which saw so much shipping, and perceiued vs to be enemies, gathered themselues together, three or foure ensignes of men, esteemed to the number of some sixe hundred at the least. These came to the fort or platforme lying ouer against the entry of the harborow, and there attended our landing: but before our admirall set forward with his boats, he gaue expresse order to all that had charge of gouerning the boats or galley, to run them with such violence against the shore, that they should be all cast away without recouery, and not one man to stay in them, whereby our men might haue no maner of retreat to trust vnto, but onely to God and their weapons.

Now was the time come of the flood, being about two of the clocke in the afternoone, when our admirall set forward, and entered the harborow with the small galley, and all the rest of the boats following him, the Hollanders that rode in the mouth of the harborow, nothing impeached him: but now the fort began to play with their ordinance vpon the galley and the boats; and one of their shot tooke away a great piece of our ensigne out of the galley. But our saile being set, it was no time for vs to make any stay, but with all the force we could we ranne the galley vpon the shore right vnder the fort, within a coits cast of it, with such violence, that we brake her backe; and she suncke presently: for there where we landed, went a breach of the sea, which presently cast her away. The boats comming after did the like. At our arriuall, those in the fort had laden all their ordinance, being seuen pieces of brasse, to discharge them vpon vs at our landing; which indeed they did: for our admirall leaping into the water, all the rest following him, off came these pieces of ordinance: but almighty God be praised, they in the fort, with feare to see vs land in their faces, had piked their ordinance so steepe downewards with their mouthes, that they shot all their shot in the sand, although, as I sayd before, it was not aboue a coits cast at the most betweene the place wee landed and the face of the fort: so that they only shot off one of our mens armes, without doing any more hurt; which was to vs a great blessing of God: for if those ordinances had bene well leuelled, a great number of vs had lost our liues at that instant. Our admirall seeing this, cried out, incouraging his men, Vpon them, vpon them; all (by Gods helpe) is ours: and they therewith ran to the fort with all violence. The fort of Fernambuck taken. Those foure ensignes of men that were set to defend our landing, seeing this resolution, began to go backe, and retire into certeine bushes that were by the same fort; and being followed, fledde thorowe a certaine oaze which was drie, being then but the beginning of the tide: and so abandoned the fort, and left it with their ordinance to vs. This day of our arriuall was their Good-Friday, when by custome they usually whippe themselues: but God sent vs now for a generall scourge to them all, whereby that labour among them might be well spared. The fort being taken with all their ordinance, the admirall waued to the ships, willing them to wey and come in; which they did with all speed, himselfe taking order in leauing certeine men in keeping the sayd fort, and placed the ordinance toward the high towne, from whence hee suspected the greatest danger; and putting his men in order, marched toward the low towne, which was about some fourteene score from the fort: in which towne lay all their merchandize and other goods. Approching to the towne, he entered the same, the people imbarking themselues in carauels and boats, with all the expedition they could. The base towne, of aboue an hundred houses, being thus taken, we found in it great store of merchandizes of all sorts: as Brasil-wood, sugars, Calico-cloth, pepper, cynamon, cloues, mase, nutmegs, with diuers other good things, to the great comfort of vs all. The admirall went vp and downe the towne, and placed at the South end of the same captaine Venner and his company, himselfe and his company in the midst of the towne, and captaine Barker and captaine Addy at the other end of the towne, giuing great charge, that no man vpon paine of great punishment and losse of his shares, should break vp or enter into any ware-house, without order and direction from the admirall. And this commandement was as well kept as euer any was kept, where so great spoile and booty was found: for it was not knowen in all the time of our being there, that any disorder was committed, or any lodge or ware-house broken open, or any spoile was made, or pillaging of any thing; which is a note much to be obserued in such an action: for common mariners and souldiers are much giuen to pillaging and spoiling, making greater account of the same then of their shares.

Order being put in all things, we kept a very sure watch this first night, and the morning being come, our admirall and captaine Venner, with the rest of the captaines, went about the towne, and gaue order for the fortifying of it with all expedition: so that within two dayes it was surrounded with posts and planks, all that part of the towne next the maine land, at least nine foot high; for (God be thanked) we found provision in the towne sufficient store for it. Now it is to be vnderstood, that this towne is enuironed on the one part by the sea, and on the back-side by a riuer that runneth behinde it; so that to come to it by land, you must enter it by a small narrow passage not aboue forty paces ouer at an high water. At this passage we built a fort, and planted in it fiue pieces of ordinance, which we tooke out of the first fort we wan at our comming into the harborow. Now we hauing the towne in possession, our admirall sent for the Hollanders by his chyrurgian, which had bene brought vp in that countrey, a man knowing their conditions, and sober and discreet of his owne cariage. At his first comming aboord of them, they seemed to stand vpon their owne guard and defence, for they were three great and strong ships: but he vsed himselfe so, that they at the last willed him to come into the greatest of their ships, which was aboue 450 tunnes. Then he declared to them our intent, of comming thither, and that they should be there as sure from any shew of violence or iniury offered them, as if they were in their owne houses, and if they should thinke so good, his admirall would fraight them for England, if they would be content with fraight reasonable, and as they should agree, and it should be at their owne choise whether to go or not, he would not force them, vnlesse it were to their benefit and good liking. Although this people were somewhat stubburne at the first, as that nation is in these causes, yet being satisfied with good words and good dealing they came aland, and after conference had with the admirall, they were so satisfied, that they went thorow with a fraight: and then we ioyned with them, and they with vs, and they serued vs as truely and as faithfully as our owne people did, both at watch and ward, by sea and all other seruices. Within two dayes after our comming in, about midnight, a great number of Portugals and Indians with them, came downe vpon vs with a very great cry and noise; but God be thanked, we were ready for them: for our admirall supposing some such assault, had prouided all our muskets with haile-shot, which did so gaule both the Indians and the Portugals, that they made them presently retreat. And this is to be noted, that there was both the horse and his rider slaine both with one of these shot. Our men followed them some fiue or sixe score, but no further. We lost in this conflict but onely one man, but had diuers hurt. What was lost of their part, we could not tell, for they had before day, after our retreat, caried away all their dead. Within three or foure dayes after our comming in appeared before the harborow 3 ships and 2 pinnesses, the pinnesses being somewhat nere, discried our flags, and one of them came in, which was a French pinnesse, declaring all the rest to be French bottoms; which our admirall willed should come in: and so they did. These were Frenchmen of war, and came thither for purchase. The captaines came aland, and were welcomed; amongst whom was one captaine Iohn Noyer of Diepe, that the yere before had taken in our admirall at the iland of Mona in the West Indies, where his ship was cast away, comming out of the East Indies. To this man our admirall offered great kindnes, and performed it, and was not vngratefull for his former benefit shewed vnto him. This captaine desired of our admirall to bestow vpon him his ships lading of Fernambuc-wood, which he granted him, and also his pinnesse, and more, gaue him a carauel of about 50 tuns, and bid him lade her with wood also; which with other benefits he gratefully receiued. To the other two captaines he granted their ladings of wood, the one captaine being of Diepe, the other of Rochel. Abraham Cocke going for the riuer of Plate, met withall. The captain of Diepe confessed that he met Abraham Cocke certein moneths before, and being distressed for want of water, gaue him some, and went with him to a watering place where he had water enough, and so departed from him, saying that his men were very weake. The comming in of these ships did much strengthen vs; for our admiral appointed both these French and the Flemings to keepe watch vpon the riuer by night with their boats, euery boat hauing in her 12 men at the least, and the boats well prouided. This was for feare of fired ships or barks to come downe; which our admirall had great care vnto, and caused our ships to ride by cables and haulsers, at all aduantages to shun them, if by that meanes they should attempt to put vs out of the harborow; giuing commandement to vs that watched in the towne, that what fires soeuer we should espy or see, not one man to start from his watch or quarter, vnlesse we were by himselfe commanded to the contrary. Now this order put in all things, and hauing viewed all the goods in the towne, and thinking our selues sufficiently fortified, we began to vnlade our ships, which came as full laden in as they went foorth, but not with so good merchandize. And this order was taken about the vnlading of them, and also the lading of goods out of the towne: our men were diuided into halues, and the one halfe wrought one day, and the other halfe the other day; always those that wrought not kept the watch with their furniture in their hands and about them, and none stept far off or wandred from his colours, and those that wrought had all their weapons in good order set and placed by them, so that at an instant euery one knew where to go to his furniture: and this was very carefully looked vnto.

The third day after our comming in, came down from the higher towne, which might be about foure miles off vpon a hill, three or foure of the principall gentlemen of the countrey, and sayd that from the bishop, themselues, and the rest, they would haue some conference with our admirall. This newes being brought to the admirall he hung downe his head for a small season; and when he had muzed a while, he answered, I must go aboord of the Flemings vpon busines that importeth me, and therefore let them stay if they will: and so he went and sate there with the Flemings from nine of the clocke till two at the afternoone. In this space diuers messengers went to the admirall, to come away, for these gentlemen stayd. To whom he gaue this answere: Are they not gone yet? And about two of the clocke he came aland, and then they tolde him they were departed. Many of the better sort of our men maruelled, and thought much, because he would not vouchsafe to come and haue conference with such men of account as they seemed to be. But the admiral made them this answere, Sirs, I haue bene brought vp among this people, I haue liued among them as a gentleman, serued with them as a souldier, and liued among them as a merchant, so that I should haue some vnderstanding of their demeanors and nature; and I know when they cannot preuaile with the sword by force, then they deale with their deceiuable tongues; for faith and trueth they haue none, neither will vse any, vnlesse it be to their owne aduantage. And this I giue you warning, that if you giue them parle, they will betray vs; and for my part, of all nations in the world, it would grieue me most to be ouertaken by this nation and the Spaniards: and I am glad it was my fortune to pay them with one of their owne fetches, for I warrant you they vnderstand me better then you thinke they do. And with this I pray you be satisfied; I hope it is for all our goods: for what shall we gaine by parle, when (by the helpe of God) we haue gotten already that we came for, should we venture that we haue gotten with our swords, to see if they can take it from vs by words and policy? there were no wisedome in so doing. You know what it hath cost vs, and how many men lie wounded that be not yet hole of this other nights hurts: and therefore from henceforth I giue this commission, that if any be taken, he be sent away with this order, although he come as a friend, that if he or any other approch vs from henceforth, he shalbe hanged out of hand: and other course then this I will not take with them. Which course was followed, for within 3 or 4 dayes after it was performed by two taken in the night: and after that we were neuer troubled with spies: and although diuers slaues came running from their men to vs, by which we vnderstood much of their working and pretences, yet the admirall would enterteine few of them.

In this meane time that we began to worke, the Portugals with the country people were not idle, for seeing vs so busie, about six nights after our comming in, they priuily in the night cast vp a trench in the sands about a sacar shot from our ships, minding there to plant ordinance, which would haue offended our ships greatly; and they would not haue bene able to haue rode there to take in their lading, which now began to go aboord of them. The admirall hearing this, about 3 of the clocke in the after noone marshalled our men, and he and all the rest of the captaines marched toward them. The Portugals and Indians perceiuing our comming, began to withdraw themselues within the trench, meaning (as it should appeare) to fight it out there: but we made no stand, neither did it behoue vs, but presently approched the trenches with our muskets and pikes, afore their trenches were thorowly finished: so that by Gods helpe we entered them. And the Portugals and Indians left the place, and left vnto vs 4 good peeces of brasse ordinance, with powder and shot and diuers other necessaries, and among the rest 5 smal carts of that countrey, which to vs were more worth then al the rest we tooke, for the lading of our goods from the towne to the water side: for without them we could not haue told what to haue done, much of our goods being so heauie, that without carts we were not able to weyld them: all these things we brought away and destroyed al those platforms that they had made, and then we had rest with them for certaine dayes, in which we went forward, deuiding our marchandize with captaine Venner according to our consort, and went daily lading them abord, euery ships company according as their turnes fell out, but only the three Dutch ships: for the goods being put into their boats their owne companies laded themselues. And this farther good chance or blessing of God we had to helpe vs, that assoone as we had taken our cartes, the next morning came in a ship with some 60 Negros, 10 Portugal women, and 40 Portugals: the women and the Negroes we turned out of the towne, but the Portugals our Admirall kept to draw the carts when they were laden, which to vs was a very great ease. For the countrey is very hote and ill for our nation to take any great trauell in.

In this towne there is no fresh water to be had, and therefore we were euery 5 or 6 dayes compelled to passe ouer the riuer into the maine land to get fresh water, which after the first or second time the Portugals kept and would haue defended our watering, so that we were driuen to water of force, and at seuerall times some of our men were hurt, and onely two or three slaine, and with this danger we were forced to get our water.

And as they molested vs in our watering, so they slept not in other deuises, but put in practise to burne our ships or remoue them out of the harbour. For within some 20 dayes after our comming in, they had prepared 5 Carauels and filled them with such things as would best take fire and burne: these they brought within a mile or little more of our ships, and there set them on fire, for neerer they could not well come because of our watch of boates, for, as is abouesaid, the Admirall had alwaies 6 boates that kept watch aboue halfe a mile from the ships for feare of such exploytes as these, which was the cause they could not fire them so neere the ships as they would haue done. But these fired Carauels had the tide with them, and also the little winde that blewe was in their favour; which caused them to come downe the streame the faster: which our boats perceiuing made to them with as much expedition as conueniently they could, but the tide and wind both seruing them, they approched toward the ships with great expedition. Our men in the towne began to be in some feare of them, yet no man mooued or started from his quarter more then if there had bene nothing to doe. Also the masters and such as were aboord, were somewhat amased to see 5 so great fires to be comming downe among their ships, but they prepared for to cleere them of it, as well as they could, being prouided afore hande and iudging that some such stratagems would be there vsed, the riuer being very fit therefore. But (God be thanked) who was alwaies with vs and our best defence in this voyage; by whose assistance we performed this so great an attempt with so small forces. Our companie in the boats so played the men when they saw the fires come neere our ships, that casting grapnels with yron chaines on them, as euery boat had one for that purpose, some they towed aground, and some they brought to a bitter or anker, where they rode till all their force was burned out, and so we were deliuered by Gods helpe from this fearefull danger. Within some 6 nights after this, which might be about the 26 day after our comming in and abode there, about 11 of the clocke at night, came driuing downe other 3 great raftes burning with the hugest fires that I haue seene. These were exceeding dangerous, for when our men approched them, thinking to clap their grapnels vpon them, as they had done vpon the Carauels the night before, they were preuented: for there stooke out of the rafts many poles which kept them from the body of the rafts, that they could not come to throw their grapnels into them: and yet they had this inconuenience worse then al the rest which most troubled vs. There stooke out among the poles certaine hollow trunks filled with such prouision of fire workes that they ceased not still (as the fire came downe to those trunks to set them on fire) to spout out such sparkles, that our boats hauing powder in them for our mens vse, durst not for feare of frying themselues with their owne powder come neere those sparkles of the raftes, but seeing them to driue neerer and neerer our ships, they wet certaine clothes and laid vpon their flaskes and bandelers and so ventured vpon them, and with their grapnels tooke holde of them, and so towed them on ground, where they stooke fast and were not burnt out the next day in the morning. Diuerse logs and timbers came driuing along by our ships, and burning, but with our boats we easily defended them. And thus (God be praysed) we escaped the second fires. A third firing was prepared, as a Negro gaue vs to vnderstand, but this we preuented by our departure. For this third firing were very great preparations: and we were credibly informed of certainetie, that this firing should be such as we should neuer be able to preuent, and assuredly these fires be dangerous things and not to be preuented vpon the sudden, vnlesse it be afore prepared for and foreseene. For when it commeth vpon the sudden and vnlooked for, and vnprouided for, it bringeth men into a great amazement and at their wits ende. And therefore let all men riding in riuers in their enemies countrey be sure to looke to be prouided before hand, for against fire there is no resistance without preparation.

Also it is a practise in these hot countreys, where there be such expert swimmers, to cut the cables of ships: and one night it was practised to cut the Admirals cable, and yet the boate rode by the cable with two men in her to watch all the night, and the bwoy onely was cut, but not the cable: but after that night, seeing then our good watch, they neuer after attempted it.

While all these things passed, our ships (God be thanked) thorow the industry of our gouernours, and diligent labour of our men, began to be wholly laden, and all the best marchandize conueyed aboord our ships, so that our Admirall went to depart that night, which was the 31 day after our entrance, or else on the next day at the farthest, and so warning was giuen to all men to make themselues readie. Our Admiral being aboord his ship the same morning, espyed in the sands right against the place where the ships rode, that there was a small banke of sand newly cast vp, vnder which he perceiued now and then some people to be: presently he tooke his boat and went to the towne and called all the Captaines together, declaring that the enemies were about some pretence right against the ships, consulting whether it were best to sally out and see what they were doing, or depart that euening according to the former determination. The Admirall was of opinion to depart that night; saying it was but folly to seeke warres since we had no neede to doe it: other affirmed, it were good to see what they did, least the winde might be contrarie and the ships not get out, and so our enemies may build vpon vs to our great disaduantage. Well, said the Admiral, the matter is not great, for there can be no danger in this sally, for where they worke it is within Falkonshot of our ships, and if any power should come against you, the ships may play vpon them with 40 pieces of ordinance at the least, so that a bird cannot passe there but she must be slaine. I am somewhat vnwilling you should go, for I haue not bene well these two dayes, and I am not strong to march vpon those heauie sands: they answered all at once, you shall not need to trouble your selfe for this seruice, for you see it is nothing and of no danger, being so neere the ships, doubt you not we will accomplish this seruice well ynough, and returne againe within this houre. The Admirall answered: the danger cannot be great, but yet you shall goe out strong for feare of the worst. And so the Admirall marshalled them 275 men French and English, which were vnder the conduct of Edmund Barker, captaine Barker of Plimmouth, Viceadmirall to captaine Venner, captaine Addy, and the three French captaines all going out together, and they were to march vpon a narrow peece of ground to the place whether they were sent vnto: in the brodest place betwixt the sea and the water on the other side, it is aboue a stones cast for it is a bank of sand lying betweene the riuer and the sea, so they needed not to feare any comming on their backs or on their sides, and before them could no man come, but he must passe by all the ships which no company of men were able to do without present death. The Admirall commanded them at their departure to go no further then the place he sent them to, and so he himselfe went aboord the ships and made readie all the ordinance for feare of the worst, not knowing what might insue, although he saw no danger might follow. Thus we marched quietly till we came to the place we were sent vnto, being right ouer against the ships: out of which place came some dozen shot, which seeing vs come, discharged and ran their wayes with such as were working within the said platforme. So that we came into it and perceiued they had begunne to lay plankes to plant ordinance vpon. Our Admiral commanded, if there were any such thing, to burne the plankes and returne in againe, which we might haue done without hurting of any mans finger: but our leaders were not content to haue performed the seruice committed them in charge, but would needes expresly and against their order march on further to fight with certaine Ensignes almost a mile off, cleane out of the reach of the ordinance of all our ships, and where lay the strength of the whole countrey. When our men began to draw neere those Ensigns of men, the Ensignes seemed to retire with great speed, which our men followed with such great hast that some outrunning other some, our order was broken, and those ensignes retyred themselues into the force of the whole countrey, so that our formost men were in the midst of their enemies yer they were aware, which were slaine yer the rest could come to succour them. The enemies incouraged by this, came also vpon the rest, which presently began to retire, and the enemies followed til they came with the reach of the ordinance of our ships, where they were beaten off and left their pursuit. In this conflict were slaine captain Barker captaine of the Salomon, captaine Cotton the Admirals Lieutenant, captaine Iohn Noyer a French captaine of Diepe, and another French captaine of Rochel, with M. Iohn Barker and other to the number of 35: for these were the formost and hottest in the pursuit of the Ensignes aforesaid, and by their forwardnes came all to perish. At our returne into the towne the Admiral came to vs much bewayling the death of so many good men as were lost, wondering what we ment to passe the expresse order that was giuen vs. With this losse our men were much danted, but our Admirall began againe to encourage them, declaring that the fortune of the warres was sometimes to win and sometimes to loose. And therewithall he wished euery man to prepare and make himselfe readie: for that night (God willing) he would depart. For all our ships were readie and laden, and he would not stay any further fortune. The euening being come, the ships began to wey and go forth of the harbour, and God be thanked of his goodnesse toward vs who sent vs a faire wind to go foorth withall, so that by 11 of the clocke in the night we were all forth in safety. The enemies perceiuing our departing, planted a peece or two of ordinance, and shot at vs in the night, but did vs no harme. We were at our comming foorth 15 sailes, that is, 3 sailes of Hollanders, the one of 450 tunnes, the other of 350 tunnes, and the third of 300 tunnes, four sailes of French and one ship which the admiral gaue the French Captain, 3 sailes of Captain Venners fleet of Plimmouth, and 4 sailes of our Admirals fleete, all these were laden with marchandizes, and that of good worth. We stayed in this harbour to passe all this businesse but onely 31 dayes, and in this time we were occupied with skirmishes and attempts of the enemie 11. times; in all which skirmishes we had the better, onely this last excepted. To God be the honour and praise of all, &c. Peranjeu 40. leagues northward of Fernambuck. The whole fleete being out in safety, the next day in the morning the Admirall gaue order to the whole fleete to saile toward Peraniew[30] a harbour lying some 40 leagues to the Northward of Fernambucke, and there to take in fresh water and to refresh themselues: and to make prouision for refreshing, our Admirall had sent thither some 6 daies before two French men in a smal pinnesse, which Frenchmen he had prouided from Diepe before his comming out of England for that purpose. For both these two spake the Indians language very perfectly: for at this port of Peraniew and an other called Potaju some 6 leagues to the Northward the Frenchmen haue had trade for brasil-wood, and haue laden from thence by the Indians meanes, who haue fet it for them some 20 leagues into the country vpon their backs, 3 or 4 ships euery yere. Thus we all sailed toward Peraniew, at which place we arriued in the night, so that we were forced to lie off and on with a stiffe gale of wind, in which we lost the most part of our fleete, and they not knowing this coast put off to the sea; and so went directly for England. Peranjeu a very good harbour. Our Admirall and some foure saile more with him put into the harborow of Peraniew, and there watered and refreshed himselfe very well, with hens, conies, hares and potatos, with other things, which the two Frenchmen had partly prouided before his comming: this is a very good harborow where ships may ride and refresh very well. But, as I am giuen to vnderstand since our comming from thence, the Portugals haue attempted the place and doe inhabite it, and haue put the French from their accustomed trade. Here hauing watered and refreshed our selues, we put to the sea, plying after the rest of our fleete which were gone before, which we neuer heard of till our arriuall in England at The downes in the moneth of Iuly, where we vnderstood the rest of our consorts to be passed vp for London, Captaine Venner and his fleete to be at Plimmouth, and the French ships to be safe arriued at Diepe, which to vs was very great comfort. At our setting sayle from The downes, according as the custome is, finding the Queenes ships there, we saluted them with certaine ordinance. The Gunner being carelesse, as they are many times of their powder, in discharging certain pieces in the gunner roome, set a barrel of powder on fire, which tooke fire in the gunner roome, blew vp the Admirals caben, slew the gunner with 2 others outright, and hurt 20 more, of which 4 or 5 died. This powder made such a smoke in the ship with the fire that burnt the gunner roome among all the fire workes, that no man at the first wist what to doe: but recalling backe their feare, they began to cast water into the gunner roome in such abundance (for the Queenes ships now and also the other ships that were in our company came presently to our helpe) that (God be praised) we put out the fire and saued all, and no great harme was done to the goods. By this may be seene that there is no sure safety of things in this world. For now we made account to be out of all danger, where behold a greater came vpon vs, then we suffered all the whole voyage. But the almightie be praysed for euer, which deliuered vs out of this and many other in this voyage. Our fire being well put out, and we taking in fresh men (God be praysed) we came to Blacke-wall in safety.

[30] Probably the mouth of the River Pirangi, in the province of Ceara.

A speciall letter written from Feliciano Cieça de Carualsho the Gouernour of Paraiua in the most Northerne part of Brasil, 1597, to Philip the second king of Spaine, answering his desire touching the conquest of Rio Grande, with the relation of the besieging of the castle of Cabodelo by the Frenchmen, and of the discouerie of a rich siluer mine and diuerse other important matters.

The king of Spaines resolution to proceed in the discouerie and conquest of Rio Grande. I receiued your Maiesties letter bearing date the ninth of Nouember 1596. whereby I vnderstande that your Maiestie doth determine to proceede in the discouerie and conquest of Rio Grande according to the relation which was sent your Maiestie by Don Francisco de Sousa, Gouernour generall of this realme of Brasilia: together with a copie of a letter, which your Maiestie sent vnto vs, bearing date the two and twentieth of March 1596. Moreouer I receiued another letter from your Maiestie bearing date the 15 of March 1597. Both which letters were to one effect. It may please your Maiestie to vnderstand that there are diuerse Gentlemen in these countreys of as good abilitie as my selfe, which seeke to liue at home onely for their ease and pleasure, and are not wont to hazard nor venture their bodies, liues, and goods so often times in your Maiesties seruice as I haue done and commonly doe; and can keepe their goods and riches, and not spend nor wast them as I haue done, and dayly doe so wilfully: yet neuerthelesse being spent in your Maiesties seruice, I am very glad thereof. For I and they are always readie at your Maiesties commandement.

The Captaineship of Paraiua standeth in sixe degr. 45 min. of Southerly latitude. And as concerning your Maiesties commandement in commanding me that I should put to my helping hand in the conquest of Rio Grande: although this Captaineship of Paraiua and countrey where I doe gouerne doth want abilitie for that purpose, yet nevertheless your Maiestie shall always finde me readie to doe your Maiestie the best seruice I can: for it is very well knowen how forward I haue bene alwayes and am in this conquest, and still doe put to my helping hand, as partly your Maiestie doth vnderstand by a letter which I wrote to your Maiesty by my sonne, bearing date the 19 of March 1596 wherein your Maiestie may vnderstand what good seruice I haue alreadie done therein, and always will be readie to my power to doe the like in furthering of the said enterprise.

It may please your Maiestie to vnderstand that the third of Iuly there was brought vnto me a Frenchman a prisoner, who presented himselfe vnto me. And I examining of him, he tolde me that he came running away from certaine French ships men of warre, which came vpon this coast: and he tolde me that he had serued your Maiestie in the warres of France. The castle of Cabodelo besieged by the French. Likewise he told me that he left me seuen great ships Frenchmen of warre riding at an anker in Rio Grande, and that there were 13 French ships of warre more, which had giuen battery to the castle of Cabodelo, and landed 350 soldiers all in white armour and the battery continued from Friday vntil the Munday following both by sea and land, and great store of Frenchmen were slaine, and two Captaines of the French. On our side the Captaine of the castle was slaine, and other two Portugals hurt: other harme they had none. There were but twentie Portugals in the castle, and fiue pieces of ordinance. They ment to haue kept the castle, and to haue traded with the Indian people. So seeing they could not take the castle, they hoysed sayles, and went from thence to Rio Grande: and being altogether they are in number 20 saile at an anker in Rio Grande. And some of them determine after they be new trimmed and drest, and haue taken in fresh victuals, and stayed there vntill Easter, then to depart from thence to the Honduras, and so to burne and spoyle some townes thereabout.

I certified Manuel Mascarenhas of these informations by my letters, requesting him to send me with all expedition those souldiers which were in Fernambuck to ayde me, and to defende this Captaineship from the enemie. But the Friers of The Couent would not consent thereunto nor suffer them to be sent vnto me. The countrey of Petiguar rebelleth against the Portugals. So I was forced to make shift with those souldiers only which I had in my gouernment and tooke them with me, and marched to the place where the enemies were entrenched, vpon Whitsunday in the euening about three of the clock, hauing in my company a Negro of the countrey of Petiguar, which was our guide, he brought vs where the enemies campe was; and presently I did assault them and slew great score of them, burning the villages and countrey of these rebels, which did ioine with the Frenchmen, and tooke many of them prisoners. So they told me that there were ten great French ships of warre which were at an anker in Rio Grande.

A rich siluer mine found at Copaoba within sixe dayes iourney of Paraiua.

Likewise I was informed, that there is a Frenchman called Daurmigas, which hath discouered and found great store of siluer in a place called Copaoba.[31] The siluer hath bene tried and melted, it is very good and fine siluer, and there is great quantite. The man which told me of this hath beene in the mine, and hath seene it tried and melted. And I haue bene myselfe once in the place: it is but 6 dayes iourney from this Captaineship.

[31] Perhaps Caproba.

Furthermore this Frenchman told me that one Monsieur Mifa a French Captaine, and a kinsman of the gouernour and Vice-admirall of Diepe in Normandie, had one of his armes strooken off at the siege of the castle of Cabodelo; who is departed from Rio Grande, with determination to come backe hither againe the next yeere in the moneth of Ianuarie following, and to inhabite in this countrey of Paraiba, which is 20 leagues from Fernambuck, because of the great store of siluer, which they haue alreadie found here.

Moreouer I am enformed that a noble man of France called The earle of Villa Dorca doth intend to come vpon this coast with a great fleete from Rochel. It were good that your Maiestie would send into France to knowe the certainetie thereof.

All the Canibals of Petiguar ioyne with the Frenchmen against the Portugals. The Frenchman likewise told me that all the Canibals of Petiguar have ioyned themselues in companie with certaine Frenchmen, which were cast away in two ships vpon this coast. The one of these ships which were cast away was one Rifoles, and the other ship was this mans. And those Frenchmen which came vpon this coast did ioyne themselues with those Canibals which did rebell, and did diuide themselues into two squadrons. So I sent presently to Manuel Mascarenhas that he should send me aide and munition. But he sent me word againe, that he had none to spare, and that he did purpose with all speede to goe himselfe to Rio Grande; and that he was not able to furnish himselfe so well as he could wish, nor to bring his souldiers into the field, for lacke of shot, powder, and other munition, which he did want.

Hereupon once more the 29 of Iuly I with my souldiers marched to the enemies campe, and there ioyning battell with the Indian rebels, which ioyned with the Frenchmen that were their leaders, I did set vpon them, and slew great store of them, and tooke fourteene of them prisoners. They doe report the very same newes, which the other Frenchmen did tell me as touching the ships which were in the harbour of Rio Grande; and how their pretence was to haue come and haue taken vs, and spoyled the countrey.

But now being put to flight and hauing received the overthrow, they can get no victuals to victuall their shippes: which hath bene the cause that they are mightily hindred in their intent, and dare not come any more to attempt vs. And the Indians are so dismayed, that in haste they will haue no more helpe nor aide of the Frenchmen. So by these meanes of necessitie the Indians must submit themselues vnto vs, considering they are quite spoyled and ouerthrowen for a long time. Likewise they haue enformed me touching the siluer mines which are found, that it is most true. For those French shippes which were in Rio Grande haue laden great store of the oare. Wherefore I certified Manuel de Mascarenhas of the Frenchmens newes, and howe euery thing did stand wishing him to make readie foure ships and three hundred souldiers, and so to take the harbour of Rio Grande, being now cleered and voyde of the enemie: and to search out the situation of the place, and where were best to fortifie and to build some fortes for the defence of this riuer, where neede shall require. Hereunto Mascarenhas sent me word, that when he went himselfe, and found it true which hath beene reported touching the siluer mines, that then he would send both men and ships. Therefore your Maiestie must giue order, that the rest of the Gouernours shall ayde and assist me in these warres: otherwise of my selfe I am not able to doe more then I haue alreadie done in defending of this countrey against our enemies which are many.

It may please your Maiestie to be aduertised, that from time to time I haue written vnto Don Francisco de Sousa Gouernor general of this realme, who is in Baia, as concerning these Frenchmen of warre: but he will not answere me to any purpose because I do write vnto him for such things as I doe want, which are shot, powder, men, and munition requisite for your Maiesties seruice and safegard of this captaineship. For here are neither shot, powder, nor any thing els to defend vs from our enemies; nor any that wil put to their helping hands for the defence of this countrey, and the service of your Maiestie. And therefore it were needful that your Maiesty should committ the charge and gouernement into the hands of Diego Sierua, with expresse charge that all the captaines and commanders vpon paine of death obey him and be readie at all times to aide and assist him in your seruice. Otherwise this countrey cannot be kept and maintained, hauing so great warres continually as we haue, and are troubled withall. For this Diego Sierua is a very good souldier, and hath good experience; and is fit to gouerne this countrey. Your Highnesse is also to send his Commission with expresse commandment to follow these wars; otherwise this countrey cannot be kept, but daily they will rebell. For here are none that will serue your Maiestie so iustly as he will do: who will haue a great care in any thing which shal concerne you Maiesties seruice touching the estate of this countrey. For the Gouernour Sousa doth spend your Maiesties treasure in building his owne ingenios or sugar milles.

And those Captaines which your Maiestie intendeth to send hither must bring with them shot, powder, and all kind of weapons, furniture, and munition for the defence and safegarde of this countrey, and for the conquest of Rio Grande. For there is no kind of munition in al this countrey to be had, if occasion should serue. It were also good that your Maiestie should send order for the building of a couple of Forts or Castles at Cabadelo, for they be very needefull for the defence of the enemie, which dayly doth warre against this Captaineship. The countrey of Paraiua in danger dayly to be lost. For that man which shall gouerne this countrey, if he be no more fortunate then I haue bene hitherto, shall not misse one time or another, but he shall lose all the countrey. If Don Francisco de Sousa had sent me those two hundred and fiftie souldiers which I did send for, which were in garison in the castle of Arrecife, which doe nothing but spend your Maiesties victuals and treasure, and had not sent them to Baiha, where there was no neede, these warres of Petiguar had bene ended long agone, and had saued your Maiesty a great deale of charges which you had spent in folowing of this conquest of Rio Grande. I haue chosen one Captaine Iohn de Matas Cardoso to be Gouernour of Cabodelo, who is a very sufficient man.

A great controuersie touching the gouernment of the Indian townes.

Furthermore, it may please your Maiestie to vnderstand, that the chiefest Friers of this Monasterie of S. Antonie haue complained on me to the lord Gouernour generall, and haue caused great strife and debate beetweene him and me touching the gouernment and rule of these Indian townes. For the Friers would command and gouerne both the Indians and their townes as well in Ecclesiasticall as Temporall causes, as touching the punishment of the bodies of such as are offenders. But I haue resisted them in your Maiesties name, and haue alleaged, that none but your Maiestie must rule and gouerne them and their countrey, and that the townes appertaine to your Maiestie, and not vnto the Friers. But the Gouernour hath written a letter vnto me, signifying that he hath pronounced a sentence against me in the Friers behalfe, which is this. The King our master hath sent a decree and certaine statutes touching the good gouernment and orders to be executed and kept in those Indian townes: and that vpon sight hereof I shall presently banish all the Mamalukes and white men which dwell in any of those Indian townes with all speede, and that none of them from hence forward shall enter into the said villages, without commandement and consent of the said Friers. So this sentence was presented vnto me by the Reuerend father Custodio, Prior of Sant Anton of Brasil, with a further postcript of the gouernour importing these words: I doe likewise charge and commaund you the Gouernour of Paraiua, that presently vpon sight hereof you shall restore those villages and houses which you haue burned and destroyed in the last warres, and likewise the towne of S. Augustine, and that you shall build them againe at your owne proper cost and charges: for the Friers alleage that these townes were giuen them, by a decree sent them from Pope Pius Quintus, that the said Friers should gouerne and rule them.

On the other side I haue pronounced another sentence against the said Friers in your Maiesties name, and for your Maiestie, alleaging that those townes, villages, and subiects appertaine and belong vnto your Maiestie, and that in temporall causes I am to punish those offenders, which shall rebell against your Maiestie: and as touching ecclesiasticall causes that the Vicar of this Cathedrall church shall rule, gouerne and instruct them in the Christian religion. So we both haue appealed vnto your Maiestie herein, and your Maiestie may peruse all our writings, and then determine that which shall be best and most profitable for your Maiesties seruice and enlargement of your crowne. For through these broyles the inhabitants of this Pariaua forsake their houses and dwelling places, and so do some of the Friers, because they cannot be suffered to rule and gouerne.

Also the Indians haue complayned against me, because I haue burned their villages in this last rebellion. Wherefore if your Maiestie doe not send some order for this countrey and see into these cases, it will breed great dissension and rebellion among vs, and we shall be readie to cut one anothers throat before it be long.

Thus I thought good, according to my humble bounden dutie, and for the seruice of your Maiestie and quietnesse of this realme, to certifie your Maiestie the truth of the whole matter; hoping in short time that your Maiestie will send some good order to qualifie these broyles: for there is great hatred and malice among vs. Iesus Christ preserve and keepe the royall person of your Maiestie with long health, as it pleaseth him. From the Captaineship of Paraiua this present 20 of August. 1597.

Feliciano Cieça de Carualsho.

A special note concerning the currents of the sea betweene the Cape of Buena Esperança and the coast of Brasilia, giuen by a French Pilot to Sir Iohn Yorke knight, before Sebastian Cabote; which Pilot had frequented the coasts of Brasilia eighteene voyages.

Memorandum, that from Cabo de buena Esperança vnto Brasilia the Sunne hath the like dominion ouer the tides there, as the Moone hath ouer our tides here.

And that whensoeuer the Sunne is in any of these signes he gouerneth the tides as followeth.[32]

The Sunne being in {Taurus, Gemini, Cancer} the tide hath his course Northwest.

The Sunne being in {Leo, Virgo, Libra} no current.

The Sunne being in {Scorpio, Sagittarius, Capricorne} the tide hath his course Southeast.

The Sunne being in {Aquarius, Pisces, Aries} no current.

[32] It may be as well to point out that the truth as to the currents of the South Atlantic is as follows:—

From the Cape of Good Hope the current flows North along the West Coast of Africa till it reaches a point somewhat North of the Congo, when it turns to the West. North of Ascension it divides. One portion, the South Equatorial Current, flows North West into the Gulf of Mexico, while the other subdivides, and whilst part flows South West down the coast of South America, the remainder returns by the South of Tristan d'Acunha to the Cape of Good Hope.

A ruttier or course to be kept for him that will sayle from Cabo Verde to the coast of Brasil, and all along the coast of Brasil vnto the riuer of Plate: and namely first from Cabo Verde to Fernambuck.

The ship that goeth from Cabo Verde to Brasil, must goe Southsoutheast: and when she is within 5 or 6 degrees of the Equinoctial she must go Southeast and by South. And if she haue the ternados, that is thundrings and lightnings, then thou must go altogether South, or that way and by that boord that doth profit thee most. And take this for aduise, that hauing the general winds, and if the wind be at South or Southeast, then go Southwest, or westsouthwest. Ye that will sayle to Brasil, must not come within 60 or 70 leagues of the coast of Guinea. And if the winde be South, then goe Southwest, and by this way but little, for it is not a way for thy profit, because the more thou goest this way, the more will be thy trouble, because thou mayest not come neerer the coaste of Guinea then 60 or 70 leagues vnto the sholde called Os baixos de Santa Anna. And being this distance from the same, thou shall cast about the other way towards Brasil, and the wind will be large.

Thou shalt vnderstand that the ship that keepeth this course to Fernambuck, and goeth in October or after, and chanceth to goe to windward of the Isle of Fernando de Loronha, when thou commest to 8 degrees, or 8 and ½, [Ed: Of Southerly latitude] then thou shalt go West and beare with the land. Thou must take this for a warning, that if going West in 8 degrees thou see land, then looke to the Northward, and thou shalt see certaine white cliffes. Then I aduise thee that thou goe well to the Southward. And this is to bee vnderstoode from October forward, for then the time is most subiect to Northeast, and Eastnortheast winds. And if thou find thy selfe in the sayd height aboue mentioned, and seest cliffes, and seest a cape to the Southward, and seest no more land to the South, then make accompt that thou art at Capiguoari: and from thence to Fernambuck thou hast sixe leagues, and hast a good port.

Thou shalt take this for a warning, that if in 8 degrees and a halfe thou see land lying all flat, thou mayest goe neerer it, and be bold till thou come in tenne or twelue fadomes: And then thou shalt see a great grosse land along the sea-coast which is called Capitagua: And being East and West with this land, and, as I haue sayd, in tenne or twelue fadomes water; and the time being from October to Februarie, then thou needest not to feare any thing: but looke to the South and thou shalt see the cape of S. Augustine: and looke to the North and thou shalt see a point, and to the Southeast a point called Punta de Olinda, where Aponiquay standeth. And the land from the cape to the poynt called Punta Olinda lieth North and South.

I aduise thee that if thou be East and West with the cape of Saint Augustine, thou shalt see within the land an high hill, hauing as it were a saddle vpon it like to a camel: And thou shalt see to the Southwards three hills along the sea, and then presently thou shall see the coaste to lie Northeast and Southwest.

The height of the cape of S. Augustine, of Olinda and Fernambuck.

Thou shalt vnderstand that from this cape of Saint Augustine, to the towne of Olinda, thou hast nine leagues to the North. And this cape standeth in eight degrees and two third parts, and Olinda standeth in eight degrees and a quarter, and Fernambuck standeth in eight degrees. And this course is to be vnderstood to be obserued and kept, if thou depart from Lisbon in October or Nouember.

In what height they shall seeke land that depart from Lisbon in February or March. Take this aduise, that if thou depart in February or March from Lisbone, then thou shalt goe to beare with the land in nine degrees, because that from March forwards raigne most commonly Southeast and Southwest windes. And if by this height and course thou bring thyselfe nigh to the shore, feare not to bring thy ship into 18 or 20 fadomes, for all the coast is cleane: and there are no more dangers, but such as the sea doth breake vpon.

How to know the cape of S. Augustine. And if after thy fall with the land thou haue occasion to goe to the Northward, and so going seest certaine sholdes, doubt not to come for the North, and thou shalt see the cape of Saint Augustine, which lyeth as it were sloaping to the seaward, and hath as it were a Whales head, and hath vpon it a round hill, with many hilles round about it. And if thou come along the sea coast much about the depth aboue mentioned, thou shalt see a little Island called Saint Alexio: And from this Island to the cape of Saint Augustine are foure leagues, and it standeth in eight degrees and three quarters.

The course that a man must keepe to the bay called A Bahia de Todos os Santos, that is to say, The bay of all Saints, which lieth on the foresayd coast of Brasil.

If thou goe for Bahia de Todos os Santos, thou must keepe the course which I haue already set downe, and shalt obserue the time from March forwards, as also from October forwards. *The height of Bahia de Todos os Santos in 13 degrees and one third part.* Thou shalt vnderstand that the Bahia de Todos os Santos standeth in 13 degrees and ⅓: and if thou goe in October or after October, then goe to fall with the land in 12 degrees or 12 and a halfe.

And take this for a warning, that when thou seest a white land, and long bankes of white sand, which shew much like linnen cloth when it is in whiting, then thou must go along from the North to the South vntill this white land doe end: and thou needest not to feare to goe along the coast, for there are no sholds. Before thou be cleane past the white land or white sands, thou shalt haue sight of an Island that standeth along the bay, I say on the Northside of the bay, which is called Tapaon:[33] and here the land lieth West and by South.

The situation of the Isle of Tapaon. When thou art so farre shot as Tapaon, thou shalt see a certaine great tree which is round, and standeth neere the sea vpon the very point of the entrance into Bahia on the Northside.

When a man may beare in with Bahia. And marke well that if thou looke to the Southward, and seest no white grounds such as I wrote of before, but that they be all behind thee to the Northward; then when thou seest none to the Southward, thou mayest bee bold to beare in with Bahia. And if when thou goest into Bahia to the Northwest, and seest the sea to breake, feare nothing: for it is the breach of a certaine banke, whereon thou shalt haue alwayes 5 or 6 fadomes water: and this be sure of.

Thou shalt vnderstand that if thou come for this place from March to the end of April, I would wish thee not to fall to the Southward of 13 degrees and a halfe. *The distance of O morro de San Paulo from Bahia.* And falling with the land, and not seeing the white sands, thou shalt striue to goe to the Northward. And seeing the land in 13 degrees and a halfe, thou shalt haue sight of an hill along the sea: And if thou be nigh the land, and cannot make it certaine what land it is: thou shalt marke if it bee a round high hill along the sea, that it is O morro de San Paulo, or, The hill of Saint Paul: and it lieth blacke and bare on the top. And from thence to Bahia is tenne leagues.

[33] Itaparica.

Rio de Tinsare a very good riuer. And here along this hill on the Northwest side there is a great riuer called Tinsare: and it is a very good riuer. And in the entrance of Bahia there are sixe or seuen fadomes water in the chanell. And I aduise thee that being in the height of 13 degrees and a halfe, thou come not neere the land, for it hath a bay very dangerous.

And if thou goe from Bahia to Fernambuck, then I aduise thee that thou take good heede of the coast on the Northeast and Southwest, and thou shalt goe East, if the winde will suffer thee to goe East: and so goe thirtie or forty leagues off to the sea.

The height of the bay called A Enseada de Vazabaris. I aduise thee that thou beare not in with the land of Fernambuck, but in the height of 9 or 10 degrees, because that in 11 degrees thou shalt fall with the bay called A Enseada de Vazabaris. Also if thou come from Portugal and fallest with the land in eleuen degrees, beare not in with it, neither come neere it, for thou mayest hurt thy selfe in so doing: but thou shalt shunne it, and goe to the Southward. For if thou lie to the North thou shalt bring thy selfe into some trouble.

Baia de todos Santos in 13 degrees. This Bay of All Saints standeth in thirteene degrees. And from thence to Fernambuck thou hast a hundreth leagues: and the coast lyeth Northeast and Southwest. And from thence to Rio das Ilhas,[34] that is, the riuer of the Islands the coast runneth Northeast and Southwest, I meane taking a quarter of the North and South.

[34] At the mouth of the Caxoeira River.

The course for Baia das Ilhas, that is, The bay of the Islands, which lie on the sayd coast of Brasil, and the marks for the finding of them.

Baia das Ilhas lieth in 15 degrees lacking a quarter. If thou goe for Baia das Ilhas thou must looke for it in fifteene degrees lacking a quarter.

If thou be minded as I sayd to goe for these Isles, if it bee from March forward, thou shalt fall with the land in 15 degrees and a halfe, and though it be in 15 degrees and ⅔, it is all the better.

And if thou haue sight of certaine high hilles, that seeme to reach to the skie, these hilles are called As Serras Raiemores. Then hauing sight of these hilles, thou shalt goe along the coast; and feare nothing, for there are no sholdes along to the North. And when thou seest the Islands, thou mayest make accompt they be these which thou seekest, for there are no other on al this coast, and thou shalt see a round hil along the sea. Thou shalt vnderstand that on the North side of this hill is the going in of the riuer. But if it chance that thou finde thy selfe in a time that will not suffer thee to goe in, then goe along the Islands giuing them a bredth off. And thou mayest well come to an ankor hard aboord them, for all is cleane ground. And thou shalt finde eight or nine fadomes, and from thence thou mayest goe into the riuer hard aboord the shore. And if it chance that thou goe from the North to the South all along the great Island, thou must keepe thy selfe from the land: and when thou hast brought it Eastnortheast, then thou mayest ankor two cables length from the shore: for all is cleane ground.

In what height a man must fall with this place in time of the Northeast winds. If thou chance to arriue on this coast in the time of the Northeast windes, thou shalt seeke to fall with the land in foureteene degrees. And if thou see a lowe land, thou mayest make accompt it is the land called Ciemana, and then thou shalt see Mangues: And also thou shalt come along this coast to the South: and when thou seest an ende of the lowe land, then thou shalt finde an high land along the sea like the other that I haue made mention of before, that is, all sandie along the sea coast.

And thou must vnderstand, that where the high land beginneth, there is a little riuer called Rio das Contas, but enter not into it: it hath for a marke to be knowen by as it were a white mouth. And from thence to the Islands thou hast nine leagues. And at the ende of this high land to the Southward of it thou shalt find a great bay within the land, and then thou shalt looke to the Westsouthwest, and shalt see another high land, which lieth as it were in the middest of the bay, and thou shalt there see certaine white houses which are the Ingenios or houses wherein they make sugar of Lucas Giraldo. From thence thou shalt see the Isles being so farre shotte as Rio de Contas. And thou shalt see within the land a round hill which is like Monte de laude, and it hath another copple[35] on the South side.

[35] Summit.

The course to sayle to Porto Seguro, that is to say, The safe hauen, lying on the foresayd coast of Brasil, and the markes to know the same by.

To auoide Os baixos dos Abrolhos. If thou goe for Porto Seguro and goest in the time of the Southeast windes, which is from March forwards, I aduise thee that thou fall not in more degrees then sixteen and a halfe, because of the sholdes called Os baixos dos Abrolhos, which are very dangerous, and stretch very farre into the sea. And also going West from them, that thou keepe thy lead going and be often sounding. And if thou chance to see the land, and an high hill and long withall, much like to The pike, it is the hill that is called Monte Pasqual. And from thence thou must goe to the North, and when thou hast brought it Southwest of thee, then thou mayest beare with the land, but with great care to looke about thee.

Marke when thou seest the land and commest to see a red cliffe, then looke to the Southward, and thou shall see a great smooth coast along the sea, and then on the North side thou shalt descrie Porto Seguro. The place of comming to an ankor before Porto Seguro, which standeth in 16 deg. and one third. And going along the coast thou shalt see the towne of Porto Seguro standing vpon the toppe of an hill; which hill is a white rocke: and on the North side of the sayd rocke there is a very hie land. I aduise thee that when thou art East and West with the sayd land, I meane with this rocke, that then thou looke to the Northward, and thou shalt see certaine rocks lying two leagues off into the sea, whereon the sea doth breake, and to the Southward of them thou mayest come to an ankor against the towne, and hast a good place to ride in thirteen fadomes in sight of the towne.

A dangerous riuer in 16 degrees. And if it be thy chance to arriue in the time of the Northeast winds, and commest in the height of fifteene degrees and two third parts, and seest not certaine hilles, then thou must goe along the coast being in 16 degrees, and vnder the first hie land that thou shalt descrie, thou shalt see certaine sandie bayes along the sea coast: And if thou haue sight of a riuer in this height,[36] put not thy selfe into it, neither beare with the land, for it hath many sholdes. And off them lie certaine sunken grounds, called Os Baixos de Santo Antonio. And from hence to the Southward lyeth Porto Seguro.

[36] Santa Cruz.

I aduise thee that going along the coast to the Southward, and seeing such sholdes, and the sea to breake vpon them, as the other which I last spake of, thou shall runne along them a sea boord of them: and when thou art at the ende of them, then the towne will beare West of thee: and then thou mayest goe to thine ankoring place as is abouesayd, giuing these sholds a good birth.

The course to the hauen named Baia do Spirito Santo, that is to say, The bay of the holy Ghost, lying on the sayde coast of Brasil, and the markes thereof.

Monzoins are certaine set winds with which the tides set. Thou shall vnderstand that the ship that goeth for Spirito Santo,[37] when it hath doubled the sholdes called Os Baixos dos Abrolhos, and hath brought it selfe in 20 or 19 degrees and a halfe, then it may hall with the land in 18 or 19 degrees and a halfe, and in twentie. And the sayd shippe must goe in this height, because on this coast there are no Monçoins.

[37] A bay to the North of Victoria.

Marks on the North side of Spirito Santo. If thou chance to come in the height of 19 degrees ½ and seest lowe land to the Northwest off thee, then thou art on the North side of Spirito Santo, and thou mayest make accomp that it is the land lying ouer Criquare, and ouer the riuer called Rio dolce, that is the riuer of sweete or fresh water. If thou come along the land thou shalt find certaine high hilles: but trust not the first that thou seest only.

The situation of la Sierra de Mestre Aluaro. For besides the rest thou shalt see a round hie hill which is at the capes end, which is called la Sierra de mestre Aluaro.

Rio dos Reyes magos. Take heede that going for this land thou looke to the North and thou shalt see a riuer called Rio dos Reyes Magos: that is, The riuer of the three kings. And comming to the Southward thou shalt see presently the mouth of the bay to open. At the end of this hill on the South side, thou hast a point of a rocke, which is called A punta do Tubaron. And on the South side of the bay it hath two or three blacke hie hilles, and in the middest of the bay thou shalt goe in westward.

I aduise thee that in going in thou take heede of a sholde which lieth in the mouth of the bay: thou must leaue it to the Southward of thee, and then plie to double a certaine Island which lieth within, and thou must leaue it to the Northward of thee: and when it beareth on the North or Northeast; thou mayest come to an ankor: for all is cleane ground.

A Sierra de Gusriparim in 20 degrees. And if thou chance to come by this course, and fallest in 20 degrees, and seest many hilles, and one among the rest very high and craggie: it is called A Sierra de Guariparim, that is, the hill of Guaraparim, and seest another hill on the North side, which is called A Sierra de Pero Cam: both these lie on the South side of Spirito Santo. And from these hils thou shalt see a little hill named Guaipel. And when thou seest these hilles, thou shalt see three little Islands together, lying to the

Southward: And then from these thou shalt see another rockie, bare and round Island: and to the land off this Island thou shalt see a great bay. If thou wilt thou mayest ankor here safely. And if thou wilt go in, thou shalt bring thy selfe East and West with the hill, and so thou mayest go in. And thou shalt leaue a lowe land to the North of thee, which is called A Ilha de Repouso, that is, the Isle of rest: and this Isle lieth along the coast: and thou mayest be bold to ride betwixt it and the maine, giuing it a breadth off.

From these three Islands to Spirito Santo are 12 leagues: and running Northwards to come to Spirito Santo, thou shalt see another Island, and shalt go a seaboord of it, and by and by the mouth of the bay will open toward thee. And this bay standeth in 20 degrees.

The course from the bay de Spirito Santo to the bay of S. Vincent, and the markes thereof. Also the course from Saint Vincent to the riuer of Plate.

Sailing from Spirito Santo for Saint Vincent, thou mayest goe along the coast, keeping seuen or eight leagues off, and must goe to seeke Cabo Frio, that is, The cold cape. And as thou commest toward Cabo Frio, thou hast a very great bay called Bahia de Saluador, that is, The bay of our Sauiour. And from thence thou hast twelue leagues to Cabo Frio.

And before thou commest to Cabo Frio, thou hast two small Islands. Thou mayest go safely either a sea boord of them, or else betweene them. Thou shalt vnderstand that Cabo Frio hath as it were an Island in the midst of the face or shew thereof, that doth cut off the cape.[38] Thou mayest ride safely on the West side thereof for all is cleane ground.

Understand that Cabo Frio standeth in 23 degrees: and from it to Rio de Ienero are twelue leagues, And this riuer of Ienero hath in the mouth thereof 3 or 4 Islands. And if thou wilt go into this riuer de Ienero, thou mayest well goe in betweene two Islands which stand in the entrance of the riuer on the South side: neere vnto this riuer there is a great hill seeming to bee a man with long haire.

And take this for aduice, that if thou be in the height of this riuer, thou shalt see certaine high hilles within the land, which be like vnto organs. And when thou seest these organs, then make accompt thou art right against the riuer: and comming neere the land thou shalt see a certaine Island very round, which lieth to the Southward, and is hie and bare in the top. Thou must know that the mouth of this riuer standeth in 23 degrees and one third part. And from this riuer to Angra, that is to say, The open hauen, thou hast 15 leagues. Goe not neere the land there, except necessitie compell thee.

I aduise thee, that from this riuer that I spake of, I meane from the entrance thereof, thou must goe Westsouthwest, and Southwest, and West and by South. And thou shalt see a great Island called Isla de San Sebastiano, and to the Southward thereof another small Island very high, called the Island of Alcatrarzas, that is to say, The Island of Pellicanes: but come not neere it, for it hath dangerous shoalds. And from hence thou mayest go West, and so thou shalt fall right with the mouth of Saint Vincent, and thou shalt see an Island.[39] And if thou meane to goe into Saint Vincent thou must leaue this Island to the Westward. And vnderstand that Saint Vincent lieth in foure and twentie degrees. And when thou art in the mouth of this bay, or art neere the mouth of it, then thou shalt see many other Islands, and one among the rest to the seaward. And hauing these sights, thou hast the best markes that bee for these Islands, that I haue told thee of: and this Island lieth Northwest and Southeast with the mouth of S. Vincent.

[38] Papagayos Island.

[39] Saint Amaro.

From San Francisco to Boca de Ouerniron are 26 leagues, and the coast lieth North and South. Also thou must marke that the riuer of San Francisco hath a great entrance, and 3 small Islands, and to seaward it hath a good road; and the main is high and craggie.

From this Boca de Ouerniron to Ilha de Aruoredo thou hast no great markes be obserued: but this Boca is a very great bay, and this bay is deepe within the Island, and is a good road, and hath many islands, and standeth in 28 degrees. And to the North of this Island vnder the point there is a good road: and there is no other road hereabout but this, and it is vnder the Island.

From hence thou shalt haue sight of the Isle called Santa Catharina, which is a great Island about eight or nine leagues long, and lieth North and South. And hard by euen with this Iland is Porto de Patos, which standest in 29 degrees. And from Porto de Patos to Porto de Don Roderigo are ten or eleuen leagues: and the coast lieth North and South. And from Porto de Don Roderigo to Laguna are 5 leagues. And this is a good harbour for all winds, except the Northeast wind.

From the Laguna to the riuer called Rio de Martin de Sousa are 42 leagues. And the coast is something high, and lieth Northeast and by North, and

Southwest and by South: and it hath an Island 2 leagues into the sea, where ships may ride well. And from the Riuer of Martin de Sousa to Rio de San Pedro are 52 leagues, and the coast lieth Northeast and Southwest.

From this riuer of San Pedro there lieth a point of sand a good league off and more, and it lyeth on the Southwest side of the port. And from thence to Cabo de Santa Maria are 42 leagues: and the coast lieth Northeast and Southwest, and all is lowe land.

Also on the Southeast side of Cabo de Santa Maria there lyeth an Isle two leagues off into the sea, and it hath a good harborough betwixt it and the mayne. And note that the mayne is lowe land.

The cape of Santa Maria standeth in 35 degrees, and at the point thereof it hath an Island a league into the sea.

Hereafter followeth a Ruttier from the sayd riuer of Plate to the Streight of Magelane.

The cape of Santa Maria is in 35 degrees. From thence to the Cape de Santo Antonio, which is on the other side of the riuer, are 30 leagues Northnortheast, and Southsouthwest. And this is the broadest place of the riuer. And this cape is in 36 degrees and a halfe, and it is a blacke grosse land. And thou must marke that 25 leagues a seaboord the mouth of the riuer there lie certaine sands, which he called Baixos de los Castellanos.

He that falleth with the Cape of Santa Maria must take good heede to go Southeast vntill he be in 36 degrees, and from thence Southsoutheast vntill 36 degrees and a halfe, giuing the sayd sholds de los Castellanos a breadth: and also taking heede of the flats of the cape. And when he findeth 40 or 45 fadomes, and russet sand, then he must goe Southwest and by South, vntill he be in 40 degrees: where hee shall finde great store of weeds, which come from the coast, and a man may goe 20 leagues from the shore in this sounding.

Cabo de Arenas Gordas. From the Cape de Santo Antonio to the cape de Arenas Gordas are eight and forty leagues, and the coast lieth Northeast and Southwest, and by East and by West: Rio de S. Anna. and in the first eighteene leagues is the riuer called Rio de Santa Anna, which hath at the entrance certaine flats and sholds, giue them a good breadth, and come not nigh them by much, but keepe thy selfe in forty fadomes to goe surely.

> Cape de S. André.

From the cape de Arenas Gordas to the cape of Sant André are one and thirty leagues: it lieth Northeast and by East, and Southwest by West: I meane when thou art in the middest with an equall distance from them both. And between both the capes are many bayes and riuers, but all full of sandie sholdes.

> Baia Anegada.

From the cape of Sant Andres to the bay called Anegada, that is, The sunken bay, are 30 leagues Eastnortheast, and Westsouthwest. It standeth in 40 degrees, rather lesse then more.

> Punta de Tierra Ilana.

From the bay called Baia Anegada to The point of the plaine land are 25 leagues Northnortheast, and Southsouthwest.

> Baia sin fondo.

This point lyeth in 41 degrees and a halfe, And from this point to Baia sin fondo, that is to say the bottomlesse bay, are 35 leagues Eastnortheast and Westsouthwest This bay standeth in 42 degrees and a halfe, rather lesse then more.

> Cabo redondo. Puerto de los leones.

And from Baia sin fondo to Cabo Redondo, and Puerto de los leones, are 37 leagues Northnortheast and Southsouth west, somewhat to the North and South. And if thou meane to go out from thence with a compasse about after the maner of a halfe circle or an arch, so thou mayest passe through the Baia sin fondo along the shore: for there is water enough.

Note that from the riuer of Plate to this place is neuer a good harbour for great shipping.

> Puerto de los leones in 44 degrees and better.

From this place to Puerto de los leones the coast is cleane, and a man may come nigh vnto the land: And it is a lowe land with white cliffes. This harbour is in 44 degrees.

> Take good heede of these little rocks.

And as a man goeth thither, after he bee in 43 degrees or more, hee must haue a care to looke out for certaine small rockes which lie neere the land, and lie North of the harbour.

> Cabo de Matas.

From this harbour to Cabo de Matas, or the cape of shrubs, are 30 leagues North and South, halfe a point to the East, and to the West: and betwixt them there is a great bay very long: And to the Northwest 18 leagues from

Cabo redondo is a riuer lying East and West: ⁝ Rio de Camarones. ⁝ and it is called Rio de Camarones, or, The riuer of shrimps. You shall know when you fall with this riuer, by seeing many white spots vpon the water, and they are small shrimps.

⁝ Cabo redondo in 45 degrees and a halfe large. ⁝ From this riuer to Cabo redondo the coast lieth Northwest and by North, and Southeast and by South. This cape is in 45 degrees and a halfe large.

⁝ Cabo Blanco and Barancas Blancas in 47 degrees. ⁝ From this sayd cape to Cabo Blanco and Barancas Blancas that is to say, to The white cape and white cliffes are 32 leagues lying North and by East and South and by West: and they stand in 47 degrees.

From this Cape the coast lyeth towards the North side Northwest about three leagues all full of white cliffes steepe vp: and the last cliffe is the biggest both in length and height, and sheweth to be the saile of a ship when it is vnder saile. These white cliffes are 6 in number, and this Cape hath in the face thereof a certaine round land that sheweth to bee an Island afarre off: and it hath certaine poynts of rockes hard by it. And two Cables length from the land is 25 fathomes water. Aboue these white cliffes the land is plaine and euen: and it hath certaine woods. There is much people in the countrey: of whom I wish thee to take good heed.

From this Cape the land lyeth North and South; which is the first fall of the Cape: and in the face thereof it hath a poynt of rocks, which shewe themselues. ⁝ A good harbour. ⁝ And on the South side of this Cape is a good harbour and road, and there is a Bay in the middest.

⁝ The port of Saint Iulian. ⁝ From Cabo and Blanco to Puerto de San Iulian are 37 leagues, and the coast lyeth North and by East and South and by West. This harbour of S. Iulian hath in the entrance certaine high hilles, which afarre off seeme to be towers. On the South part of the entrance the chanell is deepest in the middest: and thou must borrow neerer the North side then to the South. Within the harbour are two Islands: thou must come to an anker hard to them. This hauen lyeth in 49. degrees. ⁝ Islas de Ascensaom. ⁝ And betweene Cabo Blanco and this The Islands of Ascension, and they be eight. ⁝ Morro de Santo Yues, in 50 degrees large. ⁝ From this said harbour to the hill of S. Yues are 35 leagues; the coast lyeth Northeast and Southwest: it is a low land and euen and hath onely one hil, and it is a plaine from one part to the another, and hath certaine cliffes to seaward, and to the Southward, and to the South side it hath certaine little copples: it standeth in 50 degrees large.

From the hill of S. Yues to Rio de Cruz are 8 leagues, Northeast and Southwest: and on the Northside of the riuer it hath a very dry land, and in the toppe it is plaine and lyeth two leagues broad layd out along North and South, and the downefall on both sides hath as it were saddles. This Cape hath many poynts of rockes lying 4 leagues into the sea: and when thou hast sight of this land, it is goode for thee to keepe from it a good bredth off. And going from thence thou mayest runne in sight of the land in 25 fathoms.

Rio de Galegos and the marks thereof. From Rio de Cruz to Rio de Galegos are 25 leagues, Northeast and Southwest; and it standeth in 52 degrees and ⅙ of a degree. It hath a certaine high land: and in the highest of the sayd land it is plaine, and to the Northeast it is a pike vp, and hath certaine white cliffes: and on the toppe and something downewarde it is blacke: at the foote of this high land to the Eastward thereof it hath certaine steps like a lather: and to the sea it hath a sharpe poynt that lyeth into this Cape almost halfe a league. To the Southward of this Cape where the lather is, there is a little Bay, which is the entrance of Rio de Galegos, it ebbeth and floweth here 12 fathomes. A man must haue a great care how he goeth in here for the cause abouesaid: but he must keepe himselfe out and not anker in it.

From Rio de Galegos to the Streits of Magelan the coast lyeth Northnorthwest and Southsoutheast: 8 leagues vnto Cabo de la virgin Maria, which is the entrance into the Streit: and 4 leagues before a man come to this Cape there are white cliffes with certaine blacke spots in them; and they be caused with the falling downe of the water. Ciudad de Nombre de Iesus called by M. Candish Port Famine because he found al the Spaniards famished, and the towne it selfe vtterly abandoned and ruined. Here is water inough, and thou mayest come to an anker hard aboord the shore, and hast a good defence for a Southwest wind. And the Cape it selfe is the highest land of all, and is like to Cape Saint Vincent in Spaine: and it hath on the east side a ledge of rockes, and a poynt of sand, with diuers sands which shewe themselues at a lowe water: thou must take great heede heere and giue them a good breadth halfe a league or a quarter of a league off, vntill thou bring the Cape Westnorthwest, and then thou mayest stirre away Southwest. And when thou commest to the lower land

and into tenne or twelue fathoms, then art thou ouer against la Purificacion. Where Nombre de Iesus stood. And halfe a league within the land the citie of Nombre de Iesus was builded, East and West with the sayd cape right against a cliffe, which commeth from the sayd Cape, and goeth within the Streits. This Cape standeth in 52 degrees iust.

Southwest winds raigne much here in Sommer. And this is to be taken for a warning, that he that commeth neere this Cape, and passeth by it as I haue said with the wind at Northeast, or any other wind off the sea inclining to the Southeast, must not come to anker, but presently be sure to passe by: because in Sommer this place is much subiect to Southwest winds, which blow right in: and they put a man from his tackle, and make him to loose his voyage. From March forward the winds are fauorable for the Streits. And from March forwards there blow favourable winds from the sea to goe from this Cape to enter into the Streits, from this said Cape the Streits go in to the Northwest 14 leagues: and the chanell waxeth narrower and narrower vnto the first Streit which runneth Eastnortheast, and Westsouthwest. And comming out of the mouth thereof a man must keepe himselfe a poynt to the Northward, because there be rocks and shoalds. The Indians about Cape de San Gregorio in the Streits are very trecherous. And if you see beds of weeds, take heed of them, and keepe off from them: and after you be past this Streight you must stirre Westsouthwest 8 leagues vnto Cabo de San Gregorio, which is a high white cliffe, and is a good road for any wind from the Northwest to the Southwest. But men must beware and not trust the Indians of this Cape: for they be subtill and will betray a man.

From this Cape beginneth the second Streit which is called Nuestra Sennorà de Gracia, and lyeth Eastnortheast and Westsouthwest 3 leagues. And comming out of this Streit thou shalt see 3 little Islands, lying West off this Streit: thou mayest go betweene them, for there is no danger: prouided alwayes that thou keepe well off from the bayes on both sides, lest thou bee imbayed. Rincones. And from these Islands thou must keepe forwards in the channell Westsouthwest two leagues: and then the coast lyeth North and South vnto 53 degrees and a halfe, vnto a place called Punta de Santa Anna: La Ciudad del Don Philippe: which is now vtterly ruined. and to the Northwest thereof, in a corner or nooke (which is one of the rincones or nookes) was the towne builded called La Ciudad del Don Philippe. Thou must come to an anker to the Northward thereof, after thou art past the castle and a great tree.

TWO VOYAGES

OF CERTAINE ENGLISHMEN TO THE RIUER OF PLATE SITUATE IN 35 DEGREES OF SOUTHERLY LATITUDE: TOGETHER WITH AN EXACT RUTTIER AND DESCRIPTION THEREOF, AND OF ALL THE MAINE BRANCHES, SO FARRE AS THEY ARE NAVIGABLE WITH SMALL BARKES. BY WHICH RIUER THE SPANIARDS OF LATE YEERES HAVE FREQUENTED AN EXCEEDING RICH TRADE TO AND FROM PERU, AND THE MINES OF POTOSSI, AS ALSO TO CHILI, AND OTHER PLACES.

A report of a Voyage of two Englishmen in the company of Sebastian Cabota, intended for the Malucos by the Streights of Magellan, but perfourmed onely to the riuer of Plate in April 1527. Taken out of the information of M. Robert Thorne to Doctor Ley Ambassador for King Henry the eight, to Charles the Emperour, touching the discouery of the Malucos by the North.

This was the fleete wherein Cabot discouered the riuer of Plate, 1526.

Two Englishmen went with Cabot in this discouery. In a flote of three ships and a carauel that went from this citie of Siuil armed by the merchants of it, which departed in Aprill last past, I and my partner haue one thousand foure hundred duckets that wee employed in the sayd fleete, principally for that two Englishmen, friendes of mine, which are somewhat learned in Cosmographie, should goe in the same ships, to bring me certaine relation of the situation of the countrey, and to be expert in the nauigation of those seas, and there to haue informations of many other things, and aduise that I desire to know especially. Seeing in those quarters are ships and mariners of that countrey, and cardes by which they saile, though much vnlike ours: that they should procure to haue the sayd cards, and learne how they understand them, and especially to know what nauigation they haue for those Islands Northwards and Northeastward.

The Islands of the Malucos. The New found Ilands discouered by the English. For if from the said Islands the sea doth extend without interposition of land to saile from the North point to the Northeast point one thousand seuen hundred or one thousand eight hundred leagues, they should come to The new found Islands that we discouered, and so we should be neerer to the said Spicerie by almost 200 leagues then the Emperour, or the king of Portugall are.

An extract out of the discourse of one Lopez Vaz a Portugal, touching the fight of M. Fenton with the Spanish ships, with a report of the proceeding of M. Iohn Drake after his departing from him to the riuer of Plate.

Vpon the relation of Pedro Sarmiento concerning the streits of Magellan, that they might be fortified, and for that the king heard, that there were ships in England preparing for the same streits, he commanded Diego Flores de Valdes a noble man of Spaine, to passe thither with 23 ships, and 3500 men to stoppe the passage of the Englishmen.

Fiue ships of this fleete cast away on the coast of Spaine. There went in this fleete the gouernour of Chili, with 500 olde souldiers that came out of Flanders: but this was the vnhappiest fleet of ships that euer went out of Spaine: for before they came from the coast of Spaine a storme tooke them, and cast away fiue of the fleete and in them aboue 800 men, and the rest came into Cadiz. But the king sent them word that they should proceede: and so there went out on the voyage 16 of the shippes, for two more of their fleete were much spoyled by the storme which they had.

In these sixeteene shippes Pedro Sarmiento was sent to bee gouernour in the straites, and had assigned vnto him 500 men to stay there with him, and hee carried with him, all kinde of Artificers to make him forts, and other necessaries, with great store of ordinance and other munition.

This fleete because it was late, did winter on the coast of Brasil, in the riuer of Ienero: and from thence they went when the winter was past, and about the height of 42 degrees they had a sudden storme, so that Diego Flores beat it vp and downe 22 dayes, in which time hee lost one of the best ships he had, which had in her 360 men and 20 women, that went to inhabit the

Streits: and in this ship also was most part of the munition which should haue bene left in the Streits, so in the ende the storme grew to bee so great, that the ships were not able to endure it any longer, but were put backe vnto an Island called Santa Catelina:[40] and there he found a barke wherein were some fryers going for the riuer of Plate: M. Fenton took these fryers. which friers told him of two great English ships, and a pinnesse, which had taken them, but tooke nothing from them, nor did them any harme, but onely asked them for the king of Spaines ships.

Hereupon Diego Flores knowing that these English ships would goe for the Streits, determined to goe thither, although it was in the moneth of Februarie, and choosing 10 ships of the 15 that were left, hee left two ships that were not in case to goe to sea at the Iland, and into the other three ships which were old, and shaken with the storme hee put all the women, and sicke men in all the fleete, and sent them to the riuer of Ienero, and he with the other 10 returned againe for the Streits.

The three ships in which the sicke men and women were, went to Brasil, and there they found within the port of S. Vincent the two ships before mentioned.

A fight betwixt our 2 English ships and three Spanish ships. They woulde haue had the English men to haue gone out of the harbour, and thereupon they fell to fight, and because that these three ships were weake with the storme, and the men that they had were the worst in all the fleete, the Englishmen easily put them to the worst, and sunke one of them, and might haue sunke another, if the Englishmen would: but they minded not the destruction of any man: for that is the greatest vertue that can be in a man, that when hee may doe hurt, yet he will not doe it. They victual at Spirito Santo. So the Englishmen went from this port to Spirito Santo, where they had victuals for their merchandise, and so they went backe for England, without doing of any harme in the Countrey.

[40] Santa Catherina.

The cause why these English shippes vnder the conduct of M. Fenton went not to the streits, I know not: but some say that they were put backe by foule weather: other some say that it was for feare of the kings ships.

Iohn Drake proceedeth on to the riuer of Plate. But the pinnesse of these two ships went from them, in which was Captaine Iohn Drake: the cause why they parted I know not, but the pinnesse came into the riuer of Plate, and within fiue leagues of Seale Island, not farre from the place where the Earle of Cumberlands shippes did take in fresh water, shee was cast away vpon a ledge of rockes: but the men were saued in their boat, which were in number 18, who went ashore on the Northside, and went a dayes iourney into the land, and met with the Sauages which are no men-eaters, but take all the Christians that they can, and make them slaues.

But the Englishmen fought with them and the Sauages slew fiue of them, and tooke 13 aliue, which were with the Sauages about 15 moneths. Richard Faireweather remayneth in the riuer of Plate. But the Master of the pinnesse, whose name was Richard Faireweather being not willing to indure the misery that hee was in, and hauing knowledge that there was a towne of Christians on the other side of the riuer, he in a night called Iohn Drake, and another yong man which was with them, and tooke a very little Canoa, which had but two oares, and so passed to the other side of the riuer, which is about 19 leagues broade, and were three dayes before they could get ouer without meat: and comming to land, they hit vpon an high way that went towardes the Christians: and seeing the footing of horses, they followed it, and at last came to an house where there was corne sowed, and there they met with Indians seruants vnto the Spaniards, which gaue them meate, and clothes to couer them, for they were all naked, and one of the Indians went to the towne, and told them of the Englishmen: so the Captaine sent foure horsemen, who brought them to the towne behind them.

This Captaine clothed them, and prouided lodging for them, and Iohn Drake dieted at the Captaines table, and they were all very well intreated, the Captaine purposing to send them for Spaine. Iohn Drake sent to the Viceroy of Peru. But the Viceroy of Peru hauing newes hereof, sent for them, and so Iohn Drake was sent to him, but the other two were kept there, because they were married in the countrey, so that I know no more of their affaires.

Vpon this comming of the Englishmen, there were prepared 50 horsemen to goe ouer the riuer to seeke the rest of the Englishmen, and also certaine Spaniards that were among the Sauage people, but I am not certaine, whether they went forward or not.

A ruttier which declareth the situation of the coast of Brasil from the Isle of Santa Catelina vnto the mouth of the riuer of Plata, and all

along vp within the sayd riuer, and what armes and mouthes it hath to enter into it, as farre as it is nauigable with small barks.

The Isle of Santa Catelina. Rio Grande. From the Isle of Santa Catelina, (which is in 28 degrees of Southerly latitude) vnto Rio Grande is fortie leagues. This riuer by another name is called Ygai. The Island of Santa Catelina is sixe leagues in length: It hath two small Ilands on the North side betweene the maine land and it: and on the South side it hath a shoald of rockes, which lyeth hidden very neere vnto the poynt of the Isle. You are to passe betweene the firme land and the poynt of the Isle.

Puerto de Biaza, or Laguna. From Santa Catelina to the hauen of Biaça, which by another name is called la Laguna, are twelue leagues: it is a good hauen within: but you must stay the full sea to enter into it, because it hath shoaldes in the mouth, and it may be knowen by a small Island which lyeth a league into the sea which is called La Isla de Raparo, that is The Island of succour or defence, and you must ride there to search the chanell.

From this harbour vnto the riuer before named there is no hauen for a ship to harbour it selfe. And Rio Grande hath many shoals in the mouth thereof. It is a riuer that none but very small shippes can enter into. And this riuer diuideth the countrey of the people called Carios from other nations which are called Guauaes. *Certaine Ilands 12 leagues distant from the mouth of the riuer of Plate, which are 3 in number.* And from this riuer vnto the entrance of the mouth of the riuer of Plate it is al a plaine land, and very low: you must saile all along two or three leagues into the sea from the shore, vntill you come to certain Islands[41] which lye twelue leagues from the mouth of the riuer of Plate.

[41] Castillos and Palmarones.

From Rio Grande vnto these Islands are 68 leagues. And from these Islands vnto the Cape of Saint Marie the coast runneth Northeast and Southwest, somewhat inclining a poynt to the South. The Islands are three, and may be knowen as you come from the sea by two poynts, which shew like the eares of a conie: you may ride betweene them and the maine.

Isla de Lobos. From Rio Grande to the Cape of Saint Marie are 80 leagues: and the Cape may be knowne by one Island which lyeth from it a league and an halfe into the sea. You may sayle betweene the maine and that Island, because there is aboue 8 or 9 fathoms water. The Cape of Saint Mary standeth in 35 degrees of Southerly latitude.

The Cape of Santa Maria vpon the poynt thereof hath a little hill which standeth ouer against the Isle of Seales. *The way to enter into the riuer of Plate.* From this coast of Santa Maria you must coast along the land alway on the North shore, and along the same are certaine Bayes. From the Cape vnto the riuer of Solis are tenne leagues, the coast runneth East and West. There standeth an Island ouer against the mouth thereof. From this riuer of Solis vnto Los tres Mogotes which are on the maine land is three leagues. And from Los Mogotes vnto the Isles of Saint Grauiel are other 8 or 9 leagues more; all this distance runneth East and West. These are fiue small Islands: to ride here you must keepe somewhat neere the maine within an harquebuze shot halfe a league before you come at the Islands, and straightway you shall see a crosse standing on the said land, and there is an harbour for some winds.

From Saint Grauiel vnto the riuer of Sant Iuan going along the same coast, I say on the North shore, are three leagues: it is very well knowen by the broken cliffe which it hath, which is a white hill. The entrance into this riuer is very dangerous; because it is shallow, and none but very small shippes can enter into the same: the entrance thereof is on the West side very neere the land, great Carackes may ride within the harbour. From this riuer vnto the Isle of Martin Garçia are three leagues: it is one Island alone, and you must sayle along the coast on the North shore: and after you be come vnto the Island, I say, ouer against the same, you shall haue three fathoms water, and on the West side it hath a little creeke where you may ride.

He that desireth to crosse ouer the riuer of Plate vnto the riuer de Buenos Aëres from the Isles of Saint Grauiel, must shape his course Southwest: and the cut ouer is sixeteene leagues and vpon his arriuall on the South shore of the riuer, hee must seeke a chanell of three fathomes water, and straite he must goe along the coast vntill hee come to a broken cliffe and a poynt like vnto the firme land, which is distant from this chanell three or foure leagues: and when thou seest this broken cliffe, keepe thee a league from it. *The first Spanish colonie was planted in the riuer of Buenos Aëres.* Here vpon this riuer of Buenos Aëres was the first Colonie that Don Pedro de Mendoça planted. This riuer lieth very much hidden: because it is not seene, it is very shallow at a low sea, wherefore you must come in with the first of the flood.

From the Isle of Martin Garçia vnto certaine small Islands which are called the Isles of Saint Lazarus is two leagues, these are shoalds: and to goe thither you must goe hard aboord the maine, for there goeth the chanell: all this is to be passed on the North shore, and with small barkes, and with good heede.

From the Isle of Martin Garçia to the mouthes of the riuer are eight leagues in passing along on this side to seeke one of the mouthes of the riuer Parana, as it is hereafter described. But you had need first to harbour in a bay, which is in the very cliffe or Barranca, and you must stay for the full sea. *Rio Vruay.* And if you fall into the mouth of the riuer which is called Vruay,[42] you must leaue it on the right hand, I say on the North side. *Parana is the great riuer.* And foorthwith leauing the said mouth forward toward the West, you may enter into the first mouth although it seeme narrow; or rather you may enter into any of the mouthes: for all of them meete together in Parana, which is the maine riuer.

[42] River Uruguay.

Rio de las Palmas. And hee that desireth to goe from the Isle of Martin Garçia to the riuer of Palmas, which is the best of all these armes, or mouthes to speake more properly, is to shape his course to the West, and comming ouer to the other shore, and sayling along the coast Northnorthwest hee shall discouer the mouth of this riuer of Palmas: and hee must enter hard by Los Iuncales, which lye on the South side: and afterward within is very deepe sounding. All these mouthes of this riuer which are 5, are full of sholds towards the East aboue the space of two leagues. And if the course of the water were not swift there, you could not enter into them, as I haue already sayd, and you must passe all along with much heede and foresight.

Cape Blanco on the South side of the mouth of the riuer of Plate a very low and euen land. And if peradventure you haue passed Cape Saint Marie and are come ouer to Cape Blanco, consider it, that it is so euen and smooth a land, that you can scarcely discerne it a league from the maine, vnlesse it be a very cleare day: and after this sort the coast lieth low vnto the riuer de Buenos Aeres. And from thence the coast lyeth somewhat high vnto the entrance of the riuer de Palmas: all the coast runneth as I sayd before. *Man-eaters vpon the south shore.* And all along this coast are naughty people, which eate those which they kill, and many Tygers.

From the Isle of Martin Garçia vnto Saint Saluador is nine or tenne leagues. This is an Island which standeth two leagues within the first mouth: where Sebastian Cabota tooke possession. And this countrey is very well peopled by a people called Carios; and you most beware of all these people: for they are your deadly enemies. The most Southerly mouth of Parana called Rio de Palmas is sixteene leagues long, and it hath many turnings, and many palme or date-trees growing neere it, whereupon it is called The riuer of palme trees: and forthwith it entreth into the riuer Parana, as soone as these sixteene leagues are finished. All the other armes containe likewise sixteene leagues in length, sauing one small or narrow arme, which is called The riuer de los Beguaes; for this containeth fortie leagues in length. From this you must enter by the mouth of the riuer of Palmas vnto Santo Spirito, the way is fiftie leagues: you are to passe still along the cliffes. As you enter on the left hand which is on the West shore vp this riuer there are many Isles, lakes and small riuers, and many Indians which are your enemies.

From Santo Spirito vnto a people which are called Los Tenbuis is fifteene leagues. This is by the narrow arme whereby they passe into the riuer Parana: it is the more because it is the longer way. From the Tenbuis by this narrow arme vpward vnto the Quiloacas, which is another nation, are twentie leagues; and all vp this riuer is great store of people.

From the Quiloacas, to a place where the Spaniards now haue builded a towne, are fifteene leagues. This towne perhaps may be the towne of Santa Anna, 15. leagues. From this towne vnto the people called Los Mequaretas is twentie leagues. Here are many sholds which continue thirtie leagues. All these thirtie leagues are sunken lands: where are many Isles, flats, and nations, which are our enemies.

From the Mequaretas vnto the people called Mepenes ate these thirtie leagues. And from hence begin the coasts of the firme land vnto the mouth of the riuer Paraguai; sauing that there are eight leagues more of sunken ground.

From the Mepenes vnto the month of the riuer of Paraguai are thirtie leagues: it is a riuer that cannot be mistaken although it hath many armes and Islands and dangers, it hath a marke two leagues beneath the mouth on the East side, to wit, an high land, where are 7 points, which we call the 7 currents: and immediately aboue these currents there is an Island as you passe vp the riuer ouer against the poynt aforesaid standeth the mouth of Paraguai. The towne of Piquiri or Picora 170 leagues vp the riuer of Parana. This mouth is very plaine to be found in seeking whereof a man cannot be deceived. From this mouth the riuer of Parana is diuided, which is a very great riuer: and it goeth vnto the towne of Piquiri, which is an hundred and seuentie leagues: and it runneth all this space North and South, and in the way are many flats and shoalds; and great store of people, which are a bad nation, although they be diuided. The citie of Assumption, or Ascension 60 leagues from the mouth of Paraguai. From the place where these two riuers are diuided, that is to say, from the mouth of Paraguai are sixtie leagues vnto the citie of Assumption. This is a good riuer, and better to sayle then all the rest of the riuers, which are in this countrey. 200 leagues from Assumption subiect to the Spaniard, to the citie of Xaraes. And from this towne to Los Xaraes[43] are 200. leagues, very well inhabited with people of diuers nations, which serue the Spanyards.

[43] North of Lake Uberaba, in latitude 17 degrees South, and longitude 52 ½ West.

Nauigations, Voyages, Traffiques and Discoueries of the English Nation.

VOL. XIV.

PART III.

THE FIRST AND SECOND DISCOUERY

OF THE GULFE OF CALIFORNIA, AND OF THE SEA COAST ON THE NORTHWEST OR BACK-SIDE OF AMERICA, LYING TO THE WEST OF NEW MEXICO, CIBOLA AND QUIUIRA, TOGETHER WITH SIR FRANCIS DRAKES LANDING AND TAKING POSSESSION VPON NOUA ALBION IN THE BEHALFE OF THE CROWNE OF ENGLAND, AND THE NOTABLE VOYAGE OF FRANCIS GAULE; WHEREIN AMONGST MANY OTHER MEMORABLE MATTERS IS SET DOWNE THE HUGE BREDTH OF THE OCEAN SEA FROM CHINA AND IAPAN TO THE NORTHWEST PARTS OF AMERICA, IN THE 38. AND 40. DEGREES.

A relation of the discouery, which in the Name of God the Fleete of the right noble Fernando Cortez Marques of the Vally, made with three ships; The one called Santa Agueda of 120. tunnes, the other the Trinitie of 35. tunnes, and the thirde S. Thomas of the burden of 20. tunnes. Of which Fleete was Captaine the right worshipfull knight Francis de Vlloa borne in the Citie of Merida. Taken out of the third volume of the voyages gathered by M. Iohn Baptista Ramusio.

Chap. 1.

Francis Vlloa a captaine of Cortez departeth with a Fleete from the port of Acapulco, and goeth to discouer vnknowen lands, he passeth by the coast of Sacatula and Motin, and by tempest runneth to the riuer of Guajaual, from whence he crosseth ouer to the hauen of Santa Cruz, along the coast whereof he discouereth 3. smal Ilands, and within two dayes and an halfe returning to the maine land he discouereth the riuer called Rio de san Pedro y san Pablo, and not far distant from thence two other riuers as big or greater then that of Guadalquiuir which runneth by Siuil, together with their head springs.

Acapulco in 17. degrees of latitude. We imbarked our selues in the hauen of Acapulco on the 8. of Iuly in the yeere of our Lord 1539, calling vpon almighty God to guide vs with his holy hand vnto such places where he might be serued, and his holy faith aduanced. And we sailed from the said port by the coast of Sacatula and Motin, which is sweete and pleasant through the abundance of trees that grow thereon, and riuers which passe through those countries, for the which wee often thanked God the creatour of them. So sailing along we came to the hauen of S. Iago in the province of Colima: but before we arriued there, the maine mast of our ship called Santa Agueda was broken by a storme of winde that tooke vs, so as the ship was forced to saile without her mast vntil we arriued in the said hauen. From the port of Acapulco to this hauen of Colima wee were sayling the space of 20. dayes. Here we stayed to mende our mast and to take in certaine victuals, water, and wood, the space of 27. dayes. And wee departed from the saide hauen the 23. of August, and sayling by the Isles of Xalisco the 27. or 28. of the saide moneth wee were taken with an extreame tempest wherein wee thought we should have perished, and being tossed and weather-beaten, wee ranne as farre as the riuer of Guajalua in the Prouince of Culiacan. Santa Cruz in the point of California. In this storme wee lost the pinnessee called Sant Thomas, and because wee had lost her wee crossed ouer to the port of Santa Cruz in California: for while wee were so beaten in the former tempest, the pilot of the Barke signified vnto vs, that he perceiued she beganne to leake, and that already she had received in much water, insomuch that she beganne to founder: whereupon, to helpe her neede, and that we might meete together in a knowen hauen, if by chance the tempest should separate vs, as it did indeed, we willed him to repaire to the hauen of Santa Cruz, where we meant to repaire his harmes and our owne. Wherefore being all arriued in this place of Santa Cruz, wee stayed there fiue dayes and tooke in water, wherein we heard no newes of our Barke which we had lost: Whereupon the Captaine resolued to follow on our voyage; wherefore we set saile the 12. of September, and as we sailed wee saw along the coast of the said hauen 3. Islands, whereof the Captaine made no great accompt, thinking there coulde be no great good found in any of them. These Islands seemed not to be great; wherefore he commanded the Masters and pilotes to proceed on their voyage, and not to leese time without any profit. Rio de san Pedro y san Pablo. So sailing ouer the gulfe of California, in two dayes and an halfe we came to the riuer of S. Peter and S. Paul, finding before we entered into the same a small Island in the mouth of the Riuer, being 4. or 5. miles distant from the maine. On both sides of the Riuer wee beheld goodly and pleasant great plaines full of many green and beautiful trees, and farther within the land we beheld certaine exceeding high mountaines full of woods very pleasant to beholde. From this riuer wee sailed still along the coast the space of 15 leagues, in which course wee found two other Riuers in our iudgement as great or greater then Guadalquiuir the Riuer of Siuilia in Spaine. Al the coast by these Riuers is plaine as the other which we had passed, with many woods: likewise within the lande appeared great mountaines couered with woods very beautifull to beholde, and beneath in the plaine appeared certaine lakes of water. From these Riuers we sailed 18 leagues, and found very pleasant plaines, and certaine great lakes whose mouthes opened into the Sea: here our Capitane thought good throughly to discouer what those lakes were, and to search whether there were any good hauen for his ships to ride in, or to harbour themselues, if any tempest should arise; and so he commaunded a boat to be hoised out into the Sea, with a Master and fiue or sixe men to view them, and to sound the depth, and bottom of them: who went thither, and found the coast very sholde, and the mouthes of the lakes; whereupon they made no accompt of them, onely because the shore was so shallow, for otherwise the land was very pleasant. Here at euening we saw on the shore 10. or 12. Indians and fires. The aforesaide two Riuers are two leagues distant the one from the other little more or lesse, and are great, as I haue saide, and being in the last of them we went vp to the ship-top, and saw many lakes, and one among the rest exceeding great, and wee supposed that they had their springs out of this great lake, as other Riuers also haue from other lakes, for wee sawe the course of them seuerally each by themselues, hauing goodly woods growing all along their bankes. The currents of these Riuers might be discerned three leagues within the Sea: and at the mouthes of them were many small stakes set vp for markes: the shore here is plaine and sandie, and the countrey very pleasant.

Chap. 2.

Sailing along the coast from the two aforesaid great Riuers, they discouer three mouthes of lakes and a goodly Countrey, they come vnto Cabo Roxo, and take possession of those countreys for the Emperours Maiesty. A discourse of the faire hauens that are on those coastes, and of very many Islands which they saw, before they came to the Cape called Capo de las Plaias.

This day wee sailed along the coast the space of 16. leagues, and in the midst of this voyage, there is a Bay very faire of 4. or 5. leagues, hauing certaine bankes or fences in it, in beholding whereof we tooke great pleasure. The night following we road in 20. fadome water. The coast runneth Northward. The next day we followed our voyage toward the North, and hauing sailed 3. or 4. leagues we saw 3. mouthes of lakes which entred into the land, where they became like standing pooles. Wee road a league distance from these mouthes in 6. fadome water, to see what they were, and sent our boat with certaine men, to see if there were any entry for our ships: for halfe a league from shore we had not past one or two fadome water. Here our men saw 7. or 8. Indians, and found sundry sorts of greene herbes somewhat differing from those of Nueua Espanna. The Countrey is plaine, but farre within the land they saw great and small hils extending themselues a great way, and being very faire and pleasant to behold. The day following we proceeded on our voyage sayling alwayes in sight of the plaine coast toward the Northwest, in 10. or 15. fadome water. And hauing sailed 6. good leagues we found a Bay on the coast within the land of about 5. leagues ouer, from whence the coast trendeth Northwest, and this day we sailed about 16 leagues. All this coast is plaine, and not so pleasant as that which we had passed: here are certaine small hilles, but not so high as those which we had found before. Thus we sailed all night Northwest, and vntil the next day at noone, at which time we fell with a headland of white sand, where by the height which we tooke that day we found our selues to be in the latitude of 27. degrees and ¾. This cape we called Capo Roxo. All the coast is plaine and faire and cleane sand, and we saw within land some few trees not very great, with certaine mountaines and woods 3. or 4. leagues distant from the said cape: and here likewise appeared a mouth of a riuer, which (as far as we could discerne) made certaine lakes vp within the land: from the mouth whereof for the space of a league into the sea it seemed to be very sholde, because the sea did breake very much. Here we saw within the land 3. or 4. riuers. *The coast runneth Northward.* In this sort we sailed on our voiage to the Northward, and because we had not good weather we road that night in a great hauen lying in our way, where on the shore wee saw certaine plaines, and vp within the land certaine hilles not very high: and continuing our course toward the North about 3. leagues from this hauen, we found an Iland of about one league in circuite lying before the mouth of the said hauen. And sailing forward we found an hauen which hath two mouthes into the Sea, into which we entered by the Northermost mouth, which hath 10. or 12. fadome water, and so decreaseth till it come to 5. fadome, where we anckered in a poole which the Sea maketh, which is a strange thing to beholde, for there are so many entrances and mouths of streames and hauens, that we were all astonied at the sight thereof: and these hauens are so excellently framed by nature, as the like are not to bee seene in the world, wherein we found great store of fish. Here we anckered, and the Captaine went on shore, and tooke possession, vsing all such ceremonies as thereunto belong. *Fishing weares like those of Virginia.* Here also wee found certaine weares to catch fish made by the Indians, and certaine small cottages, wherein were diuers pieces of earthen pots as finely made as those in Spaine. Here by commandement of the Captaine a Crosse was erected vpon an hil, and it was set vp by Francis Preciado. In this place we saw the Countrey full of fresh and greene grasse, howbeit differing from that of New Spaine, and vp within the Countrey we saw many great and very greene mountaines. This Countrey seemed very goodly and delightsome to all of vs, in regard to the greennesse and beautie thereof, and we iudged it to be very populous within the land. From this hauen we departed and kept our way toward the Northwest with good weather, and began to finde hard by the sea-shore exceeding high mountaines spotted with white, and in them we saw many foules which had their nestes in certaine holes of those rocks, and sailed 10. leagues vntil night, all which night we were becalmed. The next day we followed our course Northwest with good weather: and from that day forward we began to see on the Westerne shore (whereon the foresaid hauen of S. Cruz standeth) certaine Islands or high lands, whereat we reioyced not a little. And so sayling forward we met with an Island about two leagues in bignesse, and on the East shore hauing still the maine land and Islands in sight, we sailed 15. leagues vntil the euening, alwayes finding hard by the sea-coast exceeding high mountaines bare of trees, the land appearing still more plainely vnto vs on the Westerne shore. *Some take the land of California to be nothing but Islands.* Whereupon wee began to be of diuers opinions, some thinking that this coast of Santa Cruz was a firme land, and that it ioyned with the continent of Nueua Espanna, others thought the contrary, and that they were nothing else but Islands, which were to the Westward. And in this sort we proceeded forward, hauing the land on both sides of vs, so farre, that we all began to wonder at it. This day we sailed some 15. leagues, and called this Cape Capo de las Plaias.

Chap. 3.

Of the Streight which they discouered on the coast of Capo de las Plaias, and of the pleasant Countrey which they found before they came to the rockes called Los diamantes. Of the wonderfull whitenesse of that Sea, and of the ebbing and flowing thereof: and of the multitude of Islands and lands, which extend themselues Northward from the hauen of Santa Cruz.

The day following we sailed vntil night with so good weather, that we ran about 20. leagues. All this coast along the shore is full of little hilles without grasse or trees: and that night we anckered in 20. fadome water. *A Streight of 12. leagues broad, of exceeding depth.* The next day we followed our voyage beginning to saile before breake of day Northwestward, and we came into the midst of a Streight or mouth which was 12 leagues broad from one land to the other, which Streight had two Ilands in the midst thereof being 4. leagues distant the one from the other: and here we discerned the countrey to be plaine, and certaine mountaines, and it seemed that a certaine gut of water like a brooke ran through the plain. This streight (as far as we could perceiue) was very deep, for we could finde no botome: and here we saw the land stretching afarre off from the one shore to the other, and on the Westerne shore of the hauen of S. Cruz, the land was more high with very bare mountaines. *The Streight here runneth Northward.* The day following we passed on our way toward the North, and sailed some 15. leagues and in the midst of our way we found a circuit or bay of 6. leagues into the land with many cooues or creeks, and the next day following continuing our course we sailed some 10. leagues, and the coast in this dayes iourney was all of high mountaines naked and bare without any tree. It is very deepe hard by the shore, and that night we were constrained to stay by reason of the contrary winde. The next morning before breake of day we sailed still along the coast to the Northwest vntil euening, and ranne about some 15. leagues. All along this shore wee sawe very goodly mountaines within the land, and many plaines and downes with some few trees, and the sea-shore was all sandy. *Small rocks called Los Diamantes.* In the midst of this dayes course we found certaine small rockes in the sea 4 leagues distant from the maine, were the said land maketh a great point into the sea, and here we stayed the rest of the night, where we had a very great shower of raine. The day following we proceeded on our voyage, and sailed vntill night by a compasse or turning, some 8. or 9. leagues, and saw within land a few mountaines hauing no trees vpon them, but the Sunne shining alwayes very cleare, as farre as we could descry, they were very great, on the Westerne shore of the hauen of Santa Cruz. Here we stayed all night because we found very shallow water and sawe the sea very white, and in a maner like to chalke, so that we all beganne to marueile thereat. The day following wee went forward againe along the coast Northwestward, and sailed eight leagues, and saw another land which stretched Northwest, and was full of high mountaines. And still continuing this course we searched very diligently to see if there were any passage through betweene both the landes, for right forward wee saw no land. And thus sayling we alwayes found more shallow water, and the Sea thicke, blacke, and very muddie, and came at length into fiue fadome water: and seeing this, wee determined to passe ouer to the land which wee had seene on the other side, and here likewise wee found as little depth and lesse, whereupon we rode all night in fiue fadome water, and wee perceiued the Sea to runne with so great a rage into the land, that it is a thing much to be marueilled at, and with the like fury it returned backe againe with the ebbe: during which time wee found 11. fadome water, and the floode and ebbe continued from sixe to sixe houres.

The day following the Captaine and Pilote went vp to the shippes top, and sawe all the lande full of sand in a great round compasse, and ioyning it selfe with the other shore and it was so low, that whereas wee were a league from the same wee could not well discern it, and it seemed that there was an inlet of the mouthes of certaine lakes, whereby the Sea went in and out. There were diuers opinions amongst vs and some thought that that current entered into those lakes, and also that some great Riuer there might be the cause thereof. And when we could perceiue no passage through, nor could discerne the countrey to be inhabited, the Captaine accompanied with certaine of vs went to take possession thereof. The same day with the ebbe of the Sea wee fell downe from the other coast from the side of Nueua Espanna, though alwayes we had in sight the firme land on the one side of vs, and the other Islands on our left hande, on the side of the port of Santa Cruz situate on the Westerne shore: for on that side there are so many Islands and lands, so farre as we could descry, that it was greatly to be wondered at: for from the said hauen of Santa Cruz, and from the coast of Culiacan we had alwayes in a maner land on both sides of vs, and that so great a countrey, that I suppose if it should so continue further inwarde, there is countrey ynough for many yeeres to conquer. This day wee had the winde contrary, and cast ancker vntil the flood increased which was in the afternoone, and then wee set saile likewise with contrary winde vntill midnigt, and then cast ancker.

The next day wee departed, shaping our course along the coast Southwest, vntill midnight with little winde, and wee sawe within the land high mountaines with some openings, and wee made way some three leagues, and all the next night wee were becalmed, and the next day we continued our course but a little while, for we sailed not aboue fiue leagues, and all the night were becalmed, and sawe the land full of bare and high mountaines, and on our left hande wee descried a plaine countrey, and saw in the night certaine fires.

Chap. 4.

They land vpon an Island to discouer the same, and there they see many fires, which issue out of certaine mountaines, and many Seale-fishes. Here they take an Indian, and can not vnderstand his language. Running along they discouer another Island, and take possession thereof for the Emperours Maiestie, and a great hauen in the firme land, which they call Ancon de Sant Andres, or The hauen of S. Andrew.

The next day following our course we saw a great hauen with an Island in the sea, within a crossebow shoote of the firme land, and in this Island and on the firme land were seene many smokes by the iudgement of all the company; wherefore the captaine thought good that wee should goe on land to know the certainty of these smokes and fires, himselfe taking ten or twelue of vs with a boate in his company: ┆Burning mountaines.┆ and going on shore in the Island, we found that the smokes proceeded out of certaine mountaines and breaches of burned earth, whereout ascended into the aire certaine cinders and ashes which mounted vp to the middle region of the aire, in such great quantitie, that we could not esteeme lesse then twenty lodes of wood to bee burned for the causing of euery of these smokes, whereat wee were all not a little amazed.

In this Island were such abundance of Seales, as it was wonderful. Here we stayed that day, and killed a great number of these Seales, with whom we had some trouble: for they were so many, and ayded one another so well, that it was strange to behold; for it fell out, that while we were occupied in killing some of them with staues, they assembled twentie or thirty together, and lifting themselues vp assayled vs with their feete in a squadron, and ouerthrew two or three of our company on the ground: whereupon letting goe those which they had in their hands, they and the others escaped vs and went into the sea, howbeit wee killed good store of them, which were so fatte as it was wonderfull: and when we opened some of them to haue their liuers, we found certaine small blacke stones in their bodies, whereat we much marueiled. The next day wee rode at anker here for lacke of good weather to sayle withall: whereupon the Captaine determined to goe on shore with nine or ten of his company, to see whether there were any people there, or any signe of people that had bene there, and they found on the maine land seuen or eight Indians like to Chichimecas, which were gone a fishing, and had a raft of canes; who so soone as they espied vs ranne away and betooke themselues to flight, but being pursued by vs, in the end we tooke one of them, whose language was so strange that wee could by no meanes vnderstand him; his clothing was nothing at all, for he was starke naked. These people caried their water in bottels made of beasts skins, they fished with hookes of bone, and wee found good store of their fishes, whereof we tooke three or foure dozen.

The Indian which we had taken seeing himselfe in our hands did nothing but weepe, but the Captaine called him, and made much of him, giuing him certaine beades, with a hat and certaine hookes of ours, and then let him goe. And it seemed that after hee was returned to his companions, he declared vnto them how we had done him no harme at all, showing them the things which wee had giuen him: whereupon they also determined to come vnto vs to our boate, but because it was now night, and that our shippes were farre from vs, we forced not to stay for them, especially because it was a bad place and a dangerous. This countrey hath on the sea coast high and bare mountaines with certaine grasse in some places like vnto our broomes, or like vnto woods of rosemary.

The next day wee sayled neere to the coast on the same side, with very scarce winde, and in a manner calme, and ranne not aboue fiue leagues, and all the night following we lay becalmed, and we saw on the shore fiue or sixe fires. Ancon de S. Andres, or The hauen of S. Andrew in 32 degrees. The land is high with very high mountaines without grasse, hauing certaine caues in them: the next day also, and part of the night following we were becalmed: and the morrow after we followed our course along the sayd coast, and passed betweene a great Island full of exceeding high mountaines, and the maine land, where we saw a very great hauen in the firme land in which wee ankered to see what it was, and being come to an anker, the Captaine and some of vs went on land the same day to see if there were any people and fresh water, and wee found certaine small cottages couered with drie grasse, with certaine little staues layd ouerthwart, and we went a little way into the countrey which was very baren, by certaine small and streight pathes, and found a little pond or pit, but drie and without water; and here the Captaine tooke possession for the Marques of the valley[44] in the name of his Maiestie, and after this we returned to our ship, and that night we sawe foure or fiue fires on the land. The next day the Captaine determined, because hee had seene these fires, to goe on shore, and so with our two boates we went fifteene or twenty of vs vnto certaine crooked strands two leagues from the place where our ships rode, and where we had seene the fires, and we found two Indians of exceeding huge stature, so that they caused vs greatly to wonder; they caried their bowes and arrowes in their hands, and as soone as they saw vs leap on shore they ran away, and wee followed them vnto their dwellings and lodgings, which were certaine cottages and bowers couered with boughs, and there we found great and small steps of many people, but they had no kind of victuals but onely cuttle fishes which wee found there. The countrey toward the sea side seemed but barren, for we saw neither trees nor greene grasse there, yet were there certaine smal pathes not well beaten, and along the sea coast we saw many tracts of dogges, hares, and conies, and to certaine small Islands neere vnto the maine we saw Seale-fishes. This hauen is called Ancon de Sant Andres.

[44] Hernando Cortez.

Chap. 5.

They discouer a mountainous Island very great, and neere vnto it certaine other Islands with a goodly greene and pleasant countrey. They haue sight of certaine Indians in Canoas of canes, whose language sounded like the Flemish tongue, with whome they could not haue any traffique.

A great Island. The next day we proceeded on your voyage, sayling betweene the maine and an Island, which we suppose to be in circuit about a hundreth or eighty leagues, sayling sometimes within one, and sometimes within two leagues of the maine. The soile of this Island is of certaine mountaines not very steepe with caues in them, and as farre as wee could descrie by the coast, there appeared no signe of any plaine countrey. Here from this day forward wee began to bee afraid, considering that wee were to returne to the port of Santa Cruz; for it was supposed, that all along this mighty gulfe from the entrance in at Culiacan vntil the returning backe vnto the said hauen, was all firme land, and also because wee had the firme land alwayes on our right hand and it goeth round circle-wise vnto the sayd hauen; but many thought and hoped that we should finde some mouth or out-let, whereby we might passe through vnto the other coast. What our successe was we will declare in the relation following.

They returne from the bottome of the gulf of California. The next day being Thursday wee sayled with scant winde, for it was almost calme, and passed beyond that great Island, hauing firme land alwayes on our right hand, and coasting (as I sayd) very neere vnto it. The next day likewise we sayled with little winde, it being in a manner calme, and passed neere vnto the shore by certaine round baies, and certaine points which the land made, which was pleasant to behold being somewhat greene, and there seemed to be some creeke there. This Friday at night wee sayled altogether with a fresh gale, and at breake of day wee were betweene the maine land, and an Island on our left hand which was somewhat big, as farre as we could discerne. Here was a great bay in the firme land, and before it was a point which stretched farre into the sea. The firme land seemed to bee much fresher and pleasanter then those lands which we had passed, hauing many bankes and hilles of indifferent height, and beautifull to behold.

The countrey (as farre as wee could discerne) was so pleasant and delightfull, that wee all desired to goe on shore, and to search vp into it two or three dayes iourney, to see whether it were inhabited or not. Wee saw within the land of that bay two fires. The night following being Saturday we sailed, continually with a prosperous and fresh gale, and the wind was so great that we drew our bonet to our maine sayle, and sayled so till the morning.

On Sunday the twelfth of October we found our selues altogether inclosed with land, on the right hand with the maine, which compassed vs before and behinde, and on the left hand with an Island of a league and a halfe; and betweene the maine and the Island in the midst of the sea there lay a small Islet, and also betweene the sayd maine and the Island there were two mouthes, through which there appeared, a passage whereby afterward we passed through. This maine was much more fresh and greene then the other which wee had passed, and had certaine plaines and points of mountaines of pleasant view, and full of greene grasse. Here all this night we saw two or three villages which were very great, and at breake of day we saw a Canoa or boate made of canes, which came from the land out of a creeke, and wee stood still vntill it came neere vnto vs in the ship, and they began to speake in their language which no man vnderstood, whose pronuntiation was like to the Flemings, and being called they returned with great haste vnto the shore, and we were very sory because our boate had not followed them.

Here happened vnto vs a very strange thing, which was, that as this Indian returned to the shore in certaine of these creekes where a number of his fellow Indians were, as wee viewed that part, we sawe fiue Canoas issue foorth, which came toward vs: whereupon wee stayed to see what they would doe. In the meane while our Admirall came vp vnto vs, which was neere the shore, for he also had seene them, and so being come together we cast anker, expecting what those Canoas would doe. In the meane while our Generall commanded vs to make ready our boate, and to furnish the same with oares and men, to try if we could by any meanes take some of them, that we might come to some knowledge of them, and that wee might giue them some of our trifles, and specially of our hookes and beads to winne their friendship. The Indians with their fiue Canoas approached within one or two stones cast of vs, and then began to speake very loude vnto vs in a very strange language, always standing vpon their guard to retire themselues with speede. When our Captaine saw this, and that they would not come, neere vs, but rather retired, he commanded six mariners to goe into the boate from the sterne of the ship, and himselfe also went with them with all possible haste toward the Indians. The Indians returned to the shore with so great celeritie, that they seemed to flie in those little Canoas of canes. Neuerthelesse our men vsed such diligence that one of the Canoas was boarded and taken; but the Indian in the Canoa seeing himselfe now taken leapt into the water, and our men followed with their boat to take him, but seeing himselfe within their reach, he ducked with his head vnder their boate, and so deceiued them, and then rose vp againe, and, with their oares and with staues they gaue him certaine blowes, to amaze him, but nothing would serue them; for as they were about to lay handes vpon him hee still diued vnder water, and with his hands and feete got neere to the shore: and as hee rose, vp aboue the water, he called to his felowes which stood on the shore to behold, crying Belen with a loud voyce, and so they pursued him, and strooke him sometimes being very neere the shore, and he alwayes went calling the rest of his fellowes to come and helpe him, whereupon within a short while after three other Canoas came foorth to succour him, being full of Indians with bowes and arrowes in their handes, crying with a loude voyce, that wee should come on shore: these Indians were of great stature and saluage, fat also and well set, and of a browne colour. Our Captaine perceiuing this, least they should wound any of our people with their arrowes, returned backe, and commanded vs immediately to set sayle, and so foorthwith wee departed.

This day the wind skanted, and we returned to anker in the foresayd place, and our Admirall rode from the firme land toward the Island, and wee which were in the ship called The Trinitie lay neere vnto the maine, and before breake of day wee departed with a fresh gale. And before we disemboqued out of that chanell we saw certaine grasse very high and greene vpon the maine: whereupon a mariner, and the Pilot went vp into the top, and saw the <u>mouth of a riuer which ranne</u> through that greene countrey into the sea. <u>Port Belen is a very good hauen.</u> But because our Admirall was vnder all her sayles farre from vs, we could not tell them of this riuer, where wee would haue taken water, where of we had some neede, and because it was a very good hauen to goe on shore to take it, and therefore without watering we followed our course. On Monday we departed from this hauen which is like vnto a lake, for on all sides we were compassed with land, hauing the continent before, behinde vs, and on our right side, and the Island on our left side, and we passed foorth at those mouthes before mentioned, which shewed an out-let into the open sea. Thus wee sayled along still viewing the situation of the countrey, reioycing all of vs at the sight thereof, for it alwayes pleased vs more and more, still appearing more greene and pleasant, and the grasse which wee found neere vnto the shore was fresh and delectable, but not very high, being (to all our iudgements) not past a spanne long. Likewise the hills which we saw, which were many, and many downes made a very pleasant prospect, especially because we iudged, that there were many valleys and dales betweene them.

Chap. 6.

They discouer a very great bay with foure small Islands in it, whereas they take possession. As they sayle along and discouer diuers Islands they come at length to the port of Santa Cruz, where not being able to get any knowledge of those Indians, although they lay in waite for them at a place called The well of Grijalua, they departed thence. They haue a perilous and long tempest, which, ceased, after they had seene a light on their shrowdes.

At our comming out of these openings we began to finde a Bay with a very great hauen, enuironed with diuers small hilles hauing vpon them greene woods and pleasant to behold. In this bay and strand were two small Islands neere vnto the shore, one of the which was like vnto a table about halfe a league in bignes, and the other was a round hill almost as big as the former. These Islands serued vs onely to content our sight, for we passed by them without staying, hauing but a slacke winde on Munday morning: all which day we followed our course with the foresayd slacke winde, and within a while after it became flat contrary, so that we were constrained to anker at the sayd point of the sayd hauen; and on Tewsday at breake of day we set sayle, but made but little away all the day, because the winde continued contrary, although but very weake. The night following wee were becalmed a little beyond the point of this hauen; but about midnight wee began to haue a fresh gale, and on Wednesday in the morning wee were seuen leagues distant from that point. This countrey shewed (as it was indeede) more plaine then the rest, with certaine small woody hilles, and within the other point which was before descried, the situation seemed to be more pleasant and delightsome then the rest which we had passed. And at the vttermost end of the point were two small Islets. The sayd Wednesday about nine of the clocke the winde blew a good gale, and we sayled by euening between seuen and eight leagues, and came ouer against a land not very high, where wee saw certaine creekes or breaches not very ragged, into euery of which a riuer seemed to fall, because the soyle was very greene, and had certaine trees growing on it farre bigger then those which we had found before. Here the Captaine with fiue or sixe men went on shore, and taking possession passed vp one of those riuers, and found the footing of many Indians vpon the sand. On the bankes of that riuer they saw many fruitful trees, as cherry-trees and little apple-trees, and other white trees: they found also in the wood three or foure beasts called Adibes, which are a kind of dogs. The same night we set sayle with the winde off the land, which blew so freshly, that it made vs to strike our foresayle; and on the sixteenth of October at nine of the clocke we came neere vnto a point of certaine high mountaines, on which day being Thursday we made little way, because the winde ceased, but it rose againe in the night, whereupon by the breake of day on Friday wee came before the sayd point being sixe or seuen leagues off. The land seemed to be very mountainous with certaine sharpe points not greatly clad with grasse, but somewhat bare. On our left hand wee saw two Islands, the one of a league and a halfe, the other not so much, and it seemed that we drew neere to the port of Santa Cruz, whereat we were sory because we were alwaies in good hope to find some out-let into the maine Ocean in some place of that land, and that the same port was the same out-let, and also that by the sayd coast we might returne to the foresayd hauen of Santa Cruz, and that we had committed a great error, because we had not certainely sought out the secret, whether that were a Streit or a riuer, which wee had left behind vs vnsearched at the bottome of this great sea or gulfe.

All Friday and the night following we sayled with a scant winde, and on Saturday at breake of day we were betweene two points of land which make a bay, wherein we saw before and behinde foure or fiue great and small Islands. The lande was very mountainous, part whereof was couered with grasse, and part was voide. Within the land appeared more mountaines and hils, and in this place we were come neere vnto the hauen of Santa Cruz, which is all firme land, except it be diuided in the very nooke by some streite or great riuer which parteth it from the maine, which because we had not throughly discouered, all of vs, that were imployed in this voyage were not a little grieued. And this maine land stretcheth so farre in length, that I cannot well expresse it: for from the hauen of Acapulco, which standeth in seuenteene degrees and twentie minutes of latitude, wee had always the coast of the firme land on our right hande, vntill we came to the great current of the white and red sea: This current is in 32 degrees and the sea is white and red. and here (as I haue said) we knew not the secret of this current, whether it were caused by a riuer or by a streit: This returne is mentioned cap. 5. and so supposing that the coast which wee had on our right hand was closed vp without passage, wee returned backe againe, alwayes descending Southward by our degrees, vntill wee returned vnto the sayd hauen of Santa Cruz, finding still along the coast a goodly and pleasant countrey, and still seeing fires made by the Indians, and Canoas made of Canes.[45] We determined to take in fresh water at the hauen of Santa Cruz, to runne along the outward Westerne coast, and to see what it was, if it pleased God. Here we rested our selues, and eat of the plummes and fruits called Pithaias: and wee entred into the port of Santa Cruz on Sunday the 18 of October and stayed there eight daies to take in wood and water resting our selues all that while, that our men might strengthen and refresh themselues. Our captaine determined to diuide amongst vs certaine garments of taffata, with clokes and saies, and a piece of taffata, and likewise ordained, that wee should goe on land to catch a couple of Indians, that they might talke with our interpreter, and that we might come to the knowledge of their language. Wherevpon thirteene of vs went out of our ship by night, and lay in ambush in a place which is called The well of Grijalua, where we stayed vntill noone betweene certaine secret wayes, and could neuer see or descrie any one Indian: The Spaniards vse mastiues to take the Indians. wherefore we returned to our ships, with two mastiue-dogs which we carried with vs to catch the Indians with more ease: and in our returne we found two Indians hidden in certaine thickets, which were come thither to spie what wee did: but because wee and our dogs were weary, and thought not on them, these Indians issued out of the thickets, and fled away, and wee ranne after them, and our dogges saw them not: wherefore by reason of the thicknes of the wilde thistles, and of the thornes and bryars, and because we were weary, we could neuer ouertake them: Read more of these staues cap 10. they left behinde them certaine staues so finely wrought that they were very beautiful to behold, considering how cunningly they were made with a handle and a corde to fling them.

[45] This voyage up the great Gulf of California, with the discovery of the mouth of the River Colorado, is so accurate in its details, that, with a good map, every portion of the voyager's course can be followed.

The nine and twentieth of October being Wednesday, we set sayle out of this hauen of Santa Cruz with little winde, and in sayling downe the chanell our shippe called the Trinitie came on ground vpon certaine sholdes: this was at noone at a low water, and with all the remedy that we could vse wee could not draw her off, whereupon wee were constrained to vnderprop her, and to stay the next tide: and when the tide began to increase wee vsed all diligence to draw her off, and could not by any meanes, whereat all the company and the Captaine were not a little grieued: for wee thought wee should haue lost her there, although wee ceased not with all our might to labour with both our boates, and with our cable and capsten. In the ende it pleased God about midnight at a full sea with the great force which wee vsed to recouer her, that we drew her off the sand, for which we gaue God most hearty thankes, and rode at anker all the rest of the night, wayting for day light for feare of falling into any further danger or mishap. When day was come, wee set forward with a fresh gale, and proceeded on our voyage, directing our prows to the maine sea, to see whether it would please God to let vs discouer the secret of this point. But whether it pleased not his great goodnesse, or whether it were for our sinnes, wee spent eight dayes from this port, before we could double the poynt,[46] by reason of contrary winds, and great raine, and lightning and darknesse euery night: also the windes grew so raging and tempestuous, that they made us all to quake, and to pray continually vnto God to ayde vs. And hereupon wee made our cables and ankers ready, and the chiefe Pilot commanded vs with all speede to cast anker, and in this sorte we passed our troubles: and whereas wee rode in no securitie, he caused vs foorthwith to weigh our ankers, and to goe whither the wind should driue vs. And in this sorte wee spent those eight dayes, turning backe by night the same way that wee had gone by day, and sometimes making good in the night that which wee had lost in the day, not without great desire of all the company to haue a winde which might set vs forward on our voyage, being afflicted with the miseries which wee indured by reason of the thunders, lightnings, and raine, wherewith we were wet from toppe to toe, by reason of the toyle which we had in weighing and casting of our ankers, as neede required.

[46] Cape St. Lucas.

And on one of these nights, which was very darke and tempestuous with winde and raine, because we thought we should haue perished, being very neere the shore, we prayed vnto God that he would vouchsafe to ayde and saue vs, without calling our sinnes to remembrance. And straightway wee saw vpon the shrowdes of the Trinity as it were a candle, which of itselfe shined, and gaue a light, whereat all the company greatly reioyced, in such sort that wee ceased not to giue thankes vnto God. Whereupon we assured our selues, that of his mercie hee would guide and saue vs, and would not suffer vs to perish, as indeede it fell out; for the next day wee had good weather, and all the mariners sayd, that it was the light of Saint Elmo[47] which appeared on the shrowdes, and they saluted it with their songs and prayers. These stormes tooke vs betweene the Isles of Saint Iago and Saint Philip, and the Isle called Isla de perlas lying ouer against the point of California supposed to be firme land.

[47] St. Elmo's light, as it is called, is by no means an unusual phenomenon. It is merely caused by the Electricity in the air.

Chap. 7.

Sayling on their way they discouer a pleasant Countrey, and in their iudgement greatly inhabited, and finde the Sea-coast very deepe. They went to discouer or viewe the Isle of perles. And by a current one of their ships is separated from the other, and with great ioy after three dayes they had sight again of her, and following their voyage they discouer certaine great, greene, and pleasant plaines.

We began to sayle along the coast the seuenth or eight of Nouember the land always shewing very greene with grasse pleasant to behold, and certaine plaines neere the shore, and vp within the countrey many pleasant hils replenished with wood, and certaine valleys, so that wee were delighted aboue measure, and wondered at the greatnes and goodly view of the countrey: and euery night we saw fires, which shewed that the countrey is greatly inhabited. From hence forward they saile on the westerne or back-side of California. Thus we proceeded on our Voyage vntill the tenth of the sayd month of Nouember, hauing always the coast of the maine Ocean on our right hand, and the farther we sailed, wee always found the countrey more delightsome and pleasant, as well in beholding the greennes therof, as also in that it shewed certaine plaines and deepe valleys, through which riuers did fall downe into the land, within certaine mountaines, and hilles full of great woods which were not very high, and appeared within the countrey. Here we were 54 leagues distant from California little more or lesse, always toward the Southwest, seeing in the night three or foure fires, whereby it appeareth that the countrey is inhabited, and full of people, for the greatnes of the countrey argueth no lesse: and we supposed that there must needs bee great townes inhabited within the land, although in this poynt we were of diuers opinions. The sea is so deepe on all this coast that we could scarce find ground in 54 fadomes. On the greatest part of the coast there are hilles of very white sand, and it seemeth to be a dangerous coast, because of the great and swift tides which goe there, for the sand sheweth so much for the space of ten or twelue leagues, for so the Pilots affirmed. Isla de perlas. This day being Saturday the winde increased, and wee had sight of the Isle of Perles, which on this side of the gulfe appeareth with a deepe valley all couered ouer with trees, and sheweth much fairer then on the other side, and wee entred into the Porte of Santa Cruz. From the ninth of Nouember to the fifteenth we sayled not aboue tenne leagues, because we had contrary winds, and great showres; and besides this we had another mischance which did not a little grieue vs; for wee lost company of the ship called The Trinitie, and could neuer see her for the space of three dayes, whereupon wee suspected that shee was returned home vnto New Spaine, or that she was seuered from our company: wherefore we were grieued out of measure to see our selues so left alone, and the Captaine of all others was most sad, though he ceased not to encourage vs to proceede on our voyage, saying that notwithstanding all this wee ought not to leaue off this enterprise which we had begunne, and that though we were left alone we should deserue the greater commendation and credite: whereupon wee all answered him, that wee would not haue him thinke that any of vs would euer be discouraged, but that we would follow him vntill hee should thinke it reasonable that we should not proceede any further in the enterprise, and that we were in danger of perishing, and that vntill then wee would bee at his commandement: but withall we perswaded him that after he had seene any great difficulty to proceede any further, hee should doe well to returne backe to make relation of our successe to the R. H. lord the Marques de Valle. Hereupon he made an Oration vnto vs wherein he told vs, that he could not beleeue, much lesse could imagine, wherefore the shippe called the Trinitie should returne into Newe Spaine, nor why she should willingly depart from vs, and goe vnto any other place, and that he thought by all reason, that some current had caried her out of our sight, and that through contrary weather and tempests she could not fetch vs vp, and that notwithstanding all that which we had done in the voyage, he had an instruction, that if by chance we were separated one from the other, wee were to take this course to meete again together, namely to returne backe eight or tenne leagues to seeke one another, beyond certaine head lands which lay out into the sea, and that therefore we should doe well to returne to seeke her vp. This sentence pleased vs all, and so returning to seeke her, we espied her two leagues distance from vs, comming toward us with a fresh gale of winde, whereat we greatly reioyced.

Thus being come together we ankered for that day, because the weather seemed very contrary, and the Captaine chid them for their negligence in sayling, because they had in such sort lost our company; and they excused themselues, that they could doe no lesse, because a current had carried them away aboue three leagues, whereby they could neuer reach vnto vs. The next day being the sixteenth of Nouember wee set forward, but sayled very little, for the North and Northwest winds were against vs. Here we discouered certaine plaines, in my iudgement very great and greene, and right before vs we could not discerne any mountaines or woods, whereat wee marueiled to see so great a countrey. And wee met an Indian in a Canoa on the shore whereon the sea did breake, who stayed to beholde vs a great while, and oftentimes he lifted vp himselfe to view vs the better, and then returned backe along the coast: we vsed all diligence to see whether he would come out further from the shore, to giue him chase, and to try whether we could catch him, but he very cunningly viewed vs without comming neere vnto vs, and returned to the shore with his Canoa. Heere we saw in the euening but one fire, and wist not whether it were done by the cunning of the Indians, because they would not haue vs know that there were people there, or that it was so indeede. From the said 16 day of Nouember vntill the 24 of the same moneth we could not proceede on our way aboue 12 or 15 leagues: and looking into our Sea-chart, we found our selues distant from the Xaguges of the Port of Santa Cruz about 70 leagues. Now on the 24 day being Munday very early in the morning we beganne to take very good view of that Countrey, and all along the coast we saw many faire plaines with certaine furrowes made in the midst like vnto halfe plaines, the said plaine still appearing vp into the Countrey, with pleasant champions, because the grasse which grew there was very beautifull, short, and greene, and good pasture for cattell. Howbeit because we rode so farre off, we could not perfectly iudge what kind of grasse it was, but it shewed very short and greene, and without thornes. These plaines on the right hand made a bay into a valley which seemed to be a piece of a mountaine: the rest shewed to be al plaines without any thistles or weedes, but full of grasse good for cattel very green and faire as I haue saide.

Chap. 8.

One of their ships by tempest was separated from the other, and afterward meeting with her consort she reporteth that the land stretcheth to the West by the mouth of the great lake. The Pilots are of diuers iudgements touching the state of this coast inhabited by Chichimecas. They enter into an hauen to take in fresh water, and are suddenly assayled by two squadrons of Indians. They defend themselues valiantly, and the Captaine with some of his souldiers are grieuously wounded.

The 26 of this moneth being Wednesday at night the North wind took vs, which still increased more and more so greatly that it put vs to much trouble, for it continued two dayes, in which the Sea was always boisterous; and this night againe we lost the Trinity being beaten with the North winde aforesaid (and we had sight of her on Munday the 24) wherewith we were all of vs greatly agrieued, both Captaine, Souldiers and Mariners, because we saw we were left alone, and our ship called Santa Agueda wherein we were, was but badly conditioned, and this grieued vs more then the trouble which we had with the boisterousnesse of the Sea, imagining that if we should leese the Trinity, or if any mishap should fall vnto vs, we should not be able to follow our voyage according to our Captaines and our owne desire. :Land running towards the Northwest.:
This said 24 day being Munday we saw a Countrey with high mountaines toward the Northwest, and it seemed that the land stretched on still forward, whereat we exceedingly reioyced, because we iudged that the lande grew always broader and broader, and that wee should meete with some speciall good thing. Whereupon we desired that it would please God to send vs good weather for our voyage, which hitherto we found always contrary, so that in 26 dayes we sayled not aboue 70 leagues, and that with much trouble, sometimes riding at anker and sometimes sayling, and seeking the remedies and benefite of the shore to auoide perils. In this Countrey which we discouered the 26 day we always saw (as I haue said) along the shore, and within the land, goodly plaines without any tree, in the midst wherof was a lake or gathering together of the Sea-water, which (to our iudgment) was aboue 12 leagues in compasse, and the sea-coast reached to the mountaines before mentioned. And this day we saw our ship called the Trinitie, which rode 2 leagues distant from vs, which so soone as she saw vs, set saile, and we came together and reioyced greatly. :A wonderfull:

fishing place like Newfoundland. They brought vs great quantity of gray fishes, and of another kinde: for at the point of those mountaines they found a fishing which was very wonderfull, for they suffered themselues to be taken by hand: and they were so great that euery one had much adoe to finde roome to lay his fish in. They found also on the said point a fountaine of fresh water which descended from those hilles, and they told vs that at the same place they had found a narrow passage, whereby the Sea entered into the said lake. They comforted vs much with the report of these things, and telling vs, that the lande trended to the West; for the chiefe Pilot thought, and the other Pilot was of the same opinion, that we shoulde finde a good Countrey. This night we set saile to goe to that point to take in fresh water which we wanted, and to see this lake, and to put some men on shore; and after midnight the winde came vpon vs so forcibly at the North that we could not stay there: whereupon wee were constrained to put further into the Sea, and returned the same way backe againe vnto the shore with much adoe, and came to an anker a great way short of the place from whence we were driuen: and there we rode vntill Thursday at noone with this bitter North winde, and on Friday about noone, when we most thought it would haue ceased, it beganne to increase againe, which grieued vs not a little seeing the weather so contrary, hoping alwayes that it would cease and that some winde would blow from the shore, whereby we might recouer the point of land to take in fresh water, and to search whether there were any people about that lake. Here we lay from the 26 of the saide moneth till the 29, driuing vp and downe the Sea, winding in by little and little vntill we had gotten vnder the shelter of those mountaines: which being obtayned wee rode the sayd 29 of the moneth halfe a league from those wooddy mountaines, which we had seene in the Sea. We stayed in this place at our ease all the Sunday, and Iuan Castilio the chiefe Pilot went that day in the bote on shore with seuen in his company, and they landed neere the Sea, and on a certaine low ground they found foure or fiue Indians Chichimecas of great stature, and went toward them, who fled away like Deere that had beene chased. After this the Pilot went a little way along the Sea-shore, and then returned to his boate, and by that time he was entered thereinto, he saw about fifteen Indians of great stature also, with their bowes and arrowes which called vnto him with a loude and strong voice, making signes with their bowes: but the Pilot made no account of their gesture, but rather returned to the shippes, and declared what had passed betweene him and the Indians. The same day the Captaine commaunded that our caske should be made readie against the next morning to take in water, for in both the shippes there were about fiue and twentie buttes emptie. The first of December, and the second day in the morning the Captaine went with both the barkes on shore with some dozen souldiers, and the greatest part of the Mariners which laboured in filling of water, leauing in the shippes as many as were needefull, and as soone as we were come on shore at the watering place the Captaine caused the buttes to be taken out, to the ende they might be filled with water, and while they returned to fetch the barrels and hogsheads of the shippe, the Captaine walked a turne or two vpon the shore for the space of one or two crossebow shoots, and afterwarde we went vp to certaine of those mountaines, to view the disposition of the countrey, and in trueth we found it in that place very bad to our iudgement, for it was very ragged, full of woods and caues, and so stonie, that we had much adoe to goe. Being come vnto the top we found certaine small hilles full of woods, and cliffes that were not so craggie, although very troublesome to climbe vp; and while we looked from these little hilles, we could not discerne any more mountaines, but rather iudged that from that place forward there were great plaines. The Captaine would not suffer us to goe any farther, because in those places we had seene certaine Indians which seemed to be spies, and warning vs thereof he commanded vs to retire vnto the shore, where we were to take in water, and to dispatch our businesse quickly, and appointed vs to make certaine pits, that our buts might more easily be filled with water. And setting our Guardes or Centinels, we beganne to fill water. In the meane while the Captaine tooke certaine souldiers, and went to the top of an high hill, from whence he descryed a great part of the Sea, and a lake which is within the land: for the Sea entereth in the space of a league, and there is a good fishing place round about: and the lake was so great, that it seemed vnto vs to be very neere 30 leagues in compasse, for we could not discerne the end thereof. Then we came downe with no lesse trouble then wee had mounted vp vnto the hill, by reason of the steepenesse of the place, and some tumbled downe with no small laughter of the rest. And being come somewhat late to our watering place (for it was then past noone) we set our selues to dinner, alwayes appointing some of our company in Centinell, vntill we were called to dinner, and when some were called two others were appointed in their roomes. *A sudden assalt of the Indians with stones, arrows and staues.* And about two of the clocke after dinner, the Captaine and the rest suspecting no danger of assalt of Indians, both because the place seemed not to be fit for it, as also for that we had set our Centinels at the passages; two squadrons of Indians came vpon vs very secretly and couertly, for one came by the great valley through which the water ranne which we tooke, and the other came by a part of that great hill which we had ascended to see the lake, and all of them came so couertly, that our Centinels could neither see nor heare them; and wee had not perceiued them, if a souldier by chance lifting vp his eyes had not sayde, Arme, Arme, my maisters, for many Indians come vpon vs. When we heard this the Capitane leapt vp in a great rage, because the guards were changed out of their place: and with his sword and target, being followed by a souldier, whose name was Haro, and afterward by the rest, he and the said souldier went toward a little gate of certaine stones, whither the rest of vs were to follow him: for if the Indians had gotten that place from vs, we should haue incurred great danger, and the greatest part of vs had like to haue beene slaine, and none could haue escaped but such as by chance could haue leapt into the boates, and the tide went so high, that none could be saued but such as were most excellent swimmers. But at length the Captaine bestirred himselfe very nimbly, vsing all celeritie that was possible. Therefore when he and Haro had wonne the gate, the rest of the souldiers gate vp after them, and the Captaine and Haro turned themselues to the Indians and made head against them, and the Indians assailed them with such numbers of stones, arrowes, and iauelins (which was a very strange thing) that they brake in pieces the target which the Captaine had on his arme, and besides that wounded him with an arrow in the bending of his knee, and though the wound was not great, yet was it very painefull vnto him. While they thus stood to withstand their assalt, they strooke Haro which was on the other side so forcibly with a stone, that they threw him flat vpon the ground: and by and by another stone lighted vpon him which shiuered his Target, and they hit the Captaine with another arrow, and shot him quite through one of his eares. Another arrow came and strooke a souldier called Grauiello Marques in the legge, of which he felt great paine and went halting. In the meane space Francis Preciado, and certaine other souldiers came vp and ioyned himselfe with the rest on the left hand of the Captaine, saying vnto him, Sir, withdrawe your selfe, for you be wounded, but be you not dismayed, for they are but Indians and cannot hurt vs. In this wise we beganne to rush in, among them vpon the side of a rocke alwayes gayning ground of them, which greatly encouraged our mindes, and when we beganne to inforce them to retire, we wanne a small wooddy hill, where we sheltered our selues, whereas before they shot vpon vs from aloft, for they were on the higher ground vnder couert in safetie, and then by no meanes we could offend them, but by running forcibly vpon them with our targets on our armes, and our swords in our hands. On the other side, to approach and seeke to ouertake them was a vaine thing, seeing they were as swift as wilde goates. By this time Haro was gotten vp on foot, and hauing clapt a woollen cloth vpon his head, which had bled extremely, he ioyned himselfe vnto vs, of whom we receiued no small aide. In the meane space the Indians fortified themselves on the cragge of a rocke, from whence they did not a little molest vs, and we likewise fortified our selues vpon an hillocke, whereby we descended into their Fort, and there was a small valley betweene them and vs, which was not very deepe from the vpper part. The Spaniards vse mastiues in their warre against the Indians.

Read more hereof cap. 12. There we were 6 souldiers and two Negroes with the Captaine, and all of vs were of opinion that it was not good to passe that place, least the Indians being many might destroy vs all, for the rest of our souldiers which were beneath at the foote of the hill, making head against the other squadron of the Indians, kept them from hurting those which tooke in water on the strand and from breaking the buts of water, and being but few, we concluded to stay here, and so we stood still fortifying our selues as well as we could, especially considering that we had no succour on any side; for Berecillo our Mastiue-dogge which should haue aided vs was grieuously wounded with 3 arrowes, so that by no meanes we could get him from vs: this mastiue was wounded in the first assault when the Indians came upon vs, who behaued himselfe very wel, and greatly aided vs; for he set vpon them, and put 8 or 10 of them out of array, and made them run away, leauing many arrowes behind them: but at length (as I haue said) he was so wounded, that by no meanes we could get him to goe from vs to set any more vpon the Indians, and the other two mastiues did vs more harme then good: for when they went against them, they shot at them with their bowes, and we received hurt and trouble in defending them. The Captaines legge when he waxed cold was so swolne, that we lapped it vp in a wollen cloth, and he halted much of it: and while the Indians thus stood still, one part of them beganne to dance, sing and shout, and then they began all to lade them selues with stones, and to put their arrowes into their bowes, and to come downe toward vs verie resolutely to assalt vs, and with great out-cries they beganne to fling stones and to shoot their arrowes. Then Francis Preciado turned him to the Captaine and said: Sir, these Indians know or thinke, that we be affeard of them, and in truth it is a great falt to giue them this encouragement, it were better for vs resolutely to set vpon them with these dogs, and to assalt them on this hill, that they may know vs to be no dastards, for they be but Indians and dare not stande vs; and if we can get their Fort vpon the hill, God will giue vs victory in all the rest. The Captaine answered, that he liked well of the motion, and that it was best so to doe, although for any further pursuit vp the hill, he thought we were to take another course. By and by Francis Preciado getting his target on his arme, and his sword in his hand, ranne vnto the other side of the valley, which on that part was not very steepe, crying S. Iago, vpon them my masters, and after him leapt Haro, Tereça, Spinosa, and a Crossebow-man called Montanno, and after them followed the Captaine, though very lame, with a Negro and a souldier which accompanied him, incouraging and comforting them, willing them not to feare. Thus we draue them to the place where they had fortified themselues, and from whence they descended, and we tooke another hill ouer against them within a darts cast of them. And hauing breathed our selues a little, the Captaine came vnto vs, and said Go too my maisters, vpon them before they strengthen themselues on this hill, for now we see plainely that they be affeard of vs, seeing we chase them continually from their Forts: and suddenly 3 or 4 of vs went toward them well couered with targets, vnto the foot of their Fort where they were assembled, and the rest of our company followed vs: the Indians beganne to make head against vs, and to fling many stones vpon vs, and shoot many arrowes, and we with our swords in our hands rushed vpon them in such sort, that they seeing how furiously we set vpon them, abandoned the fort, and ranne downe the hill as swift as Deere, and fled vnto another hill ouer against vs, where the other squadron of the Indians stood, of whom they were rescued, and they began to talke among themselues, but in a low voyce, and ioyned together 6 and 6 and 8 and 8 in a company, and made a fire and warmed themselues, and we stood quietly beholding what they did.

Chap. 9.

After the skirmish the Captaine being wounded, and the rest of the souldiers seeing the Indians depart, returned vnto their ships. The next day taking in fresh water at the saide place he sent mariners to sound the mouth of the lake. Departing thence they came to the port called Baya de Sant Abad, and indured a dangerous storme at sea. And afterward comming neere the shore to take fresh water in the said hauen, they see certaine peaceable Indians.

By this time it was late and the night approched, and the Indians seeing this, whithin a short while after determined to get them packing, and ech of them or the greatest part tooke firebrandes in their hands, and got them away into craggy places. When the Captaine saw this he commanded vs to returne aboord our boats, it being now darke night, thanking vs all for the good seruice we had done him. And being not able to stand vpon his legge, he leaned with his arme vpon Francis Preciado; and thus we returned to our boats, where with much adoe we got aboord, by reason of the great tide and roughnesse of the sea, so that our boats were filled with euery waue. Thus very weary, wet, and some wounded (as is aforesaid) each man returned vnto his ship, where our beds which we found, and our refreshing, and the cheere we had at supper did not greatly comfort vs in regard of our former trauels. We passed that night in this sort, and the next day being Tuesday the Captaine found himselfe greatly payned with his wounds, and chiefly with that on his leg, because it was greatly swolne with his going vpon it. We lacked 12 buts to fill with water, and the barrels in both the ships, and the Captaine would haue gone out to cause them to be filled, but we would not suffer him, and therefore we left off the businesse for that day. But he appointed that the crossebowes should be made readie, and two speciall good harquebuzes, and the next day being Wednesday very early, he commanded Iuan Castilio chiefe Pilot to goe out with both the botes and with all the souldiers and mariners that he could make, hauing the day before commanded the Trinitie to go as neere the shores as she might, and to make ready some of her ordinance, that if the Indians should shew themselues, they might affright them, and doe them as much hurt as they could. Wherefore on the Wednesday al we that were souldiers, sauing the wounded persons, went on shore with certaine mariners in the best order that we could, and tooke the first hill, where we had fortified our selues, standing all vpon our guard vntill the water was filled, and vntill we were called, during which time not one Indian shewed himselfe. Thus we went aboord when we thought good our selues, at least without any suspition of the Indians, although the tide of the Sea went so high that it put vs to great trouble, for oftentimes with great waues it beat into our boats. This was on the Wednesday the 3 of December. And to auoide losse of time the Captaine commanded Juan Castilio the chiefe Pilot to take a boat and certaine mariners as he should thinke good, and to view the mouth of the lake to see whether the entrance were deepe enough for to harbour the ships. A special good hauen. He taking the boat of the Admirall with 8 mariners, and ours of the Trinity, went and sounded the mouth, and on the shallowest place of the barre without they found 3 fadome depth, and farther in 4, and vp higher 5, always increasing vnto 10 or 12 fadomes, when they were come into the two points of the said lake, which was a league broad from one point to the other, and all their sounding was exceeding good ground. Then they went ouer to the southeast point, and there they saw a great boat or raft which they indeuoured to take to carrie vnto their ships. In the meane while they espied certaine cottages, which the Pilot determined to goe and see. And being come neere they saw 3 other raftes with 3 Indians on them distant from the cottages one or two crossbowes shot, and he leapt on land with 4 or 5 mariners in his companie: and while they behelde those cottages, they saw many Indians descending downe a small hill in warlike manner with their bowes and arrowes, whereupon they determined to retire to their boats, and to returne to their ships, and they were not gone from the sea-shore scarse a stones cast, but the Indians were come vpon them to shoot at them with their arrowes, and because they were vnarmed, they would not fight with them, hauing gone on shore for no other purpose, but to sound the mouth and enterance of that lake. Baya del Abad is 100 leagues from the point of California. On Thursday the 4 of December we set saile with a fresh gale of winde, and sayled some 8 or 10 leagues, and came vnto certaine mouthes or inlets which seemed to all of vs as though they had beene Ilands, and we entered into one of them, and came into an hauen which we called Baya del Abad all inclosed and compassed with land, being one of the fairest hauens that hath beene seene: and about the same, especially on both sides the lande was greene and goodly to behold; we descryed certaine riuers on that part which seemed greene, and therefore we returned backe, going out at the mouth whereby we came in, always hauing contrary wind: yet the Pilots vsed their best indeuour to make way: and we saw before vs certaine wooddy hils, and beyond them certaine plaines; this we saw from the Friday the 5 of the said moneth, vntill the Tuesday, which was the ninth. As we drew neere to these woods they seemed very pleasant, and there were goodly and large hilles and beyond them towardes the sea were certaine plaines, and through all the countrey we saw these woods. Many great smokes, of which also Francis Gualle maketh mention. From the day before, which was the Conception of our Lady, we saw many great smokes, whereat we much maruelled, being of diuerse opinions among our selues, whether those smokes were made by the inhabitants of the countrey or no. Ouer against these woods there fell euery night such a dew, that euery morning when we rose, the decke of the ship was so wet, that vntill the sunne was of a good height, we alwaies made the decke durtie with going vpon it. We rode ouer against these woods from the Tuesday morning when we set saile, vntill Thursday about midnight, when a cruell Northwest winde tooke vs, which, whither we would or no, inforced vs to way our anker: and it was so great, that the ship Santa Agueda began to returne backe, vntill her cable broke, and the ship hulled, and suddenly with a great gust the trinket and the mizen were rent asunder, the Northwest winde still growing more and more: within a short while after the maine saile was rent with a mighty flaw of winde, so that we were inforced, both souldiers, captaine, and all of vs, to doe our best indeuor to mend our sailes; and the Trinitie was driuen to do the like, for she going round vpon her anker, when she came a-head of it, her cable broke, so that there we lost two ankers, each ship one. We went backe to seeke Baya del Abad, for we were within 20 leagues of the same, and this day we came within foure leagues of it, and being not able to reach it by reason of contrary windes, we rode vnder the lee of certaine mountaines and hilles which were bare, and almost voide of grasse, neere vnto a strand full of sandie hilles. Neere vnto this road wee found a fishing place vnder a point of land, where hauing let downe our lead to see what ground was there, a fish caught it in his month, and began to draw it, and he which held the sounding-lead crying and shewing his fellowes that it was caught, that they might helpe him, as soone as he had got it aboue the water, tooke the fish, and loosed the cord of the sounding lead, and threw it againe into the sea, to see whether there were any good depth, and it was caught againe, whereupon he began to cry for helpe, and all of vs made a shout for ioy; thus drawing the fish the rope of the sounding-lead being very great was crackt, but at length we caught the fish which was very faire. Here we stayed from Friday when we arriued there, vntill the Munday, when as it seemed good to our Captaine, that we should repaire to the watering place, from whence we were some sixe leagues distant, to take in 12 buttes of water, which wee had drunke and spent, because he knew not whither we should from thenceforth finde any water, or no; and though we should finde water, it was doubtfull whither wee should be able to take it by reason of the great tide that goeth vpon that coast. We drewe neere to that place on Munday at night, when as we sawe certaine fires of the Indians. And on

Tuesday morning our Generall commaunded that the Trinitie should come as neere our ship and to the shore as it could, that if we had neede, they might helpe vs with their great ordinance: and hauing made 3 or 4 bourds to draw neere the shore, there came 4 or 5 Indians to the sea-side; who stood and beheld while we put out our boat and ankcr, marking also how our bwoy floated vpon the water; and when our boat returned to the ship, two of them leapt into the sea, and swamme vnto the bwoy, and beheld it a great while; then they tooke a cane of an arrow, and tyed to the sayd bwoy a very faire and shining sea-oyster of pearles, and then returned to the shore, neere to the watering place.

Chap. 10.

They giue vnto the Indians many trifles which stand vpon the shore to see them, and seeke to parley with them by their interpreter, which was a Chichimeco, who could not vnderstand their language. They go to take fresh water. Francis Preciado spendeth the time with them with many signes, and trucking and being afeard of their great multitude, retireth himselfe wisely with his companions, returning with safety to the ships.

When the Captaine and we beheld this we iudged these Indians to be peaceable people; whereupon the Captaine tooke the boat with 4 or 5 mariners carrying with him certain beades to truck, and went to speake with them. In the meane while he commanded the Indian interpreter our Chichimeco, to be called out of the Admirall that he should parley with them. And the Captaine came vnto the boy, and laid certaine things vpon it for exchange, and made signes vnto the Sauages to come and take them; and an Indian made signes vnto our men with his hands, his armes, and head, that they vnderstood them not, but signified that they should go aside. Whereupon the Captaine departed a smal distance from that place with his boat. And they made signes againe that he should get him further; whereupon we departing a great way off, the saide Indians leapt into the water, came vnto the boy, and tooke those beades, and returned backe againe to land, and then came vnto the other three, and all of them viewing our things, they gaue a bowe and certaine arrowes to an Indian, and sent him away, running with all haste on the shore, and made signes vnto vs that they had sent word vnto their lord what things we had giuen them, and that he would come thither. Within a while after the said Indian returned, running as he did before, and beganne to make signes vnto vs, that his Lord was comming. And while we stayed here, we saw on the shore ten or twelue Indians assemble themselues, which came vnto the other Indians, and by and by we saw another company of 12 or 15 more appeare, who assembled themselues all together. And againe they began to make signes vnto vs, to come foorthwith to our boates, and shewed vs many Oysters of pearles on the top of certaine canes, making signes that they would giue them vs. When we beheld this, the Captaine commanded vs to make readie our boate, and went aboord it with the said mariners, and rowed to a certaine stone in forme of a rocke, which lay in the sea neere vnto the shore. And hither came first 2 or 3 Indians, and layd downe one of those Oysters, and a garland made of Parats feathers, or sparrowes feathers painted red; they layd downe also certaine plumes of white feathers, and others of blew colour. In the mean while we sawe continually Indians assemble to the shore by tenne and tenne, and so by little and little they came in squadrons; anyone of them assoone as hee sawe the boat beganne to leape forward and backeward with so great nimblenesse, that doubtlesse he seemed to all of vs a man of great agilitie, and we tooke no small pleasure while we beheld him fetching those gambols: but the rest of the Indians which stood at the mouth of the fresh water ranne toward him, and cryed vnto him, forbidding him to vse those gestures, because we were come thither in peaceable sort, and by this meanes he came with the rest to the watering place, where by little and little in this manner there assembled aboue a hundred of them all in order, with certaine staues with cordes to fling them, and with their bowes and arrowes, and they were all painted. In the meane while our Chichimeco interpreter borne in the Ile of California, was come vnto vs, and the Captaine againe commanded a mariner to strippe himselfe, and to swimme and laye vpon the said rocke certaine belles, and more beades, and when he had layd them there, the Indians made signes that he should goe away; and so they came thither and tooke them, and our men drew neere with their boat. The Captaine commanded the Indian our Chichimeco to speake vnto them, but they could not vnderstand him, so that we assuredly beleeue, that they vnderstand not the language of the Ile of California. This day being Tuesday vntil night the Indians stayed at this watering place, taking some of our beades, and giuing vnto vs their feathers and other things, and when it was very late they departed. The morrow following being Wednesday very early the Captaine commanded that our buttes should be made ready, that before breake of day, and before the Indians should take the hill, which stood ouer the watering place, we might be landed in good order: which was put in execution: for we went on shore with as many as could goe, sauing those that had charge to take in the water, and such as were to stay on ship-boord, which in all were about fourteene or fifteene persons, in as good order as we could deuise: for we were foure crossebowes, two harquebuziers, and eight or nine targets, and the most part of vs carried very good slings, and eueryone eighteene riuer stones, which weapon the Captaine inuented, because the Indians at the first had handled vs very shrewdly with the multitude of stones which they flang at vs: we had nothing to defende vs sauing our targets, and to seeke to winne the fortes from whence they indamaged vs; he therefore thought with these slings, that we might offend them, and we, likewise thought well of his opinion, for making tryall of them, we threw very well with them, and much farther than we thought we could haue done: for the slings being made of hempe, we flung very farre with them. Nowe being come to the watering place the sayd Wednesday by breake of day we tooke the fort of the fountaine, which were certaine cragges or rockes hanging ouer the same, betweene which there was an opening or deepe valley through which this water runneth, which is no great quantitie, but a little brooke not past a fadome broad. So standing all in order, other foure or fiue Indians came thither, who as soone as they sawe vs to be come on shore, and to haue gotten the toppe of the watering place, they retired vnto a small hill on the other side, for the valley was betweene them and vs: neither stayed they long before they beganne to assemble themselues as they had done the day before by 10 and 10, and 15 and 15, ranging themselues on this high hill, where they made signes vnto vs. And Francis Preciado craued license of the Generall to parley with these Indians, and to giue them some trifles; wherewith he was contented, charging him not to come too neere them, nor to goe into any place where they might hurt him. Whereupon Francis went vnto a plaine place, vnder the hill where the Indians stood, and to put them out of feare he layd downe his sword and target, hauing onely a dagger hanging downe at his girdle, and in a skarfe which he carried at his necke, certaine beades to exchange with them, combs, fishinghooks and comfits. And be began to goe vp the hill, and to shew them diuerse of his merchandise. The Indians as soone as he had layd those things on the ground, and gone somewhat aside, came downe from the hill and tooke them, and carried them vp, for it seemed that their Lord was among them, to whom they carried those trifles. *Truck and traffique with the Indians for mother of pearle, and other things.* Then they came downe againe, and layd to giue vnto him in the said place, an oyster of pearles, and two feathers like haukes feathers, making signes to Preciado that he should come and take them; which he did, and againe layde there a string of belles, and a great fishhooke, and certaine beades; and they taking the same, layd there againe another oyster of pearle, and certaine feathers: and he layd downe other beads, two fishhookes, and more comfits, and the Indians came to take them vp, and approched much neerer vnto him, then at other times, and so neere that a man might haue touched them with a pike, and then they began to talke together: and 7 or 8 more came downe, vnto whom Francis Preciado made signes, that they should come downe no lower, and they incontinently layd their bowes and arrowes on the ground, and hauing layd them downe came somewhat lower, and there with signes, together with them which came first, they began to parle with him, and required mariners breeches and apparel of him, and aboue all things a red hat pleased them highly, which the saide Francis ware on his head, and they prayed him to reach it vnto them, or to lay it in the place; and after this certaine of them made signes vnto him to knowe whether he would haue a harlot, signifying with their fingers those villanies and dishonest actions, and among the rest they set before him an Indian of great stature dyed wholly with black, with certaine shels of the mother of pearle at his necke, and on his head, and speaking by signes to Francis Preciado touching the foresaid act of fornication, thrusting their finger through a hole, they said vnto him, that if hee would haue a woman, they would bring him one; and he answered, that he liked well of it, and that therefore they should bring him one. In the meane space on the other side where the Generall stood with his company, another squadron of Indians shewed themselues, whereupon the Generall and his company made a stirre, and put themselues in battell array: whereupon Francis Preciado was inforced to come downe from them, to ioyne with the General and his company: and here the Indians which came last began to make signes that we should lay downe something to truck, and that they would giue us some of their shels of mother of pearle, which they brought vpon certaine small stickes, and herewithall they came very neere vnto vs, wherewith we were not well content. And Francis Preciado said vnto the Captaine, that if it pleased him, hee would cause all the Indians to come together and to stay vpon that high hill; and he answered, that it was best to draw them all together, for by this time our men had taken in all their water, and stayed for the boat: whereupon Francis taking a crowne of beades went toward the valley, through which the water ran toward the Indians, and made signes vnto them to call the rest, and to come all together, because he would goe to the olde place, to lay things on the ground for exchange, as at the first; and they answered that he should doe so, and that they had called the others, and that they would doe, as he would haue them, and so they did, for they caused them to come vnto them, which they did, and Francis likewise went alone towards them, in which meane space the Generall commanded his people to get into the boat. Francis comming vnto the place beganne to lay downe his merchandise of traffique, and afterwards made signes vnto them to stay there, because he would goe to the ships to bring them other things, and so he returned to the place where the Captaine was, and found them all got into the boates, sauing the Generall and three or foure others, and the Generall made as though he had giuen other trifles to Preciado to carry vnto the Indians, and when he was gone a little from him, he called him back againe, and all this while the Indians stood still, and being come vnto him, wee went faire and softly to our boates, and got vnto them at our ease, without any thronging, and thence we came aboord our ship.

The Indians seeing vs thus gone aboord came downe to the strand where the brooke of water was, and called vnto vs to come foorth with our boates, and to come on shore, and to bring our beades, and that they would giue vs of their mother of pearles: but we being now set at dinner made no account of them: whereupon they beganne to shoot arrowes at the ship, and although they fell neere vs, yet they did not reach vs. In the meane season certaine mariners went out in the boat, to wey the anker, whereupon the Indians seeing them comming towards them, and bringing them nothing, they beganne in scorne to shew them their buttockes, making signes that they should kisse their bums: and these seemed to be those that came last. The Generall seeing this, commanded a musket to be once or twise shot off, and that they should take their iust ayme. They seeing these shot to be made readie, some of them rose and went to shoot their arrowes at our mariners, which were gone to weigh the ankers, then the Generall commanded the great ordinance speedily to be shot off, whereupon three or foure bullets were discharged, and we perceiued that we had slaine one of them, for we assuredly saw him lye dead vpon the shore: and I thinke some of the rest were wounded. They hearing this noyse, and seeing him dead ranne away as fast as euer they could, some along the shore, and some through the vallies, dragging the dead Indian with them, after which time none of them appeared, saue ten or twelue, which peeped vp with their heads among those rocks; whereupon another piece of ordinance was discharged aloft against the place where they were, after which time we neuer saw any more of them.

Chap. 11.

At the point of the Trinitie they spend three dayes in fishing, and in other pastimes: after which setting sayle they discouer pleasant countries, and mountaines voide of grasse, and an Iland afterward called Isla de los Cedros, or the Ile of Cedars, neere which they suffer sharpe colde and raine, and to saue themselues they returne thither.

Immediatly we set saile to ioyne with the ship Santa Agueda, which was aboue halfe a league in the high sea from vs, and this was on the Wednesday the seuenteenth of December. Being come together because the windes were contrary, we drew neere to a headland, which wee called Punta de la Trinidad, and here wee stayed fishing, and solacing our selues two or three dayes, although we had always great store of raine. Afterward we beganne to sayle very slowly, and at night we rode ouer against those mountaines where we had left our ankers, and vpon knowledge of the place we receiued great contentment seeing we had sailed some fiue and thirtie leagues from the place where we had taken in water: neither was it any maruell that wee so reioyced, because that the feare which we had of contrary windes caused vs to be so well appayd of the way which we had made. The day of the holy Natiuitie of our Lord, which was on the Thursday the fiue and twentieth of the said moneth, God of his mercy beganne to shew vs fauour in giuing vs a fresh winde almost in the poope, which carried vs beyond those mountaines, for the space of tenne or twelue leagues, finding the coast alwayes plaine: and two leagues within the land, which we coasted along, and betweene these mountaines, there was a great space of plaine ground, which we might easily discerne with our eyes, although others were of another opinion. We beganne from Christmas day to saile slowly with certaine small land-windes, and sayled from morning to night and about seuen or eight leagues, which wee esteemed no small matter, always praying to God to continue this his fauour toward vs, and thanking him for his holy Natiuitie, and all the dayes of this feast the Frier sayd masse in the Admirall, and the father Frier Raimund preached vnto vs, which gaue vs no small comfort, by incouraging vs in the seruice of God.

On Saturday at night being the 27. of the said moneth we ankored neere vnto a point which seemed to be plaine land all along the shore, and within the countrey were high mountaines with certaine woods, which woods and mountaines ranne ouerthwart the countrey, and continued along with certaine small hilles sharpe on the toppe, and certaine little vallies are betweene those mountaines. Great appearance of gold and siluer. And in truth, to me which with diligent eyes beheld the same both in length and in the breadth thereof, it could not chuse but be a good countrey, and to haue great matters in it, as well touching the inhabiting thereof by the Indians, as in golde and siluer; for there was great likelihood that there is store thereof. This night we saw a fire farre within the lande towards those mountaines, which made vs thinke that the countrey was throughly inhabited. The next day being Sunday and Innocents day, the 28 of the said moneth, at breake of day we set sayle, and by nine or ten of the clocke had sayled three or foure leagues, where we met with a point which stretched towarde the West, the pleasant situation whereof delighted vs much. From the eight and twentieth of December we ranne our course vntill Thursday being Newyeares day of the yeere 1540, and we ran some 40 leagues, passing by certaine inlets and bayes, and certaine high mountains couered with grasse in colour like rosemary: but toward the sea-side very bare and burned, and toward the top were certaine cragges somewhat of a red colour, and beyond these appeared certaine white mountaines, and so all the countrey shewed vnto a point which appeared beyond those burnt white and red mountaines which haue neither any grasse nor tree vpon them, whereat we maruelled not a little. This Newyeares day we sawe neere the maine two small Ilands, and reioyced greatly to see them; for we stood in great feare, that contrary windes would driue vs as farre backe in one day, as we had sayled in tenne, which if they had taken vs, we could not haue withstood them. Wee ranne from the first of Ianuary untill Munday which were fiue dayes, and the land alwayes stretched Northwest from the mountaines aforesaid.

And on the Sunday we saw a farre off a-head of vs a high land somewhat seuered from the maine shore, and all of vs beganne to dispute whether it were the land which trended toward the Northwest, for that way the Pilots hoped to discouer a better countrey: and the said Munday the fift of Ianuarie we came to this high land beforesaid, and it was two Ilands the one a small one and the other a great one: we coasted these two Ilands some sixe leagues, which were greene, and had on the toppe of them many high slender trees; and the great Iland was twentie leagues in compasse. Isla de los Cedros mentioned in the 13 chap. We coasted in 6 leagues in length without seeing or discouering any other things, but we saw before vs high land which stretched eight or tenne leagues Northward, where we rode on Munday at night. From Thursday being Newyeares day vntill the next Munday we sayled about 35 leagues. The land trendeth here Northwest 35 leagues. And in this course we felt great cold, which grieued vs much, especially being assailed by two or three windie showers, which pinched vs much with colde. We rode ouer against this land two or three nights, hauing it neere vnto vs, always keeping watch by equall houres, one while mariners, and another souldiers, all the night long with great vigilancie. On Tuesday being Twelfe day we came within two or three leagues of this land, which we had descryed the day before, seeming to vs very pleasant for it shewed greene with greene trees of an ordinary bignesse, and we saw many vallies, out of which certaine small mists arose, which continued in them for a long time, whereupon we gathered that they rose out of certaine riuers. The same morning, to our great comfort we saw great smokes, though we were about foure leagues distant from them, and the Captaine made no great reckoning to approach neere vnto them, nor to seeke nor serch what the matter was, and perchance because he was not then in the Santa Agueda, but was aboord the Trinitie, as his maner was to come and stay there two or three dayes, as well to passe the time, as to giue order for things that were needfull. In this countrey the winter and raine seemed to be like that of Castile. We rode al night two or three leagues distance from shore, and toward euening we saw fiue or sixe fires, whereat we all reioyced, but did not maruell thereat, because the situation of that countrey shewed to be habitable, being farre, pleasant, and all greene, and likewise because the Iland which we had left behinde vs being (as I haue said) twenty leagues in circuit, made shewe that it was well peopled. On the Wednesday we were 3 or 4 leagues at sea from the land, and began to see two fires more, and therefore we assured our selues that the countrey was very well inhabited; and the farther we sayled, we always found it more ciuill. Floting weeds for fifty leagues. And for the space of fifty leagues before we came hither we always found swimming on the sea certaine flotes of weedes of a ships length, and of the bredth of two ships, being, round and full of gourds, and vnder these weedes were many fishes, and on some of them were store of foules like vnto white sea-meawes. We supposed that these floting weeds did grow vpon some rocke under the water. We were now in 30 degrees of Northerly latitude. Twenty leagues beyond the Ile of Cedar. We sailed from the 7 of Ianuary vntill the 9 still with contrary windes: and on Fryday about noone there rose a North and Northeastern winde, which forced vs to returne vnder the shelter of that Iland which we left behind vs, from whence we had sayled about twentie leagues. And that Friday at night somewhat late we had sayled backe about twelue leagues of the same, and because it was night wee stayed in the sea, where we and our shippes were not a little troubled, so that all that night none of vs slept a winke, but watched euery one. The next morning betimes being Saturday we proceeded on our voyage, and gate vnder the shelter of the said Iland, riding in thirtie fadome water: and on that side where we ankored we found high and closed mountaines, with heapes of a certaine earth which was all ashes and burned, and in other places skorched and as blacke as coles, and like the rust of yron, and in other places whitish, and here and there small blacke hilles, whereat we maruelled exceedingly, considering that when we passed by, it seemed vnto vs an habitable countrey full of trees, and now we saw not a sticke growing on this side.

All of vs supposed that on the other side toward the firme lande the trees grewe which we sawe, although (as I haue sayde) wee sayled foure or fiue leagues distant from the same.

We stayed here vnder the shelter of these mountaines Saturday, Sunday, and Munday, alwayes hauing the Northren winde so strong, that we thinke if it had caught vs in the sea, wee should haue bene cast away.

Chap. 12.

They enuiron and land vpon the Iland of Cedars, to discouer the same, and to seeke water and wood. They are assailed of the Indians, and many of them wounded with stones: but at length getting the vpper hand, they goe to their cottages, and ranging farther vp into the Iland they find diuerse things which the Indians in their flight had left behind them.

On Friday the 13 of Ianuary the Captaine commanded vs to hoise out our boates, and to goe on shore, which was done accordingly, and we did row along the shore for the space of a good halfe league and entered into a valley: for (as I said) all this countrey was full of high and bare hils, of such qualitie as I mentioned before: and in this and other small valleys we found some water which was brackish, and not farre from thence certaine cottages made of shrubs like vnto broome: likewise we found the footings of Indians both small and great; whereat we much maruelled that in so rough and wilde a countrey (as farre as we could discerne) there should be people. Here we stayed all day, making foure or fiue pits to take in water which we wanted, which though it were bad, and in small quantitie we refused not; and so the euening being come, we returned to our boates, and so came vnto our ships which rode a good league from the shore. The next day being Wednesday the fourteenth of the said moneth our Generall commanded vs to set saile, and we sailed about the said Iland on the same side which we coasted when we came from Nueua Espanna: for when we arriued on the coast we saw fiue or sixe fires; wherefore he desired to see and learne whether it were inhabited; and at the farthest ende of this inlet or bay where we rode there came out before vs a Canoa, wherein were foure Indians which came rowing with certaine small oares, and came very neere vs to see what we were: whereupon we tolde our Generall, that it were best to send some of vs out with our boates to take these Indians or some one of them to giue them something that they might thinke vs to be good people: but hee would not consent thereto, because he minded not to stay, hauing then a prety gale of winde, whereby he might saile about this Iland, hoping that afterward we might finde and take some others to speake with them, and giue them what we would to carry on shore; and as we sayled neere the land, we saw a great hill full of goodly trees of the bignesse of the trees and Cypresses of Castile. We found in this Iland the footing of wilde beasts and conies, and saw a peece of pine tree-wood, wherof we gathered, that there was store of them in that countrey. Thus sayling neere vnto the shore, we sawe another Canoa comming toward vs with other foure Indians, but it came not very neere vs, and as we looked forward, we sawe toward a point which was very neere before vs, three other Canoas, one at the head of the point among certaine flattes, and the other two more into the sea, that they might descry vs without comming ouer neere vs. Likewise betweene certaine hilles which were neere the point, there appeared here three and there foure of them, and afterward we saw a small troope of some twentie of them together, so that all of vs reioyced greatly to behold them. On this side the land shewed greene with pieces of plaine ground which was neere the sea, and likewise all those coasts of hils shewed greene, and were couered with many trees, although they grew not very thicke together. Here at euening we rode neere the shore hard vpon the said point, to see if we could speake with those Indians, and likewise to see if we could get fresh water, which now we wanted, and still as soone as we were come to an anker, we saw the Indians shew themselues on land neere vnto their lodgings, comming likewise to descry vs in a Canoa, by sixe and seuen at a time, whereat we maruelled, because we neuer thought that one of those Canoas would hold so many men. In this wise we stayed looking still what would be the successe, and in the place where we rode we were two small leagues distant from the shore, where we found these Indians in their Canoas: whereupon we maruelled not a little to see so great an alteration in so small a distance of countrey, as well because we still discouered pleasant land with trees (whereas on the other side of the isle there were none) as also because it was so well peopled with Indians, which had so many Canoas made of wood, as we might discerne, and not raftes or Balsas, for so they call those floats which are made all flat with canes.

The next day being Thursday the fifteenth of the said moneth about breake of day foure or fiue Indians shewed themselues at the head of that point, who as soone as they had spyed vs retired behind the point, and hid themselues among the bushes vpon certaine small hilles that were there, from whence they issued forth, and couered all the greene hils and mountaines, which were along that coast; whereupon we gathered that they had their dwellings there, in regard of the commoditie of the water and the defence against ill weather and the benefite of fishing. At sun-rising we saw the Indians appeare in greater companies, going vp vnto the hilles in small troopes, and from thence they stood and beheld vs. Immediately we saw fiue or sixe Canoas come out into the sea a good distance from vs, and those which were in them stood often on their tip-toes, to view and descry vs the better. On the other side we stirred not at all for all these their gestures, but stood still riding at anker; and the Generall seemed not to be very willing to take any of them, but this day in the morning very early commanded the Masters mate to conueigh him to our other shippe called the Trinitie. Things passed in this sort, when about ten of the clocke we saw three Canoas lanch farre into the sea to fish very neere vnto vs, whereat we tooke greate pleasure. At 12 of the clocke the Generall returned from the Trinitie and commanded the boat and men to be made readie, as well souldiers as mariners, and that we should goe on shore to see if we could get any wood and water, and catch one of those Indians to vnderstande their language if it were possible: and so all the men that were readie went into the Admirals boate, and went toward the Trinitie which by this time with the other ship had a small gale of winde, wherewith they entered farther within the point, and we discouered the lodgings and houses of the Indians, and saw neere the waters side those fiue or sixe Canoas which at the first came out to view vs, drawen on shore, and ouer against this place the ships cast anker in 30 and 35 fadome water, and we were very neere the land: whereat we maruelled much to find so great depth of water so neere the shore. Being gone abord our botes, we made toward the shore ouer against a village of the Indians, who as soone as they saw vs about to come on land, left an hill whereon they stood to behold what we did, and came downe to the shore, where we were prepared to come on land: but before they came against vs they caused their women and children to fly into the mountaines with their goods, and then came directly towards vs, threatning vs with certaine great staues which they carried in their hands some 3 yardes long and thicker then a mans wrest: *A skirmish of the Indians fighting with stones.* but perceiuing that for all this we ceased not to come neere the sea-shore to come on land, they began to charge vs with stones and to fling cruelly at vs, and they hit 4 or 5 men, among whom they smote the Generall with two stones. In the meane while the other bote landed a little beneath, whereupon when they saw that they were forced to diuide themselues to keepe the rest of our company from comming on land, they began to be discouraged, and did not assaile the Generals boate so fiercely, who began to cause his people to goe on shore with no small trouble; for albeit he was neere the land, yet as soone as they leapt out of the boat they sunke downe, because they could find no fast footing; and thus swimming or otherwise as they could, first a souldier called Spinosa got on land, and next to him the General, and then some of the rest, and began to make head against the Indians, and they came hastily with those staues in their hands, for other kinds of weapons we saw none, sauing bowes and arrowes of pinetree. *The great vse of targets against arrowes or stones.* After a short combate they brake in pieces the targets of the Generall, and of Spinosa. In the meane while those of the other boat were gotten on land, but not without much difficultie, by reason of the multitude of stones which continually rained downe vpon them, and they stroke Terazzo on the head a very shrowd blow, and had it not bene for our targets, many of vs had beene wounded, and in great distresse, although our enemies were but few in number. In this maner all our company came on shore with swimming and with great difficultie, and if they had not holpen one another, some of them had bene drowned. Thus we landed, and within a while after those of the other bote were come on land, the Indians betooke themselues to flight, taking their way toward the mountaines, whether they had sent their women, children and goods: on the other side we pursued them, and one of those Indians which came to assaile the Generals boat, was slaine vpon the strand, and two or three others were wounded, and some said more. The vse of mastiues in the warre against Indians. While we pursued them in this maner our mastiue dogge Berecillo ouertooke one of them not farre from vs (who because we were so wet could not run very fast) and pulled him downe, hauing bitten him cruelly, and doubtlesse he had held him till we had come, vnlesse it had happened that another of his companions had not followed that Indian which the dogge had pulled downe, who with a staffe which he had in his hands gaue the dogge a cruell blow on the backe, and without any staying drew his fellow along like a Deere, and Berecillo was faine to leaue him for paine; neither had he scarse taken the dogge off on him but the Indian got vp, and fled so hastily towarde the mountaine, that within a short while hee ouertooke his fellowe which had saued him from the pawes of the dogge, who (as it appeared) betooke him lustily to his heeles, and thus they came vnto their fellowes which descended not downe to the shore being about some twentie, and they were in all about fiftie or sixtie.

After we had breathed our selues a while, we viewed their houses where they stood, which were certaine cottages couered with shrubs like broome and rosemary, with certaine stakes pight in the ground; and the Generall willed vs to march all together without dispersing of our selues, a little way vp those mountaines, to see if there were any water and wood, because we stood in great neede of them both. And while we marched forward, we saw in certaine little vallies the goods which the women had left there behind them in their flight: for the Indians as soone as they saw vs pursue them ouertooke the women, and for feare charged them to flie away with their children leauing their stuffe in this place. We went vnto this booty, and found good store of fresh-fish, and dried fish, and certaine bags containing aboue 28 pound weight full of dried fish ground to pouder, and many seal skins, the most part dressed with a faire white graine vpon them, and others very badly dressed. There were also their instruments to fish withall, as hookes made of the prickes of certaine shrubs and trees. Here we tooke the said skins without leauing any one in the place, and then we returned to the sea, because it was now night, or at least very late, and found our botes waiting for vs.

Chap. 13.

A description of the Canoas of the Indians of the Ile of Cedars, and how coasting the same to find fresh water they found some, and desiring to take thereof they went on shore, and were diuersely molested with the weapons of the Indians. They christen an old Indian, and returne vnto their ships.

The Canoas which they had were certaine thicke trunkes of Cedars, some of them of the thicknesse of two men, and three fadome long, being not made hollow at all, but being laid along and fastened together, they shoue them into the sea, neither were they plained to any purpose, for we found no kind of edge-toole, sauing that there were certaine sharp stones, which we found vpon certaine rockes that were very keene, wherewith we supposed that they did cut and flea those seales. And neere the shore we found certaine water, wherewith we filled certaine bottles made of the skins of those seales, contayning ech of them aboue a great paile of water. The next day our Generall commanded vs to set saile, whereupon sailing with a fresh gale about 2 leagues from the shore of this Island, trending about the same to see the end thereof, and also to approch neere the firme land, to informe our selues of the state thereof, because we had seene 5 or 6 fires we compassed the same about: for by this meanes we performed 2 or three good actions, namely, we returned to our right course, and searched whether any riuer fell out of the coast of the firme land, or whether there were any trees there, or whether any store of Indians did shew themselues or no.

In this maner proceeding on our way all the Friday being the 16 of January at euening, and seeking to double the point of the Iland, so fierce and contrary a Northren winde encountered vs, that it draue vs backe that night ouer against the lodgings and habitations of the Indians, and here we stayed all Saturday, what time we lost the Trinitie againe, but on Sunday-night being the 18 we saw her againe, and beganne to proceede on our way to compasse that Iland, if it pleased God to send vs good weather.

Isla de los Cedros, or the Ile of Cedars in 28 deg. and a quarter.

On Sunday, Munday, and Tuesday (which was the twentieth, of the said moneth of Ianuarie) wee sailed with scarce and contrary windes, and at length came to the cape of the point of the Iland, which we called Isla de los Cedros or the Ile of Cedars, because that on the tops of the mountaines therein, there growes a wood of these Cedars being very tall, as the nature

of them is to be.[48] This day the Trinitie descryed a village or towne of the Indians, and found water: for on Sunday night we had newly lost her, and had no sight of her vntill Tuesday, whenas we found her riding neere the shore, not farre from those cottages of the Indians. And as soone as we had descryed her, we made toward her, and before we could reach her, we espied three Canoas of Indians which came hard aboord the said ship called the Trinitie, so that they touched almost the side of the ship, and gaue them of their fish, and our people on the other side gaue them certaine trifles in exchange, and after they had spoken with them, the Indians went backe to the shore, and at the same instant we came vp vnto the Admirall and rode by them, and they all saluted vs, saying that the Indians were neere them, and telling what had passed betweene them, whereat the Generall and we receiued great contentment. They told vs moreouer, that they had found fresh water, whereby they increased our great ioy, because we stood in much neede thereof, for at the other place of the Indians we could get but a little.

[48] The Island still bears this name.

These mighty deepe and high weedes are described in the end of this treatise. While we thus rode at ankor, we saw a Canoa with 3 Indians put out into the sea from their cottages, and they went vnto a fishing place, among certaine great and high weedes, which grow in this sea among certaine rockes, the greatest part of which weedes groweth in 15 or 20 fadome depth; and with great celeritie they caught seuen or eight fishes, and returned with them vnto the Trinity, and gaue them vnto them, and they in recompense gaue the Indians certaine trifles. After this the Indians stayed at the sterne of the ship, viewing the same aboue three houres space, and taking the oares of our boat they tryed how they could rowe with them, wherat they tooke great pleasure; and we which were in the Admirall stirred not a whit all this while, to giue them the more assurance, that they should not flie away, but should see that we ment to do them no harme, and that we were good people. As soone as we were come to anker, and beheld all that had passed betweene the Indians and those of the Trinity, after the Indians were gone to the shore in their Canoas made of the bodies of trees, the Generall commanded the boat which was without to be brought vnto him: and when it was come, he, and Francis Preciado, and two others went into it, and so we went aboord the Trinity. The Indians seeing people commingout of the other ship into the Trinitie, sent two Canoas vnto the sterne of the ship, and brought vs a bottle of water and we gaue vnto them certain beads, and continued talking with them a little while; but euening approching the aire grew somewhat cold. The Indians returned on shore to their lodgings, and the General and we to our ship. The next day being

Wednesday in the morning, the General commanded certaine of vs to take the bote and goe ashore, to see if we could find any brooke or well of fresh water in the houses of the Indians, because he thought it impossible for them to dwell there without any water to drinke. The father frier Raimund likewise went out in our company, because the day before seeing the Indians came to the sterne of the shippe parlying with vs, he thought he might haue spoken a little with them, with the like familiarity. In like sort many mariners and souldiers went out in the boat of the Trinity, and going altogether with their weapons toward the shore, somewhat aboue the lodgings of the Indians, very early in the morning they watched the boats, and perceiued that we would come on land, wherevpon they sent away their women and children with certaine of them, who caried their goods vp into certaine exceeding steepe mountaines and hilles, and 5 or 6 of them came toward vs, which were excellently well made, and of a good stature. Two of them had bowes and arrowes, and other two 2 bastonadoes much thicker then the wrist of a mans hand, and other two with 2 long staues like iauelins with very sharpe points, and approched very neere vs being nowe come on shore. And beginning by signes very fiercely to braue vs, they came so neere vs, that almost they strooke with one of those staues one of our souldiers called Garcia a man of good parentage, but the General commanded him to withdraw himselfe, and not to hurt any of them. In the meane season the General and frier Raimund stept foorth, the frier lapping a garment about his arme, because they had taken vp stones in their hands, fearing that they would do them some mischiefe. Then began both of them to speake vnto them by signes and words, to be quiet, signifying, that they ment them no harme, but only were come to take water; and the frier shewed them a drinking cup; but nothing would serue to make them leaue that bragging and flinging of stones; and the General continuing still in a mind not to hurt them, commanded his men gently to come neere vnto them, and that by signes they should all shew them, that they meant in no wise to hurt them, but that we were come on land onely to take water.

The great vse of mastiues in pursuit of the Indians. On the other side refusing vtterly to take knowledge of these things they still insulted more and more: whereupon Francis Preciado counselled the General to giue him leaue to kill one of them, because all the rest would flee away, wherby at our ease we might take water: but he replied that he would not haue it so, but willed them to looze the two mastiues Berecillo and Achillo: wherefore the dogs were let loose, and as soone as they saw them, they vanished immediately, betaking them to their heels, and running vp those cliffes like goates. Also others which came from the mountains to succour them, betooke themselues to flight. The dogs ouertooke two of them, and bit them a little, and we running after, laid hold on them, and they seemed as fierce as wild and vntamed beasts for 3 or 4 of vs held either of them, to cherish and pacifie them, and to seeke to giue them some thing: but we auailed not, for they bit vs by the hands, and stooped downe to take vp stones for to strike vs with them. We led them a while in this maner, and came vnto their lodgings, where the Generall gaue a charge, that no man should touch any thing of theirs, commanding Francis Preciado to see that this order was observed, in not taking any thing from them, although in very deed there was little or nothing there, because the women and Indians which were fled had caried al away. Here we found an old man in a caue so extreamly aged as it was wonderful, which could neither see nor go, because he was so lame and crooked. The father frier Raimund sayd, it were good (seeing he was so aged) to make him a Christian; whereupon we christened him. The captaine gaue the Indians which we had taken two paire of eare-rings, and certaine counterfeit diamonds, and making much of them, suffered them to depart at their pleasure, and in this sort faire and softly they returned to the rest of their fellowes in the mountaine. We tooke the matter of that village which was but a small quantity, and then the Generall commanded vs to resume to our ship, because we had eaten nothing as yet, and after our repast we sayled towards a bay which lay beyond that village, where we saw a very great valley, and those of the Trinitie sayd, that they had seene there good store of water, and sufficient for vs; wherefore wee ankered neere vnto that valley. And the Generall went on shore with both the boates, and the men that went on land in the morning with the two fathers frier Raimund, and frier Antony: and passing vp that valley a crossebow shot, we found a very small brooke of water which neuertheless supplied our necessity for we filled two buts thereof that euening, leauing our vessels to take it with on shore vntill the next morning: and we reioyced not a little that we had found this water, for it was fresh, and the water which we had taken vp before was somewhat brackish, and did vs great hurt both in our bodies and in our taste.

Chap. 14.

They take possession of the Isle of Cedars for the Emperours Maiestie, and departing from thence they are greatly tossed with a tempest of the sea, and returne to the Island, as to a safe harbour.

The next day being the two and twentieth of Ianuary very early the General commanded vs to go on shore, and that we should haue our dinner brought vs, and should take in the rest of our water, which we did, and filled 17 buts without seeing any Indian at al. The next day going out to fill 8 or 9 vessels which were not yet filled, a great winde at Northwest tooke vs, whereupon they made signes to vs from the ships, that with all haste wee should come on board againe, for the wind grew still higher, and higher, and the Masters were affraid that our cables would break, thus we were in the open sea. Chap. 12. Therefore being come aboord againe not without great trouble we returned backe ouer against the village of the Indians, where we had slaine the Indian, and because the wind grew more calme about midnight, the Pilots did not cast anker, Isle de los Cedros is the greatest of the 3 Isles of S. Stephan. but hulled vnder the shelter of this Island, which (as I haue said) is called The Isle of Cedars, and is one of the 3 Isles of. S. Stephan, the greatest and chiefest of them, where the General tooke possession. While we hulled here, about midnight, the next Friday being the 23 of the moneth, without our expectation we had a fresh gale of wind from the Southeast, which was very fauourable for our voyage, and the longer it continued, the more it increased; so that betweene that night and the next day being Saturday the 24 of the said moneth we sailed 18 great leagues. Read cap. 11 about the end. While we were thus on our way, the winde grew so contrary and so tempestuous, that to our great grief we were constrained to coast about with our ships, and returned twenty leagues backe againe, taking for our succour the second time, the point of the lodgings of the Indians, where the foresayd Indian was slaine, and here we stayed Munday, Tewsday, and Wednesday, during which time the Northwest and the North wind blew continually, whereupon we determined not to stirre from thence vntill we saw good weather, and well setled for our voyage: for in this climate these winds doe raigne so greatly, that we feared they would stay vs longer there then we would; and we were so weary of staying, that euery day seemed a moneth vnto vs. Vnder this shelter we rode Thursday, Friday, and Saturday vntill noone, which was the last of Ianuary in the yeere 1540. About noone the wind began to blow softly at Southwest, whereupon the General told the Pilots, that we should doe well to put ouer to the maine land, where with some wind off the shore we might by the grace of God saile somewhat farther. Thus we hoised our sailes, and sailed vntil euening three or foure leagues, for the wind scanted, and wee remained becalmed. February. The night being come there arose a contrary winde, and we were inforced of necessitie to retire the third time to the same shelter of the Isle of Cedars, where we stayed from the first of February vntil Shrouesunday, in the which meane time we tooke in two buts of water which we had spent. During the space of these eight dayes we sought to make sayle two or three times, but as we went out a little beyond the point of this Isle, we found the wind so boystrous and contrary, and the sea so growen, that of force we were constrained to returne vnder the succour of the Island, and often times wee were in great feare that we should not be able to get in thither againe. During this time that we could not proceed on our iourney, we imployed our selues in catching a few fishes for the Lent. From Shrouesunday being the 8 of February, on which day we set sayle, we sayled with a very scant wind, or rather a calme, vntil Shrouetewsday, on which we came within kenne of the firme land, from whence we were put backe these twenty leagues (for in these two dayes and a halfe wee sayled some 20 small leagues) and we lay in sight of the said poynt of the firme land. And on the Tewsday we were becalmed, waiting till God of his mercy would helpe vs with a prosperous wind to proceed on our voyage.

On Shrouesunday at night, to make good cheere withall wee had so great winde and raine, that there was nothing in our ships which was not wet, and very colde ayre. On Ashwednesday at sun-rising we strooke saile neere a point which we fel somewhat short withall in a great bay running into this firme land: and this is the place where we saw fiue or sixe fires, and at the rising of the sunne being so neere the shore that we might well descrie and viewe it at our pleasure we saw it to bee very pleasant, for wee descried as farre as wee could discerne with our eyes, faire valleys and small hilles, with greene shrubs very pleasant to behold, although there grew no trees there. The situation shewed their length and breadth. This day was little winde, it being in a manner calme, to our no small griefe: and the father frier Raimund sayd vs a drie masse, and gaue vs ashes, preaching vnto vs according to the time and state wherein we were: with which sermon we were greatly comforted. The point of Santa Cruz otherwise called Punta de Balenas. After noonetide we had contrary wind, which still was our enemie in all our iourney, at the least from the point of the port of Santa Cruz. Here we were constrained to anker in fiue fadome of water, and after wee rode at anker wee began to viewe the countrey, and tooke delight in beholding how goodly and pleasant it was, and neere vnto the sea wee iudged that wee saw a valley of white ground. At euening so great a tempest came vpon vs of winde and raine, that it was so fearfull and dangerous a thing that a greater cannot be expressed: for it had like to haue driuen vs vpon the shore, and the chiefe Pilot, cast out another great anker into the sea yet all would not serve, for both these ankers could not stay the ship. Whereupon all of vs cryed to God for mercy, attending to see how he would dispose of vs; who of his great goodnesse, while we were in this danger, vouchsafed a little to slake the tempest, and with great speede the chief Pilot commanded the mariners to turne the capsten, and the Generall commanded and prayed all the souldiers to helpe to turne the capsten, which they were nothing slow to performe: and thus we beganne to weigh our ankers, and in weighing of one which was farre greater then the other, the sea was so boisterous that it forced the capsten in such sorte, that the men which were at it could not rule the same, and it strooke a Negro of the Generals such a blowe, that it cast him downe along vpon the decke, and did the like vnto another mariner and one of the barres strooke our firefurnace so violently, that it cast it ouerboord into the sea. Yet for all these troubles wee weighed our ankers, and set sayle, and albeit we had great tempests at sea, yet made we no account thereof in respect of the ioy which we conceiued to see our selues freed of the perill of being cast on that shore with our ships, especially seeing it fell out at midnight, at which time no man could haue escaped, but by a meere myracle from God.

Wee sayled vp and downe the sea all Thursday, and vntill Friday in the morning being the fourteeneth day of February, and the waues of the sea continually came raking ouer our deckes. At length, on Saturday morning at breake of day we could finde no remedy against the contrary windes, notwithstanding the Generall was very obstinate to haue vs keepe out at sea, although it were very tempestuous, least we should be driuen to put backe againe, but no diligence nor remedie preuailed: for the windes were so boysterous and so contrary, that they could not be worse, and the sea went still higher, and swelled more and more, and that in such sorte, that we greatly feared wee should all perish. Whereupon the Pilot thought it our best course to returne to the Isle of Cedars, whither wee had repaired three or foure times before by reason of the selfe same contrary windes, for wee tooke this Island for our father and mother, although we receiued no other benefite thereby saue this onely, namely, to repaire thither in these necessities, and to furnish our selues with water, and with some small quantitie of fish.

Being therefore arriued at this Island; and riding vnder the shelter thereof, the contrary windes did alwayes blow very strongly, and here we tooke water which we drunke, and wood for our fewel, and greatly desired, that the windes would bee more fauourable for proceeding on our iourney. And though we rode under the shelter of the Isle, yet felt wee the great fury of those windes, and the rage of the sea, and our ships neuer ceased rolling.

At breake of day the twentieth of February, wee found the cable of the Admirall cracked, whereupon, to our great griefe, we were constrained to set sayle, to fall downe lower the space of a league, and the Trinitie came and rode in our company.

Chap. 15.

They goe on land in the isle of Cedars, and take diuers wilde beastes, and refresh and solace themselues. They are strangely tossed with the Northwest winde, and seeking often to depart they are forced, for the auoiding of many mischiefes, to repaire thither againe for harbour.

The two and twentieth of February being the second Sonday in Lent, the General went on shore with the greatest part of his people and the friers, neere vnto a valley which they sawe before them. And hearing masse on land, certaine souldiers and mariners, with certaine dogges which we had in our company went into the said valley, and we met with certaine deere, whereof we tooke a female, which was little, but fat, whose haire was liker the haire of a wild goat then of a deere, and we found her not to be a perfect deere, for she had foure dugs like vnto a cowe full of milke, which made vs much to marueile. And after we had flayed off her skinne, the flesh seemed more like the flesh of a goate, then of a deere. We killed likewise a gray conie, in shape like vnto those of Nueua Espanna, and another as blacke as heben-wood. In the cottages at the shelter aboue, where we brake our cable, we found many pine-nuts opened, which (in mine opinion) the Indians had gathered together to eate the kernels of them. On Munday the 23 of the said moneth we rode at anker, taking our pleasure and pastime with fishing. And the Northwest winde began to blow, which waxed so great a little before midnight, as it was wonderfull: so that although we were vnder the shelter of the Island, and greatly defended from that wind, yet for all that it was so furious, and the sea became so raging and boisterous, that it greatly shook our ships, and we were in great feare of breaking our cables, whereof (to say the trueth) we had very much neede: for hauing spent longer time in this voyage then we looked for, wee had broken two, and lost two of our best ankers. This furious winde continued vntill the next being Tewsday the 24 when as we went on shore with the friers, who sayd vs masse, recommending our selues to God, beseeching him to vouchsafe to succour and help vs with some good weather that we might proceede on our voyage, to the aduancement of his seruice. And still the winds were so high and outragious, that the deuill seemed to be loosed in the aire. Whereupon the Pilots caused all the masts to be let downe, least they should be shaken with the wind, and tooke off all the shrowds, and likewise caused the cabbens in the sterne to be taken away, that the winds might haue more free passage, for the safetie of the ships: yet for al this they ceased not to be in great trouble. On Tewsday the second of March, about midnight or somewhat after, riding vnder the Island in this distresse, there came a gust of Northwest winde, which made the cable of the Admirall to slip, and the Trinitie brake her cable, and had bene cast away, if God of his mercy had not prouided for vs, together with the diligence which the Pilots vsed, in hoising the sailes of the trinkets and mizzen, wherewith they put to sea, and rode by another anker vntill day, when the men of both the ships went with their boats to seeke the anker vntill noone, which at length they found and recouered, not without great paines and diligence which they vsed in dragging for it, for they were till noone in seeking the same, and had much adoe to recouer it. After this we set vp our shrowdes, and all things necessary to saile, for to proceede on our voyage, if it pleased God, and not to stay alwayes in that place, as lost and forlorne. Thus on the Wednesday two or three houres after dinner wee set saile, with a scarce winde at Southeast, which was fauourable for our course and very scant; and our Pilots and all the rest of vs were in no small feare, that it would not continue long. We began therefore to set forward, although we seemed to see before our eies, that at the end of the Island we should meete with contrary winde at North and Northwest. This day about euening when our ships had discouered the point of this Isle of Cedars, wee began to perceiue those contrary windes, and the sea to go so loftily, that it was terrible to behold. And the farther we went, the more the winds increased, so that they put vs to great distresse, sayling alwayes with the sheates of our mainesaile and trinket warily in our hands, and with great diligence we loosed the ties of all the sailes, to saue them the better, that the wind might not charge them too vehemently. For all this the mariners thought it best to returne backe, and that by no means we should runne farre into the sea, because we were in extreame danger. Whereupon wee followed their counsel, turning backe almost to the place from whence we departed, whereat we were al not a little grieued, because we could not prosecute our voyage, and began to want many things for the furniture of our ships. The 8 of March being Munday about noone the Generall commanded vs to set saile; for a small gale of winde blew from the West, which was the wind whereof we had most need, to follow our voyage, whereat wee were all glad for the great desire which wee had to depart out of that place. Therefore we began to set saile, and to passe toward the point of the Island, and to shape our course toward the coast of the firme land, to view the situation thereof. And as we passed the Island, and were betwixt it and the maine, the Northwest being a contrary wind began to blow, which increased so by degrees, that we were constrained to let fall the bonets of our sailes, to saue them, striking them very low. And the Trinitie seeing this bad weather returned forthwith vnto the place from whence we departed, and the Admiral cast about all night in the sea, vntill the morning;

and the chiefe Pilot considering that by no means we could proceed farther without danger, if we should continue at sea any longer, resolued that we should retire our selues againe to that shelter, where we rode at anker vntill Thursday. And on Friday about noone we set saile againe with a scarce winde, and in comming forth vnto the point of the Island, we met againe with contrary winde at Northwest: whereupon running all night with the firme land, on Saturday in the morning being S. Lazarus day and the 13 of March, we came in sight thereof, in viewing of the which we all reioyced, and we souldiers would very willingly haue gone on shore. This night fel great store of raine like the raine in Castilia, and we were all well wet in the morning, and we tooke great pleasure in beholding the situation of that firme land, because it was greene, and because we had discouered a pleasant valley and plaines of good largenes, which seemed to bee enuironed with a garland of mountains. At length for feare of misfortunes, seeing the sea so high, we durst not stay here or approch neere the land, and because we had great want of cables and ankers, we were again constrained to put to sea; and being in the same, and finding the said contrary windes, the Pilots iudged that we had none other remedie, but againe to retire our selues to our wonted shelter. And thus we returned, but somewhat aboue the old place. On Sunday we rode here to the great grief of all the company, considering what troubles we indured, and could not get forward; so that this was such a corrasiue, as none could be more intollerable. This day being come to an anker wee had a mighty gale of wind at Northwest, which was our aduersary and capital enemie, and when day was shut in, it still grew greater and greater, so that the ships rouled much. And after midnight, toward break of day, the Trinitie brake her two cables, which held the two ankers which she had, and seeing her selfe thus forlorne, she turned vp and downe in the sea vntill day, and came and rode neere vs, by one anker which shee had left. This day all of vs went to seeke these lost ankers, and for all the diligence which wee vsed, wee could find but one of them. We rode at anker all day vntill night, when the Trinitie againe brake a cable, which certaine rocks had cut asunder: whereupon the General commanded that she should ride no longer at anker, but that shee should turne vp and downe, as she had done before in sight of vs, which she did al day long, and at night she came to an anker ouer against a fresh water somewhat lower, and wee went and rode hard by her. On Palmesunday we went on shore with the fathers, which read the passion vnto vs and said masse, and we went in procession with branches in our hands. And so being comforted, because we had receiued that holy Sacrament, we returned to our ships.

Chap. 16.

Returning to the Isle of Cedars weather-beaten, and with their ships in euil case, they conclude, that the ship called Santa Agueda or Santa Agatha should returne vnto Nueua Espanna. Of the multitude of whales which they found about the point of California: with the description of a weede, which groweth among the Islands of those seas.

Here we continued vntill the Wednesday before Easter being the foure and twentieth of March, on which day wee consulted together, that because the ships were ill conditioned, and wanted necessary furniture to proceede any further, it were best for vs to returne backe to New Spaine, as also because our clothes were consumed: but the Generall seemed not willing to returne, but to proceed on his voyage: and in fine it was resolued, that seeing both the ships could not proceede forward, as well because they had lost their necessary furnitures, as also that the Santa Agatha had neede of calking, because she receiued much water, and was the worst furnished of the twaine, that shee should returne backe to aduertise the Marques of our successe in this voyage, and what hindred our proceeding, and in what case wee stoode, and howe wee were bereft of our necessary furniture. And because the Trinitie was the swifter ship, and better appointed then the other, it was concluded, that it should be prouided in the best maner that might be, and that the General should proceed on his iourney in her with such companie as he should make choise of, and that the rest should returne at their good leisure. Wherefore vpon this determination we went vnder a point of this Island, because it was a fit place to carene the ship: and in recouering the same we spent Wednesday, Thursday, and Friday till noone, and yet for all that wee could not wel double it, vntil Easter day about noone. Here we ankered very neere the shore and in a valley we found very excellent fresh water, whereof we made no smal account, and here stayed all the Easter holidayes, to set our selues about the furnishing vp of the Trinity: and after the worke was taken in hand by the two Masters which were very sufficient calkers (one of which was Iuan Castiliano chiefe Pilot, and the other Peruccio de Bermes) they finished the same so well in fiue dayes, as it was wonderfull; for no man could perceiue how any droppe of water could enter into any of the seames. Afterward they mended the other ship from Saturday till Munday, during which time all those were shriuen that had not confessed, and receiued the communion, and it was resolued by charge of the confessors, that all those seale-skins which they had taken from the Indians should bee restored againe; and the Generall gaue charge to Francis Preciado to restore them all, charging him on his conscience so to doe. Thus they gathered them together, and deliuered them into the hands of the fathers, to bee kept vntill they returned to the place, where they were to restore them. *The Santa Agueda returneth for Newspaine the 5. of April.* After this maner on Munday before noone we tooke our leaues of the Generall Francis Vlloa, and of the people that stayed with him, who at our departure shed no small number of teares, and we chose for our captaine in the Santa Agueda master Iuan Castiliano the chiefe pilot, as well of the ship, as of vs all, and set saile the same day being the fift of April, hauing our boat tied at our sterne, till we came ouer against the cottages, whence wee had taken the seale-skins. *The Isle of Cedars 300 leagues from Colima.* From the countrey of the Christians and the port of Colima we were now distant some three hundreth leagues, which is the first port where wee determined to touch at. And hauing sailed a league from the Trinitie the captaine Iuan Castiliano commanded vs to salute them with three pieces of great Ordinance, and she answered vs with other three, and afterward we answered one another with two shot apiece.

The sixt of Aprill. We sailed on Munday and Tewsday til noone with contrary wind in sight of the Island, and at noone we had a fresh gale in the poupe, which brought vs ouer against the cottages of the Indians where we tooke away those seal-skins; and there certain souldiers and mariners with the father frier Antony de Melo leapt on shore with the boat, carying the skins with them, and flung them into the sayd cottages out of which they were taken, and so returned to their ship. *The 7 of April. They saile from the Isle of Cedars to the point of Santa Cruza or California in sixe daies.* This day the weather calmed, whereupon we were driuen to cast anker, fearing that we should foorthwith be distressed for want of victuals, if we should stay there any long time: but God which is the true helper prouided better for vs then we deserued or imagined; for as we rode here, after midnight the Wednesday following before ten of the cloke wee had a fauourable gale of winde from the Southeast, which put vs into the sea; whither being driuen, wee had the wind at Northwest so good and constant, that in six dayes it brought vs to the cape of the point of the port of Santa Cruz: for which so great blessing of God we gaue vnto him infinite thankes. And here we began to allow our selues a greater proportion of victuals then wee had done before, for wee had eaten very sparingly for feare our victuals would faile vs. :Punta de Balenas.: Before we came to this point of the hauen of Santa Cruz by sixe or seuen leagues we saw on shore between certaine valleys diuers great smokes. And hauing passed the point of this port, our captaine thought it good to lanch foorth into the maine Ocean: yet although we ran a swift course, aboue 500 whales came athwart of vs in 2 or 3 skulles within one houres space, which were so huge, as it was wonderfull, and some of them, came so neere vnto the ship, that they swam vnder the same from one side to another, whereupon we were in great feare, lest they should doe vs some hurt, but they could not because the ship had a prosperous and good winde, and made much way, whereby it could receiue no harme, although they touched and strooke the same.

:Read more of these weedes cap. 13.: Among these Islands are such abundance of those weedes, that if at any time wee were inforced to sayle ouer them, they hindred the course of our ships. They growe fourteene or fifteene fadome deepe vnder the water, their tops reaching foure or fiue fadome aboue the water. They are of the colour of yellow waxe, and their stalke groweth great proportionably. This weede is much more beautifull then it is set foorth, and no maruell, for the naturall painter and creator thereof is most excellent.

This relation was taken out of that which Francis Preciado brought with him. :Sant Iago de Buena esperanza in 19 degrees.: After this ship the Santa Agueda departed from the Generall Vlloa, and returned backe the 5 of April, she arriued in the port of Sant Iago de buena esperança the 18 of the said moneth, and after she had stayed there foure or fiue dayes, she departed for Acapulco: howbeit vntill this present seuenteenth of May in the yeere 1540, I haue heard no tidings nor newes of her.

:Cabo del Enganno in 30 degrees and a halfe.: Moreouer after the departure of the Santa Agueda for Nueua Espanna, the General Francis Vlloa in the ship called the Trinitie proceeding on his discouery coasted the land vntill he came to a point called Cabo del Enganno standing in thirty degrees and a halfe of Northerly latitude, and then returned backe to Newspaine, because he found the winds very contrary, and his victuals failed him.

The true and perfect description of a voyage performed and done by Francisco de Gualle a Spanish Captaine and Pilot, for the Vice-roy of New Spaine, from the hauen of Acapulco in New Spaine, to the Islands of the Luçones or Philippinas, vnto the Hauen of Manilla, and from thence to the Hauen of Macao in China, and from Macao backe againe to Acapulco, accomplished in the yeere of our Lord, 1584.

Chap. 1.

The tenth of March in the yeere of our Lorde 1582 wee set sayle out of the Hauen of Acapulco, lying in the countrey of New Spaine, directing our course towards the Islands of the Luçones, or Philippinas West Southwest, running in that maner for the space of twentie fiue leagues, till wee came vnder sixteene degrees, so that wee might shunne the calmes by sayling close by the shoare. From thence forward we held our course West for the space of 30 leagues, and being there, we ran West, and West and by South, for the space of 1800 leagues, to the Iland called Isla del Enganno, which is the furthest Iland lying in the South parts of the Ilands called De los Ladrones, that is, The Ilands of rouers, or Islas de las Velas, vnder 13. degrees and ½. in latitude Septentrionall, and 164. degrees in longitude Orientall, vpon the fixed Meridionall line, which lyeth right with the Iland of Terçera. From thence we helde our coarse Westward for the space of 280. leagues, till we came to the point called El capo de Espirito Santo, that, is, The point of the holy Ghost, lying in the Iland Tandaya, the first Iland of those that are called Philippinas, Luçones, or Manillas, which is a countrey with fewe hilles, with some mines of brimstone in the middle thereof. From the point aforesayde, wee sailed West for the space of eighteene leagues to the point or entrie of the chanell, which runneth in betweene that Iland and the Iland of Luçon. This point or entrie lieth scarce vnder 12. degrees. All the coast that stretcheth from the entrie of the chanel to the point of El capo del Spirito santo, is not very faire.

Eight leagues from the sayde point lyeth a hauen of indifferent greatnesse, called Baya de Lobos, that is, The Bay of Woolues, hauing a small Iland at the mouth thereof: and within the chanell about halfe a league from the ende of the sayd Iland lyeth an Iland or cliffe, and when you passe by the point in the middle of the chanell, then you haue fiue and twentie fathom deepe, with browne sand: there we found so great a streame running Westward, that it made the water to cast a skum as if it had beene a sande, whereby it put us in feare, but casting out our lead, wee found fiue and twentie fathom deepe.

From the aforesayd entrie of the chanell North, and North and by East about tenne leagues, lyeth the Island of Catanduanes, about a league distant from the lande of Luçon, on the furthest point Eastward, and from the same entrie of the chanell towards the West and Southwest, lyeth the Iland Capuli about six leagues from thence, stretching Westsouthwest, and Eastnortheast, being fiue leagues long, and foure leagues broad: and as wee past by it, it lay Northward from vs vnder twelue degrees and ¾. and somewhat high lande. Foure leagues from the aforesayd Iland of Capuli Northwestward lie the three Ilands of the hauen of Bollon in the Iland of Luçones, stretching North and South about foure leagues, distant from the firme lande halfe a league, whereof the furthest Southward lieth vnder thirteene degrees; In this chanell it is twentie fathome deepe, with white sand, and a great streame, running Southeast: we passed through the middle of the chanell. From this chanell wee helde our coarse Southwest, and Southwest and by West, for the space of twentie leagues, vntill wee came to the West ende of the Iland of Tycao, which reacheth East and West thirteene leagues. This point or hooke lyeth vnder 12. degrees and ¾. In the middle betweene this Iland and the Iland Capuli there lie three Ilands called the Faranias, and we ranne in the same course on the Northside of all the Ilands, at the depth of 22. fathom with white sand.

From the aforesayd West point of the Iland Tycao to the point of Buryas it is East and West to sayle about the length of a league or a league and a halfe: we put into that chanell, holding our course South, and South and by West about three leagues, vntill we were out of the chanell at sixteene fathome deepe, with halfe white and reddish sande in the chanell, and at the mouth thereof, whereof the middle lyeth vnder 12. degrees and ⅔. and there the streames runne Northward.

The Isle of Masbate. The Iland of Buryas stretched Northwest and Southeast, and is low lande, whereof the Northwest point is about three leagues from the coast of Luçon, but you cannot passe betweene them with any shippe, but with small foistes and barkes of the countrey. This shallow channell lieth vnder twelue degrees: and running thorow the aforesayd chanell betweene the Ilands Tycao and Buryas, as I sayd before, we sayled Southward about two leagues from the Iland of Masbate, which stretcheth East and West 8. leagues long, being in bredth 4. leagues, and lyeth vnder 12. degrees and ¼. in the middle thereof, and is somewhat high land.

From the sayd chanell betweene Tycao and Buryas, wee helde our course Westnorthwest for thirteene leagues, leauing the Iland Masbate on the Southside, and the Iland Buryas on the North side: at the ende of thirteene leagues wee came by an Iland called Banton, which is in forme like a hat, vnder twelue degrees and ⅔. when we had sayled the aforesayd thirteene leagues and eight leagues more, on the South side wee left the Iland called Rebuiam, which stretcheth Northwest, and Northwest and by North, and Southeast, and Southeast and by South, for the space of eight leagues, being high and crooked lande, whereof the North point lyeth vnder twelue degrees and ⅔. and there you finde 35 fathom deepe, with white sand.

From the aforesayd Iland of Banton Southward nine leagues, there beginne and followe three Ilandes, one of them being called Bantonsilla, which is a small Iland in forme of a sugar loafe: the second Crymara, being somewhat great in length, reaching East and West about two leagues: the third Itaa, or the Ile of Goates, hauing certaine houels. By all these Ilands aforesayd you may passe with all sortes of shippes, whereof the foremost lyeth Southward vnder twelue degrees and ¼. From the Iland of Bantonsilla, or small Banton, wee helde our course Northwest for the space of foure leagues, to the chanell betweene Ilands called de Vereies, and the Iland of Marinduque, the Vereies lying on the South side vnder twelue degrees and ¾. (which are two small Ilands like two Frigats) and the Iland Marinduque on the North side vnder twelue degrees, and ¼. which is a great Iland, stretching Westnorthwest, and Eastsoutheast, hauing in length 12. and in bredth 7. leagues. On the North side, with the Iland Luçon it maketh a long and small chanell, running somewhat crooked, which is altogether full of shallowes and sandes, whereby no shippes can passe through it. The furthest point Westward of the same Iland lyeth vnder thirteene degrees and ¼. It is high lande, on the East side hauing the forme of a mine of brimstone or fierie hill, and on the West side the land runneth downewarde at the point thereof being round like a loafe of bread: in the chanell betweene it and the Vereies, there are 18. fathom deepe with small black sand.

From the aforesaid chanell of Vereies and Marinduque, wee helde our course Westnorthwest twelue leagues to the lande of Mindora, to the point or hooke called Dumaryn, lying full vnder thirteene degrees: Fiue leagues forward from the sayde chanell on the South side wee left an Iland called Isla de maestro del Campo, that is, The Iland of the Colonell, lying vnder twelue degrees and ¾. which is a small and flat Iland: In this course we had 45 fathom deep white sand.

By this point or end of the Iland Marinduque beginneth the Iland of Myndoro, which hath in length East and West fiue and twentie leagues, and in bredth twelue leagues, whereof the furthest point Southward lyeth vnder thirteene degrees, and the furthest point Northward vnder thirteene degrees and ⅔. and the furthest point Westward vnder thirteene degrees. This Iland with the Iland of Luçon maketh a chanell of fiue leagues broad, and ten or twelue fathom deepe with muddie ground of diuers colours, with white sande. Fiue leagues forward from Marinduque lyeth the riuer of the towne of Anagacu, which is so shallowe, that no shippes may enter into it. From thence two leagues further lie the Ilands called Bacco, which are three Ilands lying in a triangle, two of them being distant from the land about three hundred cubits, and between them and the land you may passe with small shippes: And from the lande to the other Iland, are about two hundred cubites, where it is altogether shallowes and sandes, so that where the shippes may passe outward about 150. cubites from the lande, you leaue both the Ilands on the South side, running betweene the third Iland and the riuer called Rio del Bacco, somewhat more from the middle of the chanell towardes the Iland, which is about a league distant from the other; the chanell is tenne fathom deepe, with mud and shelles vpon the ground: the riuer of Bacco is so shallowe, that no ships may enter into it. From this Iland with the same course two leagues forward, you passe by the point called El Capo de Rescaseo, where we cast out our lead, and found that a man may passe close by the lande, and there you shall finde great strong streames: and halfe a league forward with the same course, lyeth the towne of Mindoro, which hath a good hauen for shippes of three hundred tunnes. Three leagues Northward from the same hauen lyeth the Iland called Cafaa, stretching from East to West, being hilly ground.

From the sayde towne of Myndora, wee helde our course Westnorthwest eight leagues, till wee came to the poynt or hooke of the sandes called Tulen, lying vpon the Iland of Luçon, which sande or banke reacheth into the Sea halfe a league from the coast: you must keepe about an hundred cubites from it, where you finde eight fathom water, muddie and shellie ground: you runne along by those sandes North, and North and by West for the space of two leagues, till you come to the riuer called Rio de Anasebo: all the rest of the coast called De los Limbones to the month or entrie of the Bay called Manilla, (which are foure leagues) is sayled with the same course. The Limbones (which are Ilands so called) are high in forme like a paire of Organs, with good hauens for small shippes, running along by the Limbones: and two leagues beyond them on the South side, wee leaue the Ilands of Fortan, and foure Ilands more, but the three Ilands of Lubao, which are very low, lie vnder 13. degrees and $\frac{1}{3}$. and the Limbones lie in the mouth or entrie of the Bay of Manilla vnder 14. degrees and $\frac{1}{4}$.

From thence we ranne Northwest for the space of sixe leagues to the hauen of Cabite, keeping along by the land lying on the West side, where it is shallowe, and is called Los Baixos del Rio de Cannas, The shallowes of the riuer of Reedes: all along this Bay in the same course, there is from ten to foure fathom deepe.

Being by the point or hooke of Cabite, then wee kept but an hundred paces from it, running Southwest, southsouthwest, and South, vntill we discouered the whole mouth or entrie of the Bay, where we might anker at foure fathom about two hundred cubites from the lande, and then the towne of Manilla was two leagues Northward from vs.[49]

[49] The Philippine Islands are an archipelago of about 1400 islands, forming a dependency of Spain, lying between 4 deg. 40 min and 20 deg. N. lat., and 116 deg. 40 min. and 126 deg. 30 min. E. lon., and having the China Sea on the west, and the Pacific Ocean on the East. They are very imperfectly known at present, but are estimated to have a total area of 114,000 square miles, and a population of about 10,000,000. The principal islands of the many hundreds of large and small forming the group are— Luzon, Mindanao, Palawan, Mindoro, Panay, Negros, Zebu, Leyte, and Samar.

The Philippines were discovered by Fernando Magalhaens in 1521, in the reign of Philip II, after whom they were named; and in 1564 the Spaniards made a settlement on one of the islands, and founded Manila in 1571. They obtained the possession of this important group almost without bloodshed; and they have preserved it by the extensive diffusion of the Roman Catholic religion among the Malays, who form the greater part of the population. The Spaniards have retained the island ever since, except from 1762 to 1764, during which the English held Manila, and for the release of which the Spaniards paid a ransom of £1,000,000.

Chap. 2.

The course and voyage of the aforesayd Francisco Gualle out of the hauen or roade of Manilla, to the hauen of Macao in China, with all the courses and situations of the places.

Sayling out of the hauen of Cabite, lying in the Bay of Manilla, wee helde our course Westwarde for the space of eighteene leagues, to the point called El Cabo de Samballes: and when wee were eight leagues in our way, wee left the two Ilands Maribillas on the South side, and sailed about a league from them: the point of Samballes aforesayde lyeth vnder foureteene degrees, and ⅔. being low land, at the end of the same coast of Luçon, on the West side.

From the hooke or point aforesayde, wee ranne North, and North and by West, for the space of fiue and twentie leagues (aboue a league from the coast of Luçon) to the point called Cabo de Bullinao: all this coast and Cape is high and hilly ground, which Cape lyeth vnder sixteene degrees and ⅔. From this Cape de Bellinao we helde our course North, and North and by East, for 45. leagues to the point called El Cabo de Bojador, which is the furthest lande Northwarde from the Iland Luçon lying vnder 19. degrees.

The Cape de Bullinao being past the lande maketh a great creeke or bough, and from this creeke the coast runneth North to the point of Bojador, being a land full of cliffes and rockes that reach into the Sea, and the land of the hooke or point is high and hilly ground.

From the point of Bojador, wee helde our course Westnorthwest an hundred and twentie leagues, vntill we came to the Iland called A Ilha Branca, or the white Iland, lying in the beginning of the coast and Bay of the riuer Canton vnder two and twentie degrees, hauing foure and twentie fathom browne muddie ground.

From the Iland Ilha Branca, wee helde the aforesayde course of Westnorthwest, for the space of sixteene leagues, to the Iland of Macao lying in the mouth of the riuer of Canton, and it maketh the riuer to haue two mouths or entries, and it is a small Iland about three leagues great.

Chap. 3.

The Nauigation or course of the aforesayd Francisco Gualle out of the hauen of Macao to Newe Spaine, with the situation and stretchings of the same, with other notable and memorable things concerning the same voyage.

When we had prepared our selues, and had taken our leaues of our friends in Macao, we set saile vpon the foure and twentieth of Iuly, holding our course Southeast, and Southeast and by East, being in the wane of the Moone: for when the Moone increaseth, it is hard holding the course betweene the Ilands, because as then the water and streames run very strong to the Northwest; wee trauailed through many narrowe channels by night, hauing the depth of eight or ten fathom, with soft muddie ground, vntill wee were about the Iland Ilha Branca, yet we saw it not, but by the height we knew that we were past it.

Being beyond it, we ranne Eastsoutheast an hundred and fiftie leagues, to get aboue the sands called Os Baixos dos Pescadores, and the beginning of the Ilands Lequeos on the East side, which Ilands are called As Ilhas fermosas,[50] that is to say, The faire Ilands. This I vnderstoode by a Chinar called Santy of Chinchon, and hee sayde that they lie vnder one and twentie degrees and ¾. there it is thirtie fathom deepe: and although wee sawe them not, notwithstanding by the height and depth of the water we knew we were past them.

[50] Formosa.

Being past As Ilhas fermosas, or the faire Ilands, wee helde our course East, and East and by North, for two hundred and sixtie leagues, vntill we were past the length of the Ilands Lequeos,[51] sayling about fiftie leagues from them: the said Chinar tolde me, that those Ilands called Lequeos are very many, and that they haue many and very good hauens, and that the people and inhabitants thereof haue their faces and bodies painted like the Bysayas of the Ilands of Luçon or Philippinas and are apparelled like the Bysayas, and that there also are mines of gold: Hee sayd likewise that they did often come with small shippes and barkes laden with Bucks and Harts-hides, and with golde in graines or very small pieces, to traffique with them of the coast of China, which hee assured mee to bee most true, saying that hee had bene nine times in the small Ilands, bringing of the same wares with him to China: which I beleeued to bee true, for that afterwarde I enquired thereof in Macao, and upon the coast of China, and found that hee sayde true. The furthest or vttermost of these Ilands stretching Northwarde and Eastwarde, lie vnder nine and twentie degrees.

[51] The Lu-Tchu (*Chinese*) or Liu-Khiu (*Japanese*) Islands are a chain of 52 Islands belonging to Japan, and stretching S.W. to Formosa.

Being past these Ilands, then you come to the Ilands of Iapon, whereof the first lying West and South, is the Iland of Firando, where the Portugals vse to traffique: they are in length altogether an hundred and thirtie leagues, and the furthest Eastward lieth under two and thirtie degrees: we ranne still East, and East and by North, vntill we were past the sayd hundred and thirtie leagues.

All this information I had of the aforesaid Chinar, as also that there I should see some mines of brimstone or fierie hilles, being seuentie leagues beyond them,[52] and thirtie leagues further I should finde four Ilands lying together, which I likewise found, as hee had tolde mee: Other Ilands Eastward of Iapon. And that being in Iapon, he sayd hee had there seene certaine men of a very small stature, with great rolle of linnen cloth about there heads, that brought golde in small pieces, and some white Cangas of cotton, (which are pieces of cotton-linnen so called by the Chinars) as also salte-fish like the Spanish Atun, or Tunney, which hee sayde came out of other Ilands Eastward from Iapon: and by the tokens and markes which hee shewed mee, I gessed whereabout those Ilands should bee, and found them not farre from whence he sayd they lay. Hee sayd likewise that all the Ilands of Iapon haue good hauens and chanels, being a Countrey full of Rice, Corne, Fish, and flesh, and that they are indifferent and reasonable people to traffique with, and that there they haue much siluer.

[52] This probably refers to Fusyiama, which can be seen from Tokio, 80 miles away. Its last eruption took place in 1707.

Running thus East, and East and by North about three hundred leagues from Iapon, wee found a very hollowe water, with the streame running out of the North and Northwest, with a full and very broad Sea, without any hinderance or trouble in the way that wee past: and what winde soeuer blewe, the Sea continued all in one sort, with the same hollow water and streame, vntill wee had passed seuen hundred leagues. Iapon 900. leagues distant from the coast of America in 37 degrees and an halfe. About two hundred leagues from the coast and land of newe Spaine wee beganne to lose the sayd hollow Sea, and streame: whereby I most assuredly thinke and beleeue, that there you shall finde a chanell or straight passage, betweene the firme lande of newe Spaine, and the Countreys of Asia and Tartaria.

Likewise all this way from the aforesayde seuen hundred leagues, we found a great number of Whale-fishes and other fishes called by the Spaniards Atuns or Tunnies, whereof many are found on the coast of Gibraltar in Spaine, as also Albacoras and Bonitos, which are all fishes, which commonly keepe in chanels, straights, and running waters, there to disperse their seede when they breede: which maketh mee more assuredly beleeue, that thereabouts is a chanel or straight to passe through.

: Read Francis Vlloa chap. 16. : Being by the same course vpon the coast of newe Spaine, vnder seuen and thirtie degrees and ½. wee passed by a very high and faire lande with many trees, wholly without snowe, and foure leagues from the lande, you finde thereabouts many drifts of rootes, leaues of trees, reeds, and other leaues like figge leaues, the like whereof wee found in great abundance in the countrey of Iapon, which they eate: and some of those that wee found, I caused to bee sodden with flesh, and being sodden, they eate like Coleworts: there likewise wee found great store of Seales: whereby it is to bee presumed and certainely to bee beleeued, that there are many riuers, bayes, and hauens along by those coastes to the hauen of Acapulco.

From thence wee ranne Southeast, Southeast and by South, and Southeast and by East, as wee found the winde, to the point called El Cabo de Sant Lucas, which is the beginning of the lande of California, on the Northwest side, lying vnder two and twentie degrees, being fiue hundred leagues distant from Cape Mendoçino.

: Hauens lately found out. : In this way of the aforesayde fiue hundred leagues along by the coast, are many Ilands: and although they bee but small, yet without doubt there are in them some good hauens, as also in the firme land, where you haue these hauens following, now lately found out, as that of the Ile of Sant Augustine, lying vnder thirtie degrees and ¾. and the Iland called Isla de Cedros, scarce vnder eight and twenty deg. and ¼. and the Iland lying beneath Saint Martyn, vnder three and twentie degrees and ½. All this coast and countrey, as I thinke, is inhabited, and sheweth to be a very good countrey: for there by night wee sawe fire, and by day smoke, which is a most sure token that they are inhabited.

From the poynt or hooke of Saint Lucas, to the Southeast side of California, wee helde our course Eastsoutheast, for the space of 80. leagues, to the point called El cabo de las corrientes, that is, the Cape of the streames lying vnder 19. degrees and ⅔. And running this course, Northward about a league from vs wee sawe three Ilands called Las tres Marias, (that is to say, The three Maries) running the same course. About foure leagues from the other Ilands, there are other Ilands, reaching about two or three leagues: All this way from the mouth or gulfe of California aforesayd, for the space of the sayd fourescore leagues, there are great streames that run Westward.

From the point or Cape de las Corrientes, we ranne Southeast, and sometimes Southeast and by East, for the space of an hundred and thirtie leagues to the hauen of Acapulco. In this way of an hundred and thirtie leagues, being twentie leagues on the way, we had the hauen of Natiuidad, that is, of the birth of the Virgin Mary: and other eight leagues further, the hauen of Saint Iago, or Saint Iames; and six leagues further, the sea Strand called La Playa de Colima, that is, the Strand of Colima. All this coast from California to the hauen of Acapulco is inhabited by people that haue peace and traffique with the Spaniards, and are of condition and qualities like the people of the other places of new Spaine.

The conclusion of the Author of this last voyage.

All this description and nauigation haue I my selfe seene, prooued, and well noted in my voyage made and ended in the yeere of our Lord 1584. from great China out of the hauen and riuer of Canton, as I will more at large set it downe vnto your honour, with the longitudes and latitudes thereof, as God shall permit mee time and leysure, whom I beseech to send you long and happie dayes.

And the same was truly translated out of Spanish into lowe Dutch verbatim out of the Originall copy, (which was sent vnto the Viceroy of the Portugall Indies) by Iohn Huyghen Van Linschoten.

The relation of the nauigation and discouery which Captaine Fernando Alarchon made by the order of the right honourable Lord Don Antonio de Mendoça, Vizeroy of New Spaine, dated in Colima, an hauen of New Spaine.

Chap. 1.

Fernando Alarchon after he had suffered a storme, arriued with his Fleete at the hauen of Saint Iago, and from thence at the hauen of Aguaiaual: he was in great perill in seeking to discouer a Bay, and getting out of the same he discouered a riuer on the coast with a great current, entring into the same, and coasting along he descried a great many of Indians with their weapons: with signes hee hath traffique with them, and fearing some great danger returneth to his ships.

On Sunday the ninth of May in the yeere 1540. I set saile with two ships, the one called Saint Peter being Admirall, and the other Saint Catherine, and wee set forward meaning to go to the hauen of Saint Iago of good hope: but before wee arriued there wee had a terrible storme, wherewith they which were in the ship called Saint Catherine, being more afraid then was neede, cast ouer boord nine pieces of Ordinance, two ankers and one cable, and many other things as needfull for the enterprise wherein we went, as the ship it selfe. Assoone as we were arriued at the hauen of Saint Iago I repaired my losse which I had receiued, prouided my selfe of things necessary, and tooke aboord my people which looked for my comming, and directed my course toward the hauen of Aguaiauall. And being there arriued I vnderstood that the Generall Francis Vazquez de Coronado was departed with all his people: whereupon taking the ship called Saint Gabriel which carried victuals for the armie I led her with mee to put in execution your Lordships order. Afterward I followed my course along the coast without departing from the same, to see if I could find any token, or any Indian which could giue me knowledge of him: and in sailing so neere the shore I discouered other very good hauens, for the ships whereof Captaine Francis de Vllua was General for the Marquesse de Valle neither sawe nor found them. These shoalds are the bottome of mar Bermejo, or the Bay of California. And when we were come to the flats and shoalds from whence the foresaid fleete returned, it seemed as well to me as to the rest, that we had the firme land before vs, and that those shoalds were so perilous and fearefull, that it was a thing to be considered whither with our skiffes we could enter in among them: and the Pilotes and the rest of the company would haue had vs done as Captaine Vllua did, and haue returned backe againe. But because your Lordship commanded mee, that I should bring you the secret of that gulfe, I resolued, that although I had knowen I should haue lost the shippes, I would not haue ceased for any thing to haue seene the head thereof: and therefore I commanded Nicolas Zamorano Pilote maior, and Dominico del Castello that eche of them should take a boate, and their lead in their hands, and runne in among those shoalds, to see if they could find out the chanell whereby the shippes might enter in: to whom it seemed that the ships might saile vp higher (although with great trauell and danger) and in this sort I and he began to follow our way which they had taken, and within a short while after wee found our selues fast on the sands with all our three ships, in such sort that one could not helpe another, neither could the boates succour vs, because the current was so great that it was impossible for one of vs to come vnto another: whereupon we were in such great ieopardie that the decke of the Admirall was oftentimes vnder water, and if a great surge of the sea had not come and driuen our ship right vp, and gaue her leaue as it were to breath a while, we had there bin drowned: and likewise the other two shippes found themselues in very great hazard, yet because they were lesser and drewe lesse water, their danger was not so great as ours: Nowe it pleased God vpon the returne of the flood that the shippes came on flote, and so wee went forward. And although the company would haue returned backe, yet for all this I determined to goe forwarde, and to pursue our attempted voyage: and we passed forward with much adoe, turning our stemmes now this way, now that way, to seeke to find the chanel. *The bottome of the Bay of California.* And it pleased God that after this sort we came to the very bottoms of the Bay: where we found a very mightie riuer, which ranne with so great fury of a streame, that we could hardly saile against it.[53] In this sort I determined as wel as I could to go vp this riuer, and with two boates, leauing the third with the ships, and twenty men, my selfe being in one of them with Roderigo Maldonado treasurer of this fleet, and Gaspar de Castilleia comptroller, and with certaine small pieces of artillerie I began to saile vp the river, and charged all my company, that none of them should stirre nor vse any signe, but he whom I appointed, although wee found Indians. *They goe vp the riuer of Buena guia the 26. of August.* The same day, which was Thursday the sixe and twentieth of August, following our voyage with drawing the boats with halsers we went about some 6 leagues; and the next day which was Friday by the breake of day thus following our way vpward, I saw certaine Indians which went toward certaine cottages neere vnto the water, who assoone as they saw vs, ten or twelue of them rose vp furiously, and crying with a loud voyce, other of their companions came running together to the number of 50 which with all haste carried out of their cottages such things as they had, and layd them vnder certaine shrubs and many of them came running toward that part whether wee approched, making great signes vnto vs that we should goe backe againe, vsing great threatnings against vs, one while running on this side and an other while on that side. I seeing them in such a rage, caused our boates to lanch from the shore into the middes of the riuer, that the Indians might be out of feare, and I rode at anker, and set my people in as good order as I could, charging them that no man should speake, nor make any signe nor motion, nor stirre out of his place, nor should not be offended for anything that the Indians did, nor should shewe no token of warre: and by this meanes the Indians came euery foote neere the riuers side to see vs: and I gate by little and little toward them where the riuer seemed to be deepest. In this meane space there were aboue two hundred and fiftie Indians assembled together with bowes and arrowes, and with certaine banners in warrelike sort in such maner as those of New Spayne doe vse: and perceiuing that I drewe toward the shore, they came with great cryes toward vs with bowes and arrowes put into them, and with their banners displayed. And I went vnto the stemme of my boate with the interpreter which I carried with me, whom I commanded to speake vnto them, and when he spake, they neither vnderstood him, nor he them, although because they sawe him to be after their fashion, they stayed themselues: and seeing this I drewe neerer the shore, and they with great cryes came to keepe mee from the shore of the riuer, making signes that I should not come any further, putting stakes in my way betweene the water and the land: and the more I lingered, the more people still flocked together. Which when I had considered I beganne to make them signes of peace, and taking my sword and target, I cast them downe in the boate and set my feete vpon them, giving them to vnderstand with this and other tokens that I desired not to haue warre with them, and that they should doe the like: A very good course taken to appease vnknowen Sauages. Also I tooke a banner and cast it downe; and I caused my company that were with mee to sit downe likewise, and taking the wares of exchange which I carried with mee, I called them to giue them some of them: yet for all this none of them stirred to take any of them, but rather flocked together, and beganne to make a great murmuring among themselues: and suddenly one came out from among them with a staffe wherein certayne shelles were set, and entred into the water to giue them vnto mee, and I tooke them, and made signes vnto him that hee should come neere me, which when he had done, I embraced him, and gaue him in recompence certaine beades and other things, and he returning with them vnto his fellowes, began to looke vpon them, and to parley together, and within a while after many of them came toward me, to whom I made signes to lay downe their banners, and to leaue their weapons: which they did incontinently, then I made signes that they should lay them altogether, and should goe aside from them, which likewise they did: and they caused those Indians which newly came thither to leaue them, and to lay them together with the rest. After this I called them vnto me, and to all them which came I gaue some smal trifle, vsing them gently, and by this time they were so many that came thronging about mee, that I thought I could not stay any longer in safety among them, and I made signes vnto them that they should withdraw themselues, and that they should stand al vpon the side of an hill which was there betweene a plaine and the riuer, and that they should not presse to me aboue ten at a time. And immediately the most ancient among them called unto them with a loud voyce, willing them to do so: and some ten or twelue of them came where I was: whereupon seeing my selfe in some securitie, I determined to goe on land the more to put them out of feare: and for my more securitie, I made signes vnto them, to sit downe on the ground which they did: but when they saw that ten or twelue of my companions came a shore after me, they began to be angry, and I made signes vnto them that we would be friends, and that they should not feare, and herewithal they were pacified, and sate down as they did before, and I went vnto them, and imbraced them, giuing them certain trifles, commanding mine interpreter to speake vnto them, for I greatly desired to vnderstand their maner of speech, and the cry which they made at mee. And that I might knowe what maner of foode they had, I made a signe vnto them, that wee would gladly eate, and they brought mee certaine cakes of Maiz, and a loafe of Mizquiqui, and they made signes vnto mee that they desired to see an harquebuse shot off, which I caused to be discharged, and they were all wonderfully afraid, except two or three olde men among them which were not mooued at all, but rather cried out vpon the rest, because they were afrayd: and through the speach of one of these olde men, they began to rise vp from the ground, and to lay hold on their weapons: whom when I sought to appease, I would haue giuen him a silken girdle of diuers colours, and hee in a great rage bitte his nether lippe cruelly, and gaue mee a thumpe with his elbowe on the brest, and turned in a great furie to speake vnto his company. After that I saw them aduance their banners, I determined to returne my selfe gently to my boates, and with a small gale of wind I set sayle, whereby wee might breake the current which was very great, although my company were not well pleased to goe any farther. In the meane space the Indians came following vs along the shore of the riuer, making signes that I should come on land, and that they would giue mee food to eate, some of them sucking their fingers, and others entred into the water with certaine cakes of Maiz, to giue me them in my boate.

[53] Rio Colorado.

Chap. 2.

Of the habite, armour and stature of the Indians. A relation of many others with whom he had by signes traffique, victuals and many courtesies.

Good forecast. In this sort we went vp two leagues, and I arriued neere a cliffe of an hill, whereupon was an arbour made newly, where they made signes vnto me, crying that I should go thither, shewing me the same with their handes, and telling mee that there was meate to eate. But I would not goe thither, seeing the place was apt for some ambush, but followed on my voyage, within a while after issued out from thence aboue a thousand armed men with their bowes and arrowes, and after that many women and children shewed themselues, toward whom I would not goe, but because the Sunne was almost set, I rode in the middest of the riuer. These Indians came decked after sundry fashions, some came with a painting that couered their face all ouer, some had their faces halfe couered, but all besmouched with cole, and euery one as it liked him best. Others carried visards before them of the same colour which had the shape of faces. They weare on their heads a piece of a Deeres skinne two spannes broad set after the maner of a helmet, and vpon it certaine small sticks with some sortes of fethers. Their weapons were bowes and arrowes of hard wood, and two or three sorts of maces of wood hardened in the fire. This is a mightie people, well feitured, and without any grossenesse. They haue holes bored in their nostrels whereat certaine pendents hang: and others weare shelles, and their eares are full of holes, whereon they hang bones and shelles. All of them both great and small weare a girdle about their waste made of diuerse colours, and in the middle is fastened a round bunch of feathers, which hangeth downe behind like a tayle. Likewise on the brawne of their armes they weare a streit string, which they wind so often about that it becommeth as broad as ones hand. They weare certaine pieces of Deeres bones fastened to their armes, wherewith they strike off the sweate, and at the other certaine small pipes of canes. Pipes and bagges of tobacco. They carry also certaine little long bagges about an hand broade tyed to their left arme, which serue them also instead of brasers for their bowes, full of the powder of a certaine herbe, whereof they make a certaine beuerage. They haue their bodies traced with coles, their haire cut before, and behind it hangs downe to their wast. The women goe naked, and weare a great wreath of fethers behind them, and before painted and glued together, and their haire like the men. There were among these Indians three or foure men in womens apparell. Nowe the next day being Saturday very early I went forward on my way vp the riuer, setting on shore two men for eache boate to drawe them with the rope, and about breaking foorth of the Sunne, wee heard a mightie crie of Indians on both sides of the riuer with their weapons, but without any banner. I thought good to attend their comming, aswell to see what they woulde haue, as also to try whither our interpreter could vnderstand them. When they came ouer against vs they leapt into the riuer on both sides with their bowes and arrowes, and when they spake, our interpreter vnderstoode them not: whereupon I beganne to make a signe vnto them that they should lay away their weapons, as the other had done. Some did as I willed them, and some did not, and those which did, I willed to come neere me and gaue them some things which we had to trucke withall, which when the others perceiued, that they might likewise haue their part, they layd away their weapons likewise. I iudging my selfe to be in securitie leaped on shore with them, and stoode in the middest of them, who vnderstanding that I came not to fight with them, began to giue some of those shels and beades, and some brought me certaine skinnes well dressed, and others Maiz and a roll of the same naughtily grinded, so that none of them came vnto me that brought mee not something, and before they gaue it me going a little way from mee they began to cry out amayne, and made a signe with their bodies and armes, and afterward they approached to giue me that which they brought. And now that the Sunne beganne to set I put off from the shore, and rode, in the middest of the riuer. The next morning before break of day on both sides of the riuer wee heard greater cries and of more Indians, which leaped into the riuer to swimme, and they came to bring mee certaine gourdes full of Maiz, and of those wrethes which I spake of before. *A notable policie.* I shewed vnto them Wheate and Beanes, and other seedes, to see whether they had any of those kindes: but they shewed me that they had no knowledge of them, and wondred at all of them, and by signes I came to vnderstand that the thing which they most esteemed and reuerenced was the Sunne: and I signified vnto them that I came from the Sunne. Whereat they maruelled, and then they began to beholde me from the toppe to the toe, and shewed me more favour then they did before; and when I asked them for food, they brought me such aboundance that I was inforced twise to call for the boates to put it into them, and from that time forward of all the things which they brought me they flang vp into the ayre one part vnto the Sunne, and afterward turned towards me to giue mee the other part: and so I was alwayes better serued and esteemed of them as well in drawing of the boats vp the riuer, as also in giuing me food to eat: and they shewed me so great loue, that when I stayed they would have carried vs in their armes vnto their houses: and in no kind of thing they would breake my commandment: and for my suretie, I willed them not to carry any weapons in my sight: and they were so careful to doe so, that if any man came newly thither with them, suddenly they would goe and meete him to cause him to lay them downe farre from mee: and I shewed them that I tooke great pleasure in their so doing: Swarmes of people. and to some of the chiefe of them I gaue certaine little napkins and other trifles; for if I should haue giuen somewhat to euery one of them in particular, all the small wares in New Spayne would not haue sufficed. Sometimes it fell out (such was the great loue and good wil which they shewed me) that if any Indians came thither by chance with their weapons, and if any one being warned to leaue them behind him, if by negligence, or because he vnderstood them not at the first warning, he had not layd them away, they would runne vnto him, and take them from him by force, and would breake them in pieces in my presence. Afterward they tooke the rope so louingly, and with striuing one with another for it, that we had no need to pray them to doe it. Wherefore if we had not had this helpe, the current of the riuer being exceeding great, and our men that drew the rope being not well acquainted with that occupation, it would haue beene impossible for vs to haue gotten vp the riuer so against the streame. When I perceiued that they vnderstood mee in all things, and that I likewise vnderstoode them, I thought good to try by some way or other to make a good entrance to find some good issue to obtaine my desire: And I caused certaine crosses to be made of certaine small sticks and paper, and among others when I gaue any thing I gaue them these as things of most price and kissed them, making signes vnto them that they should honour them and make great account of them, and that they should weare them at their necks: giuing them to vnderstand that this signe was from heauen, and they tooke them and kissed them, and lifted them vp aloft, and seemed greatly to reioyce thereat when they did so, and sometime I tooke them into my boate, shewing them great good will, and sometime I gaue them of those trifles which I caried with me. And at length the matter grew to such issue, that I had not paper and stickes ynough to make crosses. In this matter that day I was very well accompanied, vntill that when night approched I sought to lanch out into the riuer, and went to ride in the middest of the streame, and they came to aske leaue of me to depart, saying that they would returne the next day with victuals to visite me, and so by litle and litle they departed, so that there stayed not aboue fiftie which made fires ouer against vs, and stayed there al night calling vs, and before the day was perfectly broken, they leapt into the water and swamme vnto vs asking for the rope, and we gaue it them with a good will, thanking God for the good prouision which he gaue vs to go vp the riuer: for the Indians were so many, that if they had gone about to let our passage, although we had bene many more then wee were, they might haue done it.

Chap. 3.

One of the Indians vnderstanding the language of the interpreter, asketh many questions of the originall of the Spaniards, he telleth him that their Captaine is the child of the Sunne, and that he was sent of the Sunne vnto them, and they would haue receiued him for their king. They take this Indian into their boat, and of him they haue many informations of that countrey.

A wise deuise. In this manner we sailed vntill Tuesday at night, going as we were wont, causing mine interpreter to speak vnto the people to see if peraduenture any of them could vnderstand him, I perceiued that one answered him, whereupon I caused the boates to be stayed, and called him, which hee vnderstoode, charging mine interpreter that hee should not speake nor answere him any thing else, but onely that which I said vnto him: and I saw as I stood still that that Indian began to speake to the people with great furie: whereupon all of them beganne to drawe together, and mine interpreter vnderstood, that he which came to the boate sayd vnto them, that he desired to knowe what nation we were, and whence wee came, and whither we came out of the water, or out of the earth, or from heauen: And at this speech an infinite number of people came together, which maruelled to see mee speake: and this Indian turned on this side and on that side to speake vnto them in another language which mine interpreter vnderstood not. Whereas he asked me what we were, I answered that we were Christians, and that we came from farre to see them: and answering to the question, who had sent me, I said, I was sent by the Sunne, pointing vnto him by signes as at the first, because they should not take mee in a lye. He beganne againe to ask mee, how the Sunne had sent me, seeing he went aloft in the skie and never stoode still, and seeing these many yeeres neither he nor their olde men had euer seene such as we were, of whome they euer had any kind of knowledge, and that Sunne till that houre had neuer sent any other. I answered him that it was true that the Sunne made his course aloft in the skie, and did neuer stand still, yet neuertheless that they might well perceiue that at his going downe and rising in the morning hee came neere vnto the earth, where his dwelling was, and that they euer sawe him come out of one place, and that hee had made mee in that land and countrey from whence hee came, like as hee had made many others which hee had sent into other parties, and that nowe hee had sent me to visitie and view the same riuer, and the people that dwelt neere the same, that I should speake vnto them, and should ioyne with them in friendshippe, and should giue them things which they had not, and that I should charge them that they should not make warre one against another. Whereunto he answered, that I should tell him the cause why the Sunne had not sent mee no sooner to pacifie the warres which had continued a long time among them, wherein many had beene slaine. I tolde him the cause hereof was, because at that time I was but a child. Then he asked the interpreter whether wee tooke him with vs perforce hauing taken him in the war, or whether he came with vs of his own accord. He answered him that he was with vs of his owne accord, and was very wel appaid of our company. He returned to enquire, why we brought none saue him onely that vnderstood vs, and wherefore we vnderstood not all other men, seeing we were the children of the Sunne: he answered, that the Sunne also had begotten him, and giuen him a language to vnderstand him, and me, and others: that the Sunne knew well that they dwelt there, but that because he had many other businesses, and because I was but yong hee sent me no sooner. And he turning vnto me sayd suddenly: Comest thou therefore hither to bee our Lord, and that wee should serue thee? I supposing that I should not please him if I should haue said yea, answered him, not to be their Lord, but rather to be their brother, and to giue them such things as I had. He asked me, whether the Sunne had begotten me as he had begotten others, and whether I was his kinsman or his sonne: I answered him that I was his sonne. He proceeded to aske me whether the rest that were with me were also the children of the Sunne, I answered him no, but that they were borne all with me in one countrey, where I was brought vp. Then he cryed out with a loud voyce and sayd, seeing thou doest vs so much good, and wilt not haue vs to make warre, and art the child of the Sunne, wee will all receiue thee for our Lord, and always serue thee, therefore wee pray thee that thou wilt not depart hence nor leaue vs: and suddenly hee turned to the people, and beganne to tell them, that I was the childe of the Sunne, and that therefore they should all chuse me for their Lord. Those Indians hearing this, were astonied beyond measure, and came neerer still more and more to behold me. That Indian also asked mee other questions, which to auoyd tediousnesse I doe not recite: and in this wise we passed the day, and seeing the night approch, I began by all meanes I could deuise to get this fellow into our boat with vs: and he refusing to goe with vs, the interpreter told him that wee would put him on the other side of the riuer, and vpon this condition he entred into our boate, and there I made very much of him, and gaue him the best entertaynement I could, putting him alwayes in securitie, and when I iudged him to be out of all suspition, I thought it good to aske him somewhat of that countrey. And among the first things that I asked him this was one, whether hee had euer seene any men like vs, or had heard any report of them. Newes of *bearded and white men.* Hee answered mee no, sauing that hee had sometime hearde of olde men, that very farre from that Countrey there were other white men, and with beardes like vs, and that hee knewe nothing else. I asked him also whether hee knewe a place called Ceuola, and a Riuer called Totonteac, and hee answered mee no. Whereupon perceiuing that hee coulde not giue mee any knowledge of Francis Vazquez nor of his company, I determined to aske him other things of that countrey, and of their maner of life: and beganne to enquire of him, whether they helde that there was one *God, creator of heauen and earth*, or that they worshipped any other Idol. *The Sunne worshipped as God.* And hee answered mee no: but that they esteemed and reuerenced the Sunne aboue all things, because it warmed them and made their croppes to growe: and that of all things which they did eate, they cast a little vp into the ayre vnto him. I asked him next whether they had any Lorde, and hee sayde no: but that they knewe well, that there was a great Lorde, but they knewe not well which way hee dwelt. And I tolde him that hee was in heauen, and that hee was called Iesus Christ, and I went no farther in diuinitie with him. I asked him whether they had any warre, and for what occasion. Hee answered that they had warre and that very great, and vpon exceeding small occasions: for when they had no cause to make warre, they assembled together, and some of them sayd, let vs goe to make warre in such a place, and then all of them set forward with their weapons. I asked them who commanded the armie: he answered the eldest and most valiant, and that when they sayd they should proceede no farther, that suddenly they retired from the warre. I prayed him to tell me what they did with those men which they killed in battell: he answered me that they tooke out the hearts of some of them, and eat them, and others they burned; and he added, that if it had not bene for my comming, they should haue bin now at warre: and because I commanded them that they should not war, and that they should cease from armes, therefore as long as I should not command them to take armes, they would not begin to wage warre against others, and they said among themselues, that seeing I was come vnto them, they had giuen ouer their *intention of making warre*, and that they had a good mind to liue in peace. *Certaine warlike people behind a mountaine.* He complained of certaine people which dwelt behind in a mountaine which made great war vpon them, and slew many of them: I answered him, that from henceforward they should not need to feare any more, because I had commanded them to be quiet, and if they would not obey my commandement I would chasten them and kill them. He enquired of me how I could kill them seeing we were so few, and they so many in number. And because it was now late and that I saw by this time he was weary to stay any longer with me, I let him goe out of my boat, and therewith I dismissed him very well content.

Chap. 4.

Of Naguachato and other chiefe men of those Indians they receiue great store of victuals, they cause them to set vp a crosse in their countreys, and hee teacheth them to worship it. They haue newes of many people, of their diuers languages, and customes in matrimony, how they punish adultery, of their opinions concerning the dead, and of the sicknesses which they are subiect vnto.

The next day betimes in the morning came the chiefe man among them called Naguachato, and wished me to come on land because he had great store of victuals to giue me. And because I saw my selfe in securitie I did so without doubting; and incontinently an olde man came with rols of that Maiz, and certaine litle gourds, and calling me with a loud voyce and vsing many gestures with his body and armes, came neere vnto me, and causing me to turne me vnto that people, and hee himselfe also turning vnto them sayd vnto them, Sagueyca, and all the people answered with a great voyce, Hu, and hee offred to the Sunne a little of euery thing that he had there, and likewise a little more vnto me (although afterward he gaue me all the rest) and did the like to all that were with me: and calling out mine interpreter, by meanes of him I gaue them thanks, telling them that because my boats were litle I had not brought many things to giue them in exchange, but that I would come againe another time and bring them, and that if they would go with me in my boates vnto my ships which I had beneath at the riuers mouth, I would giue them many things. They answered that they would do so, being very glad in countenance. Here by the helpe of mine interpreter I sought to instruct them what the sign of the crosse meant, and willed them to bring me a piece of timber, wherof I caused a great crosse to be made, and commanded al those that were with mee that when it was made they should worship it, and beseech the Lord to grant his grace that so great a people might come to the knowledge of his holy Catholike faith: and this done I told them by mine interpreter that I left them that signe, in token that I tooke them for my brethren, and that they should keepe it for me carefully vntill I returned, and that euery morning at the Sunne rising they should kneele before it. And they tooke it incontinently, and without suffering it to touch the ground, they carried it to set it vp in the middest of their houses, where all of them might beholde it; and I willed them always to worshippe it because it would preserue them from euill. They asked me how deep they should set in the ground, and I shewed them. These people are greatly inclined to learne the

Christian faith. Great store of people followed the same, and they that stayed behinde inquired of mee, how they should ioyne their handes, and how they should kneele to worship the same; and they seemed to haue great desire to learne it. *The Riuer in diuers places full of shelfes.* This done, I tooke that chiefe man of the Countrey, and going to our boates with him, I followed my iourney vp the Riuer, and all the company on both sides of the shoare accompanied me with great good will, and serued me in drawing of our boates, and in halling vs off the sands whereupon we often fel: for in many places we found the riuer so shoald, that we had no water for our boats. As wee thus went on our way, some of the Indians which I had left behind me, came after vs to pray mee that I would throughly instruct them, how they should ioyne their hands in the worshipping of the crosse: others shewed me whether they were well set in such and such sort, so that they would not let me be quiet. Neere vnto the other side of the riuer was greater store of people, which called vnto me very often, that I would receiue the victuals which they had brought me. And because I perceiued that one enuied the other, because I would not leaue them discontented, I did so. And here came before me another old man like vnto the former with the like ceremonyes and offrings: and I sought to learne something of him as I had done of the other. This man said likewise to the rest of the people, This is our lord. Now you see how long ago our ancesters told vs, that there were bearded and white people in the world, and we laughed them to scorne. I which am old and the rest which are here, haue neuer seene any such people as these. And if you wil not beleeue me, behold these people which be in this riuer: let vs giue them therefore meate, seeing they giue vs of their victuals: let vs willingly serue this lord, which wisheth vs so well, and forbiddeth vs to make warre, and imbraceth all of vs: and they haue mouth, handes and eyes as we haue, and speake as we doe. I gaue these likewise another crosse as I had done to the others beneath, and said vnto them the selfe same words: which they listened vnto with a better will, and vsed greater diligence to learne that which I said. *Another nation.* Afterward as I passed farther vp the riuer, I found another people, whom mine interpreter vnderstood not a whit: wherefore I shewed them by signes the selfe same ceremonies of worshipping the crosse, which I had taught the rest. And that principal old man which I tooke with me, told me that farthur vp the riuer I should find people which would vnderstand mine interpreter: and being now late, some of those men called me to giue me victuals, and did in all poynts as the others had done, dauncing and playing to shew me pleasure. *People of 23. languages* dwelling along this riuer. I desired to know what people liued on the banks of this riuer: and I vnderstood by this man that it was inhabited by 23 languages, and these were bordering vpon the riuer, besides others not farre off, and that there were besides these 23. languages, other people also which hee knewe not, aboue the riuer. I asked him whether euery people were liuing in one towne together: and he answered me, No: but that they had many houses standing scattered in the fieldes, and that euery people had their Countrey seuerall and distinguished, and that in euery habitation there were great store of people. Acuco as Gomara writeth is on a strong mountaine. He shewed me a towne which was in a mountaine, and told me that there was there great store of people of bad conditions, which made continual warre vpon them: which being without a gouernour, and dwelling in that desert place, where small store of Maiz groweth, came downe into the playne to buy it in trucke of Deeres skinnes, wherewith they were apparelled with long garments, which they did cutte with rasors, and sewed with needles made of Deeres bones: and that they had great houses of stone. I asked them whether there were any there of that Countrey; and I found one woman which ware a garment like a little Mantle, which clad her from the waste downe to the ground, of a Deeres skin well dressed. Then I asked him whether the people which dwelt on the riuers side, dwelt alwayes there, or els sometime went to dwell in some other place: he answered me, that in the summer season they aboade there, and sowed there; and after they had gathered in their croppe they went their way, and dwelt in other houses which they had at the foote of the mountaine farre from the riuer. And hee shewed me by signes that the houses were of wood compassed with earth without, and I vnderstood that they made a round house, wherein the men and women liued all together. I asked him whether their women were common or no: he tolde me no, and that hee which was married, was to haue but one wife only. I desired to know what order they kept in marying: and he tolde me, that if any man had a daughter to marry, he went where the people kept, and said, I haue a daughter to marry, is there any man here that wil haue her? And if there were any that would haue her, he answered that he would haue her: and so the mariage was made. Dancing and singing at mariages of the Sauages. And that the father of him which would have her, brought something to giue the yong woman; and from that houre forward the mariage was taken to be finished, and that they sang and danced: and that when night came, the parents tooke them, and left them together in a place where no body might see them. And I learned that brethren, and sisters, and kinsfolk married not together: and that maydes before they were married conuersed not with men, nor talked not with them, but kept at home at their houses and in their possessions, and wrought: and that if by chance any one had company with men before she were married, her husband forsooke her, and went away into other Countreyes: and that those women which fell into this fault, were accompted naughty packs. And that if after they were maried, any man were taken in adultery with another woman, they put him to death: and that no man might haue more that one wife, but very secretly. They burne their dead. They tolde mee that they burned those which dyed: and such as remayned widowes, stayed halfe a yeere, or a whole yeere before they married. I desired to know what they thought of such as were dead. Hee told me that they went to another world, but that they had neither punishment nor glory. The greatest sicknesse that this people dye of is vomiting of blood by the mouth: and they haue Physicions which cure them with charmes and blowing which they make. Pipes to drinke Tabacco with. The apparell of these people were like the former: they carried their pipes with them to perfume themselues, like as the people of New Spaine vse Tabacco. I inquired whether they had any gouernour, and found that they had none, but that every family had their seuerall gouernour. Maize, gourds, Mill. These people haue besides their Maiz certaine gourds, and another corne like vnto Mill: Grindestones, earthern pots, good fish. they haue grindstones and earthern pots, wherein they boyle those gourds, and fish of the riuer, which are very good. My interpreter could goe no farther then this place: for he said that those which we should find farther on our way, were their enemies, and therefore I sent him backe very well contented. Not long after I espied many Indians to come crying with a loude voice, and running after me. This riuer ouerfloweth his banks at certaine seasons. I stayed to know what they would haue; and they told me that they had set vp the crosse which I had giuen them, in the midst of their dwellings as I had appointed, but that I was to wit, that when the riuer did ouerflow, it was wont to reach to that place, therefore they prayed mee to giue them leaue to remove it, and to set it in another place where the riuer could not come at it, nor carry it away: which I granted them.

Chap. 5.

Of an Indian of that countrey they haue relation of the state of Ceuola, and of the conditions and customes of these people, and of their gouernour: and likewise of the countreys not farre distant from thence, whereof one was called Quicoma, and the other Coama: of the people of Quicoma, and of the other Indians not farre distant they receiue courtesie.

Thus sayling I came where were many Indians, and another interpreter, which I caused to come with me in my boat. And because it was cold, and my people were wet, I leapt on shore, and commanded a fire to be made, and as we stood thus warming our selues, an Indian came and strooke me on the arme, pointing with his finger to a wood, out of which I saw two companies of men come with their weapons, and he told me that they came to set vpon vs: and because I meant not to fall out with any of them, I retired my company into our boats, and the Indians which were with me swam into the water, and saued themselues on the other side of the riuer. In the meane season I inquired of that Indian which I had with me, what people they were that came out of the wood: and he told me that they were their enemies, and therefore these others at their approch without saying any word leapt into the water: and did so, because they meant to turne backe againe, being without weapons, because they brought none with them, because they vnderstood my wil and pleasure, that they should cary none. I inquired the same things of this interpreter which I had done of the other of the things of that countrey, because I vnderstood that among some people one man vsed to haue many wiues, and among others but one.

Ceuola 40 dayes iourney from thence by the riuer. Now I vnderstood by him, that he had bin at Ceuola, and that it was a moneths iourney from his country, and that from that place by a path that went along that riuer a man might easily trauel thither in xl. daies, and that the occasion that moued him to go thither, was only to see Ceuola, because it was a great thing, and had very hie houses of stone of 3. or 4. lofts, and windowes on ech side; that the houses were compassed about with a wall conteining the height of a man and an halfe, and that aloft and beneath they were inhabited with people, and that they vsed the same weapons, that others vsed, which we had seene, that is to say, bowes and arrowes, maces, staues and bucklers:

Turqueses in Ceuola. and that they had one gouernor, and that they were apparelled with mantles, and with oxe-hides, and that their mantles had a painting about them, and that their gouernour ware a long shirt very fine girded vnto him, and ouer the same diuers mantles: and that the women ware very long garments, and that they were white, and went all couered: and that euery day many Indians wayted at the gate of their gouernour to serue him, and that they did weare many Azure or blew stones, which were digged out of a rocke of stone, and that they had but one wife, with whom they were maried, and that when their gouernors died, all the goods that they had were buried with them. And likewise all the while they eate, many of their men waite at their table to court them, and see them eate, and that they eate with napkins, and that they haue bathes. On Thursday morning at breake of day the Indians came with the like cry to the banke of the riuer, and with greater desire to serue vs, bringing me meat to eat, and making me the like good cheere, which the others had done vnto me, hauing vnderstood what I was: and I gaue them crosses, with the self same order which I did vnto the former. And going farther vp the riuer I came to a country where I found better gouernment: for the inhabitants are wholly obedient vnto one only. But returning againe to conferre with mine interpreter touching the dwellings of those of Ceuola, he tolde me, that the lord of that countrey had a dog like that which I caried with me. This was the Negro that went with Frier Marco de Niza. Afterward when I called for dinner, this interpreter saw certaine dishes caried in the first and later seruice, whereupon he told me that the lord of Ceuola had also such as those were, but that they were greene, and that none other had of them sauing their gouernour, and that they were 4, which he had gotten together with that dogge, and other things, of a blacke man which had a beard, but that he knew not from what quarter he came thither, and that the king caused him afterward to be killed, as he heard say. I asked him whether he knew of any towne that was neere vnto that place: he tolde me that aboue the riuer he knew some, and that among the rest there was a lord of a towne called Quicoma, and another of a towne called Coama: and that they had great store of people vnder them. And after he had giuen me this information, he craued leaue of me to returne vnto his companions. From hence I began againe to set saile, and within a dayes sayling I found a towne dispeopled: where assoone as I was entred, by chance there arriued there 500. Indians with their bowes and arrowes, and with them was that principal Indian called Naguachato, which I had left behind, and brought with them certaine conies and yucas: and after I had friendly interteined them all, departing from them, I gaue them license to returne to their houses. As I passed further by the desert, I came to certain cotages, out of which much people came toward me with an old man before them, crying in a language which mine interpreter wel vnderstood, and he said vnto those men: Brethren, you see here that lord; let vs giue him such as we haue, seeing he dooth vs pleasure, and hath passed through so many discourteous people, to come to visit vs. And hauing thus said, he offred to the Sunne, and then to me in like sort as the rest had done. These had certaine great bags and well made of the skins of fishes called Sea-bremes. And I vnderstood that this was a towne belonging vnto the lord of Quicoma, which people came thither onely to gather the fruit of their haruest in summer; and among them I found one which vnderstood mine interpreter very well: whereupon very easily I gaue them the like instruction of the crosse which I had giuen to others behind. These people had cotton, but they were not very carefull to vse the same: because there was none among them that knew the arte of weauing, and to make apparel thereof. They asked me how they should set vp their crosse when they were come to their dwelling which was in the mountaine, and whether it were best to make an house about it, that it might not be wet, and whether they should hang any thing vpon the armes therof. I said no; and that it sufficed to set it in a place where it might be seene of all men, vntill I returned: and lest peraduenture any men of warre should come that way, they offred mee more men to goe with me, saying that they were naughty men which I should finde aboue; but I would haue none: neuerthelesse 20. of them went with me, which when I drew neere vnto those which were their enemies, they warned mee thereof: and I found their centinels set vpon their guarde on their borders. On Saturday morning I found a great squadron of people sitting vnder an exceeding great arbour, and another part of them without: and when I saw that they rose not vp, I passed along on my voyage: when they beheld this an old man rose vp which said vnto me, Sir, why doe you not receiue victuals to eate of vs, seeing you haue taken food of others? I answered, that I tooke nothing but that which was giuen me, and that I went to none but to such as requested me. Here without any stay they brought me victuals, saying vnto me, that because I entred not into their houses, and stayed all day and all night in the riuer, and because I was the sonne of the Sunne, all men were to receiue me for their lord. I made them signes to sit down, and called that old man which mine interpreter vnderstood, and asked him whose that countrey was, and whether the lord thereof was there, he said yes: and I called him to me; and when he was come, I imbraced him, shewing him great loue: and when I saw that all of them tooke great pleasure at the friendly interteinment which I gaue him, I put a shirt vpon him, and gaue him other trifles, and willed mine interpreter to vse the like speaches to that lord which he had done to the rest; and that done, I gaue him a crosse, which he receiued with a very good wil, as the others did: and this lord went a great way with me, vntill I was called vnto from the other side of the riuer, where the former old man stood with much people: to whom I gaue another crosse, vsing the like speach to them which I had vnto the rest, to wit, how they should vse it. Then following my way, I mette with another great company of people, with whom came that very same olde man whom mine interpreter vnderstood; and when I saw their lord which he shewed vnto me, I prayed him to come with me into my boat, which he did very willingly, and so I went still vp the riuer, and the olde man came and shewed me who were the chiefe lords: and I spake vnto them always with great courtesie, and all of them shewed that they reioyced much thereat, and spake very wel of my comming thither. At night I withdrew my selfe into the midst of the riuer, and asked him many things concerning that country: and I found him as willing and wel disposed to shew them me, as I was desirous to know them. Ceuola a goodly thing. I asked him of Ceuola: and he told me he had bin there, and that it was a goodly thing, and that the lord thereof was very wel obeyed: and that there were other lords thereabout, with whom he was at continual warre. I asked him whether they had siluer and gold, and he beholding certain bels, said they had metal of their colour. Gold and siluer in a mountaine neere Ceuola. I inquired whether they made it there and he answered me no, but that they brought it from a certain mountaine, where an old woman dwelt. This riuer seemeth to bee Northward by the colde. I demanded whether he had any knowledge of a riuer called Totonteac, he answered me no, but of another exceeding mighty riuer, wherein there were such huge Crocodiles, that of their hides they made bucklers, and that they worship the Sunne neither more nor lesse then those which I had passed: and when they offer vnto him the fruits of the earth, they say: Receiue hereof, for thou hast created them, and that they loued him much, because he warmed them; and that when he brake not foorth, they were acolde. Herein reasoning with him, he began somewhat to complaine, saying vnto me, I know not wherefore the Sunne vseth these termes with vs, because he giueth vs not clothes, nor people to spin nor to weaue them, nor other things which he giueth to many other, and he complayned that those of that country would not suffer them to come there, and would not giue them of their corne. I told him that I would remedie this, whereat he remayned very well satisfied.

Chap. 6.

They are aduertised by the Indians, wherefore the lorde of Ceuola killed the Negro, which went with Frier Marco, and of many other things: And of an old woman called Guatazaca, which liueth in a lake and eateth no food. The description of a beast, of the skinne whereof they make targets. The suspition that they conceiue of them, that they are of those Christians which were seene at Ceuola, and how they cunningly saue themselues.

The next day which was Sunday before breake of day, began their cry as they were woont: and this was the cry of 2. or 3. sorts of people, which had lyen all night neere the riuers side, wayting for me: and they tooke Maiz and other corne in their mouth, and sprinkled me therewith, saying that that was the fashion which they vsed when they sacrificed vnto the Sunne: afterward they gaue me of their victuals to eat, and among other things, they gaue me many white peason. I gaue them a crosse as I had done to the rest: and in the meane season that old man tolde them great matters of my doing, and poynted me out with his finger, saying, this is the lord, the sonne of the Sunne: and they made me to combe my beard, and to set mine apparel handsomely which I ware vpon my backe. And so great was the confidence that they had in me, that all of them told me what things had passed, and did passe among them, and what good or bad mind they bare one toward another. I asked them wherefore they imparted vnto me all their secrets, and that old man answered mee: Thou art our lord, and we ought to hide nothing from our lord. After these things, following on our way, I began againe to inquire of him the state of Ceuola, and whether he knewe that those of this countrey had euer seene people like vnto vs: he answered me no, sauing one Negro which ware about his legs and armes certain things which did ring. *The Negro that went with Frier Marco de Niza slaine.* Your lordship is to cal to mind how this Negro which went with frier Marco was wont to weare bels, and feathers on his armes and legs, and that he caried plates of diuers colours, and that it was not much aboue a yeere agoe since he came into those parts. *The cause wherefore Stephan Dorantez the Negro was slaine.* I demanded vpon what occasion he was killed; and he answered me, That the lord of Ceuola inquired of him whether he had other brethren: he answered that he had an infinite number, and that they had great store of weapons with them, and that they were not very farre from thence. Which when he had heard, many of the chiefe men consulted together, and resolued to kil him, that he might not giue newes vnto these his brethren, where they dwelt, and that for this cause they slew him, and cut him into many pieces, which were diuided among all those chiefe lords, that they might know assuredly that he was dead: and also that he had a dogge like mine, which he likewise killed a great while after. I asked him whether they of Ceuola had any enemies, and he said they had. And he reckoned vnto me 14. or 15. lords which had warre with them: and that they had mantles, and bowes like those aboue mentioned: howbeit he told me that I should find going vp the riuer a people that had no warre neither with their neighbors, nor with any other.

Antonio d'Espejo speaketh of such a great lake. He told me that they had 3. or 4. sorts of trees bearing most excellent fruite to eate: and that in a certaine lake dwelt an olde woman, which was much honoured and worshipped of them: and that shee remayned in a litle house which was there, and that she neuer did eate any thing: and that there they made things which did sound, and that many mantles, feathers and Maiz were giuen vnto her. I asked what her name was, and he tolde me that she was called Guatuzaca, and that thereabout were many lords which in their life and death, vsed the like orders which they of Ceuola did, which had their dwelling in the summer with painted mantles, and in the winter dwelt in houses of wood of 2. or 3. lofts hie: and that he had seene all these things, sauing the old woman. And when againe I began to aske him more questions, he would not answere me, saying that he was wearie of me: and many of those Indians comming about me, they said among themselues: Let vs marke him well, that we may knowe him when he commeth back againe. The Monday following, the riuer was beset with people like to them, and I began to request the old man to tell me what people were in that countrey, which told me he thought I would soone forget them: and here he reckoned vp vnto me a great number of lords, and people at the least 200. And discoursing with him of their armour, he said that some of them had certaine very large targets of lether, aboue two fingers thicke. *This might be the crooke backed oxe of Quiuira.* I asked him of what beasts skinne they made them: and he discribed vnto me a very great beast, like vnto an Oxe, but longer by a great handfull, with broad feete, the legs as bigge as the thigh of a man, and the head seuen handfuls long, the forehead of three spannes, and the eyes bigger then ones fist, and the hornes of the length of a mans leg, out of which grew sharpe poynts, an handfull long, the forfeete and hinderfeete aboue seuen handfuls bigge, with a wrethed tayle, but very great; and holding vp his armes aboue his head, he said the beast was higher then that. After this hee gaue mee information of another olde woman which dwelt toward the sea side. I spent this day in giuing crosses to those people as I had done vnto the former. This old man that was with me leapt on shore, and fell in conference with another which that day had often called him; and here both of them vsed many gestures in their speach, moouing their armes, and poynting at me. *The Sauages treasons to be taken heede of.* Therefore I sent mine interpreter out, willing him to drawe neere vnto them, and listen what they said; and within a while I called him, and asked him whereof they talked, and he sayd, that he which made those gestures said vnto the other, that in Ceuola there were others like vnto vs with beards, and that they said they were Christians, and that both of them sayd that we were all of one company, and that it were a good deede to kill vs, that those others might haue no knowledge of vs, lest they might come to doe them harme: and that the old man had answered him, this is the sonne of the Sunne, and our lord, he doth vs good, and wil not enter into our houses, although we request him thereunto: he will take away nothing of ours, he wil meddle with none of our women, and that to be short, he had spoken many other things in my commendation and fauour: and for all this the other stedfastly affirmed that we were all one, and that the old man said, Let vs goe vnto him, and aske him whether he be a Christian as the other be, or els the sonne of the Sonne: and the old man came vnto me, and sayd: In the countrey of Ceuola whereof you spake vnto me doe other men like vnto you dwell. *Certaine newes of the Spanyards at Ceuola.* Then I began to make as though I wondred, and answered him, that it was impossible; and they assured me that it was true, and that two men had seene them which came from thence, which reported that they had things which did shoote fire, and swords as we had. I asked them whether they had seene them with their owne eyes? and they answered no; but that certaine of their companions had seene them. Then hee asked mee whether I were the sonne of the Sunne, I answered him yea. They said that those Christians of Ceuola said so likewise. And I answered them that it might well be. Then they asked mee if those Christians of Ceuola came to ioyne themselues with me, whether I would ioyne with them: and I answered them, that they needed not to feare any whit at all, for if they were the sonnes of the Sunne as they said, they must needes be my brethren, and would vse towards all men the like loue and courtesie which I vsed: whereupon hereat they seemed to be somewhat satisfied.

Chap. 7.

It is tolde him that they are ten dayes iourney distant from Ceuola, and that there be Christians there, which make warre against the lords of that countrey. Of the Sodomie which those Indians vse with foure young men, appoynted for that seruice, which weare womens apparel. Seeing they could not send newes of their being there to them of Ceuola, they went backe againe downe the riuer to their ships.

Ceuola tenne dayes distant from this place. A desert of ten dayes iourney.

Then I prayed them to tel me how many dayes that kingdom of Ceuola, which they spake of, was distant from that riuer: and that man answered, that there was the space of tenne dayes iourney without habitation, and that he made none accompt of the rest of the way, because there were people to be found. Vpon this aduertisement I was desirous to certifie Captaine Francis Vazquez of my being there, and imparted my mind with my souldiers, among whom I found none that was willing to goe thither, although I offered them many rewards in your lordships name, onely one Negro slaue though with an euil wil offred himselfe vnto me to go thither: but I looked for the comming of those two Indians which they tolde me of, and herewithall we went on our way vp the riuer against the streame in such sort as we had done before. Here that olde man shewed me as a strange thing a sonne of his clad in womans apparel, exercising their office: I asked him how many there were of these among them, and he told me there were foure; and that when any of them died, there was a search made of all the women with child which were in the country, and that the first sonne which was borne of them, was appoynted to doe that duetie belonging vnto women, and that the women clad him in their apparell, saying, that seeing he was to doe that which belonged to them, he should weare their apparel: these yong men may not haue carnall copulation with any woman: but all the yong men of the countrey which are to marrie, may company with them. These men receiue no kind of reward for this incestuous act of the people of that countrey, because they haue libertie to take whatsoeuer they find in any house for their food. I saw likewise certaine women which liued dishonestly among men: and I asked the old man whether they were married, who answered me noe, but they were common women, which liued apart from the married women. I came at length after these discourses to pray them to send for those Indians, which they said had bin at Ceuola, and they told me that they were eight dayes iourney distant from that place, but that notwithstanding there was one among them which was their companion and which had spoken with them, as he met them on the way, when they went to see the kingdome of Ceuola, and that they told him that he were not best to goe any farther, for he should find there a fierce nation like vs: and of the same qualities and making, which had fought much with the people of Ceuola, because they had killed a Negro of their company saying, Wherefore haue yee killed him? what did he to you? did he take any bread from you, or do you any other wrong? and such like speech. And they said moreouer, that these people were called Christians, which dwelt in a great house, and that many of them had oxen like those of Ceuola, and other litle blacke beastes with wooll and hornes, and that some of them had beasts which they rode vpon, which ran very swiftly; and that one day before their departure, from sunne rising vntill sunne setting these Christians were all day in comming thither, and all of them lodged in that place where others had lodged, and that these two met with two Christians, which asked them whence they were, and whether they had fields sowen with corne: and they told them that they dwelt in a farre country, and that they had corne, and that then they gaue each of them a litle cap and they gaue them another to cary to their other companions, which they promised to do, and departed quickly. When I vnderstood this, I spoke againe with my company, to see if any one of them would go thither, but I found them vnwilling as at the first, and they layd against me greater inconueniences.

A desert. Then I called the old man to see if he would giue me any people to goe with me, and victuals to trauel through that wildernes, but he laid before me many inconueniences and dangers, which I might incurre in that voyage, shewing me the danger that there was in passing by a lord of Cumana, which threatned to make warre vpon them, because his people had entred into the others country to take a stagge, and that I should not therefore depart thence without seeing him punished. And when I replied that in any wise I must needes goe to Ceuola, he willed me to surcease from that purpose, for they looked that that lord without a doubt would come to annoy them, and that therefore they could not leaue their countrey naked to goe with me, and that it would be better, that I would make an end of that warre betweene them, and that then I might haue their company to Ceuola. And vpon this point we grew to such variance, that we began to grow into choler, and in a rage he would haue gone out of the boat, but I stayed him, and with gentle speeches began to pacifie him, seeing that it imported mee much to haue him my friend: but for all my courtesies which I shewed him, I could not alter him from his mind, wherein he stil remained obstinate. In the meane while I sent a man away vnto my ships to giue them knowledge of the iourney that I had determined to make. After this I prayed the old man that he would fetch him backe again, because I had determined, that seeing I saw no meanes to be able to go to Ceuola, and because I would stay no longer among those people because they should not discouer me, and likewise because I meant in person to visit my ships, with determination to returne againe vp the riuer, carying with me other companions, and leaue there some which I had sicke, and telling the olde man and the rest that I would returne, and leauing them satisfied the best I could (although they alwayes said that I went away for feare) I returned downe the riuer: and that way which I had gone against the streame vp the riuer in 15 dayes and an halfe, He returneth in 2 dayes and an halfe to his ships. I made in my returne in 2 dayes and an halfe, because the streame was great and very swift. In this wise going downe the riuer, much people came to the banks, saying, Sir, wherefore doe you leaue vs? what discourtesie hath bin done vnto you? did you not say that you would remayne continually with vs, and be our Lord; And turne backe again? if any man aboue the riuer hath done you any wrong we will goe with our weapons with you and kill him; and such like words ful of loue and kindnes.

Chap. 8.

When they came to their shippes the Captaine named the coast La Campanna de la Cruz, and builded a Chapel vnto our Lady, and called the riuer El Rio de Buena Guia, and returned vp the same againe? when he came to Quicona and Coama the Lords of those places vsed him very courteously.

Vpon mine arriuall at my ships I found all my people in health, although very heauie for my long stay, and because the current had fretted fower of their cables, and that they had lost two ankers which were recouered. After we had brought our ships together, I caused them to bring them into a good harbour, and to giue the carena to the shippe called Sanct Peter, and to mend all that were needfull. And here assembling all my company together, I opened vnto them what knowledge I had receiued of Francis Vasquez; and how it might be that in those sixeteene dayes space which I was in sayling vp the riuer he might peraduenture haue some knowledge of me, and that I was minded to returne vp the riuer once againe to try if I could finde any means to ioyne myself with him: and although some spake against my determination, I caused al my boates to bee made ready, because the ships had no need of them. Mark what things the Spaniardes cary with them in newe discoueries. I caused one of them to be filled with wares of exchange, with corne and other seedes, with hennes and cockes of Castile, and departed vp the riuer, leauing order that in that prouince called Campanna de la Cruz they should build an Oratorie or Chapell, and called it the Chappell of our Lady de la Buena Guia, and that they should call this riuer Rio de Buena because that is your Lordships Deuise: I carried with me Nicolas Zamorano Pilote mayor, to take the height of the pole. And I departed on Tuesday the fourteenth of September, and on Wednesday I came vnto the first dwellings of the first Indians, which came running to hinder my passage, supposing that we had bene other people, for we caried with vs a fifer, and a drummer, and I was clad in other apparell, then I went in before, when they saw me first of all: and when they knew me they stayed, though I could not grow vnto perfect friendship with them, whereupon I gaue some of those seedes which I brought with mee; teaching them how they should sow them, and after I had sayled 3 leagues, my first interpretour came euen to my boat to seeke me with great ioy, of whom I demanded wherefore he had left me, he tolde me that certaine companions of his had led him away. I made him good countenance and better intertainment, because he should beare me companie againe, considering howe much it did importe me to haue him with me. Parrats in these parts. He excused himselfe because he stayed there to bring mee certaine feathers of Parrats, which he gaue me. Two moones to Ceuola. I asked him what people these were, and whether they had any Lord: hee answered me yea; and named three or foure vnto me, of 24 or 25 names of people which he knew and that they had houses painted within, and that they had trafficke with those of Ceuola, and that in two moones he came into the countrey. Another booke written of the particulars of that countrey. He told me moreouer many other names of Lords, and other people, which I haue written downe in a booke of mine, which I will bring myselfe vnto your Lordship. But I thought good to deliuer this brief relation to Augustine Guerriero in this hauen of Colima, that he might send it ouerland to your Lordshippe, to whom I haue many other things to imparte.

But to returne to my iourney, I arriued at Quicama, where the Indians came forth with great ioy and gladnes to receive me, aduertizing me that their Lord waited for my comming; to whom when I was come I found that he had with him fiue or six thousand men without weapons, from whom he went aparte with some two hundred onely, all which brought victuals with them, and so he came towards me, going before the rest with great authoritie, and before him and on each side of him were certaine which made the people stand aside, making him way to passe. Hee ware a garment close before and behind and open on both sides, fastened with buttons, wrought with white and blacke checker worke, it was very soft and well made, being of the skinnes of certaine delicate fishes called Sea breams. Assoone as he was come to the waters side his seruants tooke him vp in their armes, and brought him into my boate, where I embraced him and receiued him with great ioy, shewing vnto him much kindnesse: vpon which intertainment his people standing by and beholding the same seemed not a litle to reioyce. This Lord turning himselfe to his people willed them to consider my courtesie, and that he being of his owne accord come vnto me with a strange people, they might see how good a man I was, and with how great loue I had entertained him, and that therefore they should take me for their Lord, and that all of them should become my seruants, and doe whatsoever I would command them. There I caused him to sit downe, and to eat certaine conserues of sugar which I had brought with mee, and willed the interpreter to thanke him in my name for the fauour which he had done me in vouchsafing to come to see mee, recommending vnto him the worshipping of the crosse, and all such other things as I had recommended to the rest of the Indians; namely that they should liue in peace, and should leaue off warres, and should continue alwayes good friendes together: he answered that of long time they had continued in warres with their neighbours, but that from thence forward he would command his people that they should giue food to all strangers that passed through his kingdome, and that they should doe them no kinde of wrong, and that if any nation should come to inuade him, he said he would tell them howe I had commanded that they should liue in peace, and if they refused the same, he would defend himselfe, and promised me, that he would neuer goe to seeke warre, if others came not to invade him. Then I gaue him certaine trifles, as well of the seedes which I brought, as of the hens of Castile, wherewith he was not a litle pleased. And at my departure I caryed certaine of his people with me, to make friendship betweene them and those other people which dwelt aboue the Riuer: and here the interpreter came vnto me, to craue leaue to returne home: and I gaue him certaine gifts wherewith he departed greatly satisfied.

The next day I came to Coama, and many of them knew me not, seeing me clad in other aparrel, but the old man which was there as soone as he knew me leapt into the water, saying vnto me, Sir, lo here is the man which you left with me, which came forth very ioyfull and pleasant declaring vnto me the great courtesies which that people had shewed him, saying that they had strouen together who should haue him to his house, and that it was incredible to thinke what care they had at the rising of the Sunne to hold vp their hands and kneele before the Crosse. I gaue them of my seedes and thanked them hartily for the good entertainement which they had shewed my man, and they besought me that I would leaue him with them, which I granted them vntill my return, and he stayed among them very willingly.

Treason of the sauages. Thus I went forward vp the Riuer, taking that olde man in my companie, which tolde mee, that two Indians came from Cumana to enquire for the Christians, and that he had answered them that he knew none such, but that he knew one which was the sonne of the Sunne, and that they had perswaded him to ioyne with them to kill mee and my companions. I wished him to lend me two Indians, and I would send word by them, that I would come vnto them, and was desirous of their friendship, but that if they on the contrary would haue warre, I would make such a warre with them, that should displease them. And so I passed through all that people, and some came and asked me, why I had not giuen them Crosses as well as the rest, and so I gaue them some.

Chap. 9.

They goe on land, and see the people worship the Crosse which they had giuen them. The Captain causeth an Indian to make a draught of the countrey: hee sendeth a Crosse to the Lord of Cumana, and going down the Riuer with the streame, he arriueth at his ships. Of the error of the Pilots of Cortez as touching the situation of this Coast.

The next day I went on land to see certaine cottages, and I found many women and children holding vp their hands and kneeling before a Crosse which I had giuen them. When I came thither I did the like my self; and conferring with the old man, he began to informe me of as many people and Prouinces as he knew. And when euening was come I called the old man to come and lodge with mee in my boate; hee answered that hee would not goe with mee because I would wearie him with asking him questions of so many matters: I told him that I would request him nothing else but that he would set me downe in a chart as much as he knew concerning that Riuer, and what maner of people those were which dwelt vpon the banckes thereof on both sides: which he did willingly. And then he requested me that I would describe my countrey vnto him, as he had done his vnto me. And for to content him, I caused a draught of certaine things to be made for him. The next day I entred betweene certaine very high mountaines, through which this Riuer passeth with a streight chanel, and the boats went vp against the streame very hardly for want of men to draw the same. Here certaine Indians came and told me, that in the same place there were certaine people of Cumana, and among the rest an enchanter, who enquired which way we would passe; and they telling him that we meant to passe by the Riuer, he set certaine canes on both sides thereof, through which wee passed, without receiuing any kinde of domage which they intended against vs. Thus going forward I came vnto the house of the olde man which was in my company, and here I caused a very high crosse to be set vp, whereupon I engraued certaine letters to signifie that I was come thither: and this I did, that if by chance any of the people of the generall Vasquez de Coronado should come thither, they might haue knowledge of my being there. At length seeing I could not attaine to the knowledge of that which I sought for, I determined to returne backe vnto my ships. And being ready to depart there arriued two Indians, which by meanes of the interpreters of the old man, told me that they were sent to me, and that they were of Cumana, and that their Lord could not come himselfe, because he was farre from that place, but desired me to signifie vnto him what my pleasure was. I told them, that I wished that he would alwayes imbrace peace, and that I was comming to see that countrey, but being inforced to returne backe downe the Riuer I could not now doe it, but that hereafter I would returne, and that in the meane season they should giue that Crosse vnto their Lorde, which they promised me to do, and they went directly to cary him that Crosse with certaine feathers which were on the same. This Riuer ran much farther vp then he had trauelled. Of these I sought to vnderstand what people dwelt vpward vpon the bankes of the Riuer, which gaue me knowledge of many people, and told me that the Riuer went farre more vp into the land then I had yet seene, but that they knew not the head thereof, because it was very far into the countrey, and that many other Riuers fell into the same.

Hauing learned thus much the next day morning I returned downe the Riuer, and the day following I came where I had left my Spaniard, with whom I spake, and told him that all things had gone well with me, and that at this time and the former I had gone aboue 30 leagues into the countrey. The Indians of that place inquired of me what the cause was of my departure, and when I would returne: to whom I answered, that I would returne shortly. Thus sayling downe the streame, a woman leapt into the water crying vnto vs to stay for her, and shee came into our boate, and crept vnder a bench, from whence we could not make her to come out: I vnderstood that shee did this, because her husband had taken vnto him another wife, by whom hee had children, saying that she ment not to dwell any longer with him, seeing he had taken another wife. Thus shee and another Indian came with me of their owne accord, and so I came into my ships, and making them ready we proceeded home on our voyage, coasting and oftentimes going on land, and entering a great way into the countrey, to see if I could learne any newes of Captaine Francis Vasquez and his companie; of whom I could haue no other knowledge, but such as I learned in the aforesaide Riuer. I bring with me many actes of taking possession of all that Coast. And by the situation of the Riuer, and the height which I tooke, I finde that that which the Masters and Pilots of the Marquesse tooke is false, and that they were deceiued by 2 degrees, and I haue sayled beyond them aboue 4 degrees. I sayled vp the Riuer 85 leagues, where I saw and learned all the particulars before mentioned, and many other things; whereof when it shall please God to giue me leaue to kisse your Lordships hands, I will deliuer you the full and perfect relation. I thinke my selfe to haue had very good fortune, in that I found Don Luis de Castilia, and Augustine Ghenero in the port of Colima: for the Galiot of the Adelantado came vpon mee, which was there with the rest of his fleet, and commanded me to strike sayle, which seeming a strange thing vnto me, and not vnderstanding in what state things were in Nueua Espanna, I went about to defend my selfe, and not to doe it. In the meane while came Don Luis de Castilia in a boate and conferred with mee, and I lay at anchor on the other side of the hauen where the saide fleete road, and I gaue vnto him this relation (and to auoyd striffe I determined to sayle away by night) which relation I caryed about me briefly written; for I alwayes had a purpose to send the same, as soone as I should touch vpon Nueua Espanna, to aduertise your Lordship of my proceedings.

An extract of a Spanish letter written from Pueblo de los Angeles in Nueua Espanna in October 1597, touching the discouerie of the rich Isles of California, being distant eight dayes sayling from the maine.

We haue seene a letter written the eight of October 1597, out of a towne called Pueblo de los Angeles situate eighteene leagues from Mexico, making mention of the Ilands of California situate two or three hundreth leagues from the maine land of Nueua Espanna, in Mar del Sur: as that thither haue bene sent before that time some people to conquer them: which with losse of some twentie men were forced backe. After that they had wel visited and found those Islands or countreys to be very rich of gold and siluer mynes, and of very fayre Orientall pearles, which were caught in good quantitie vpon one fathome and an halfe passing in beautie the pearles of the Island Margarita: the report thereof caused the Vice-roy of Mexico to send a citizen of Mexico with two hundreth men to conquer the same. Therein also was affirmed that within eight dayes they could sayle thither from the mayne.

The course which Sir Francis Drake held from the hauen of Guatulco in the South sea on the backe side of Nueua Espanna, to the Northwest of California as far as fourtie three degrees: and his returne back along the said Coast to thirtie eight degrees: where finding a faire and goodly hauen, he landed, and staying there many weekes, and discouering many excellent things in the countrey and great shewe of rich minerall matter, and being offered the dominion of the countrey by the Lord of the same, hee tooke possession thereof in the behalfe of her Maiestie, and named it Noua Albion.

Wee kept our course from the Isle of Cano (which lyeth in eight degrees of Northerly latitude, and within two leagues of the maine of Nicaragua, where wee calked and trimmed our ship) along the Coast of Nueua Espanna, vntill we came to the Hauen and Towne of Guatulco, which (as we were informed) had but seuenteene Spaniards dwelling in it, and we found it to stand in fifteene degrees and fiftie minutes.

Assoone as we were entred this Hauen we landed, and went presently to the towne, and to the Towne house, were we found a Iudge sitting in iudgement, he being associate with three other officers, vpon three Negroes that had conspired the burning of the Towne: both which Iudges, and prisoners we tooke, and brought them a shippeboord, and caused the chiefe Iudge to write his letter to the Towne, to command all the Townesmen to auoid, that we might safely water there. Which being done, and they departed, wee ransaked the Towne, and in one house we found a pot of the quantitie of a bushell full of royals of plate, which we brought to our ship.

And here one Thomas Moone one of our companie, took a Spanish gentleman as he was flying out of the Towne, and searching him he found a chaine of Gold about him, and other jewels, which we tooke and so let him goe.

The Portugal Pilote set on land. At this place our Generall among other Spaniards, set ashore his Portugall Pilote, which he tooke at the Island of Cape Verde, out of a ship of Saint Marie port of Portugall, and hauing set them ashoore, we departed thence.

Our General at this place and time thinking himselfe both in respect of his priuate injuries receiued from the Spaniards, as also of their contempts and indignities offered to our Countrey and Prince in generall, sufficiently satisfied, and reuenged: and supposing that her Maiestie at his returne would rest contented with this seruice, purposed to continue no longer vpon the Spanish coastes, but began to consider and to consult of the best way for his Countrey.

He thought it not good to returne by the Streights, for two speciall causes: the one, least the Spaniards should there waite, and attend for him in great number and strength, whose handes he being left but one ship, could not possibly escape. The other cause was the dangerous situation of the mouth of the Streits of the South side, with continuall stormes raining and blustring, as he found by experience, besides the shoals and sands vpon the coast, wherefore he thought it not a good course to aduenture that way: he resolued therefore to auoide these hazards, to goe forward to the Islands of the Malucos, and therehence to saile the course of the Portugales by the Cape of Bona Sperança.

Vpon this resolution, he began to thinke of his best way for the Malucos, and finding himselfe, where hee now was, becalmed, hee sawe that of necessitie hee must bee enforced to take a Spanish course, namely to saile somewhat Northerly to get a good winde, and thus much we sayled from the 16 of Aprill after our olde stile till the third of Iune.

Sir Francis Drake sayled on the backe side of America, to 43 degrees of Northerly latitude. 38 degrees. The fift day of Iune being in fortie three degrees towardes the pole Arcticke, being speedily come out of the extreame heate, wee found the ayre so colde, that our men being pinched with the same, complayned of the extremitie thereof, and the further we went, the more the colde increased vpon vs, whereupon we thought it best for that time to seeke land, and did so, finding it not mountainous, but low plaine land, and we drew backe againe without landing, til we came within thirtie eight degrees towardes the line. In which height it pleased God to send vs into a faire and good Bay, with a good winde to enter the same.

In this Bay wee ankered the seuententh of Iune, and the people of the Countrey, hauing their houses close by the waters side, shewed themselues vnto vs, and sent a present to our Generall.

When they came vnto vs, they greatly wondred at the things which we brought, but our Generall (according to his naturall and accustomed humanitie) curteously intreated them, and liberally bestowed on them necessarie things to couer their nakednesse, whereupon they supposed vs to be gods, and would not be perswaded to the contrary: the presentes which they sent vnto our Generall were feathers, and cals of net worke.

A description of the people and Countrey of Noua Albion. Their houses are digged round about with earth, and haue from the vttermost brimmes of the circle clifts of wood set vpon them, ioyning close together at the toppe like a spire steeple, which by reason of that closenesse are very warme.

Their bed is the ground with rushes strawed on it, and lying about the house, they haue the fire in the middest. The men goe naked, the women take bulrushes and kembe them after the maner of hempe, and thereof make their loose garments, which being knit about their middles, hang downe about their hippes, hauing also about their shoulders a skinne of Deere, with the haire vpon it. These women are very obedient and seruiceable to their husbands.

After they were departed from vs, they came and visited vs the second time, and brought with them feathers and bags of Tabacco for presents:

And when they came to the toppe of the hil (at the bottome whereof wee had pitched our tents) they stayed themselues, where one appointed for speaker, wearied himselfe with making a long oration, which done, they left their bowes vpon the hill and came downe with their presents.

In the meane time the women remaining on the hill, tormented themselues lamentably, tearing their flesh from their cheekes, whereby we perceiued that they were about a sacrifice. In the meane time our Generall, with his companie, went to prayer, and to reading of the Scriptures, at which exercise they were attentiue and seemed greatly to be affected with it: but when they were come vnto vs they restored againe vnto vs those things which before we had bestowed vpon them.

The newes of our being there being spread through the countrey, the people that inhabited round about came downe, and amongst them the king himself, a man of a goodly stature, and comely personage, with many other tall and warlike men: before whose comming were sent two Ambassadours to our Generall, to signifie that their king was comming, in doing of which message, their speech was continued about halfe an howre. This ended, they by signes requested our Generall to send something by their hand to their king, as a token that his comming might bee in peace: wherein our Generall hauing satisfied them, they returned with glad tidings to their king, who marched to vs with a princely Maiestie, the people crying continually after their maner, and as they drewe neere vnto vs, so did they striue to behaue themselues in their actions with comelinesse.

These are like chaines of Esurnoy in Canada and Hochelage. In the fore
----
front was a man of a goodly personage, who bare the scepter, or mace before the king, whereupon hanged two crownes, a lesse and a bigger, with three chaines of a marueilous length: the crownes were made of knit work wrought artificially with feathers of diuers colours: the chaines were made of a bony substance and few be the persons among them that are admitted to weare them: and of that number also the persons are stinted, as some ten, some twelue, &c. Next vnto him which bare the scepter, was the king himselfe, with his Guarde about his person, clad with Conie skinnes, and other skinnes: after them followed the naked common sort of people, euery one hauing his face painted, some with white, some with blacke, and other colours, and hauing in their hands one thing or other for a present, not so much as their children, but they also brought their presents.

In the meane time, our Generall gathered his men together, and marched within his fenced place, making against their approching, a very warlike shewe. They being trooped together in their order, and a general salutation being made, there was presently a generall silence. When he that bare the scepter before the king, being informed by another, whome they assigned to that office, with a manly and loftie voice, proclaimed that which the other spake to him in secret, continuing halfe an houre: which ended, and a generall Amen as it were giuen, the king with the whole number of men, and women (the children excepted) came downe without any weapon, who descending to the foote of the hill, set themselues in order.

In comming towards our bulwarks and tents, the scepter bearer began a song, obseruing his measures in a dance, and that with a stately countenance, whom the king with his Garde, and euery degree of persons following, did in like maner sing and dance, sauing onely the women which daunced and kept silence. The General permitted them to enter within our bulwark, where they continued their song and daunce a reasonable time. When they had satisfied themselues, they made signes to our Generall to sit downe, to whom the king, and diuers others made seueral orations, or rather supplication, that he would take their prouince and kingdom into his hand, and become their king, making signes that they would resigne vnto him their right and title of the whole land, and become his subiects. The king resignes his crowne and kingdome to Sir Frances Drake. Great riches in Noua Albion. In which to perswade vs the better, the king and the rest, with one consent and with great reuerence, ioyfully singing a song, did set the crowne vpon his head, inriched his necke with all their chaines, and offered vnto him many other things, honouring him by the name of Hioh, adding thereunto as it seemed a signe of triumph: which thing our Generall thought not meete to reiect, because hee knewe not what honour and profite it might bee to our countrey. Wherefore in the name, and to the vse of her Maiestie, he tooke the scepter, crowne and dignitie of the said Countrey in his hands, wishing that the riches and treasure thereof might so conueniently be transported to the inriching of her kingdome at home, as it aboundeth in the same.

The common sort of the people leauing the king and his Guarde with our Generall, scattered themselues together with their sacrifices among our people, taking a diligent viewe of euery person; and such as pleased their fancie, (which were the yongest) they inclosing them about offred their sacrifices vnto them with lamentable weeping, scratching, and tearing the flesh from their faces with their nayles, whereof issued abundance of blood. But wee vsed signes to them of disliking this, and stayed their hands from force, and directed them vpwardes to the liuing God, whome onely they ought to worshippe. They shewed vnto vs their wounds, and craued helpe of them at our handes, whereupon wee gaue them lotions, plaisters, and ointments agreeing to the state of their griefes, beseeching God to cure their deseases. Euery thirde day they brought their sacrifices vnto vs, vntill they vnderstoode our meaning, that we had no pleasure in them: yet they could not be long absent from vs, but daily frequented our company to the houre of our departure, which departure seemed so grieuous vnto them, that their ioy was turned into sorrow. They intreated vs, that being absent wee would remember them, and by stelth prouided a sacrifice, which we misliked.

Our necessarie businesse being ended, our Generall with his companie traueiled vp into the Countrey to their villages, where we found heardes of Deere by a thousand in a companie, being most large and fat of body.

Abundance of strange conies. We found the whole countrey to bee a warren of a strange kinde of Conies, their bodyes in bignes as be the Barbary Conies, their heads as the heades of ours, the feet of a Want, and the taile of a Rat being of great length: vnder her chinne on either side a bagge, into the which shee gathereth her meate when she hath filled her belly abroad. The people eate their bodies, and make great account of their skinnes, for their Kings coate was made of them.

Our Generall called this countrey, Noua Albion, and that for two causes: the one in respect of the white bankes and cliffes, which lye towardes the sea: and the other, because it might haue some affinitie with our Countrey in name, which sometimes was so called.

Golde and siluer in the earth of Noua Albion. There is no part of earth heere to be taken vp, wherein there is not some special likelihood of gold or siluer.

At our departure hence our Generall set vp a monument of our being there; as also of her Maiesties right and title to the same, namely a plate nailed vpon a faire great poste, whereupon was ingrauen her Maiesties name, the day and yeere of our arriuall there, with the free giuing vp of the Prouince and people into her Maiesties hands, together with her highnesse picture and armes, in a piece of sixe pence of current English money vnder the plate, where vnder was also written the name of our Generall.

It seemeth that the Spaniards hitherto had neuer bene in this part of the countrey, neither did euer discouer the land by many degrees to the Southwards of this place.

THE DISCOVERIE

OF THE LARGE, RICH, AND BEAUTIFULL EMPIRE OF GUIANA, WITH A RELATION OF THE GREAT AND GOLDEN CITIE OF MANOA (WHICH THE SPANIARDS CALL EL DORADO) AND THE PROUINCES OF EMERIA, AROMAIA, AMAPAIA, AND OTHER COUNTRIES, WITH THEIR RIUERS ADIOYNING. PERFORMED IN THE YEERE 1595 BY SIR WALTER RALEGH KNIGHT, CAPTAINE OF HER MAIESTIES GUARD, LORDE WARDEN OF THE STANNERIES, AND HER HIGHNESSE LIEUTENANT GENERALL OF THE COUNTIE OF CORNE-WALL.

To the right Honourable my singular good Lord and kinsman Charles Howard, Knight of the Garter, Baron and Counceller, and of the Admirals of England the most renowmed: and to the right Honourable Sir Robert Cecyll knight, Counceller in her Highnesse Priuie Councils.

For your Honours many Honourable and friendly partes, I haue hitherto onely returned promises, and now for answere of both your adventures, I haue sent you a bundle of papers, which I haue deuided betwene your Lordship, and Sir Robert Cecyll in these two respects chiefly: First for that it is reason, that wastful factors, when they haue consumed such stockes as they had in trust, doe yeeld some colour for the same in their account; secondly for that I am assured, that whatsoeuer shall bee done, or written by me, shall neede a double protection and defence. The triall that I had of both your loues, when I was left of all, but of malice and reuenge, makes me still presume, that you wil be pleased (knowing what litle power I had to performe ought, and the great aduantage of forewarned enemies) to answer that out of knowledge, which others shal but obiect out of malice. In my more happy times as I did especially Hon. you both, so I found that your loues sought mee out in the darkest shadow of aduersitie, and the same affection which accompanied my better fortune, sored not away from me in my many miseries: al which though I can not requite yet I shal euer acknowledge: and the great debt which I haue no power to pay, I can do no more for a time but confesse to be due. It is true that as my errors were great, so they haue yeelded very grieuous effects, and if ought might haue bene deserued in former times to haue conterpoysed any part of offences, the fruit thereof (as it seemeth) was long before fallen from the tree, and the dead stocke onely remained. I did therefore euen in the winter of my life, vndertake these trauels, fitter for bodies lesse blasted with misfortunes, for men of greater abilitie, and for minds of better incouragement, that thereby, if it were possible, I might recouer but the moderation of excesse, and the least tast of the greatest plenty formerly possessed. If I had knowen other way to win, if I had imagined how greater aduentures might haue regained, if I could conceiue what farther meanes I might yet vse, but euen to appease so powerful displeasure, I would not doubt but for one yeere more to hold fast my soule in my teeth, till it were performed. Of that litle remaine I had, I haue wasted in effect all herein. I haue vndergone many constructions. I haue been accompanyed with many sorrows, with labour, hunger, heat, sicknes, and perill: It appeareth notwithstanding that I made no other brauado of going to the sea, then was ment, and that I was neuer hidden in Cornewall, or els where, as was supposed. They haue grosly belied me, that foreiudged, that I would rather become a seruant to the Spanish King, then returne, and the rest were much mistaken, who would haue perswaded, that I was too easefull and sensuall to vndertake a iourney of so great trauell. But, if what I haue done, receiue the gracious construction of a painefull pilgrimage, and purchase the least remission, I shall thinke all too litle, and that there were wanting to the rest many miseries. But if both the times past, the present, and what may be in the future, doe all by one grain of gall continue in eternall distaste; I doe not then know whether I should bewaile my selfe, either for my too much trauell and expence, or condemne my selfe for doing lesse then that, which can deserue nothing. From my selfe I haue deserued no thankes, for I am returned a begger, and withered, but that I might haue bettred my poore estate, it shall appeare by the following discourse, if I had not onely respected her Maiesties future Honour, and riches. It became not the former fortune in which I once liued, to goe iourneys of picory, it had sorted ill with the offices of Honour, which by her Maiesties grace I hold this day in England, to run from Cape to Cape, and from place to place, for the pillage of ordinaries prizes. Many yeeres since, I had knowledge by relation, of that mighty, rich and beautifull Empier of Guiana, and of that great and golden Citie, which the Spaniards call El Dorado, and the naturals Manoa, which Citie was conquered, reedified, and inlarged by a yonger sonne of Guainacapa Emperour of Peru, at such time as Francisco Piçarro and others conquered the said Empire, from his two elder brethren, Guascar, and Atabalipa, both then contending for the same, the one being fauoured by the Orejones of Cuzco, the other by the people of Caxamalca. I sent my seruant Iacob Whiddon the yere before, to get knowledge of the passages, and I had some light from Captaine Parker, sometime my seruant, and nowe attending on your Lordship, that such a place there was to the Southward of the great Bay of Charuas, or Guanipa: but I found that it was 600 miles farther off then they supposed, and many other impediments to them vnknowen and vnheard. After I had displanted Don Antonio de Berreo, who was vpon the same enterprize, leauing my ships at Trinidad at the Port called Curiapan, I wandred 400 miles into the said countrey by lande and riuer: the particulars I will leaue to the following discourse. The countrey hath more quantity of gold by manifolde, then the best partes of the Indies, or Peru: All the most of the kings of the borders are already become her Maiesties vassals: and seeme to desire nothing more then her Maiesties protection and the returne of the English nation. It hath another ground and assurance of riches and glory, then the voyages of the West Indies, an easier way to inuade the best parts thereof, then by the common course. The king of Spaine is not so impouerished, by taking three or foure Port townes in America, as wee suppose, neither are the riches of Peru, or Nueua Espanna so left by the sea side, as it can bee easily washt away with a great flood, or springtide, or left dry vpon the sandes on a lowe ebbe. The Port townes are fewe and poore in respect of the rest within the lande, and are of litle defence, and are onely rich, when the Fleets are to receiue the treasure for Spaine: and we might thinke the Spaniards very simple, hauing so many horses and slaues, if they could not vpon two dayes warning cary all the golde they haue into the land, and farre enough from the reach of our foote-men, especially the Indies being (as they are for the most part) so mountainous, so full of woodes, riuers, and marishes. In the Port townes of the Prouince of Veneçuela, as Cumana, Coro and S. Iago (whereof Coro and S. Iago were taken by Captaine Preston, and Cumana and S. Iosepho by vs) we found not the value of one riall of plate in either: but the Cities of Barquasimeta, Valencia, S. Sebastian, Cororo, S. Lucia, Laguna, Maracaiba, and Truxillo, are not so easely inuaded: neither doeth the burning of those on the coast impouerish the king of Spaine any one ducat: and if we sacke the riuer of Hacha, S. Marta, and Cartagena, which are the Portes of Nueuo reyno, and Popayan; there are besides within the land, which are indeed riche and populous the townes and Cities of Merida, Lagrita, S. Christophoro, the great Cities of Pamplon, S. Fe de Bogota, Tunxa and Mozo where the Esmeralds are found, the townes and Cities of Marequita, Velez, la Villa de Leua, Palma, Vnda, Angustura, the great citie of Timana, Tocaima, S. Aguila, Pasto, Iuago, the great Citie of Popaian it selfe, Los Remedios, and the rest. If we take the Ports and villages within the Bay of Vraba in the kingdom or riuers of Dariene, and Caribana, the Cities and townes of S. Iuan de Roydas, of Cassaris, of Antiocha, Caramanta, Cali, and Anserma haue gold enough to pay the kings part, and are not easily inuaded by the way of the Ocean: or if Nombre de Dios and Panama be taken in the Prouince of Castilla del oro, and the villages vpon the riuers of Cenu and Chagre; Peru hath besides those and besides the magnificent cities of Quito and Lima so many ylands, ports, cities, and mines, as if I should name them with the rest, it would seem incredible to the reader; of all which, because I haue written a particular treatise of the West Indies, I wil omit the repetition at this time, seeing that in the said treatise I haue anatomised the rest of the sea-townes, aswel of Nicaragua, Iucatan, Nueua Espanna, and the ylands, as those of the Inland, and by what meanes they may be best inuaded, as far as any meane iudgment can comprehend. But I hope it shal appeare that there is a way found to answer euery mans longing, a better Indies for her Maiestie then the King of Spaine hath any: which if it shal please her highnes to vndertake, I shall most willingly end the rest of my daies in folowing the same: if it be left to the spoile and sackage of common persons, if the loue and seruice of so many nations be dispised, so great riches, and so mighty an empire refused, I hope her maiesty wil yet take my humble desire and my labor therin in gracious part, which, if it had not bin in respect of her highnes future honor and riches, could haue laid hands on and ransomed many of the kings and Casiqui of the country, and haue had a reasonable proportion of gold for their redemption: but I haue chosen rather to beare the burden of pouerty, then reproch, and rather to endure a second traue and the chances therof, then to haue defaced an enterprise of so great assurance, vntil I knew whether it pleased God to put a disposition in her princely and royal heart either to folow or foreslow the same: I wil therefore leaue it to his ordinance that hath only power in all things, and do humbly pray that your honors wil excuse such errors, as without the defence of art, ouerrun in euery part of the folowing discourse, in which I haue neither studied phrase, forme or fashion, that you will be pleased to esteeme mee as your owne (though ouer dearly bought) and I shall euer remaine ready to do you all honour and seruice.

W. R.

¶ To the Reader.

Because there haue bin diuers opinions conceiued of the gold oare broght from Guiana, and for that an Alderman of London and an officer of her Maiesties Mint, hath giuen out that the same is of no price, I haue thought good by the addition of these lines to giue answer aswel to the said malicious slander, as to other obiections. It is true that while we abode at the yland of Trinidad, I was informed, by an Indian, that not far from the Port, where we ancored, there were found certaine mineral stones which they esteemed to be gold, and were thereunto perswaded the rather for that they had seene both English and Frenchmen gather, and imbark some quantities therof: vpon this likelyhood I sent 40. men and gaue order that each one should bring a stone of that mine to make trial of the goodnes: which being performed, I assured them at their returne that the same was Marcasite, and of no riches or value: notwithstanding diuers, trusting more to their owne sence, then to my opinion, kept of the said Marcasite, and haue tried therof since my returne in diuers places. In Guiana it selfe I neuer saw Marcasite, but al the rocks, mountains, al stones in the plaines, woods, and by the riuers side are in effect throughshining, and seem maruelous rich, which being tried to be no Marcasite, are the true signes of rich minerals, but are no other then El madre del oro (as the Spaniards terme them) which is the mother of gold, or as it is said by others the scum of gold: of diuers sorts of these many of my company brought also into England, euery one taking the fairest for the best, which is not general. For mine own part I did not countermand any mans desire, or opinion, and I could haue aforded them litle if I should haue denied them the pleasing of their owne fancies therein: but I was resolued that gold must be found either in graines separate from the stone (as it is in most of the riuers of Guiana) or els in a kind of hard stone, which we call The white spar, of which I saw diuers hils, and in sundry places, but had neither time nor men, nor instruments fit for labour. Neere vnto one of the riuers I found of the said White sparre or flint a very great ledge or banke, which I endeuoured to breake by al the meanes I could, because there appeared on the outside some smal graines of golde, but finding no meane to worke the same vpon the vpper part, seeking the sides and circuit of the said rocke, I found a clift in the same from whence with daggers, and with the head of an axe, we got out some smal quantitie therof, of which kind of white stone (wherin gold engendred) we saw diuers hils and rocks in euery part of Guiana, wherein we traueiled. Of this there haue bin made many trials, and in London it was first assaid by M. Westwood a refiner dwelling in Woodstreet, and it held after the rate of 12000. or 13000. pounds a tunne. Another sort was afterward tried by M. Bulmar and M. Dimock Assay-master, and it held after the rate of 23000 li. a tunne. There was some of it againe tried by M. Palmer comptroller of the Mint, and M. Dimock in goldsmiths hal, and it held after 26900. li. a tun. There was also at the same time, and by the same persons a trial made of the dust of the said mine which held 8. li. 6. ounces weight of gold in the 100: there was likewise at the same time a triall of an image of copper made in Guiana, which held a third part of gold, besides diuers trials made in the countrey, and by others in London. But because there came ill with the good, and belike the said Alderman was not presented with the best, it hath pleased him therefore to scandall all the rest, and to deface the enterprize as much as in him lieth. It hath also bene concluded, by diuers, that if there had bin any such oare in Guiana, and the same discouered, that I would haue brought home a greater quantitie thereof: first I was not bound to satisfie any man of the quantitie, but such only as aduentured, if any store had bin returned thereof: but it is very true that had al their mountaines bene of massie gold, it was impossible for vs to haue made any longer stay to haue wrought the same: and whosoeuer hath seene with what strength of stone the best gold oare is inuironed, hee will not thinke it easy to be had out in heapes, and especially by vs, who had neither men, instruments, nor time (as it is said before) to performe the same. There were on this discouery no lesse then 100. persons, who can all witnesse, that when we past any branch of the riuer to view the land within, and staicd from our boats but 6. houres, wee were driuen to wade to the eyes, at our returne: and if we attempted the same, the day following it was impossible either to ford it, or to swim it, both by reason of the swiftnesse, and also for that the borders were so pestred with fast woods, as neither boat nor man could find place, either to land or to imbarke: for in Iune, Iuly, August and September, it is impossible to nauigate any of those riuers: for such is the fury of the current, and there are so many trees and woods ouerflowne, as if any boat but touch vpon any tree or stake, it is impossible to saue any one person therein: and yer [ed: before] we departed the land it ranne with such swiftnes, as wee draue downe most commonly against the wind, little lesse then 100. miles a day: Besides our were no other then whirries, one little barge, a small cockboat, and a bad Galiota, which we framed in hast for that purpose at Trinidad, and those little boats had 9. or 10. men a piece, with all their victuals, and armes. It is further true, that we were about 400. miles from our ships, and had bene a moneth from them, which also we left weakly manned in an open road, and had promised our returne in 15. dayes. Others haue deuised that the same oare was had from Barbary, and that we caried it with vs into Guiana: surely the singularitie of that deuice I doe not well comprehend: for mine owne part, I am not so much in loue with these long voyages, as to deuise, therby to cozen my selfe, to lie hard, to fare worse, to be subiected to perils, to diseases, to ill sauors, to be parched and withered, and withall to sustaine the care and labour of such an enterprize, except the same had more comfort, then the fetching of Marcasite in Guiana, or buying of gold oare in Barbary. But I hope the better sort will judge me by themselves, and that the way of deceit is not the way of honour or good opinion: I have herein consumed much time, and many crownes, and I had no other respect or desire then to serue her Majestie and my country thereby. If the Spanish nation had bene of like beliefe to these detracters, we should litle have feared or doubted their attempts, wherewith we now are daily threatned. But if we now consider of the actions both of Charles the 5. who had the maidenhead of Peru, and the abundant treasures of Atabalipa, together who the affaires of the Spanish king now liuing, what territories he hath purchased, what he hath added to the acts of his predecessors, how many kingdoms he hath indangered, how many armies, garisons, and nauies he hath and doth mainteine, the great losses which he hath repaired, as in 88. aboue 100 saile of great ships with their artillery, and that no yere is lesse vnfortunate but that many vessels, treasures, and people are deuoured, and yet notwithstanding he beginneth againe like a storme to threaten shipwrack to vs all: we shall find that these abilities rise not from the trades of sacks, and Siuil oringes, nor from ought els that either Spaine, Portugal, or any of his other prouinces produce: it is his Indian gold that indangereth and disturbeth all the nations of Europe, it purchaseth intelligence, creepeth into counsels, and setteth bound loyaltie at libertie, in the greatest Monarchies of Europe. If the Spanish king can keepe vs from forren enterprizes, and from the impeachment of his trades, either by offer of inuasion, or by besieging vs in Britaine, Ireland, or elsewhere, hee hath then brought the worke of our peril in great forwardnes. Those princes which abound in treasure haue great aduantages ouer the rest, if they once constraine them to a defensiue war, where they are driuen once a yere or oftener to cast lots for their own garments, and from such shal all trades and entercourse be taken away, to the general losse and impouerishment of the kingdom and common weale so reduced: besides when our men are constrained to fight, it hath not the like hope, as when they are prest and incouraged by the desire of spoile and riches. Farther, it is to be douted how those that in time of victory seeme to affect their neighbor nations, wil remaine after the first view of misfortunes, or il successe; to trust also to the doubtfulnes of a battel, is but a fearefull and vncertaine adventure, seeing therein fortune is as likely to preuaile, as vertue. It shall not be necessary to alleage all that might bee said, and therefore I will thus conclude, that whatsoeuer kingdome shall be inforced to defend it selfe, may be compared to a body dangerously diseased, which for a season may be preserued with vulgar medicines, but in a short time, and by litle and litle, the same must needs fall to the ground, and be dissolued. I have therefore laboured all my life, both according to my smal power, and perswasion, to aduance al those attempts, that might either promise return of profit to our selues, or at least be a let and impeachment to the quiet course and plentifull trades of the Spanish nation, who in my weake judgement by such a warre were as easily indangered and brought from his powerfulnes, as any prince of Europe, if it be considered from how many kingdoms and nations his reuenues are gathered, and those so weake in their owne beings, and so far seuered from mutual succour. But because such a preparation and resolution is not to be hoped for in hast, and that the time which our enemies imbrace, cannot be had againe to aduantage, I wil hope that these prouinces, and that Empire now by me discouered shal suffice to inable her Maiestie and the whole kingdome, with no lesse quantities of treasure, then the king of Spaine hath in all the Indies East and West, which he possesseth, which if the same be considered and followed, ere the Spaniards enforce the same, and if her Maiestie wil vndertake it, I wil be contented to lose her highnesse fauour and good opinion for euer, and my life withall, if the same be not found rather to exceed, then to equal, whatsoeuer is in this discourse promised or declared. I will now referre the

Reader to the following discourse, with the hope that the perillous and chargeable labours and indeuors of such as thereby seeke the profit and honour of her Maiestie, and the English nation, shall by men of qualitie and vertue receiue such construction, and good acceptance, as themselues would looke to be rewarded withall in the like.

W. R.

¶ The discouerie of Guiana.

On Thursday the 6. of February in the yeere 1595. we departed England, and the Sunday following had sight of the North cape of Spaine, the winter for the most part continuing prosperous: we passed in sight of the Burlings, and the Rocke, and so onwards for the Canaries, and fel with Fuerte ventura the 17 of the same moneth, where we spent two or three dayes, and relieued our companies with some fresh meat. From thence we coasted by the Grand Canaria, and so to Tenerif, and stayed there for the Lions whelpe your Lordships ship, and for Captaine Amyas Preston and the rest.

The yle of Trinidad. But when after 7. or 8. dayes wee found them not, we departed and directed our course for Trinidad with mine owne ship, and a small barke of Captaine Crosses onely (for we had before lost sight of a small Galego on the coast of Spaine, which came with vs from Plimmouth) we arriued at Trinidad the 22. of March, casting ancker at point Curiapan, which the Spaniards call punta de Gallo, which is situate in 8. degrees or there abouts: we abode there 4. or 5. dayes, and in all that time we came not to the speach of any Indian or Spaniard: on the coast we saw a fire, as we sailed from the point Caroa towards Curiapan, but for feare of the Spaniards none durst come to speake with vs. I my selfe coasted it in my barge close abord the shore and landed in euery Coue, the better to know the yland, while the ships kept the chanell. From Curiapan after a fewe dayes we turned vp Northeast to recouer that place which the Spaniards call Puerto de los Espannoles, and the inhabitants Conquerabia, and as before (reuictualling my barge) I left the ships and kept by the shore, the better to come to speach with some of the inhabitants, and also to vnderstand the riuers, watering places, and ports of the yland, which (as it is rudely done) my purpose is to send your Lordship after a few dayes. From Curiapan I came to a port and seat of Indians called Parico, where we found a fresh water riuer, but saw no people. From thence I rowed to another port, called by the naturals Piche, and by the Spaniards Tierra de Brea: In the way betweene both were diuers little brookes of fresh water and one salt riuer that had store of oisters vpon the branches of the trees, and were very salt and well tasted. All their oisters grow vpon those boughs and spraies, and not on the ground: the like is commonly seene in other places of the West Indies, and else where. This tree is described by Andrew Theuet in his French Antarctique, and the forme figured in the booke as a plant very strange, and by Plinie in his 12. booke of his naturall historie. But in this yland, as also in Guiana there are very many of them.

At this point called Tierra de Brea or Piche there is that abundance of stone pitch, that all the ships of the world may be therewith loden from thence, and we made trial of it in trimming our shippes to be most excellent good, and melteth not with the Sunne as the pitch of Norway, and therefore for shippes trading the South parts very profitable. From thence wee went to the mountaine foote called Anniperima, and so passing the riuer Carone on which the Spanish Citie was seated, we met with our ships at Puerto de los Espannoles or Conquerabia.

This yland of Trinidad hath the forme of a sheephooke, and is but narrow, the North part is very mountainous, the soile is very excellent and will beare suger, ginger, or any other commoditie that the Indies yeeld. It hath store of deere, wilde porks, fruits, fish and foule: It hath also for bread sufficient maiz, cassaui, and of those rootes and fruites which are common euery where in the West Indies. It hath diuers beastes which the Indies haue not: the Spaniards confessed that they found graines of golde in some of the riuers, but they hauing a purpose to enter Guiana (the Magazin of all rich mettals) cared not to spend time in the search thereof any further. This yland is called by the people thereof Cairi, and in it are diuers nations: those about Parico are called Iaio, those at Punta de Carao are of the Arwacas, and betweene Carao and Curiapan they are called Saluajos, betwene Carao and Punta de Galera are the Nepoios, and those about the Spanish citie terme themselues Carinepagotes: Of the rest of the nations, and of other ports and riuers I leaue to speake here, being impertinent to my purpose, and meane to describe them as they are situate in the particular plot and description of the yland, three parts whereof I coasted with my barge, that I might the better describe it.

The death of Captaine Whiddon. Meeting with the ships at Puerto de los Espannoles, we found at the landing place a company of Spaniards who kept a guard at the descent, and they offering a signe of peace, I sent Captaine Whiddon to speake with them, whom afterward to my great griefe I left buried in the said yland after my returne from Guiana, being a man most honest and valiant. The Spaniards seemed to be desirous to trade with vs, and to enter into termes of peace, more for doubt of their owne strength then for ought else, and in the ende vpon pledge, some of them came abord: the same euening there stale also abord vs in a small Canoa two Indians, the one of them being a Casique or Lord of the people called Cantyman, who had the yeere before bene with Captaine Whiddon and was of his acquaintance. By this Cantyman, wee vnderstood what strength the Spaniards had, howe farre it was to their Citie, and of Don Antonio de Berreo the gouernor, who was said to be slaine in his second attempt of Guiana, but was not.

While we remained at Puerto de los Espannoles some Spaniards came abord vs to buy linnen of the company, and such other things as they wanted, and also to view our ships and company, all which I entertained kindly and feasted after our maner: by meanes whereof I learned of one and another as much of the estate of Guiana as I could, or as they knew for those poore souldiers hauing bene many yeeres without wine, a few draughts made them merrie, in which mood they vaunted of Guiana and of the riches thereof, and all what they knewe of the wayes and passages, my selfe seeming to purpose nothing lesse then the enterance or discouerie thereof, but bred in them an opinion that I was bound onely for the reliefe of those English which I had planted in Virginia, whereof the bruite was come among them: which I had performed in my returne, if extremitie of weather had not forst me from the said coast.

I found occasions of staying in this place for two causes: the one was to be reuenged of Berreo, who the yere before 1594. had betraied eight of Captaine Whiddons men, and tooke them while he departed from them to seeke the Edward Bonauenture, which arriued at Trinidad the day before from the East Indies: 8 Englishmen betrayed by Antony Berreo. in whose absence Berreo sent a Canoa abord the pinnesse onely with Indians and dogs inuiting the company to goe with them into the woods to kill a deare, who like wise men in the absence of their Captaine followed the Indians, but were no sooner one harquebuze shot from the shore, but Berreos souldiers lying in ambush had them al, notwithstanding that he had giuen his word to Captaine Whiddon that they should take water and wood safely: the other cause of my stay was, for that by discourse with the Spaniards I dayly learned more and more of Guiana, of the riuers and passages, and of the enterprise of Berreo, by what meanes or fault he failed, and how he meant to prosecute the same.

While wee thus spent the time I was assured by another Casique of the North side of the yland, that Berreo had sent to Margarita and Cumana for souldiers, meaning to haue giuen mee a cassado at parting, if it had bene possible. For although he had giuen order through all the yland that no Indian should come abord to trade with me vpon paine of hanging and quartering, (hauing executed two of them for the same, which I afterwards founde) yet euery night there came some with most lamentable complaints of his crueltie, how he had diuided the yland and giuen to euery souldier a part, that hee made the ancient Casiques which were Lords of the countrey to be their slaues, that he kept them in chaines, and dropped their naked bodies with burning bacon, and such other torments, which I found afterwards to be true: for in the citie after I entred the same there were 5. of the lords or litle kings (which they cal Casiques in the West Indies) in one chaine almost dead of famine, and wasted with torments: these are called in their owne language Acarewana, and now of the late since English, French and Spanish are come among them, they call themselues Capitaines, because they perceiue that the chiefest of euery ship is called by that name. Those fiue Capitaines in the chaine were called Wannawanare, Carroaori, Maquarima, Tarroopanama, and Aterima. So as both to be reuenged of the former wrong as also considering that to enter Guiana by small boats, to depart 400. or 500. miles from my ships, and to leaue a garison in my backe interrested in the same enterprize, who also dayly expected supplies out of Spaine, I should haue sauored very much of the asse: and therefore taking a time of most aduantage I set vpon the Corps du guard in the euening, and hauing put them to the sword, sent Captaine Calfield onwards with 60. souldiers, and my selfe followed with 40. more and so tooke their new City which they called S. Ioseph by breake of day: they abode not any fight after a fewe shot, and all being dismissed but onely Berreo and his companion, I brought them with me abord, and at the instance of the Indians I set their new citie of S. Ioseph on fire.

The Citie of S. Ioseph taken. Antony Berreo taken prisoner.

The same day arriued Captaine George Gifford with your Lordships ship, and Captaine Keymis whom I lost on the coast of Spaine with the Galego, and in them diuers gentlemen and others, which to our little armie was a great comfort and supply.

We then hasted away towards our purposed discouery, and first I called all the Captaines of the yland together that were enemies to the Spaniards: for there were some which Berreo had brought out of other countreys, and planted there to eate out and wast those that were naturall of the place, and by my Indian interpreter, which I caried out of England, I made them vnderstand that I was the seruant of a Queene, who was the great Casique of the North, and a virgine, and had more Casiqui vnder her then there were trees in that yland: that shee was an enemie to the Castellani in respect of their tyrannie and oppression, and that she deliuered all such nations about her, as were by them oppressed, and hauing freed all the coast of the Northren world from their seruitude, had sent mee to free them also, and withall to defend the countrey of Guiana from their inuasion and conquest.

I shewed them her Maiesties picture which they so admired and honoured, as it had bene easie to haue brought them idolatrous thereof.

The like and a more large discourse I made to the rest of the nations both in my passing to Guiana, and to those of the borders, so as in that part of the world her Maiestie is very famous and admirable, whom they now call Ezrabeta Cassipuna Aquerewana, which is as much as Elizabeth, the great princesse or greatest commander. This done we left Puerto de los Espannoles, and returned to Curiapan, and hauing Berreo my prisoner I gathered from him as much of Guiana as he knew.

This Berreo is a gentleman wel descended, and had long serued the Spanish king in Millain, Naples, the Low countreis and elsewhere, very valiant and liberall, and a gentleman of great assurednes, and of a great heart: I vsed him according to his estate and worth in all things I could, according to the small meanes I had.

Sir W. Ralegh passed 400. miles toward Guiana. I sent Captaine Whiddon the yeere before to get what knowledge he could of Guiana, and the end of my iourney at this time was to discouer and enter the same, but my intelligence was farre from trueth, for the countrey is situate aboue 600. English miles further from the Sea, then I was made beleeue it had bin, which afterward vnderstanding to be true by Berreo, I kept it from the knowledge of my company, who else would neuer haue bene brought to attempt the same: of which 600. miles I passed 400. leauing my ships so farre from mee at ancker in the Sea, which was more of desire to performe that discouery, then of reason, especially hauing such poore and weake vessels to transport our selues in; for in the bottom of an old Galego which I caused to be fashioned like a galley, and in one barge, two whirries, and a shipboat of the Lions whelpe, we caried 100. persons and their victuals for a moneth in the same, being al driuen to lie in the raine and weather, in the open aire, in the burning Sunne, and vpon the hard bords, and to dresse our meat, and to cary all maner of furniture in them, wherewith they were so pestered and unsauory, that what with victuals being most fish, with wette clothes of so many men thrust together, and the heat of the Sunne, I will vndertake there was neuer any prison in England, that could bee found more vnsauorie and lothsome, especially to my selfe, who had for many yeeres before bene dieted and cared for in a sort farre more differing.

If Captaine Preston had not bene perswaded that he should haue come too late to Trinidad to haue found vs there (for the moneth was expired which I promised to tary for him there ere hee coulde recouer the coast of Spaine) but that it had pleased God hee might haue ioyned with vs, and that we had entred the countrey but some ten dayes sooner ere the Riuers were ouerflowen, wee had aduentured either to haue gone to the great Citie of Manoa, or at least taken so many of the other Cities and townes neerer at hand, as would haue made a royall returne: but it pleased not God so much to fauour mee at this time: if it shall be my lot to prosecute the same, I shall willingly spend my life therein, and if any else shalbe enabled thereunto, and conquere the same, I assure him thus much, he shall perfourme more then euer was done in Mexico by Cortez, or in Peru by Piçarro, whereof the one conquered the Empire of Mutezuma, the other of Guascar, and Atabalipa, and whatsoeuer prince shall possesse it, that Prince shall be Lord of more golde, and of a more beautifull Empire, and of more Cities and people, then either the King of Spaine, or the great Turke.

But because there may arise many doubts, and how this Empire of Guiana is become so populous, and adorned with so many great Cities, townes, temples and treasures, I thought good to make it knowen, that the Emperour now reigning is descended from those magnificent princes of Peru, of whose large territories, of whose policies, conquests, edifices, and riches Pedro de Cieça, Francisco Lopez, and others haue written large discourses: for when Francisco Piçarro, Diego Almagro and others conquered the said Empire of Peru, and had put to death Atabalipa sonne to Guaynacapa, which Atabalipa had formerly caused his eldest brother Guascar to bee slaine, one of the yonger sonnes of Guaynacapa fled out of Peru, and tooke with him many thousands of those souldiers of the Empire called Oreiones, and with those and many others which followed him, he vanquished all that tract and valley of America which is situate betweene the great riuer of Amazones, and Baraquan, otherwise called Orenoque and Marannon.

The Empire of Guiana is directly East from Peru towards the Sea, and lieth under the Equinoctial line, and it hath more abundance of golde then any part of Peru, and as many or more great Cities then euer Peru had when it flourished most: it is gouerned by the same lawes, and the Emperour and people obserue the same religion, and the same forme and policies in gouernment as were vsed in Peru, not differing in any part: The statelines of Manoa. and I haue bene assured by such of the Spaniards as haue seene Manoa the Imperial Citie of Guiana, which the Spaniards call El Dorado, that for the greatnesse, for the riches, and for the excellent seat, it farre exceedeth any of the world, at least of so much of the world as is knowen to the Spanish nation: it is founded vpon a lake of salt water of 200. leagues long like vnto Mare Caspium. Fran. Lopez de Gomera hist. gen. cap. 120. And if we compare it to that of Peru, and but read the report of Francisco Lopez and others, it will seeme more then credible: and because we may iudge of the one by the other, I thought good to insert part of the 120. Chapter of Lopez in his generall historie of the Indies, wherein he describeth the Court and magnificence of Guaynacapa, ancestour to the Emperor of Guiana, whose very wordes are these. Todo el seruicio de su casa, mesa, y cozina, era de oro, y de plata, y quando menos de plata, y cobre por mas rezio. Tenia en su recamara estatuas huecas de oro, que parecian gigantes, y las figuaras al propio, y tamanno de quantos animales, aues, arboles, y yeruas produze la tierra, y de quantos peces cria la mar y aguas de sus reynos. Tenia assi mesmo sogas, costales, cestas, y troxes de oro y plata, rimeros de palos de oro, que parecissen lenna raiada para quemar. En fin no auia cosa en su tierra, que no la tuuiesse do oro contrahecha: y aun dizen, que tenian los Ingas vn vergel en vna Isla cerca de la Puna, donde se yuan a holgar, quando querian mar, que tenia la ortaliza, las flores, y arboles de oro y plata, inuencion y grandeza hasta entonces nunca vista. Allende de todo esto tenia infinitissima, cantitad de plata, y oro por labrar en el Cuzco, que se perdio por la muerte de Guascar, car los Indios lo escondieron, viendo que los Espannoles se lo tomauan, y embiauan a Espanna. That is, All the vessels of his house, table and kitchin were of gold and siluer, and the meanest of siluer and copper for strength and hardnesse of metall. He had in his wardrobe hollow statues of gold which seemed giants, and the figures in proportion and bignesse of all the beasts, birds, trees and hearbes, that the earth bringeth foorth: and of all the fishes that the sea or waters of his kingdome breedeth. He had also ropes, budgets, chestes and troughs of golde and siluer, heapes of billets of gold, that seemed wood marked out to burne. Finally, there was nothing in his countrey, whereof he had not the counterfait in gold: Yea and they say, The Ingas had a garden of pleasure in an yland neere Puna, where they went to recreat themselues, when they would take the aire of the Sea, which had all kinde of garden-hearbs, flowers and trees of golde and siluer, an inuention, and magnificence till then neuer seene. Besides all this, he had an infinite quantitie of siluer and golde vnwrought in Cuzco which was lost by the death of Guascar, for the Indians hid it, seeing that the Spaniards tooke it, and sent it into Spaine.

And in the 117. chapter Francisco Piçarro caused the gold and siluer of Atabalipa to be weyed after he had taken it, which Lopez setteth downe in these words following. Hallaron cinquenta y dos mil marcos de buena plata, y vn millon y trezientos veinte y seys mil, y quinientos pesos de oro, Which is: They found fiftie and two thousand markes of good siluer, and one million, and three hundred twenty and six thousand and fiue hundred pezos of golde.[54]

[54] These quotations show the riches of *Peru*, not of *El Dorado*. This was the name given by the Spaniards in the sixteenth century to an imaginary region somewhere in the interior of South America, between the Orinoco and the Amazon, where gold and precious stones were supposed to be in such abundance as to be had for merely picking them up. This story was communicated by an Indian cacique to Gonzalo Pizarro, brother of the conquerer, who sent Francisco Orellana down the Amazon River to discover this wonderful land. Orellana followed the course of the Amazon down to the sea, but he did not find El Dorado. The story, however, continued to be credited for many years afterwards.

Now although these reports may seeme strange, yet if we consider the many millions which are dayly brought out of Peru into Spaine, wee may easily beleeue the same: for we finde that by the abundant treasure of that countrey the Spanish king vexeth all the princes of Europe, and is become in a few yeeres, from a poore king of Castile, the greatest monarch of this part of the world, and likely euery day to increase, if other princes forslow the good occasions offered, and suffer him to adde this empire to the rest, which by farre exceedeth all the rest: if his golde now endanger vs, hee will then be vnresistable. Such of the Spanyards as afterward endeuoured the conquest thereof (whereof there haue bene many, as shall be declared hereafter) thought that this Inga (of whom this emperour now liuing is descended) tooke his way by the riuer of Amazones, by that branch which is called Papamene: for by that way followed Orellana (by the commandement of Gonzalo Piçarro, in the yere 1542) whose name the riuer also beareth this day, which is also by others called Marannon, although Andrew Theuet doeth affirme that betweene Marannon and Amazones there are 120 leagues: but sure it is that those riuers haue one head and beginning, and the Marannon, which Theuet describeth, is but a branch of Amazones or Orellana, of which I will speake more in another place. *Iuan Martinez the first that euer saw Manoa.* It was attempted by Ordas; but it is now little lesse then 70 yeres since that Diego Ordas, a knight of the order of Saint Iago attempted the same: and it was in the yeere 1542 that Orellana discouered the riuer of Amazones: but the first that euer saw Manoa was Iuan Martinez master of the munition to Ordas. At a port called Morequito in Guiana there lieth at this day a great anker of Ordas his ship; and this port is some 300 miles within the land, vpon the great riuer of Orenoque.

I rested at this port foure dayes: twenty dayes after I left the ships at Curiapan. The relation of this Martinez (who was the first that discouered Manoa) his successe and ende are to bee seene in the Chancery of Saint Iuan de Puerto rico, whereof Berreo had a copy, which appeared to be the greatest incouragement aswell to Berreo as to others that formerly attempted the discouery and conquest. Orellana after he failed of the discouery of Guiana by the sayd riuer of Amazones, passed into Spaine, and there obteined a patent of the king for the inuasion and conquest, but died by sea about the Islands, and his fleet seuered by tempest, the action for that time proceeded not. :Diego de Ordas went foorth with 600 souldiers 1531.: Diego Ordas followed the enterprise, and departed Spaine with 600 souldiers, and 30 horse, who arriuing on the coast of Guiana, was slaine in a mutiny, with the most part of such as fauoured him, as also of the rebellious part, insomuch as his ships perished, and few or none returned, neither was it certeinly knowen what became of the sayd Ordas, vntill Berreo found the anker of his ship in the riuer of Orenoque; but it was supposed, and so it is written by Lopez, that he perished on the seas, and of other writers diuersely conceiued and reported. :Fran. Lopez hist. gen. de las Ind. cap. 87.: And hereof it came that Martinez entred so farre within the land, and arriued at that city of Inga the emperour; for it chanced that while Ordas with his army rested at the port of Morequito (who was either the first or second that attempted Guiana) by some negligence, the whole store of powder prouided for the seruice was set on fire: and Martinez hauing the chiefe charge, was condemned by the Generall Ordas to be executed foorthwith: Martinez being much fauoured by the souldiers, had all the meanes possible procured for his life; but it could not be obteined in other sort than this: That he should be set into a canao alone without any victuall, onely with his armes, and so turned loose into the great riuer: but it pleased God that the canoa was caried downe the streame, and that certeine of the Guianians mette it the same euening; :The great city of Manao or El Dorado.: and hauing not at any time seene any Christian, nor any man of that colour, they caried Martinez into the land to be woondred at, and so from towne to towne, vntill he came to the great city of Manoa, the seat and residence of Inga the emperour. The emperour after he had beheld him, knew him to be a Christian (for it was not long before that his brethren Guascar and Atabalipa were vanquished by the Spanyards in Peru) and caused him to be lodged in his palace, and well interteined. Hee liued seuen moneths in Manoa, but was not suffered to wander into the countrey any where. He was also brought thither all the way blindfold, led by the Indians, vntill he came to the entrance of Manoa it selfe, and was fourteene or fifteene dayes in the passage. He auowed at his death that he entred the city at Noon, and then they vncouered his face, and that he trauelled all that day till night thorow the city, and the next day from Sun rising to Sun setting yer he came to the palace of Inga. After that Martinez had liued seuen monethes in Manoa, and began to vnderstand the language of the countrey, Inga asked him whether he desired to returne into his owne countrey, or would willingly abide with him. But Martinez not desirous to stay, obteined the fauour of Inga to depart: with whom he sent diuers Guianians to conduct him to the riuer of Orenoque, all loden with as much golde as they could cary, which he gaue to Martinez at his departure: but when he was arriued neere the riuers side, the borderers which are called Orenoqueponi robbed him and his Guianians of all the treasure (the borderers being at that time at warres, which Inga had not conquered) saue only of two great bottels of gourds, which were filled with beads of golde curiously wrought, which those Orenoqueponi thought had bene no other thing then his drinke or meat, or graine for food, with which Martinez had liberty to passe: and so in canoas hee fell downe from the riuer of Orenoque to Trinidad, and from thence to Margarita, and also to Saint Iuan de puerto rico, where remaining a long time for passage into Spaine, he died. In the time of his extreme sicknesse, and when he was without hope of life, receiuing the Sacrament at the hands of his Confessor, he deliuered these things, with the relation of his trauels, and also called for his calabaças or gourds of the golde beads which he gaue to the church and friers to be prayed for. ¦ The author of the name of El Dorado. ¦ This Martinez was he that Christened the city of Manoa by the name of El Dorado, and as Berreo informed mee, vpon this occasion: Those Guianians, and also the borderers, and all other in that tract which I haue seene are maruellous great drunkards; in which vice, I thinke no nation can compare with them: and at the times of their solemne feasts, when the emperour caroweth with his captaines, tributaries, and gouernours, the maner is thus: All those that pledge him are first stripped naked, and their bodies anointed all ouer with a kind of white balsamum (by them called curca) of which there is great plenty, and yet very deare amongst them, and it is of all other the most precious, whereof wee haue had good experience: when they are anointed all ouer, certeine seruants of the emperour, hauing prepared golde made into fine powder, blow it thorow hollow canes vpon their naked bodies, vntill they be all shining from the foot to the head: and in this sort they sit drinking by twenties and hundreds, and continue in drunkennesse sometimes sixe or seuen dayes together. ¦ Sir Robert Duddeley. ¦ The same is also confirmed by a letter written into Spaine, which was intercepted, which M. Robert Duddeley tolde me he had seene. Vpon this sight, and for the abundance of golde which he saw in the city, the images of golde in their temples, the plates, armours, and shields of gold which they vse in the warres, he called it El Dorado. After the death of Ordas and Martinez, and after Orellana, who was imployed by Gonzalo Piçarro, one Pedro de Osua a knight of Nauarre attempted Guiana, taking his way from Peru, and built his brigandines vpon a riuer called Oia, which riseth to the Southward of Quito, and is very great. This riuer falleth into Amazones, by which Osua with his companies descended, and came out of that prouince which is called Mutylonez: and it seemeth to mee that this empire is reserued for her Maiestie and the English nation, by reason of the hard successe which all these and other Spanyards found in attempting the same, whereof I will speake briefly, though impertinent in some sort to my purpose. Reade Iosephus Acosta. This Pedro de Osua had among his troups a Biscain, called Agiri, a man meanly borne, who bare no other office then a sergeant or alferez: but after certaine moneths, when the souldiers were grieued with trauels, and consumed with famine, and that no entrance could be found by the branches or body of Amazones, this Agiri raised a mutiny, of which hee made himselfe the head, and so preuailed, as he put Osua to the sword, and all his followers, taking on him the whole charge and commandement, with a purpose not onely to make himselfe emperour of Guiana, but also of Peru, and of all that side of the West Indies: he had of his party seuen hundred souldiers, and of those many promised to draw in other captaines and companies, to deliuer vp townes and forts in Peru: but neither finding by the sayd riuer any passage into Guiana, nor any possibility to returne towards Peru by the same Amazones, by reason that the descent of the riuer made so great a current, he was inforced to disemboque at the mouth of the sayd Amazones, which can not be lesse then a thousand leagues from the place where they imbarked: from thence be coasted the land till he arriued at Margarita: The voyage of sir Iohn Burgh to the West Indies. to the North of Mompatar, which is at this day called Puerto de Tyranno, for that he there slew Don Iuan de villa Andreda, gouernour of Margarita when sir Iohn Burgh landed there and attempted the Island. Agiri put to the sword all other in the Island that refused to be of his party, and tooke with him certeine Simerones, and other desperate companions. From thence he went to Cumana, and there slew the gouernour, and dealt in all as at Margarita: hee spoiled all the coast of Caracas, and the prouince of Venezuela, and of Rio de la hacha; and as I remember, it was the same yere that sir Iohn Hawkins sailed to Saint Iuan de Vllua in the Iesus of Lubeck: for himselfe tolde me that he met with such a one vpon the coast that rebelled, and had sailed downe all the riuer of Amazones. Agiri from thence landed about Sancta Marta, and sacked it also, putting to death so many as refused to be his followers, purposing to inuade Nueuo reyno de Granada, and to sacke Pamplon, Merida, Lagrita, Tunxa, and the rest of the cities of Nueuo reyno, and from thence againe to enter Peru: but in a fight in the sayd Nueuo reyno he was ouerthrowen, and finding no way to escape, he first put to the sword his owne children, foretelling them that they should not liue to be defamed or vpbraided by the Spanyards after his death, who would haue termed them the children of a traitour or tyrant; and that sithence hee could not make them princes, hee would yet deliuer them from shame and reproche. These were the ends and tragedies of Ordas, Martinez, Oreliana, Ozua, and Agiri.

1532. Gomar. cap. 84 and 86. Also soone after Ordas followed Ieronimo Ortal de Saragosa with 130 souldiers, who failing his entrance by sea, was cast with the current on the coast of Paria, and peopled about S. Miguel de Neueri. It was then attempted by Don Pedro de Silua, a Portugues of the family of Ruigomes de Silua, and by the fauour which Ruigomes had with the king, he was set out, but he also shot wide of the marke; for being departed from Spaine with his fleete, he entered by Marannon and Amazones, where by the nations of the riuer, and by the Amazones hee was vttlerly ouerthrowen, and himselfe and all his armie defeated, only seuen escaped, and of those but two returned.

After him came Pedro Hernandez de Serpa, and landed at Cumana in the West Indies, taking his iourney by and towards Orenoque, which may be some 120 leagues: but ther he came to the borders of the sayd riuer, hee was set vpon by a nation of the Indians called Wikiri, and ouerthrowen in such sort, that of 300 souldiers, horsemen, many Indians, and Negros, there returned but 18. Others affirme, that he was defeated in the very entrance of Guiana, at the first ciuil towne of the empire called Macureguarai. Captaine Preston in taking S. Iago de Leon (which was by him and his companies very resolutely performed, being a great towne, and farre within the land) held a gentleman prisoner, who died in his ship, that was one of the company of Hermandez de Serpa, and saued among those that escaped, who witnessed what opinion is held among the Spanyards thereabouts of the great riches of Guiana, and El Dorado the city of Inga. Another Spanyard was brought aboord me by captaine Preston, who told me in the hearing of himselfe and diuers other gentlemen, that he met with Berreos campe-master at Caracas, when he came from the borders of Guiana, and that he saw with him forty of most pure plates of golde curiously wrought, and swords of Guiana decked and inlayed with gold, feathers garnished with golde and diuers rarities which he carried to the Spanish king.

After Hernandez de Serpa, it was undertaken by the Adelantado, Don Gonzales Ximenes de Casada, who was one of the chiefest in the conquest of Nueuo reino, whose daughter and heire Don Antonio de Berreo maried. Gonzales sought the passage also by the riuer called Papamene, which riseth by Quito in Peru, and runneth Southeast 100 leagues, and then falleth into Amazones, but he also failing the entrance, returned with the losse of much labour and cost. I tooke one captaine George a Spanyard that followed Gonzales in this enterprise. Gonzales gaue his daughter to Berreo, taking his oth and honour to follow the enterprise to the last of his substance and life, who since, as he hath sworne to me, hath spent 300000 ducats in the same, and yet nevcr could enter so far into the land as my selfe with that poore troupe or rather a handfull of men, being in all about 100 gentlemen, souldiers, rowers, boat-keepers, boyes, and of all sorts: neither could any of the forepassed vndertakers, nor Berreo himselfe, discouer the countrey, till now lately by conference with an ancient king called Carapana, he got the true light thereof: for Berreo came about 1500 miles yer he vnderstood ought, or could finde any passage or entrance into any part thereof, yet he had experience of al these forenamed, and diuers others, and was perswaded of their errors and mistakings. Berreo sought it by the river Cassamar,[55] which falleth into a great riuer called Pato: Pato falleth into Meta, and Meta into Baraquan, which is also called Orenoque.

[55] Casanare.

He tooke his journey from Nueuo reyno de Granada where he dwelt, hauing the inheritance of Gonzales Ximenes in those parts: he was followed with 700 horse, he draue with him 1000 head of cattell, he had also many women, Indians, and slaues. How all these riuers crosse and encounter, how the countrey lieth and is bordered, the passage of Ximenes and Berreo, mine owne discouery, and the way that I entred, with all the rest of the nations and riuers, your lordship shall receiue in a large Chart or Map, which I haue not yet finished, and which I shall most humbly pray your lordship to secret, and not to suffer it to passe your owne hands: for by a draught thereof all may be preuented by other nations: for I know it is this very yeere sought by the French, although by the way that they now take, I feare it not much. A new and rich trade of the French to the riuer of Amazones. It was also tolde me yer I departed from England, that Villiers the Admirall was in preparation for the planting of Amazones, to which riuer the French haue made diuers voyages and returned much golde, and other rarities. I spake with the captaine of a French ship that came from thence, his ship riding in Falmouth the same yere that my ships came first from Virginia.

There was another this yeere in Helford that also came from thence, and had bene foureteene moneths at an anker in Amazones, which were both very rich. Although, as I am perswaded, Guiana cannot be entred that way, yet no doubt the trade of gold from thence passeth by branches of riuers into the riuer of Amazones, and so it doth on euery hand far from the countrey it selfe; for those Indians of Trinidad haue plates of golde from

Guiana, and those canibals of Dominica which dwell in the Islands by which our ships passe yerely to the West Indies, also the Indians of Paria, those Indians called Tucaris, Chochi, Apotomios, Cumanagotos, and all those other nations inhabiting neere about the mountaines that run from Paria thorow the prouince of Venezuela, and in Maracapana, and the canibals of Guanipa, the Indians called Assawai, Coaca, Aiai, and the rest (all which shall be described in my description as they are situate) haue plates of golde of Guiana. And vpon the riuer of Amazones, Theuet writeth that the people weare croissants of golde, for of that forme the Guianians most commonly make them: so as from Dominica to Amazones, which is aboue 250 leagues, all the chiefe Indians in all parts weare of those plates of Guiana. Vndoubtedly those that trade Amazones returne much golde, which (as is aforesayd) commeth by trade from Guiana, by some branch of a riuer that falleth from the countrey into Amazones, and either it is by the riuer which passeth by the nations called Tisnados, or by Carepuna. I made inquiry amongst the most ancient and best travelled of the Orenoqueponi, and I had knowledge of all the riuers betweene Orenoque and Amazones, and was very desirous to vnderstand the truth of those warlike women, because of some it is beleeued, of others not. And though I digresse from my purpose, yet I will set downe that which hath bene deliuered me for trueth of those women, and I spake with a casique or lord of people, that told me he had bene in the riuer, and beyond it also. :The seat of the: :Amazones.: The nations of these women are on the South side of the riuer in the prouinces of Topago, and their chiefest strengths and retracts are in the Islands situate on the South side of the entrance some 60 leagues within the mouth of the sayd riuer. The memories of the like women are very ancient aswell in Africa and in Asia: In Africa those that had Medusa for queene: others in Scithia nere the riuers of Tanais and Thermodon: we finde also that Lampedo and Marthesia were queenes of the Amazones: in many histories they are verified to haue bene, and in diuers ages and prouinces: but they which are not far from Guiana doe accompany with men but once in a yere, and for the time of one moneth, which I gather by their relation, to be in April: and that time all kings of the borders assemble, and queenes of the Amazones: and after the queenes haue chosen, the rest cast lots for their Valentines. This one moneth, they feast, dance, and drinke of their wines in abundance; and the Moone being done, they all depart to their owne prouinces. If they conceiue, and be deliuered of a sonne, they returne him to the father; if of a daughter they nourish it, and reteine it: and as many as haue daughters send vnto the begetters a present; all being desirous to increase their owne sex and kind: but that they cut off the right dug of the brest, I doe not finde to be true. It was farther tolde me, that if in these warres they tooke any prisoners that they vsed to accompany with those also at what time soeuer, but in the end for certeine they put them to death: for they are sayd to be very cruell and bloodthirsty, especially to such as offer to inuade their territories. These Amazones haue likewise great store of these plates of golde, which they recouer by exchange chiefly for a kinde of greene stones, which the Spanyards call Piedras hijadas, and we vse for spleene stones: and for the disease of the stone we also esteeme them. Of these I saw diuers in Guiana: and commonly euery king or casique hath one, which their wiues for the most part weare: and they esteeme them as great iewels.

But to returne to the enterprise of Bereo, who (as I haue sayd) departed from Nueuo reyno with 700 horse, besides the prouisions aboue rehearsed, he descended by the riuer called Cassanar, which riseth in Nueuo reyno out of the mountaines by the city of Tunia, from which mountaine also springeth Pato: both which fall into the great riuer of Meta: and Meta riseth from a mountaine ioyning to Pampion in the same Nueuo reyno de Grenada. These, as also Guaiare, which issueth out of the mountaines by Timana, fall all into Baraquan, and are but of his heads: for at their comming together they lose their names: and Baraquan farther downe is also rebaptized by the name of Orenoque. On the other side of the city and hilles of Timana riseth Rio grande, which falleth in the sea by Sancta Marta. By Cassanar first, and so into Meta, Berreo passed, keeping his horsemen on the banks, where the countrey serued them for to march, and where otherwise, he was driuen to imbarke them in boats which he builded for the purpose, and so came with the current downe the riuer of Meta, and so into Baraquan. After he entred that great and mighty riuer, he began dayly to lose of his companies both men and horse: for it is in many places violently swift, and hath forcible eddies, many sands, and diuers Islands sharp pointed with rocks: but after one whole yeere, iourneying for the most part by riuer and the rest by land, he grew dayly to fewer numbers: for both by sicknesse, and by encountring with the people of those regions, thorow which he trauelled, his companies were much wasted, especially by diuers encounters with the Amapians: and in all this time hee neuer could learne of any passage into Guiana, nor any newes or fame thereof, vntill he came to a further border of the sayd Amapaia, eight dayes iourney from the riuer Caroli, which was the furthest riuer that he entred. Among those of Amapaia, Guiana was famous, but few of these people accosted Berreo, or would trade with him the first three moneths of the six, which he soiourned there. This Amapaia is also maruellous rich in golde (as both Berreo confessed and those of Guiana with whom I had most conference) and is situate vpon Orenoque also. In this countrey Berreo lost 60 of his best souldiers, and most of all his horse that remained in his former yeeres trauell: but in the end, after diuers encounters with those nations, they grew to peace; and they presented Berreo with tenne images of fine golde among diuers other plates and croissants, which, as he sware to me and diuers other gentlemen, were so curiously wrought, as he had not seene the like either in Italy, Spaine, or the Low countreys: and he was resolued, that when he came to the hands of the Spanish king, to whom he had sent them by his camp-master, they would appeare very admirable, especially being wrought by such a nation as had no yron instruments at all, nor any of those helps which our goldsmiths haue to worke withall. The particular name of the people in Amapaia which gaue him these pieces, are called Anebas, and the riuer of Orenoque at that place is aboue 12 English miles broad, which may be from his out fall into the sea 700 or 800 miles.

This prouince of Amapaia is a very low and a marish ground nere the riuer; and by reason of the red water which issueth out in small branches thorow the fenny and boggy ground; there breed diuers poisonfull wormes and serpents: and the Spanyards not suspecting, nor in any sort foreknowing the danger, were infected with a grieuous kinde of fluxe by drinking thereof; and euen the very horses poisoned therewith: insomuch as at the end of the 6 moneths, that they abode their, of all there troups, there were not left aboue 120 souldiers, and neither horse nor cattell: for Berreo hoped to haue found Guiana by 1000 miles nerer then it fel out to be in the end: by meanes whereof they sustained much want and much hunger, oppressed with grieuous diseases, and all the miseries that could be imagined. I demanded of those in Guiana that had trauelled Amapaia, how they liued with that tawny or red water when they trauelled thither: and they tolde me that after the Sun was neere the middle of the skie, they vsed to fill their pots and pitchers with that water, but either before that time, or towardes the setting of the Sun it was dangerous to drinke of, and in the night strong poison. I learned also of diuers other riuers of that nature among them, which were also (while the Sun was in the Meridian) very safe to drinke, and in the morning, euening, and night woonderfull dangerous and infectiue. From this prouince Berreo hasted away assoone as the Spring and beginning of Summer appeared, and sought his entrance on the borders of Orenoque on the South side: but there ran a ledge of so high and impassable mountaines, as he was not able by any meanes to march ouer them, continuing from the East sea into which Orenoque falleth, euen to Quito in Peru: neither had he meanes to cary victuall or munition ouer those craggie, high, and fast hilles, being all woody, and those so thicke and spiny, and so full of prickles, thornes, and briers, as it is impossible to creepe thorow them: hee had also neither friendship among the people, nor any interpreter to perswade or treat with them: and more, to his disaduantage, the casiques and kings of Amapaia had giuen knowledge of his purpose to the Guianians, and that he sought to sacke and conquer the empire, for the hope of their so great abundance and quantities of golde: he passed by the mouthes of many great riuers, which fell into Orenoque both from the North and South, which I forbeare to name for tediousnesse, and because they are more pleasing in describing then reading.

Many great riuers falling into Orenoque. Berreo affirmed that there fell an hundred riuers into Orenoque from the North and South, whereof the least was as big as Rio grande, that passed betweene Popayan and Nueuo reyno de Granada (Rio Grande being esteemed one of the renowmed riuers in all the West Indies, and numbred among the great riuers of the world:) but he knew not the names of any of these, but Caroli onely; neither from what nations they descended, neither to what prouinces they led: for he had no meanes to discourse with the inhabitants at any time: neither was he curious in these things, being vtterly vnlearned, and not knowing the East from the West. But of all these I got some knowledge, and of many more, partly by mine owne trauell, and the rest by conference: of some one I learned one, of others the rest, hauing with me an Indian that spake many languages, and that of Guiana naturally. I sought out all the aged men, and such as were greatest travellers, and by the one and the other I came to vnderstand the situations, the riuers, the kingdomes from the East sea to the borders of Peru, and from Orenoque Southward as farre as Amazones or Marannon, and the religions of Maria Tamball, and of all the kings of prouinces, and captaines of townes and villages, how they stood in tearmes of peace or warre, and which were friends or enemies the one with the other, without which there can be neither entrance nor conquest in those parts, nor elsewhere: for by the dissention betweene Guascar and Atabalipa, Piçarro conquered Peru, and by the hatred that the Tlaxcallians have to Mutezuma, Cortez was victorious ouer Mexico: without which both the one and the other had failed of their enterprise, and of the great honour and riches which they atteined vnto.

The prouince of Emeria inhabited by gentle Indians. Now Berreo began to grow into dispaire, and looked for no other successe then his predecessor in this enterprise, vntill such time as hee arriued at the prouince of Emeria towards the East sea and mouth of the riuer, where he found a nation of people very fauourable, and the countrey full of all maner of victuall. The king of this land is called Carapana, a man very wise, subtill, and of great experience, being little lesse then an hundred yeeres olde: in his youth he was sent by his father into the Island of Trinidad, by reason of ciuill warre among themselues, and was bred at a village in that island, called Parico: at that place in his youth hee had seene many Christians, both French and Spanish, and went diuers times with the Indians of Trinidad to Margarita and Cumana in the West Indies (for both those places haue euer beene relieued with victuall from Trinidad) by reason whereof he grew of more vnderstanding, and noted the difference of the nations, comparing the strength and armes of his countrey with those of the Christians, and euer after temporized so, as whosoeuer els did amisse, or was wasted by contention, Carapana kept himselfe and his countrey in quiet and plenty: he also held peace with the Caribes or Canibals his neighbours, and had free trade with all nations, whosoeuer els had warre.

Berreo soiourned and rested his weake troupe in the towne of Carapana sixe weeks, and from him learned the way and passage to Guiana, and the riches and magnificence thereof: but being then vtterly disable to proceed, he determined to try his fortune another yere, when he had renewed his prouisions, and regathered more force, which hee hoped for as well out of Spaine as from Nueuo reyno, where hee had left his sonne Don Antonio Ximenes to second him vpon the first notice giuen of his entrance, and so for the present imbarked himselfe in canoas, and by the branches of Orenoque arriued at Trinidad, hauing from Carapana sufficient pilots to conduct him. From Trinidad he coasted Paria, and so recouered Margarita: and hauing made relation to Don Iuan Sermiento the gouernour, of his proceeding and perswaded him of the riches of Guiana, he obteined from thence fifty souldiers, promising presently to returne to Carapana, and so into Guiana. But Berreo meant nothing lesse at that time: for he wanted many prouisions necessary for such an enterprise, and therefore departed from Margarita, seated himselfe in Trinidad, and from thence sent his camp-master, and his sergeant-maior backe to the borders to discouer the neerest passage into the empire, as also to treat with the borderers, and to draw them to his party and loue: without which, he knew he could neither passe safely, nor in any sort be relieued with victuall or ought els. Carapana directed his company to a king called Morequito, assuring them that no man could deliuer so much of Guiana as Morequito could, and that his dwelling was but fiue dayes journey from Macureguarai, the first ciuill towne of Guiana.

> Vides the gouernour of Cumana competitor with Berreo in the conquest of Guiana.

Now your lordship shall vnderstand, that this Morequito, one of the greatest lords or kings of the borders of Guiana, had two or three yeeres before bene at Cumana and at Margarita, in the West Indies, with great store of plates of golde, which he caried to exchange for such other things as he wanted in his owne countrey, and was dayly feasted, and presented by the gouernours of those places, and held amongst them some two monethes, in which time one Vides gouernour of Cumana wanne him to be his conductour into Guiana, being allured by those croissants and images of golde which hee brought with him to trade, as also by the ancient fame and magnificence of El Dorado: whereupon Vides sent into Spaine for a patent to discouer and conquer Guiana, not knowing of the precedence of Berreos patent, which, as Berreo affirmeth, was signed before that of Vides: so as when Vides vnderstood of Berreo, and that he had made entrance into that territory, and forgone his desire and hope, it was verily thought that Vides practised with Morequito to hinder and disturbe Berreo in all he could, and not to suffer him to enter thorow his signorie, nor any of his companies; neither to victuall, nor guide them in any sort; for Vides gouernour of Cumana, and Berreo, were become mortall enemies, aswell for that Berreo had gotten Trinidad into his patent with Guiana, as also in that he was by Berreo preuented in the iourney of Guiana it selfe: howsoeuer it was, I know not, but Morequito for a time dissembled his disposition, suffered Spanyards, and a frier (which Berreo had sent to discouer Manoa) to trauell thorow his countrey, gaue them a guide for Macureguaray, the first towne of ciuill and apparelled people, from whence they had other guides to bring them to Manoa the great city of Inga: *Ten Spanyards arriue at Manoa.* and being furnished with those things which they had learned of Carapana were of most price in Guiana, went onward, and in eleuen dayes arriued at Manoa, as Berreo affirmeth for certaine: although I could not be assured thereof by the lord which now gouerneth the prouince of Morequito, for he tolde me that they got all the golde they had, in other townes on this side Manoa, there being many very great and rich, and (as he sayd) built like the townes of Christians, with many roomes.

When these ten Spaniards were returned, and ready to put out of the border of Aromaia, the people of Morequito set vpon them, and slew them all but one that swam the riuer, and tooke from them to the value of forty thousand pezos of golde: and one of them onely liued to bring the newes to Berreo, that both his nine souldiers and holy father were benighted in the said prouince. I my selfe spake with the captaines of Morequito that slew them, and was at the place where it was executed. Berreo, inraged heerewithall, sent all the strength he could make into Aromaia, to be reuenged of him, his people, and countrey. But Morequito suspecting the same, fled ouer Orenoque, and thorow the territories of the Saima, and Wikiri, recouered Cumana, where he thought himself very safe, with Vides the gouernour. But Berreo sending for him in the Kings name, and his messengers finding him in the house of one Fashardo on the sudden yer he was suspected, so as he could not then be conueyed away, Vides durst not deny him, aswell to avoid the suspition of this practise, as also for that an holy father was slaine by him and his people. *Morequito executed.* Morequito offered Fashardo the weight of three quintals in golde, to let him escape: but the poore Guianian betrayed on all sides was delivered to the camp-master of Berreo, and was presently executed.

After the death of this Morequito, the souldiers of Berreo spoiled his territorie, and tooke diuers prisoners, among others they tooke the vncle of Morequito, called Topiawari, who is now king of Aromaia (whose sonne I brought with me into England) and is a man of great vnderstanding and policy: he is aboue an hundred yeeres olde, and yet of a very able body. The Spaniards ledde him in a chaine seuenteene dayes, and made him their guide from place to place betweene his countrey and Emeria, the prouince of Carapana, aforesayd, and he was at last redeemed for an hundred plates of golde, and diuers stones called Piedras Hijadas, or Spleene-stones. The towne of Carapana is the port of Guiana. Now Berreo for executing of Morequito, and other cruelties, spoiles, and slaughters done in Armonaia, hath lost the loue of the Orenoqueponi, and all the borderers, and dare not send any of his souldiers any further into the land then to Carapana, which he called the port of Guiana: but from thence by the helpe of Carapana he had trade further into the countrey, and alwayes appointed ten Spaniards to reside in Carapanas towne, by whose fauour, and by being conducted by his people, those ten searched the countrey thereabouts, aswell for mines, as for other trades and commodities.

They also haue gotten a nephew of Morequito, whom they haue Christened, and named Don Iuan, of whom they haue great hope, endeuouring by all meanes to establish him in the sayd prouince. Some fewe Spaniards are now seated in Dissequebe. Among many other trades, those Spaniards vsed canoas to passe to the riuers of Barema, Pawroma, and Dissequebe, which are on the south side of the mouth of Orenoque, and there buy women and children from the Canibals, which are of that barbarous nature, as they will for three or foure hatchets sell the sonnes and daughters of their owne brethren and sisters, and for somewhat more, euen their owne daughters. Hereof the Spaniards make great profit: for buying a maid of twelue or thirteene yeres for three or foure hatchets, they sell them againe at Margarita in the West Indies for fifty and an hundred pezos, which is so many crownes.

The master of my shippe, Iohn Dowglas, tooke one of the canoas which came laden from thence with people to be solde, and the most of them escaped: yet of those he brought, there was one as well fauoured, and as well shaped as euer I saw any in England, afterward I saw many of them, which but for their tawnie colour may be compared to any of Europe. They also trade in those riuers for bread of Cassaui, of which they buy an hundred pound weight for a knife, and sell it at Margarita for ten pezos. They also recouer great store of Cotton, Brasill wood, and those beds which they call Hamcas or Brasill beds, wherein in hot countreyes all the Spaniards vse to lie commonly, and in no other, neither did we our selues while we were there. By meanes of which trades, for ransome of diuers of the Guianians, and for exchange of hatchets and kniues, Berreo recouered some store of golde plates, eagles of golde, and images of men and diuers birdes, and dispatched his campe-master for Spaine, with all that hee had gathered, therewith to leuie souldiers, and by the shew thereof to draw others to the loue of the enterprise. And hauing sent diuers images aswell of men as beasts, birds and fishes, so curiously wrought in gold, he doubted not but to perswade the king to yeeld to him some further helpe, especially for that this land had neuer beene sacked, the mines neuer wrought, and in the Indies their works were well spent, and the golde drawen out with great labour and charge. He also dispatched messengers to his sonne in Nueuo reyno to leuie all the forces he could, and to come downe the riuer Orenoque to Emeria, the prouince of Carapana, to meet him: he had also sent to Saint Iago de Leon on the coast of the Caracas, to buy horses and mules.

After I had thus learned of his proceedings past and purposed, I told him that I had resolued to see Guiana, and that it was the end of my iourney, and the cause of my comming to Trinidad, as it was indeed, (and for that purpose I sent Iacob Whiddon the yeere before to get intelligence with whom Berreo himselfe had speech at that time, and remembred how inquisitiue Iacob Whiddon was of his proceedings, and of the countrey of Guiana) Berreo was stricken into a great melancholy and sadnesse, and vsed all the arguments he could to disswade me, and also assured the gentlemen of my company that it would be labour lost, and that they should suffer many miseries if they proceeded. And first he deliuered that I could not enter any of the riuers with any barke or pinnesse, or hardly with any ships boat, it was so low, sandy, and full of flats, and that his companies were dayly grounded in their canoas, which drew but twelue inches water. He further sayde, that none of the countrey would come to speake with vs, but would all flie: and if we followed them to their dwellings, they would burne their owne townes: and besides that, the way was long, the Winter at hand, and that the riuers beginning once to swell, it was impossible to stem the current, and that we could not in those small boats by any means cary victuall for halfe the time, and that (which indeed most discouraged my company) the kings and lords of all the borders of Guiana had decreed that none of them should trade with any Christians for golde, because the same would be their owne ouerthrow, and that for the loue of gold the Christians meant to conquer and dispossesse them of all together.

Many and the most of these I found to be true, but yet I resoluing to make triall of all whatsoever happened, directed Captaine George Gifford my vice-admirall to take the Lions whelpe, and captaine Calfield his barke to turne to the Eastward, against the mouth of a riuer called Capuri, whose entrance I had before sent captaine Whiddon, and Iohn Dowglas the master, to discouer, who found some nine foot water or better vpon the flood, and fiue at low water, to whom I had giuen instructions that they should anker at the edge of the shoald, and vpon the best of the flood to thrust ouer, which shoald Iohn Dowglas bwoyed and beckoned for them before: but they laboured in vaine: for neither could they turne it vp altogether so farre to the East, neither did the flood continue so long, but the water fell yer they could haue passed the sands: as wee after found by a second experience; so as now wee must either give ouer our enterprise, or leauing our ships at aduenture foure hundred mile behinde vs, must run vp in our ships boats, one barge, and two wheries. But being doubtfull how to cary victuals for so long a time in such bables, or any strength of men, especially for that Berreo assured vs that his sonne must be by that time come downe with many souldiers. I sent away one King, master of the Lions whelpe, with his shipboat to trie another branch of a riuer in the bottome of the bay of Guanipa, which was called Amana, to prooue if there were water to be found for either of the small ships to enter. But when he came to the mouth of Amana, he found it as the rest, but stayed not to discouer it thorowly, because he was assured by an Indian, his guide, that the Canibals of Guanipa would assaile them with many canoas, and that they shot poisoned arrowes: so as if he hasted not backe, they should all be lost.

In the mean time, fearing the woorst, I caused all the carpenters we had, to cut downe a Galego boat, which we meant to cast off, and to fit her with banks to row on, and in all things to prepare her the best they could, so as she might be brought to draw but fiue foot, for so much we had on the barre of Capuri at low water. And doubting of Kings returne, I sent Iohn Dowglas againe in my long barge, aswell to relieue him, as also to make a perfect search in the bottome of that bay: for it hath bene held for infallible, that whatsoeuer ship or boat shall fall therein, can neuer disembogue againe, by reason of the violent current which setteth into the sayde-bay, as also for that the brize and Easterly winde bloweth directly into the same. Of which opinion I haue heard Iohn Hampton of Plymmouth, one of the greatest experience of England, and diuers other besides that haue traded to Trinidad.

I sent with Iohn Dowglas an old casique of Trinidad for a pilot, who tolde vs that we could not returne againe by the bay or gulfe, but that he knew a by-branch which ran within the land to the Eastward, and that he thought by it we might fall into Capuri, and so returne in foure dayes. Iohn Dowglas searched those riuers, and found foure goodly entrances, whereof the least was as bigge as the Thames at Wolwich; but in the bay thitherward it was shoald, and but sixe foote water: so as we were now without hope of any ship or barke to passe ouer, and therefore resolued to go on with the boats, and the bottome of the Galego, in which we thrust 60 men. In the Lions whelps boat and whery we caried 20. Captaine Calfield in his whery caried ten more, and in my barge other tenne, which made vp a hundred: we had no other meanes but to cary victuall for a moneth in the same, and also to lodge therein as we could, and to boile and dresse our meat. Captaine Gifford had with him master Edward Porter, captaine Eynos, and eight more in his whery, with all their victuall, weapons, and prouisions. Captaine Calfield had with him my cousin Butshead Gorges, and eight more. In the galley, of gentlemen and officers my selfe had captaine Thin, my cousin Iohn Greenuile, my nephew Iohn Gilbert, captaine Whiddon, captaine Keymis, Edward Handcocke, captaine Clarke, lieutenant Hewes, Thomas Vpton, captaine Facy, Ierome Ferrar, Anthony Welles, William Connocke, and aboue fifty more. We could not learne of Berreo any other way to enter but in branches, so farre to wind-ward, as it was impossible for vs to recouer: for wee had as much sea to crosse ouer in our wheries, as betweene Douer and Calais, and in a great billow, the winde and current being both very strong, so as we were driuen to goe in those small boats directly before the winde into the bottome of the bay of Guanipa, and from thence to enter the mouth of some one of those riuers which Iohn Dowglas had last discouered, and had with vs for pilot an Indian of Barema, a riuer to the South of Orenoque, betweene that and Amazones, whose canoas we had formerly taken as hee was going from the sayd Barema, laden with Cassaui-bread, to sell at Margarita. This Arwacan promised to bring me into the great riuer of Orenoque, but indeed of that which he entred he was vtterly ignorant, for he had not seene it in twelue yeeres before: at which time he was very yoong, and of no iudgement: A wonderfull confluence of streames. and if God had not sent vs another helpe, we might haue wandred a whole yere in that labyrinth of riuers, yer wee had found any way, either out or in, especially after wee were past ebbing and flowing which was in foure dayes, for I know all the earth doeth not yeelde the like confluence of streames and branches, the one crossing the other so many times, and all so faire and large, and so like one to another, as no man can tell which to take: and if wee went by the Sunne or Compasse, hoping thereby to goe directly one way or other, yet that way wee were also caried in a circle amongst multitudes of Islands, and euery Island so bordered with high trees, as no man coulde see any further then the bredth of the riuer, or length of the breach. But this it chanced, that entering into a riuer, (which because it had no name, wee called the riuer of the Red crosse, our selues being the first Christians that euer came therein) the two and twentieth of May, as wee were rowing vp the same, wee espied a small canoa with three Indians, which (by the swiftnesse of my barge, rowing with eight oares) I ouertooke yer they could crosse the riuer, the rest of the people on the banks shadowed vnder the thicke wood, gazed on with a doubtfull conceit what might befall those three which we had taken. But when they perceiued that we offered them no violence, neither entred their canoa with any of ours, nor tooke out of the canoa any of theirs, they then beganne to shew themselues on the banks side, and offered to traffique with vs for such things as they had. And as wee drew neere, they all stayed, and we came with our barge to the mouth of a little creeke which came from their towne into the great riuer.

As we abode there a while, our Indian pilot, called Ferdinando, would needs goe ashore their village to fetch some fruits, and to drinke of their artificiall wines, and also to see the place, and know the lord of it against another time, and tooke with him a brother of his, which hee had with him in the iourney: when they came to the village of these people the lord of the Island offered to lay hands on them, purposing to haue slaine them both, yeelding for reason that this Indian of ours had brought a strange nation into their territory, to spoile and destroy them. But the pilot being quicke, and of a disposed body, slipt their fingers, and ran into the woods, and his brother being the better footman of the two, recouered the creekes mouth, where we stayed in our barge, crying out that his brother was slaine: with that we set hands on one of them that was next vs, a very olde man, and brought him into the barge, assuring him that if we had not our pilot againe, we would presently cut off his head. This olde man being resolued that he should pay the losse of the other, cried out to those in the woods to saue Ferdinando our pilot: but they followed him notwithstanding, and hunted after him vpon the foot with the Deere-dogges, and with so maine a crie, that all the woods eckoed with the shout they made: but at the last this poore chased Indian recouered the riuer side, and got vpon a tree, and as we were coasting, leaped downe and swamme to the barge halfe dead with feare. But our good happe was, that we kept the other olde Indian which we handfasted to redeeme our pilot withall: for being naturall of those riuers, we assured our selues hee knew the way better then any stranger could. And indeed, but for this chance, I thinke we had neuer found the way either to Guiana, or backe to our ships: for Ferdinando after a few dayes knew nothing at all, nor which way to turne, yea and many times the old man himselfe was in great doubt which riuer to take. Those people which dwell in these broken islands and drowned lands, are generally called Tiuitiuas: there are of them two sorts, the one called Ciawani, and the other Waraweete.

A description of the mighty riuer of Orenoque or Baraquan. The great riuer of Orenoque or Baraquan hath nine branches which fall out on the North side of his owne maine mouth: on the South side it hath seuen other fallings into the sea, so it disemboqueth by sixteene armes in all, betweene Ilands and broken ground, but the Ilands are very great, many of them as bigge as the Isle of Wight, and bigger, and many lesse. From the first branch on the North to the last of the South, it is at least 100 leagues, so as the riuers mouth is 300 miles wide at his entrance into the sea, which I take to be farre bigger then that of Amazones. All those that inhabit in the mouth of this riuer vpon the seuerall North branches, are these Tiuitiuas, of which there are two chiefe lords which haue continuall warres one with the other. The Ilands which lie on the right hand, are called Pallamos, and the land on the left, Horotomaka, and the riuer by which Iohn Douglas returned within the land from Amana to Capuri, they call Macuri.

What maner of people the Tiuitiuas are. These Tiuitiuas are a very goodly people and very valiant, and haue the most manly speech and most deliberate that euer I heard, of what nation soeuer. In the Summer they haue houses on the ground, as in other places: in the Winter they dwell vpon the trees, where they build very artificiall townes and villages, as it is written in the Spanish story of the West Indies, that those people do in the low lands nere the gulfe of Vraba: for betweene May and September the riuer of Orenoque riseth thirty foot vpright, and then are those ilands ouerflowen twenty foot high aboue the leuell of the ground, sauing some few raised grounds in the middle of them: and for this cause they are inforced to liue in this maner. They neuer eat of any thing that is set or sowen: and as at home they vse neither planting nor other manurance, so when they come abroad, they refuse to feed of ought, but of that which nature without labour bringeth forth. They vse the tops of Palmitos for bread, and kill deere, fish, and porks, for the rest of their sustenance. They haue also many sorts of fruits that grow in the woods, and great variety of birds and fowle.

And if to speake of them were not tedious, and vulgar, surely we saw in those passages of very rare colours and formes, not elsewhere to be found, for as much as I haue either seene or read. Of these people those that dwell vpon the branches of Orenoque, called Capuri and Macureo, are for the most part carpenters of canoas, for they make the most and fairest canoas, and sel them into Guiana for golde, and into Trinidad for tobacco in the excessiue taking whereof, they exceed all nations: and not withstanding the moistnesse of the aire in which they liue, the hardnesse of their diet, and the great labours they suffer to hunt, fish and fowle for their liuing in all my life, either in the Indies or in Europe, did I neuer behold a more goodly or better fauoured people or a more manly. They were woont to make warre vpon all nations, especially on the Canibals, so as none durst without a good strength trade by those riuers: but of late they are at peace with their neighbours, all holding the Spaniards for a common enemy. When their commanders die, they vse great lamentation, and when they thinke the flesh of their bodies is petrified, and fallen from the bones, then they take vp the carcase againe, and hang it in the caciques house that died, and decke his scull with feathers of all colours, and hang all his golde plates about the bones of his armes, thighs, and legs. Those nations which are called Arwacas, which dwell on the South of Orenoque, (of which place and nation our Indian pilot was) are dispersed in many other places, and doe vse to beat the bones of their lords into powder, and their wiues and friends drinke it all in their seuerall sorts of drinks.

After we departed from the port of these Ciawani, wee passed vp the riuer with the flood, and ankered the ebbe, and in this sort we went onward. The third day that we entred the riuer, our galley came on ground, and stucke so fast, as we thought that euen there our discouery had ended, and that we must haue left fourescore and ten of our men to haue inhabited like rooks vpon trees with those nations: but the next morning, after we had cast out all her ballast, with tugging and halling to and fro, we got her aflote, and went on. At foure dayes end wee fell into as goodly a riuer as euer I beheld, which was called The great Amana, which ranne more directly without windings and turnings then the other: but soone after the flood of the sea left vs; and being inforced either by maine strength to row against a violent current, or to returne as wise as we went out, we had then no shift but to perswade the companies that it was but two or three dayes worke, and therefore desired them to take paines, euery gentleman and others taking their turnes to row, and to spell one the other at the houres end. Euery day we passed by goodly branches of riuers, some falling from the West, others from the East into Amana, but those I leaue to the description in the Cart of discouery, where euery one shalbe named with his rising and descent. When three dayes more were ouergone, our companies began to despaire, the weather being extreame hote, the riuer bordered with very high trees, that kept away the aire, and the current against vs euery day stronger then other: but we euermore commanded our pilots to promise an ende the next day, and vsed it so long, as we were driuen to assure them from foure reaches of the riuer to three, and so to two, and so to the next reach: but so long we laboured, that many dayes were spent, and wee driuen to drawe our selues to harder allowance, our bread euen at the last, and no drinke at all; and our men and our selues so wearied and scorched, and doubtfull withall, whether wee should euer performe it or no, the heat increasing as we drew towards the line: for wee were now in fiue degrees.

The further we went on (our victuall decreasing and the aire breeding great faintnesse) wee grew weaker and weaker, when wee had most need of strength and abilitie: for hourely the riuer ranne more violently then other against vs, and the barge, wheries, and shippes boat of captaine Gifford and captaine Calfield, had spent all their prouisions: so as we were brought into despaire and discomfort, had wee not perswaded all the company that it was but onely one dayes worke more to atteine the land where wee should be relieued of all wee wanted, and if we returned, that wee were sure to starue by the way, and that the world would also laugh vs to scorne. On the banks of these riuers were diuers sorts of fruits good to eat, flowers and trees of such variety, as were sufficient to make tenne volumes of herbals: we relieued our selues many times with the fruits of the countrey, and sometimes with fowle and fish. Wee saw birds of all colours, some carnation, some crimson, orenge-tawny, purple, watchet and of all other sorts both simple and mixt, and it was vnto vs a great good passing of the time to beholde them, besides the reliefe we found by killing some store of them with our fowling pieces: without which, hauing little or no bread, and lesse drinke, but onely the thicke and troubled water of the riuer, we had beene in a very hard case.

Our olde pilot of the Ciawani (whom, as I sayd before, wee tooke to redeeme Ferdinando) tolde vs, that if we would enter a branch of a riuer on the right hand with our barge and wheries, and leaue the galley at anker the while in the great riuer, he would bring vs to a towne of the Arwacas, where we should finde store of bread, hennes, fish, and of the countrey wine; and perswaded vs that departing from the galley at noone, we might returne yer night. I was very glad to heare this speech, and presently tooke my barke, with eight musketiers, captaine Giffords whery, with myselfe and foure musketiers and Captaine Calfield with his whery, and as many; and so we entred the mouth of this riuer: and because we were perswaded that it was so nere, we tooke no victuall with vs at all. When we had rowed three houres, we maruelled we saw no signe of any dwelling, and asked the pilot where the towne was: he tolde vs a little further. After three houres more, the Sun being almost set, we began to suspect that he led vs that way to betray vs; for hee confessed that those Spaniards which fled from Trinidad, and also those that remained with Carapana in Emeria, were ioyned together in some village vpon that riuer. But when it grew towards night; and wee demanded where the place was: hee tolde vs but foure reaches more. When we had rowed foure and foure, we saw no signe; and our poore water-men, euen heart-broken, and tired, were ready to giue up the ghost: for we had now come from the galley neere forty miles.

At the last we determined to hang the pilot; and if wee had well knowen the way backe againe by night, we had surely gone; but our owne necessities pleaded sufficiently for his safety: for it was as darke as pitch, and the riuer began so to narrow it selfe, and the trees to hang ouer from side to side, as wee were driuen with arming swords to cut a passage thorow those branches that couered the water. Wee were very desirous to finde this towne, hoping of a feast, because wee made but a short breakefast aboord the galley in the morning and it was now eight a clocke at night, and our stomacks began to gnawe apace: but whether it was best to returne or goe on, we beganne to doubt, suspecting treason in the pilot more and more: but the poore olde Indian euer assured vs that it was but a little further, but this one turning and that turning: and at the last about one a clocke after midnight wee saw a light; and rowing towards it, wee heard the dogges of the village. When we landed wee found few people; for the lord of that place was gone with diuers canoas aboue foure hundred miles off, vpon a iourney towardes the head of Orenoque to trade for golde, and to buy women of the Canibals, who afterward vnfortunately passed by vs as wee rode at an anker in the port of Morequito in the darke of the night, and yet came so neere vs, as his canoas grated against our barges: he left one of his company at the port of Morequito, by whom wee vnderstood that hee had brought thirty yoong women, diuers plates of golde, and had great store of fine pieces of cotton cloth, and cotton beds. In his house we had good store of bread, fish, hennes, and Indian drinke, and so rested that night, and in the morning after we had traded with such of his people as came downe, we returned towards our gally, and brought with vs some quantity of bread, fish, and hennes.

A most beautifull countrey. On both sides of this riuer we passed the most beautifull countrey that euer mine eyes beheld: and whereas all that we had seene before was nothing but woods, prickles, bushes, and thornes, here we beheld plaines of twenty miles in length, the grasse short and greene, and in diuers parts groues of trees by themselues, as if they had beene by all the arte and labour in the world so made of purpose: and still as we rowed, the deere came downe feeding by the waters side, as if they had beene vsed to a keepers call. *The riuer of Lagartos, or Crocodiles.* Vpon this riuer there were great store of fowle, and of many sorts: we saw in it diuers sorts of strange fishes, and of maruellous bignes: but for lagartos it exceeded, for there were thousands of those vgly serpents; and the people call it for the abundance of them, The riuer of Lagartos, in their language. I had a Negro a very proper yoong fellow, who leaping out of the galley to swim in the mouth of this riuer, was in all our sights taken and deuoured with one of those lagartos. In the meane while our companies in the gally thought we had bene all lost, (for wee promised to returne before night) and sent the Lions whelps shippes boat with captaine Whiddon to follow vs vp the riuer; but the next day, after we had rowed vp and downe some fourescore miles, we returned, and went on our way, vp the great riuer; and when we were euen at the last cast for want of victuals, captaine Gifford being before the galley and the rest of the boats, seeking out some place to land vpon the banks to make fire, espied foure canoas comming downe the riuer; Two canoas taken. and with no small ioy caused his men to trie the vttermost of their strengths, and after a while two of the foure gaue ouer, and ranne themselues ashore, euery man betaking himselfe to the fastnesse of the woods, the two other lesser got away, while he landed to lay hold on these: and so turned into some by-creeke, we knew not whither. Three Spanyards escaped. Those canoas that were taken, were loaden with bread, and were bound for Margarita in the West Indies, which those Indians (called Arwacas) purposed to cary thither for exchange: but in the lesser there were three Spanyards, who hauing heard of the defeat of their gouernour in Trinidad, and that we purposed to enter Guiana, came away in those canoas: one of them was a cauallero; as the captaine of the Arwacas after tolde vs, another a souldier, and the third a refiner.

END OF VOL. XIV.

Milton Keynes UK
Ingram Content Group UK Ltd.
UKHW040819051024
449151UK00004B/332